NEW YORK REVIEW COMICS

SLUM WOLF

TADAO TSUGE is one of alternative manga's cult stars. Debuting as a cartoonist in the rental *kashihon* market in 1959, he was a leading contributor to the legendary magazine *Garo* during its heyday in the late 1960s. He has drawn extensively for magazines like *Yagyō* and *Gentō*, often pulling from his experiences growing up in the slums of Tokyo, working for ooze-for-booze blood banks, and daydreaming while fishing. He currently lives in Chiba Prefecture, north of Tokyo, where he splits his time between cooking for his family and drawing ever stranger manga.

RYAN HOLMBERG is an art and comics historian who currently teaches at the University of Tokyo. He is a frequent contributor to *Artforum International*, *Art in America*, and *The Comics Journal*, and has edited and translated books of Japanese comics by Osamu Tezuka, Seiichi Hayashi, Baron Yoshimoto, and others.

THIS IS A NEW YORK REVIEW COMIC
PUBLISHED BY THE NEW YORK REVIEW OF BOOKS
435 Hudson Street, New York, NY 10014
www.nyrb.com

Custom fonts by Dean Sudarsky

Library of Congress Cataloging-in-Publication Data

Names: Tsuge, Tadao, 1941- author, artist. | Holmberg, Ryan, editor,
    translator.
Title: Slum wolf / by Tadao Tsuge ; edited, translated, and with an
    introduction by Ryan Holmberg.
Description: New York : New York Review Books, 2017. | Series: New York
    Review Comics |
Identifiers: LCCN 2017038763 (print) | LCCN 2017039125 (ebook) | ISBN
    9781681371757 (epub) | ISBN 9781681371740 (paperback) | ISBN 168137174X
    (paperback)
Subjects: LCSH: Comic books, strips, etc. | BISAC: COMICS & GRAPHIC NOVELS /
    Manga / General. | COMICS & GRAPHIC NOVELS / Literary. | COMICS & GRAPHIC
    NOVELS / Manga / Crime & Mystery.
Classification: LCC PN6790.J33 (ebook) | LCC PN6790.J33 T75713 2017 (print) |
    DDC 741.5/952—dc23
LC record available at https://lccn.loc.gov/2017038763

ISBN 978-1-68137-174-0
Available as an electronic book; 978-1-68137-175-7

Printed in the United States of America
10 9 8 7 6 5 4 3 2 1

SLUM WOLF

TADAO TSUGE

EDITED AND TRANSLATED BY
RYAN HOLMBERG

NEW YORK REVIEW COMICS · *New York*

CONTENTS

SENTIMENTAL MELODY

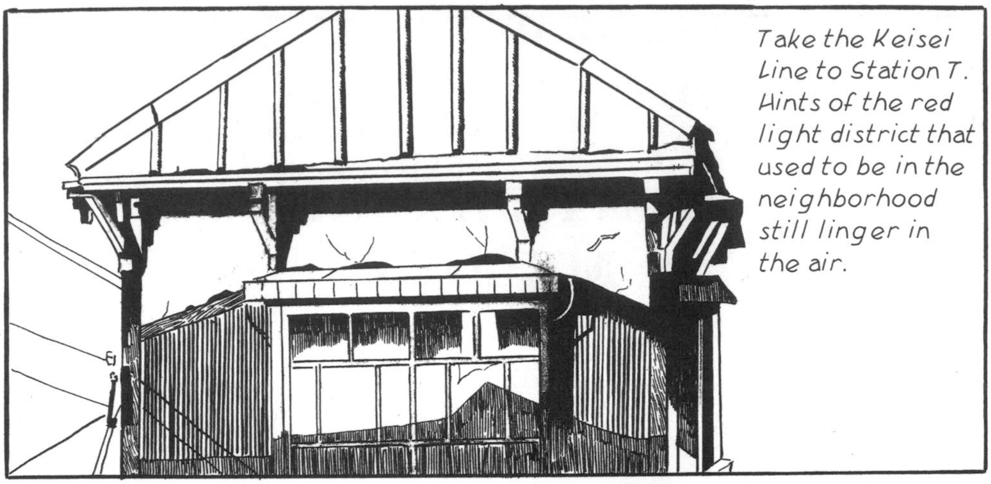
Take the Keisei Line to Station T. Hints of the red light district that used to be in the neighborhood still linger in the air.
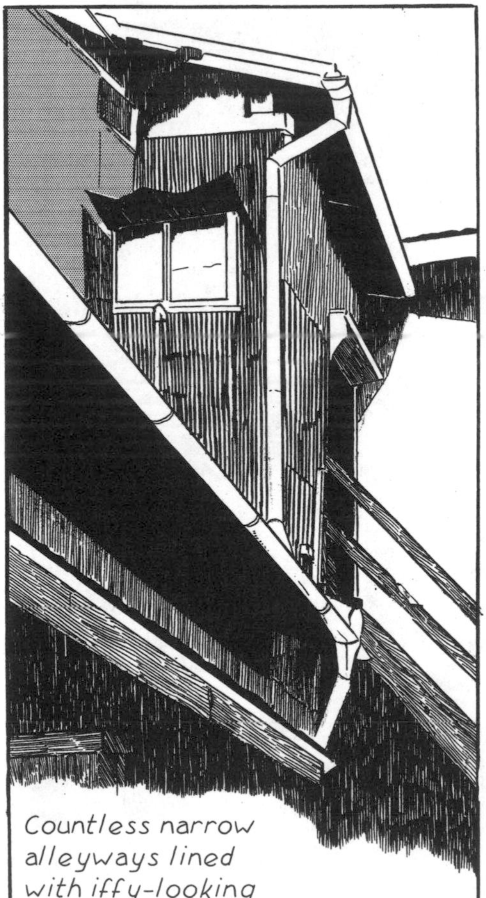
Countless narrow alleyways lined with iffy-looking houses and smelling of piss...
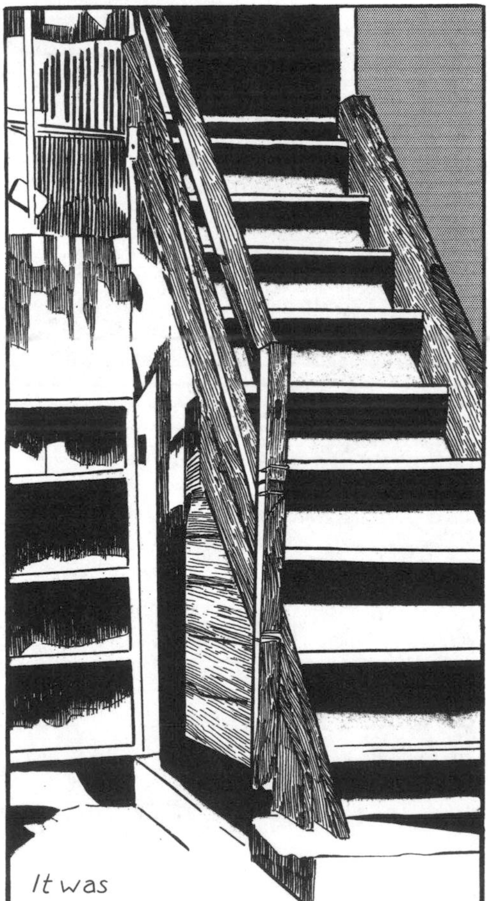
It was around 1948, 1949...

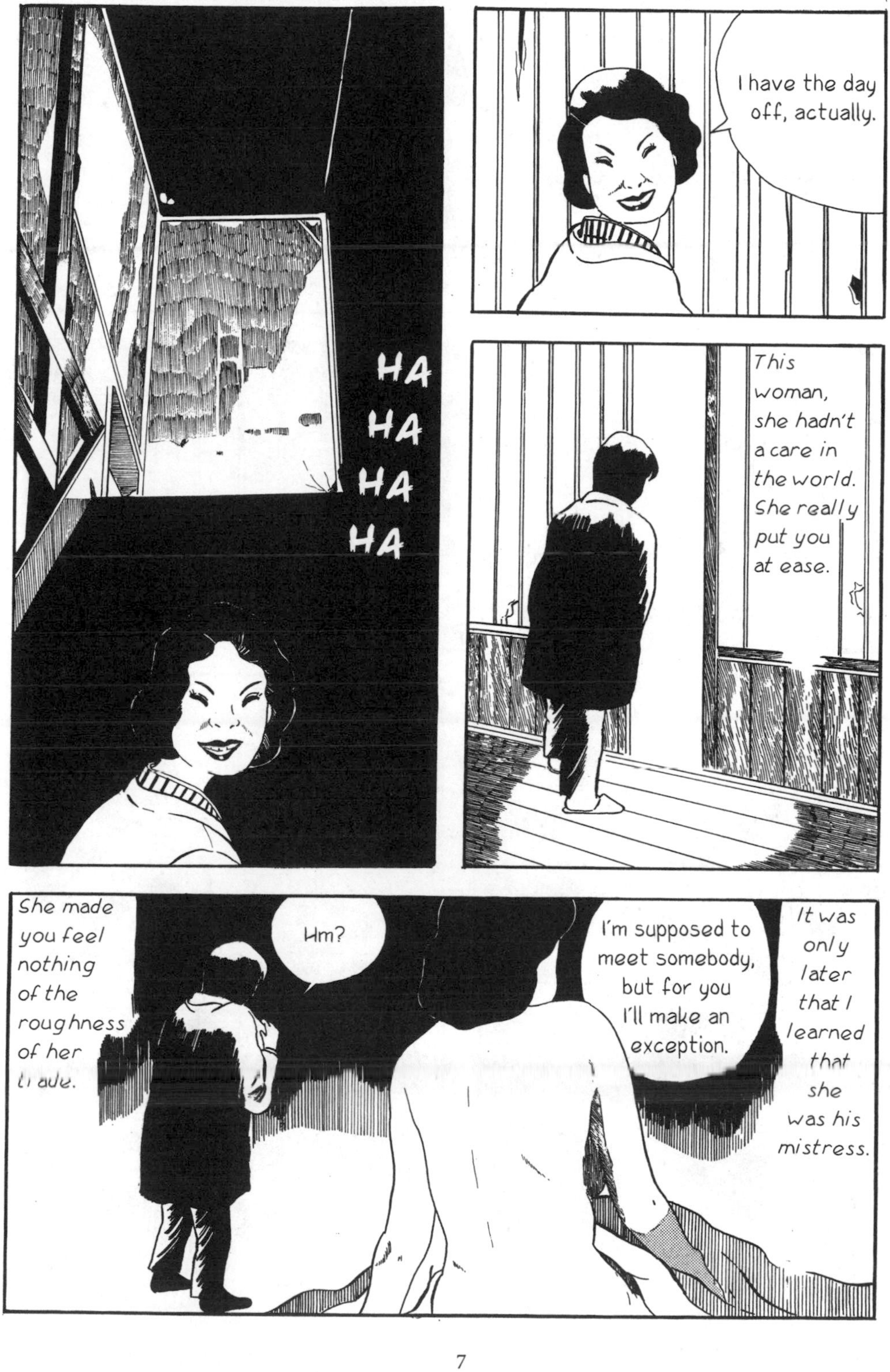
HA HA HA HA
I have the day off, actually.
This woman, she hadn't a care in the world. She really put you at ease.
She made you feel nothing of the roughness of her trade.
Hm?
I'm supposed to meet somebody, but for you I'll make an exception.
It was only later that I learned that she was his mistress.

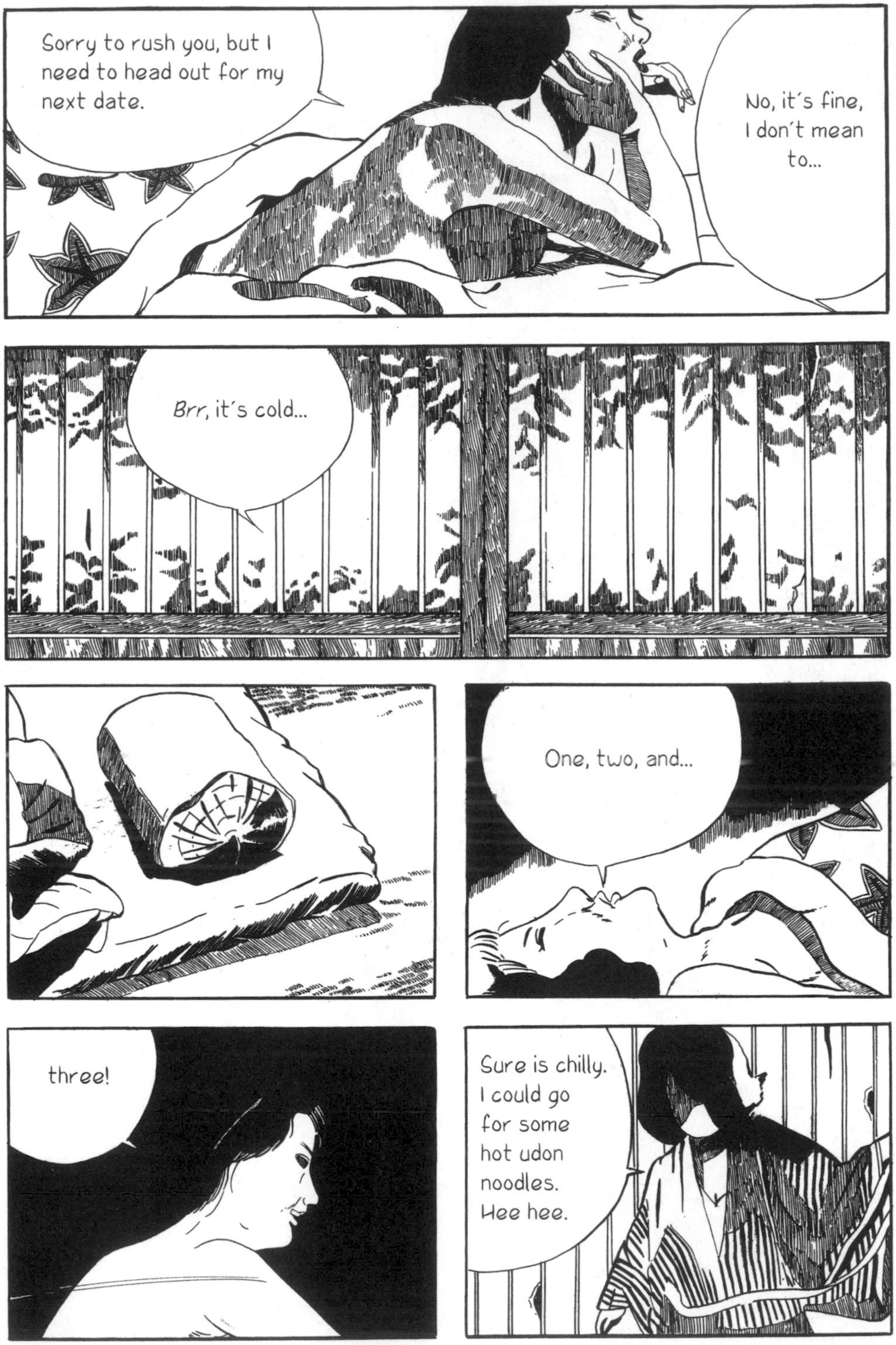
Sorry to rush you, but I need to head out for my next date.
No, it's fine, I don't mean to...
Brr, it's cold...
One, two, and...
three!
Sure is chilly. I could go for some hot udon noodles. Hee hee.

Watch your step. One customer fell down these stairs.

Oh, you're already here. Did I keep you waiting?

It's fine... Looks like I came at a bad time.

No no, this one's just leaving.

.....

Thank you, sir. We really appreciate your business.

HA HA HA

You're quite the gentleman...

9

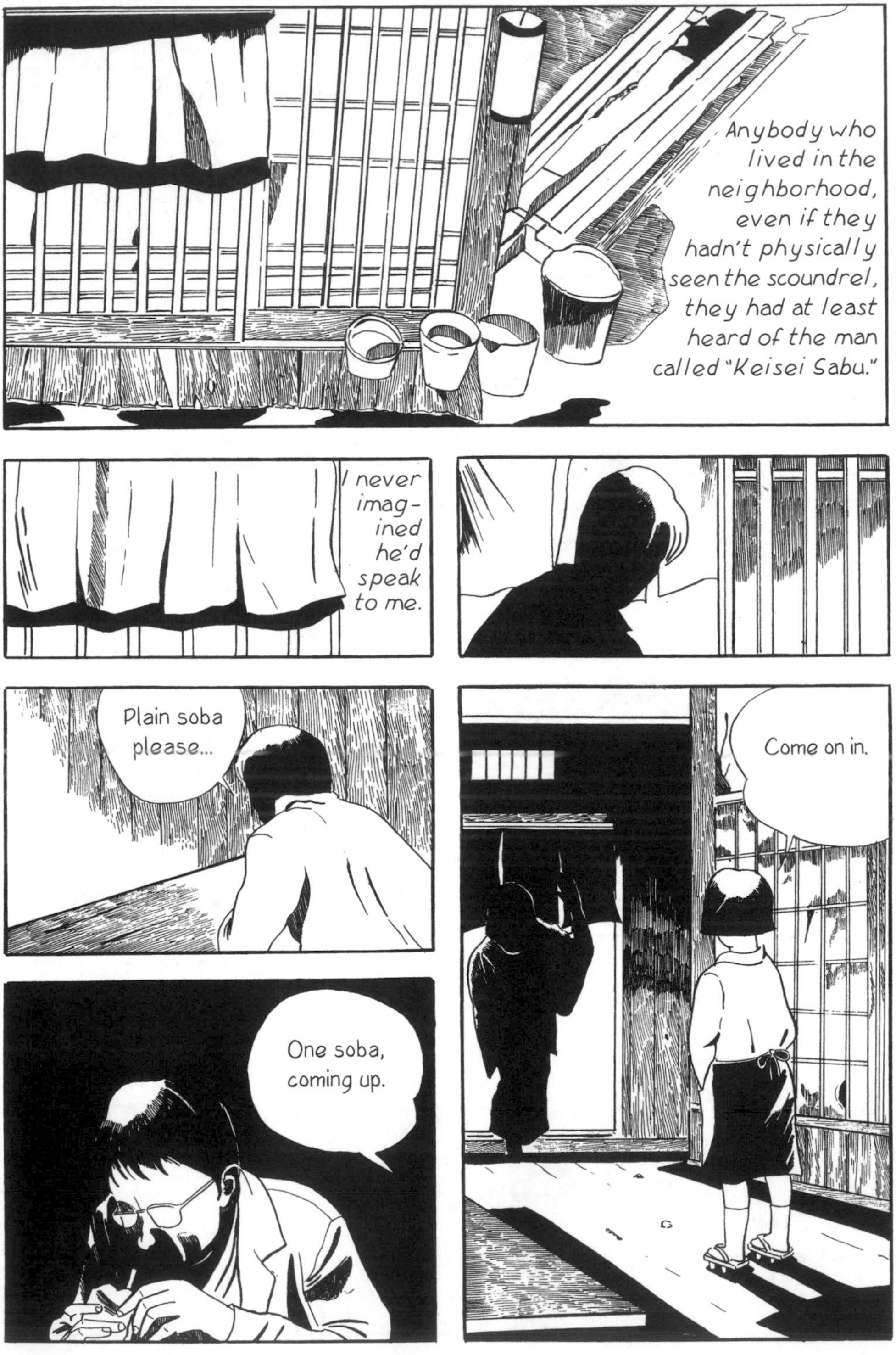
Anybody who lived in the neighborhood, even if they hadn't physically seen the scoundrel, they had at least heard of the man called "Keisei Sabu."
I never imag-ined he'd speak to me.
Plain soba please...
Come on in.
One soba, coming up.

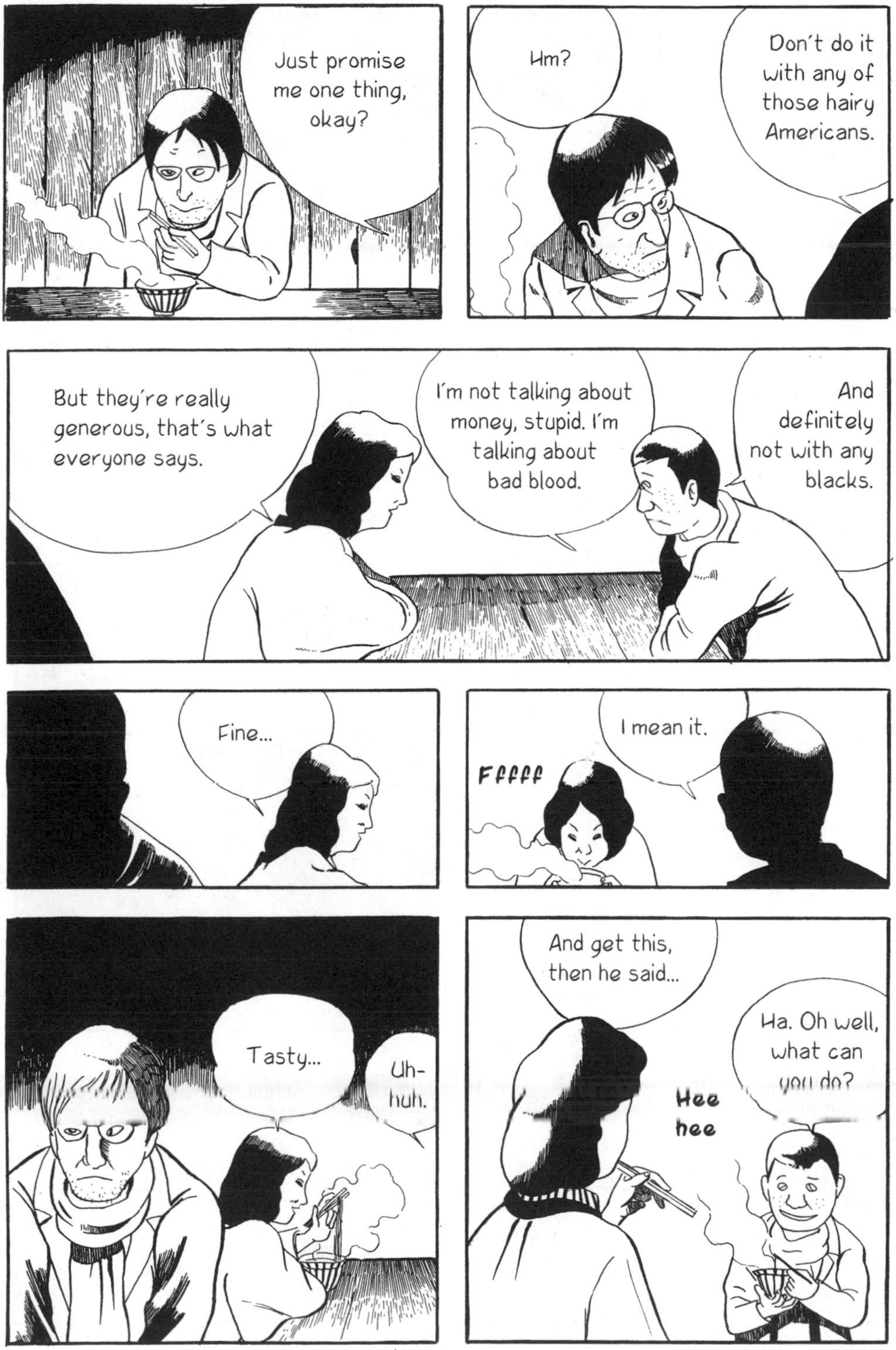
Just promise me one thing, okay?
Hm?
Don't do it with any of those hairy Americans.
But they're really generous, that's what everyone says.
I'm not talking about money, stupid. I'm talking about bad blood.
And definitely not with any blacks.
Fine...
I mean it.
Fffff
Tasty...
Uh-huh.
And get this, then he said...
Hee hee
Ha. Oh well, what can you do?

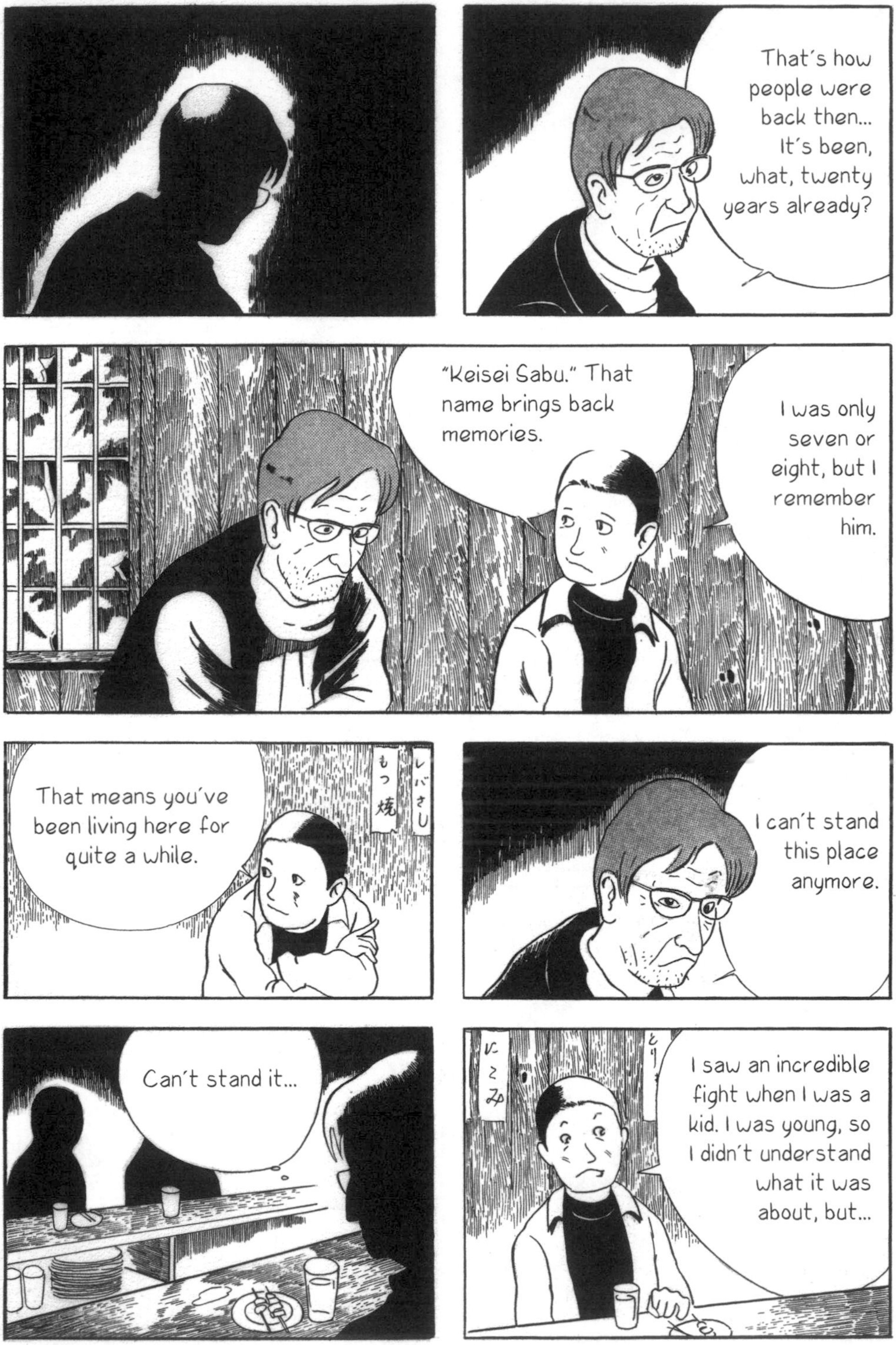
That's how people were back then... It's been, what, twenty years already?
"Keisei Sabu." That name brings back memories.
I was only seven or eight, but I remember him.
That means you've been living here for quite a while.
レバさし
もつ焼
I can't stand this place anymore.
Can't stand it...
I saw an incredible fight when I was a kid. I was young, so I didn't understand what it was about, but...

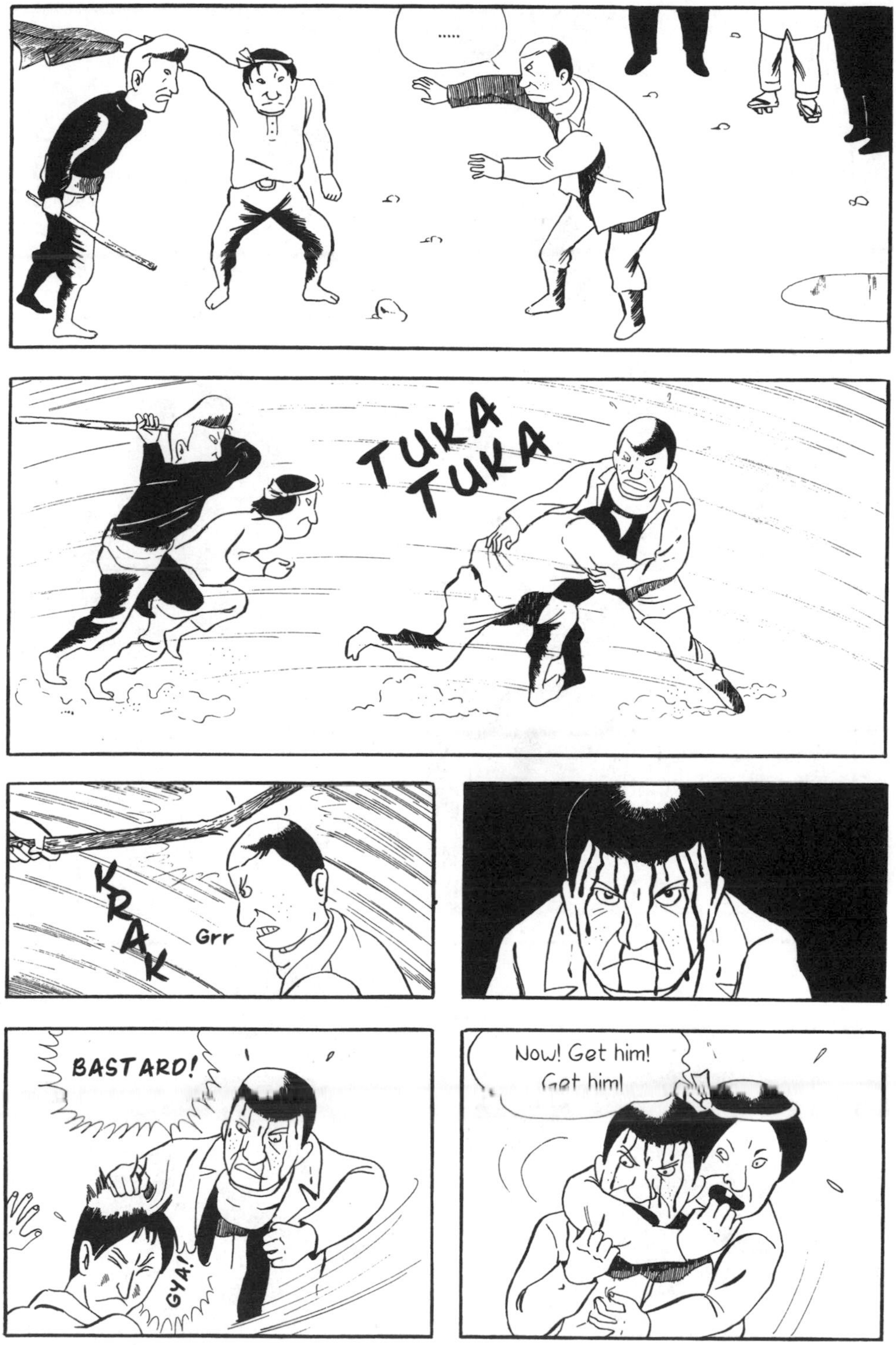
......
TUKA TUKA
KRAK
Grr
BASTARD!
GYA!
Now! Get him! Get him!

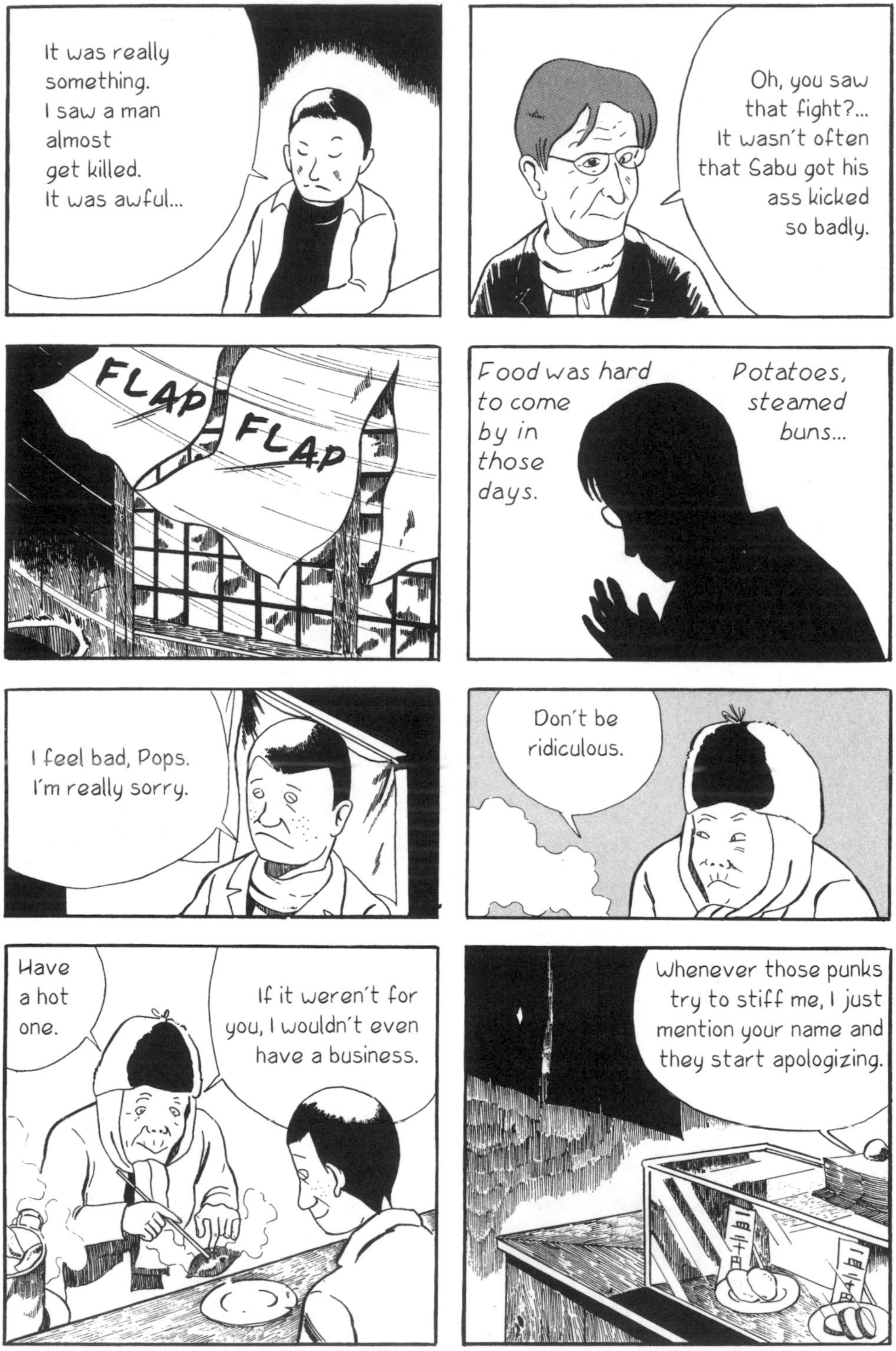
It was really something. I saw a man almost get killed. It was awful...
Oh, you saw that fight?... It wasn't often that Sabu got his ass kicked so badly.
FLAP
FLAP
Food was hard to come by in those days.
Potatoes, steamed buns...
I feel bad, Pops. I'm really sorry.
Don't be ridiculous.
Have a hot one.
If it weren't for you, I wouldn't even have a business.
Whenever those punks try to stiff me, I just mention your name and they start apologizing.

signs: 20 yen per plate

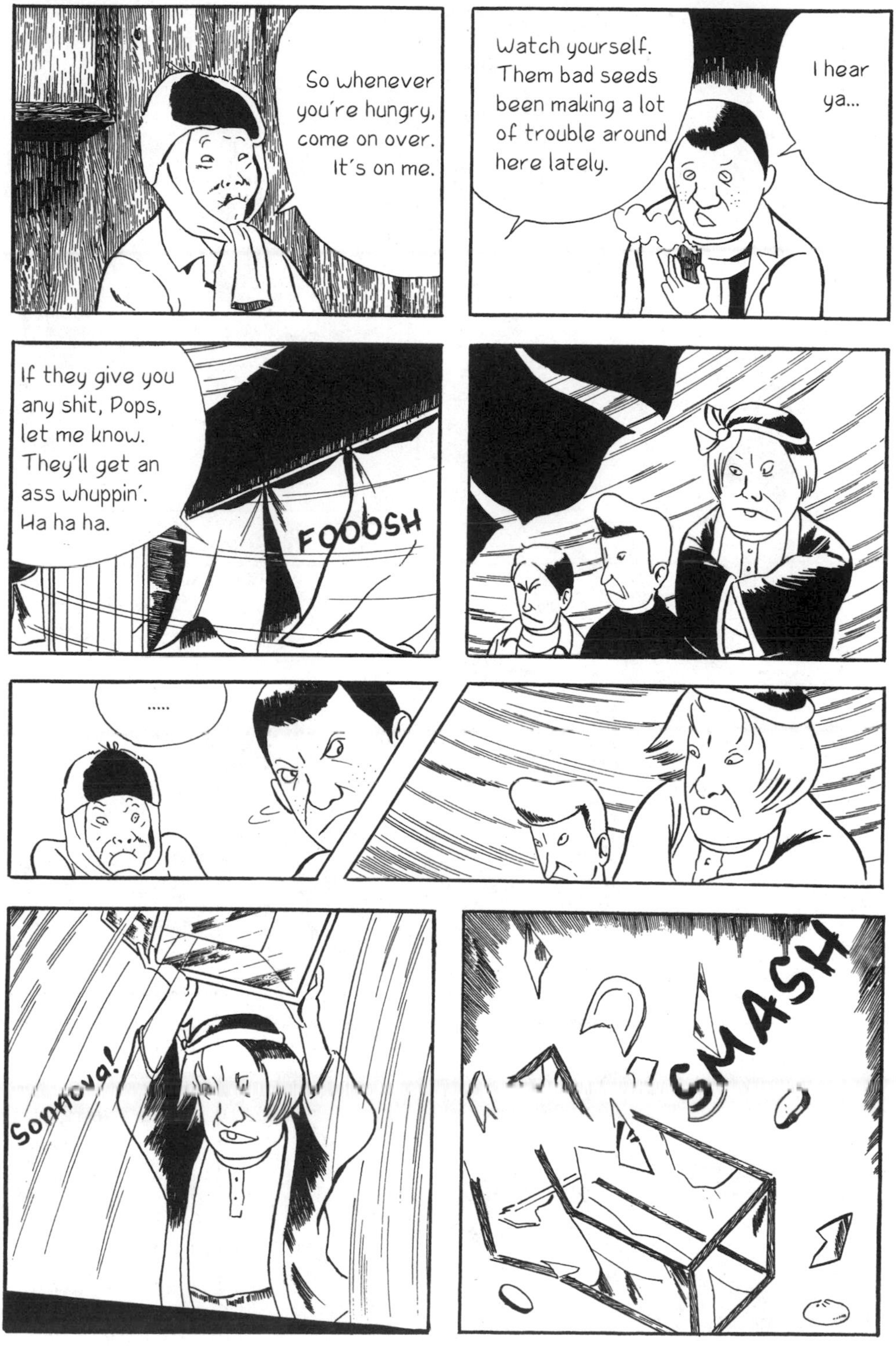
So whenever you're hungry, come on over. It's on me.
Watch yourself. Them bad seeds been making a lot of trouble around here lately.
I hear ya...
If they give you any shit, Pops, let me know. They'll get an ass whuppin'. Ha ha ha.
FOOOSH
.....
Sonnova!
SMASH

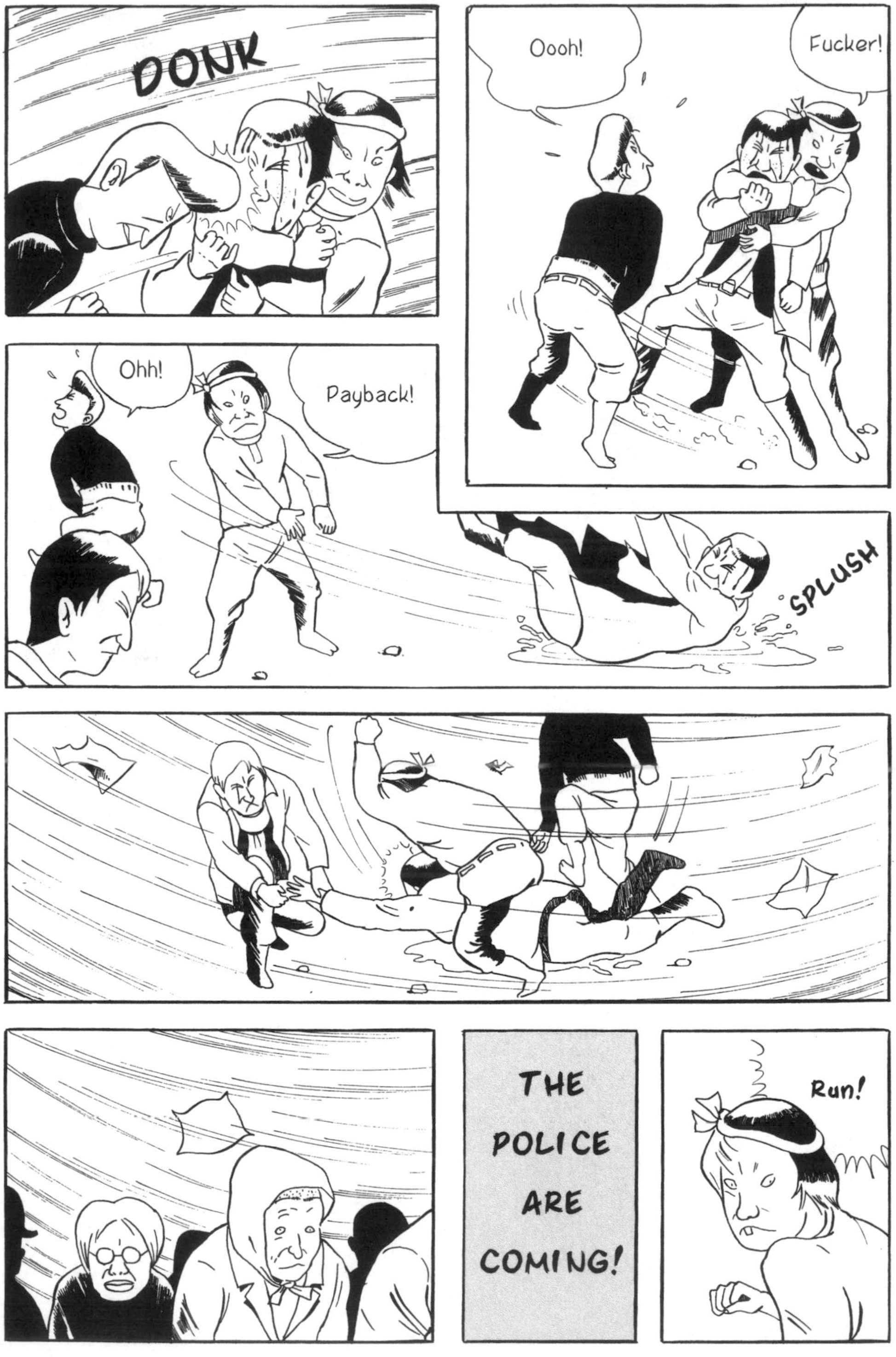
DONK
Oooh!
Fucker!
Ohh!
Payback!
SPLUSH
THE POLICE ARE COMING!
Run!

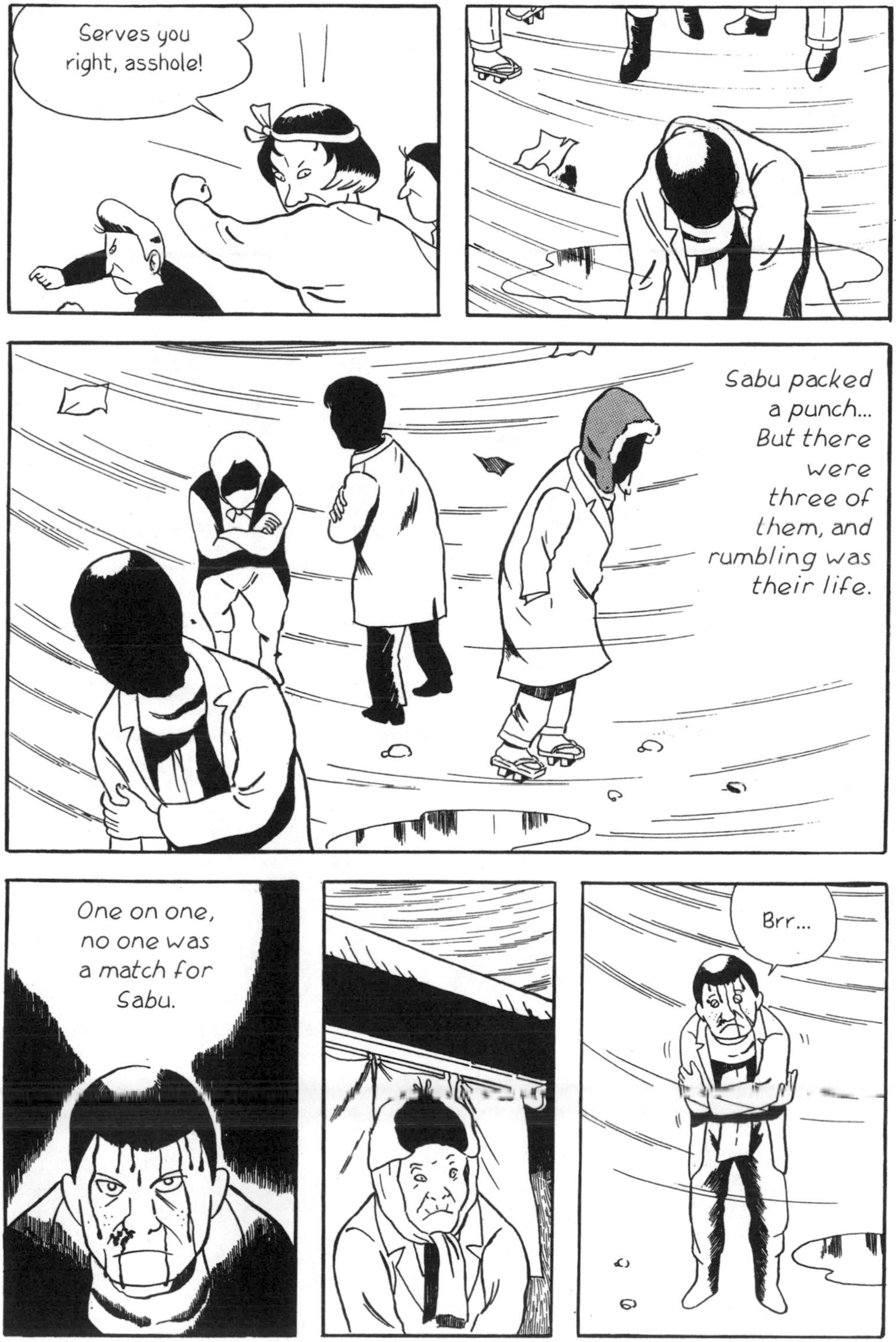
Serves you right, asshole!
Sabu packed a punch... But there were three of them, and rumbling was their life.
One on one, no one was a match for Sabu.
Brr...

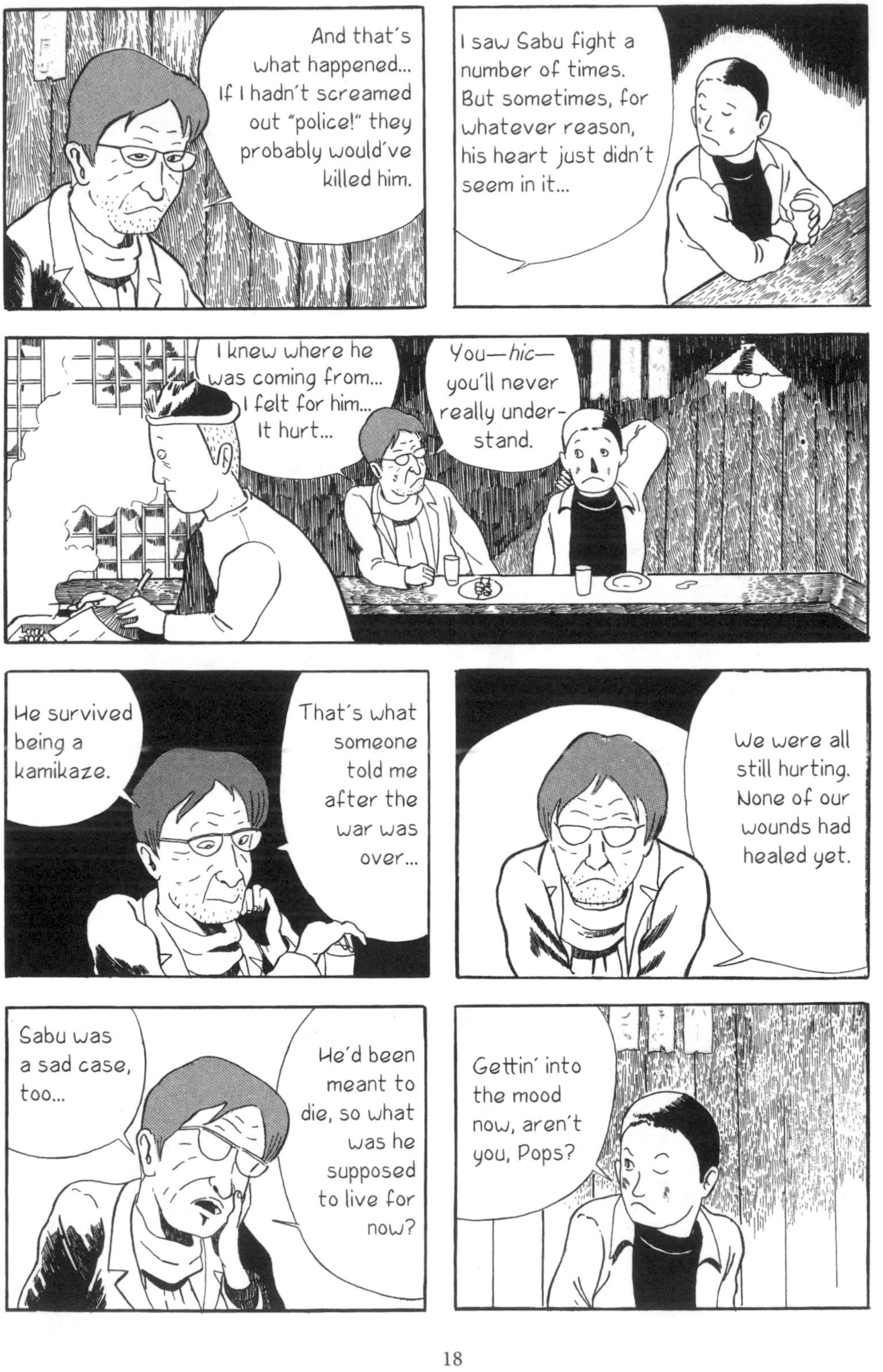
And that's what happened... If I hadn't screamed out "police!" they probably would've killed him.
I saw Sabu fight a number of times. But sometimes, for whatever reason, his heart just didn't seem in it...
I knew where he was coming from... I felt for him... It hurt...
You—*hic*—you'll never really under-stand.
He survived being a kamikaze.
That's what someone told me after the war was over...
We were all still hurting. None of our wounds had healed yet.
Sabu was a sad case, too...
He'd been meant to die, so what was he supposed to live for now?
Gettin' into the mood now, aren't you, Pops?

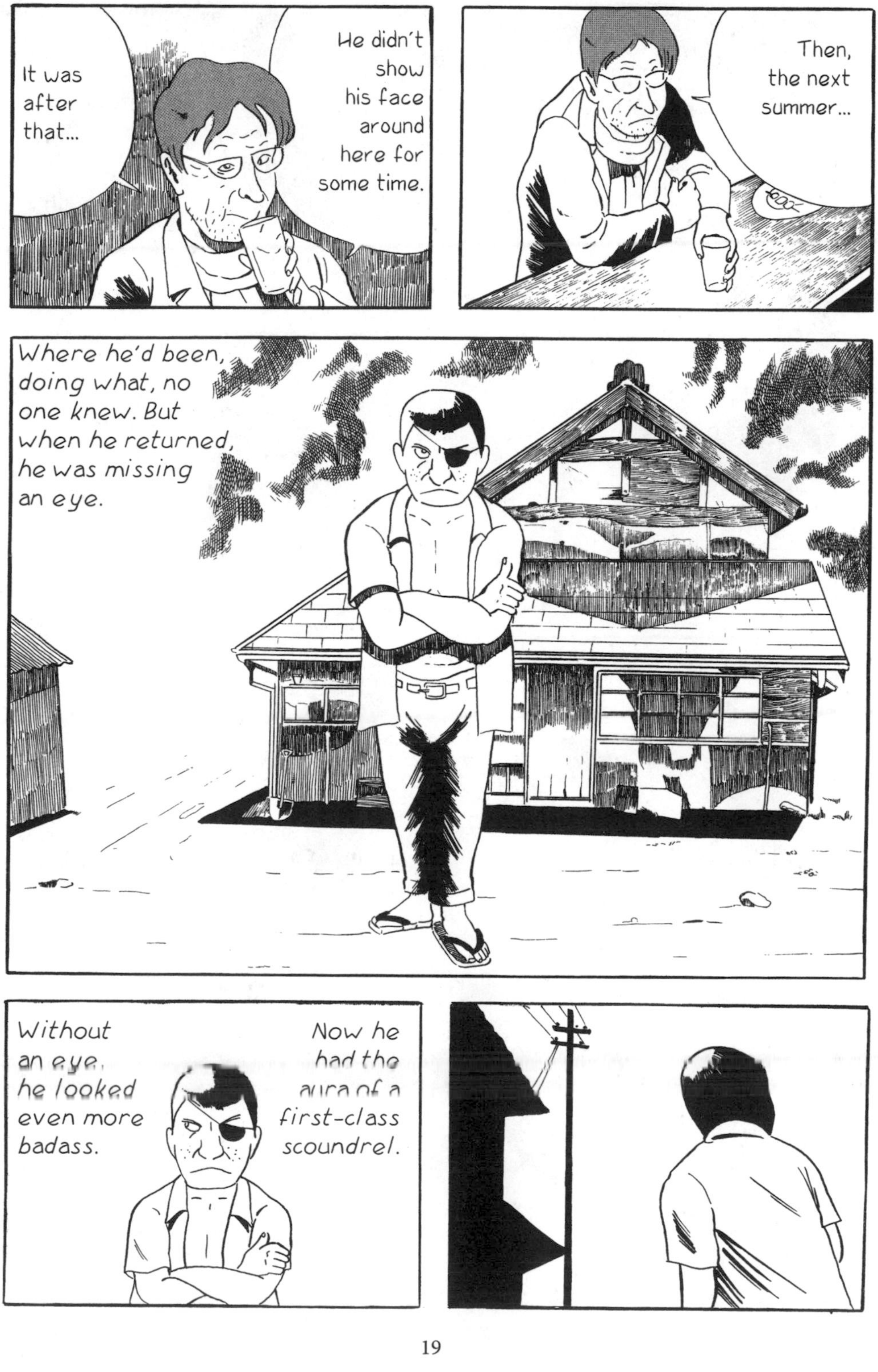
It was after that...
He didn't show his face around here for some time.
Then, the next summer...
Where he'd been, doing what, no one knew. But when he returned, he was missing an eye.
Without an eye, he looked even more badass.
Now he had the aura of a first-class scoundrel.

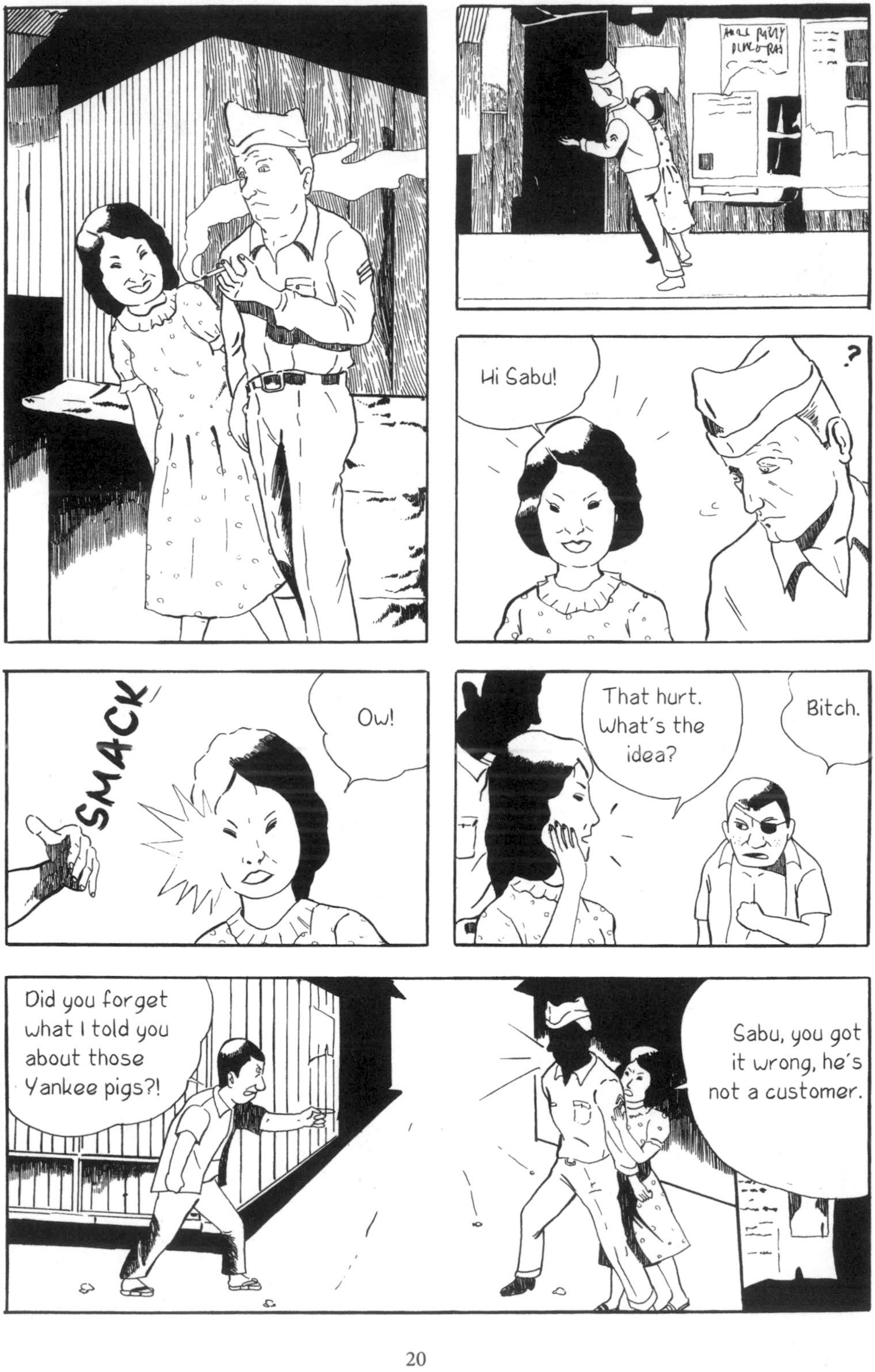
Hi Sabu!
?
SMACK
Ow!
That hurt. What's the idea?
Bitch.
Did you forget what I told you about those Yankee pigs?!
Sabu, you got it wrong, he's not a customer.

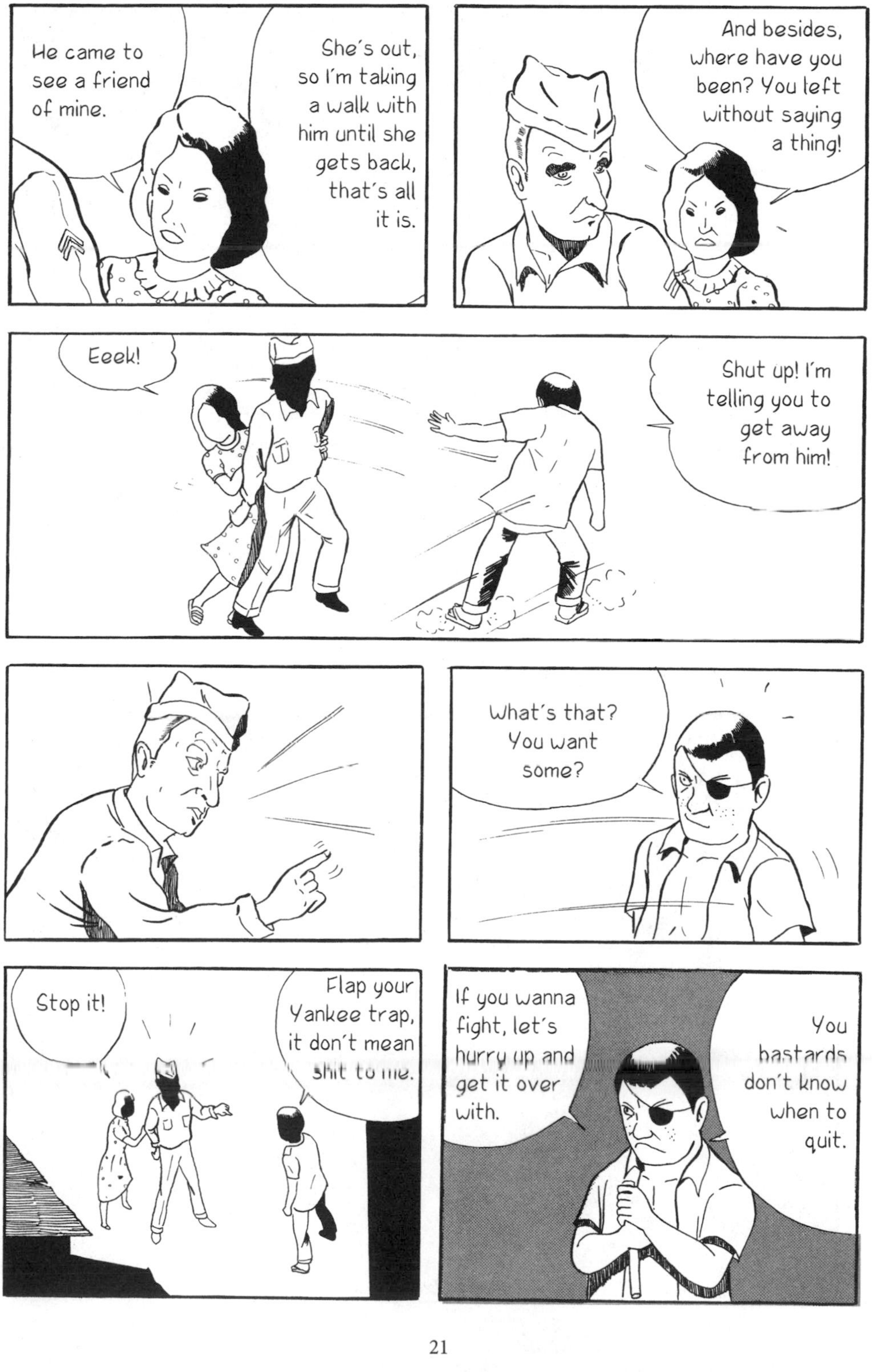
He came to see a friend of mine.
She's out, so I'm taking a walk with him until she gets back, that's all it is.
And besides, where have you been? You left without saying a thing!
Eeek!
Shut up! I'm telling you to get away from him!
What's that? You want some?
Stop it!
Flap your Yankee trap, it don't mean shit to me.
If you wanna fight, let's hurry up and get it over with.
You bastards don't know when to quit.

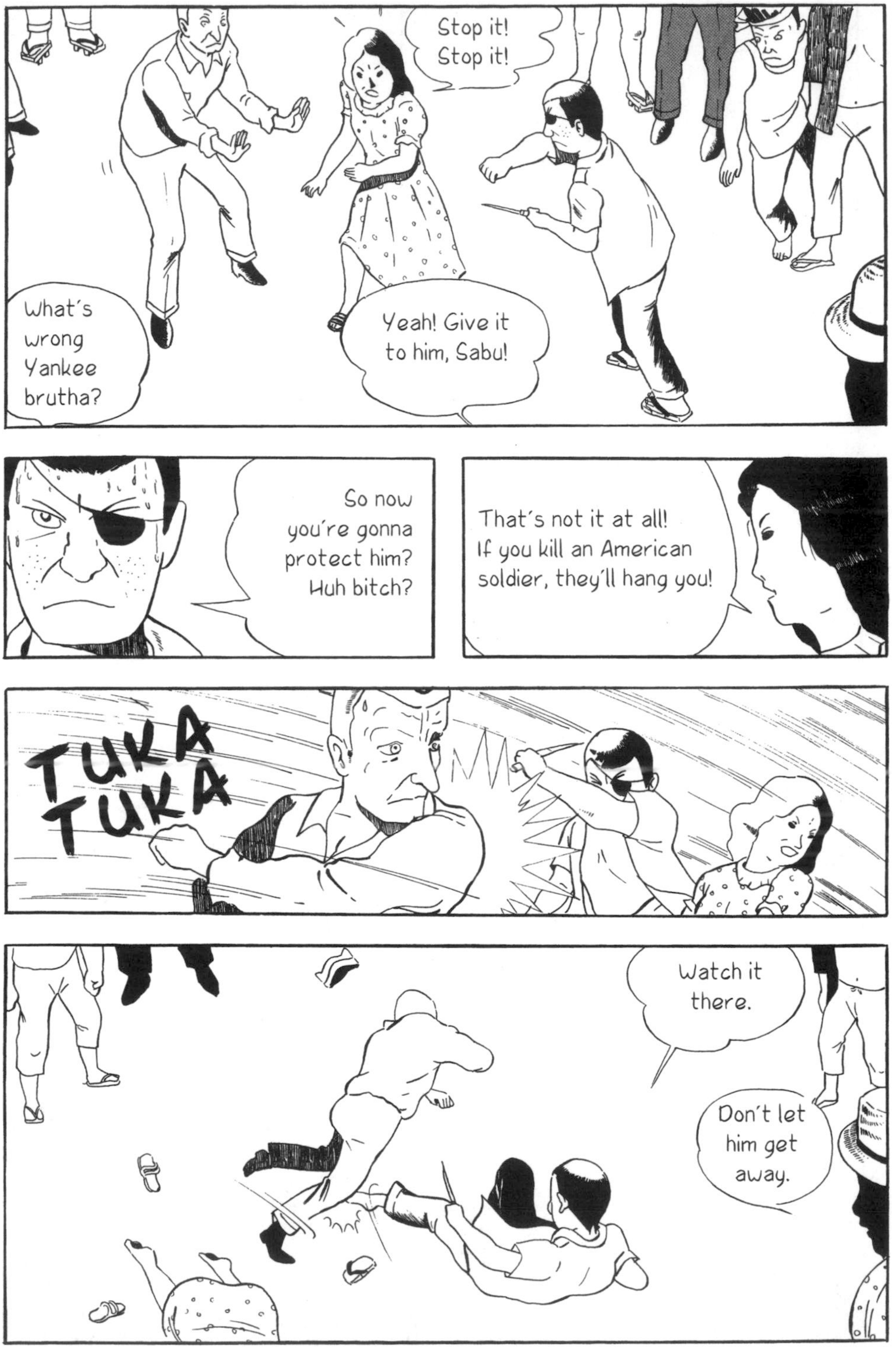
Stop it! Stop it!
What's wrong Yankee brutha?
Yeah! Give it to him, Sabu!
So now you're gonna protect him? Huh bitch?
That's not it at all! If you kill an American soldier, they'll hang you!
TUKA TUKA
Watch it there.
Don't let him get away.

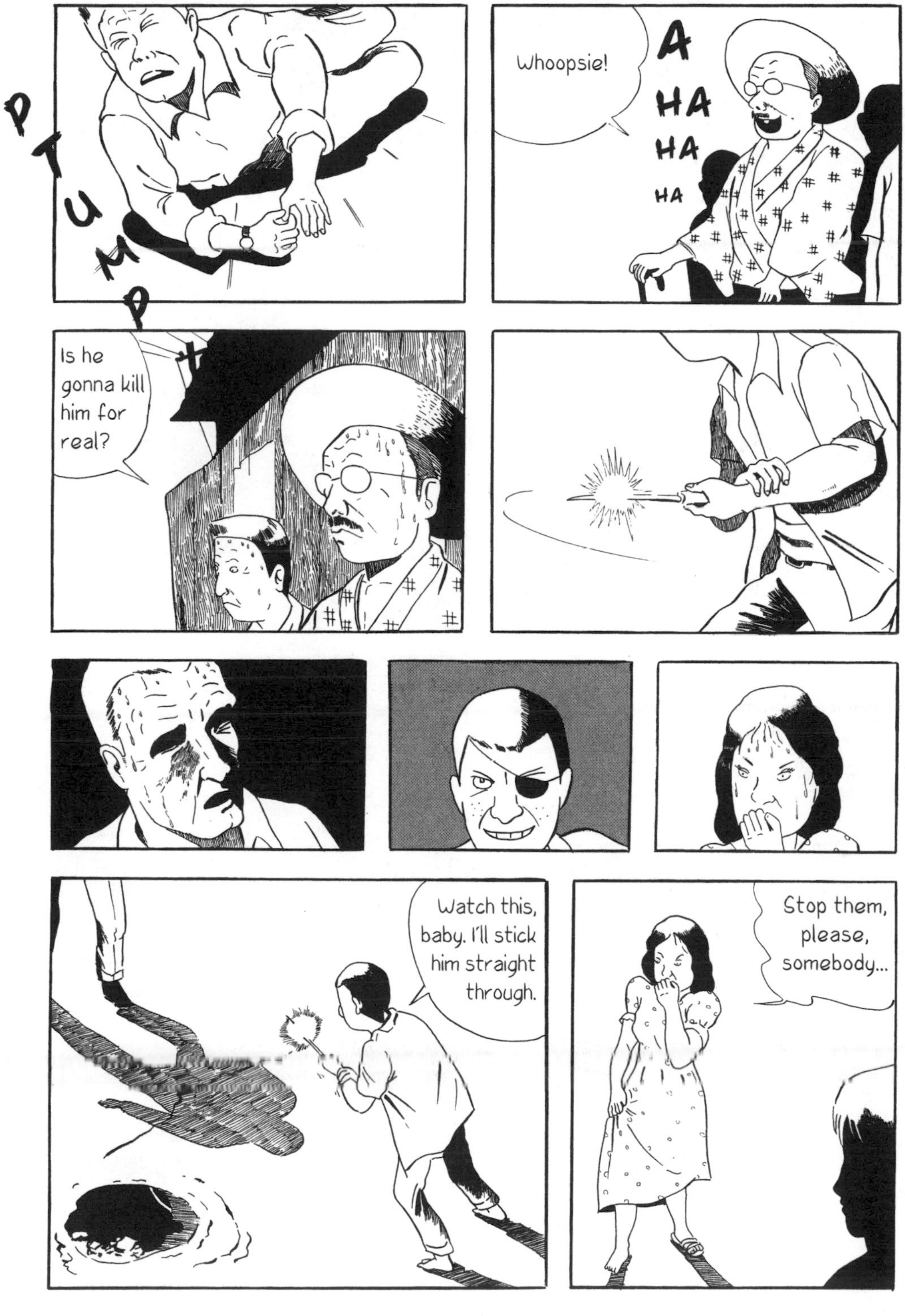
PTUMPT
Whoopsie!
A HA HA HA
Is he gonna kill him for real?
Watch this, baby. I'll stick him straight through.
Stop them, please, somebody...

What happened after that?

Nothing, ha ha ha... That was it! He didn't go through with it...

Ah man, that's it?

That can't be the end.

Don't tell me... The police again?

Yup, the police again...

How-ever

This time it wasn't me. The police really did show up.

Run!

As far as you can! Run!

Don't let them catch you! Don't ever come back!

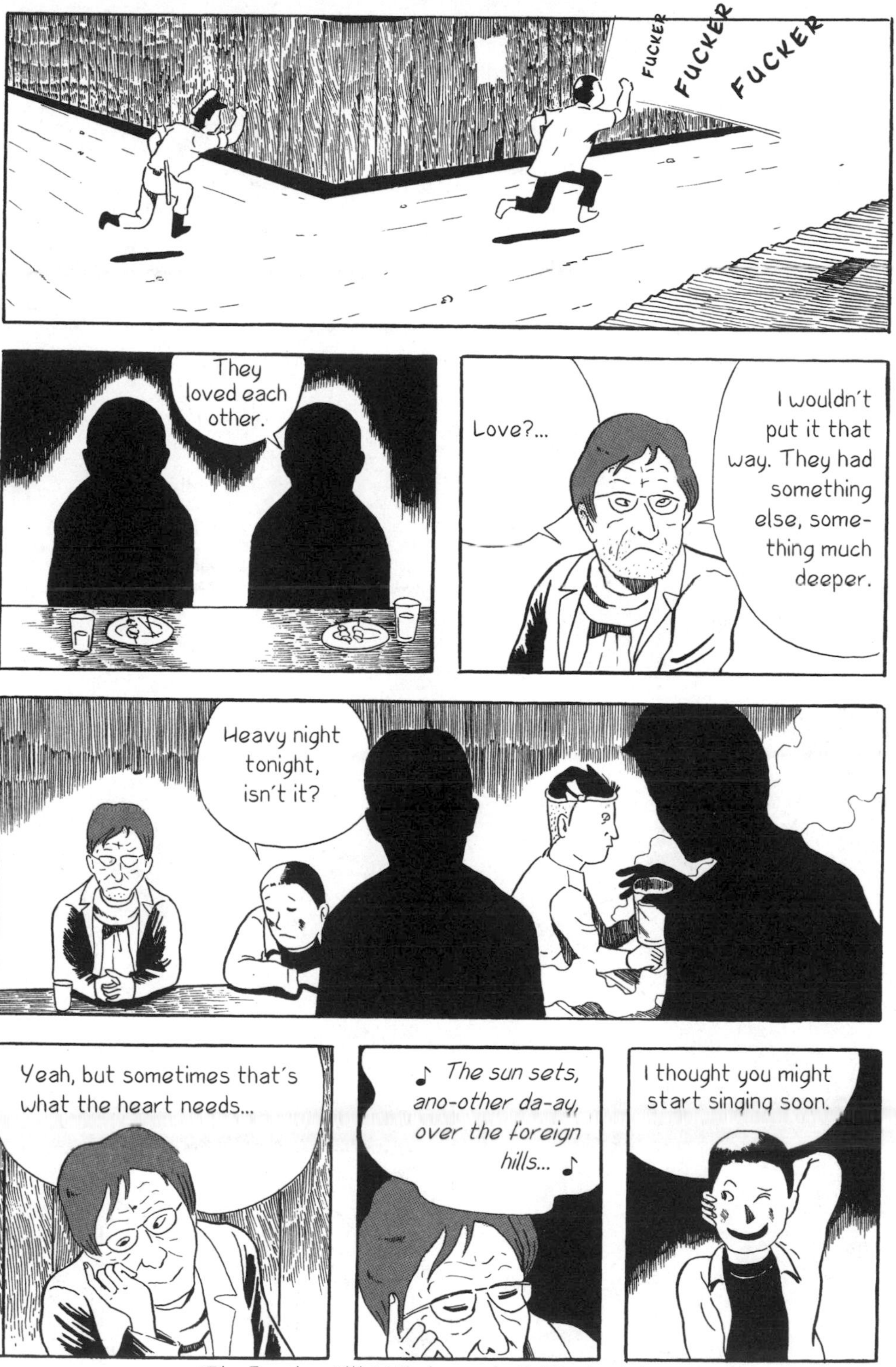
FUCKER
FUCKER
FUCKER
They loved each other.
Love?...
I wouldn't put it that way. They had something else, something much deeper.
Heavy night tonight, isn't it?
Yeah, but sometimes that's what the heart needs...
♪ The sun sets, ano-other da-ay, over the foreign hills... ♪
I thought you might start singing soon.

song: "The Foreign Hills" (Ikoku no oka, 1948), about Japanese POWs in Siberia

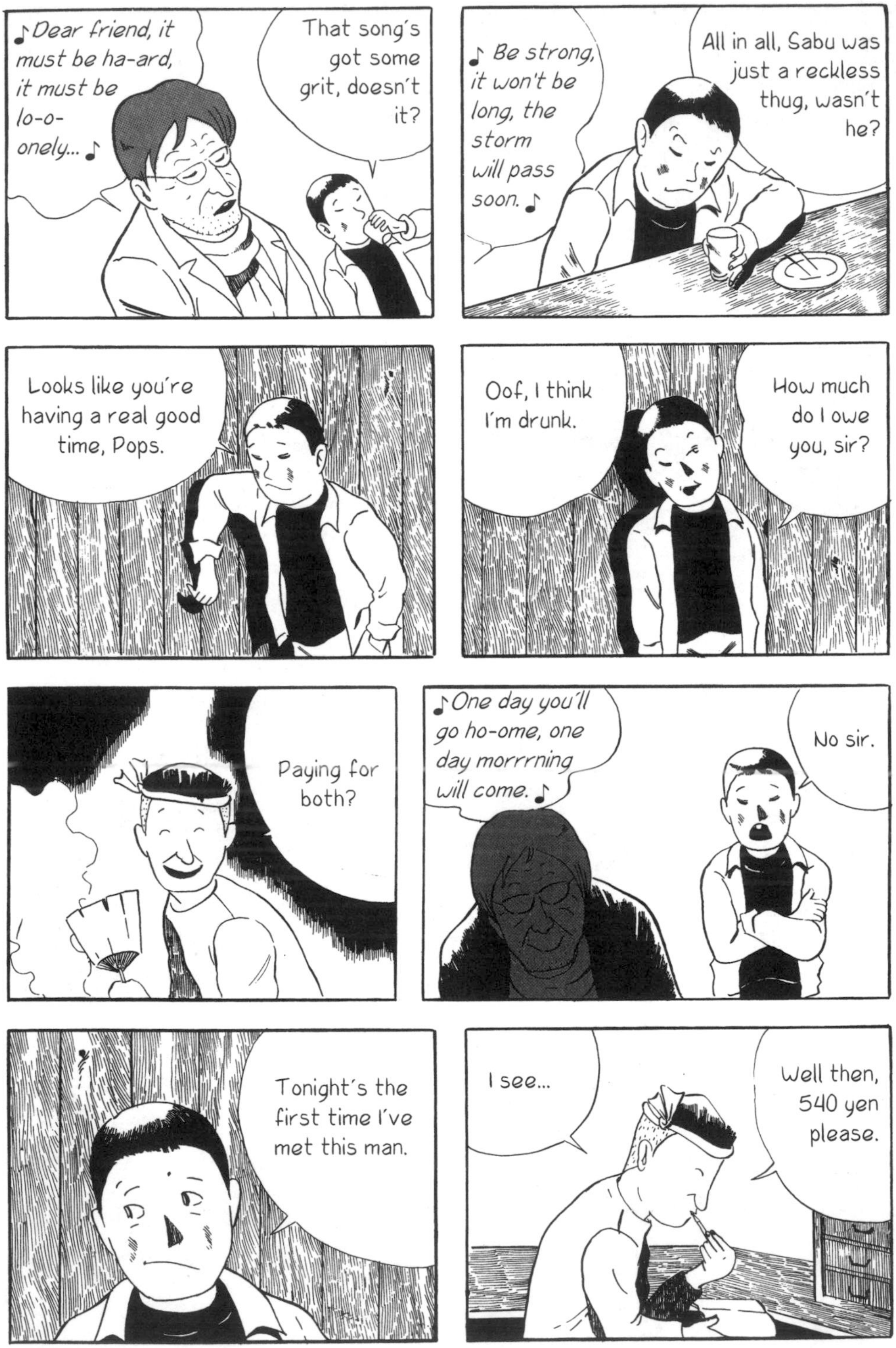
♪Dear friend, it must be ha-ard, it must be lo-o-onely... ♪
That song's got some grit, doesn't it?
♪ Be strong, it won't be long, the storm will pass soon. ♪
All in all, Sabu was just a reckless thug, wasn't he?
Looks like you're having a real good time, Pops.
Oof, I think I'm drunk.
How much do I owe you, sir?
Paying for both?
♪One day you'll go ho-ome, one day morrrning will come. ♪
No sir.
Tonight's the first time I've met this man.
I see...
Well then, 540 yen please.

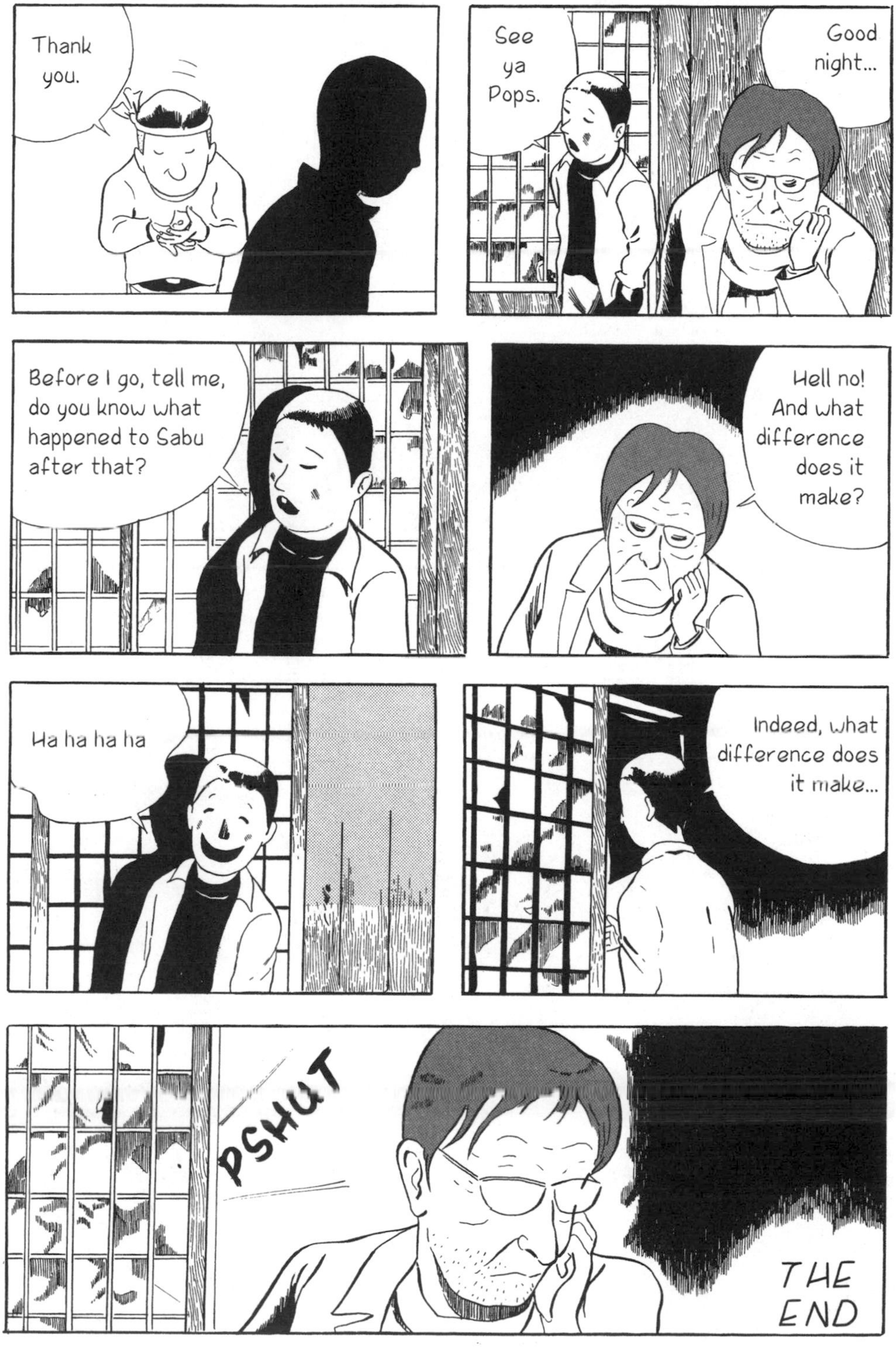
Thank you.
See ya Pops.
Good night...
Before I go, tell me, do you know what happened to Sabu after that?
Hell no! And what difference does it make?
Ha ha ha ha
Indeed, what difference does it make...
PSHUT
THE END

THE FLIGHT
OF
RYOKICHI AOGISHI

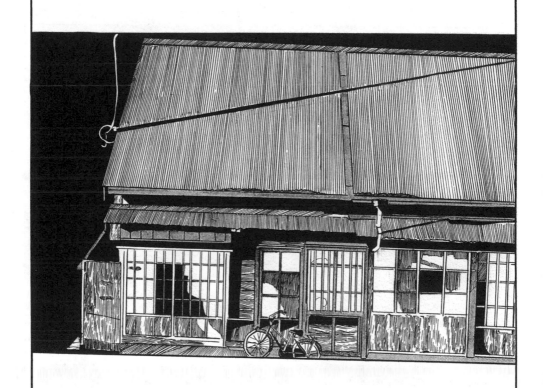

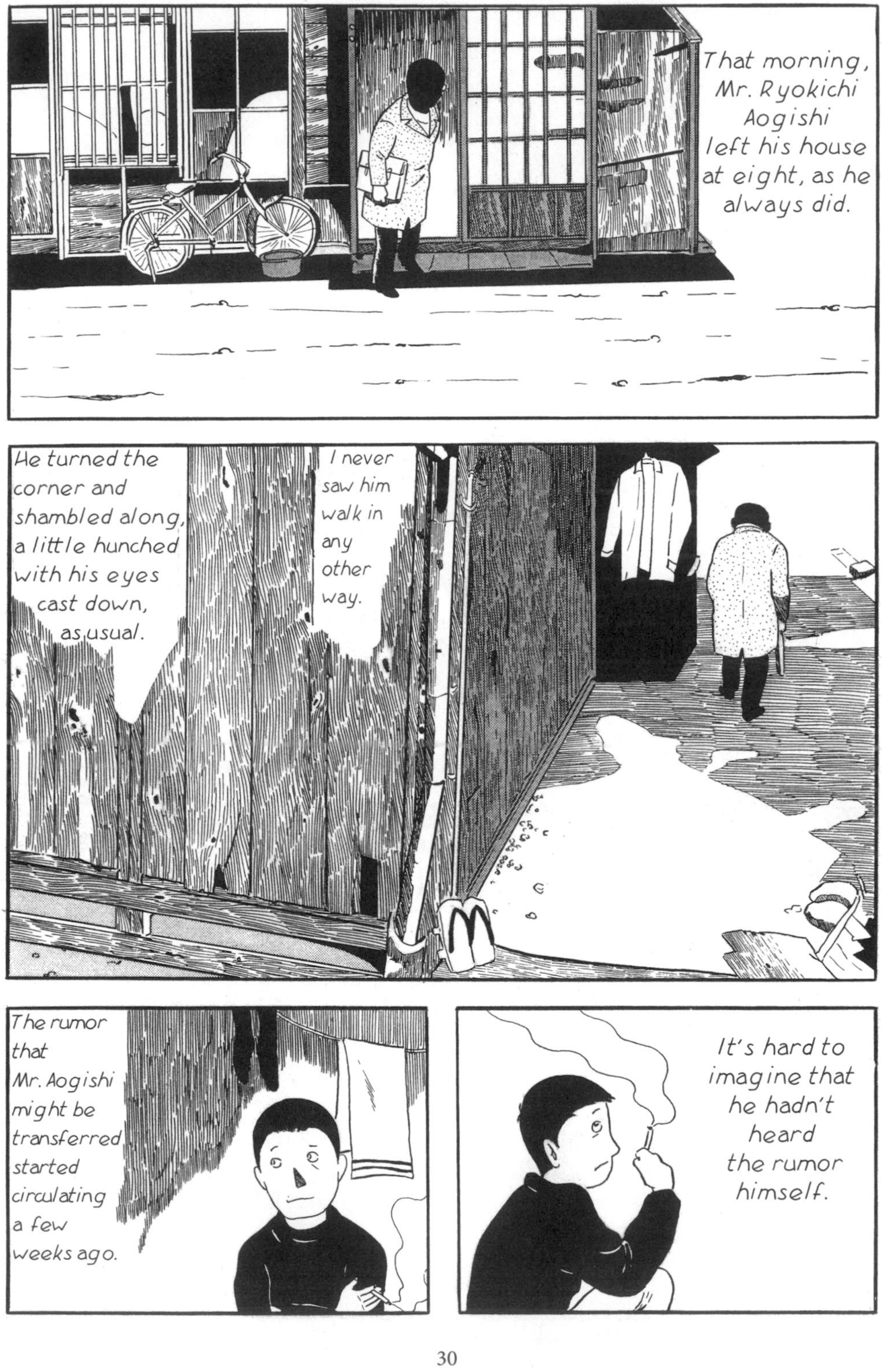
That morning, Mr. Ryokichi Aogishi left his house at eight, as he always did.
He turned the corner and shambled along, a little hunched with his eyes cast down, as usual.
I never saw him walk in any other way.
The rumor that Mr. Aogishi might be transferred started circulating a few weeks ago.
It's hard to imagine that he hadn't heard the rumor himself.

But he didn't seem fazed at all... I'll give him credit for that.

I should have a photo some- where...

Let's see, where is he...

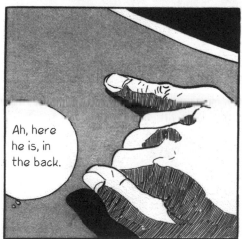

Ah, here he is, in the back.

Supervisor, Business Sales, Cosmetics Company, seventeen years' service

Forty-six years old

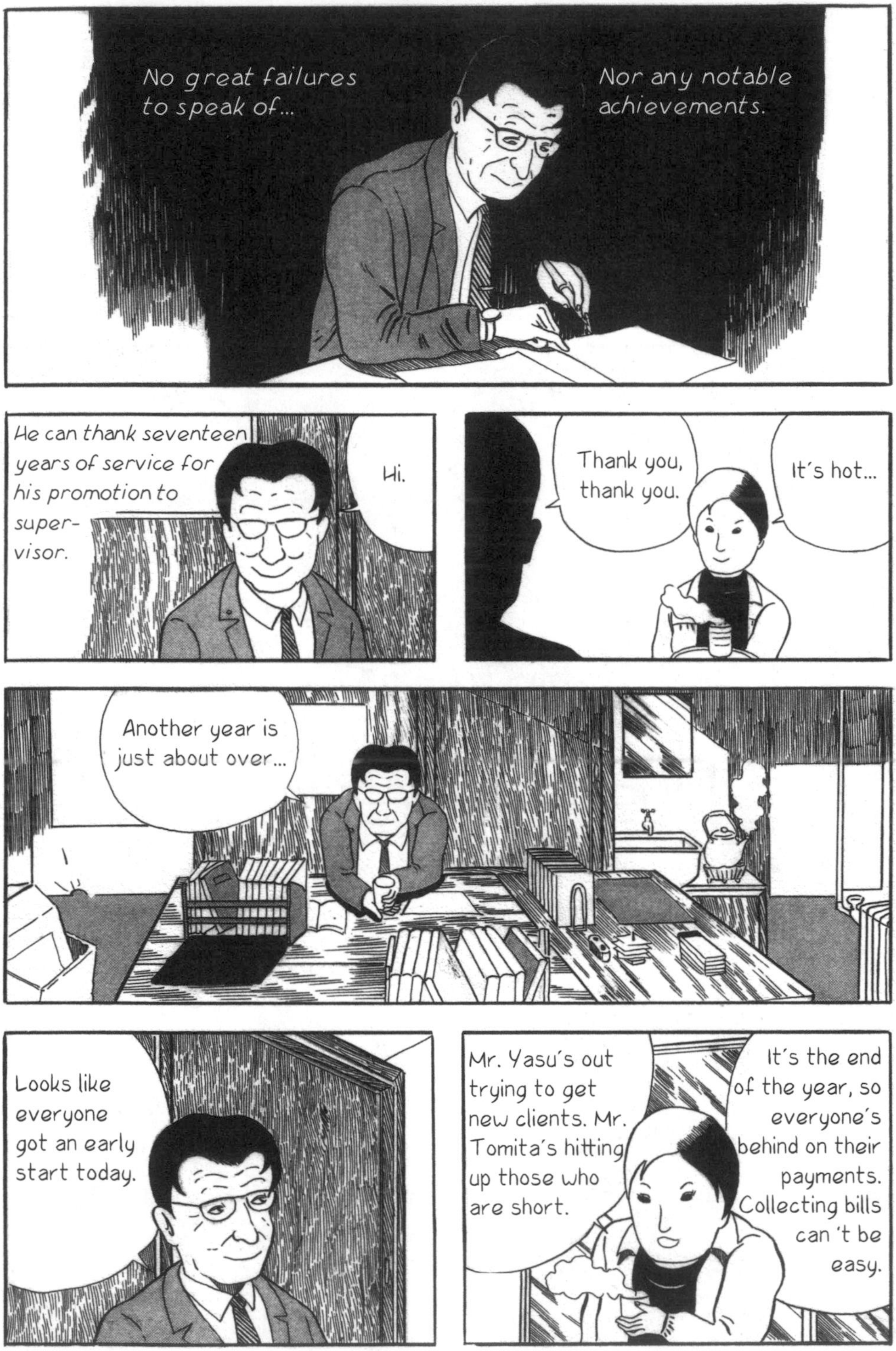
No great failures to speak of...
Nor any notable achievements.
He can thank seventeen years of service for his promotion to super-visor.
Hi.
Thank you, thank you.
It's hot...
Another year is just about over...
Looks like everyone got an early start today.
Mr. Yasu's out trying to get new clients. Mr. Tomita's hitting up those who are short.
It's the end of the year, so everyone's behind on their payments. Collecting bills can 't be easy.

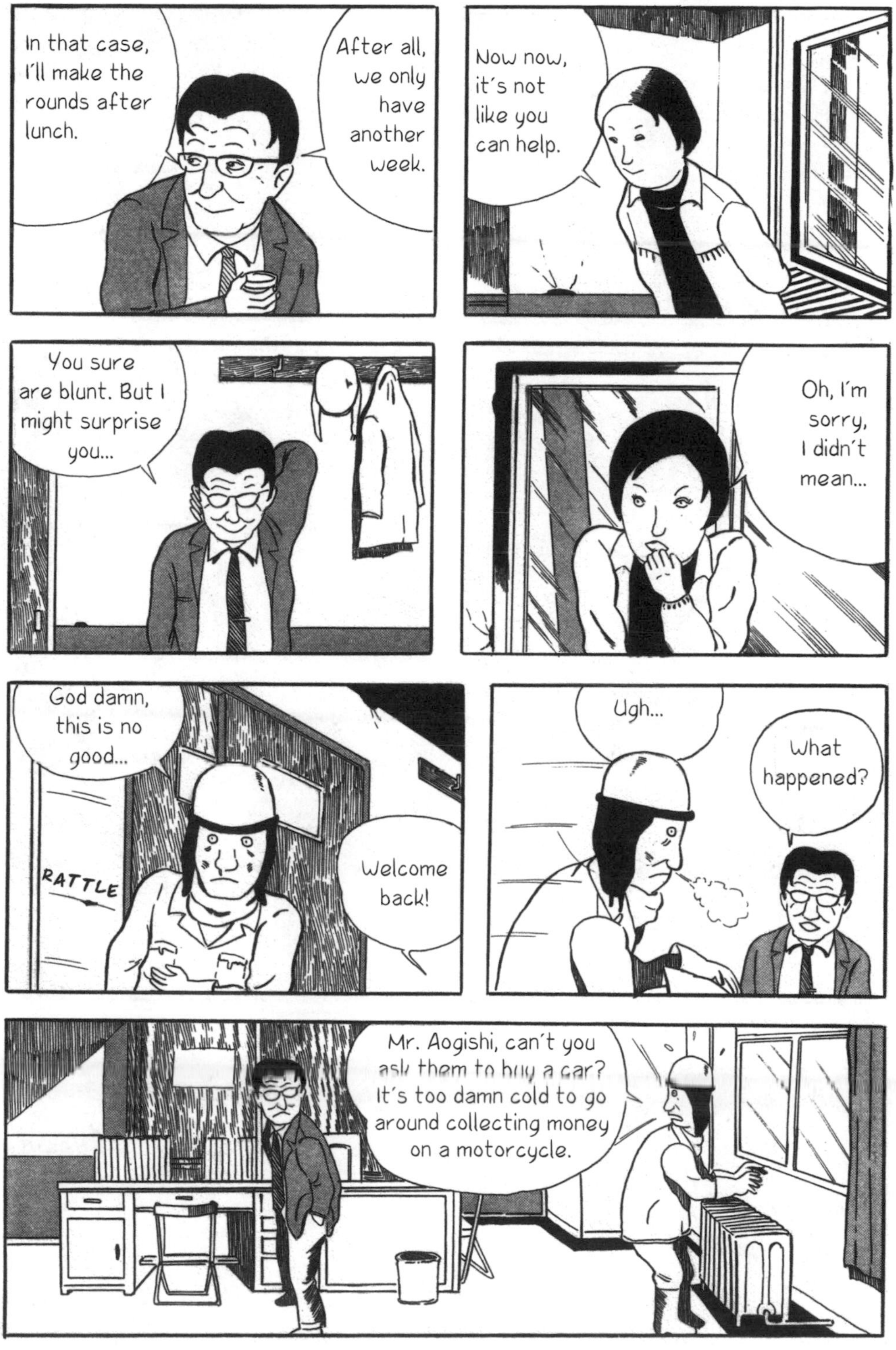
In that case, I'll make the rounds after lunch.
After all, we only have another week.
Now now, it's not like you can help.
You sure are blunt. But I might surprise you...
Oh, I'm sorry, I didn't mean...
God damn, this is no good...
RATTLE
Welcome back!
Ugh...
What happened?
Mr. Aogishi, can't you ask them to buy a car? It's too damn cold to go around collecting money on a motorcycle.

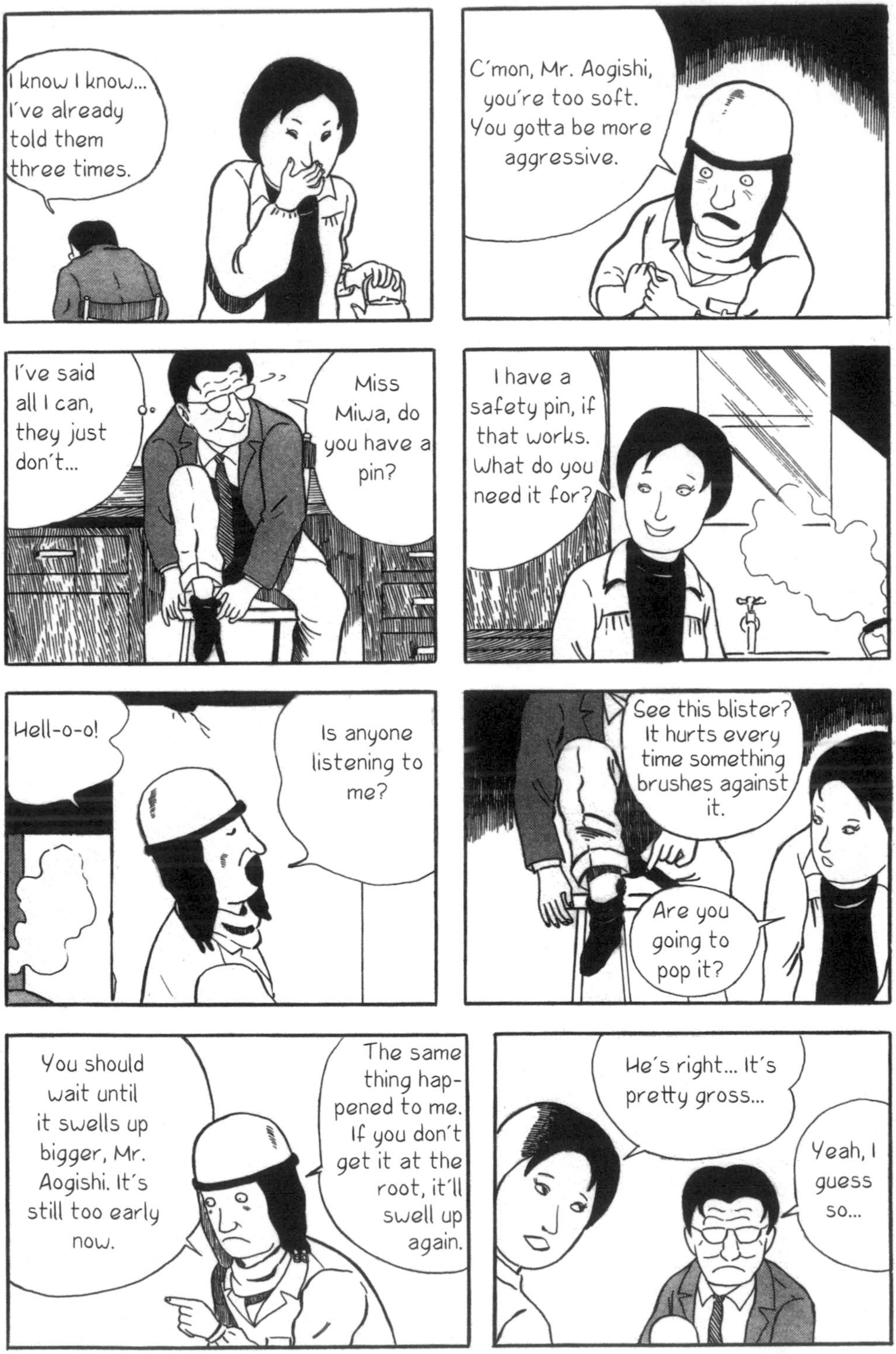
I know I know...
I've already told them three times.
C'mon, Mr. Aogishi, you're too soft. You gotta be more aggressive.
I've said all I can, they just don't...
Miss Miwa, do you have a pin?
I have a safety pin, if that works. What do you need it for?
Hell-o-o!
Is anyone listening to me?
See this blister? It hurts every time something brushes against it.
Are you going to pop it?
You should wait until it swells up bigger, Mr. Aogishi. It's still too early now.
The same thing happened to me. If you don't get it at the root, it'll swell up again.
He's right... It's pretty gross...
Yeah, I guess so...

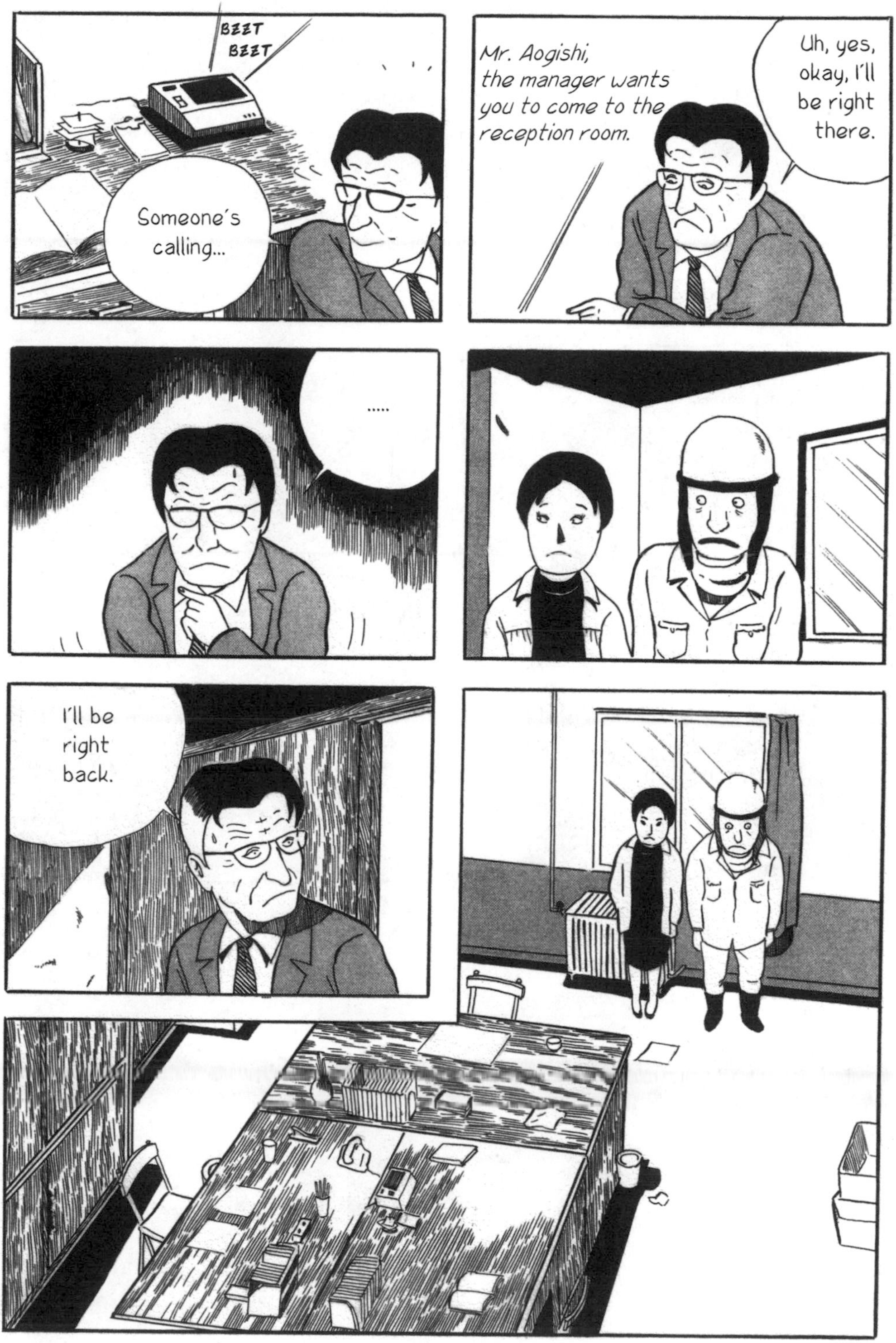
BZZT
BZZT
Someone's calling...
Mr. Aogishi, the manager wants you to come to the reception room.
Uh, yes, okay, I'll be right there.
.....
I'll be right back.

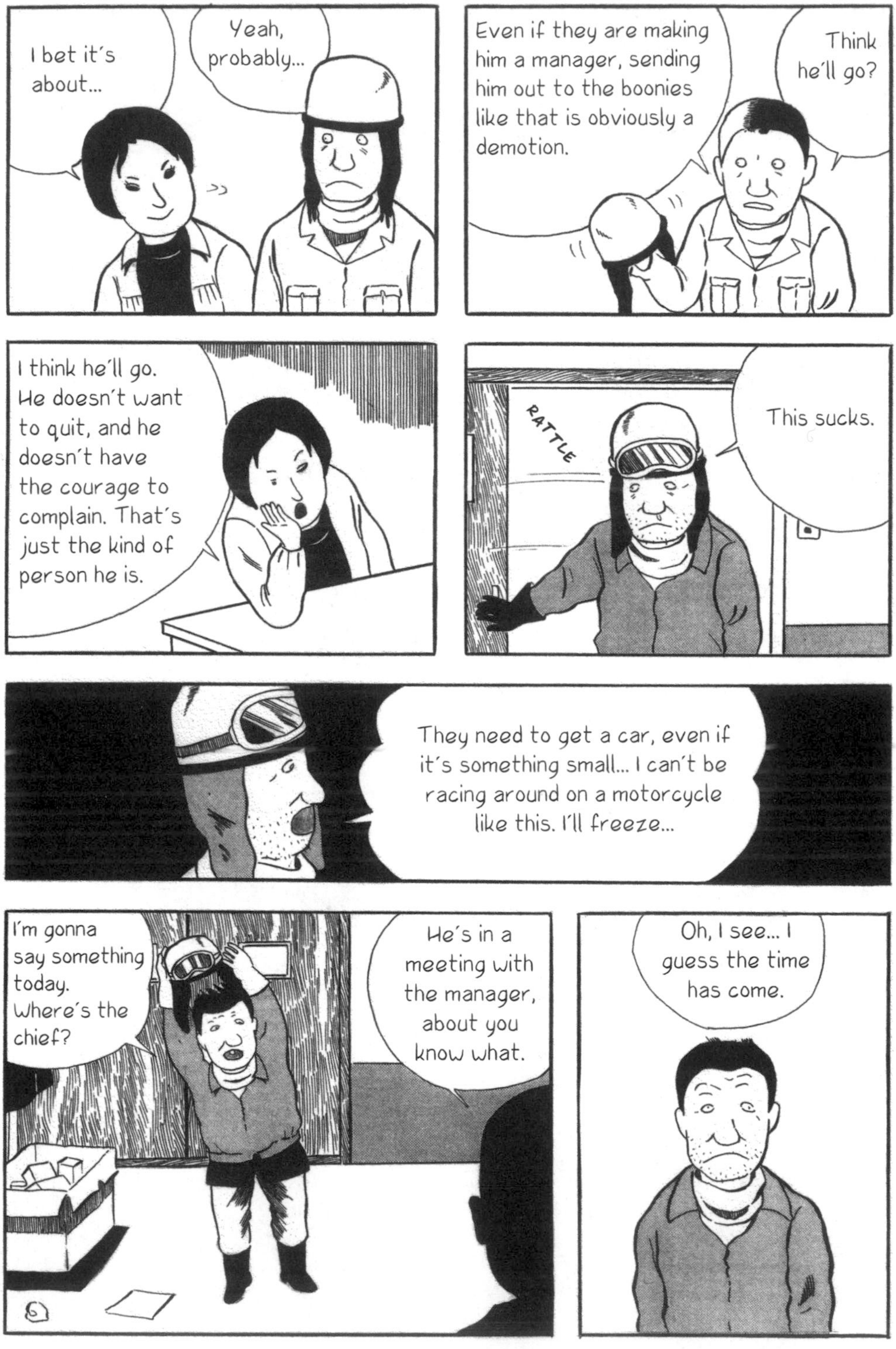
I bet it's about...
Yeah, probably...
Even if they are making him a manager, sending him out to the boonies like that is obviously a demotion.
Think he'll go?
I think he'll go. He doesn't want to quit, and he doesn't have the courage to complain. That's just the kind of person he is.
RATTLE
This sucks.
They need to get a car, even if it's something small... I can't be racing around on a motorcycle like this. I'll freeze...
I'm gonna say something today. Where's the chief?
He's in a meeting with the manager, about you know what.
Oh, I see... I guess the time has come.

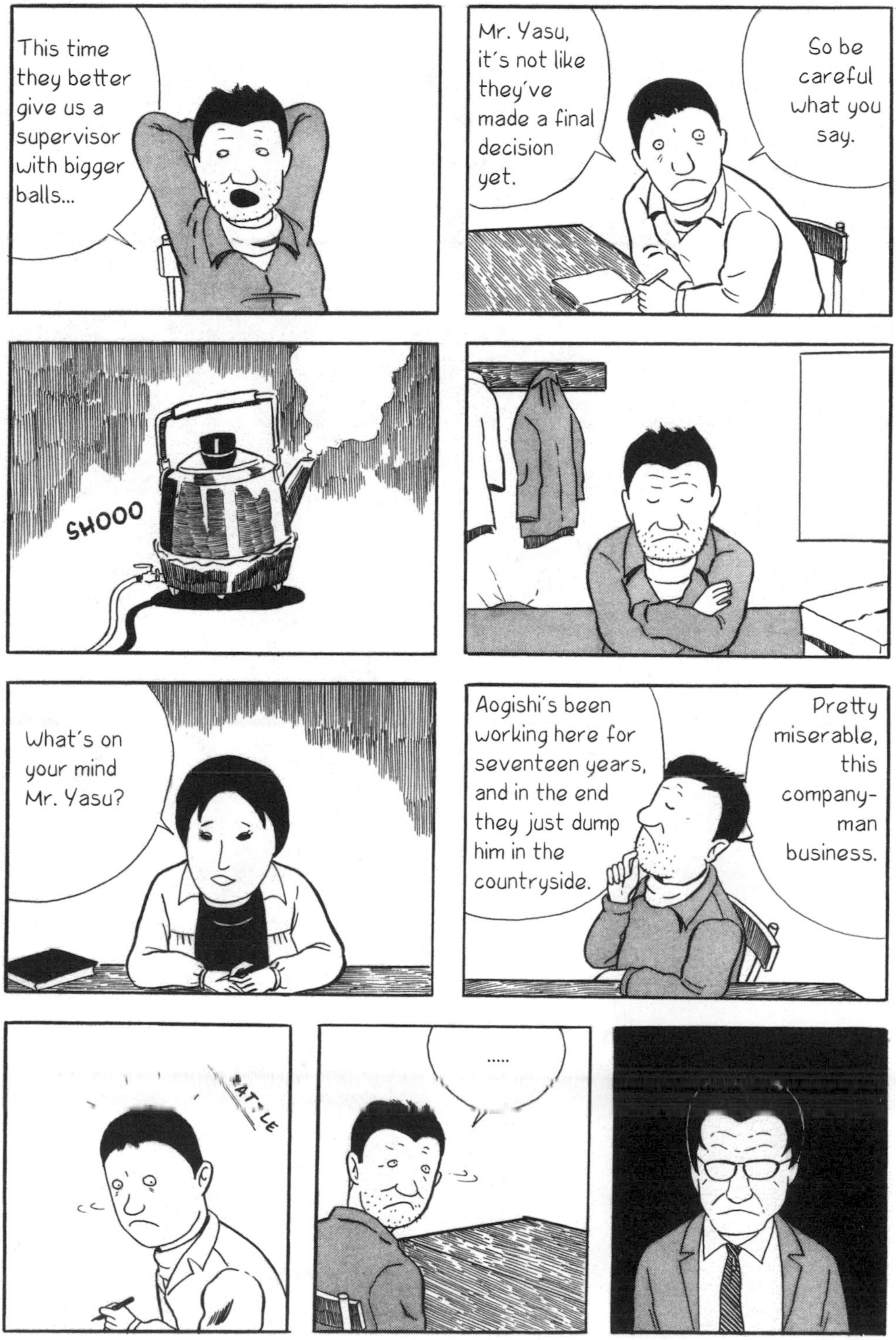
This time they better give us a supervisor with bigger balls...
Mr. Yasu, it's not like they've made a final decision yet.
So be careful what you say.
SHOOO
What's on your mind Mr. Yasu?
Aogishi's been working here for seventeen years, and in the end they just dump him in the countryside.
Pretty miserable, this company-man business.
.....

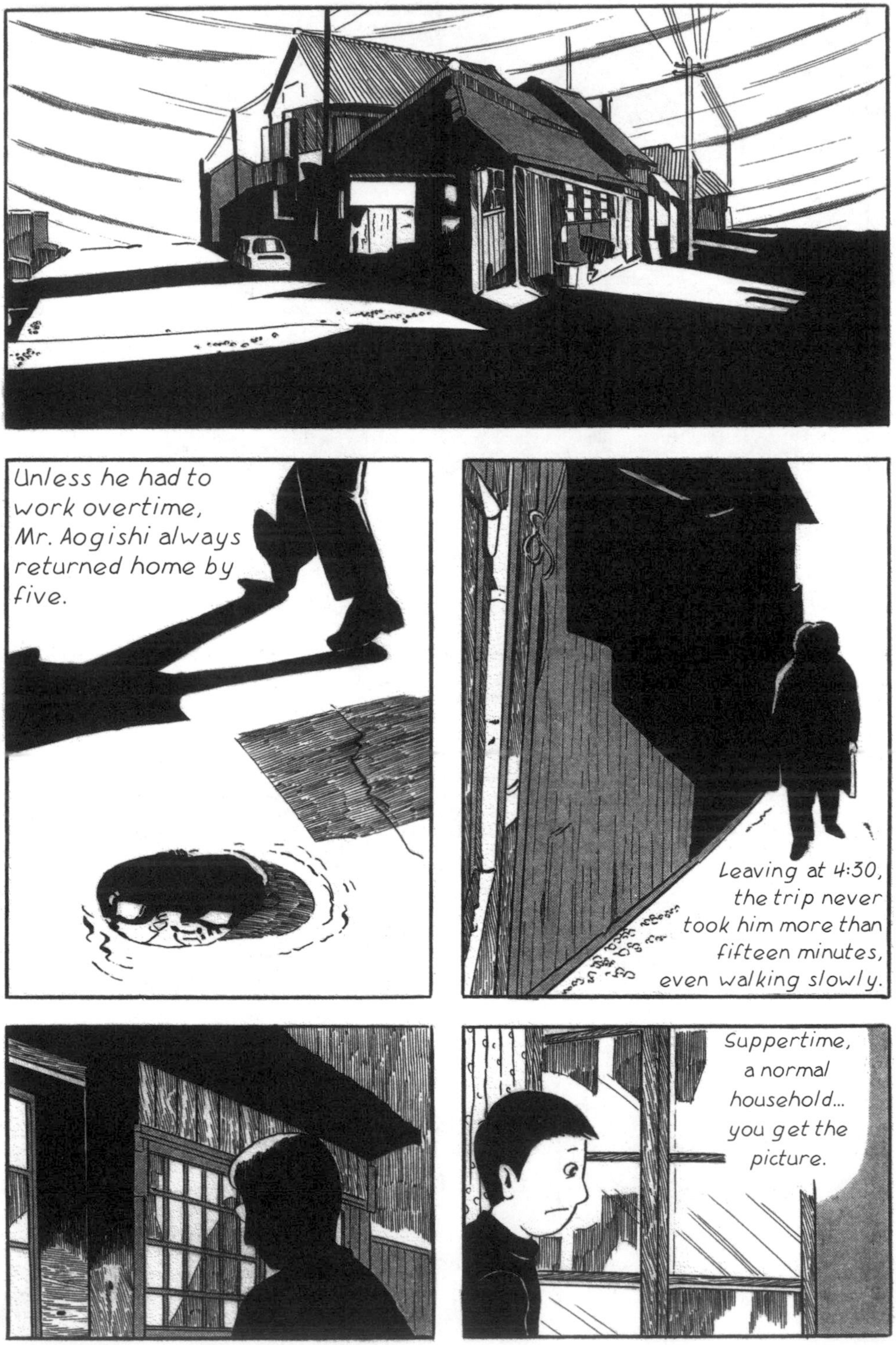
Unless he had to work overtime, Mr. Aogishi always returned home by five.
Leaving at 4:30, the trip never took him more than fifteen minutes, even walking slowly.
Suppertime, a normal household... you get the picture.

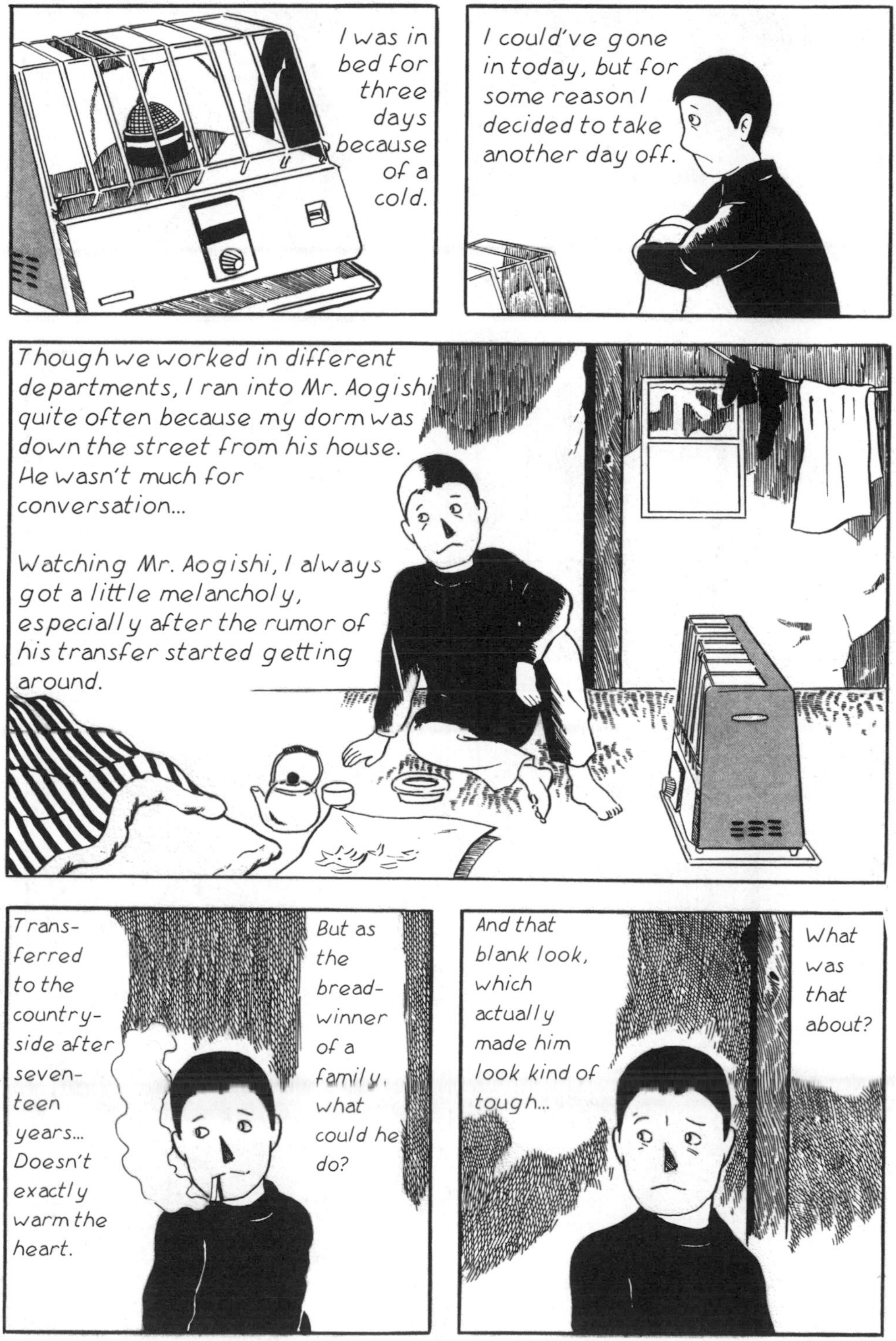

I was in bed for three days because of a cold.
I could've gone in today, but for some reason I decided to take another day off.
Though we worked in different departments, I ran into Mr. Aogishi quite often because my dorm was down the street from his house. He wasn't much for conversation...
Watching Mr. Aogishi, I always got a little melancholy, especially after the rumor of his transfer started getting around.
Trans-ferred to the country-side after seven-teen years... Doesn't exactly warm the heart.
But as the bread-winner of a family, what could he do?
And that blank look, which actually made him look kind of tough...
What was that about?

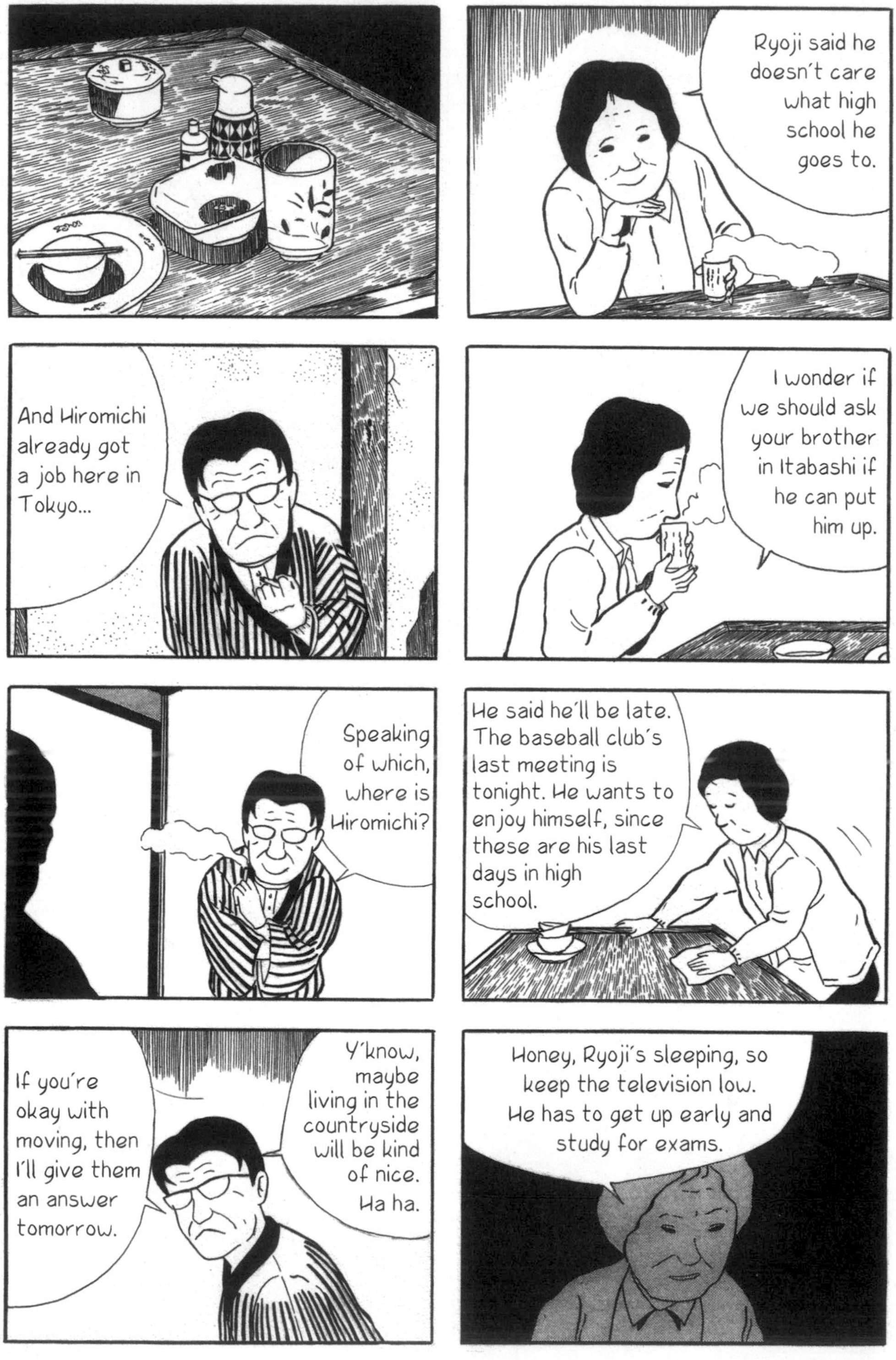
Ryoji said he doesn't care what high school he goes to.
And Hiromichi already got a job here in Tokyo...
I wonder if we should ask your brother in Itabashi if he can put him up.
Speaking of which, where is Hiromichi?
He said he'll be late. The baseball club's last meeting is tonight. He wants to enjoy himself, since these are his last days in high school.
If you're okay with moving, then I'll give them an answer tomorrow.
Y'know, maybe living in the countryside will be kind of nice. Ha ha.
Honey, Ryoji's sleeping, so keep the television low. He has to get up early and study for exams.

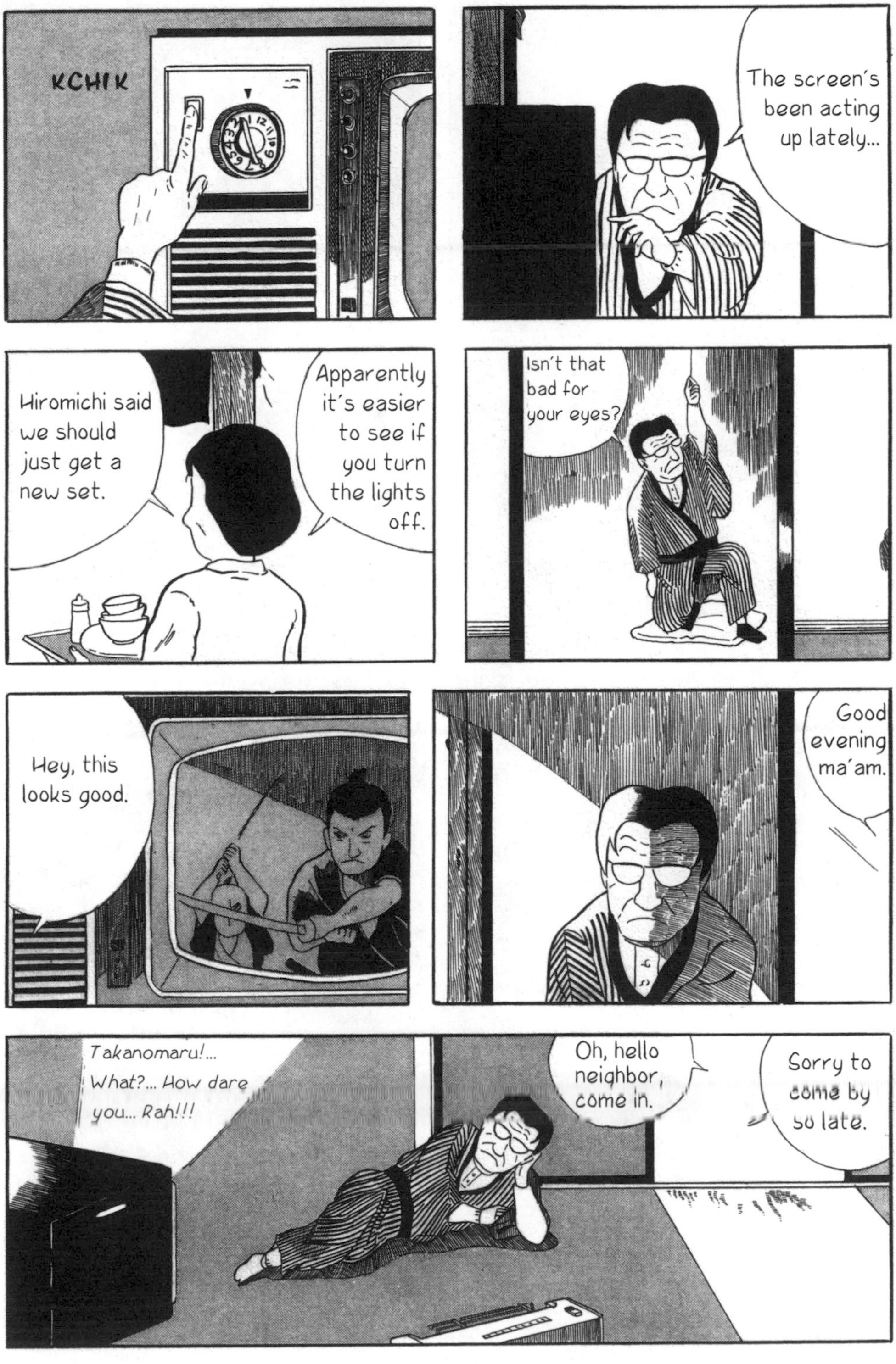
KCHIK
The screen's been acting up lately...
Hiromichi said we should just get a new set.
Apparently it's easier to see if you turn the lights off.
Isn't that bad for your eyes?
Hey, this looks good.
Good evening ma'am.
Takanomaru!... What?... How dare you... Rah!!!
Oh, hello neighbor, come in.
Sorry to come by so late.

Now you've done it...

ZZZ

ZZZ

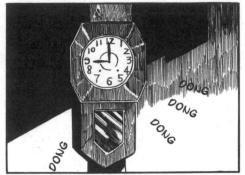

DONG

DONG

DONG

DONG

And then like this? Oh, I see...

Then through the fifth one... right, like that.

私達の昭和

第二次世界大戦

OUR SHOWA ERA

World War II

9:00

Sorry I stayed so late.

I feel bad about not saying hi to your husband.

Please give him my regards.

Sure sure, see you later.

Sorry honey... Oh!

Honey, you'll catch a cold dozing off like that!

Huh? Wha?

I fell asleep?

How embarrassing...

I'm going to check on the bath...

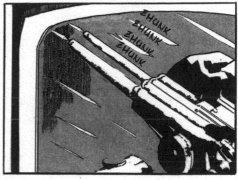

ZHUNK
ZHUNK
ZHUNK
ZHUNK

By 1945, an already dire situation had become even worse, and pounded Japan like a tsunami...

Giant B-29s rained bombs upon Tokyo...

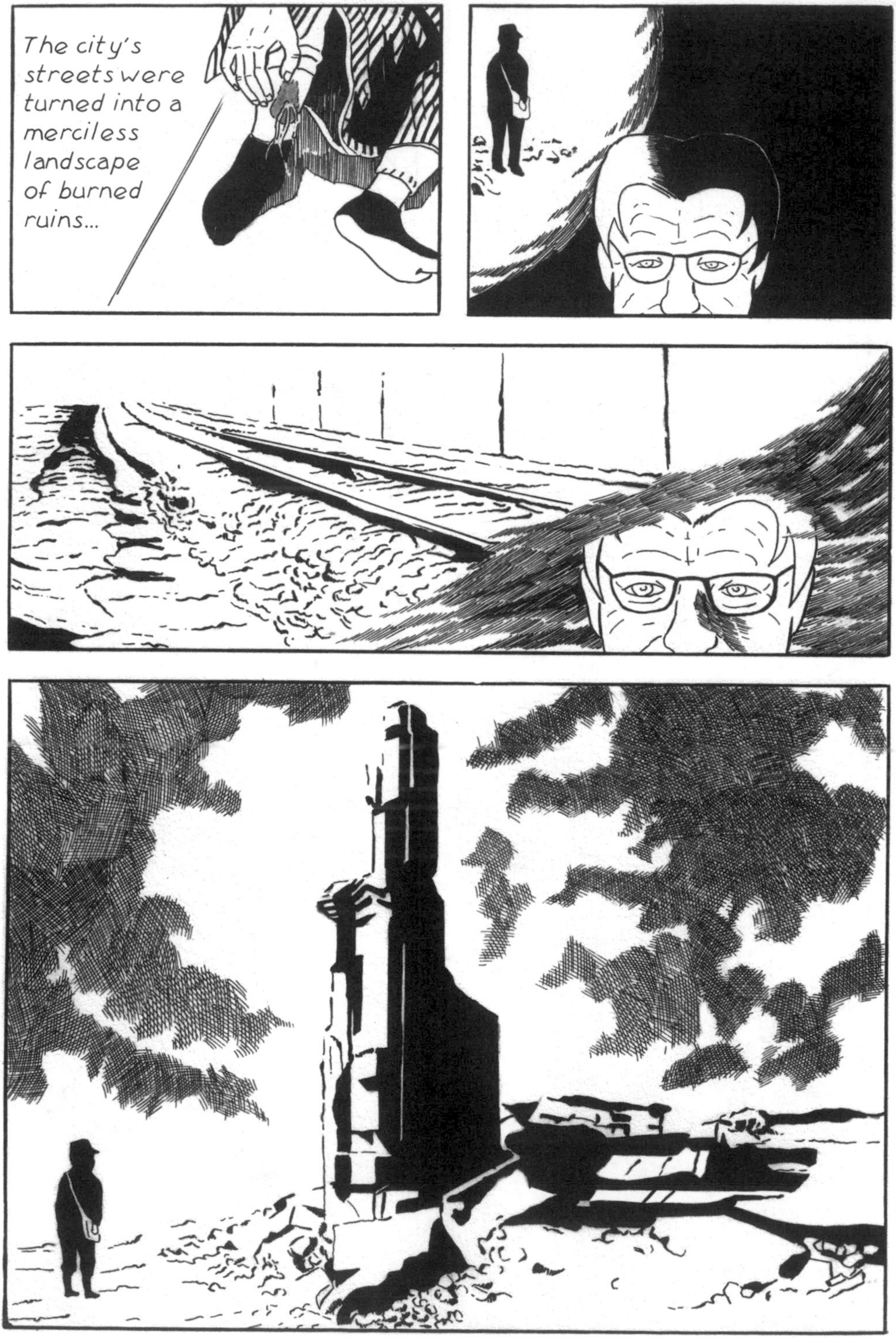
The city's streets were turned into a merciless landscape of burned ruins...

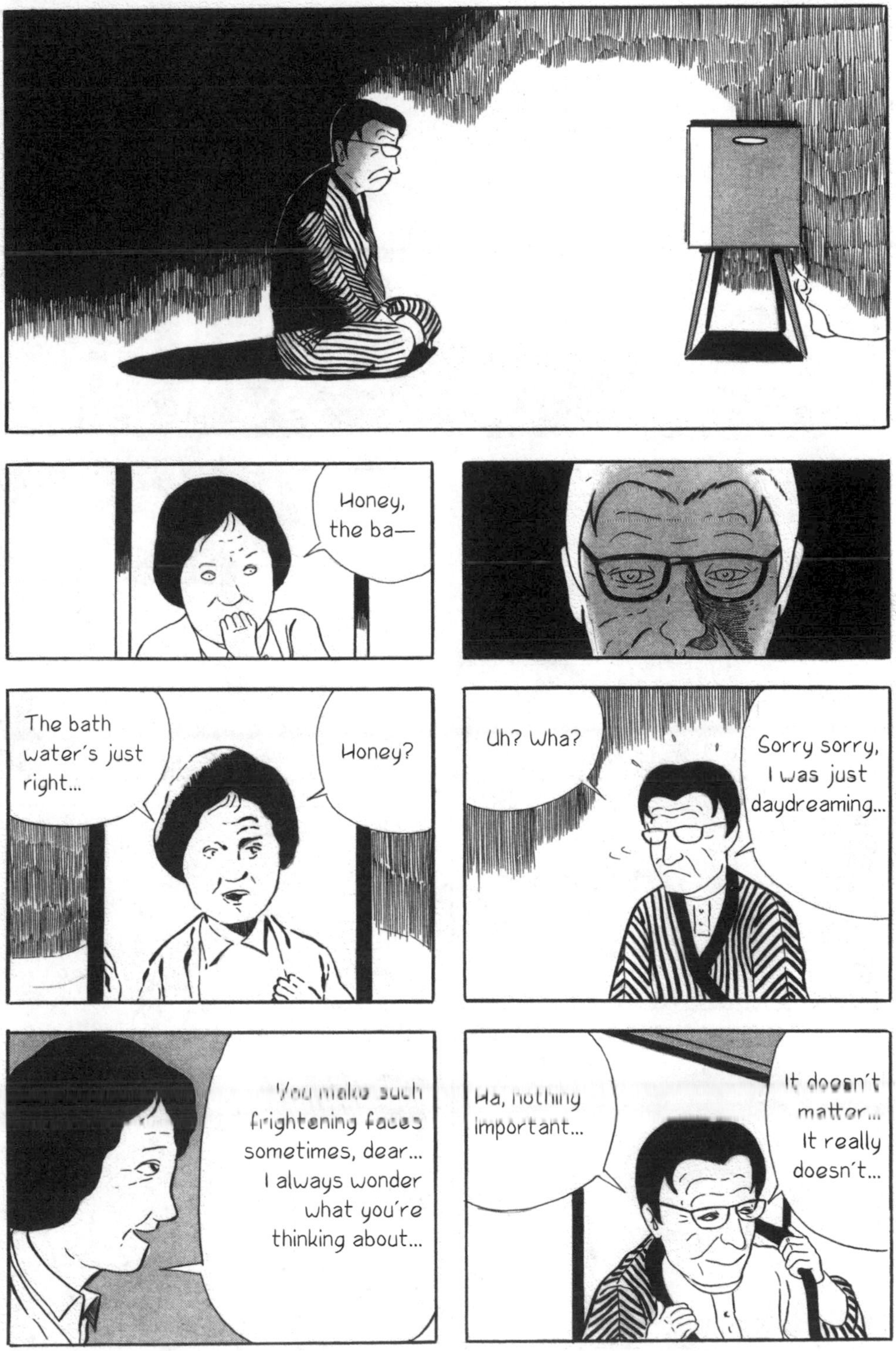
Honey, the ba—
The bath water's just right...
Honey?
Uh? Wha?
Sorry sorry, I was just daydreaming...
You make such frightening faces sometimes, dear... I always wonder what you're thinking about...
Ha, nothing important...
It doesn't matter... It really doesn't...

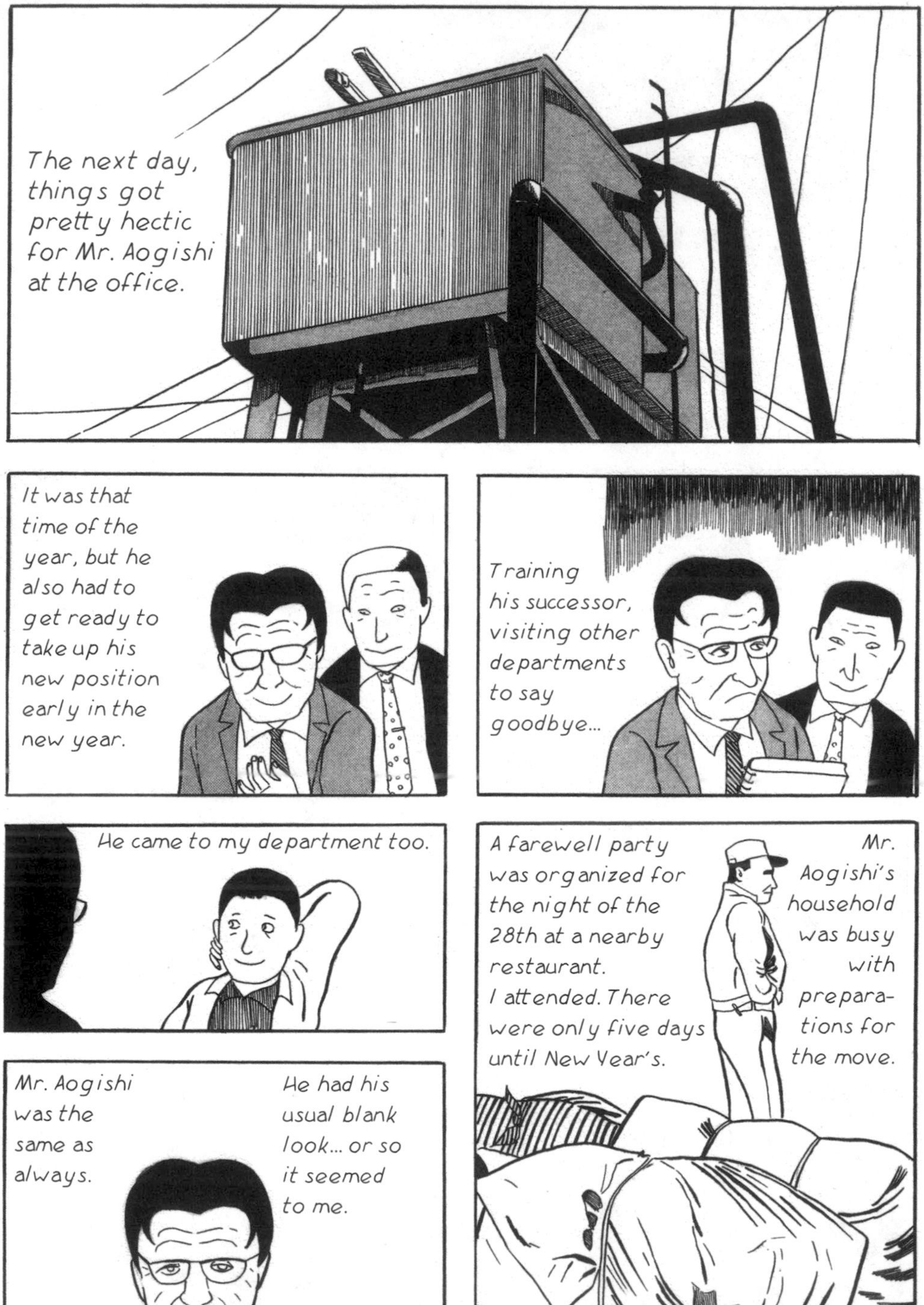
The next day, things got pretty hectic for Mr. Aogishi at the office.
It was that time of the year, but he also had to get ready to take up his new position early in the new year.
Training his successor, visiting other departments to say goodbye...
He came to my department too.
Mr. Aogishi was the same as always.
He had his usual blank look... or so it seemed to me.
A farewell party was organized for the night of the 28th at a nearby restaurant.
I attended. There were only five days until New Year's.
Mr. Aogishi's household was busy with preparations for the move.

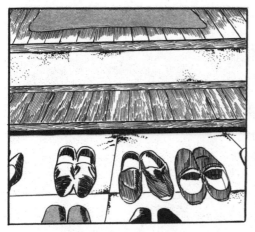

I don't think Mr. Aogishi drank much that night.

Nonetheless, his face was pretty red. I suppose he's a weak drinker.

For a farewell party, this one was really tame.

For the two hours between the plant manager's formulaic greeting and the end of the party...

People chit-chatted about nothing in particular...

I was struck by how out of it Mr. Aogishi looked.

There was no after-party to speak of. Everyone headed home, Mr. Aogishi and I in the same direction.

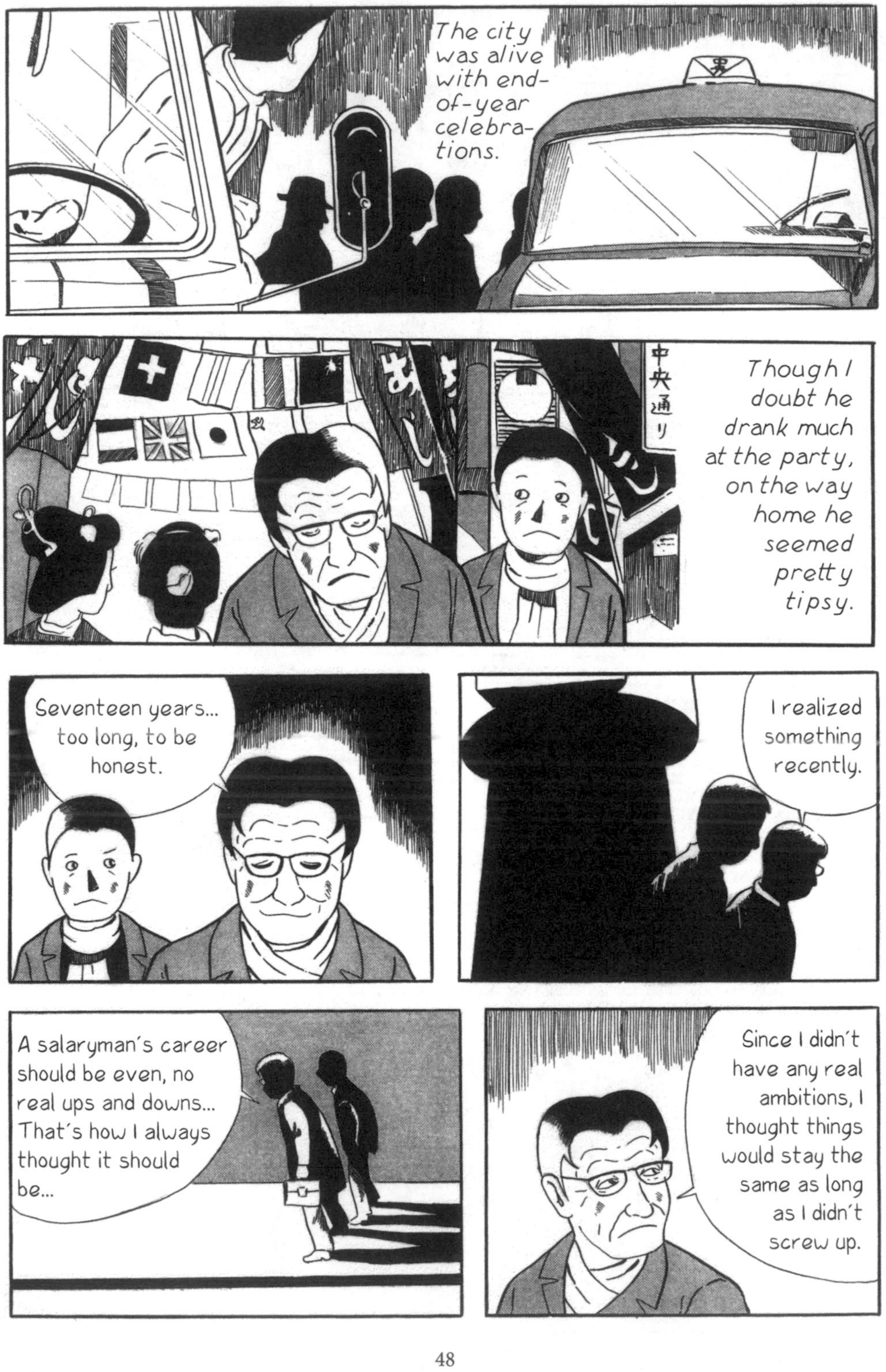
The city was alive with end-of-year celebrations.
中央通り
Though I doubt he drank much at the party, on the way home he seemed pretty tipsy.
Seventeen years... too long, to be honest.
I realized something recently.
A salaryman's career should be even, no real ups and downs... That's how I always thought it should be...
Since I didn't have any real ambitions, I thought things would stay the same as long as I didn't screw up.

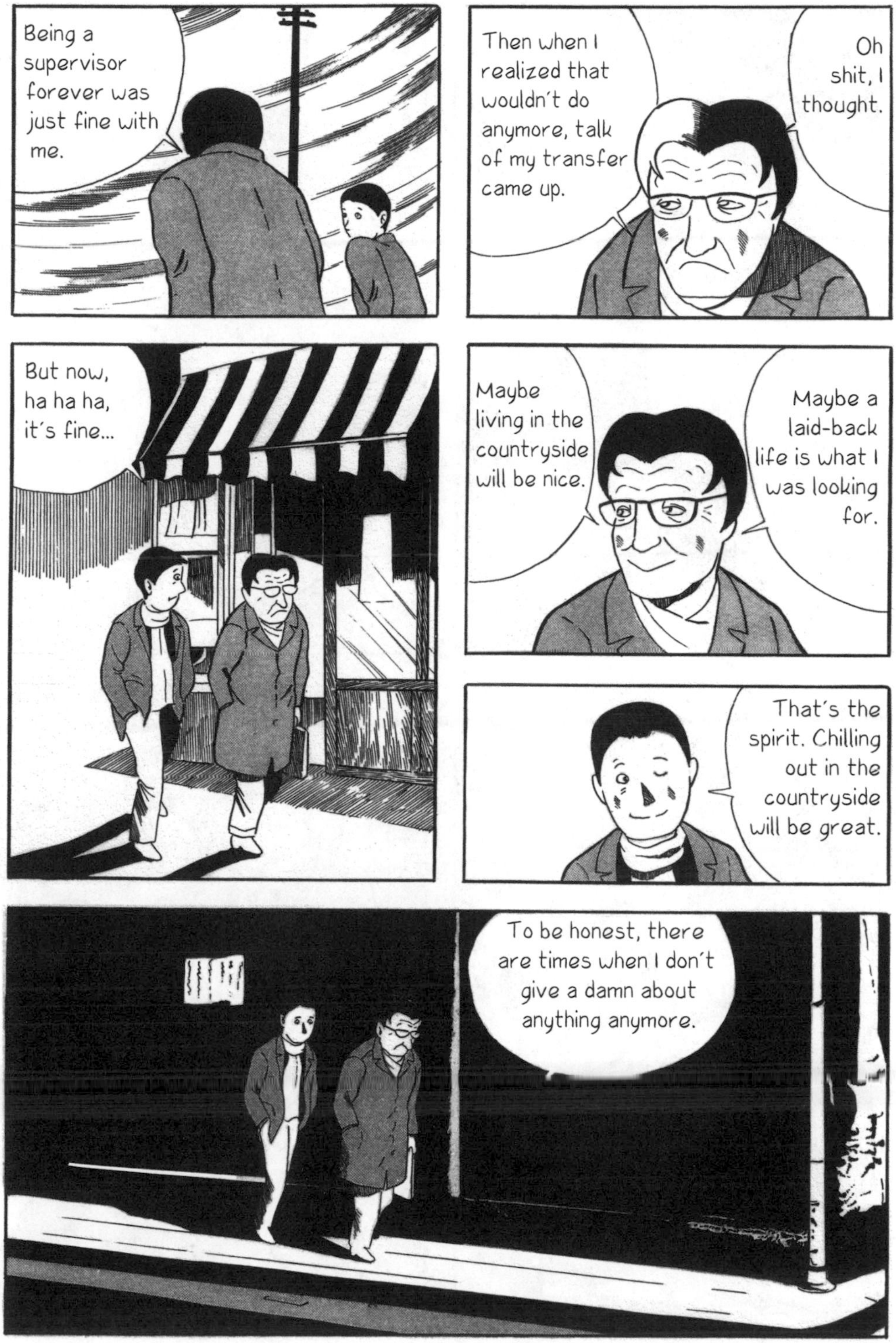
Being a supervisor forever was just fine with me.
Then when I realized that wouldn't do anymore, talk of my transfer came up.
Oh shit, I thought.
But now, ha ha ha, it's fine...
Maybe living in the countryside will be nice.
Maybe a laid-back life is what I was looking for.
That's the spirit. Chilling out in the countryside will be great.
To be honest, there are times when I don't give a damn about anything anymore.

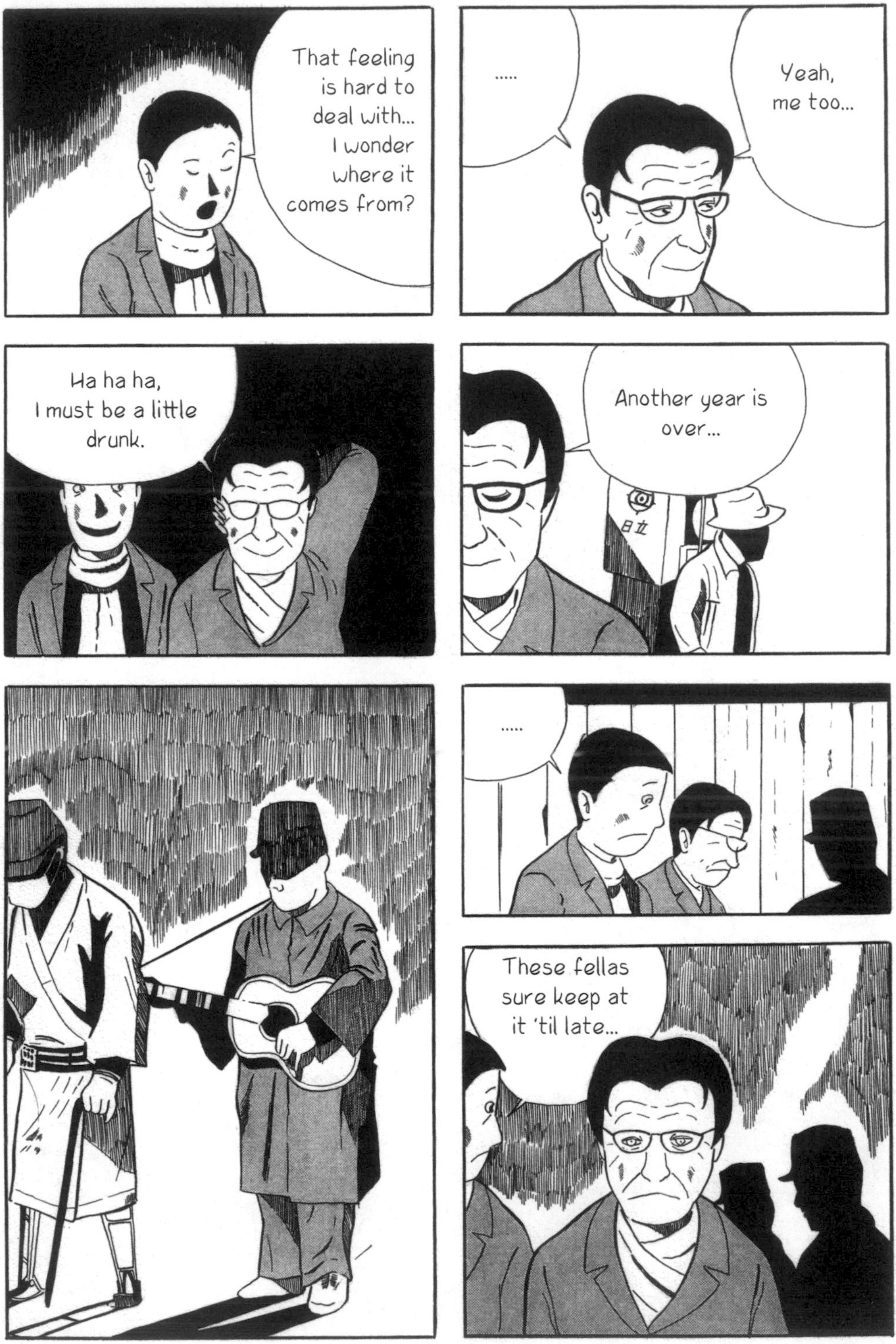
That feeling is hard to deal with... I wonder where it comes from?
.....
Yeah, me too...
Ha ha ha, I must be a little drunk.
Another year is over...
日立
.....
These fellas sure keep at it 'til late...

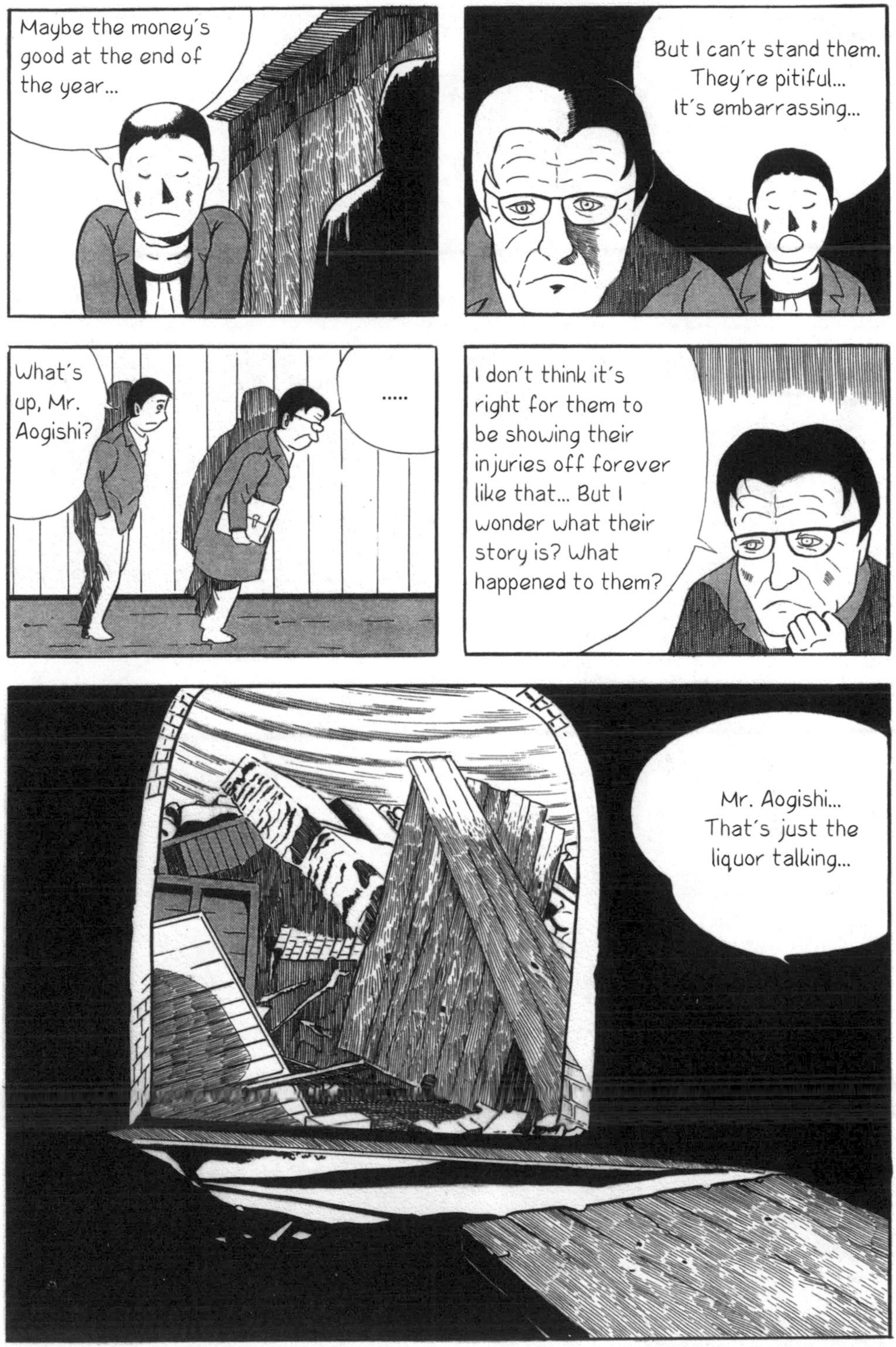
Maybe the money's good at the end of the year...
But I can't stand them. They're pitiful... It's embarrassing...
What's up, Mr. Aogishi?
.....
I don't think it's right for them to be showing their injuries off forever like that... But I wonder what their story is? What happened to them?
Mr. Aogishi... That's just the liquor talking...

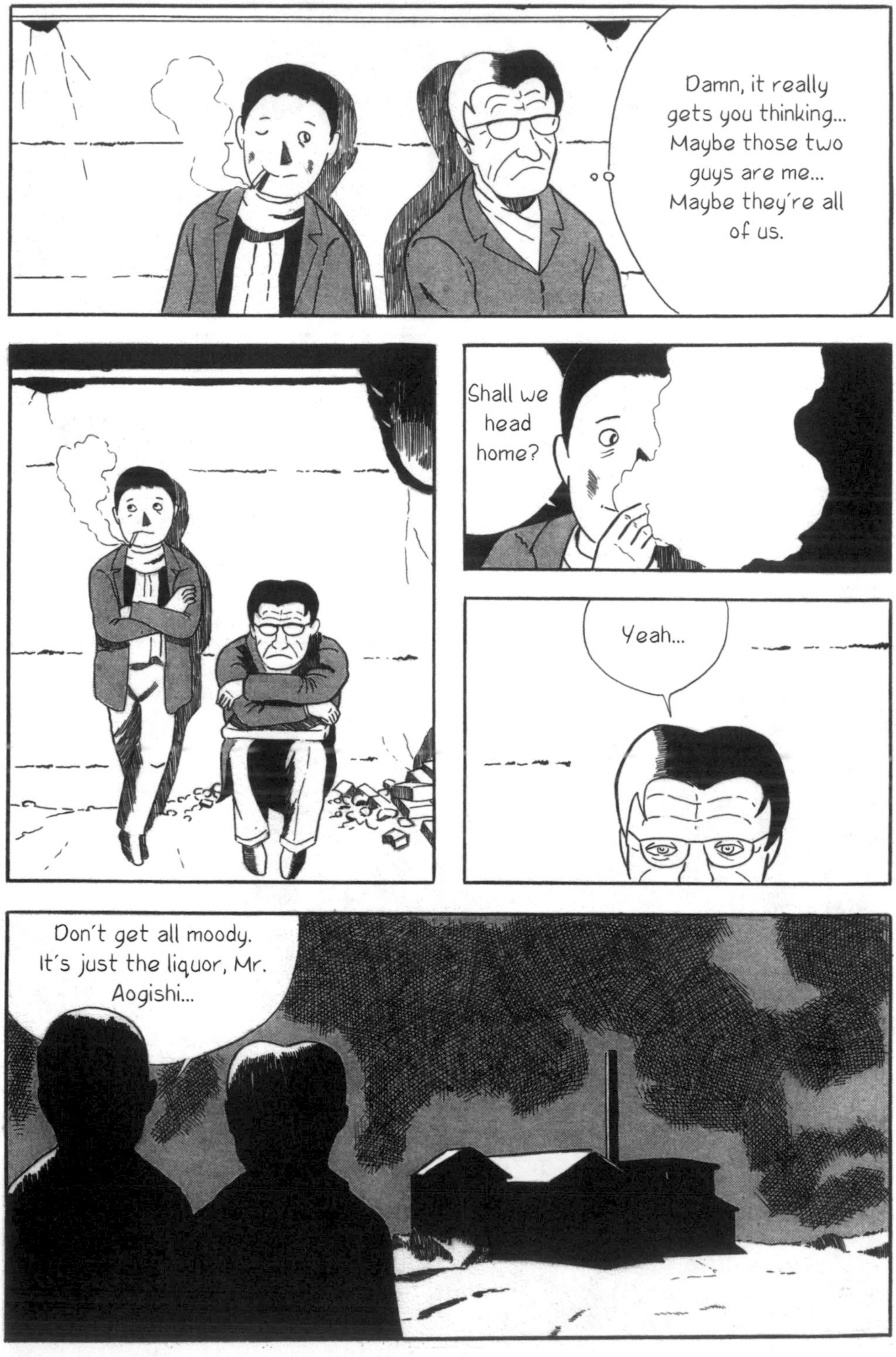
Damn, it really gets you thinking... Maybe those two guys are me... Maybe they're all of us.
Shall we head home?
Yeah...
Don't get all moody. It's just the liquor, Mr. Aogishi...

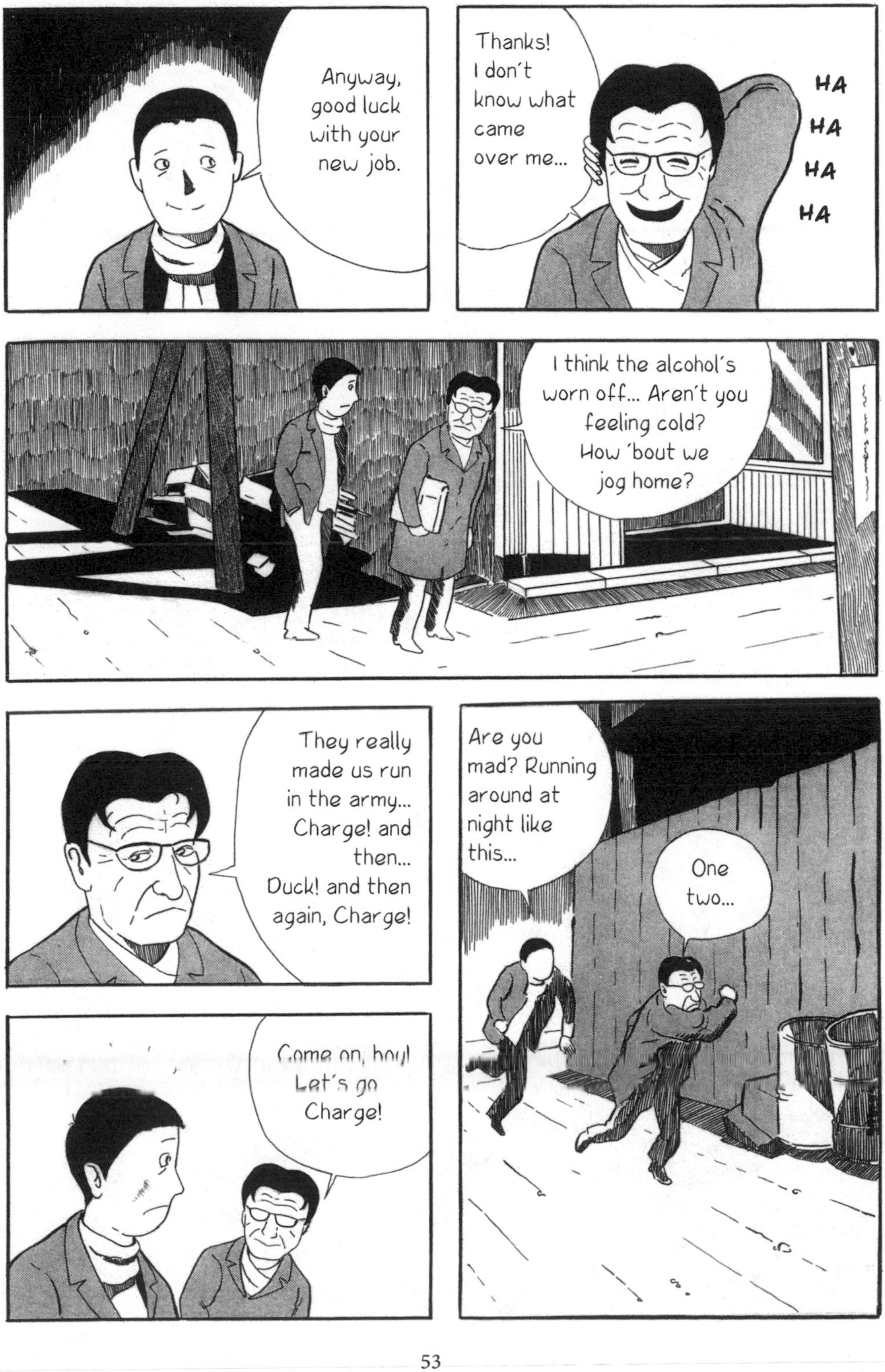
Anyway, good luck with your new job.
Thanks! I don't know what came over me...
HA HA HA HA
I think the alcohol's worn off... Aren't you feeling cold? How 'bout we jog home?
They really made us run in the army... Charge! and then... Duck! and then again, Charge!
Come on, boy! Let's go Charge!
Are you mad? Running around at night like this...
One two...

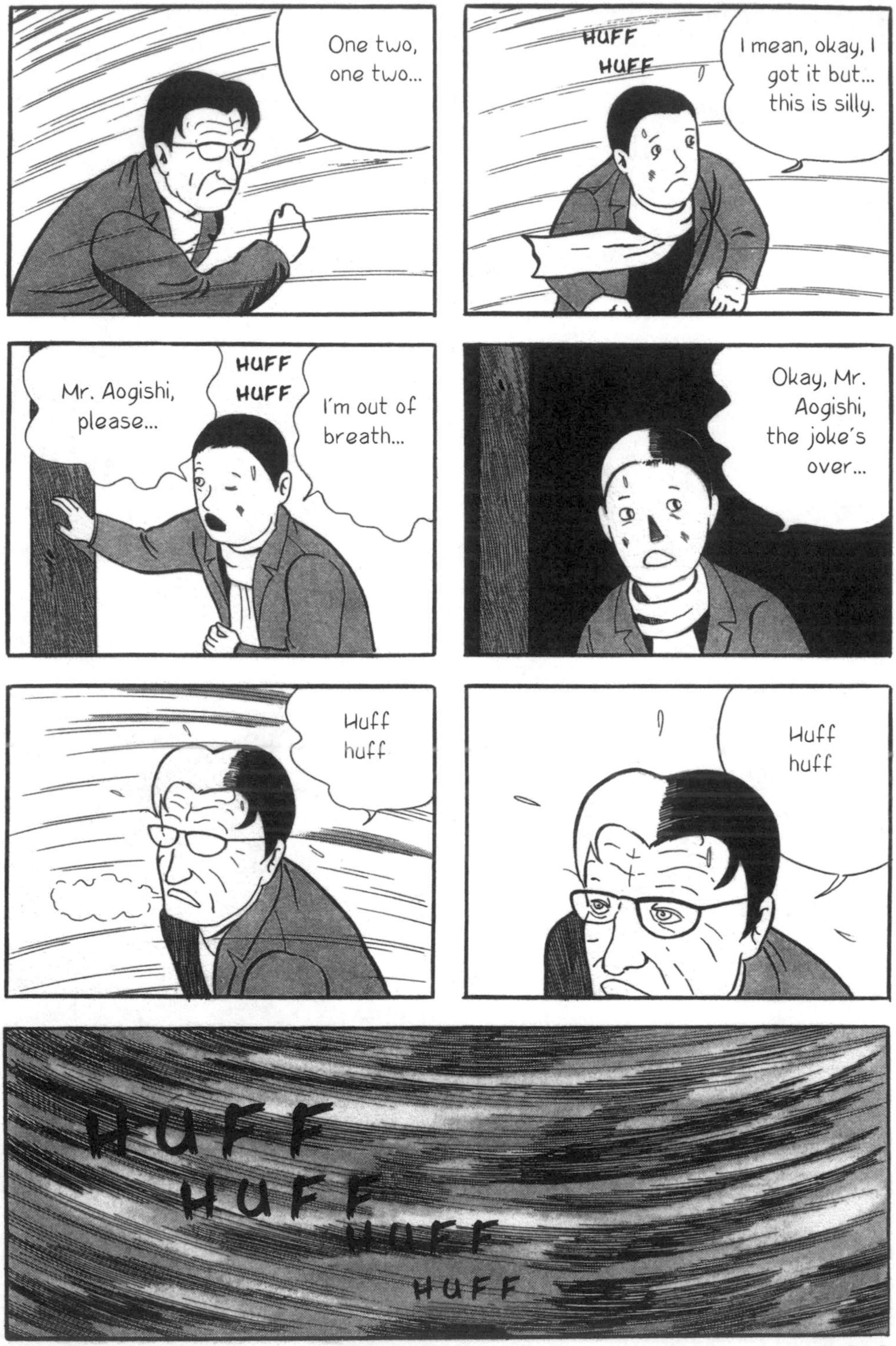
One two, one two...
HUFF HUFF
I mean, okay, I got it but... this is silly.
Mr. Aogishi, please...
HUFF HUFF
I'm out of breath...
Okay, Mr. Aogishi, the joke's over...
Huff huff
Huff huff
HUFF
HUFF
HUFF
HUFF

THE END

SOUNDS

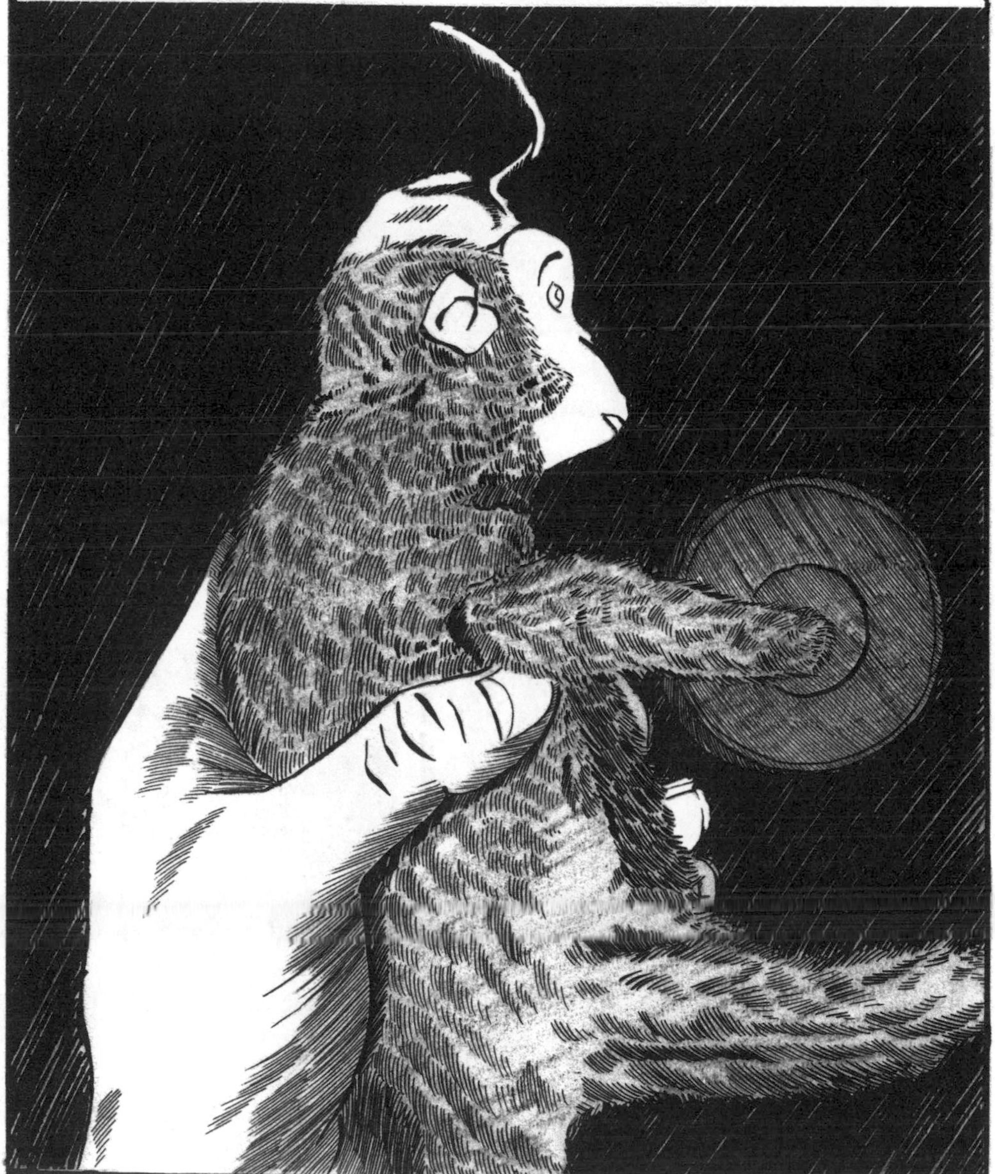

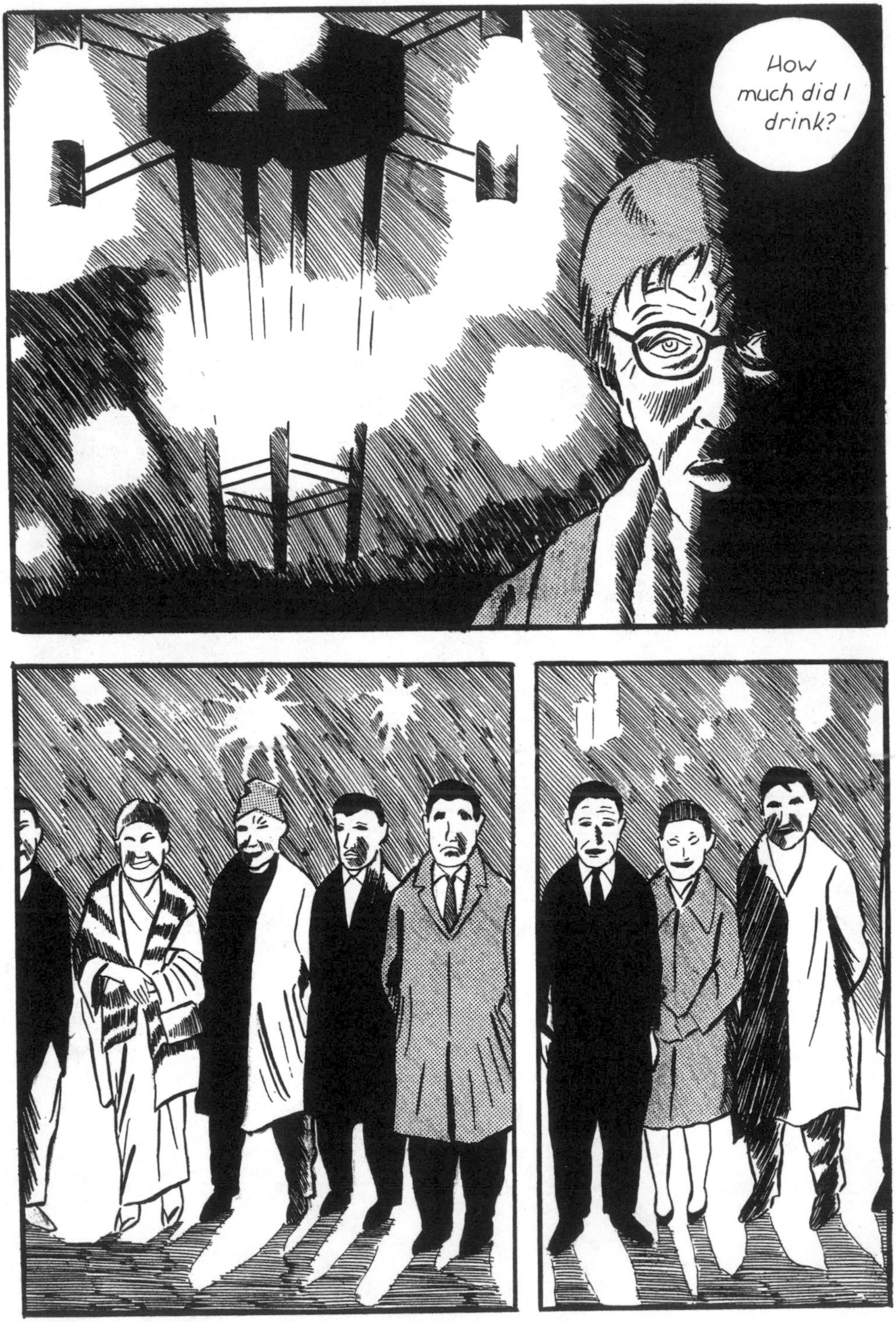
How much did I drink?

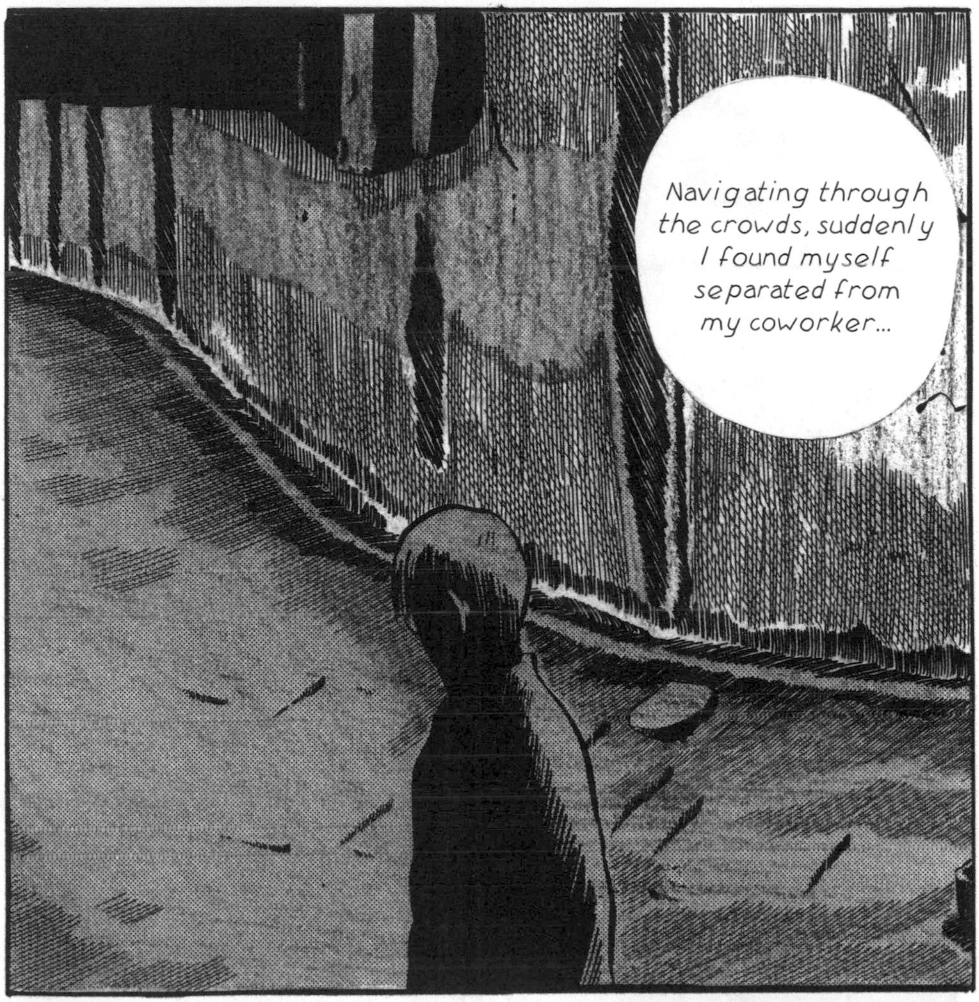
Navigating through the crowds, suddenly I found myself separated from my coworker...

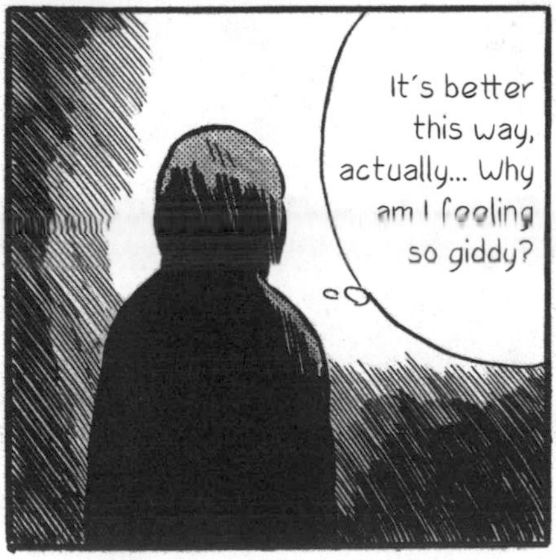
It's better this way, actually... Why am I feeling so giddy?

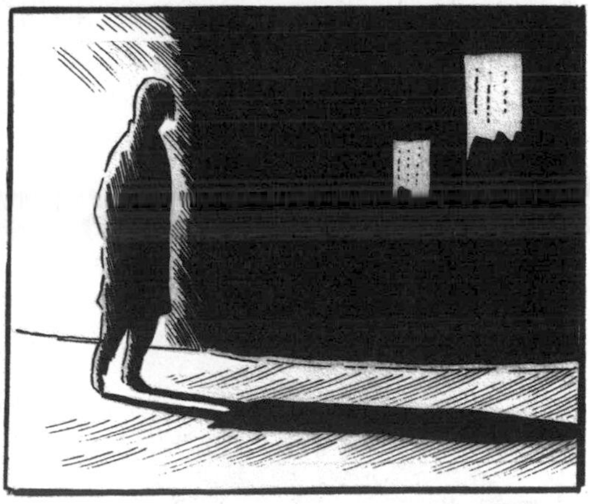

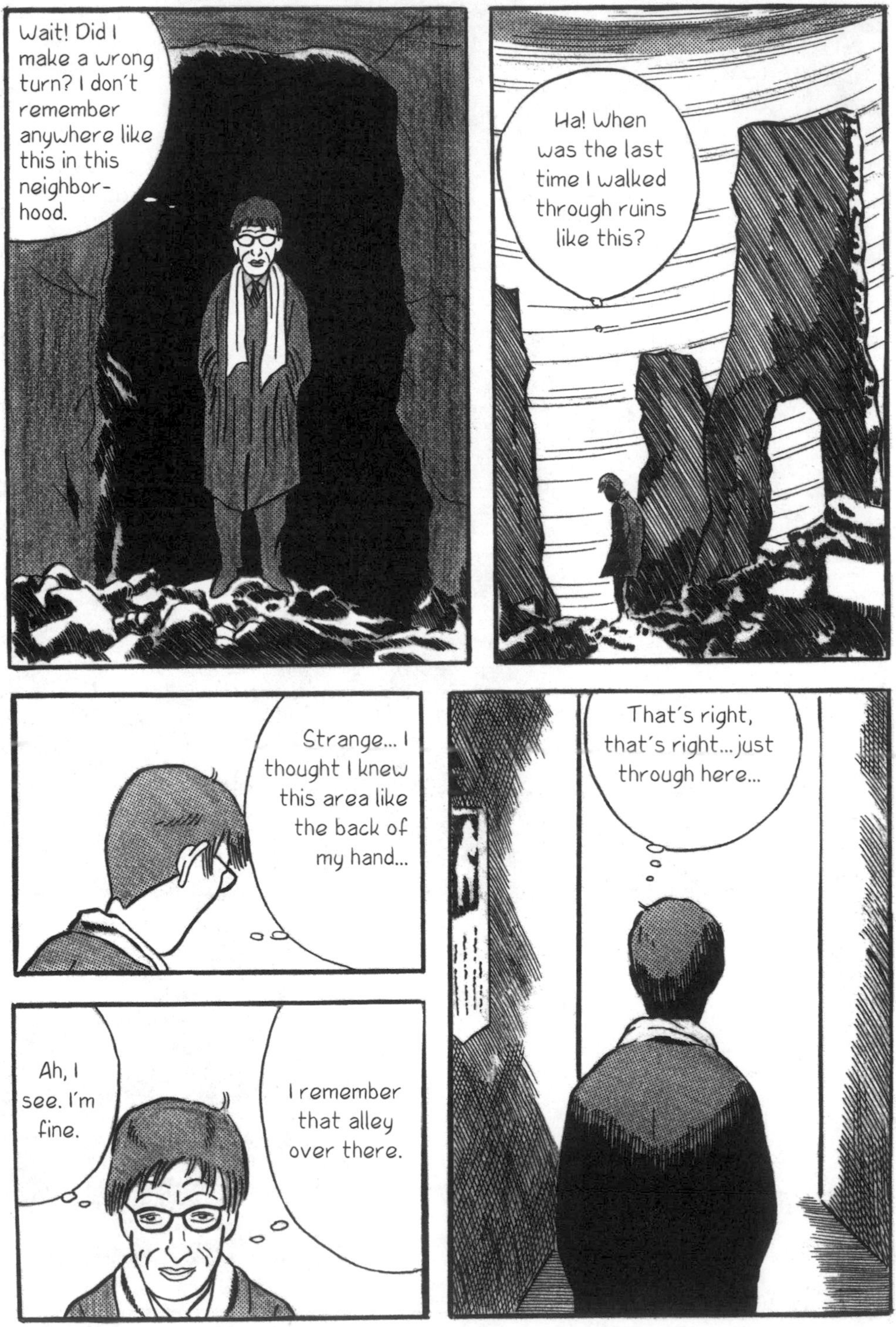
Wait! Did I make a wrong turn? I don't remember anywhere like this in this neighbor-hood.
Ha! When was the last time I walked through ruins like this?
Strange... I thought I knew this area like the back of my hand...
Ah, I see. I'm fine.
I remember that alley over there.
That's right, that's right... just through here...

SKREEEEECH

Ah!

CRASH

Get a hold of yourself, that's the first thing...

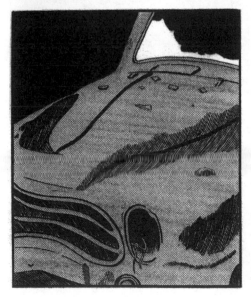

Uh...

Let's see... I'm uh...

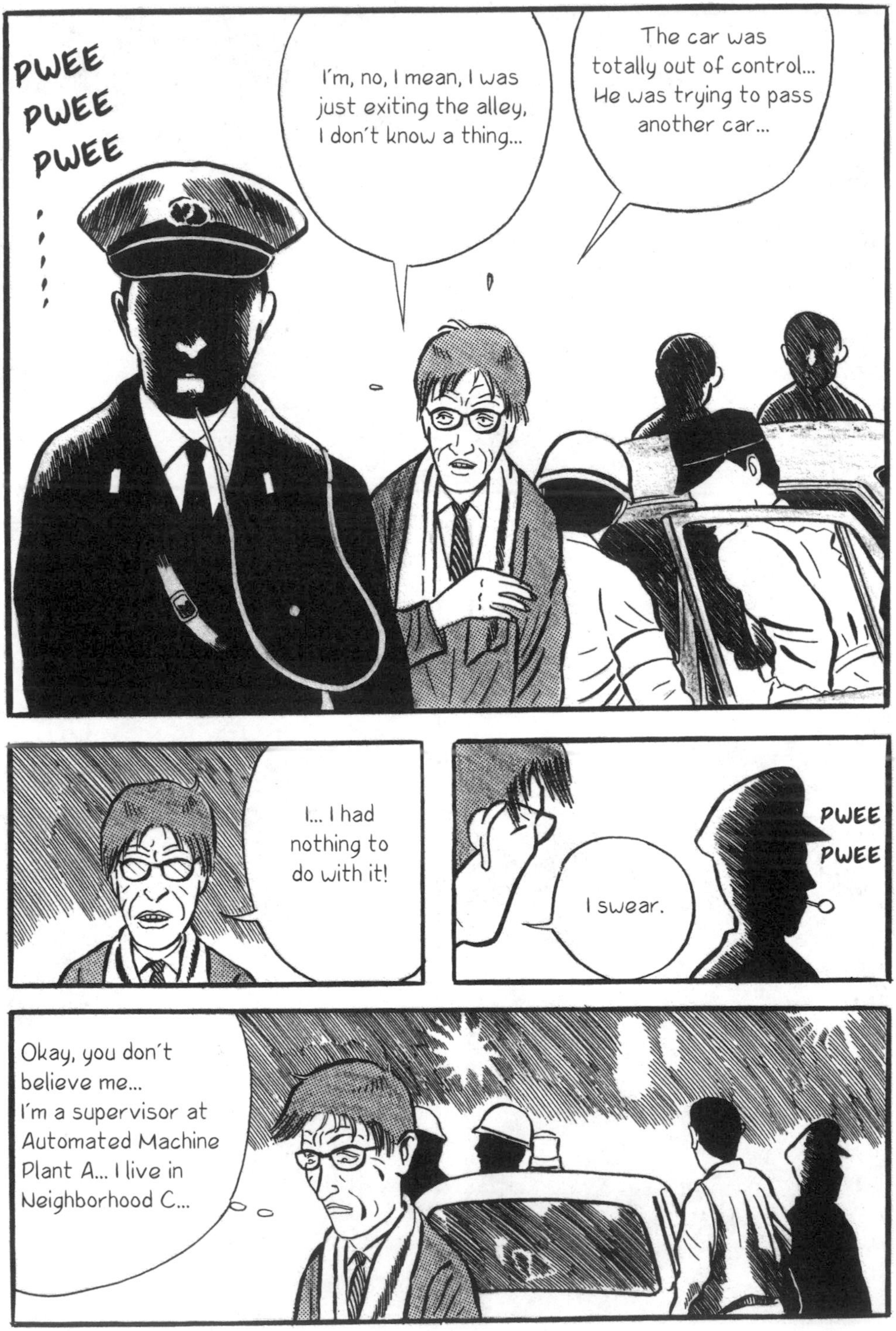
PWEE
PWEE
PWEE
I'm, no, I mean, I was just exiting the alley, I don't know a thing...
The car was totally out of control... He was trying to pass another car...
I... I had nothing to do with it!
I swear.
PWEE
PWEE
Okay, you don't believe me... I'm a supervisor at Automated Machine Plant A... I live in Neighborhood C...

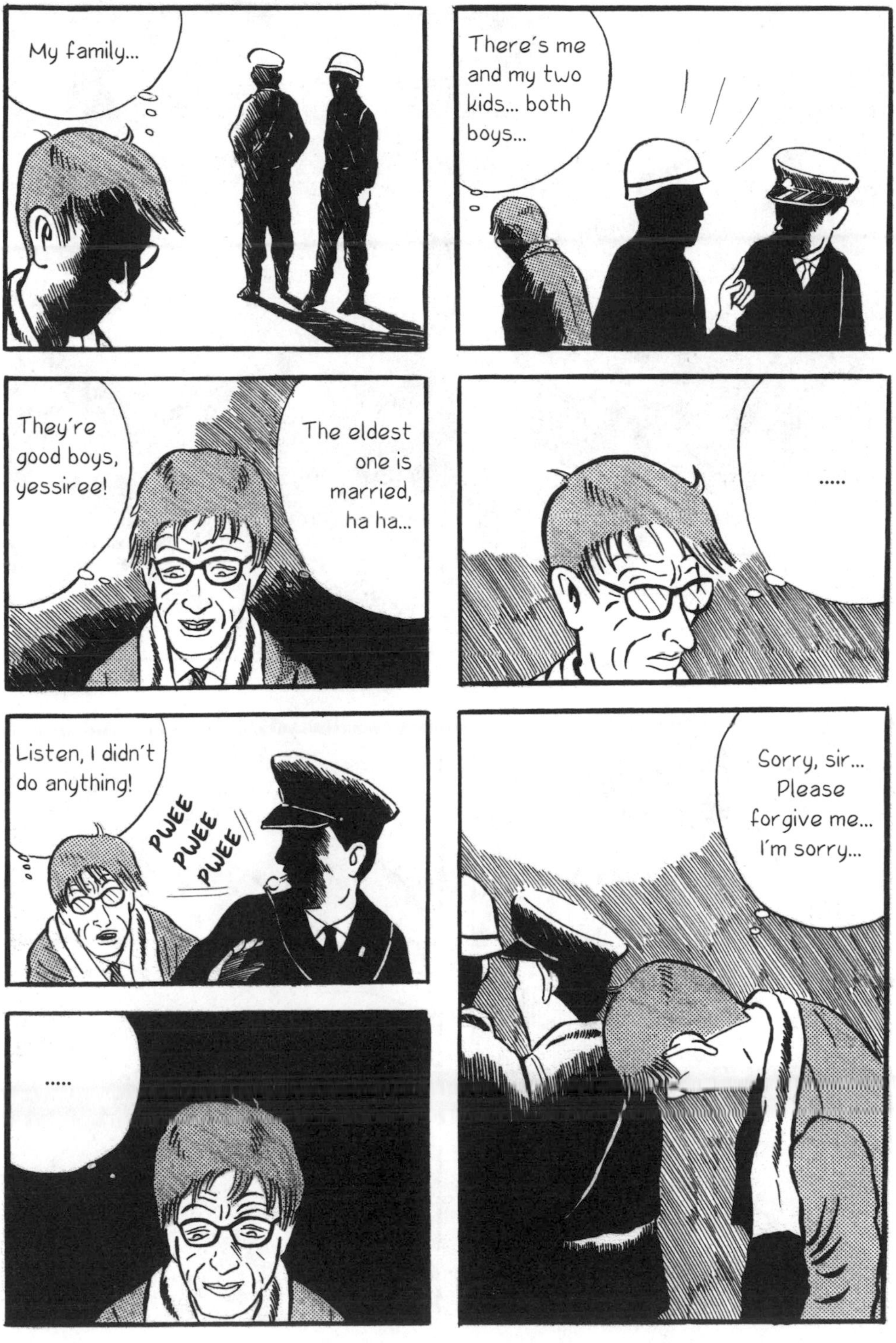

My family...
There's me and my two kids... both boys...
They're good boys, yessiree!
The eldest one is married, ha ha...
.....
Listen, I didn't do anything!
PWEE PWEE PWEE
Sorry, sir... Please forgive me... I'm sorry...
.....

Whoa, how did I weasel out of that one?
Whaddya know... ha ha ha.
What a bunch of suckers, right?
They didn't realize who I really am...

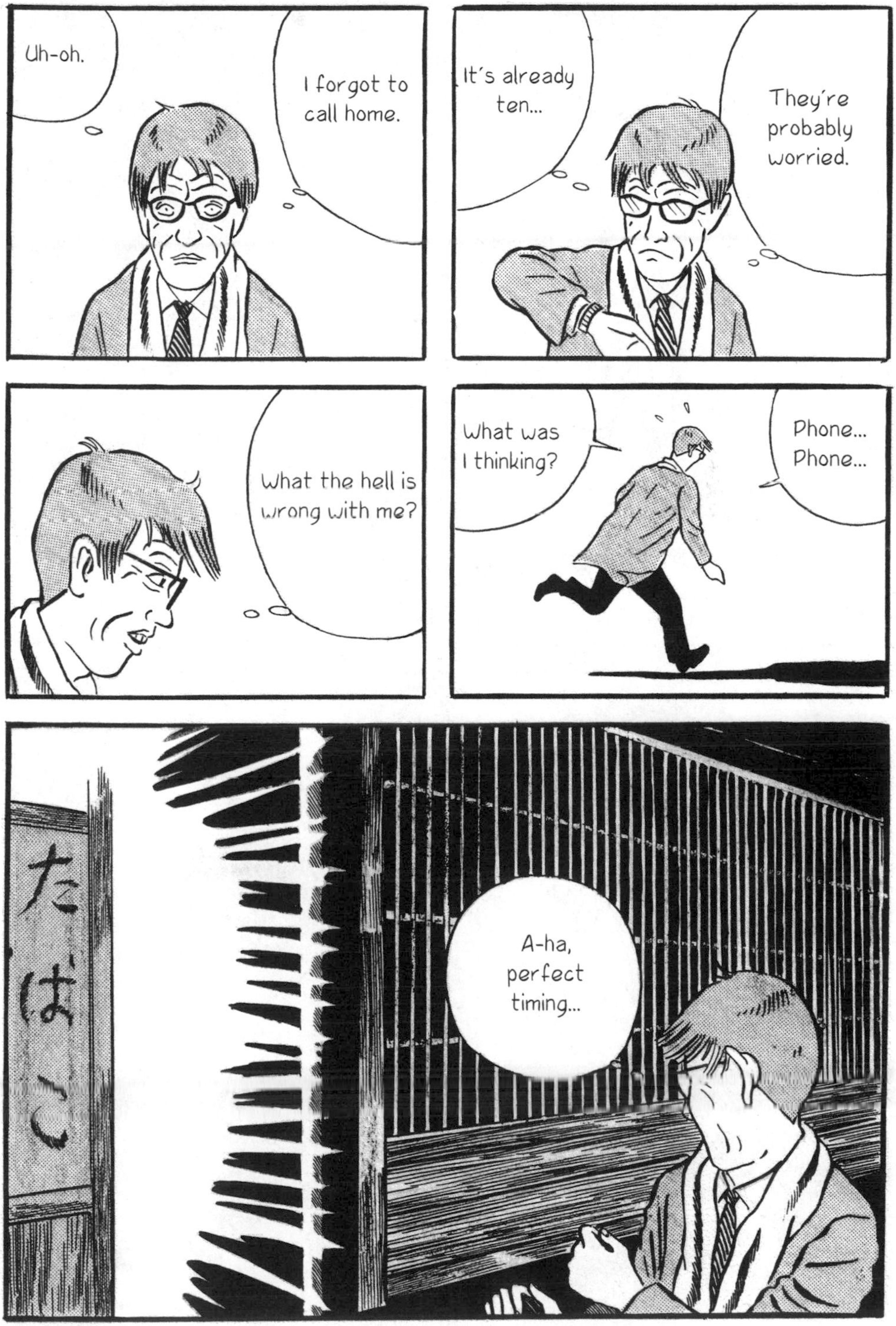
Uh-oh.
I forgot to call home.
It's already ten...
They're probably worried.
What the hell is wrong with me?
What was I thinking?
Phone... Phone...
たばこ
A-ha, perfect timing...
sign: cigarettes

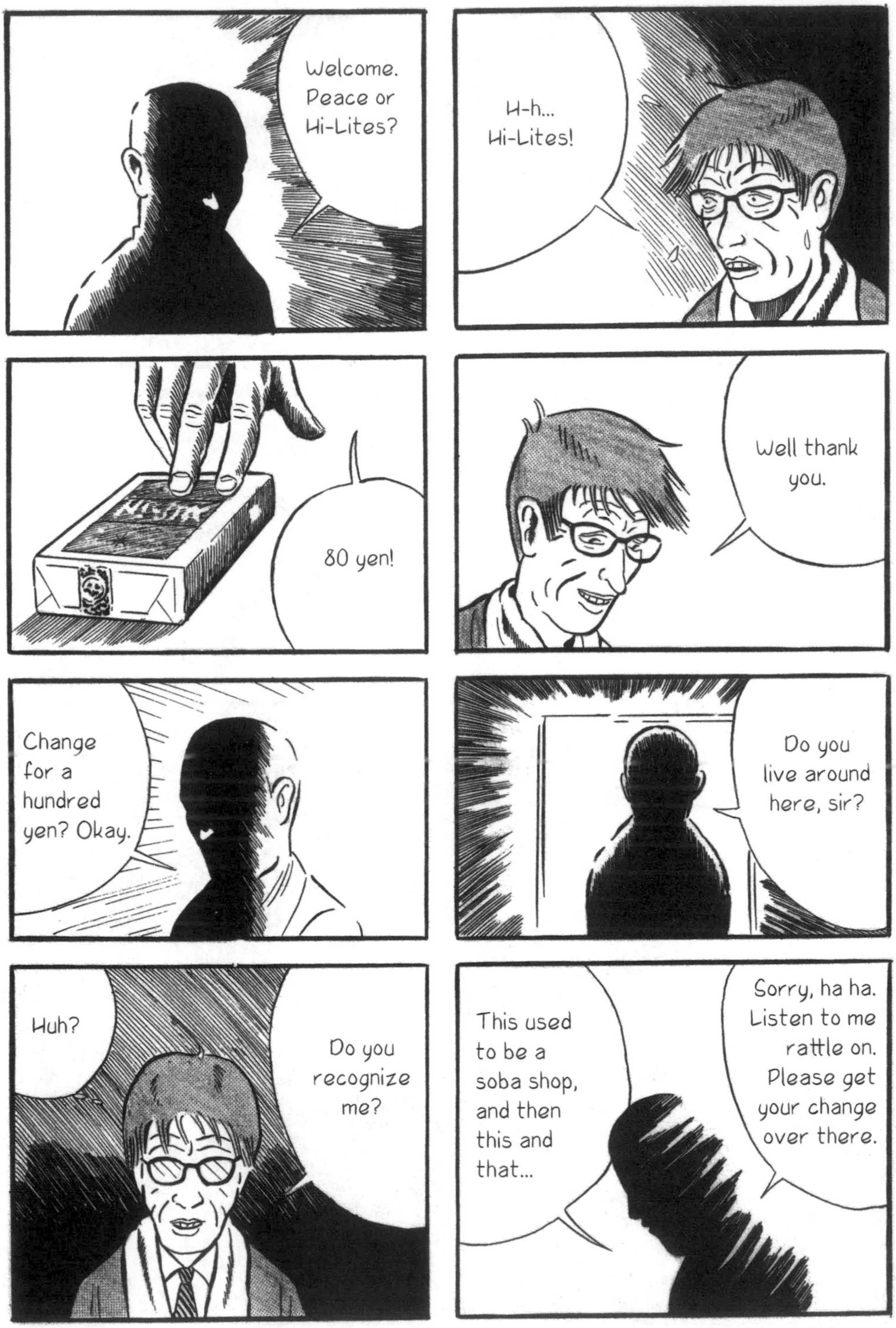
Welcome. Peace or Hi-Lites?
H-h... Hi-Lites!
80 yen!
Well thank you.
Change for a hundred yen? Okay.
Do you live around here, sir?
Huh?
Do you recognize me?
This used to be a soba shop, and then this and that...
Sorry, ha ha. Listen to me rattle on. Please get your change over there.

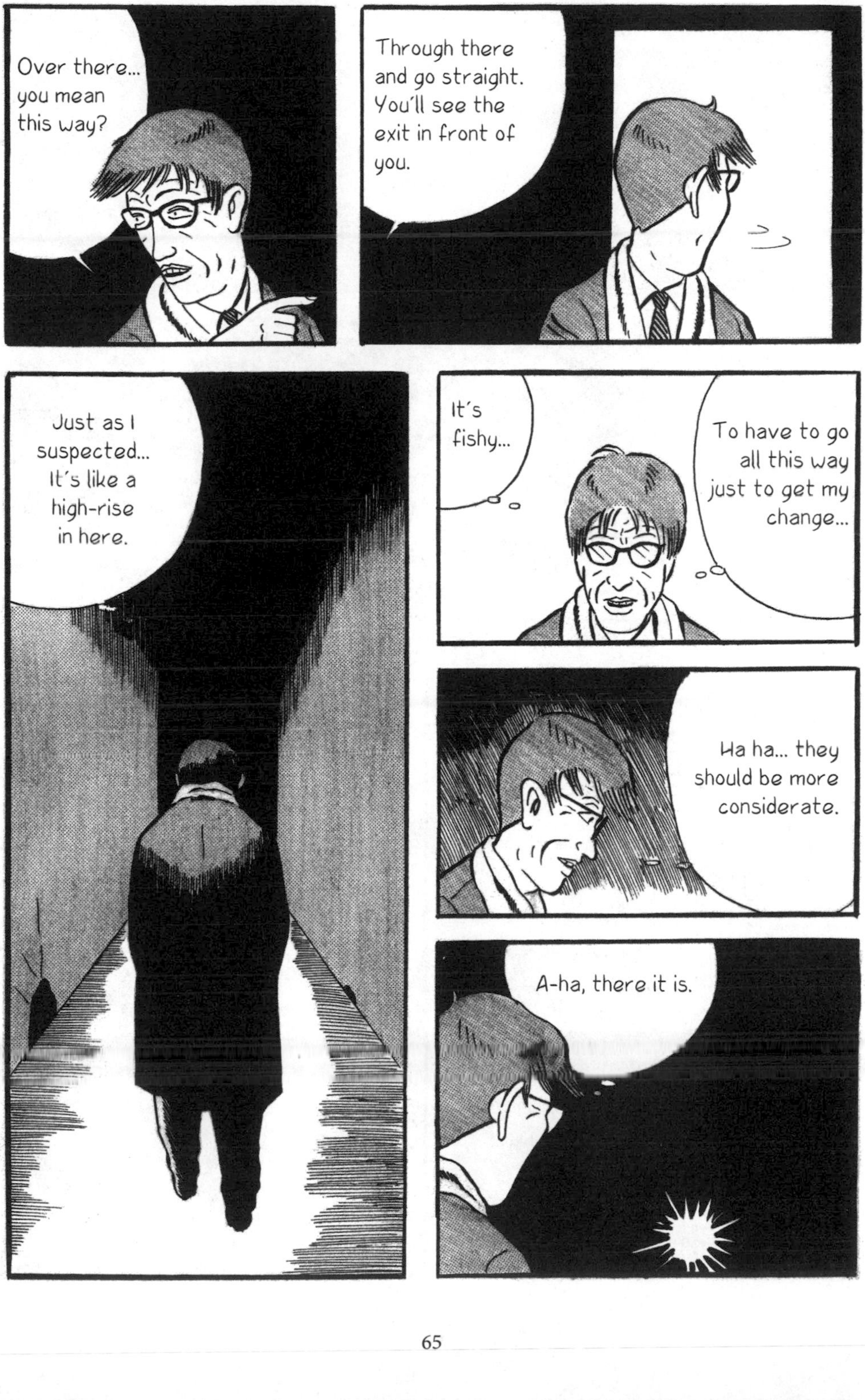
Over there... you mean this way?
Through there and go straight. You'll see the exit in front of you.
Just as I suspected... It's like a high-rise in here.
It's fishy...
To have to go all this way just to get my change...
Ha ha... they should be more considerate.
A-ha, there it is.

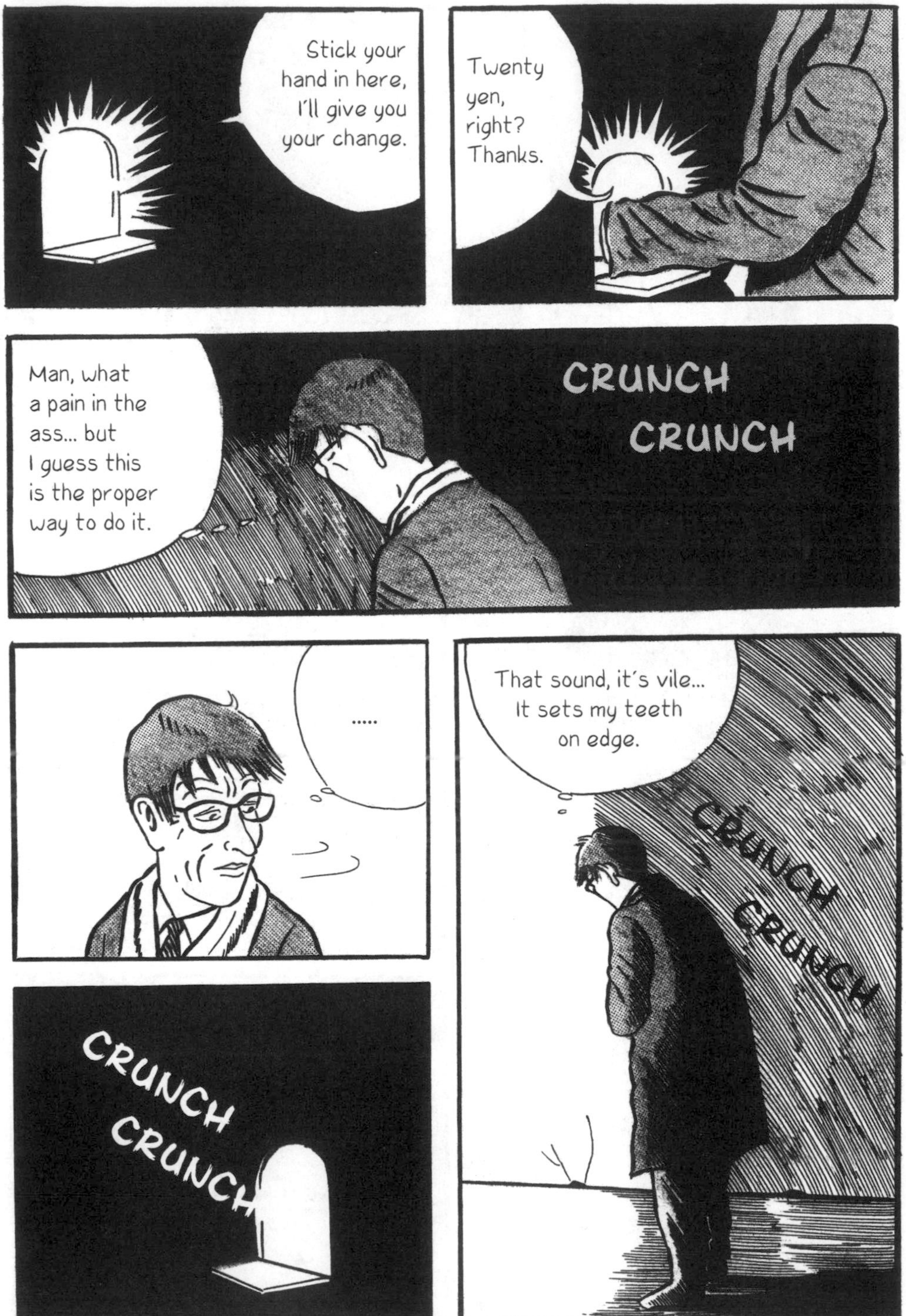
Stick your hand in here, I'll give you your change.
Twenty yen, right? Thanks.
Man, what a pain in the ass... but I guess this is the proper way to do it.
CRUNCH
CRUNCH
.....
That sound, it's vile... It sets my teeth on edge.
CRUNCH
CRUNCH
CRUNCH
CRUNCH

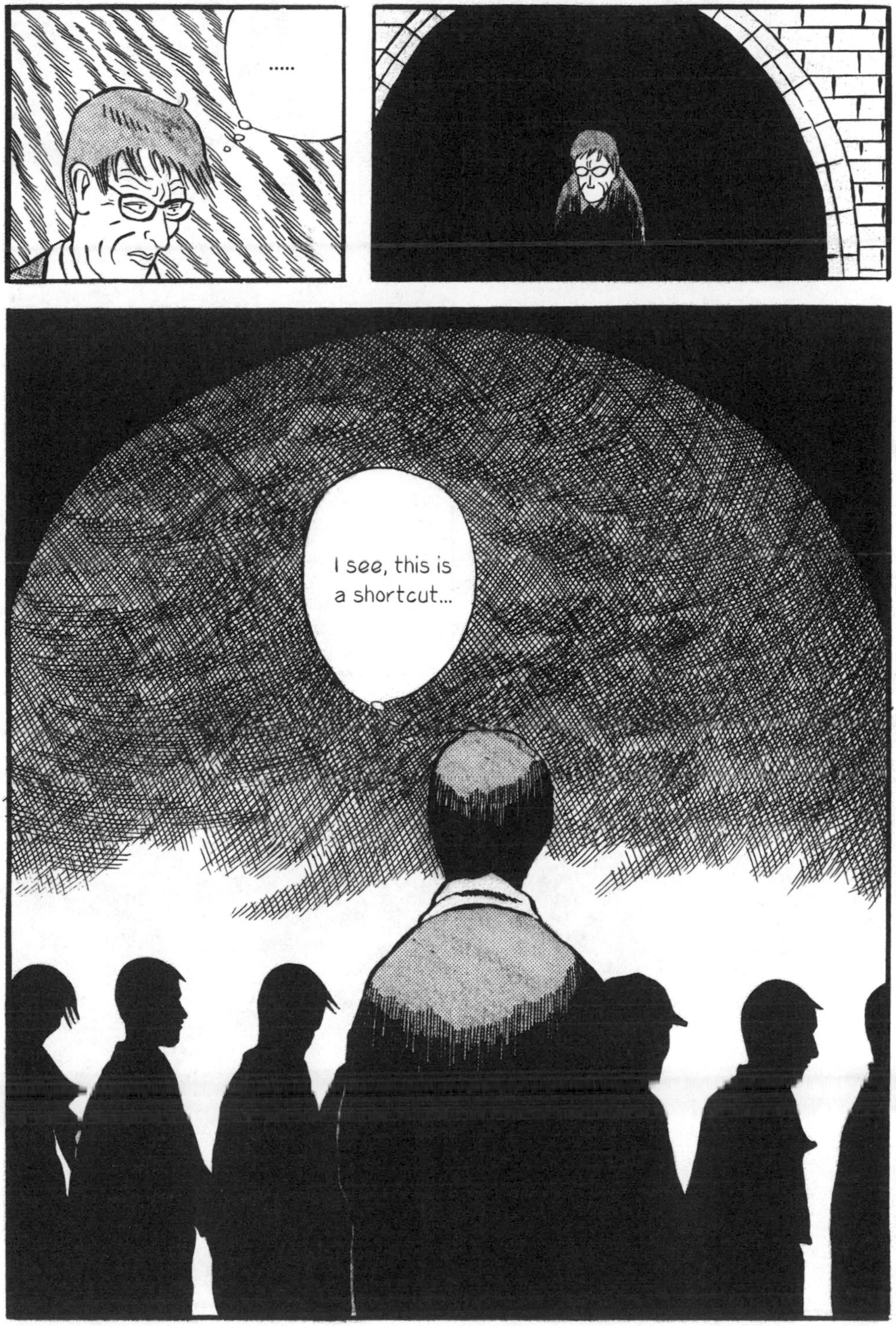
.....
I see, this is a shortcut...

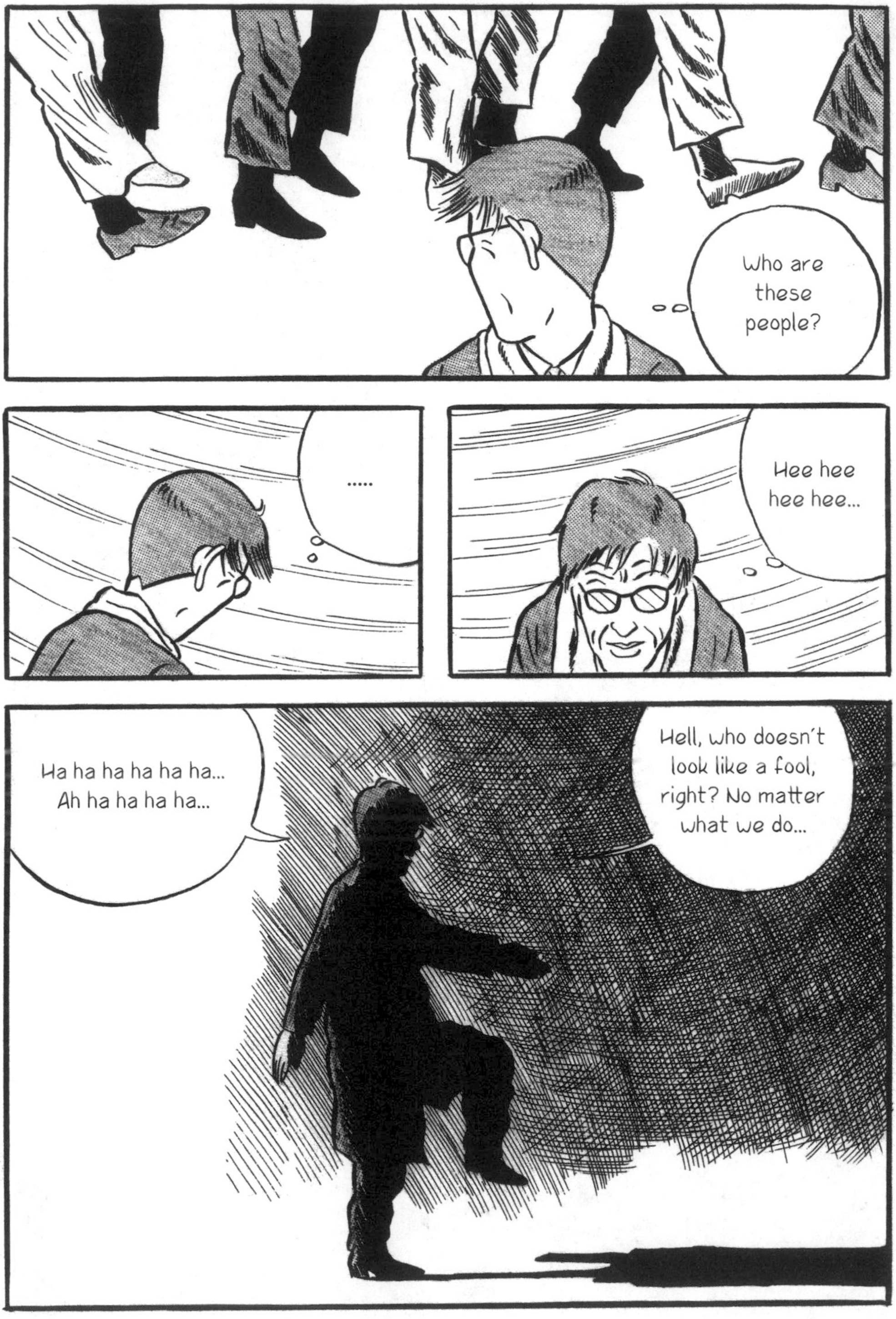
Who are these people?
.....
Hee hee hee hee...
Ha ha ha ha ha ha... Ah ha ha ha ha...
Hell, who doesn't look like a fool, right? No matter what we do...

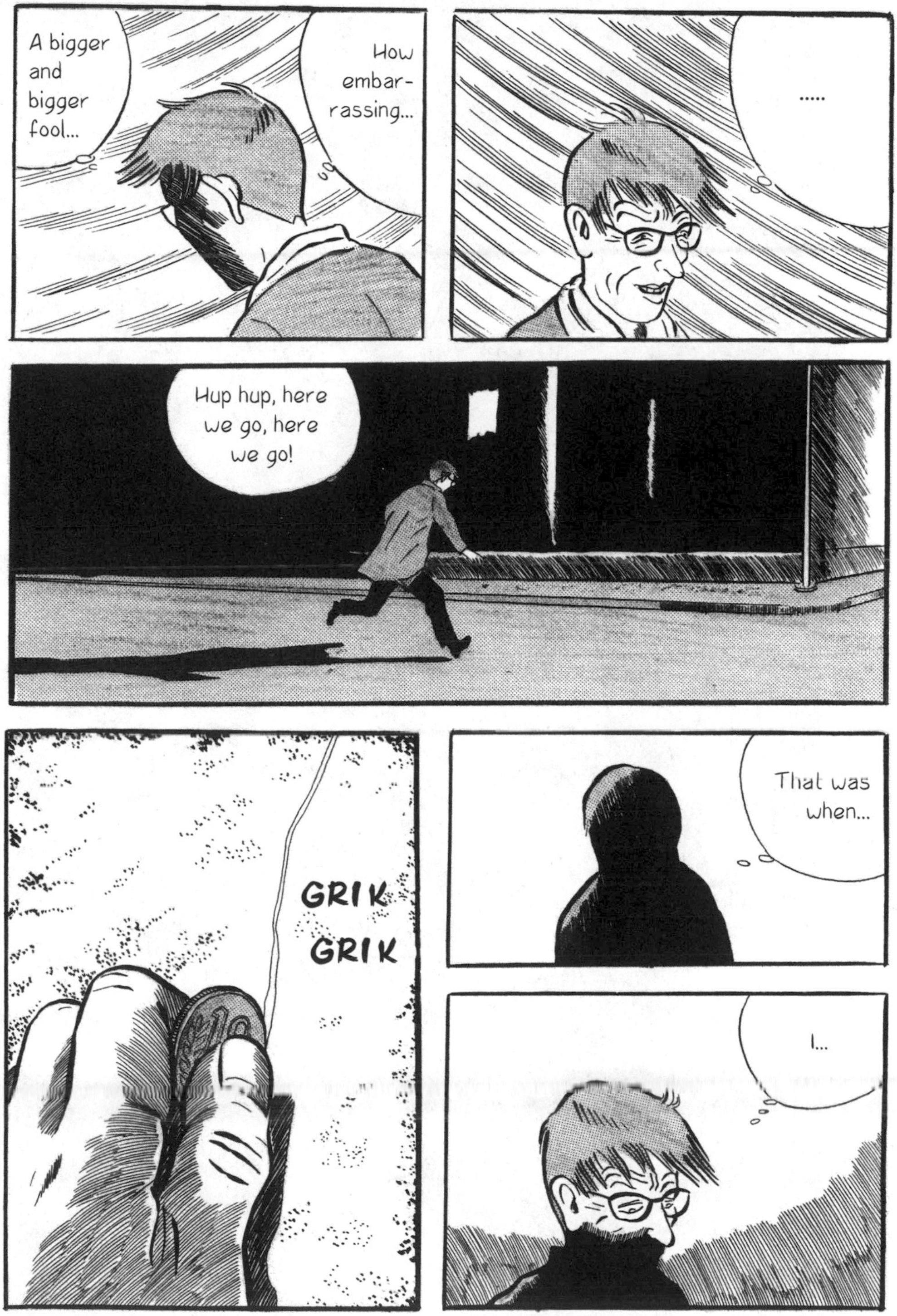
A bigger and bigger fool...
How embarrassing...
.....
Hup hup, here we go, here we go!
GRIK
GRIK
That was when...
I...

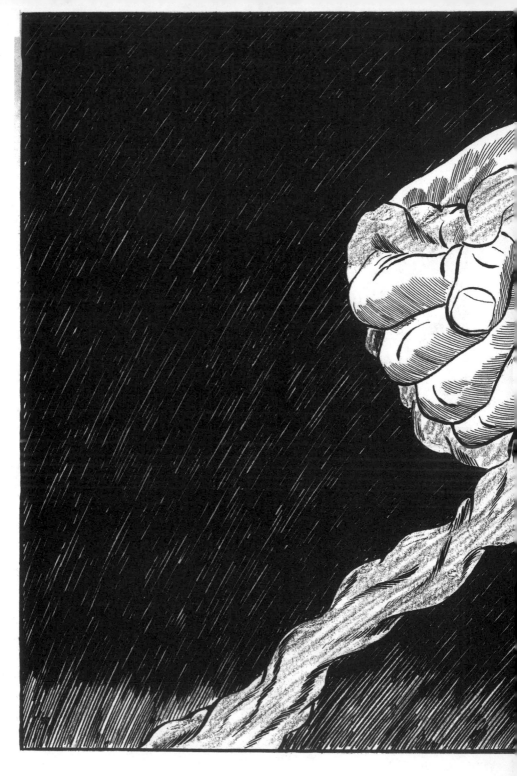

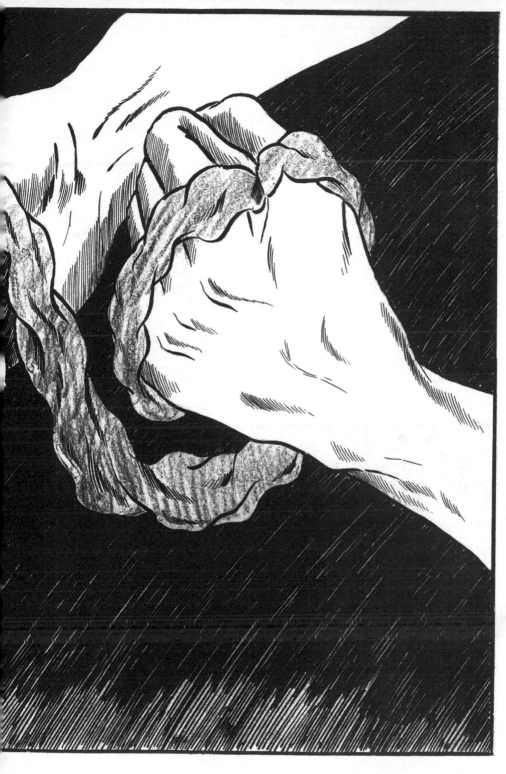

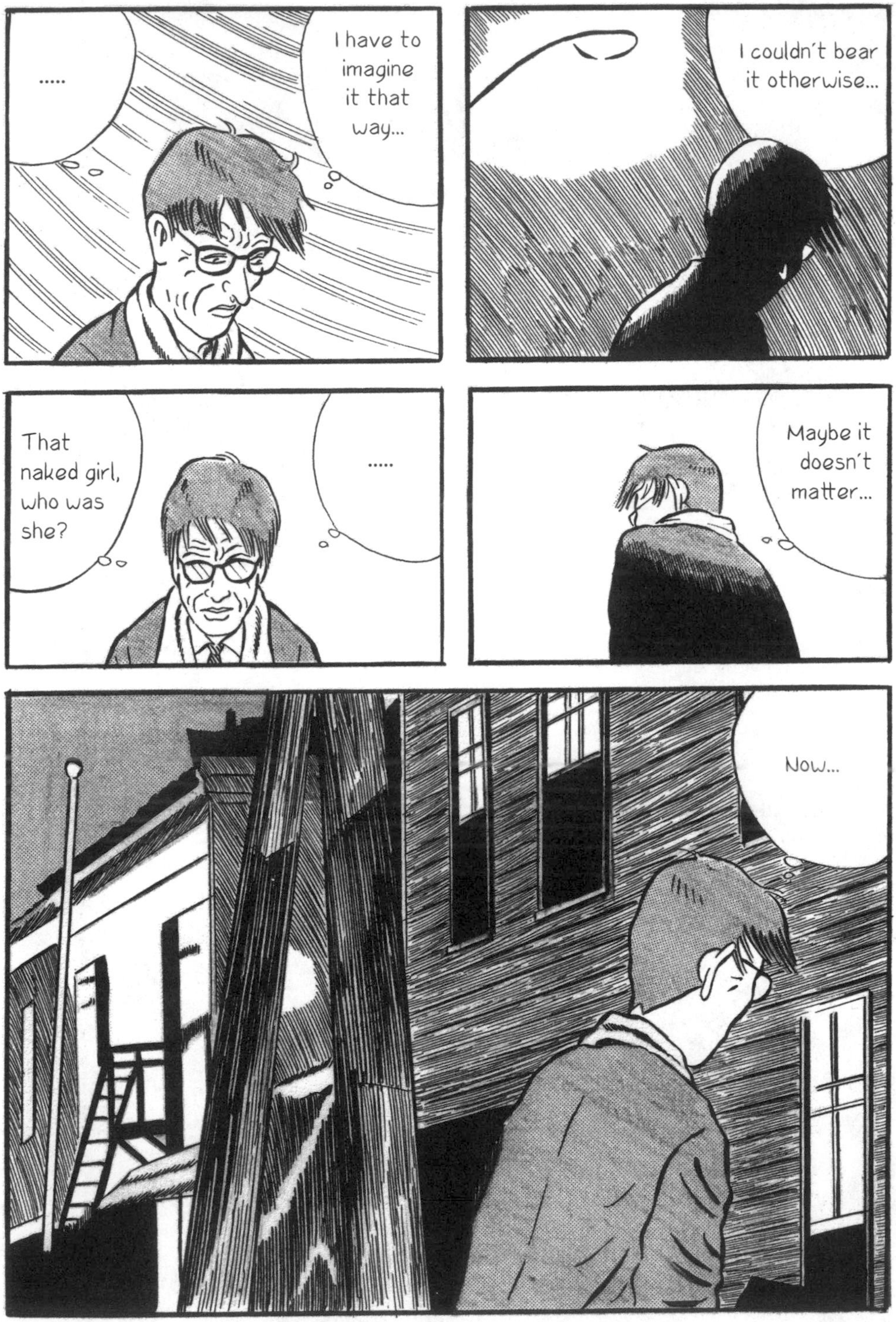
.....
I have to imagine it that way...
I couldn't bear it otherwise...
That naked girl, who was she?
.....
Maybe it doesn't matter...
Now...

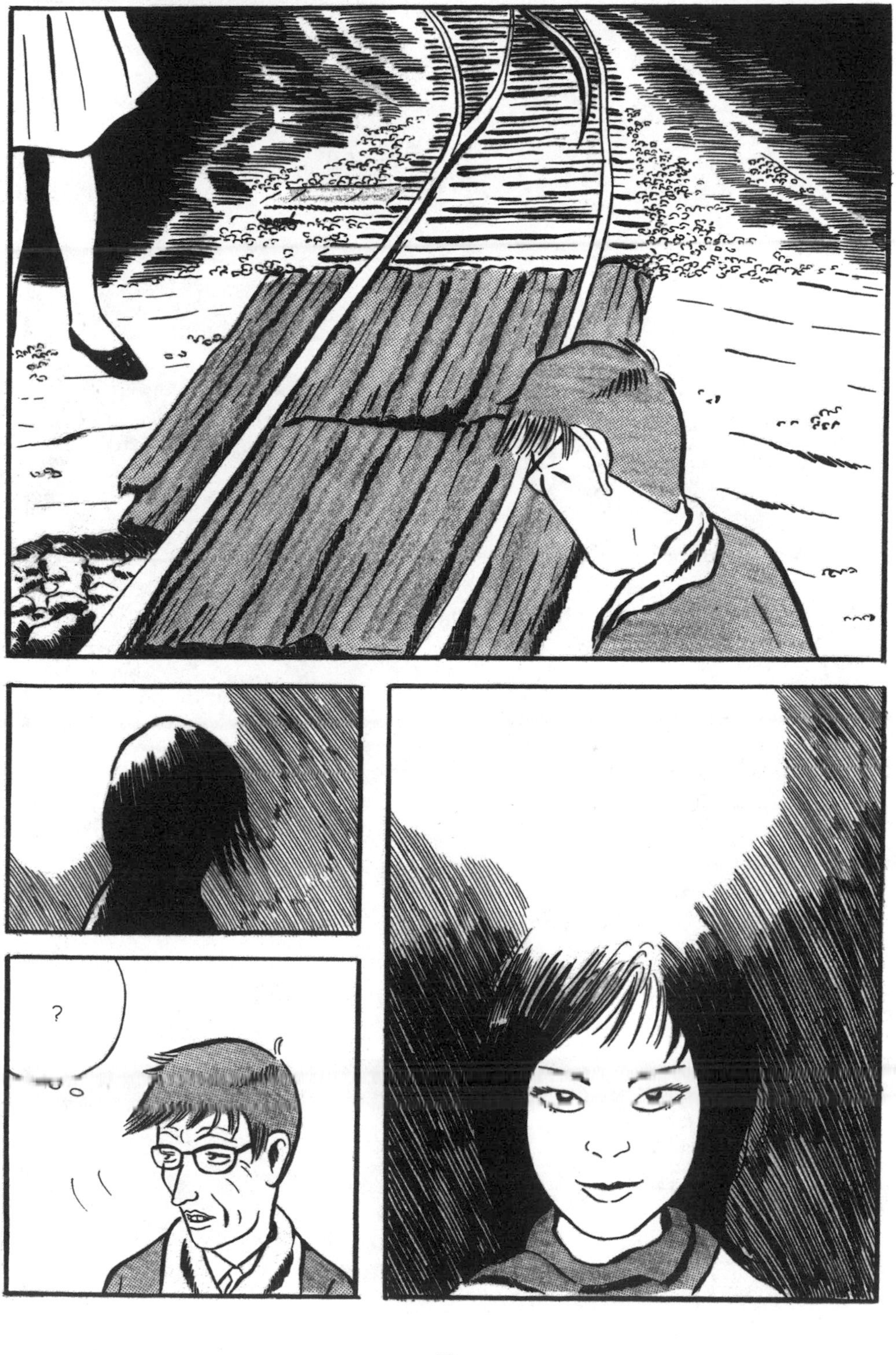
?

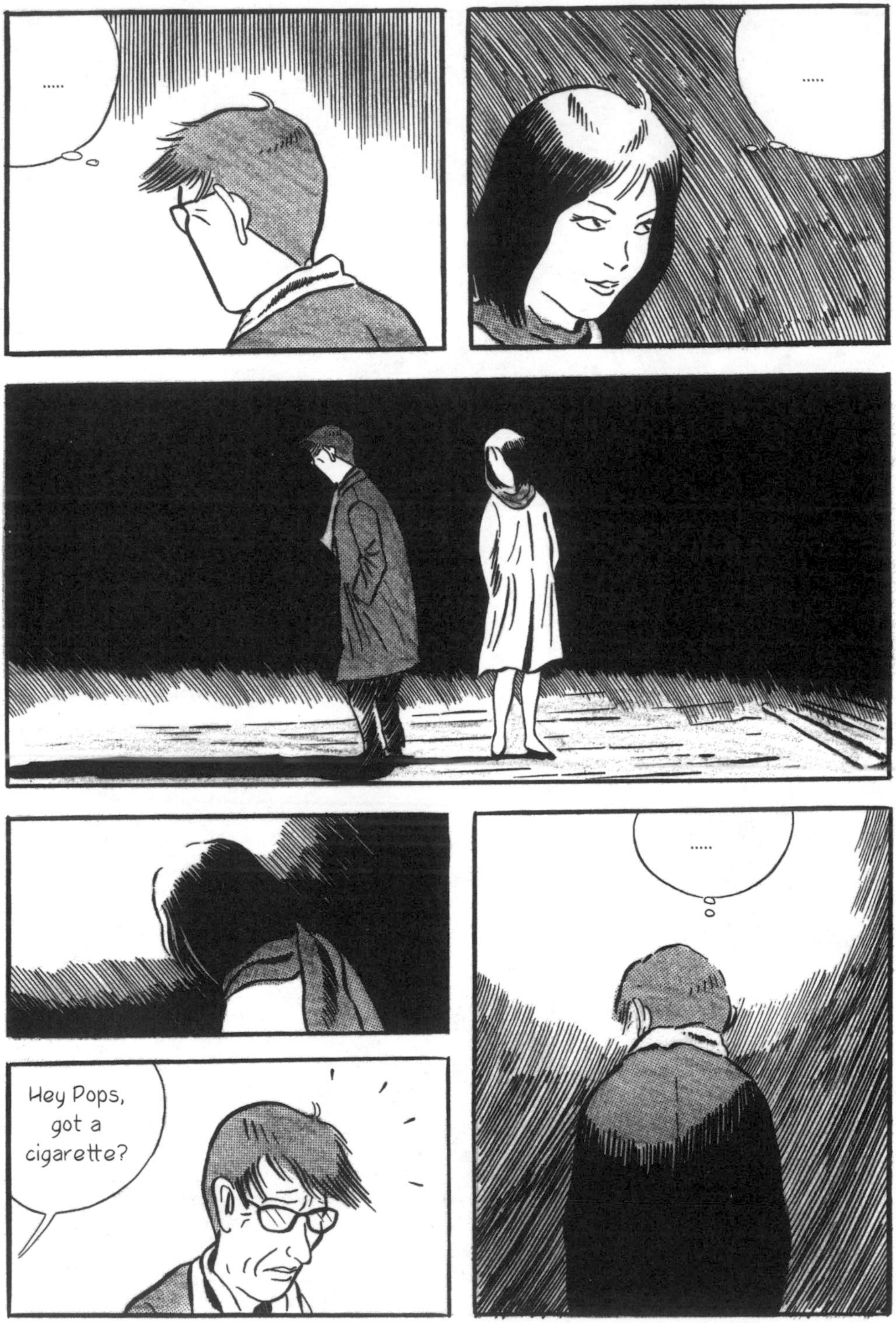
.....
.....
.....
Hey Pops, got a cigarette?

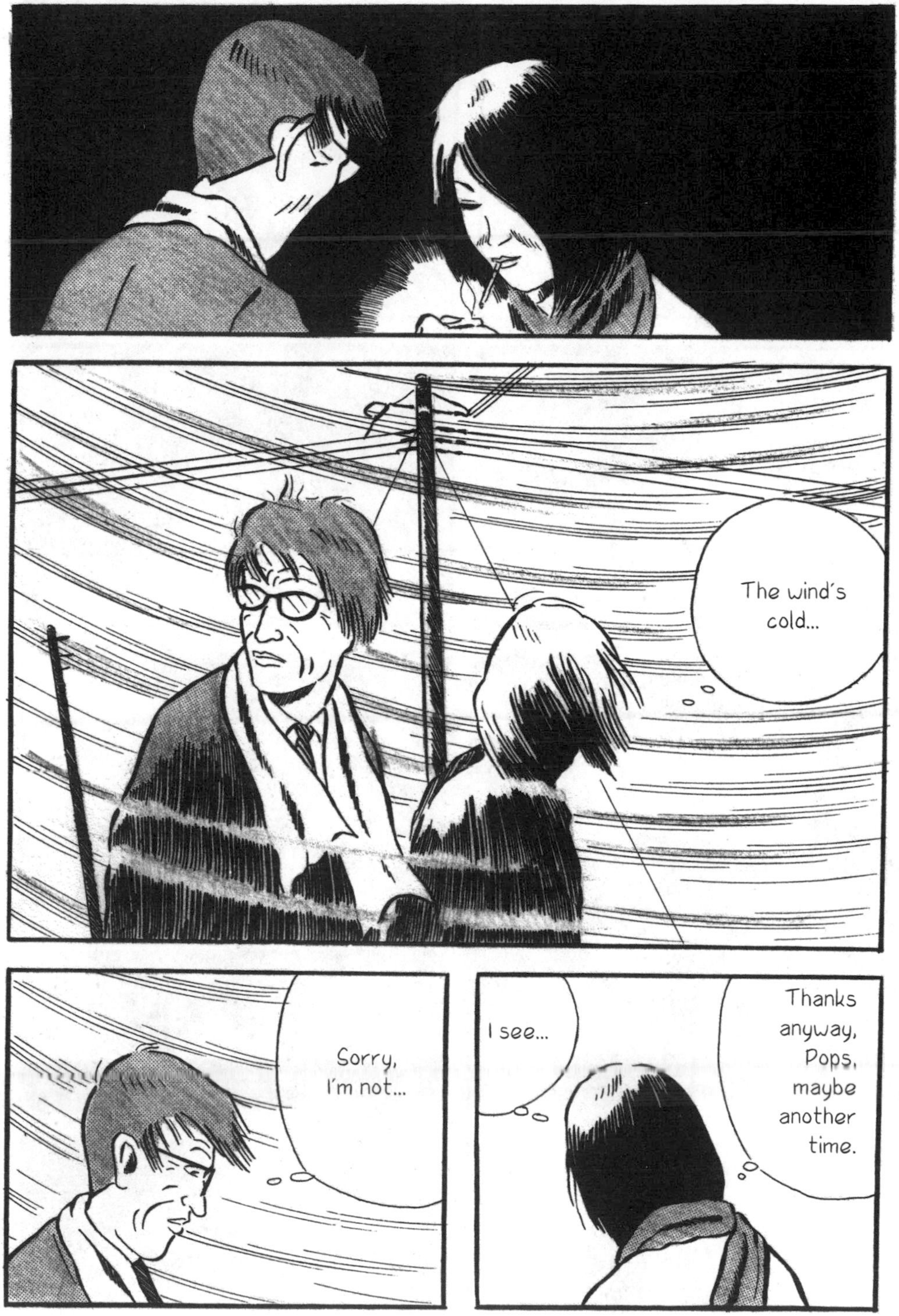
The wind's cold...
Sorry, I'm not...
I see...
Thanks anyway, Pops, maybe another time.

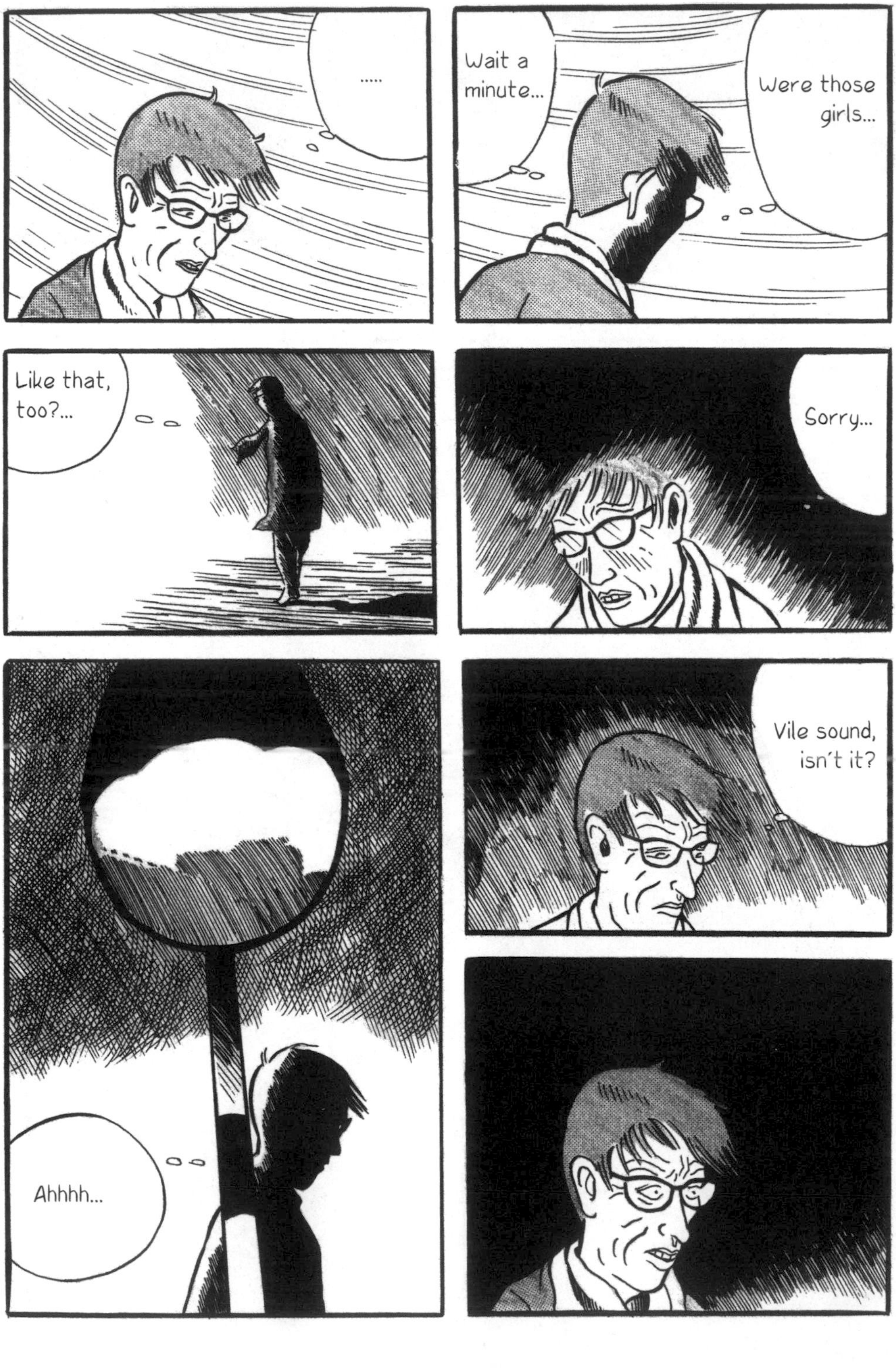
.....
Wait a minute...
Were those girls...
Like that, too?...
Sorry...
Ahhhh...
Vile sound, isn't it?

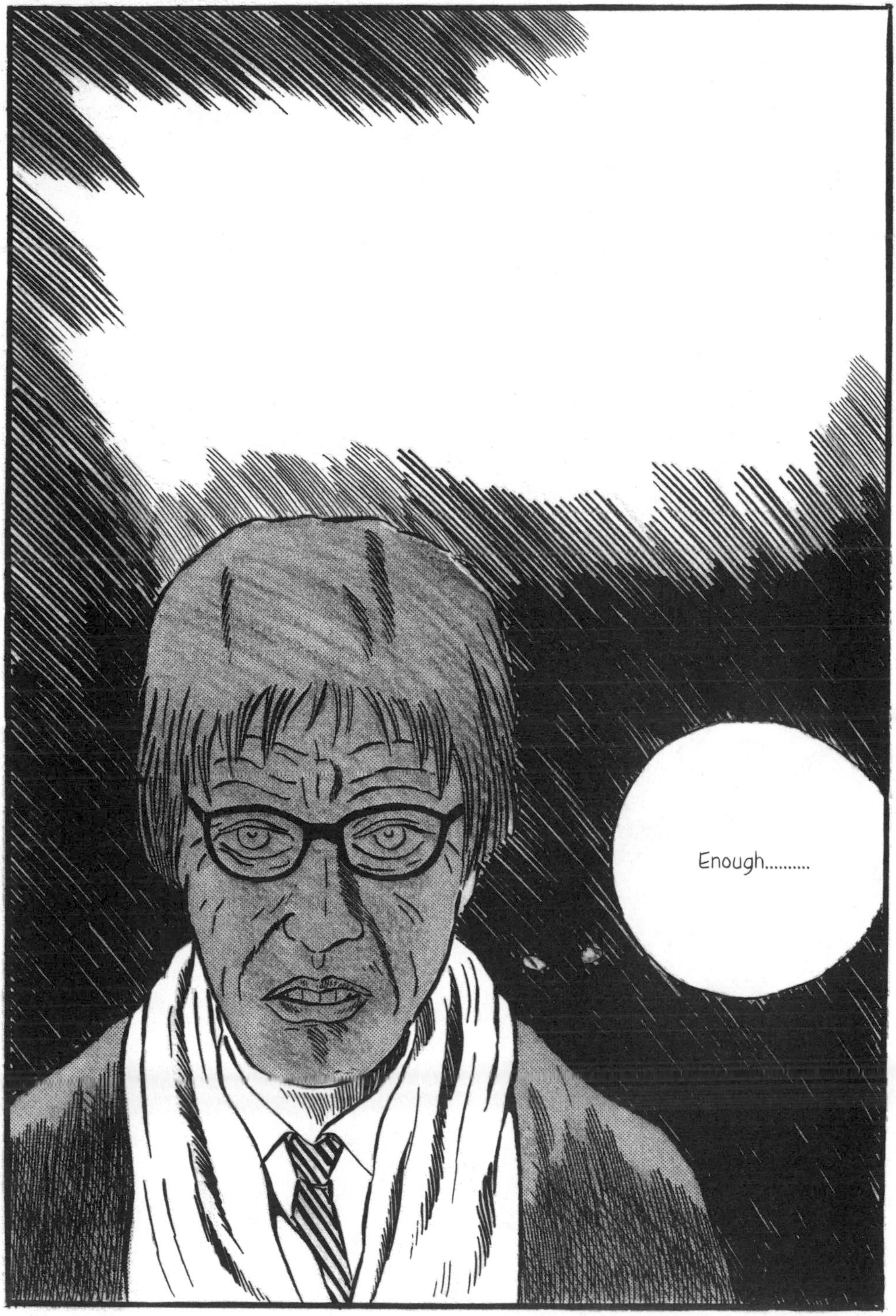
Enough..........

THE END

PUNK

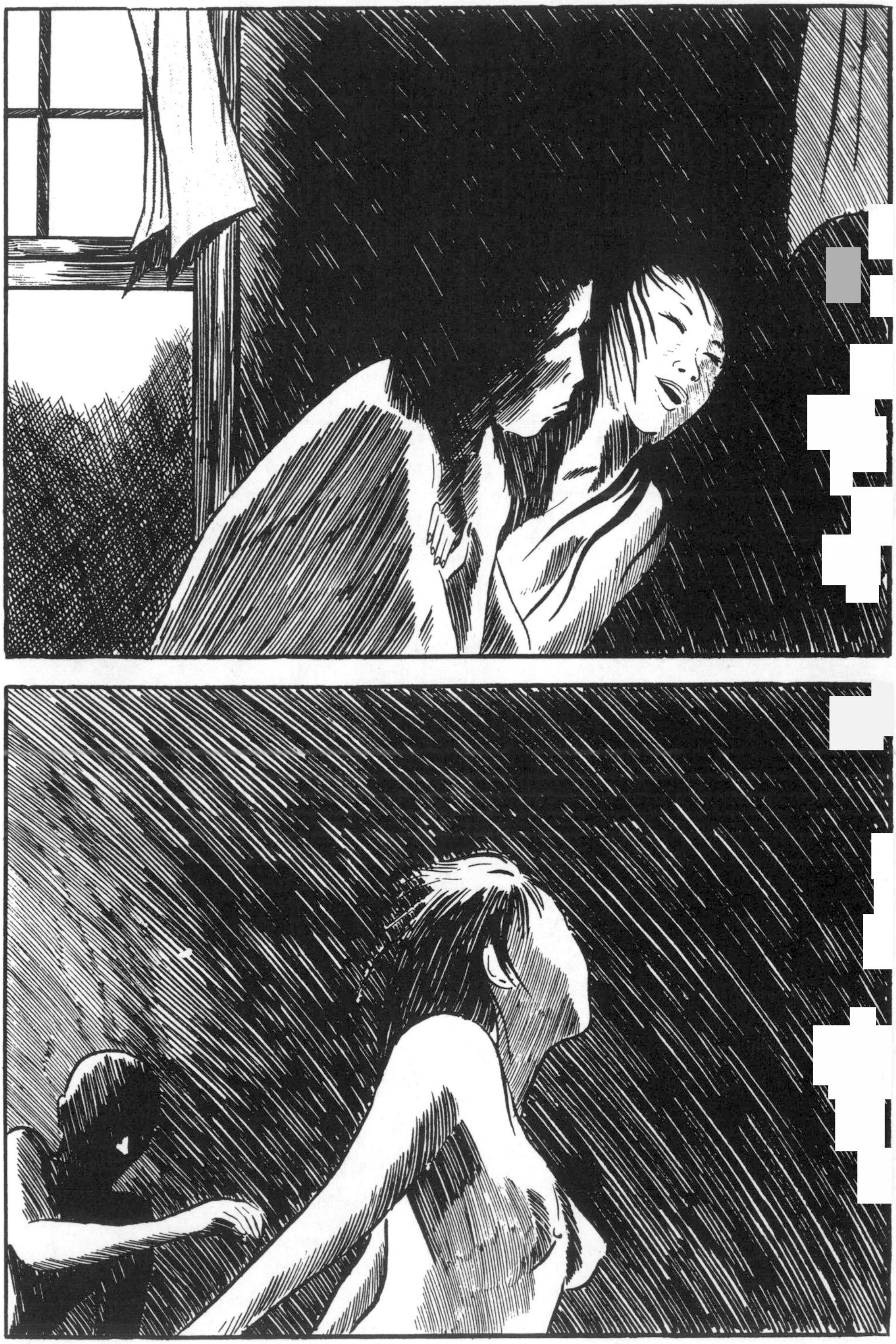

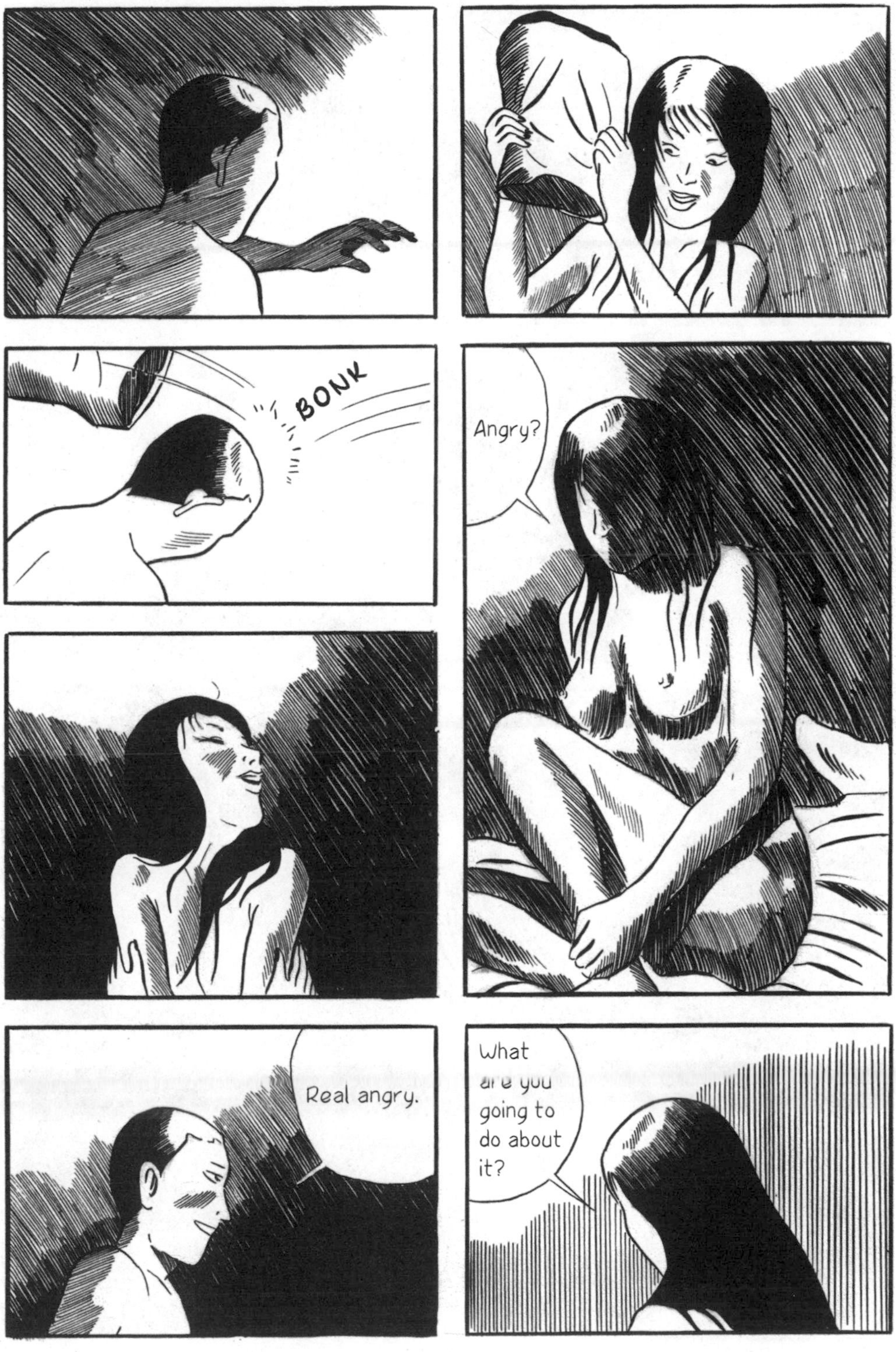
BONK
Angry?
Real angry.
What are you going to do about it?

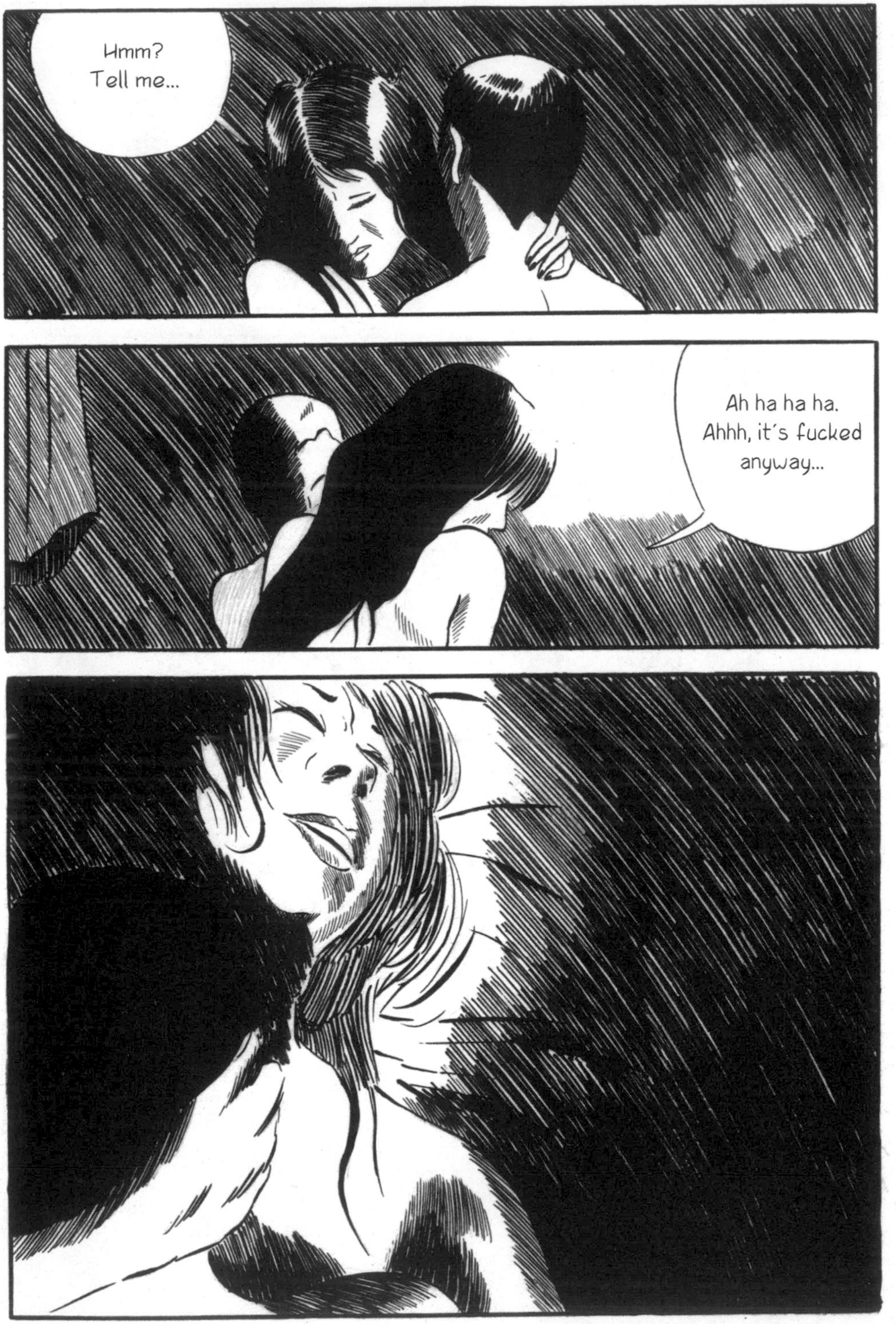
Hmm? Tell me...
Ah ha ha ha. Ahhh, it's fucked anyway...

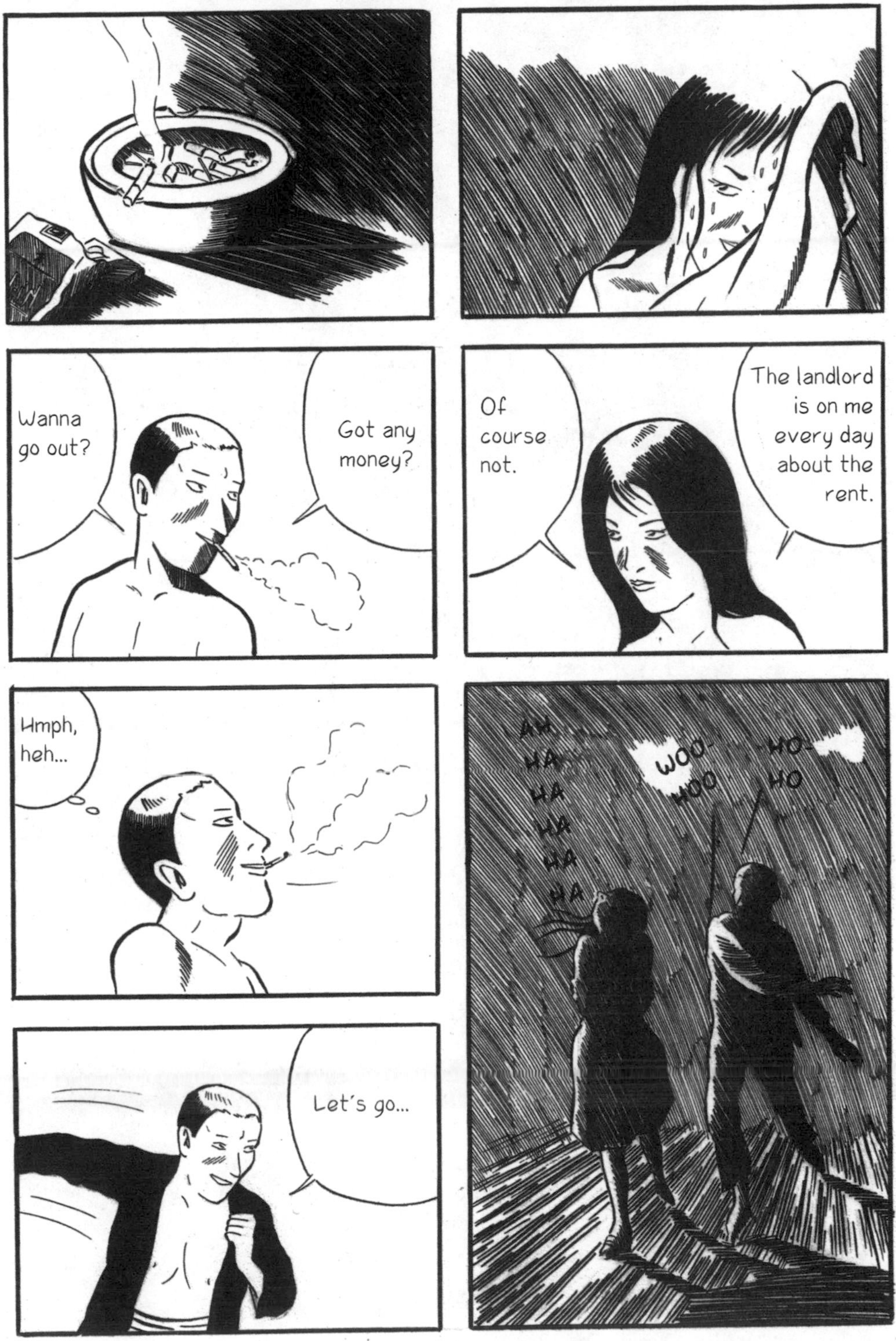
Wanna go out?
Got any money?
Of course not.
The landlord is on me every day about the rent.
Hmph, heh...
Let's go...
AH HA HA HA HA HA
WOO-HOO
HO-HO

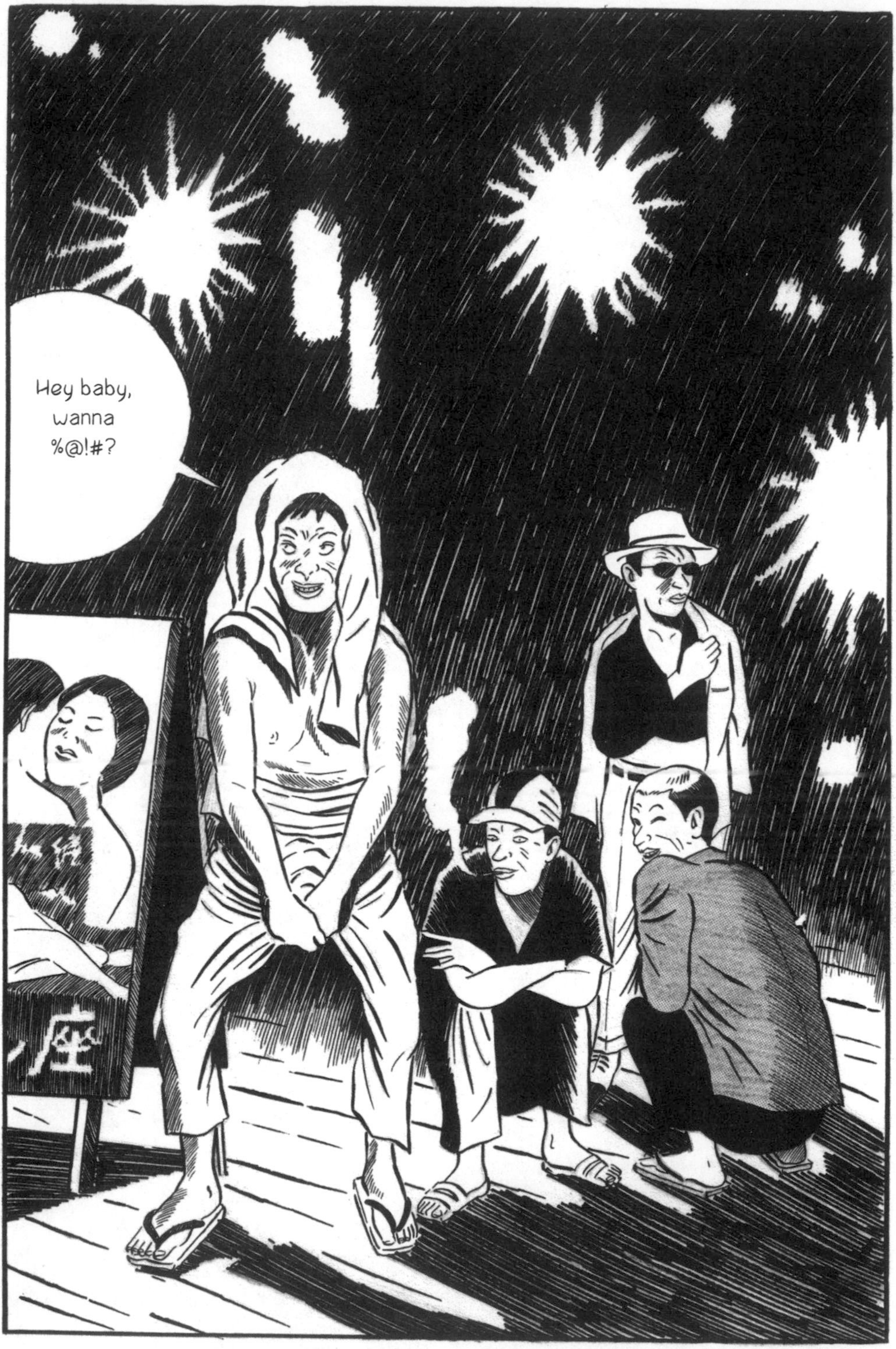
Hey baby, wanna %@!#?

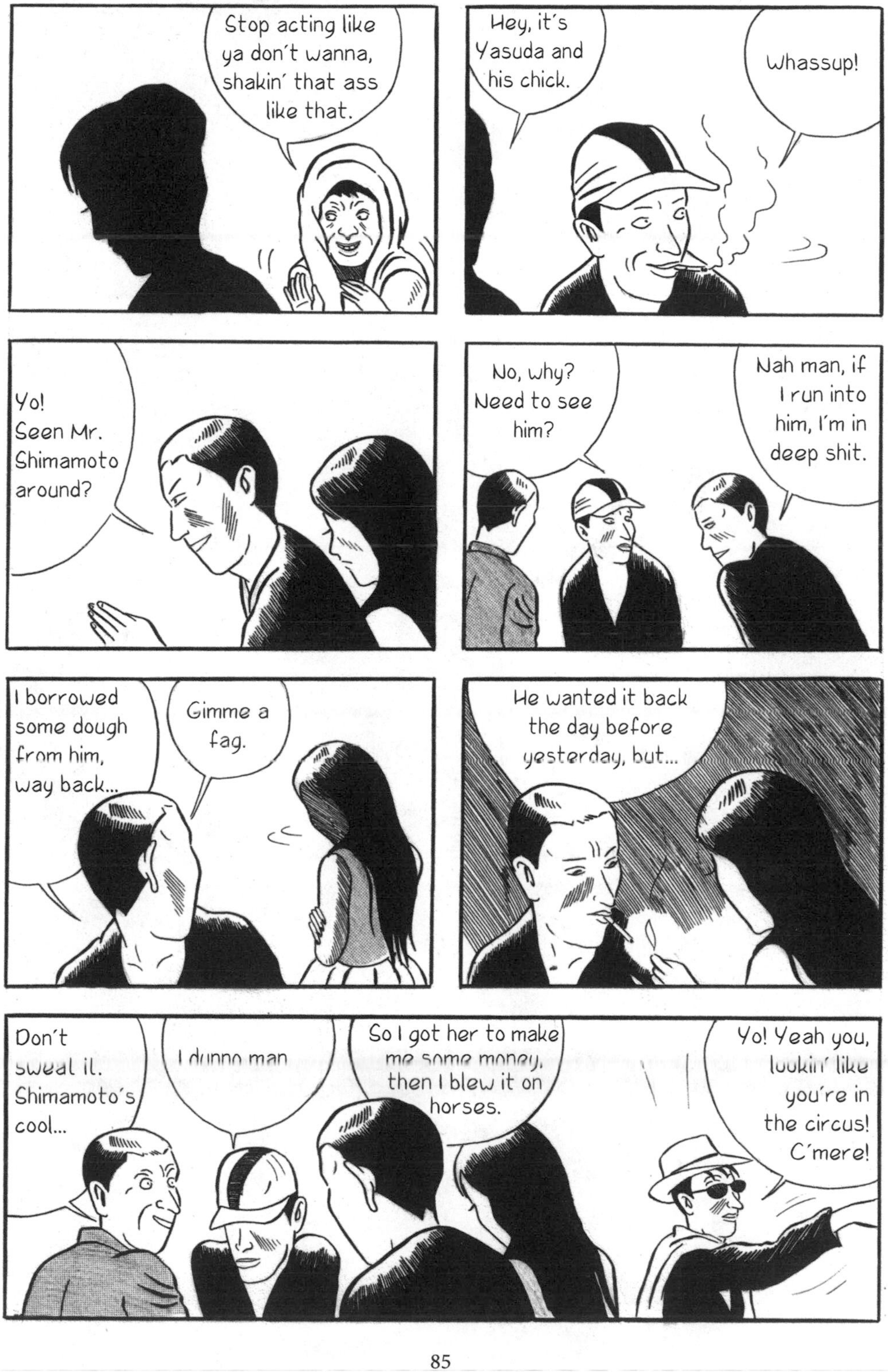
Stop acting like ya don't wanna, shakin' that ass like that.
Hey, it's Yasuda and his chick.
Whassup!
Yo! Seen Mr. Shimamoto around?
No, why? Need to see him?
Nah man, if I run into him, I'm in deep shit.
I borrowed some dough from him, way back...
Gimme a fag.
He wanted it back the day before yesterday, but...
Don't sweat it. Shimamoto's cool...
I dunno man
So I got her to make me some money, then I blew it on horses.
Yo! Yeah you, lookin' like you're in the circus! C'mere!

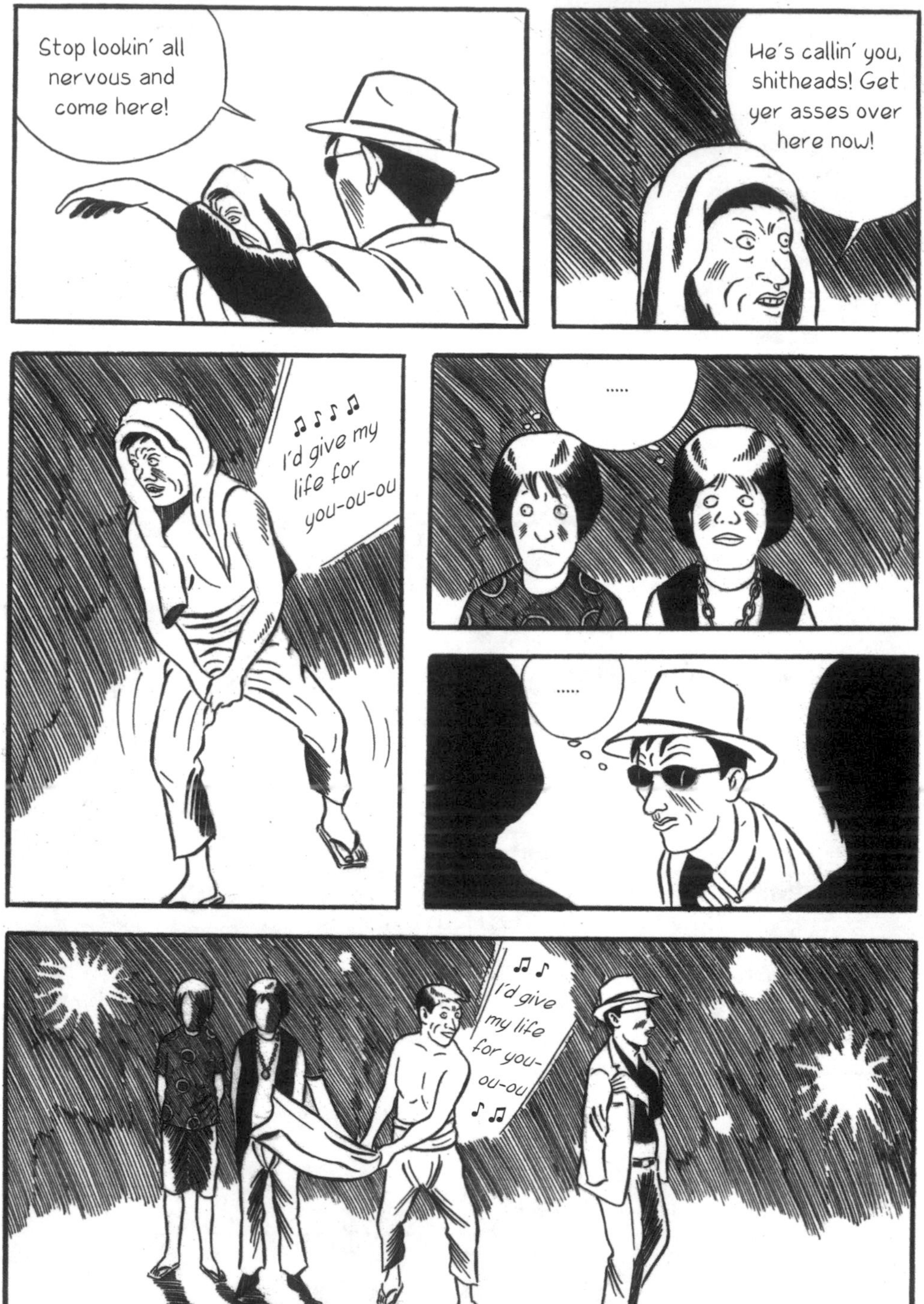
Stop lookin' all nervous and come here!
He's callin' you, shitheads! Get yer asses over here now!
♫♪♪♫ I'd give my life for you-ou-ou
.....
.....
♫♪ I'd give my life for you-ou-ou ♪♫

song: Fuji Keiko, "I'd Give My Life For You" (Inochi azukemasu, 1970)

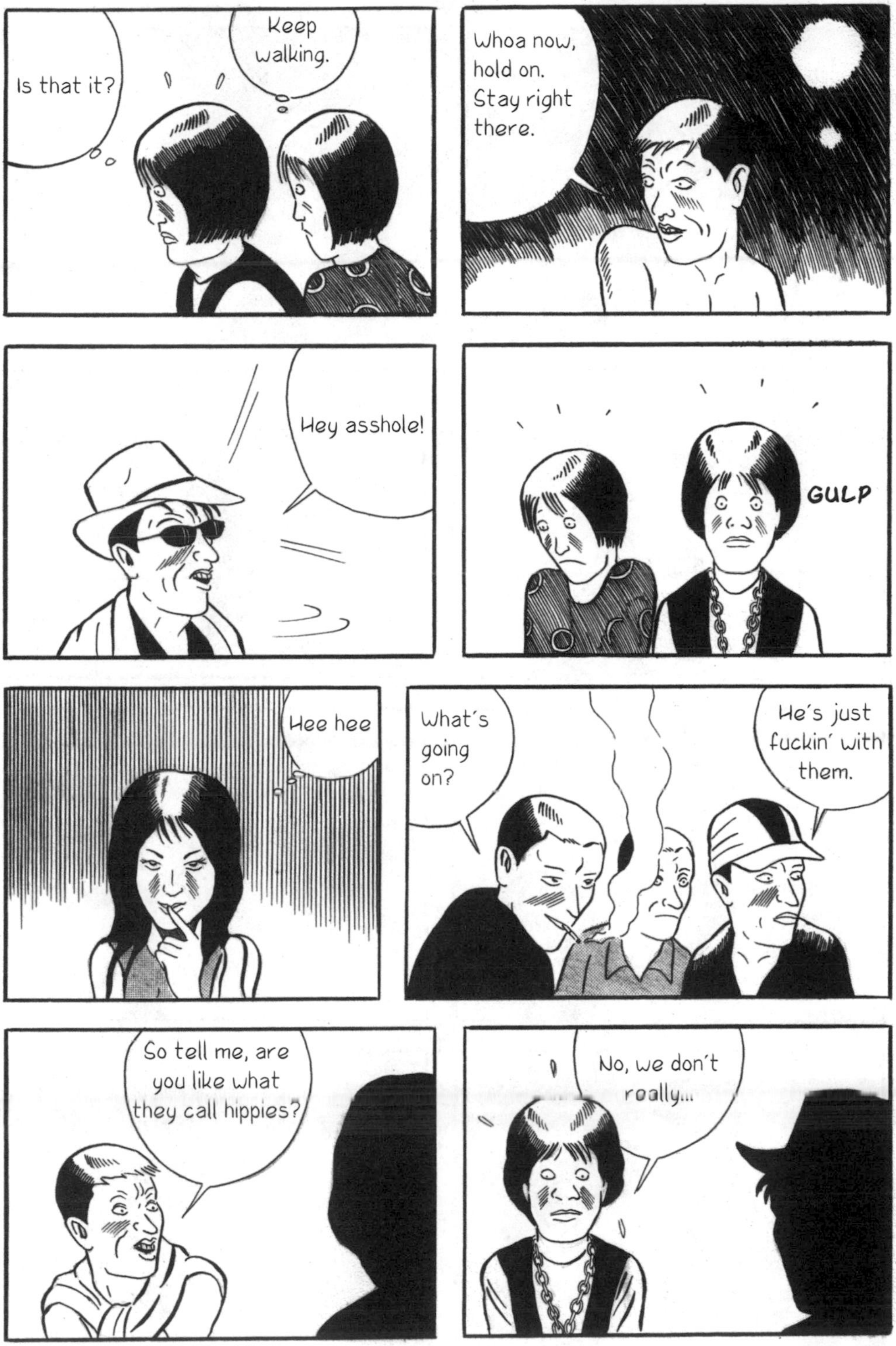
Is that it?
Keep walking.
Whoa now, hold on. Stay right there.
Hey asshole!
GULP
Hee hee
What's going on?
He's just fuckin' with them.
So tell me, are you like what they call hippies?
No, we don't really...

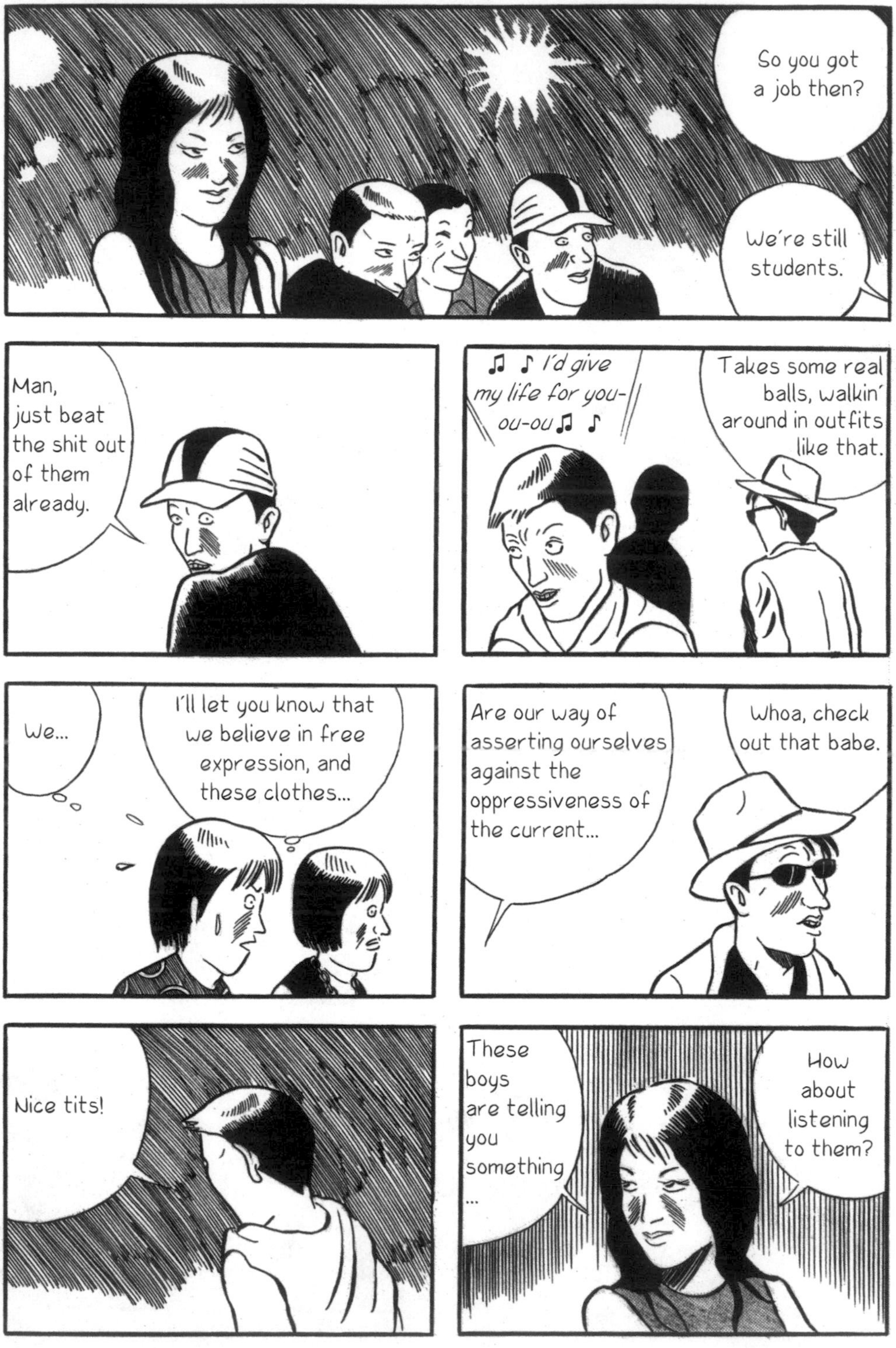
So you got a job then?
We're still students.
Man, just beat the shit out of them already.
♫ ♪ I'd give my life for you-ou-ou ♫ ♪
Takes some real balls, walkin' around in outfits like that.
We...
I'll let you know that we believe in free expression, and these clothes...
Are our way of asserting ourselves against the oppressiveness of the current...
Whoa, check out that babe.
Nice tits!
These boys are telling you something ...
How about listening to them?

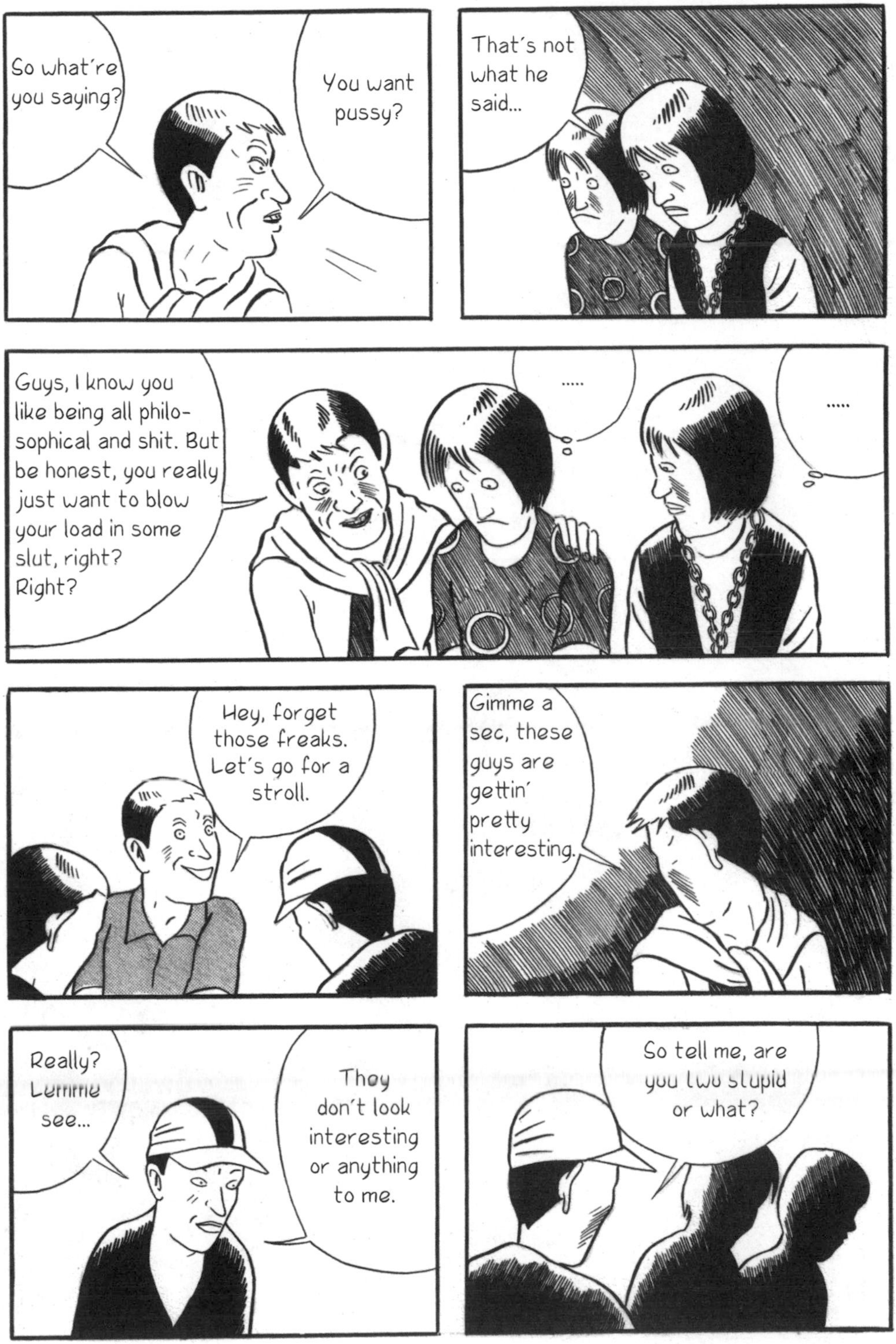
So what're you saying?
You want pussy?
That's not what he said...
Guys, I know you like being all philo-sophical and shit. But be honest, you really just want to blow your load in some slut, right? Right?
.....
.....
Hey, forget those freaks. Let's go for a stroll.
Gimme a sec, these guys are gettin' pretty interesting.
Really? Lemme see...
They don't look interesting or anything to me.
So tell me, are you two stupid or what?

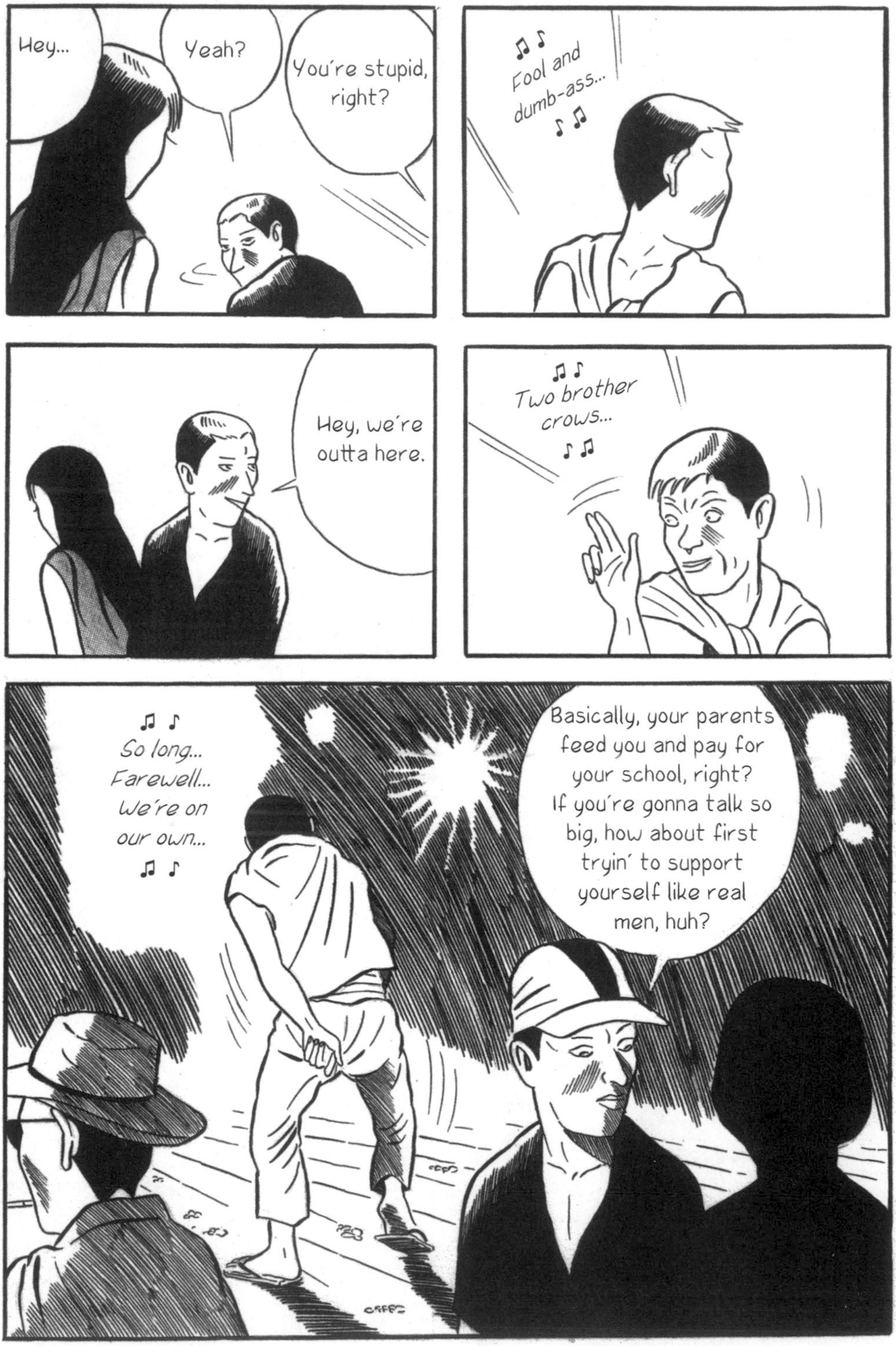
Hey...
Yeah?
You're stupid, right?
♫ ♪ Fool and dumb-ass... ♪ ♫
Hey, we're outta here.
♫ ♪ Two brother crows... ♪ ♫
♫ ♪ So long... Farewell... We're on our own... ♫ ♪
Basically, your parents feed you and pay for your school, right? If you're gonna talk so big, how about first tryin' to support yourself like real men, huh?

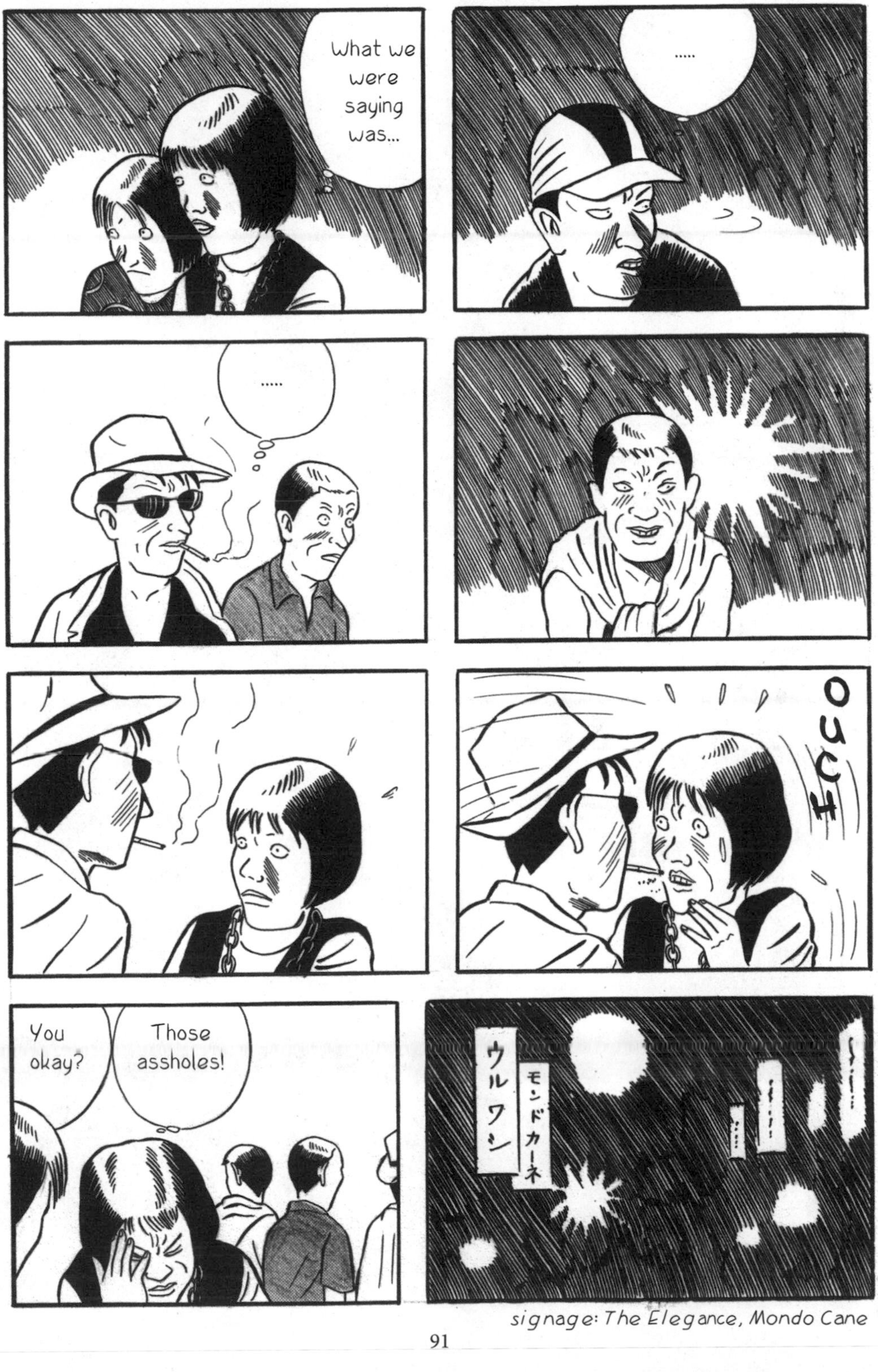
What we were saying was...
.....
.....
OUCH
You okay?
Those assholes!
ウルワシ
モンドカーネ

signage: The Elegance, Mondo Cane

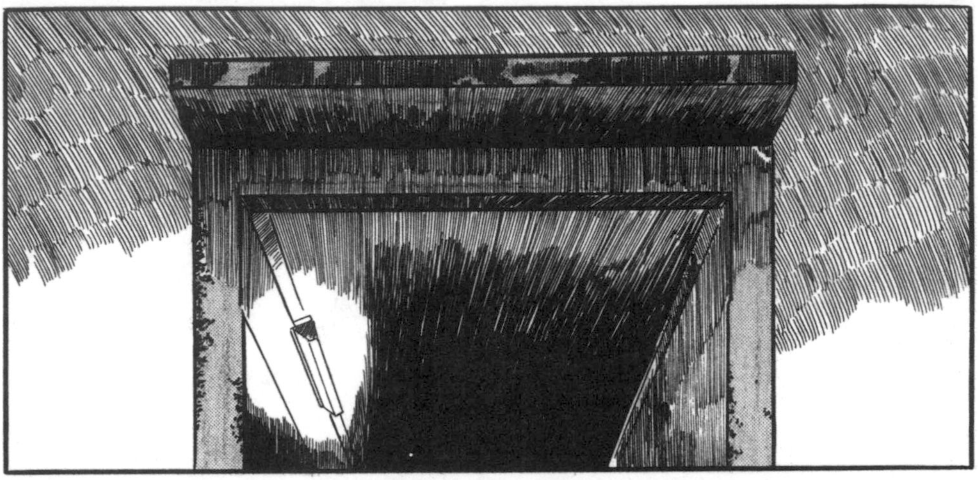

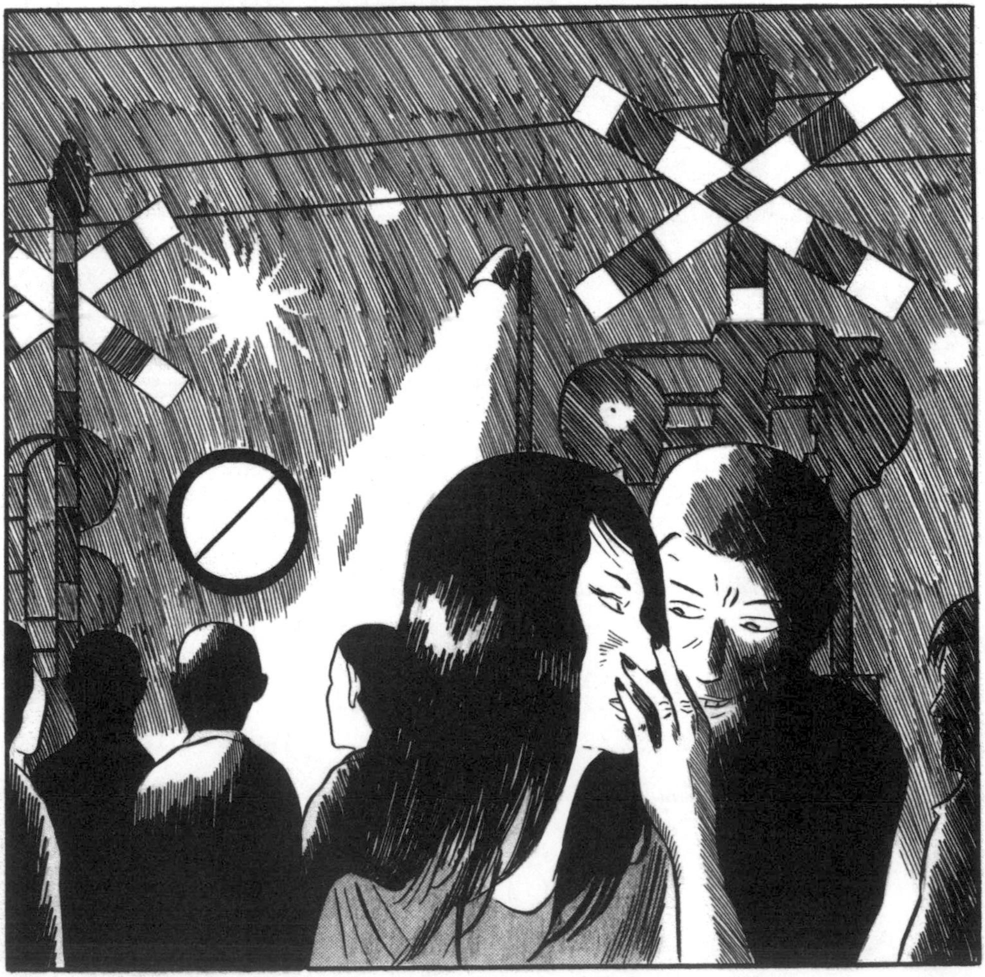

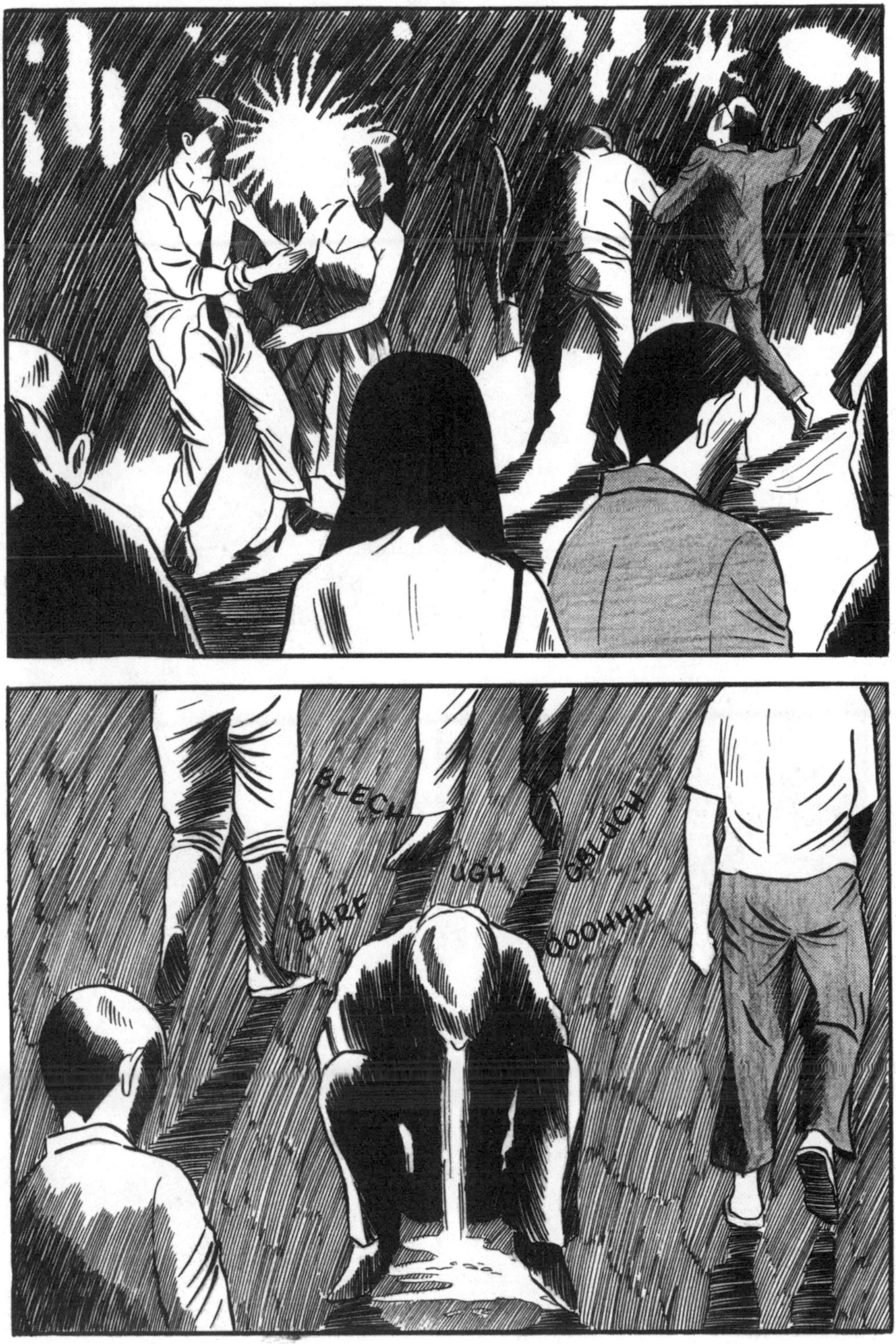
BLECH
GBLUCH
UGH
BARF
OOOHHH

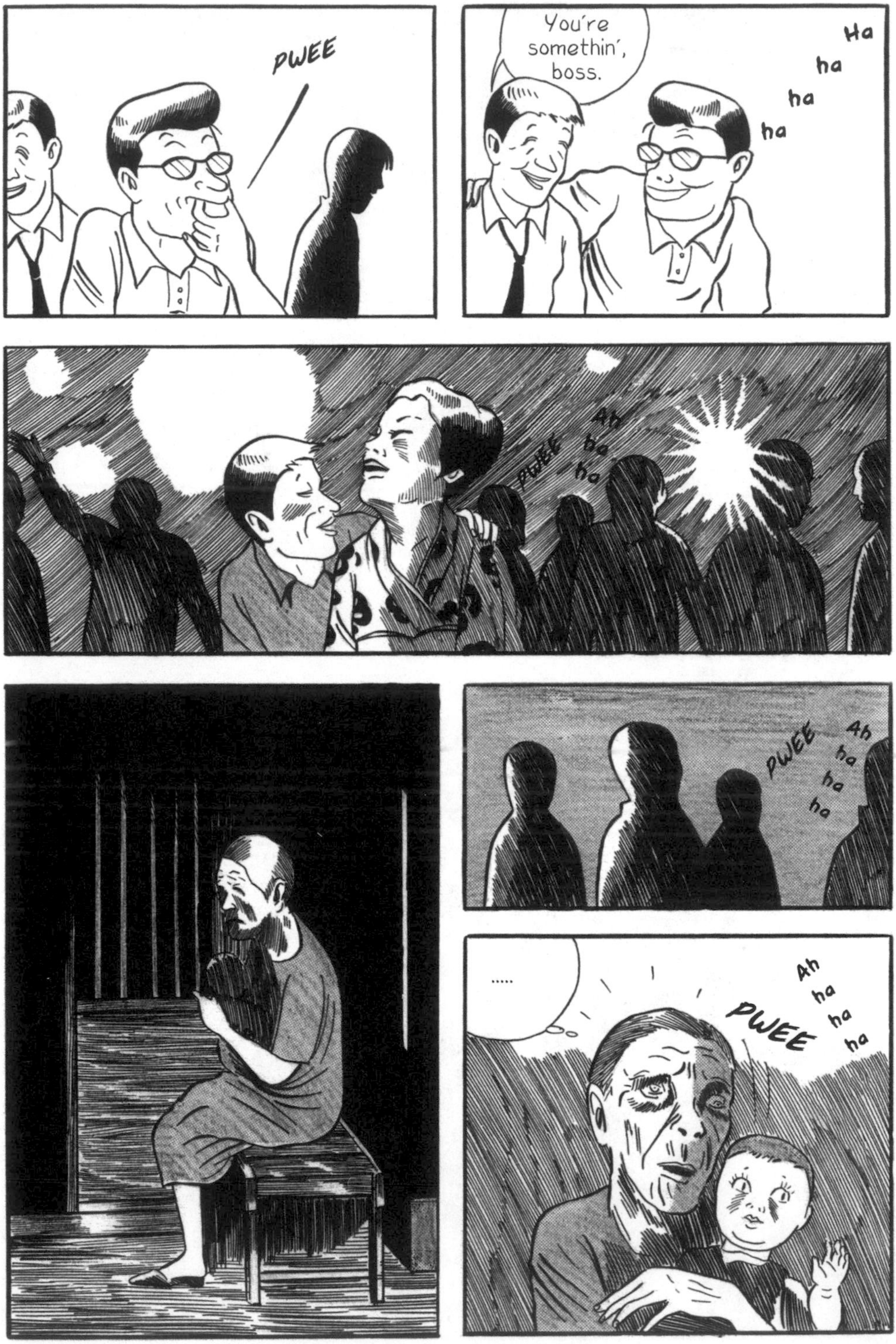
PWEE
You're somethin', boss.
Ha ha ha ha
PWEE
Ah ha ha
PWEE
Ah ha ha ha
.....
PWEE
Ah ha ha ha

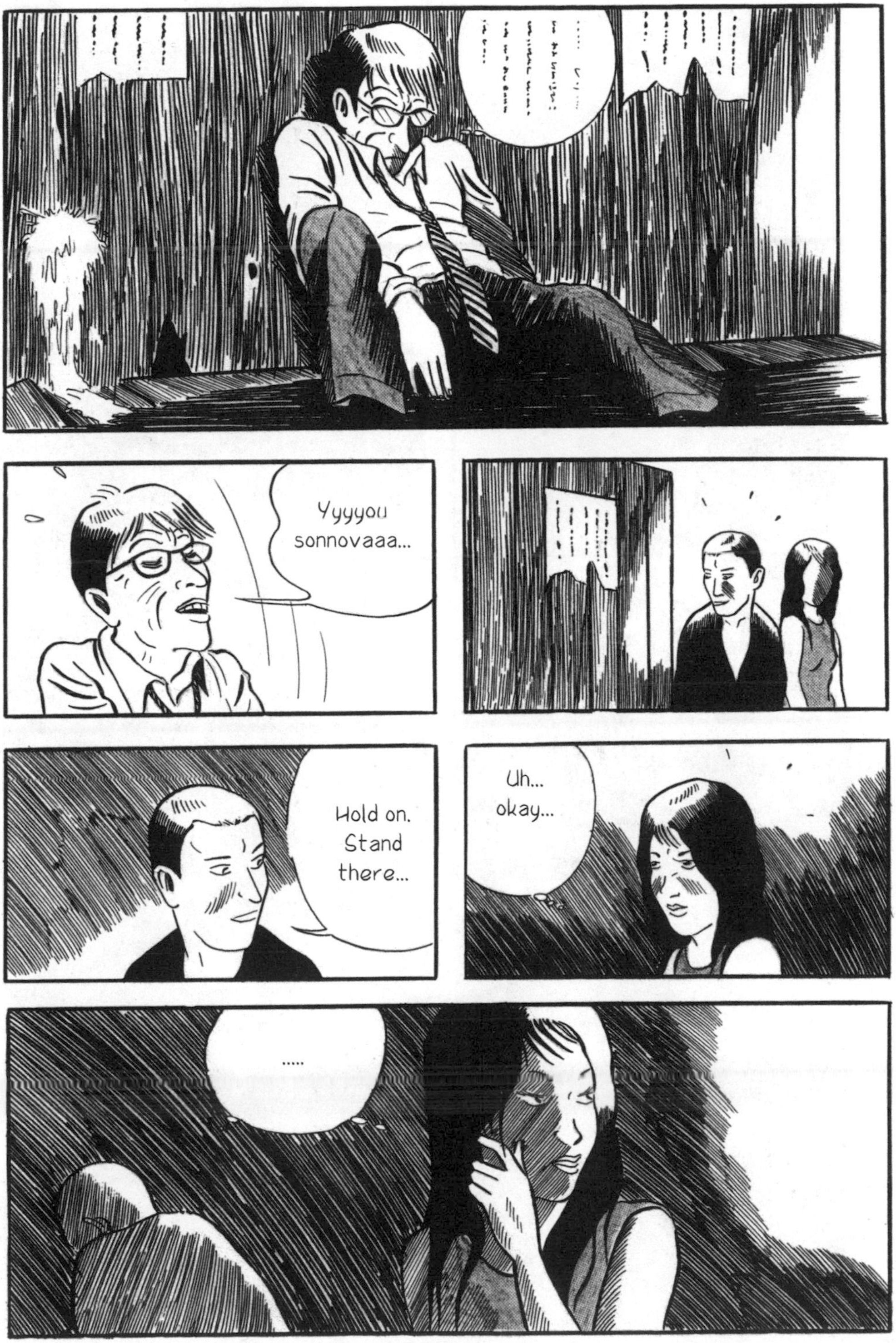
Yyyyou sonnovaaa...
Hold on. Stand there...
Uh... okay...
.....

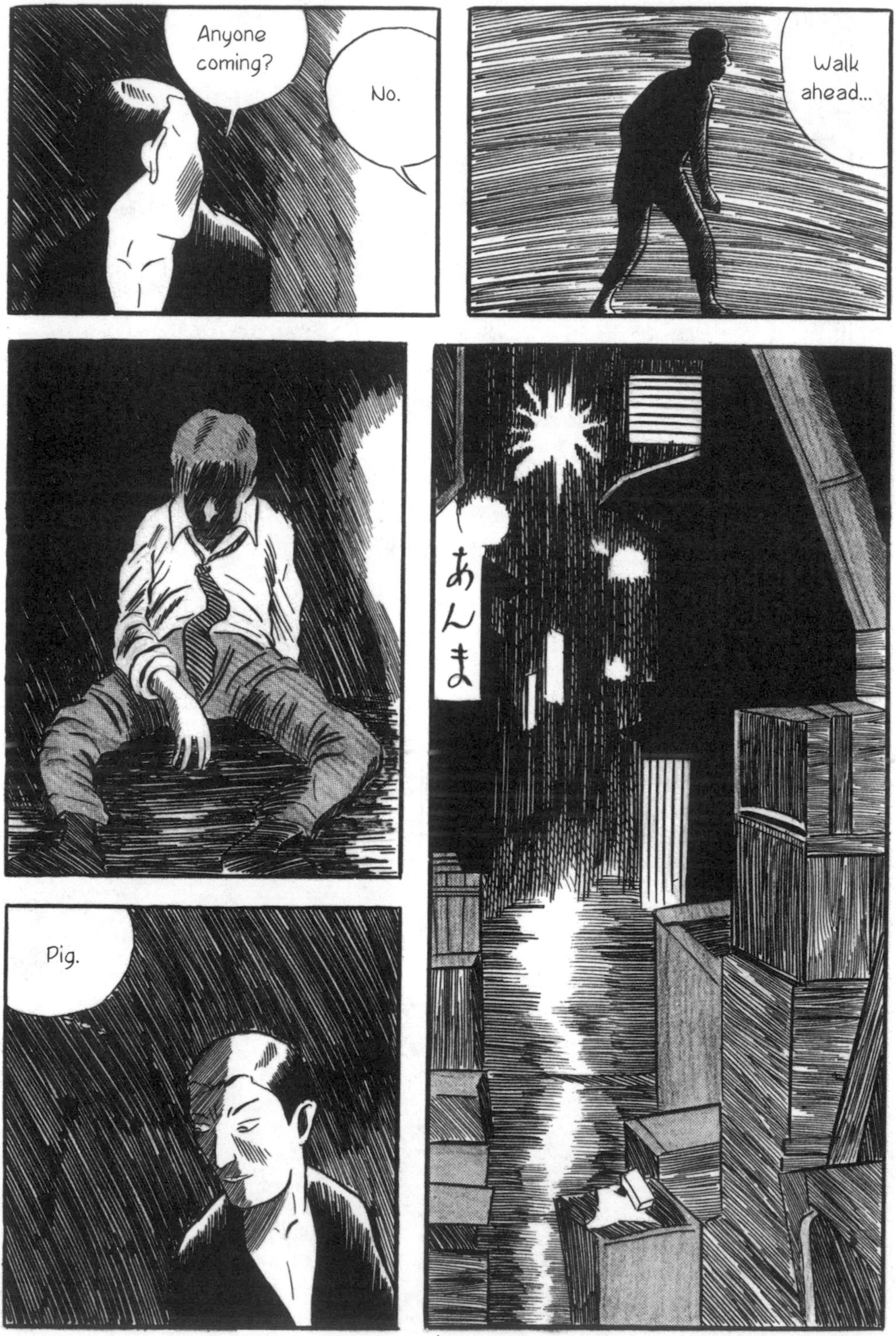
Anyone coming?
No.
Walk ahead...
Pig.
あんま

sign: massage

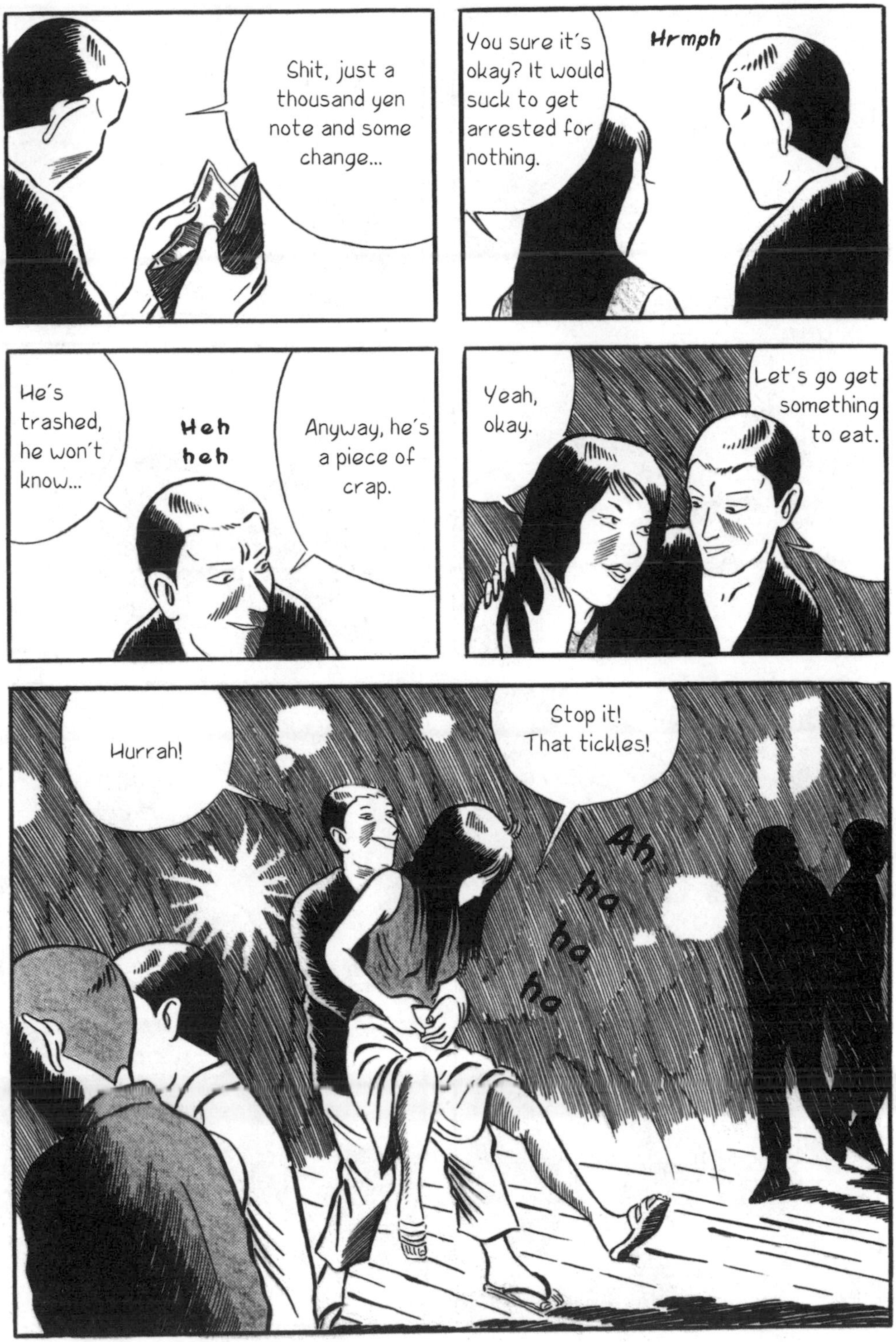
Shit, just a thousand yen note and some change...
You sure it's okay? It would suck to get arrested for nothing.
Hrmph
He's trashed, he won't know...
Heh heh
Anyway, he's a piece of crap.
Yeah, okay.
Let's go get something to eat.
Hurrah!
Stop it! That tickles!
Ah ha ha ha

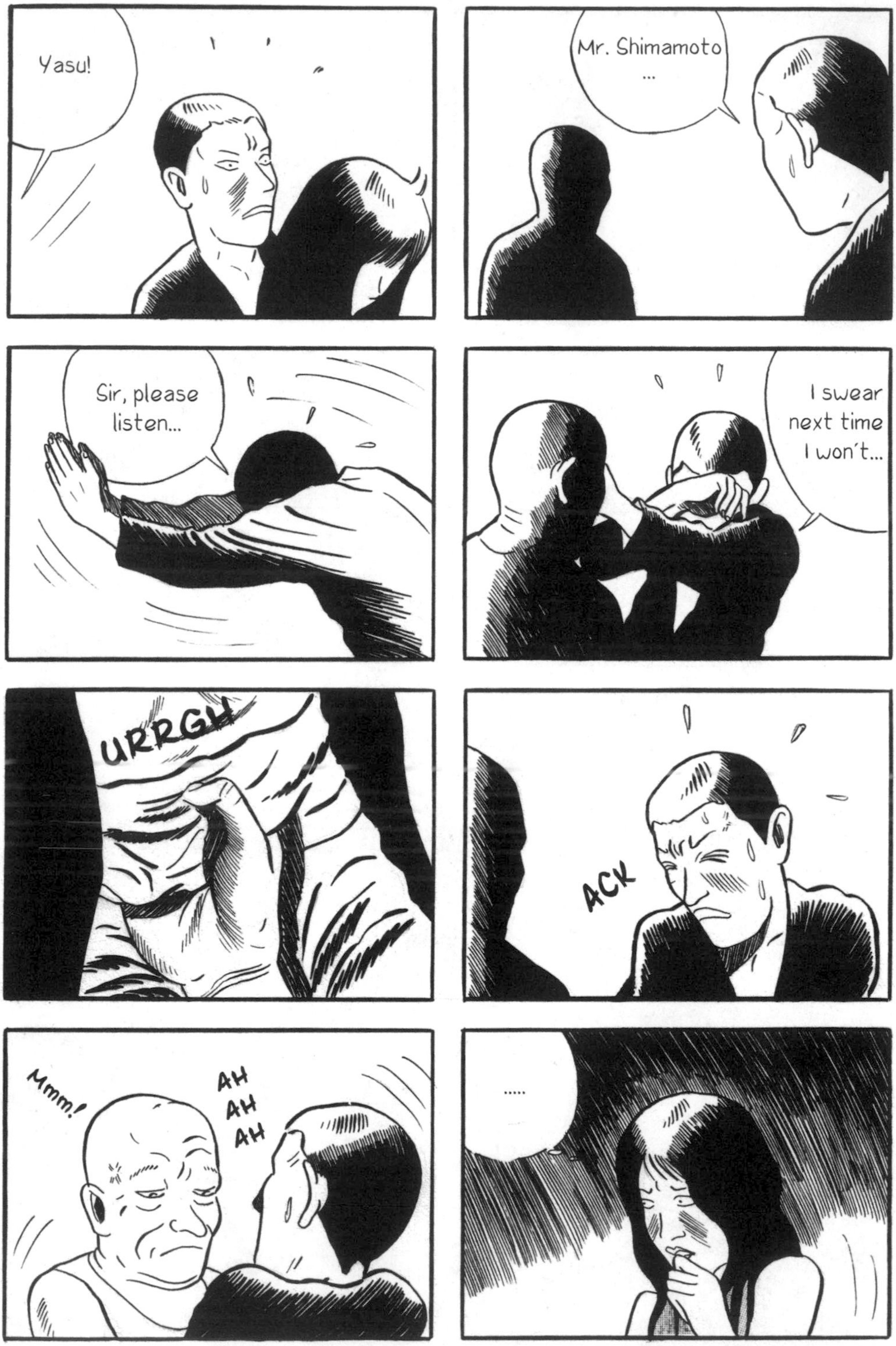
Yasu!
Mr. Shimamoto ...
Sir, please listen...
I swear next time I won't...
URRGH
ACK
Mmm!
AH AH AH
.....

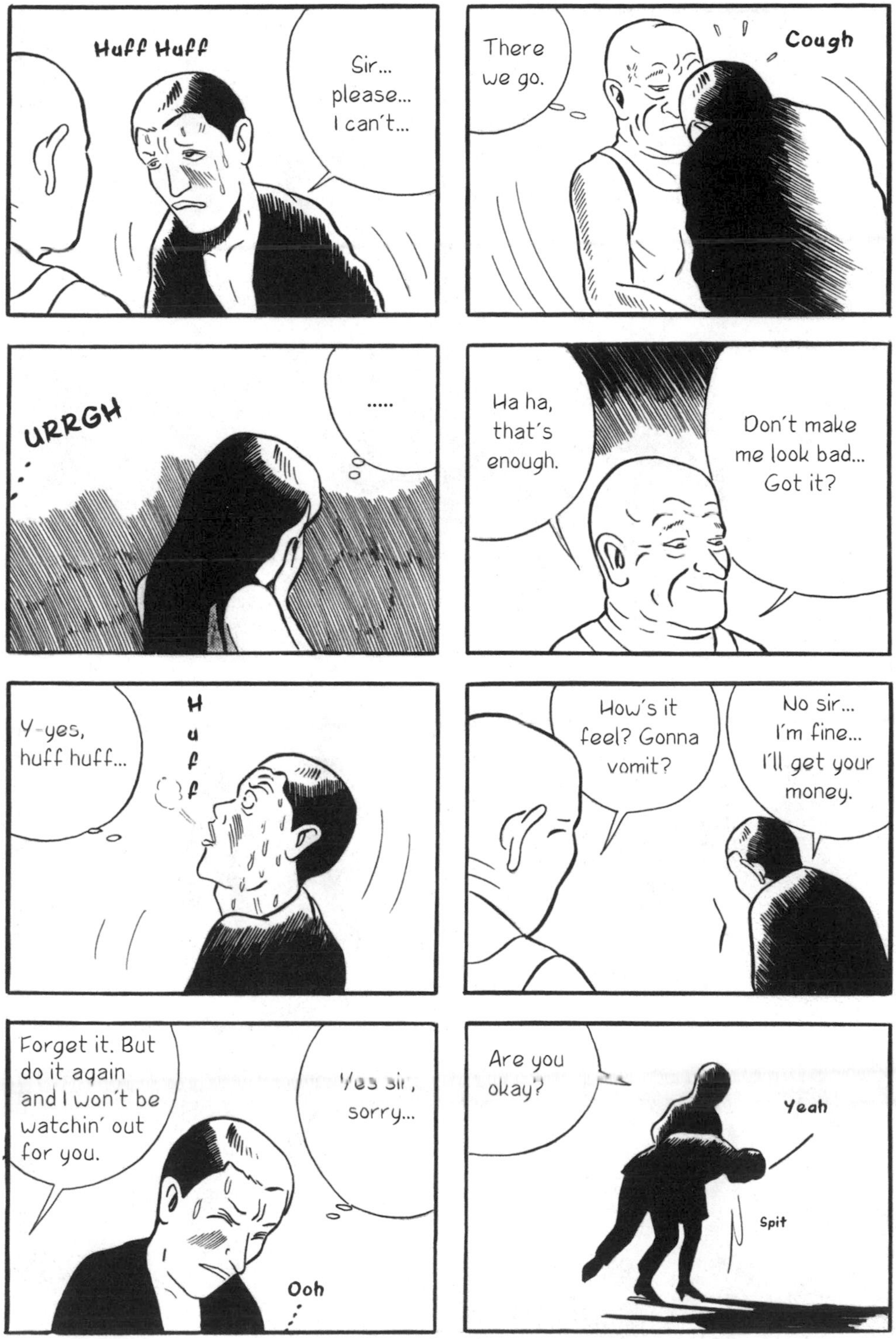
Huff Huff
Sir... please... I can't...
There we go.
Cough
URRGH
.....
Ha ha, that's enough.
Don't make me look bad... Got it?
Y-yes, huff huff...
Huff
How's it feel? Gonna vomit?
No sir... I'm fine... I'll get your money.
Forget it. But do it again and I won't be watchin' out for you.
Yes sir, sorry...
Ooh
Are you okay?
Yeah
Spit

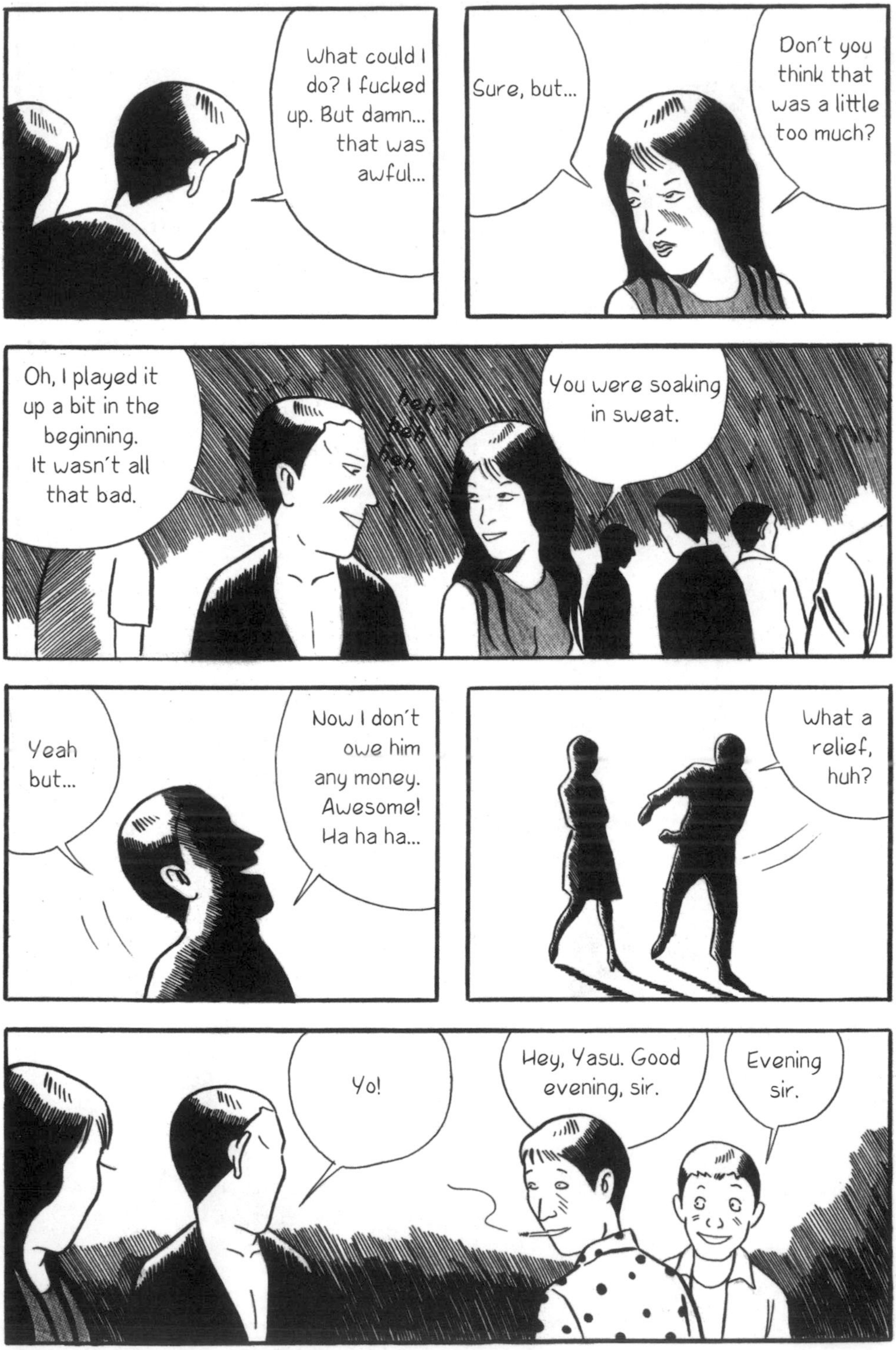
What could I do? I fucked up. But damn... that was awful...
Sure, but...
Don't you think that was a little too much?
Oh, I played it up a bit in the beginning. It wasn't all that bad.
heh heh heh
You were soaking in sweat.
Yeah but...
Now I don't owe him any money. Awesome! Ha ha ha...
What a relief, huh?
Yo!
Hey, Yasu. Good evening, sir.
Evening sir.

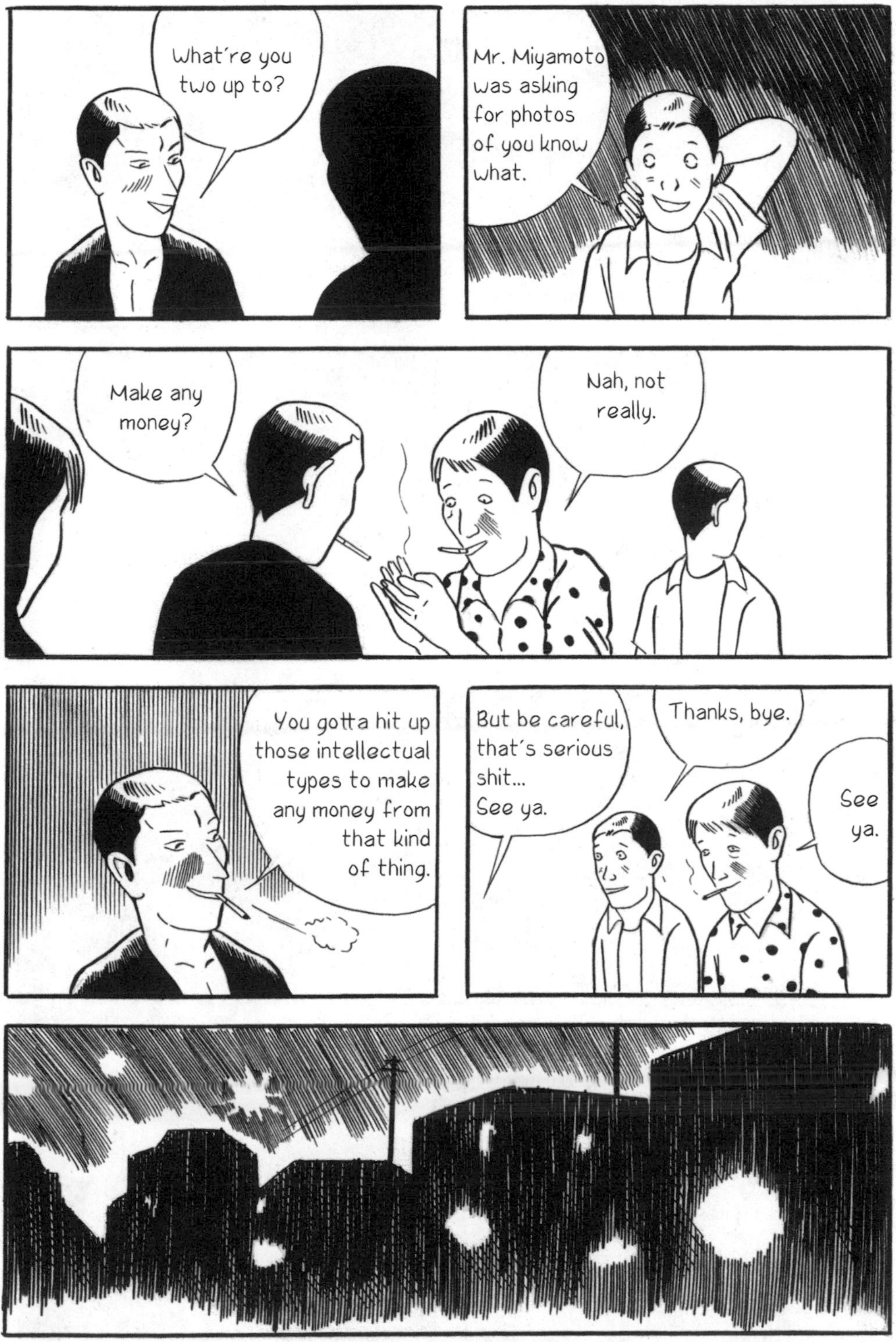
What're you two up to?
Mr. Miyamoto was asking for photos of you know what.
Make any money?
Nah, not really.
You gotta hit up those intellectual types to make any money from that kind of thing.
But be careful, that's serious shit... See ya.
Thanks, bye.
See ya.

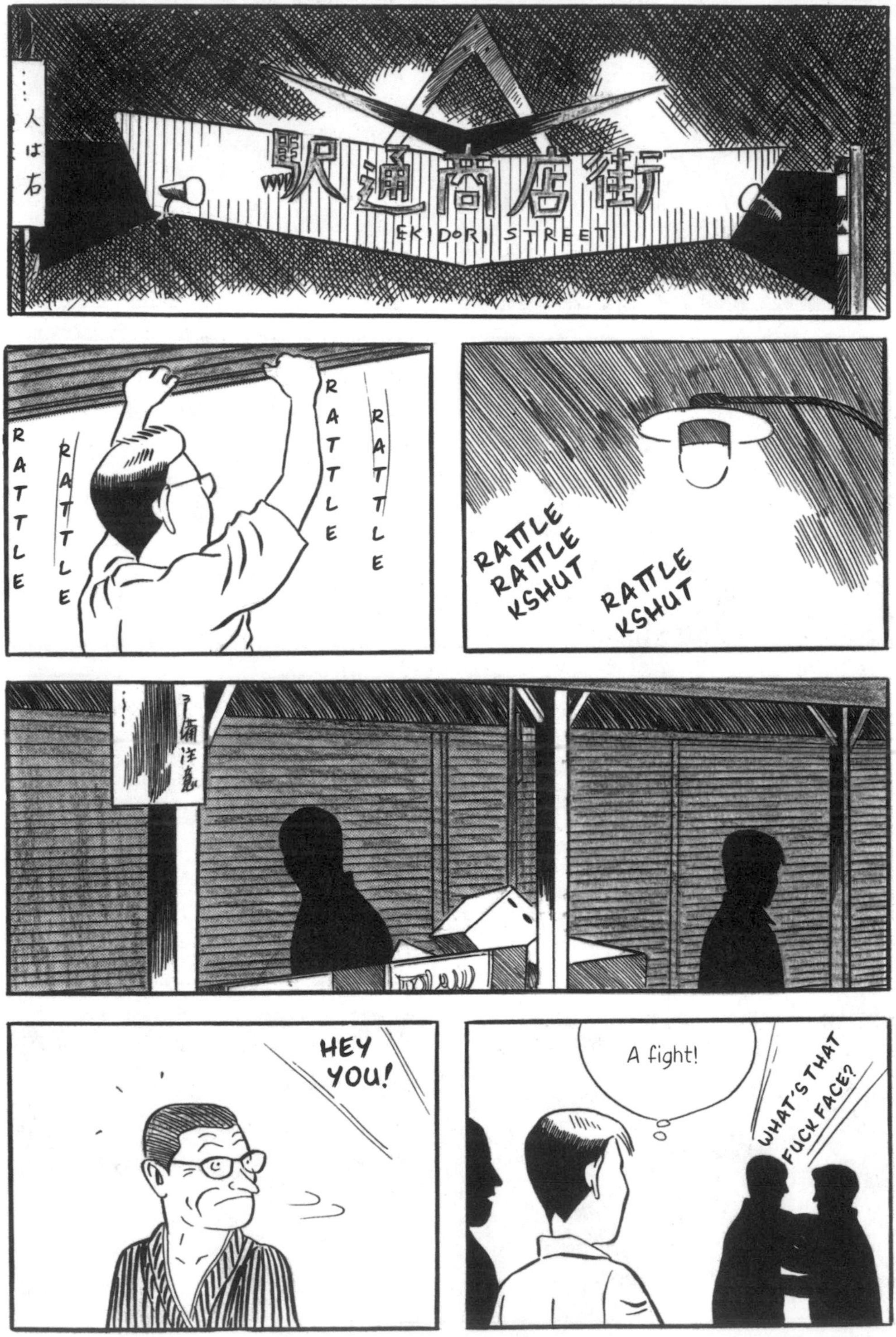

人は右
駅通商店街
EKIDORI STREET
RATTLE
RATTLE
RATTLE
RATTLE
RATTLE RATTLE KSHUT
RATTLE KSHUT
備注意
HEY YOU!
A fight!
WHAT'S THAT FUCK FACE?

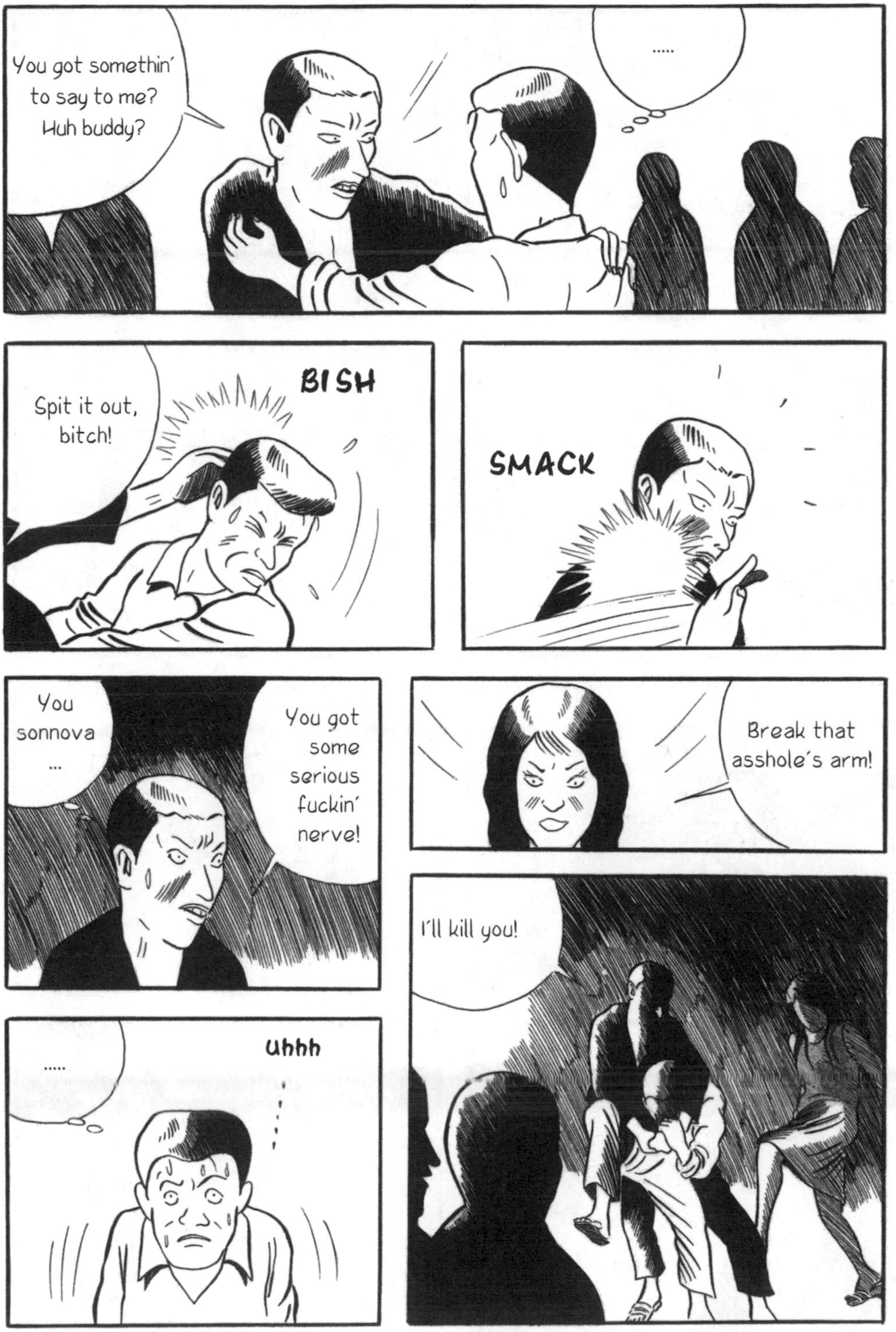

You got somethin' to say to me? Huh buddy?
.....
Spit it out, bitch!
BISH
SMACK
You sonnova ...
You got some serious fuckin' nerve!
Break that asshole's arm!
.....
uhhh
I'll kill you!

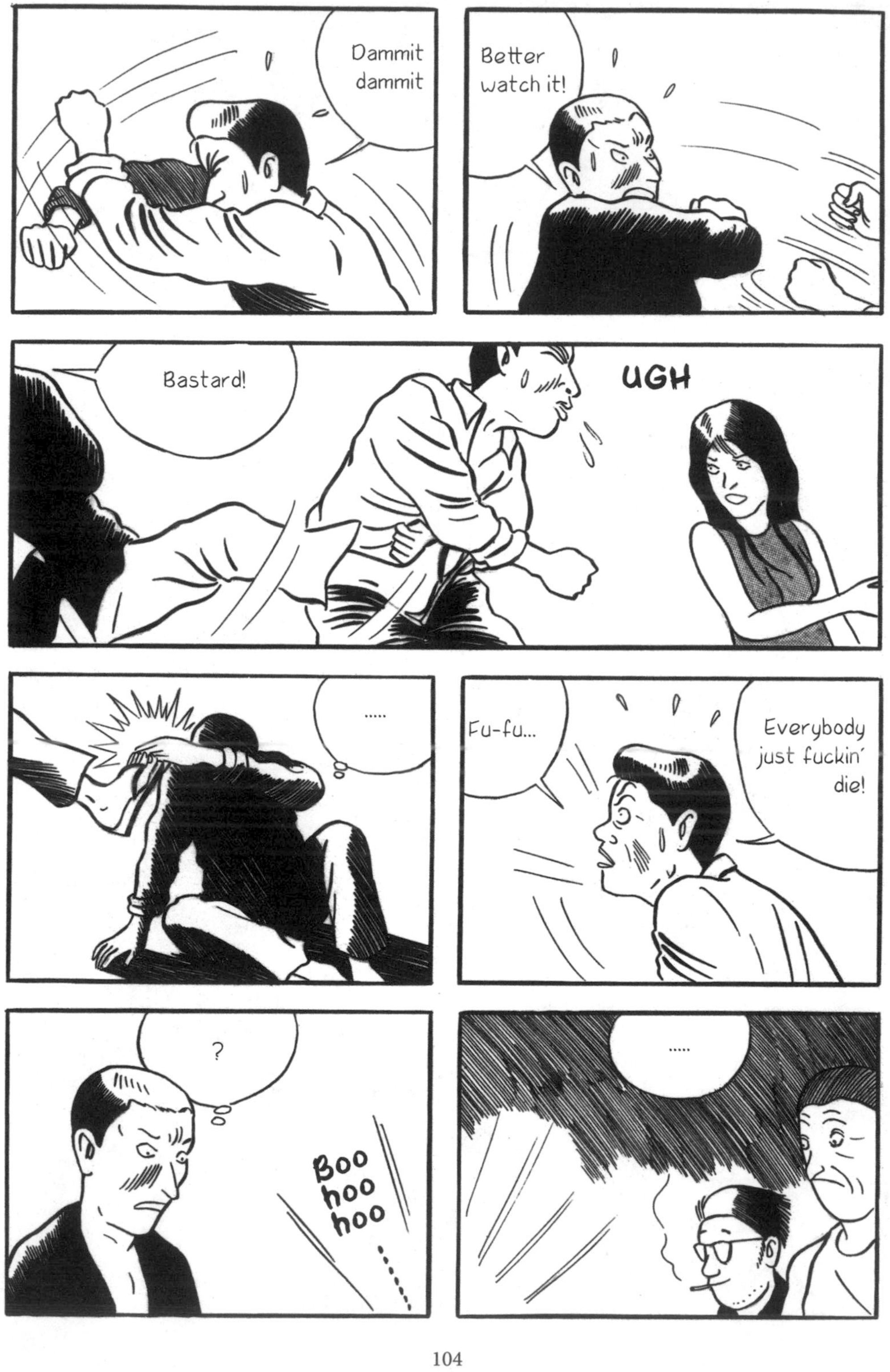
Dammit dammit
Better watch it!
Bastard!
UGH
.....
Fu-fu...
Everybody just fuckin' die!
?
Boo hoo hoo
.....

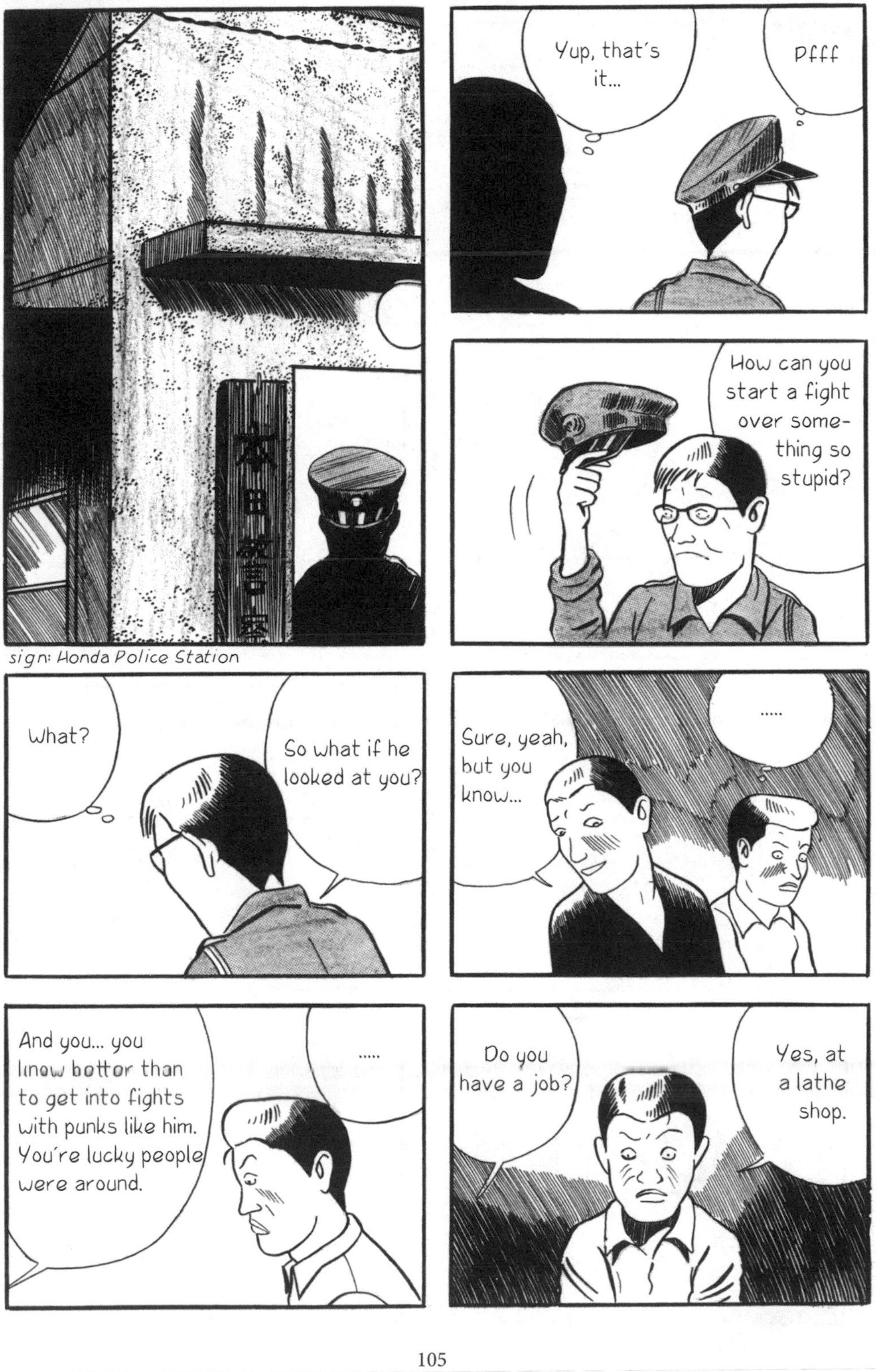
sign: Honda Police Station
Yup, that's it...
Pfff
How can you start a fight over some-thing so stupid?
What?
So what if he looked at you?
Sure, yeah, but you know...
.....
And you... you know better than to get into fights with punks like him. You're lucky people were around.
.....
Do you have a job?
Yes, at a lathe shop.

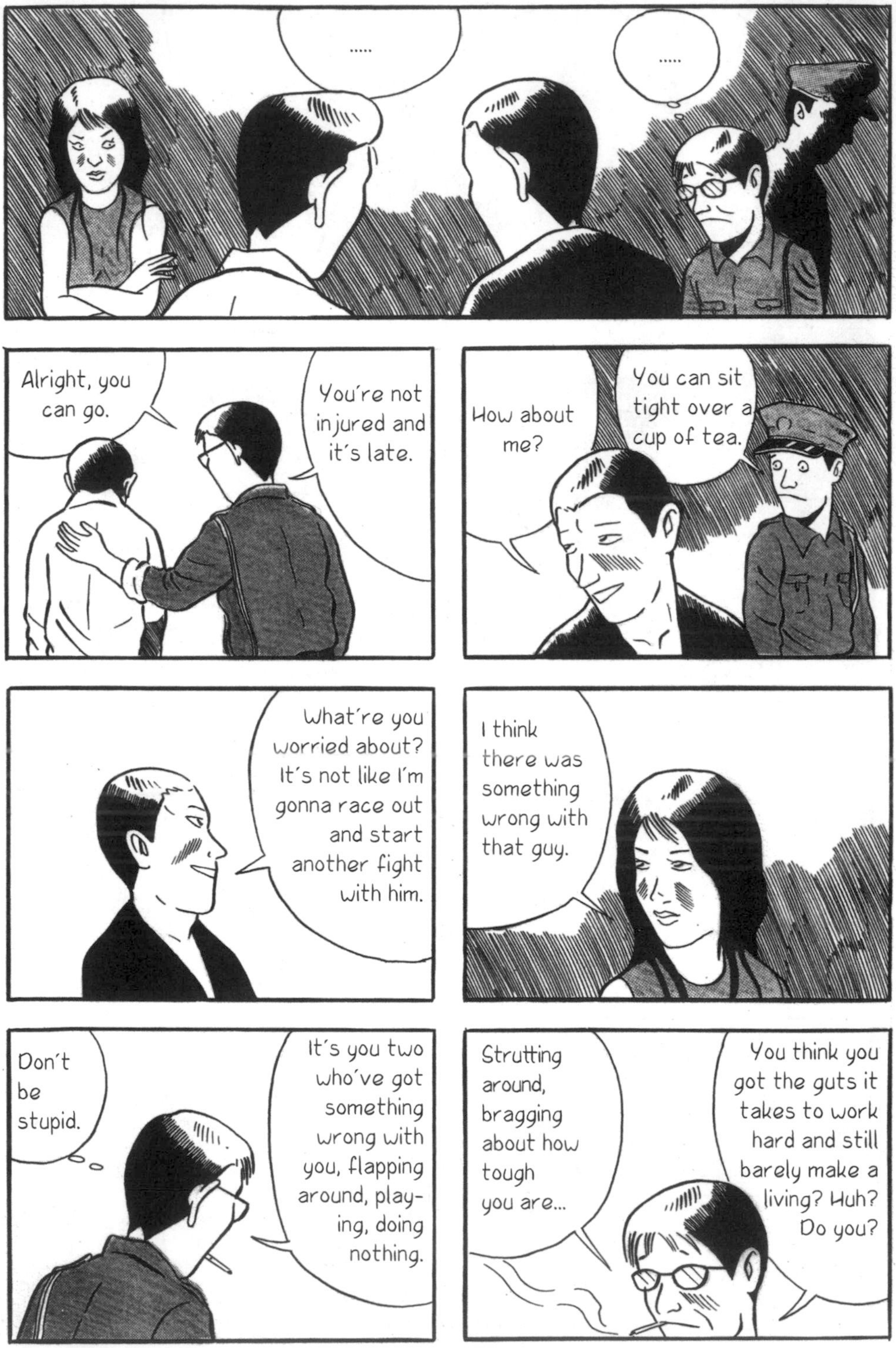
.....
.....
Alright, you can go.
You're not injured and it's late.
How about me?
You can sit tight over a cup of tea.
What're you worried about? It's not like I'm gonna race out and start another fight with him.
I think there was something wrong with that guy.
Don't be stupid.
It's you two who've got something wrong with you, flapping around, play-ing, doing nothing.
Strutting around, bragging about how tough you are...
You think you got the guts it takes to work hard and still barely make a living? Huh? Do you?

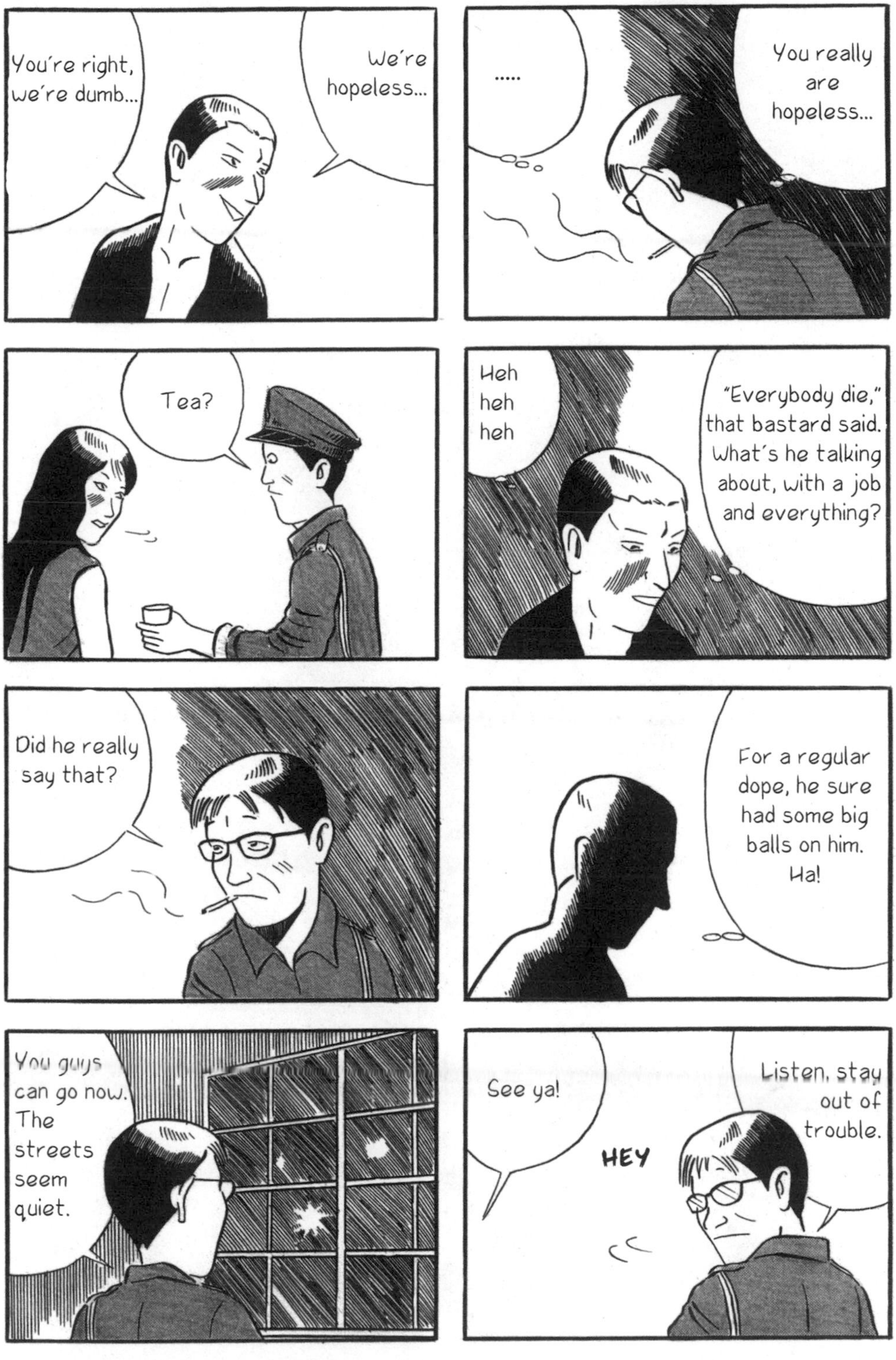
You're right, we're dumb...
We're hopeless...
.....
You really are hopeless...
Tea?
Heh heh heh
"Everybody die," that bastard said. What's he talking about, with a job and everything?
Did he really say that?
For a regular dope, he sure had some big balls on him. Ha!
You guys can go now. The streets seem quiet.
See ya!
Listen, stay out of trouble.
HEY

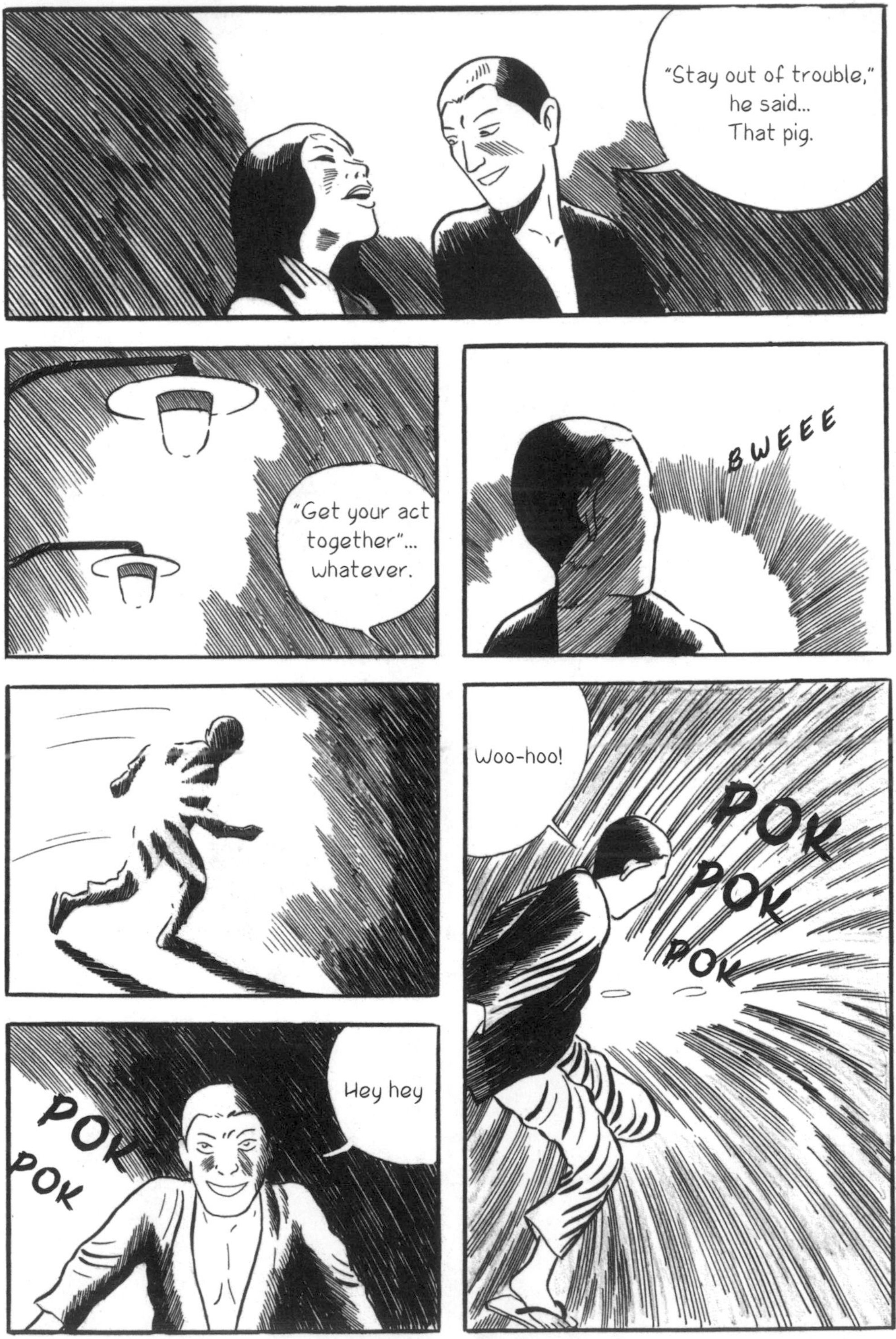
"Stay out of trouble," he said... That pig.
"Get your act together"... whatever.
BWEEE
Hey hey
POK
POK
Woo-hoo!
POK
POK
POK

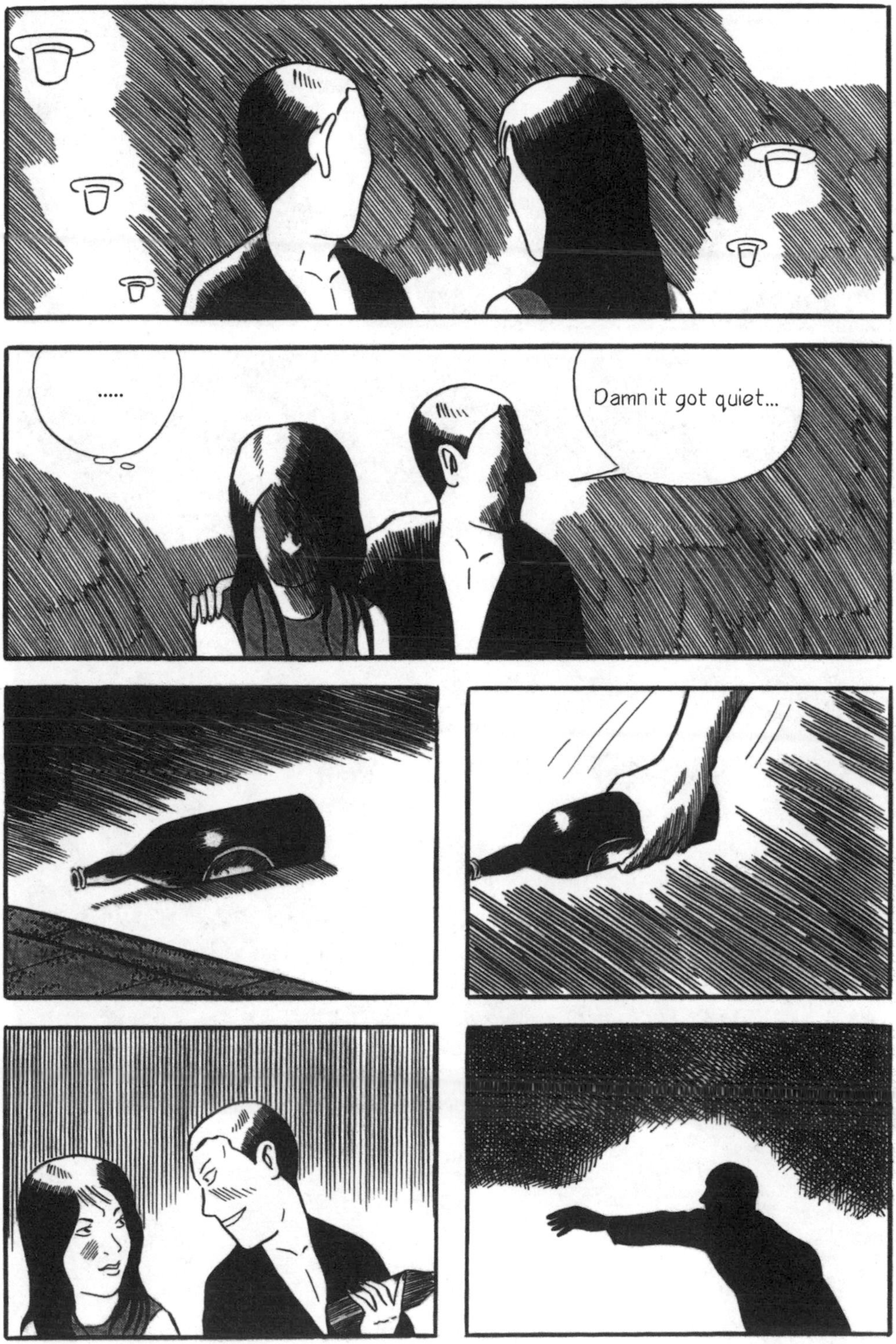
.....
Damn it got quiet...

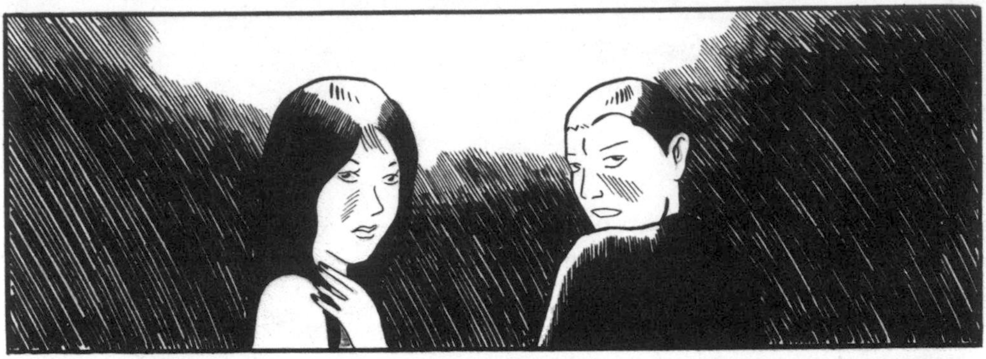

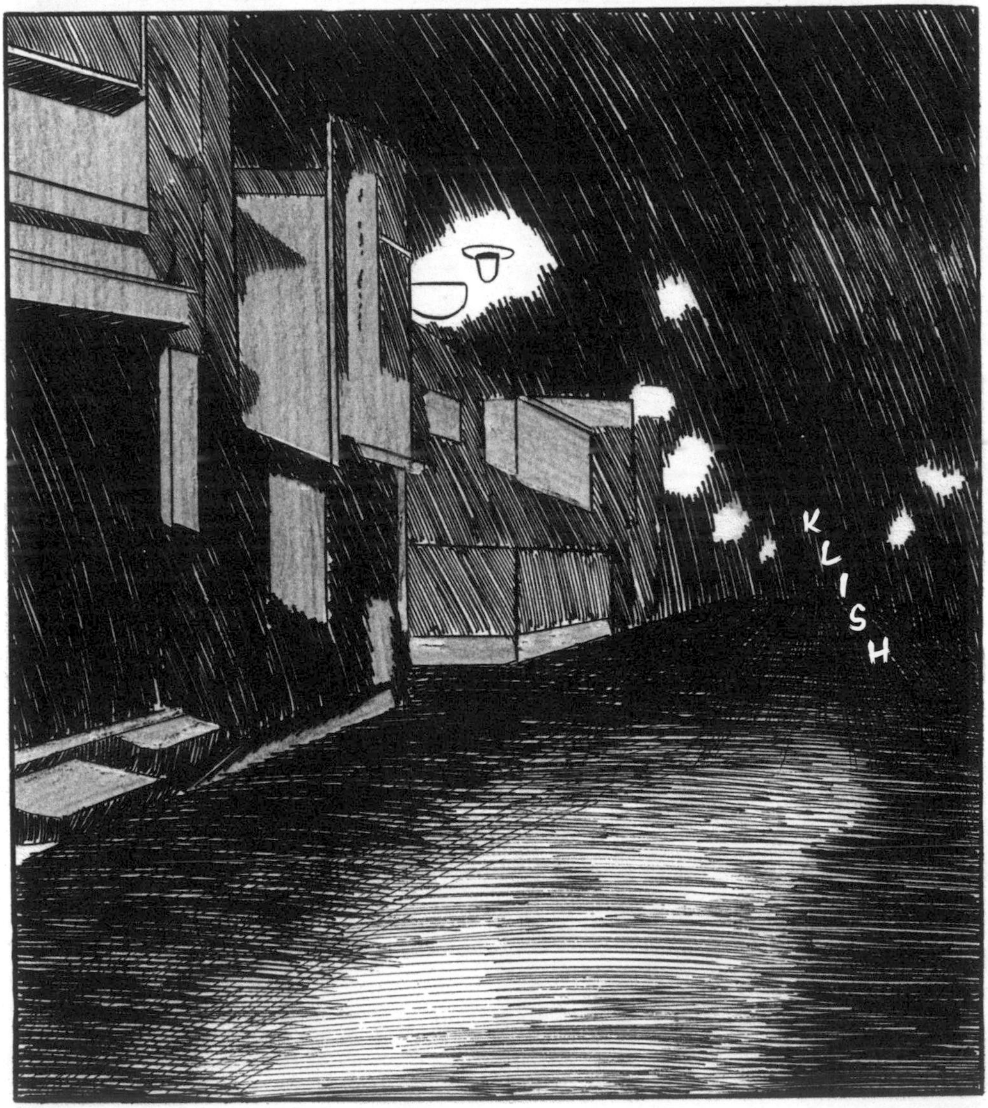
KLISH

THE END

WANDERING WOLF:
THE BLOODSPATTERED
CODE OF HONOR
AND HUMANITY

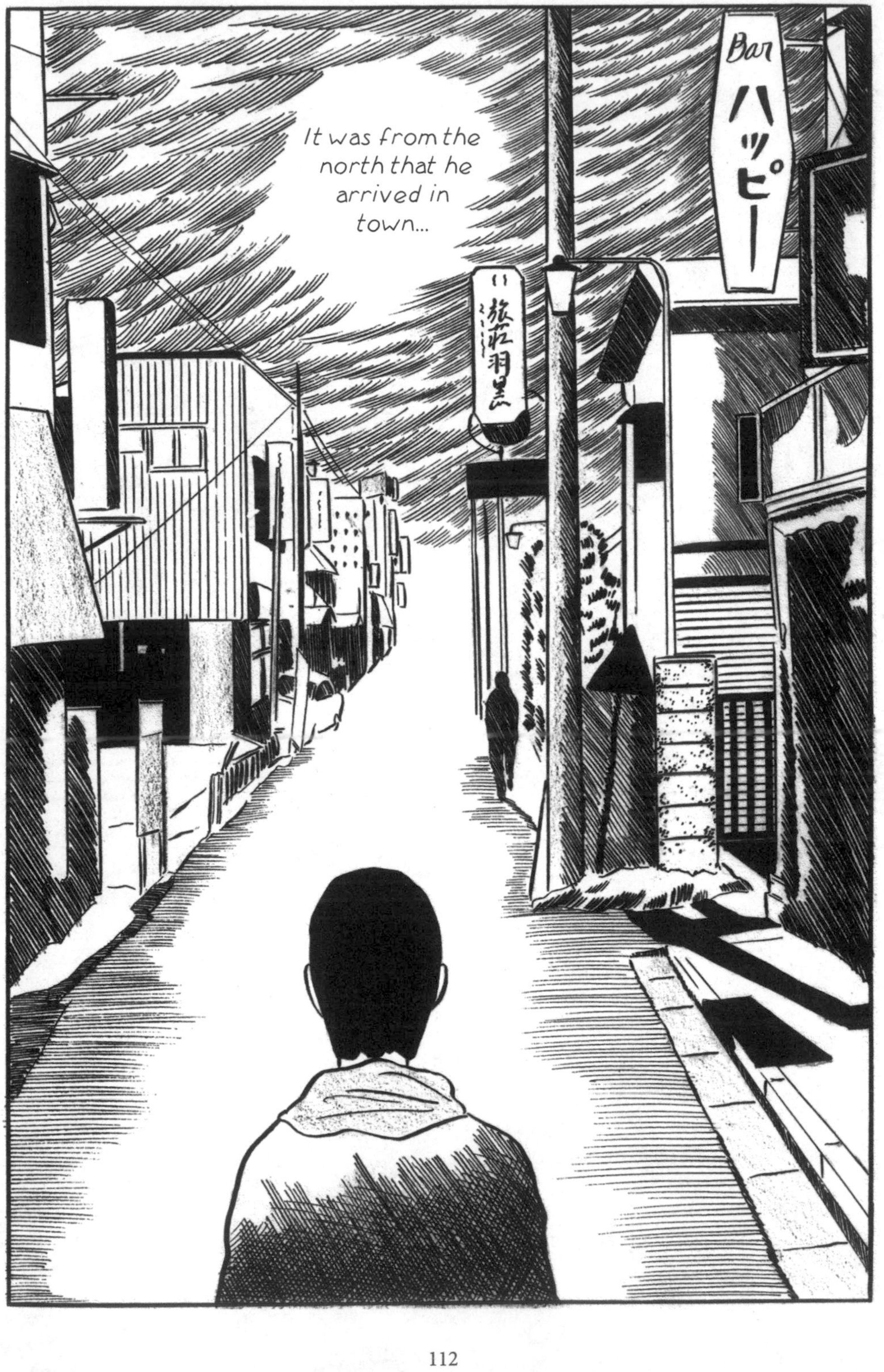
It was from the north that he arrived in town...
Bar
ハッピー
旅荘羽黒

He sported a red handkerchief around his neck, perhaps in lieu of a scarf...

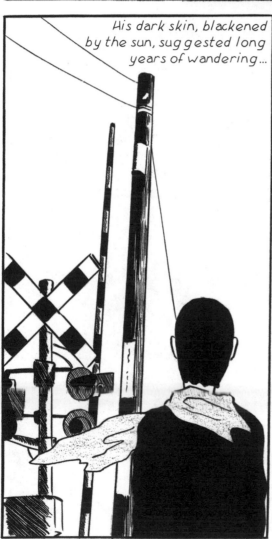

His dark skin, blackened by the sun, suggested long years of wandering...

His eyes were infinitely distant...

A gambling man, surely that's what he was...

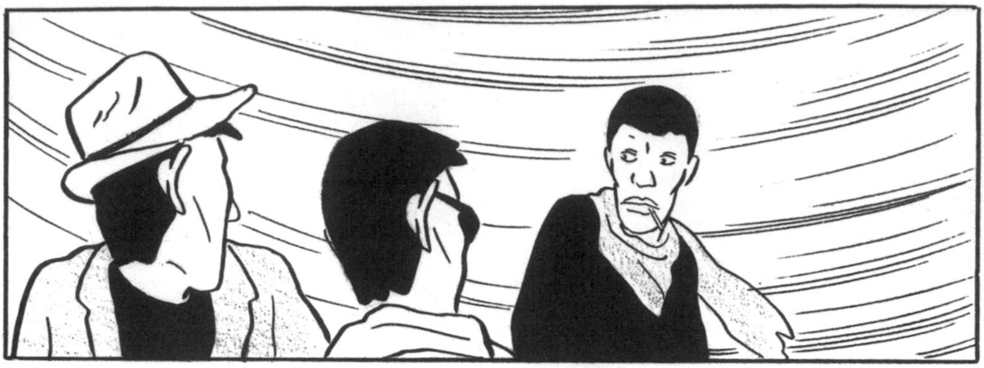

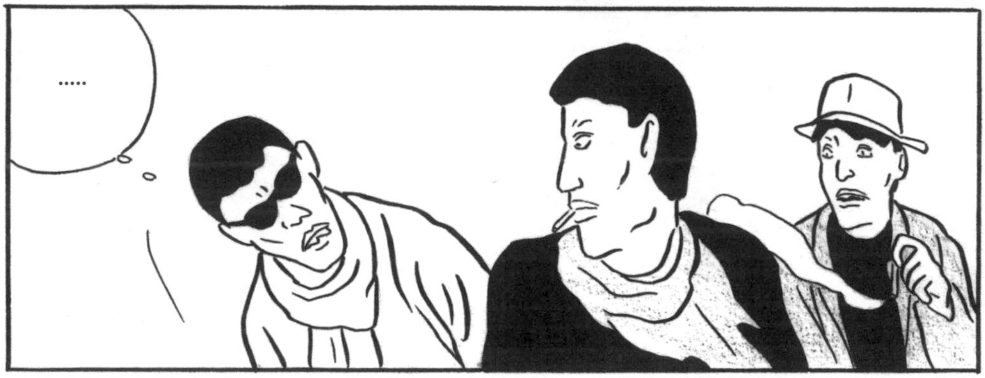
.....

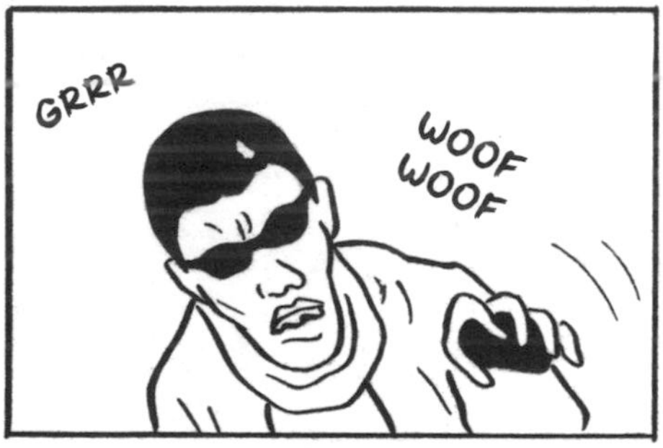
GRRR
WOOF WOOF

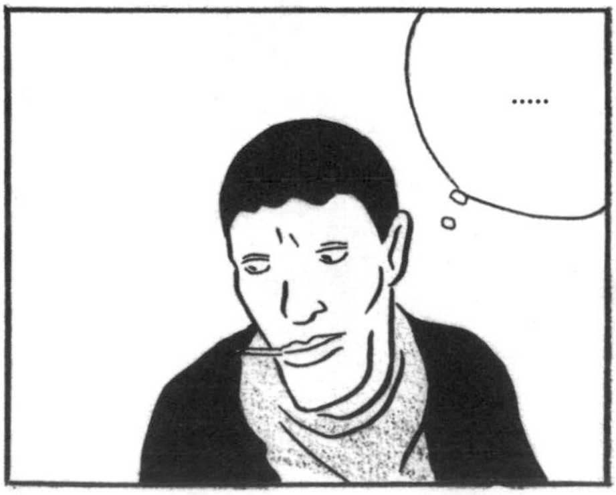
.....

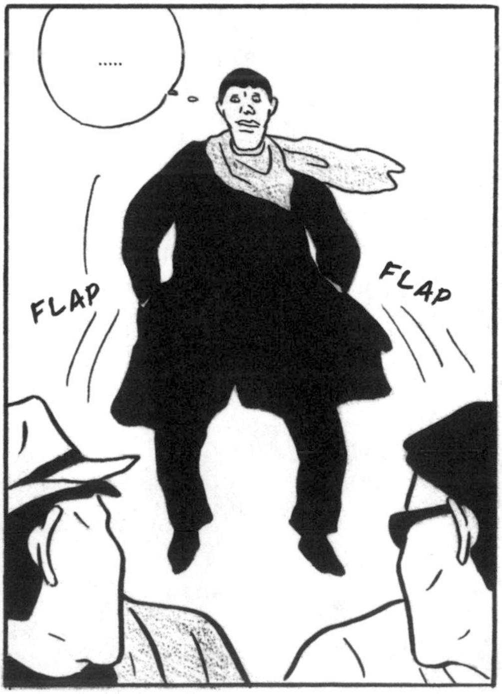
.....
FLAP
FLAP

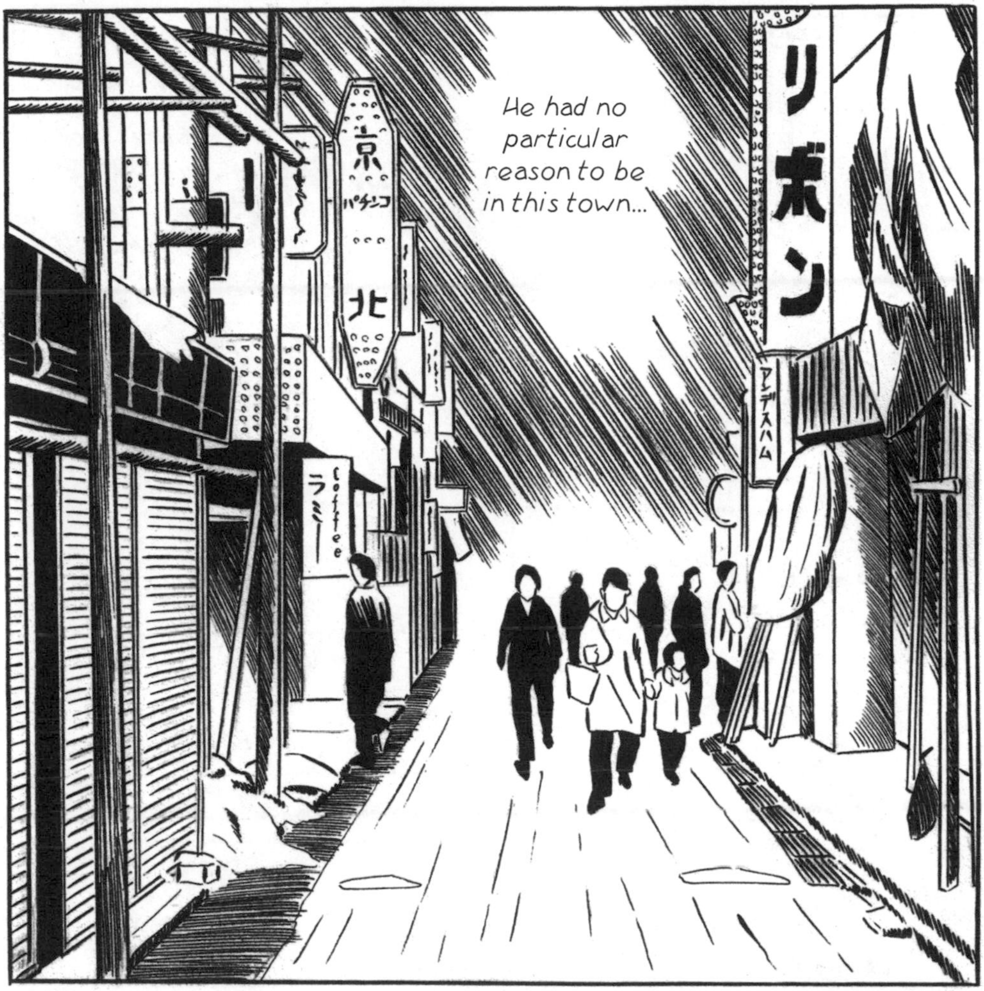
He had no particular reason to be in this town...
京
パチンコ
北
リボン
アンデスハム
ラミー
Coffee

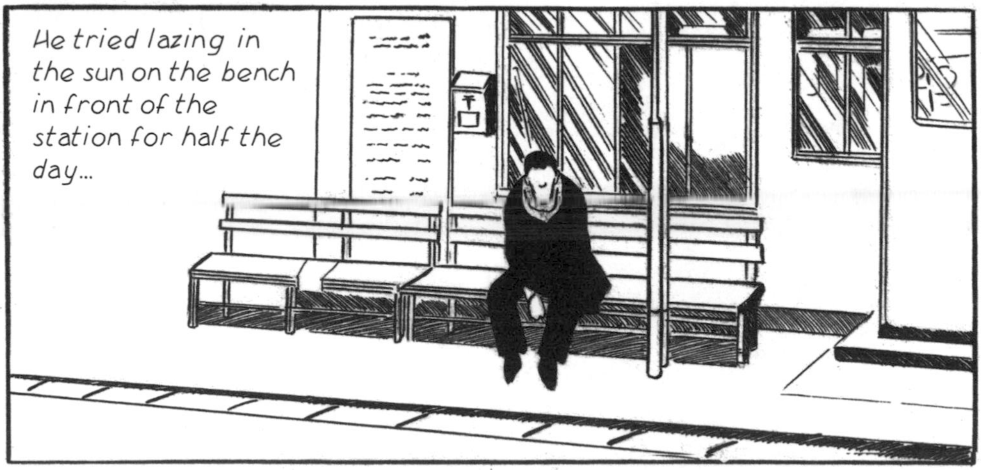
He tried lazing in the sun on the bench in front of the station for half the day...

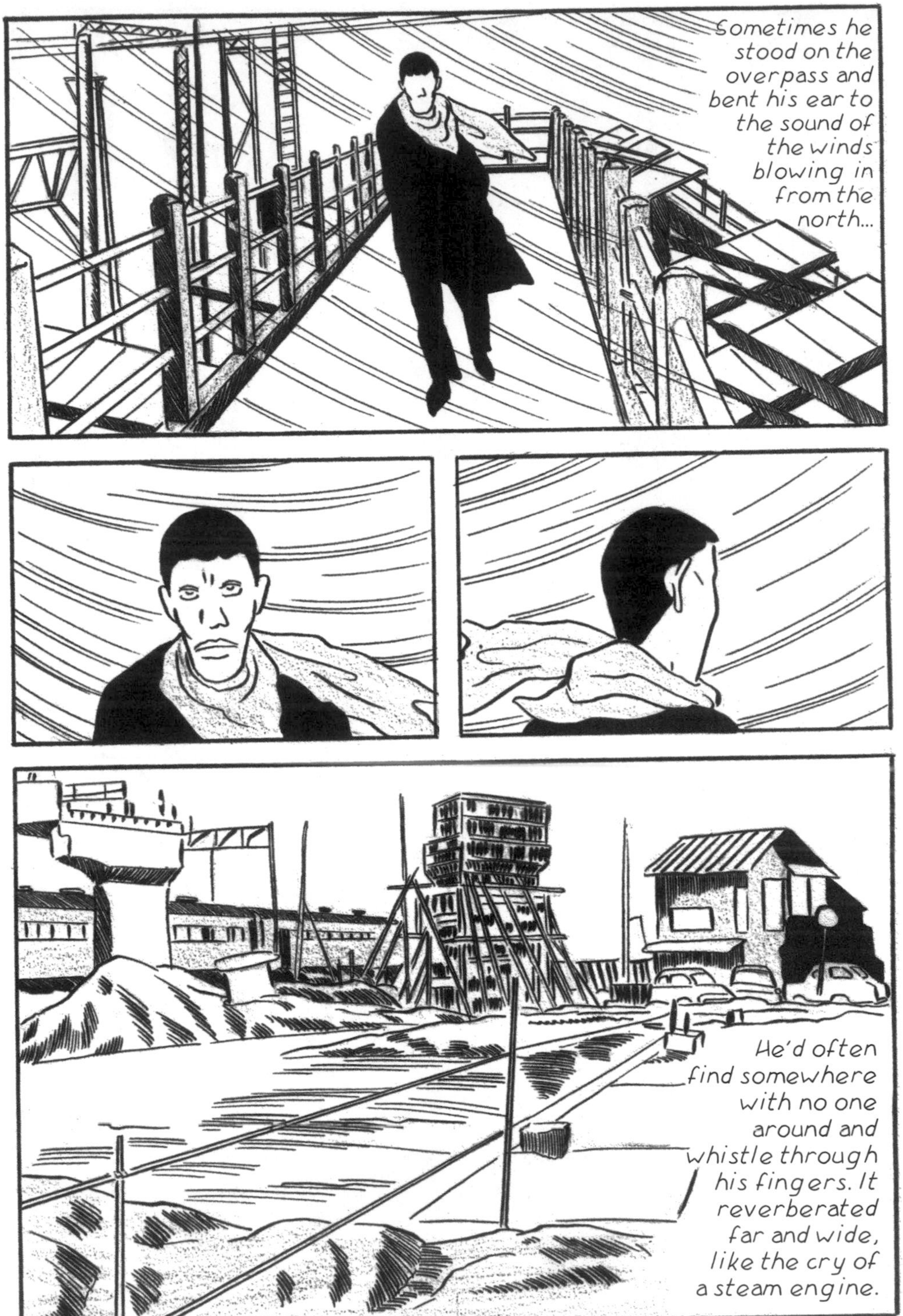
Sometimes he stood on the overpass and bent his ear to the sound of the winds blowing in from the north...
He'd often find somewhere with no one around and whistle through his fingers. It reverberated far and wide, like the cry of a steam engine.

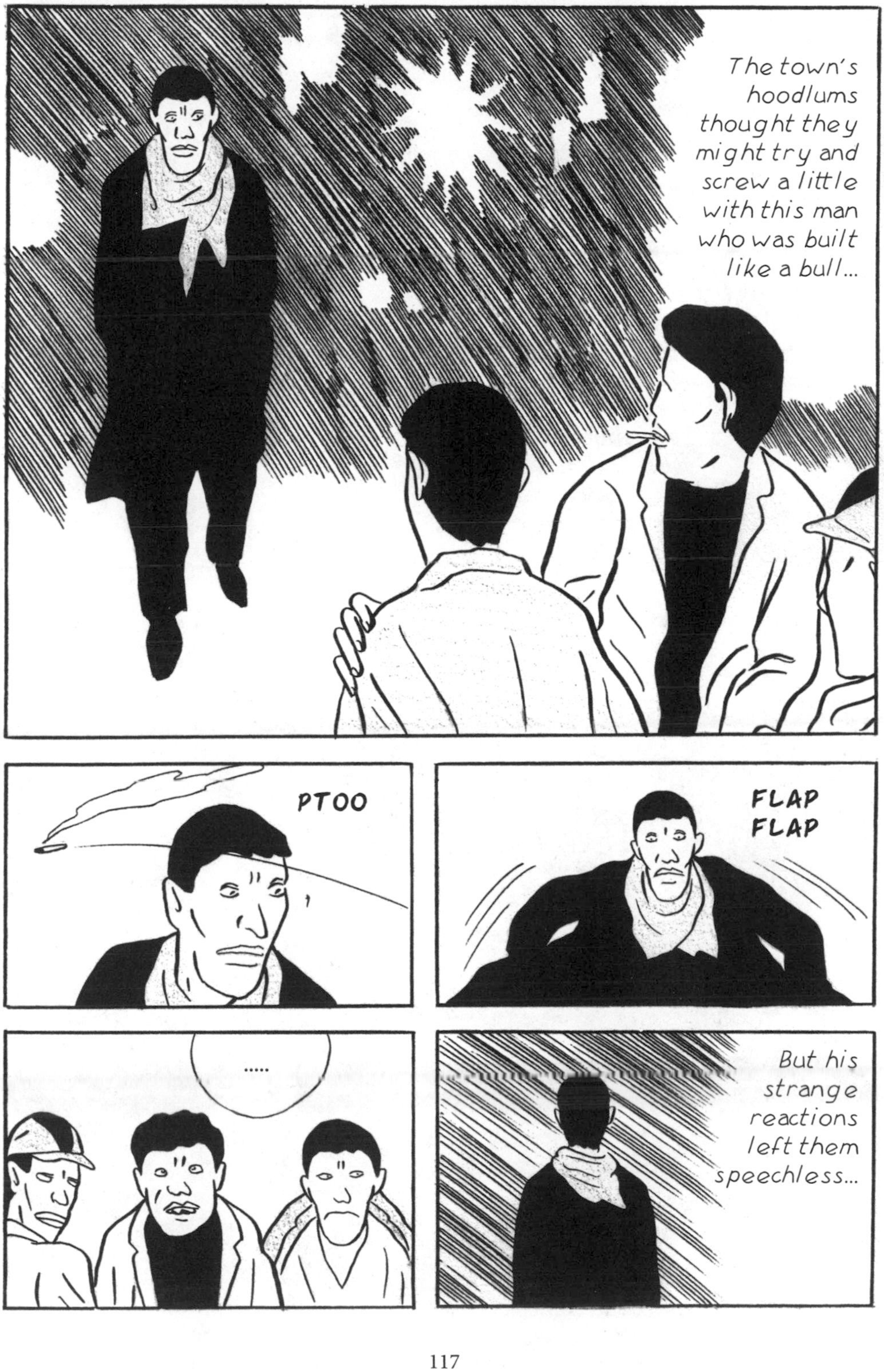
The town's hoodlums thought they might try and screw a little with this man who was built like a bull...
PTOO
FLAP FLAP
.....
But his strange reactions left them speechless...

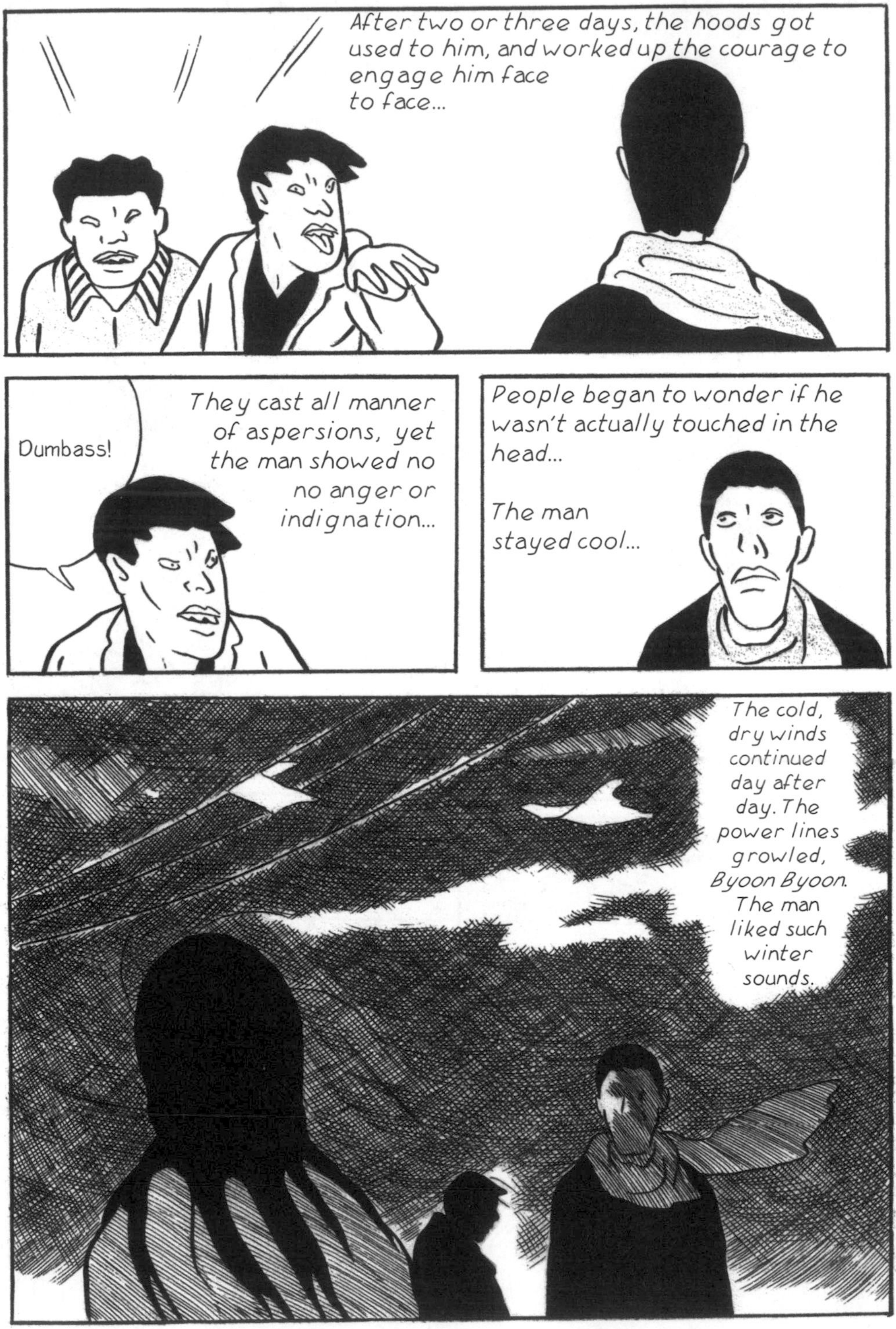
After two or three days, the hoods got used to him, and worked up the courage to engage him face to face...
They cast all manner of aspersions, yet the man showed no no anger or indignation...
Dumbass!
People began to wonder if he wasn't actually touched in the head...
The man stayed cool...
The cold, dry winds continued day after day. The power lines growled, Byoon Byoon. The man liked such winter sounds.

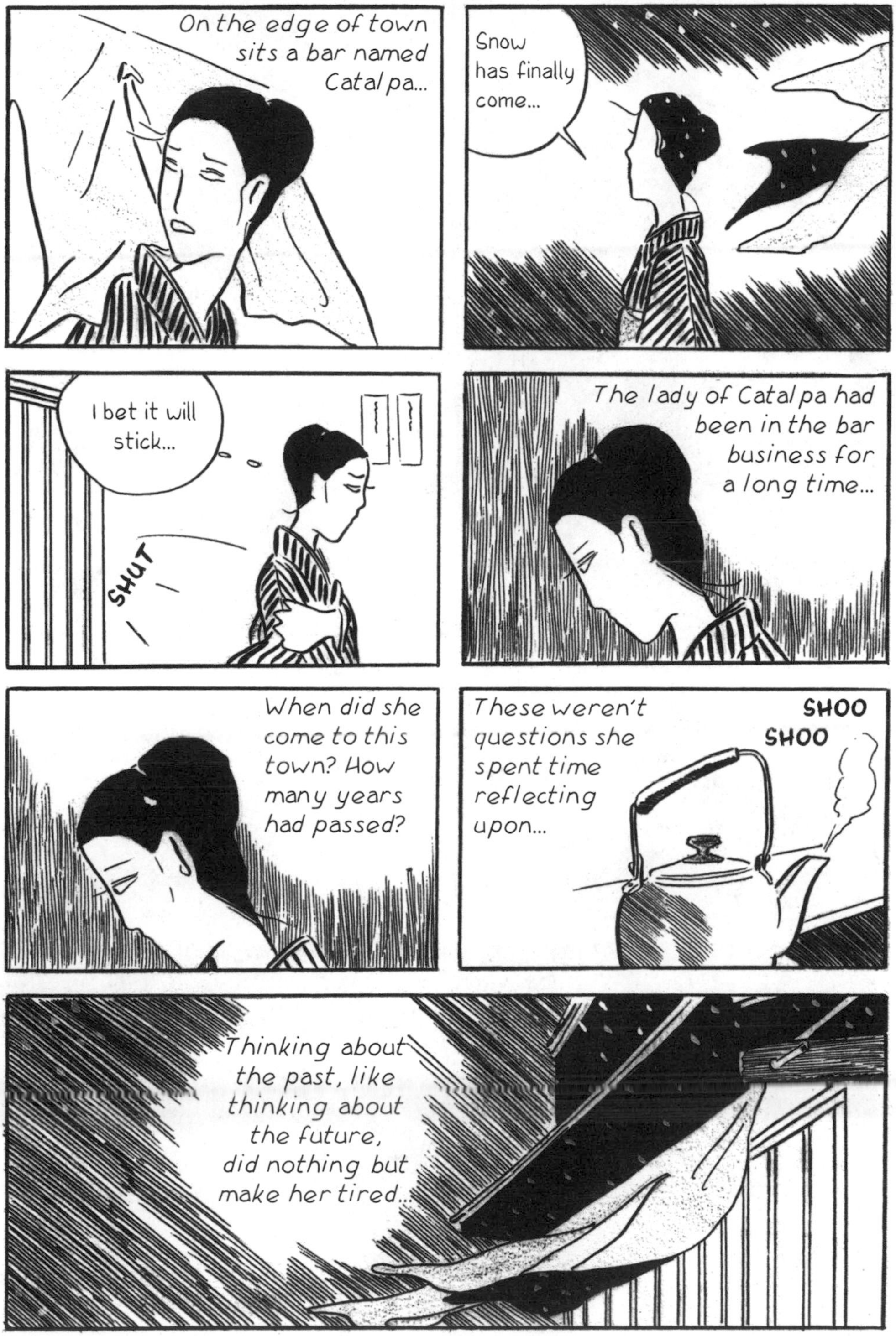
On the edge of town sits a bar named Catalpa...
Snow has finally come...
I bet it will stick...
SHUT
The lady of Catalpa had been in the bar business for a long time...
When did she come to this town? How many years had passed?
These weren't questions she spent time reflecting upon...
SHOO
SHOO
Thinking about the past, like thinking about the future, did nothing but make her tired...

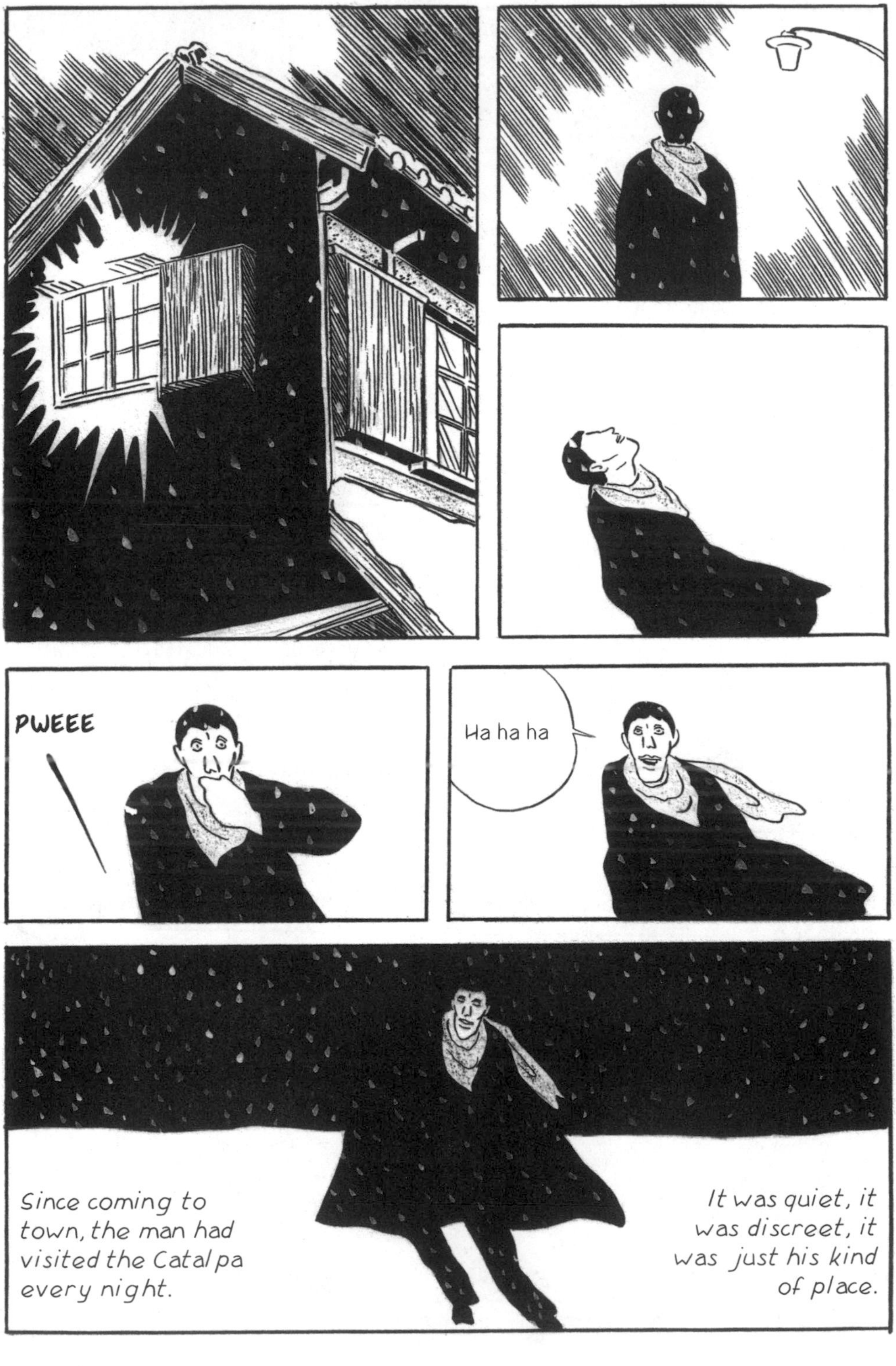
PWEEE
Ha ha ha
Since coming to town, the man had visited the Catalpa every night.
It was quiet, it was discreet, it was just his kind of place.

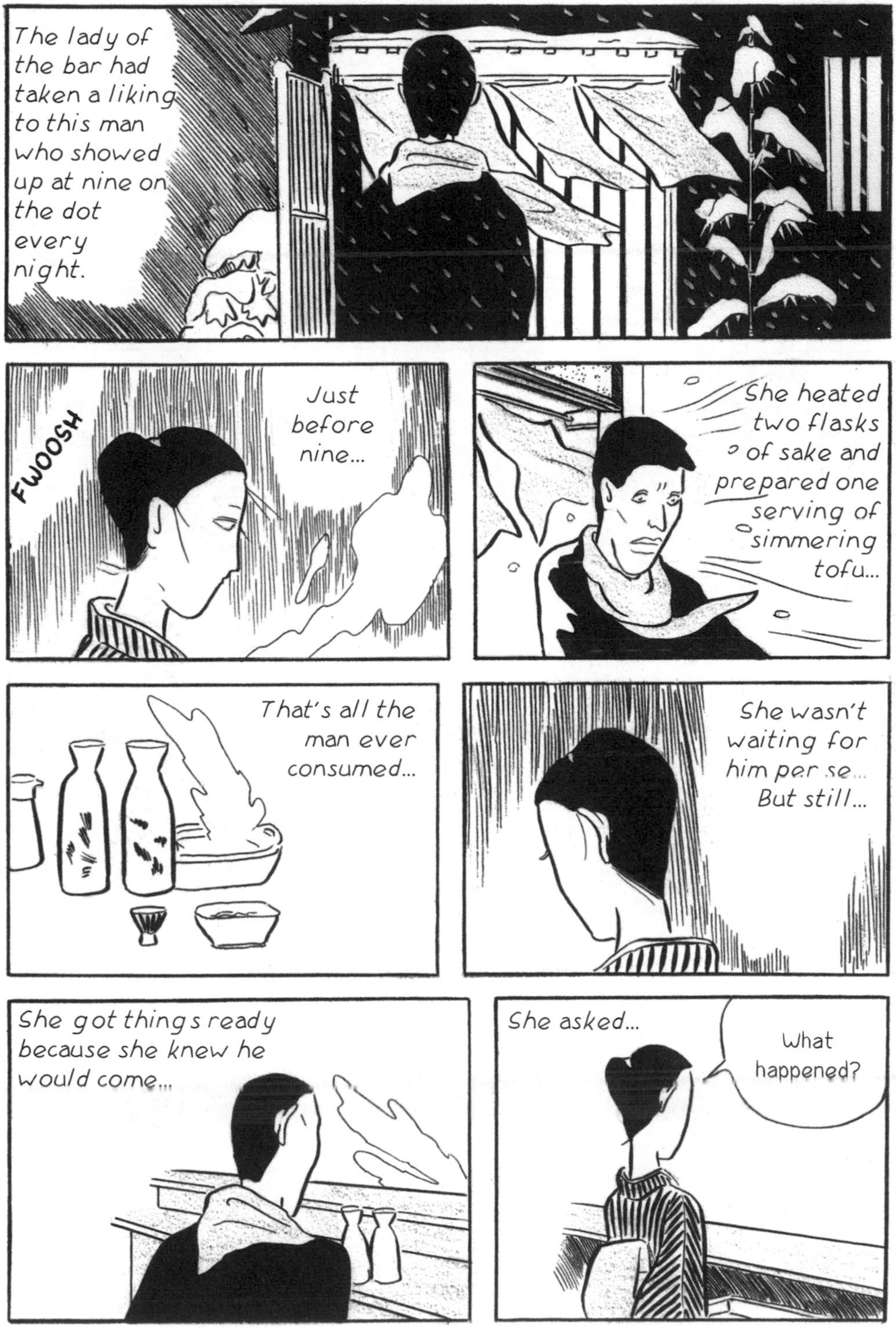
The lady of the bar had taken a liking to this man who showed up at nine on the dot every night.
FWOOSH
Just before nine...
She heated two flasks of sake and prepared one serving of simmering tofu...
That's all the man ever consumed...
She wasn't waiting for him per se... But still...
She got things ready because she knew he would come...
She asked...
What happened?

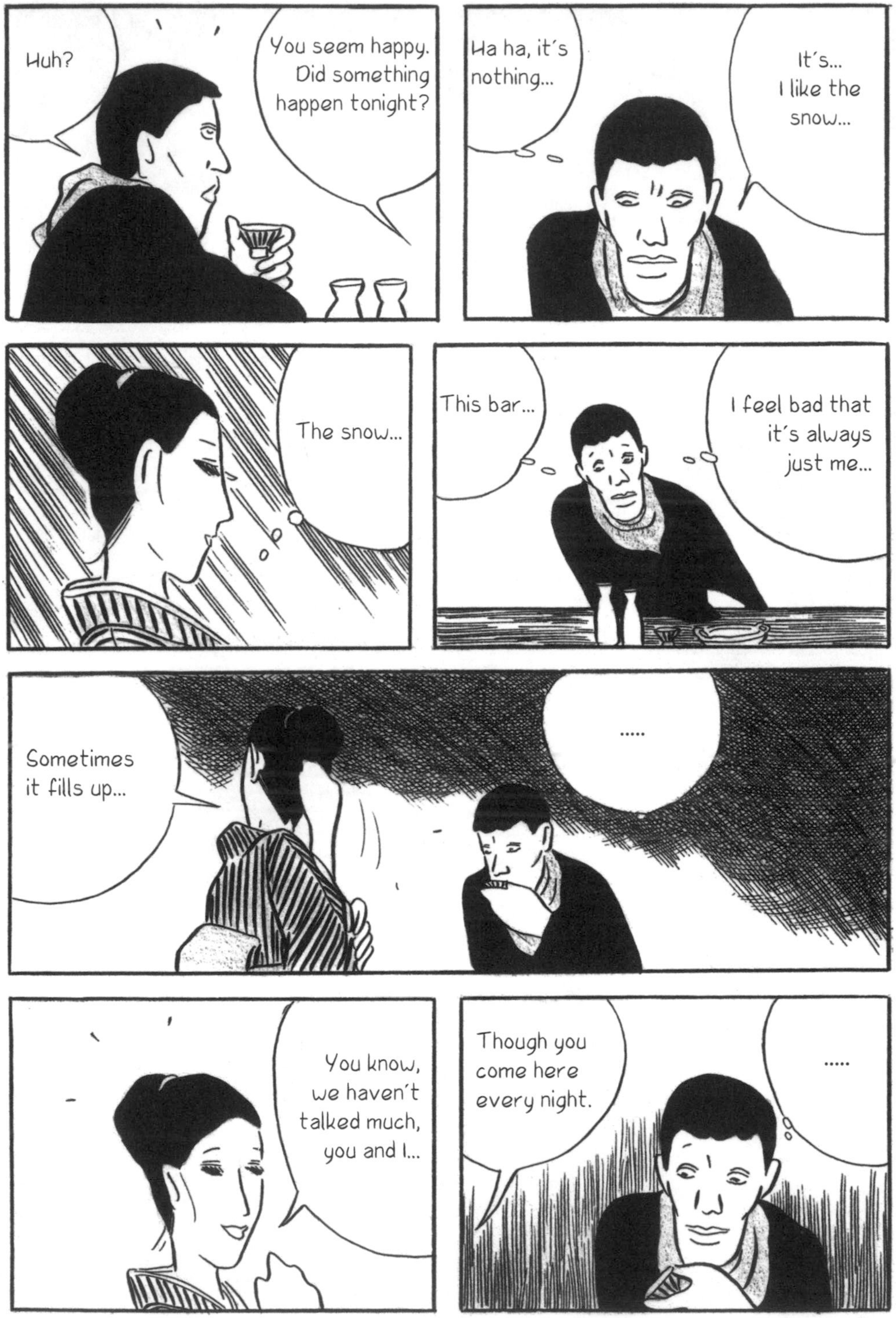
Huh?
You seem happy. Did something happen tonight?
Ha ha, it's nothing...
It's... I like the snow...
The snow...
This bar...
I feel bad that it's always just me...
Sometimes it fills up...
.....
You know, we haven't talked much, you and I...
Though you come here every night.
.....

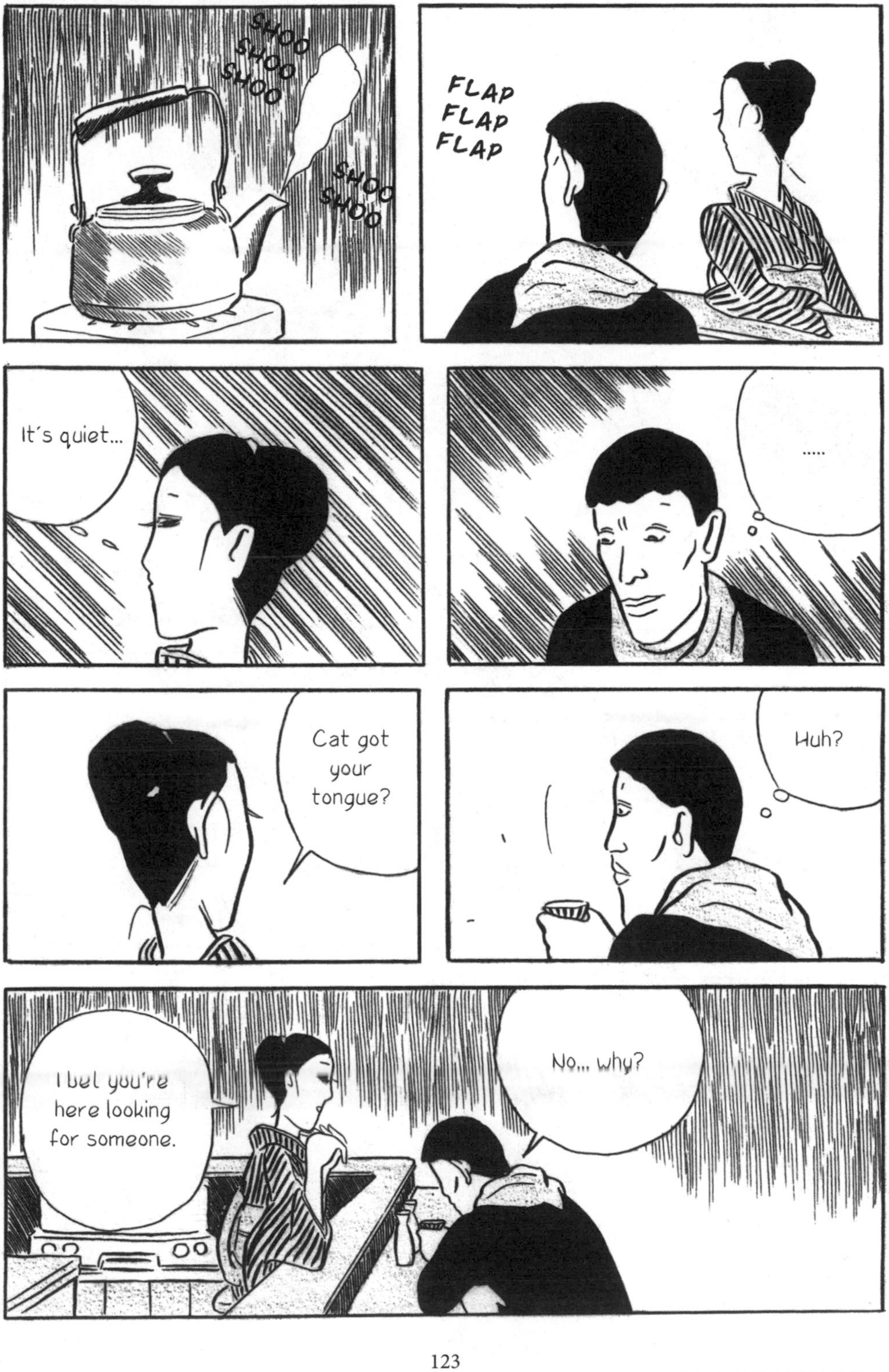
SHOO SHOO SHOO
SHOO SHOO
FLAP FLAP FLAP
It's quiet...
.....
Cat got your tongue?
Huh?
I bet you're here looking for someone.
No... why?

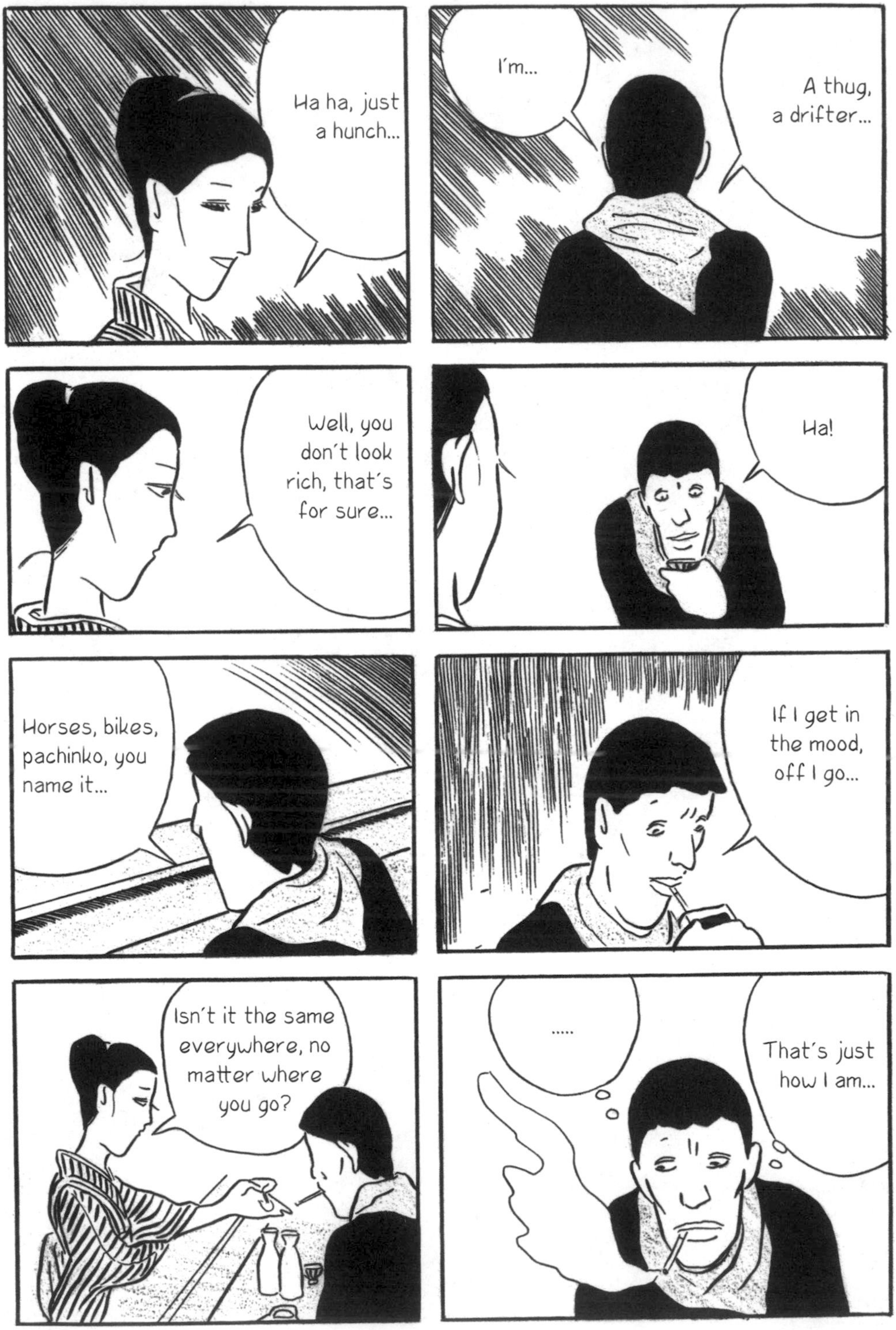
Ha ha, just a hunch...
I'm...
A thug, a drifter...
Well, you don't look rich, that's for sure...
Ha!
Horses, bikes, pachinko, you name it...
If I get in the mood, off I go...
Isn't it the same everywhere, no matter where you go?
.....
That's just how I am...

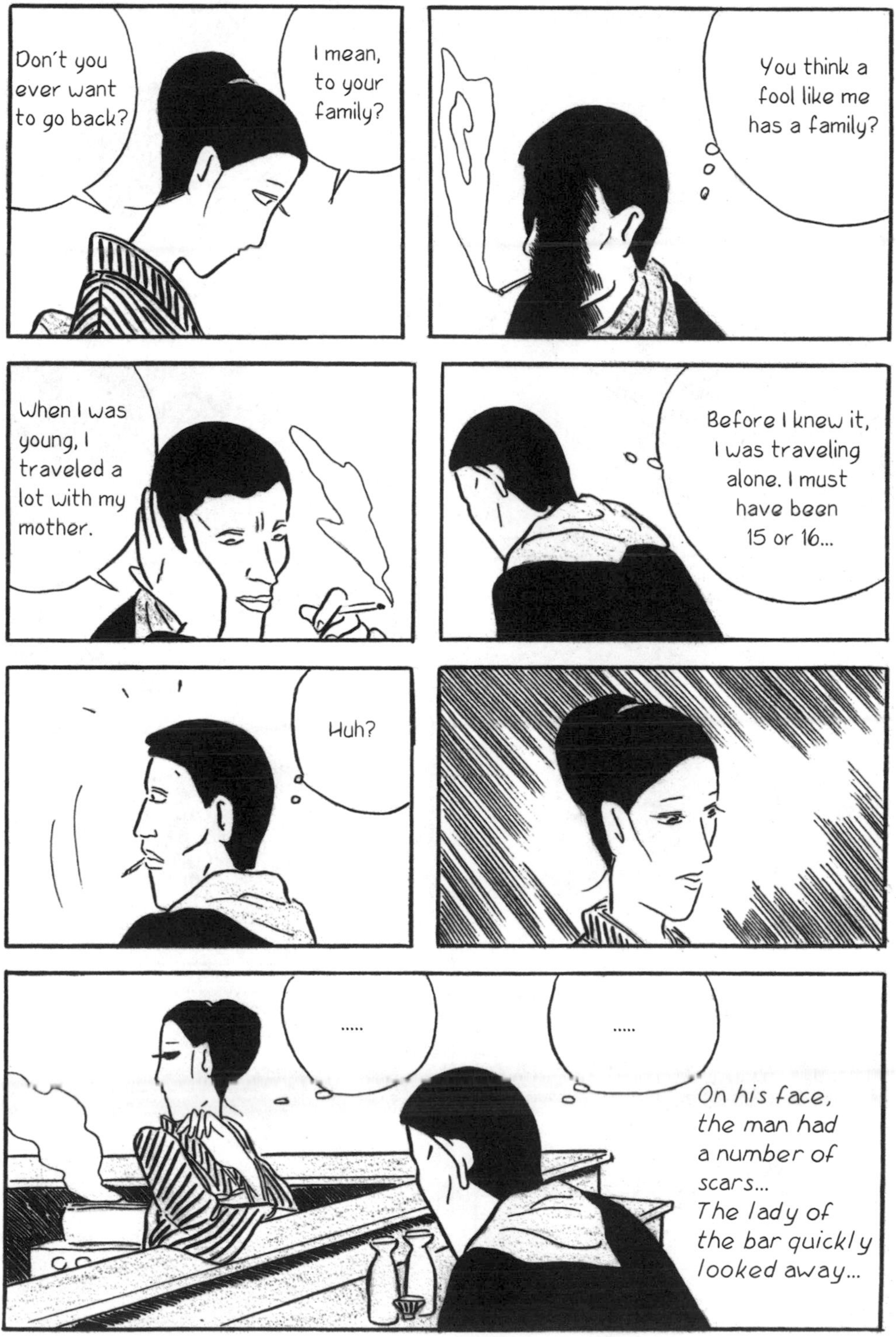
Don't you ever want to go back?
I mean, to your family?
You think a fool like me has a family?
When I was young, I traveled a lot with my mother.
Before I knew it, I was traveling alone. I must have been 15 or 16...
Huh?
.....
.....
On his face, the man had a number of scars... The lady of the bar quickly looked away...

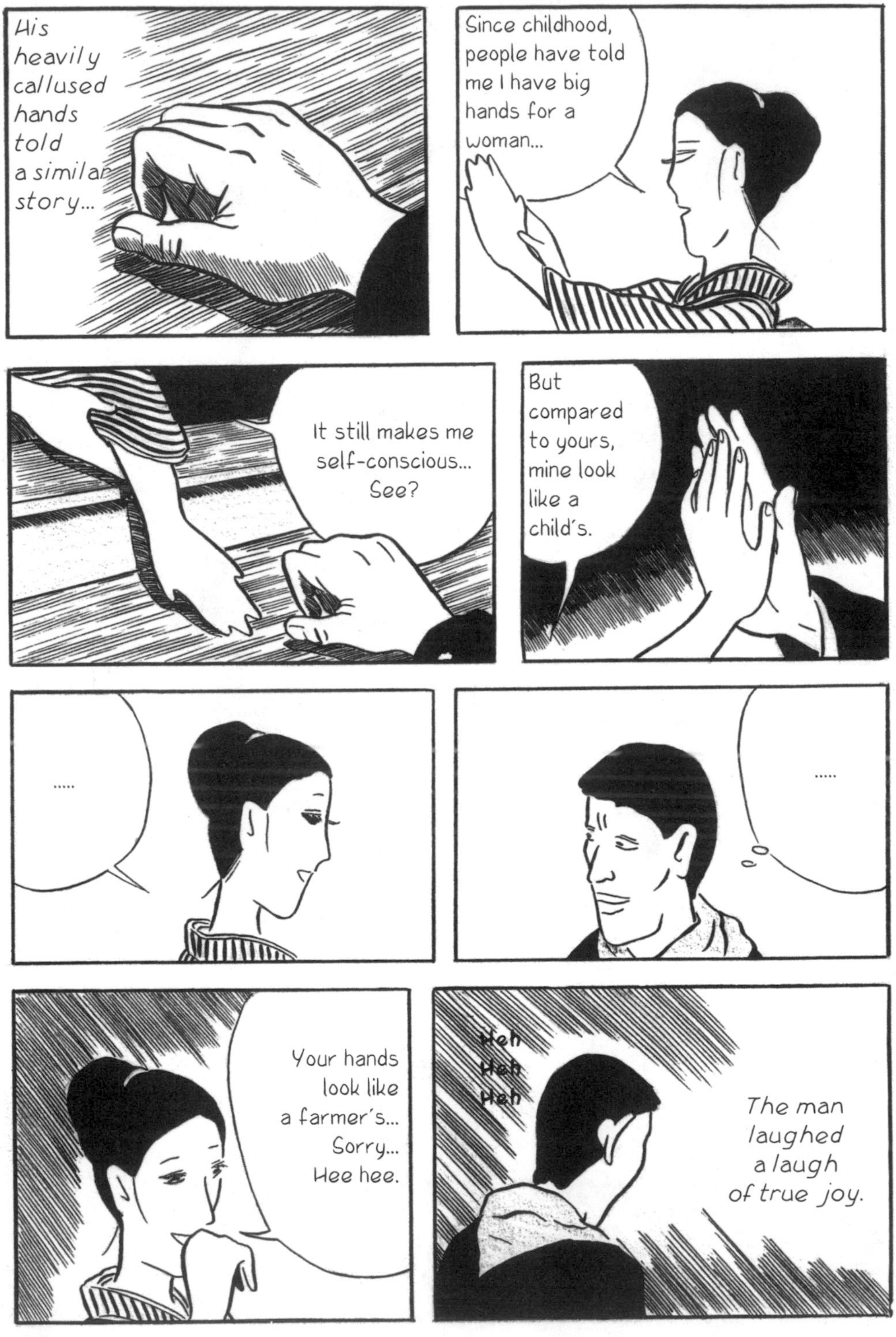
His heavily callused hands told a similar story...
Since childhood, people have told me I have big hands for a woman...
It still makes me self-conscious... See?
But compared to yours, mine look like a child's.
.....
.....
Your hands look like a farmer's... Sorry... Hee hee.
Heh Heh Heh
The man laughed a laugh of true joy.

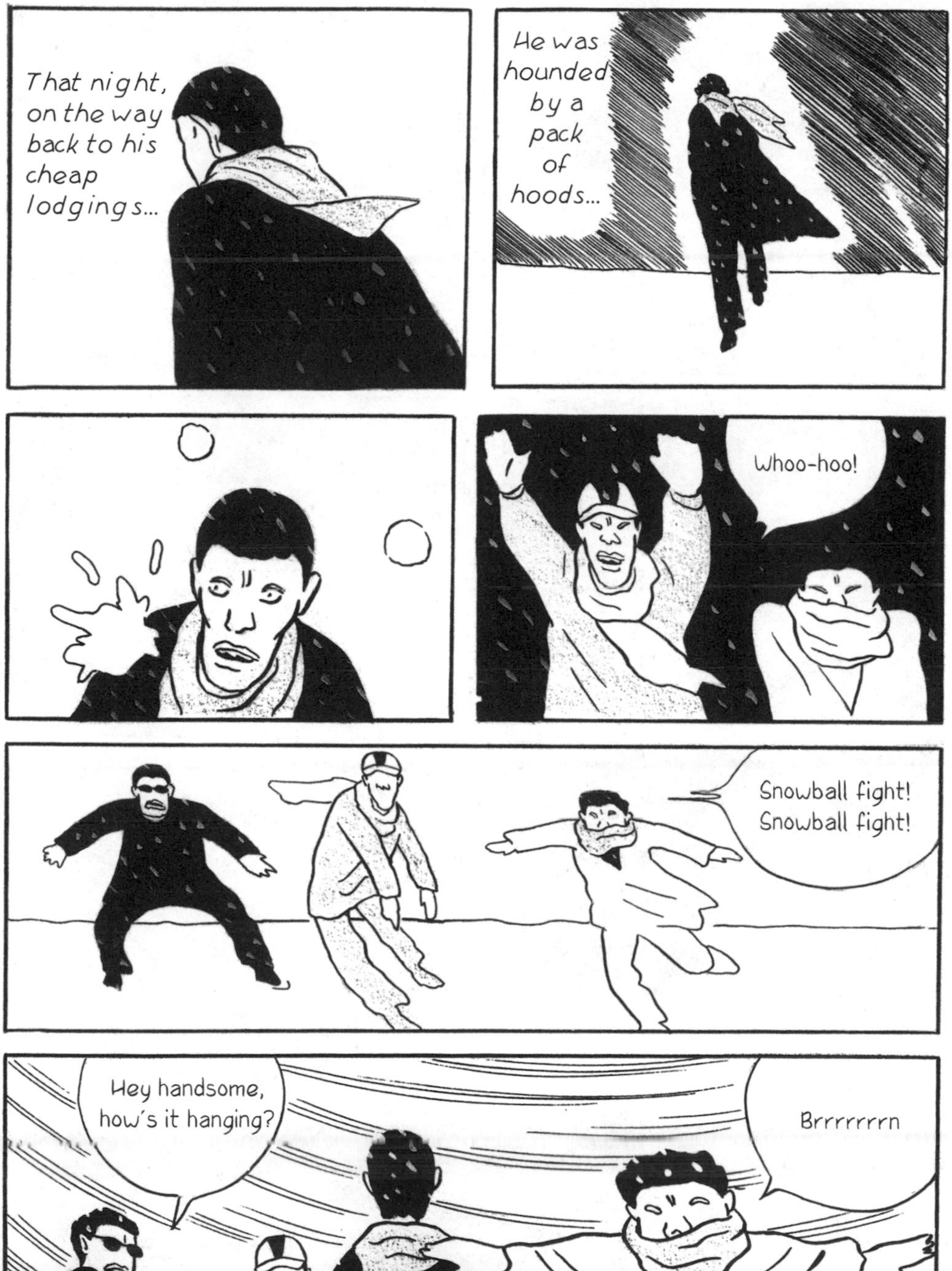
That night, on the way back to his cheap lodgings...
He was hounded by a pack of hoods...
Whoo-hoo!
Snowball fight! Snowball fight!
Hey handsome, how's it hanging?
Brrrrrrrn

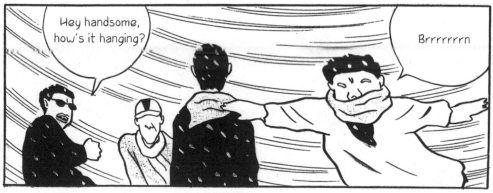

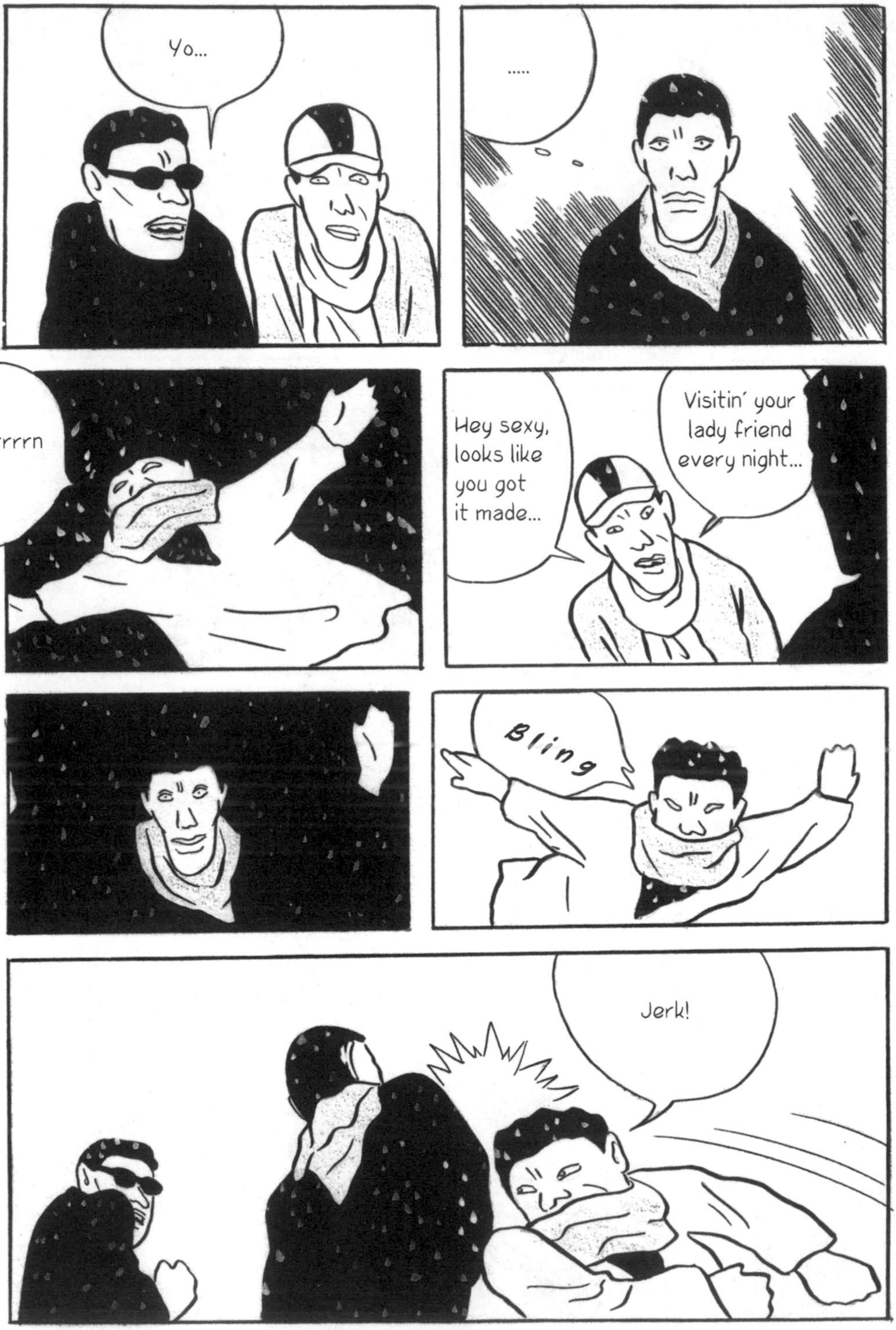
Yo...
.....
Brrrrrrrn
Hey sexy, looks like you got it made...
Visitin' your lady friend every night...
Bling
Jerk!

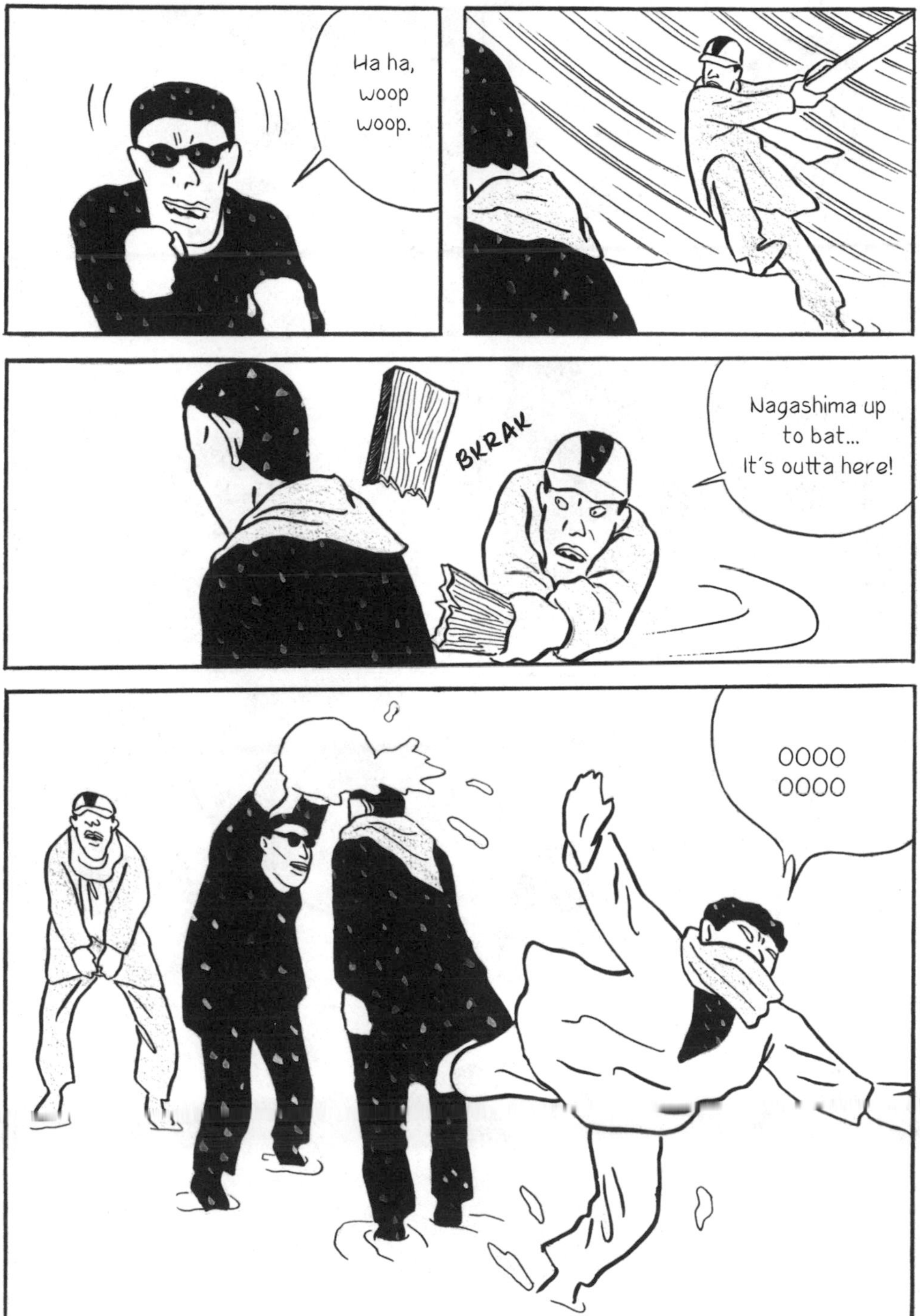
Ha ha, woop woop.
BKRAK
Nagashima up to bat... It's outta here!
OOOO OOOO

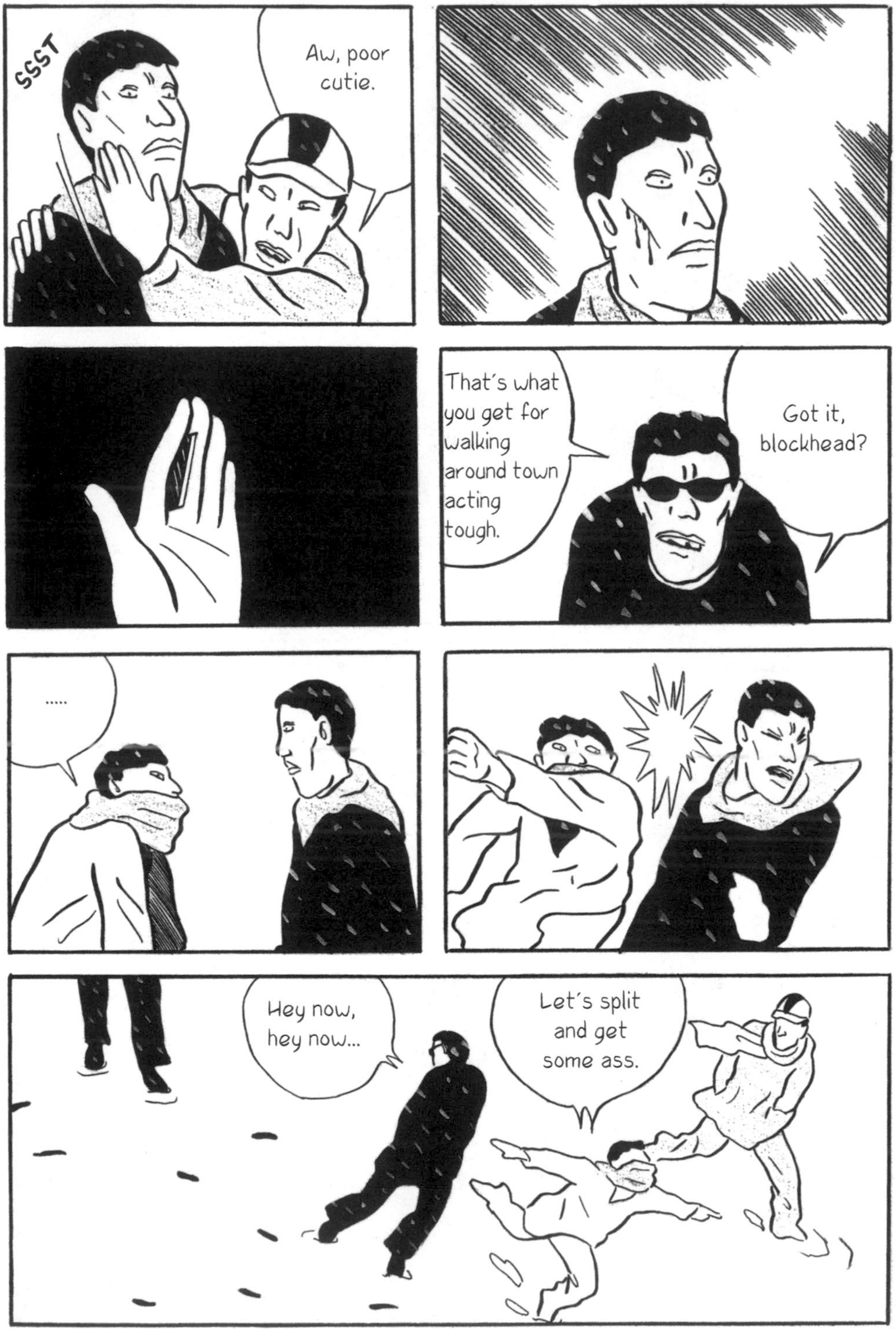
SSST
Aw, poor cutie.
That's what you get for walking around town acting tough.
Got it, blockhead?
.....
Hey now, hey now...
Let's split and get some ass.

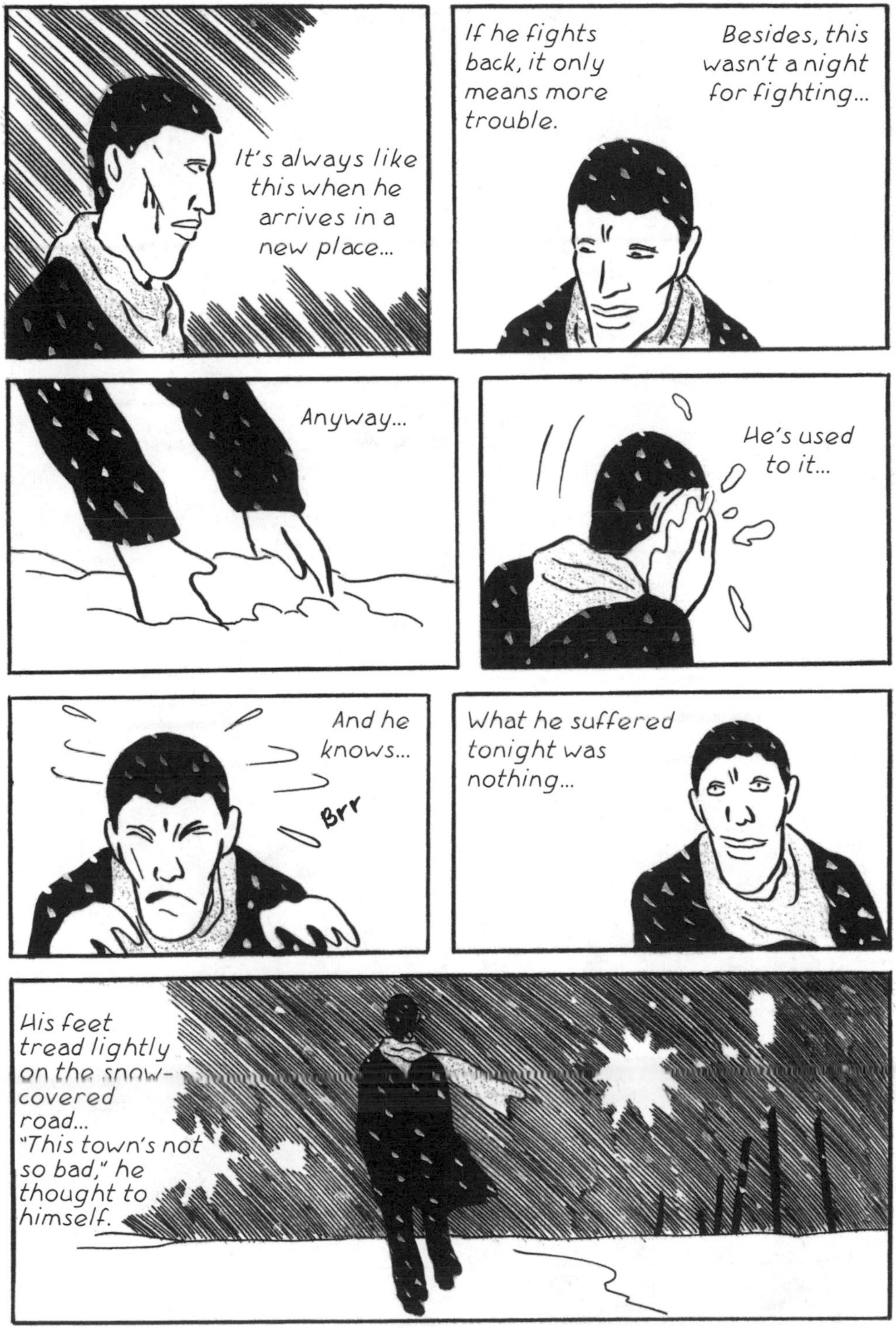
It's always like this when he arrives in a new place...
If he fights back, it only means more trouble.
Besides, this wasn't a night for fighting...
Anyway...
He's used to it...
And he knows...
Brr
What he suffered tonight was nothing...
His feet tread lightly on the snow-covered road...
"This town's not so bad," he thought to himself.

The snow kept falling...

It finally stopped the following evening...

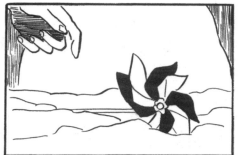

.....

KSUK KSUK

The man was feeling uneasy that night...

But he headed to the Catalpa as usual...

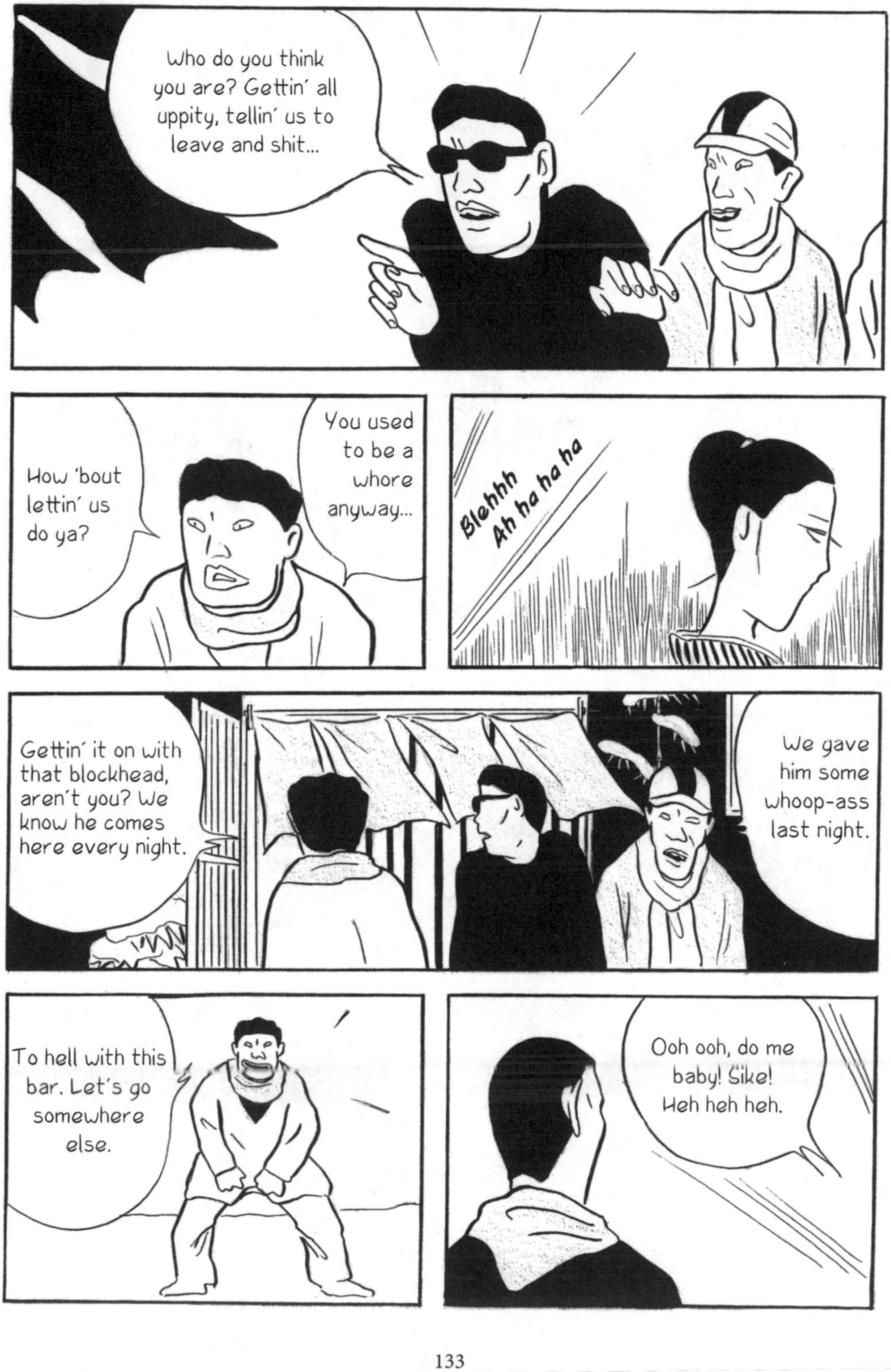

Who do you think you are? Gettin' all uppity, tellin' us to leave and shit...
How 'bout lettin' us do ya?
You used to be a whore anyway...
Blehhh
Ah ha ha ha
Gettin' it on with that blockhead, aren't you? We know he comes here every night.
We gave him some whoop-ass last night.
To hell with this bar. Let's go somewhere else.
Ooh ooh, do me baby! Sike! Heh heh heh.

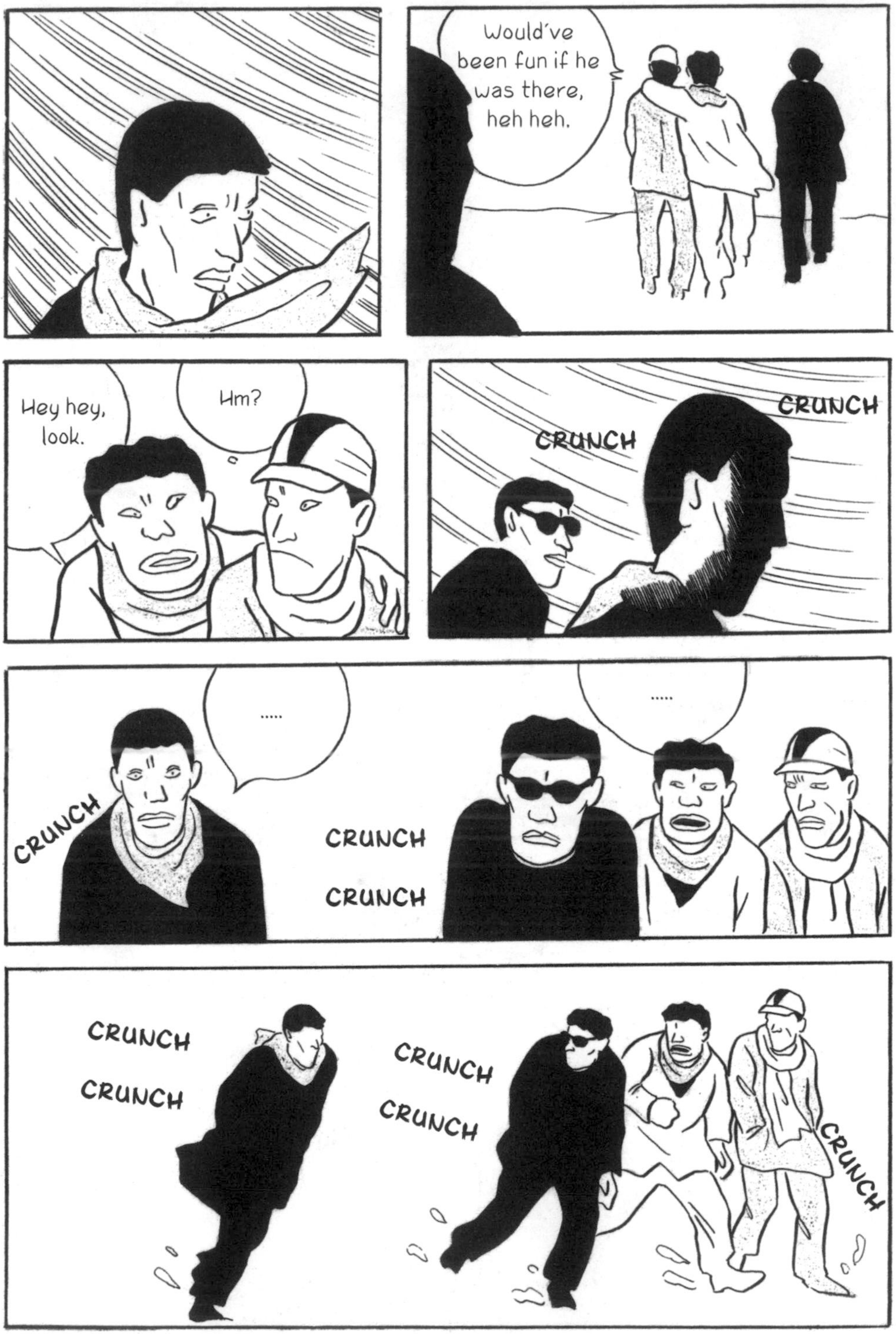
Would've been fun if he was there, heh heh.
Hey hey, look.
Hm?
CRUNCH
CRUNCH
.....
.....
CRUNCH
CRUNCH
CRUNCH
CRUNCH
CRUNCH
CRUNCH
CRUNCH
CRUNCH

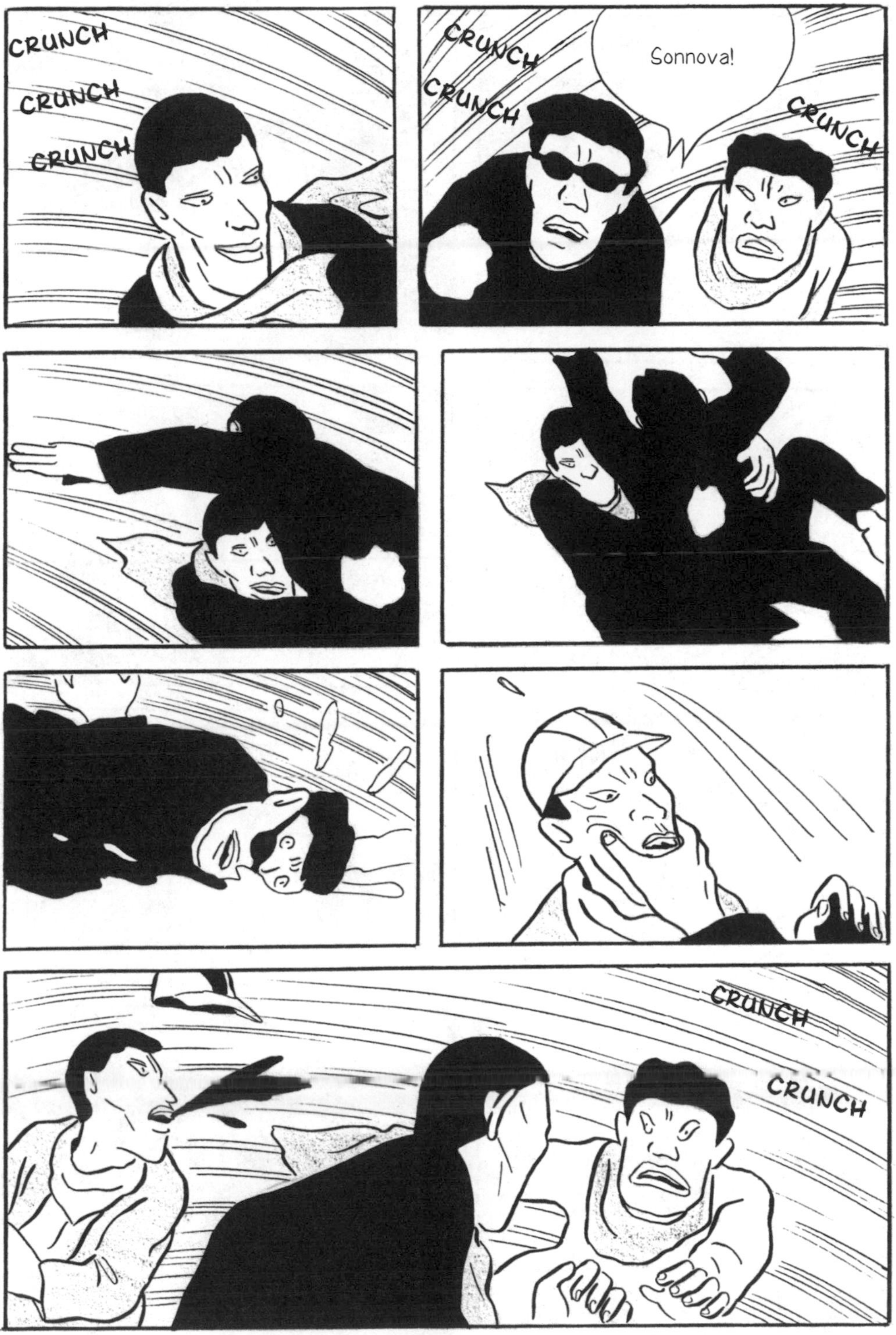
CRUNCH
CRUNCH
CRUNCH
CRUNCH
CRUNCH
Sonnova!
CRUNCH
CRUNCH
CRUNCH

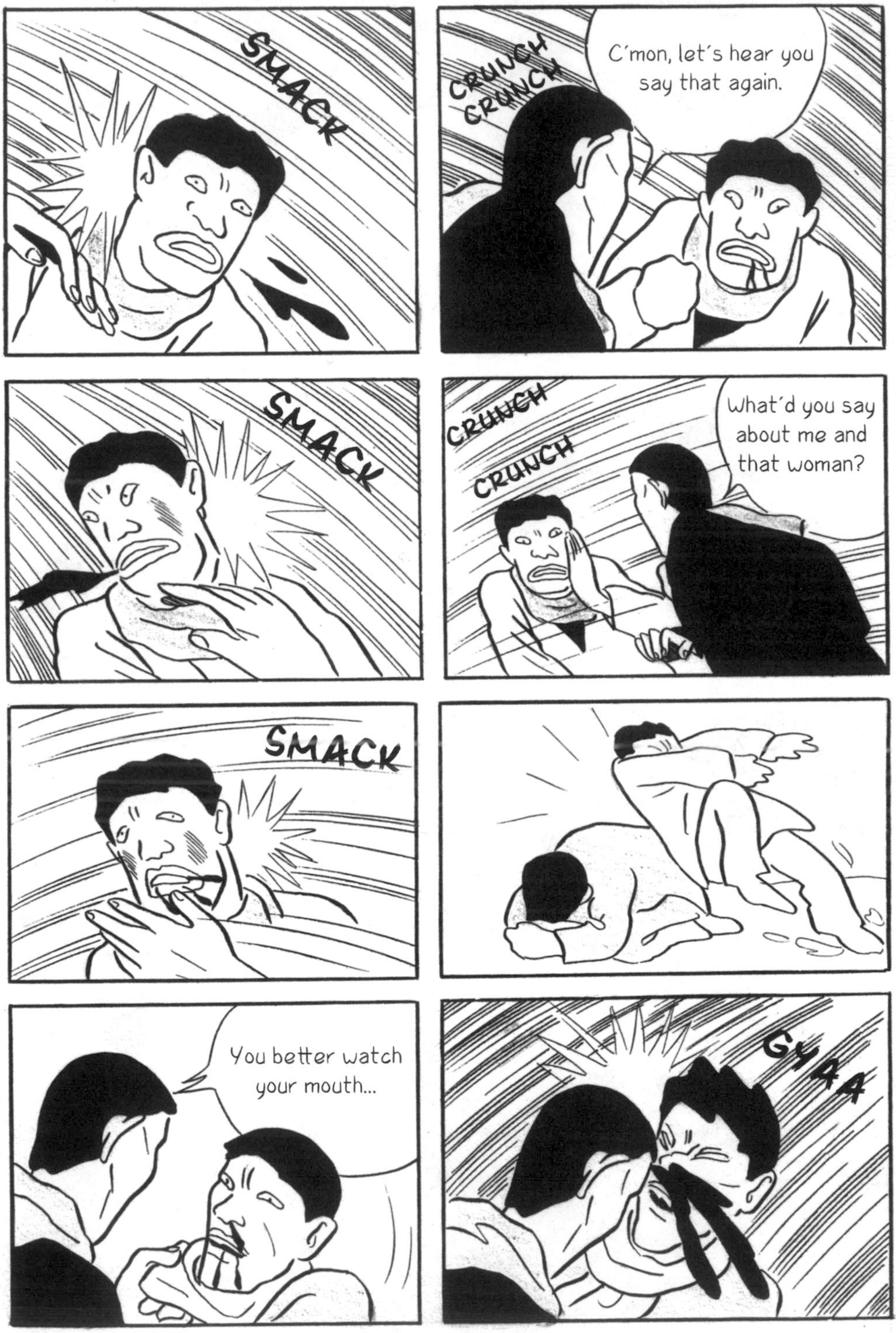
SMACK
CRUNCH
CRUNCH
C'mon, let's hear you say that again.
SMACK
CRUNCH
CRUNCH
What'd you say about me and that woman?
SMACK
You better watch your mouth...
GYAA

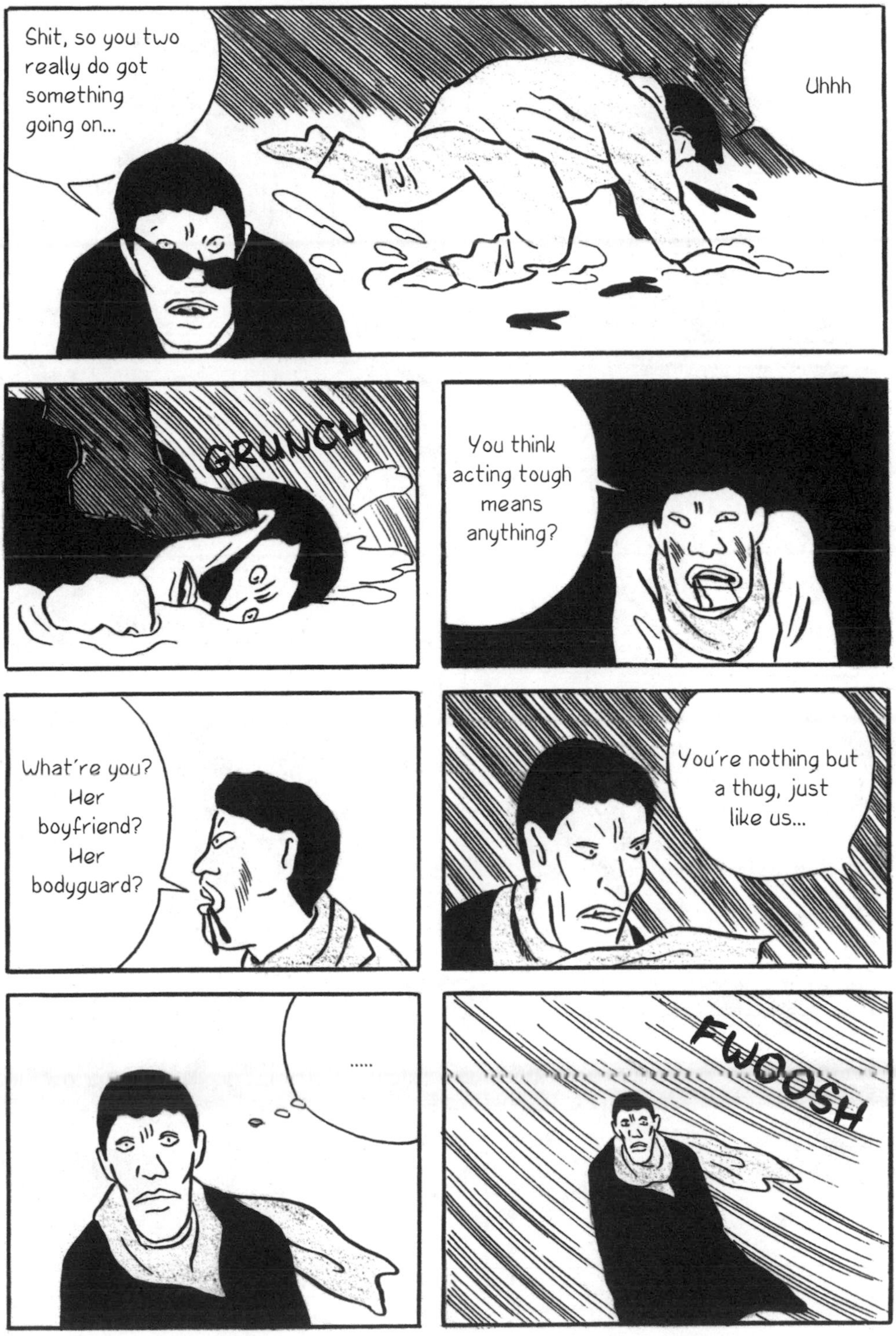
Shit, so you two really do got something going on...
Uhhh
GRUNCH
You think acting tough means anything?
What're you? Her boyfriend? Her bodyguard?
You're nothing but a thug, just like us...
.....
FWOOSH

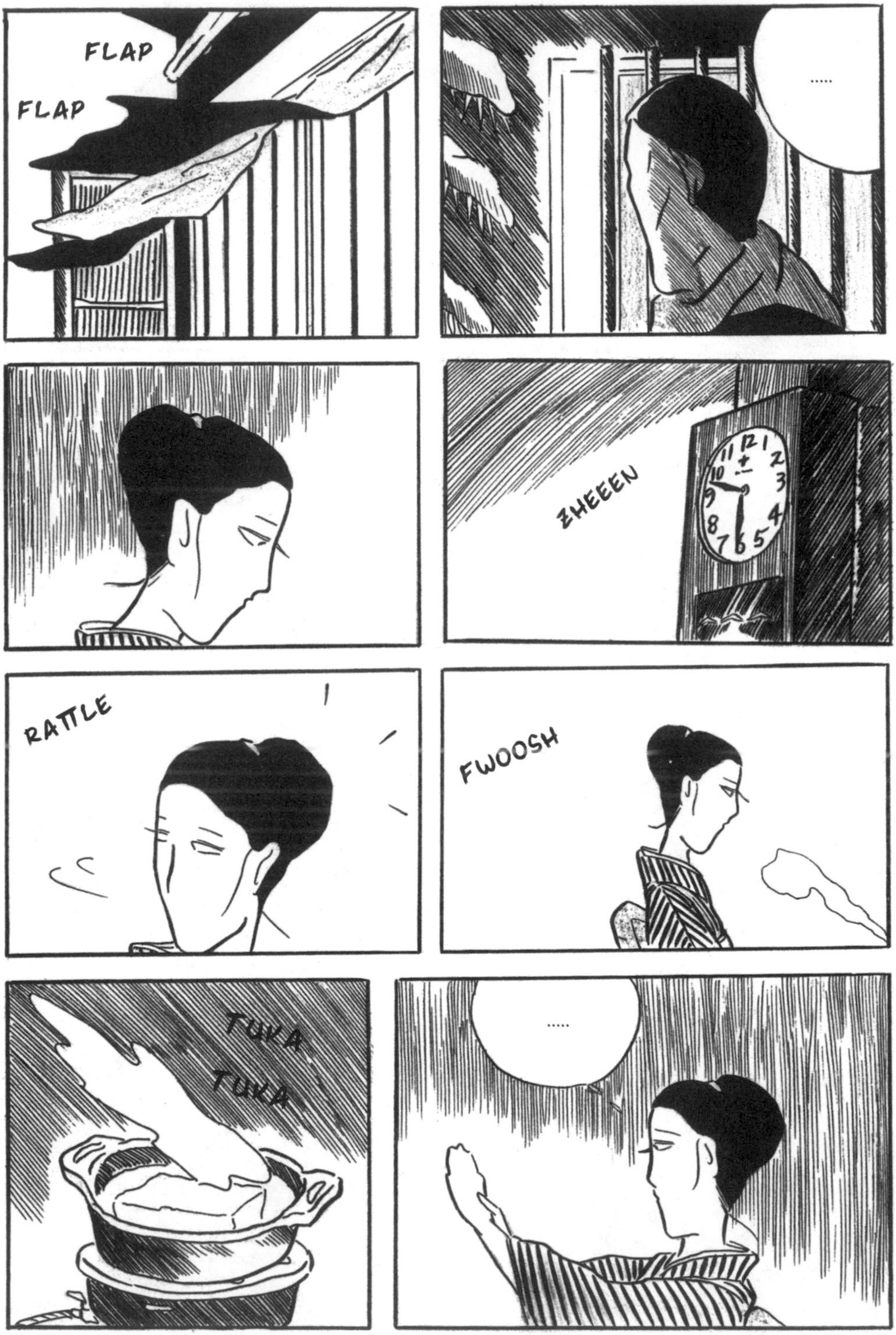
FLAP
FLAP
.....
ZHEEEN
RATTLE
FWOOSH
TUKA
TUKA
.....

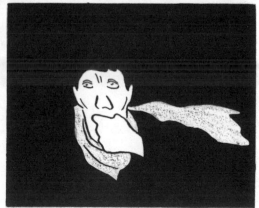

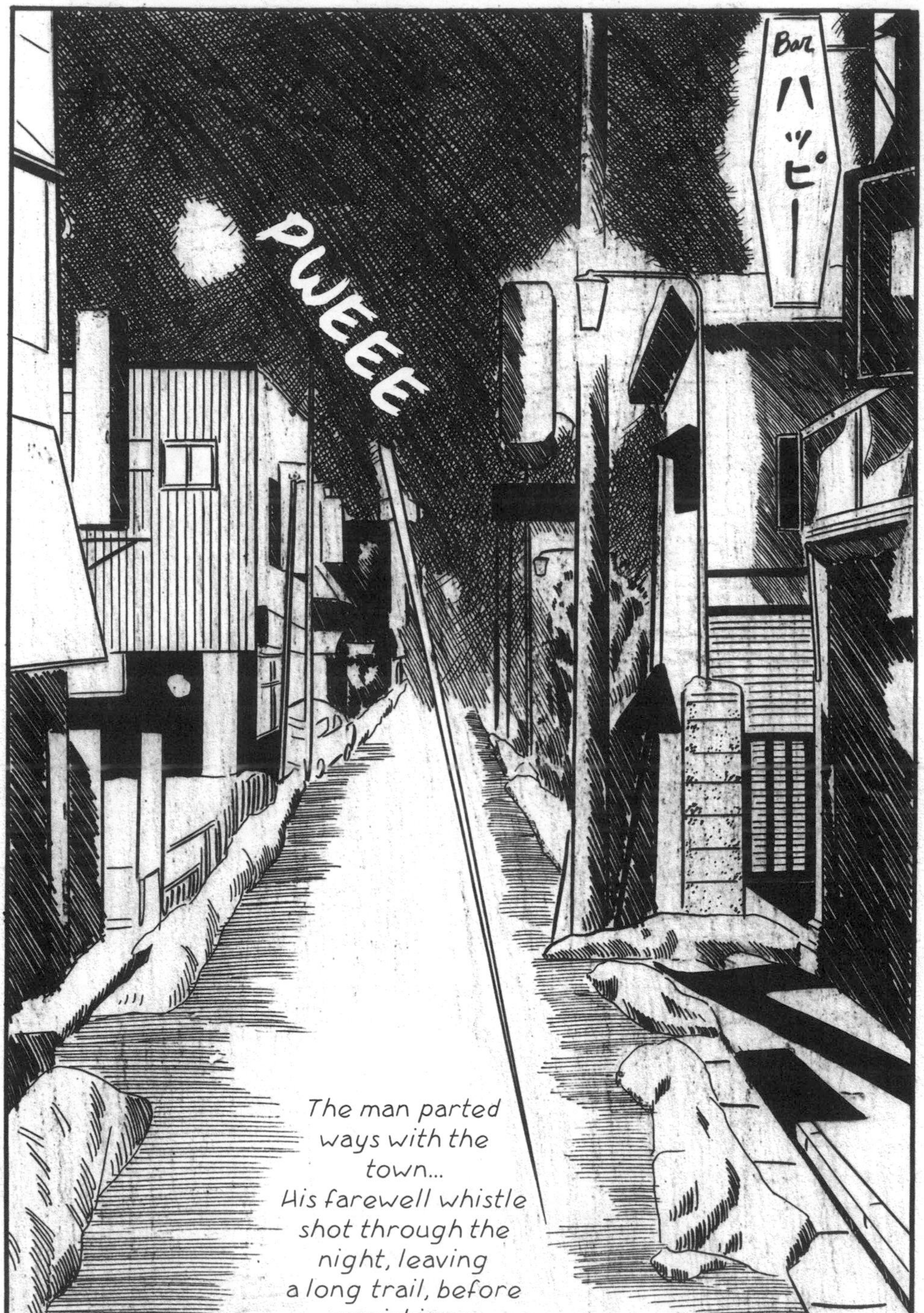
Bar
ハッピー
PWEEE
The man parted ways with the town... His farewell whistle shot through the night, leaving a long trail, before vanishing...

The End

LEGEND OF THE WOLF

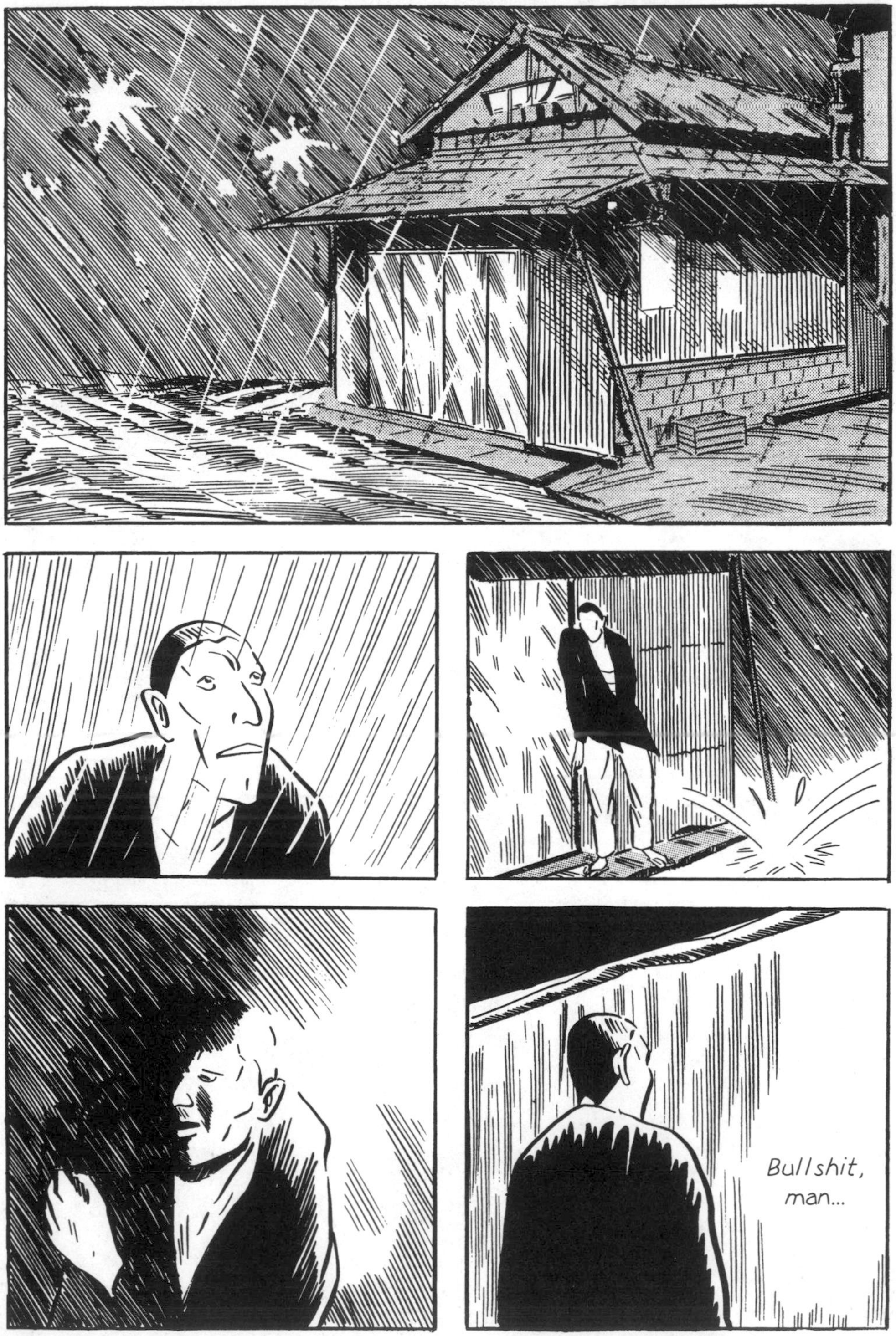
Bullshit,
man...

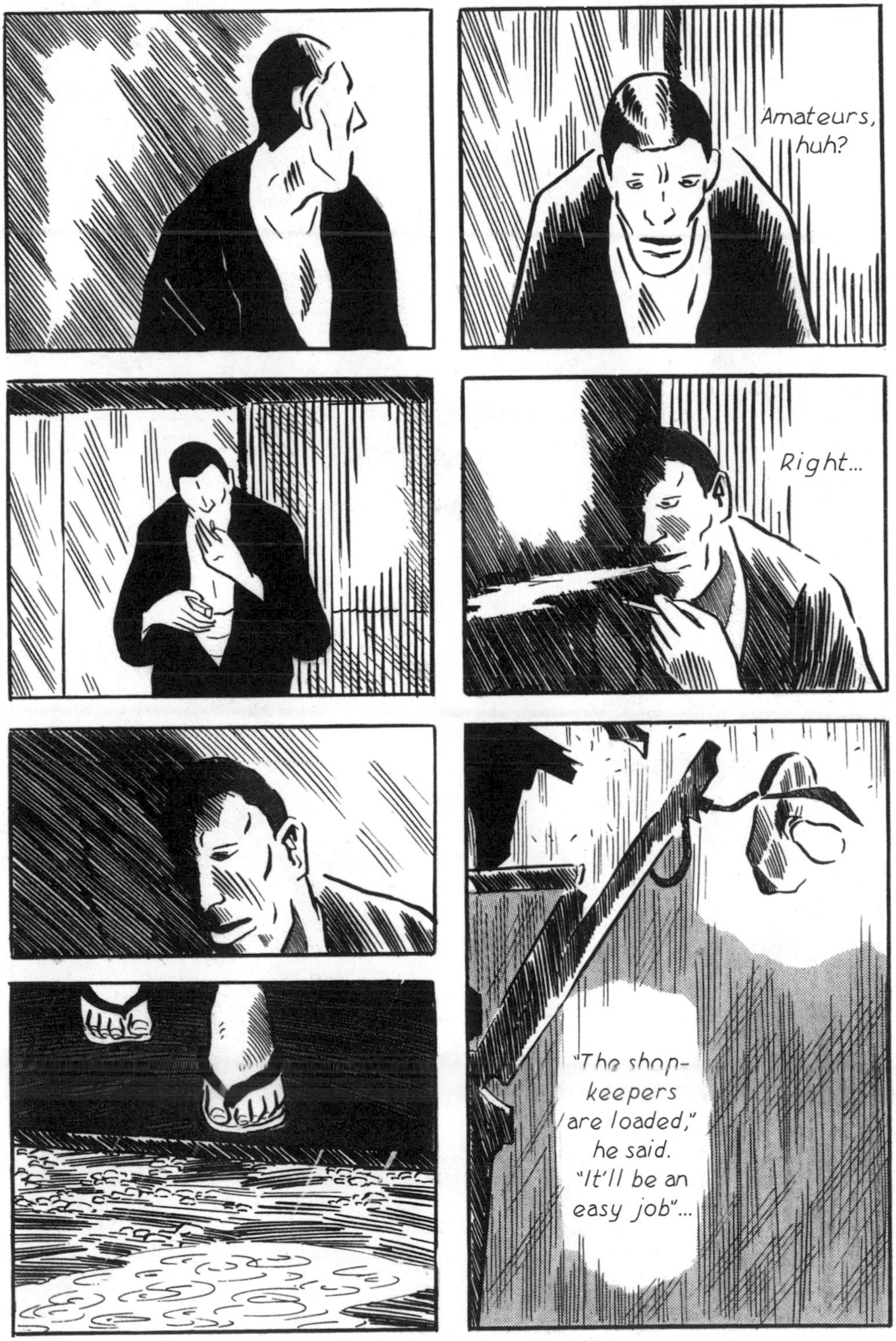
Amateurs, huh?
Right...
"The shop-keepers are loaded," he said. "It'll be an easy job"...

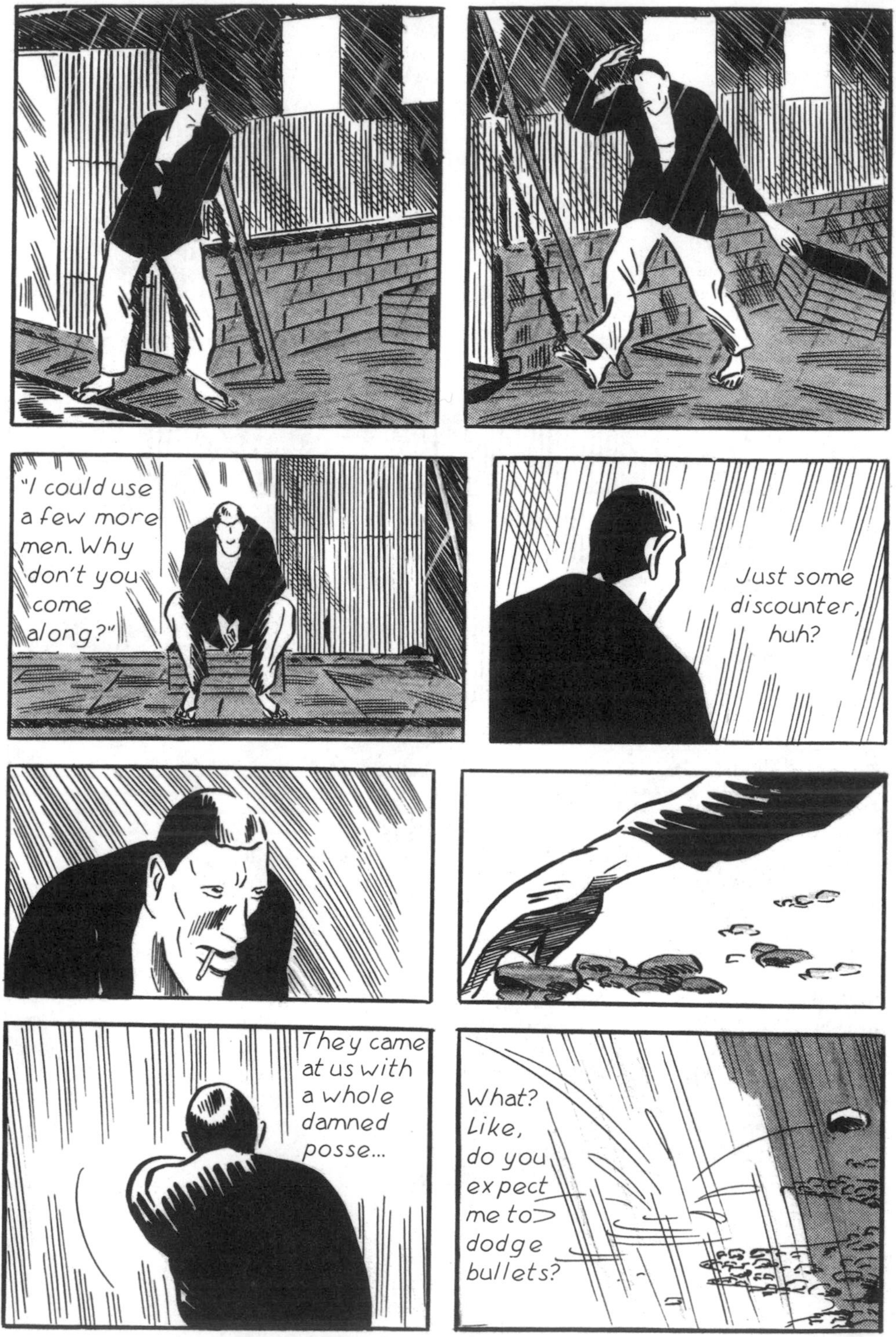
"I could use a few more men. Why don't you come along?"
Just some discounter, huh?
They came at us with a whole damned posse...
What? Like, do you expect me to dodge bullets?

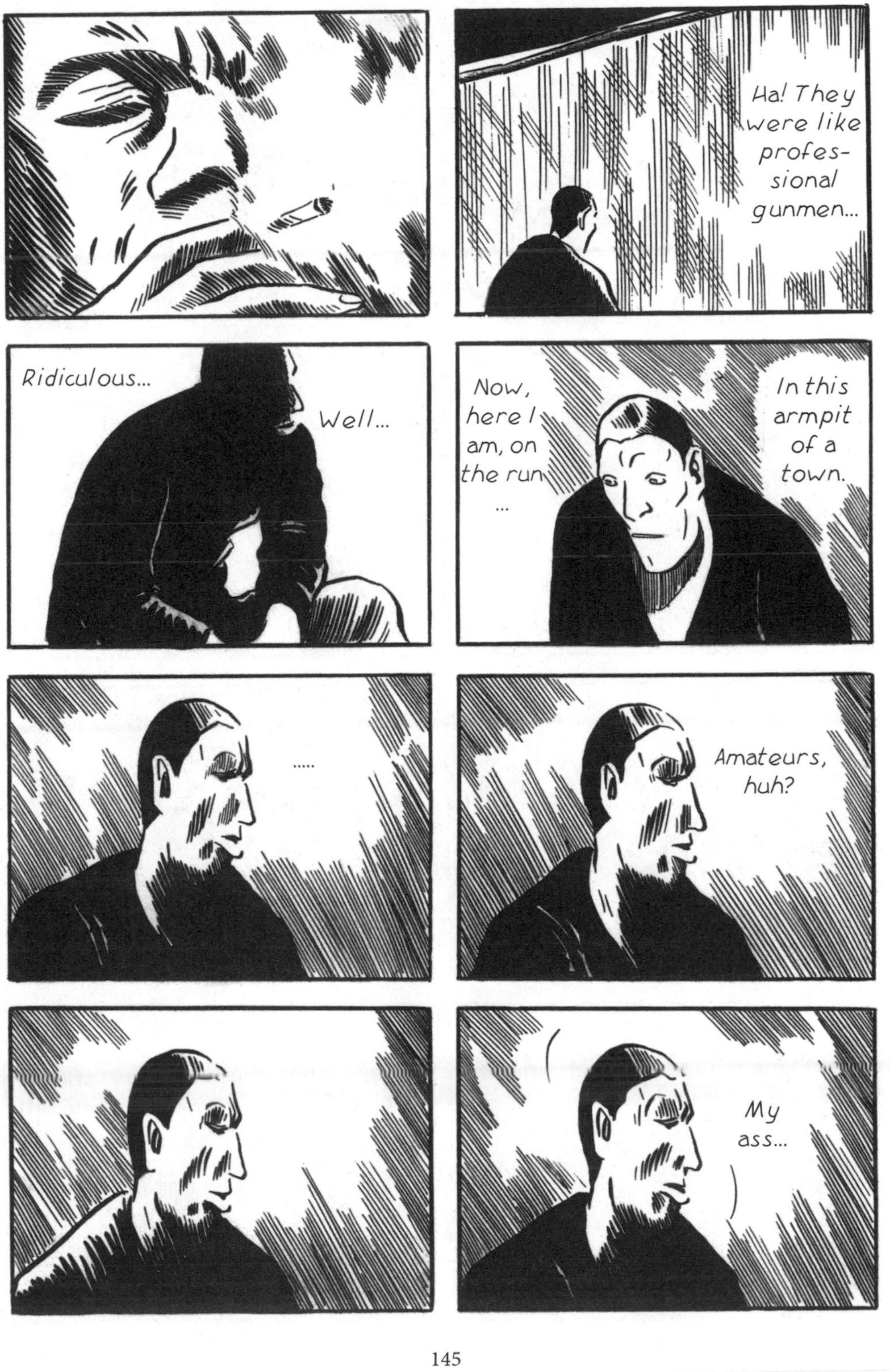
Ha! They were like profes-sional gunmen...
Ridiculous...
Well...
Now, here I am, on the run ...
In this armpit of a town.
.....
Amateurs, huh?
My ass...

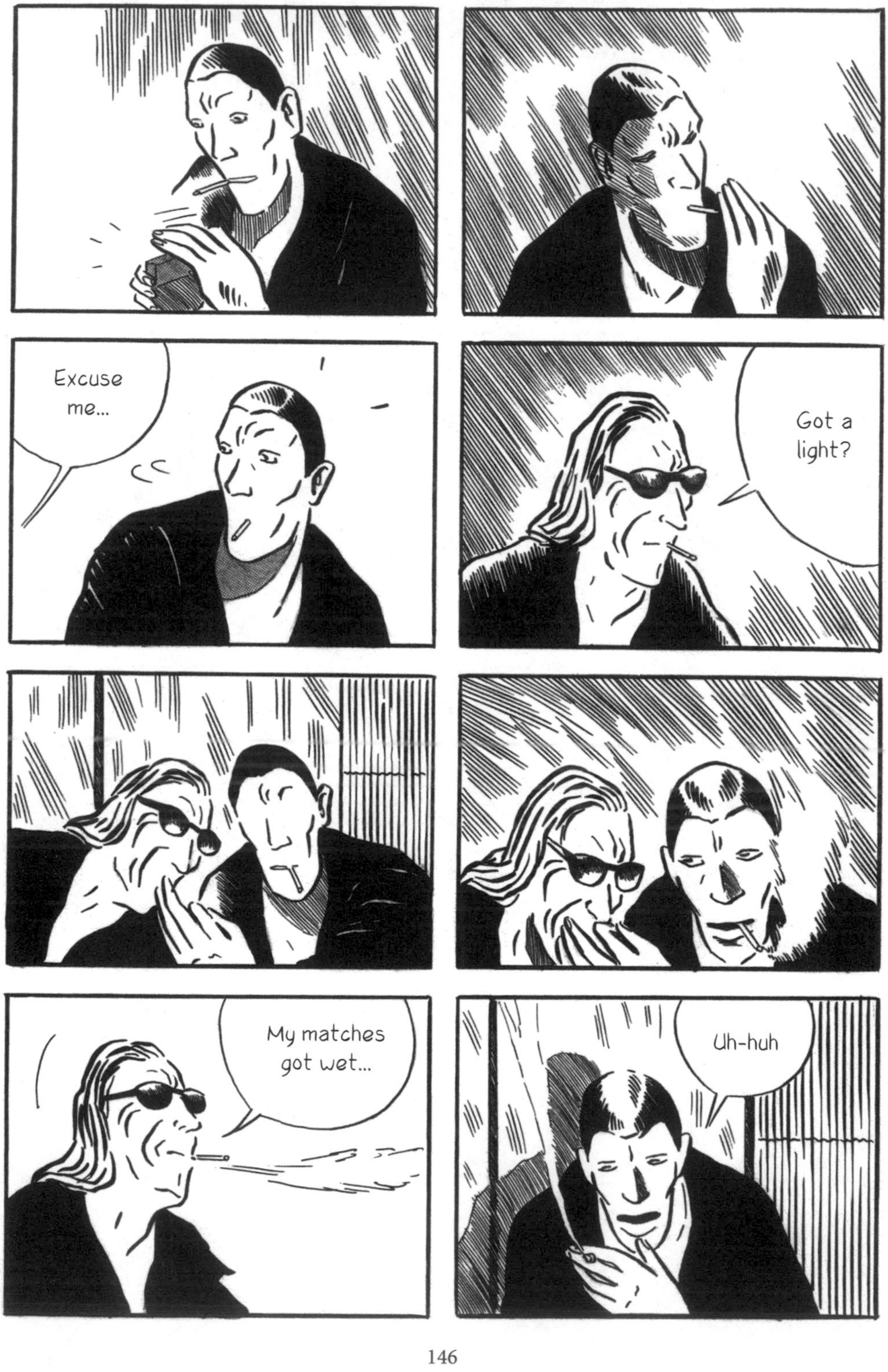
Excuse me...
Got a light?
My matches got wet...
Uh-huh

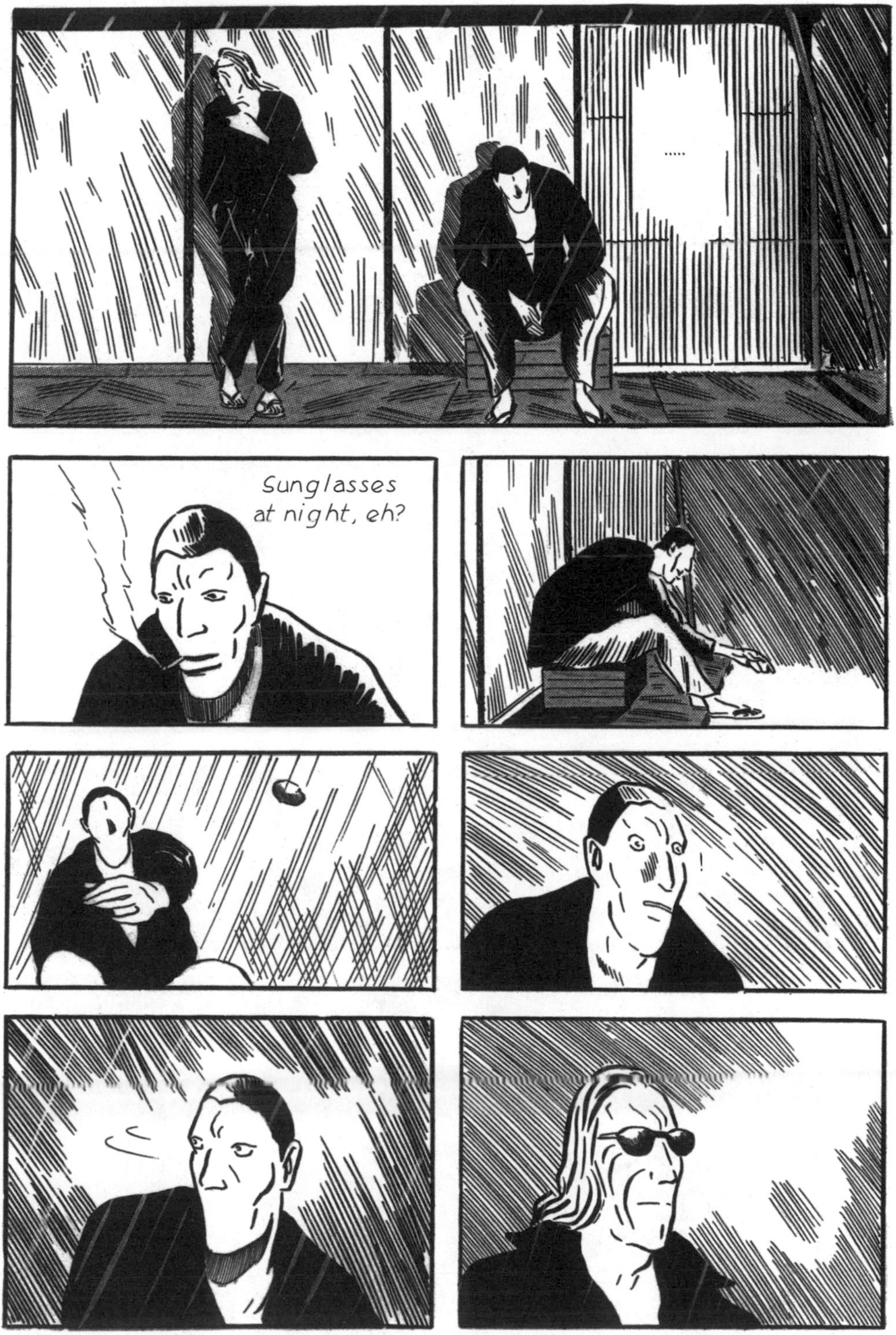
.....
Sunglasses at night, eh?

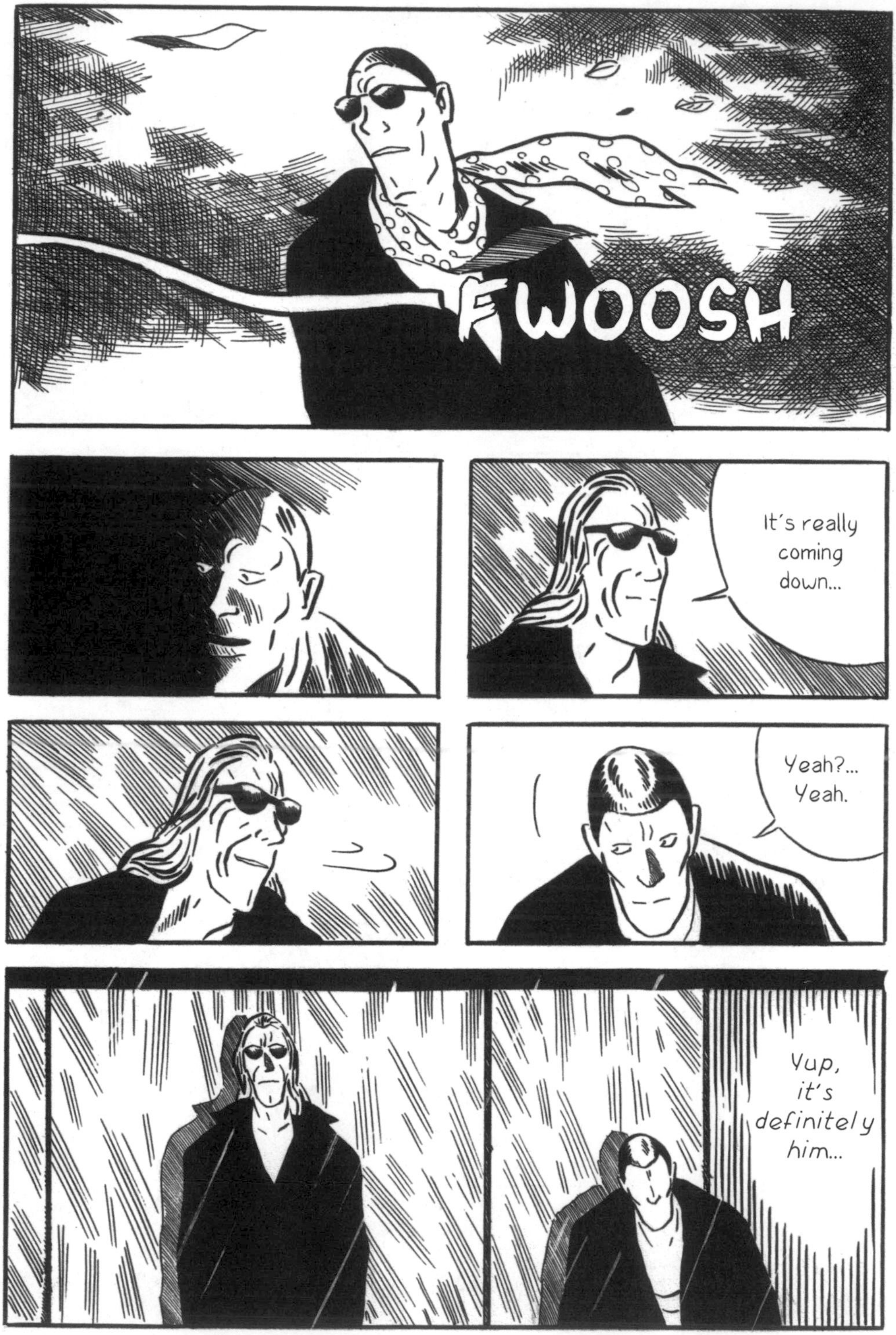
FWOOSH
It's really coming down...
Yeah?... Yeah.
Yup, it's definitely him...

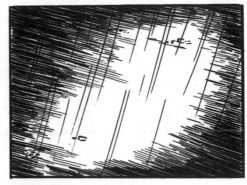

What should I say?

Why the hell is my heart thumping like this?

Want to move over there?

Mud from the cars will splash us if we stay here.

Hm?

Nah, I'm good...

I got drenched before you showed up...

Ha ha...

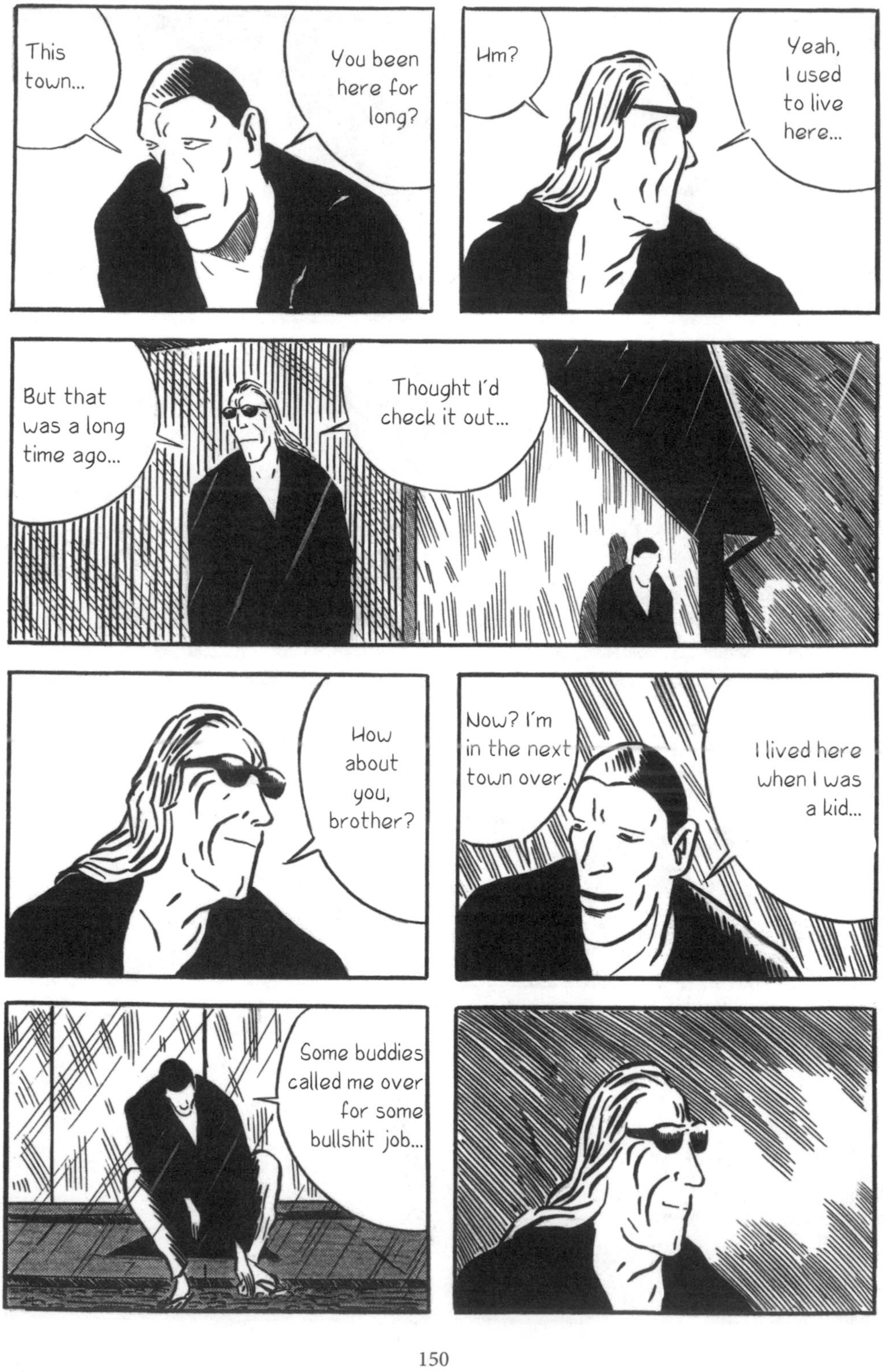
This town...
You been here for long?
Hm?
Yeah, I used to live here...
But that was a long time ago...
Thought I'd check it out...
How about you, brother?
Now? I'm in the next town over.
I lived here when I was a kid...
Some buddies called me over for some bullshit job...

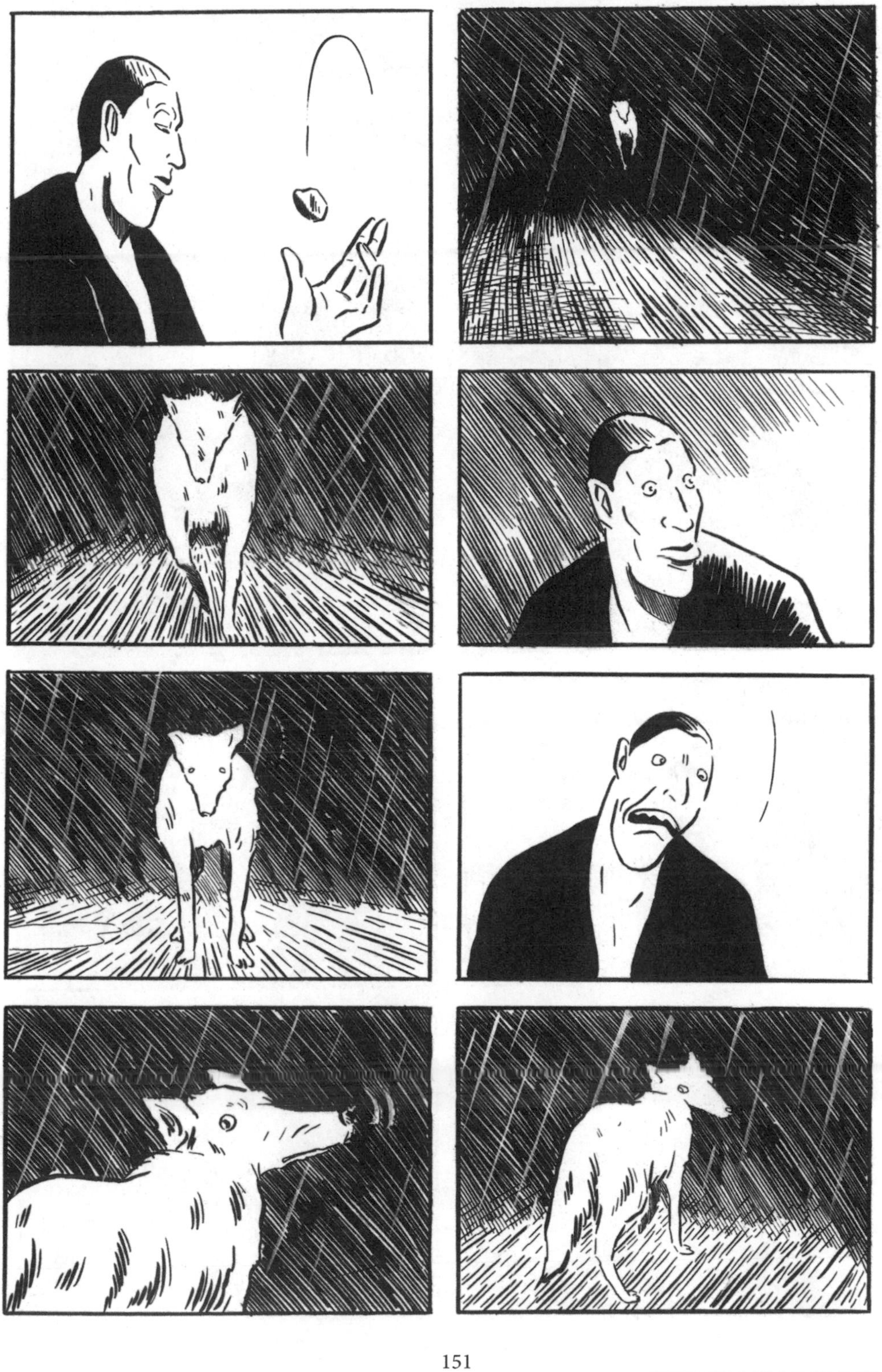

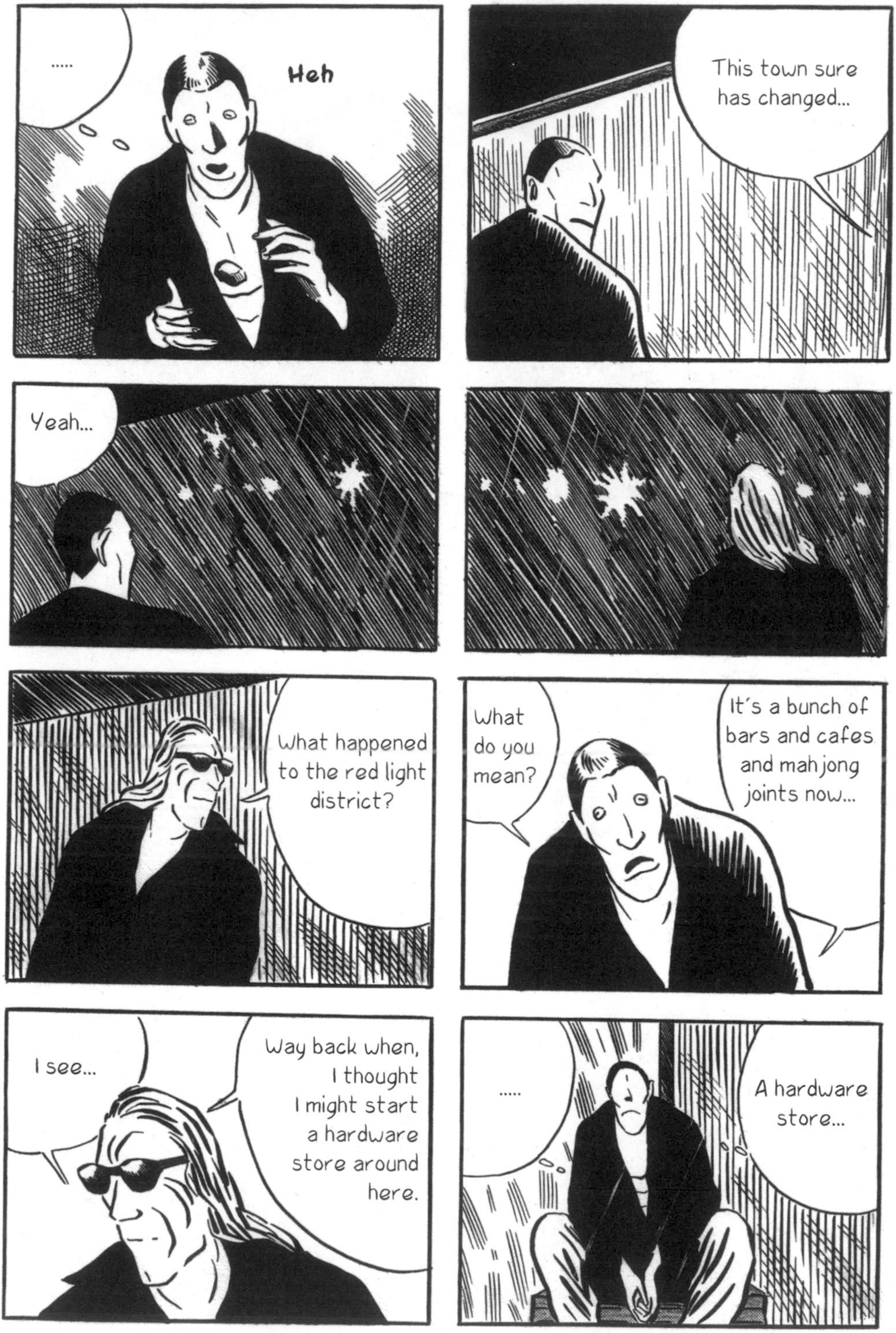
.....
Heh
This town sure has changed...
Yeah...
What happened to the red light district?
What do you mean?
It's a bunch of bars and cafes and mah jong joints now...
I see...
Way back when, I thought I might start a hardware store around here.
.....
A hardware store...

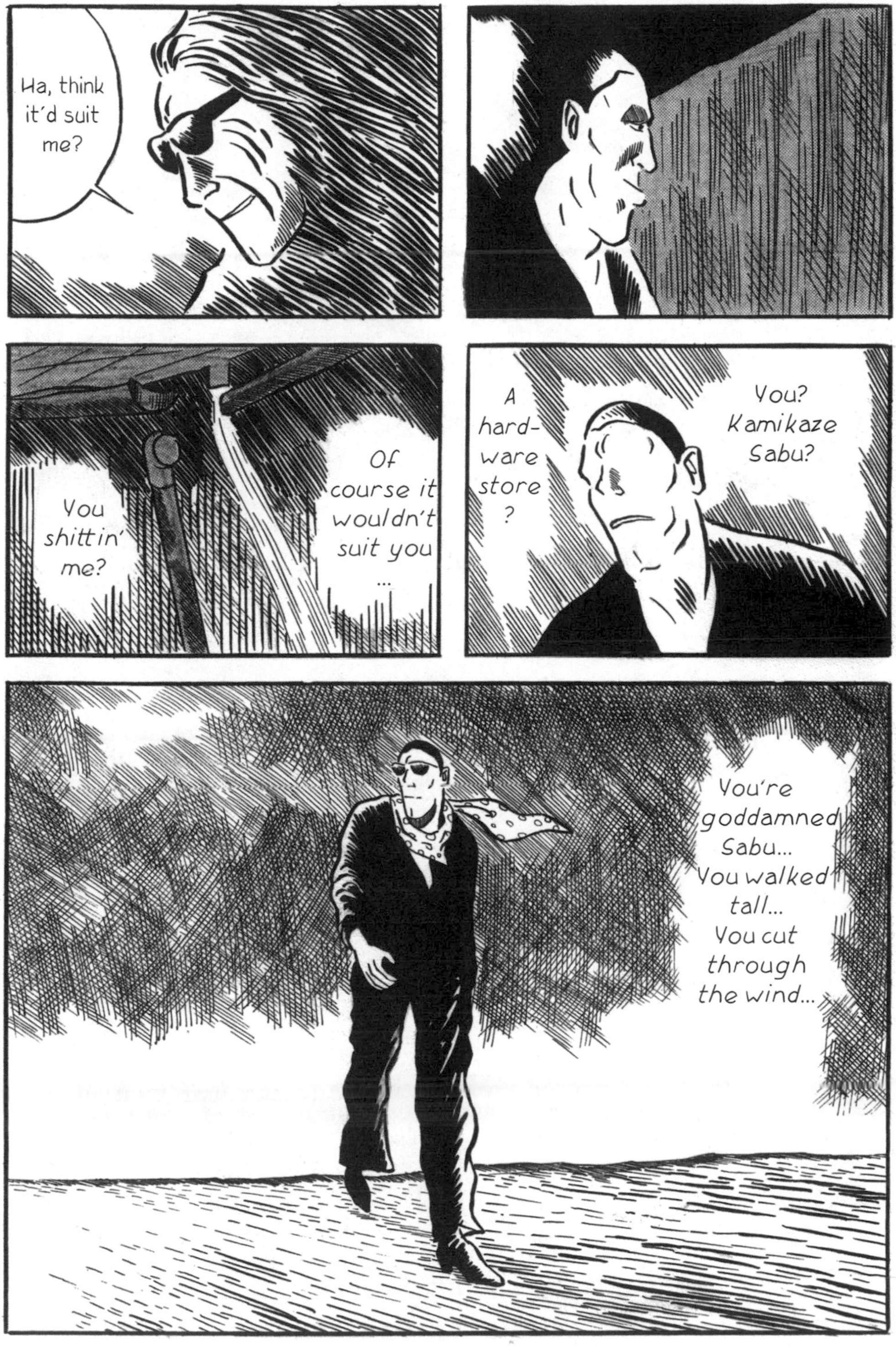
Ha, think it'd suit me?
You shittin' me?
Of course it wouldn't suit you ...
A hard-ware store ?
You? Kamikaze Sabu?
You're goddamned Sabu... You walked tall... You cut through the wind...

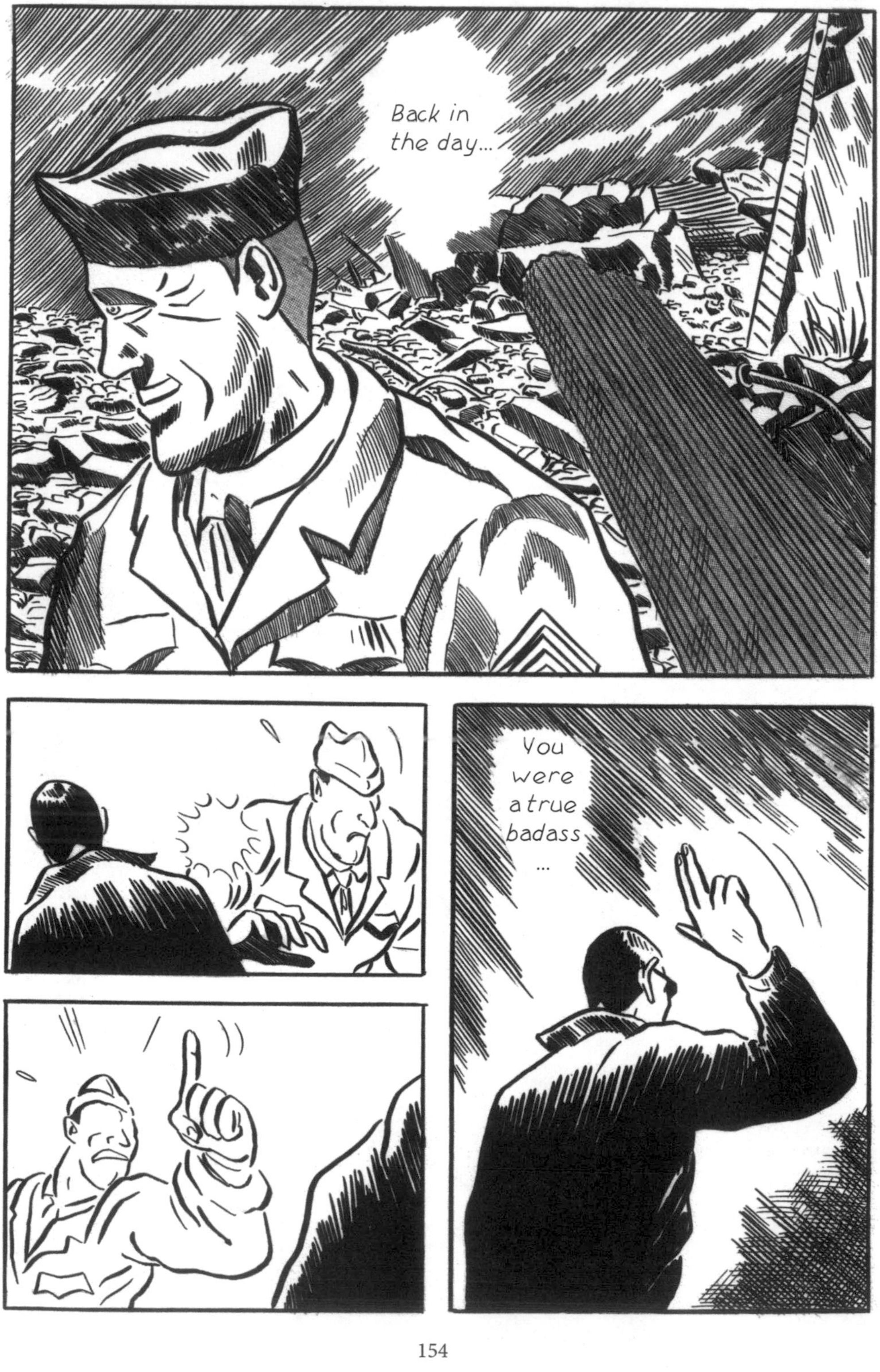
Back in the day...
You were a true badass ...

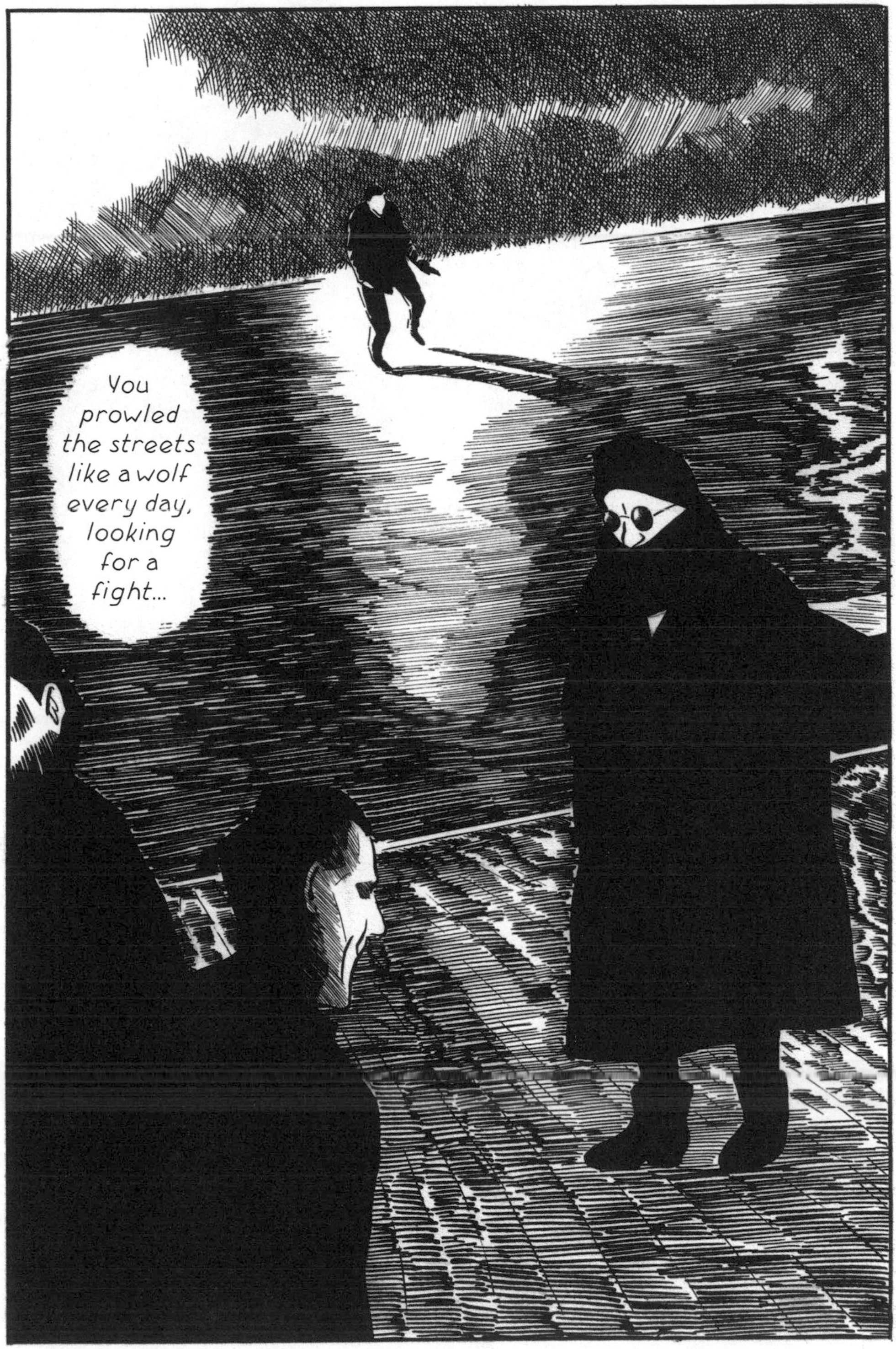
You prowled the streets like a wolf every day, looking for a fight...

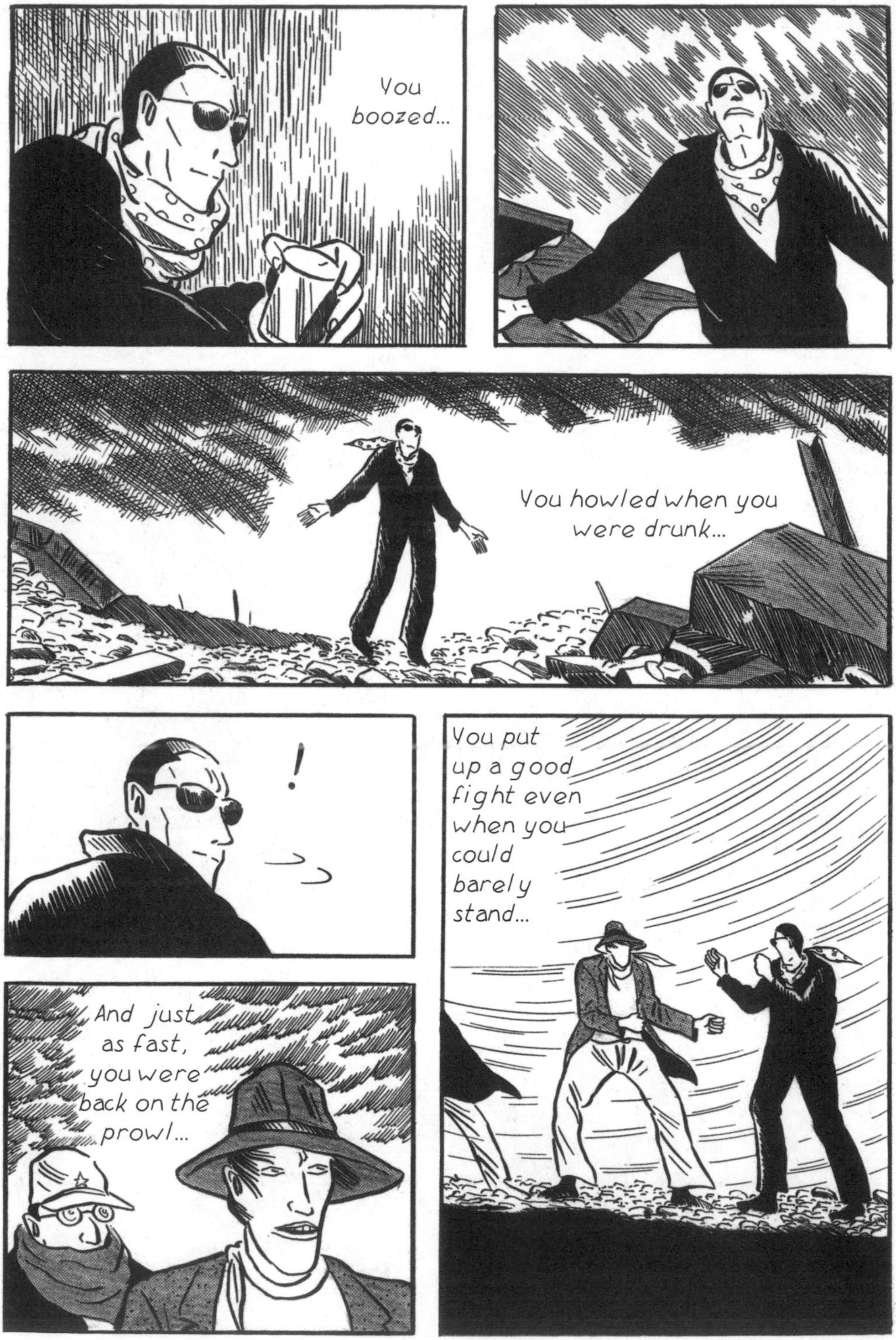
You boozed...
You howled when you were drunk...
!
And just as fast, you were back on the prowl...
You put up a good fight even when you could barely stand...

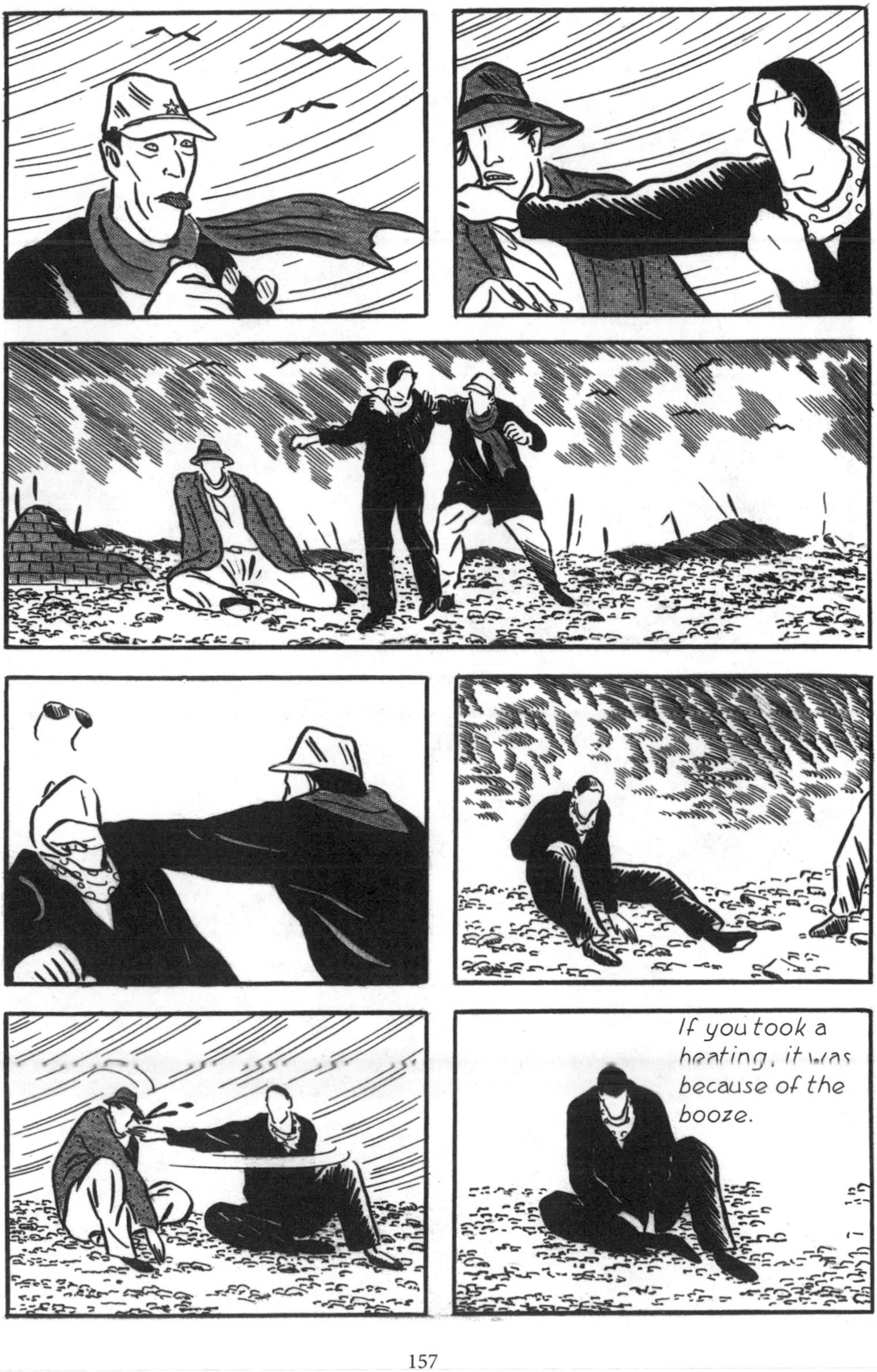
If you took a beating, it was because of the booze.

The thrashing was always mutual...

What were you fighting for?

Was it just for the hell of it?

Without a dose of pain once in a while...

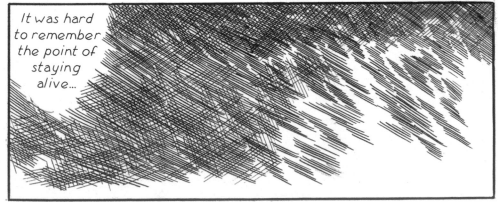

It was hard to remember the point of staying alive...

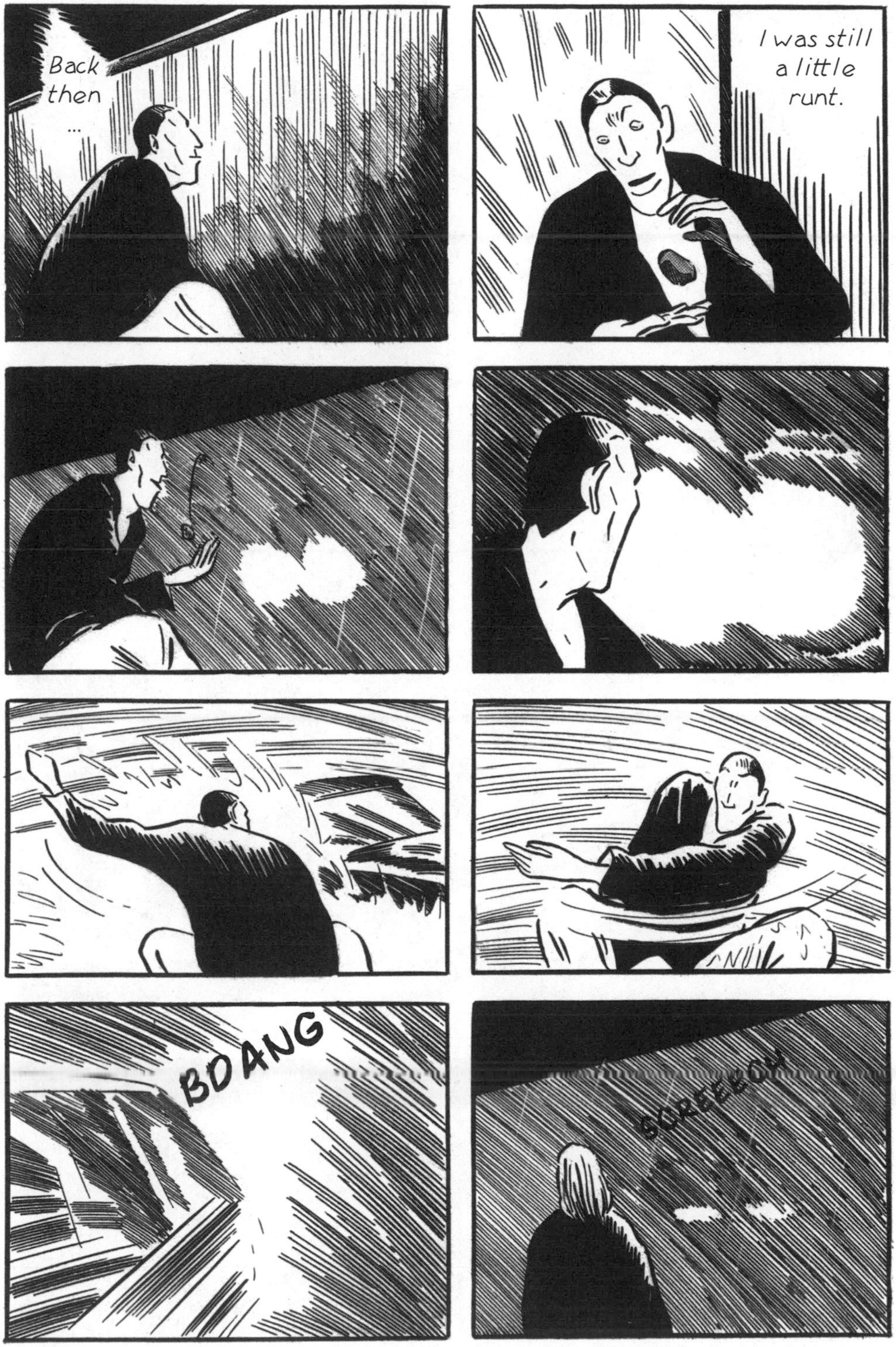
Back then ...
I was still a little runt.
BDANG
SCREEECH

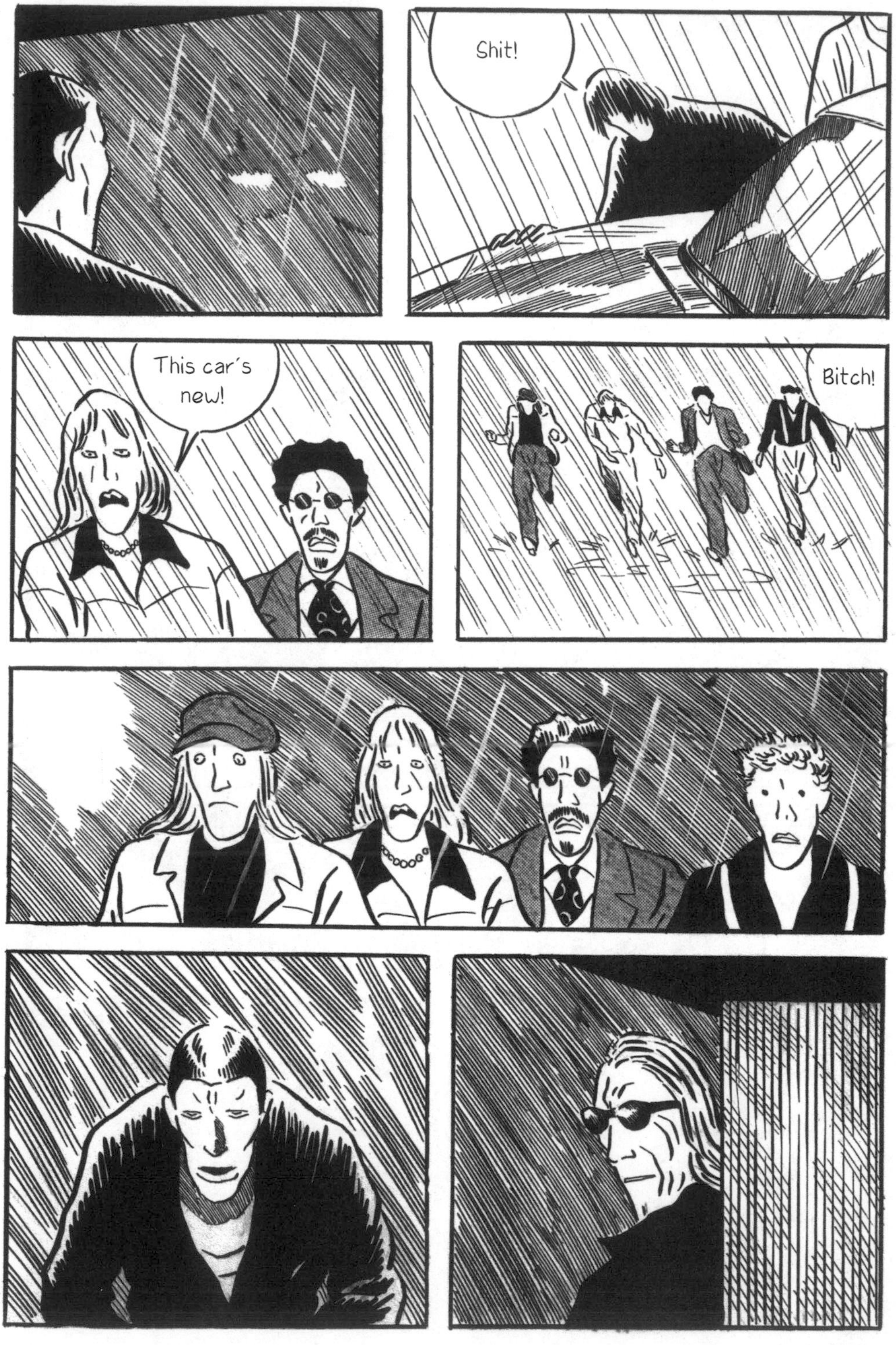

Shit!
This car's new!
Bitch!

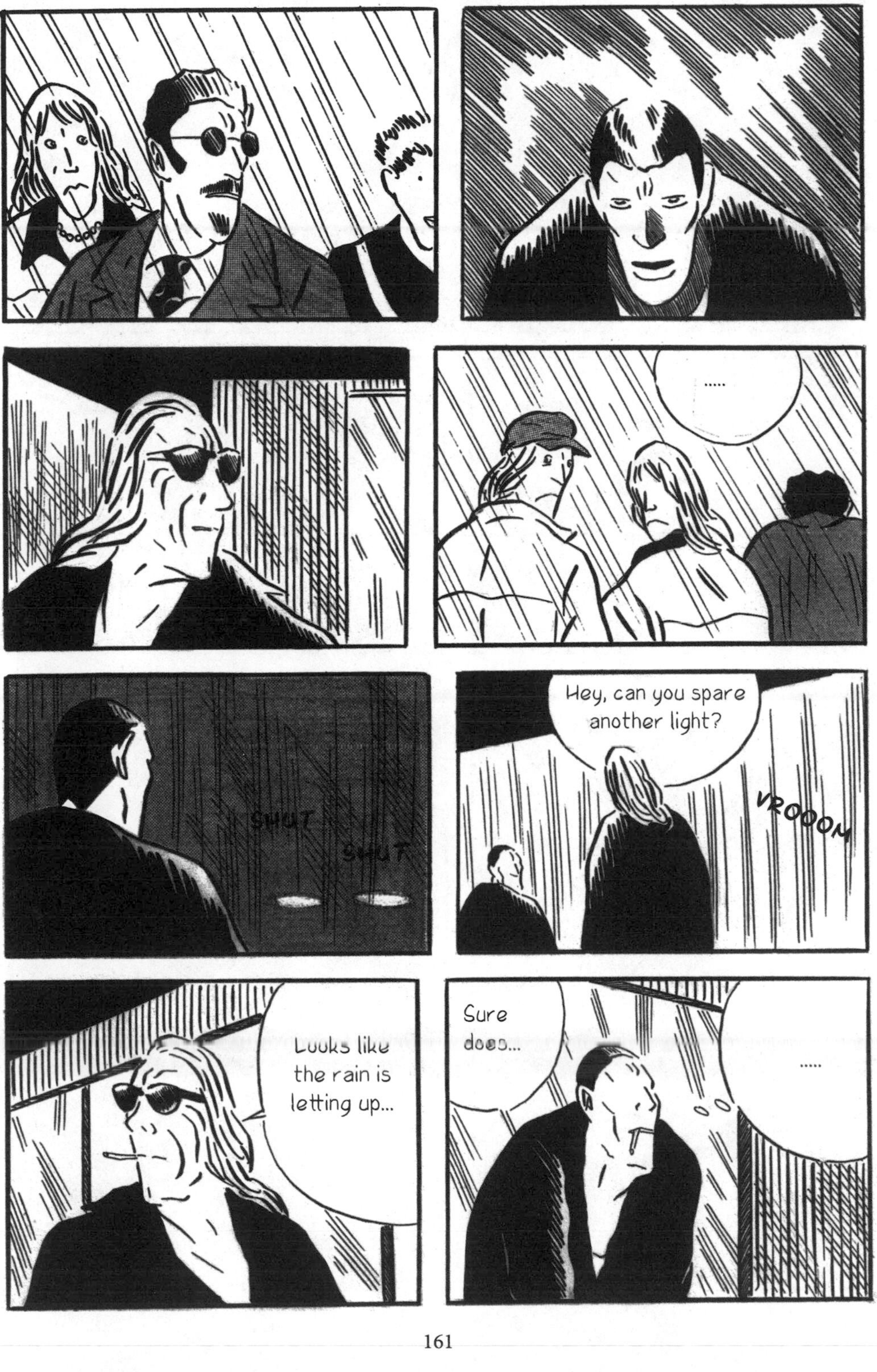
.....
SHUT
SHUT
Hey, can you spare another light?
VROOOM
Looks like the rain is letting up...
Sure does...
.....

FWOOSH

Last time I saw you...

When I was still a kid...

There was a woman...

There were some men...

You towered like a giant...

I never saw you so angry...

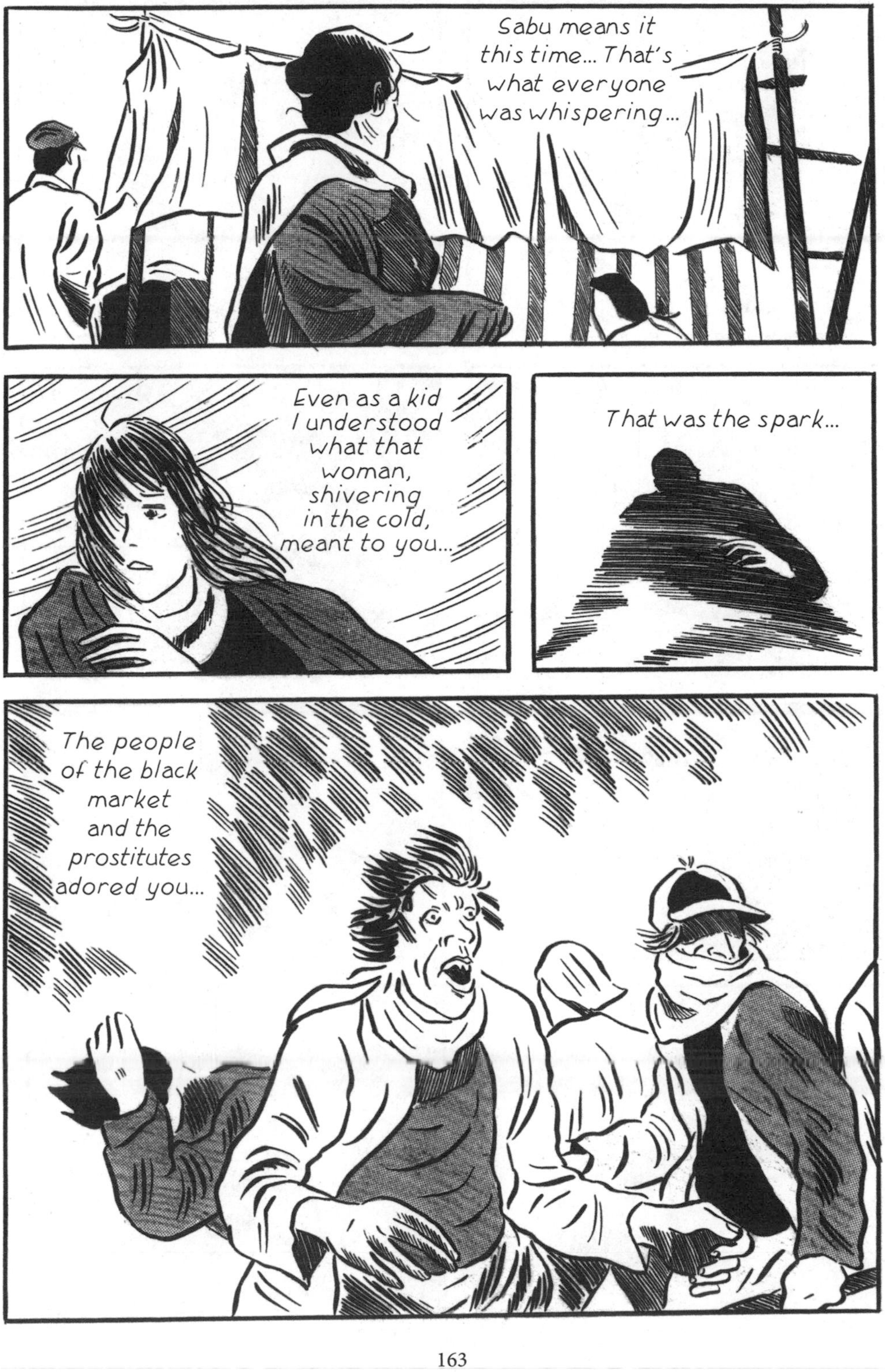
Sabu means it this time... That's what everyone was whispering...
Even as a kid I understood what that woman, shivering in the cold, meant to you...
That was the spark...
The people of the black market and the prostitutes adored you...

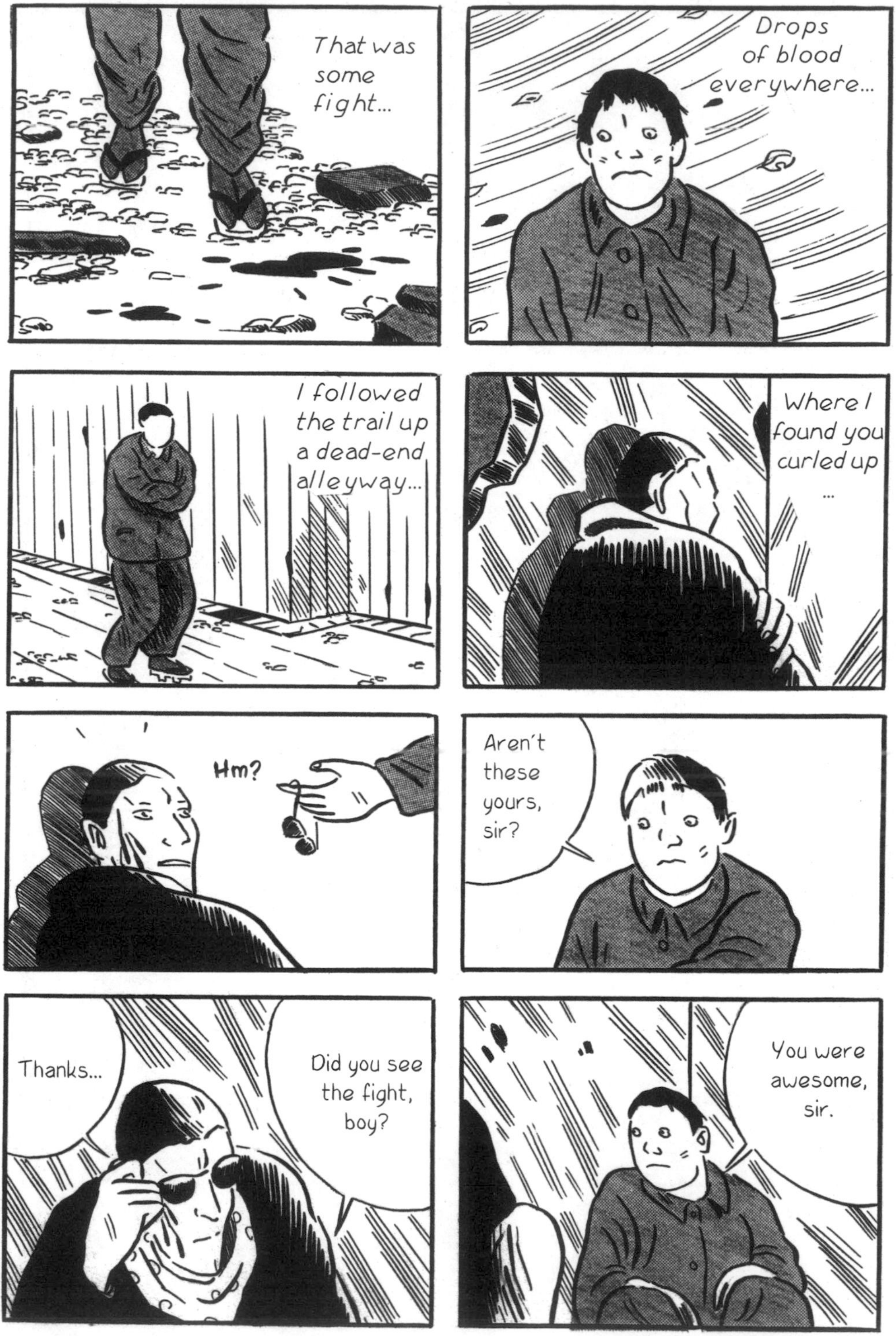
That was some fight...
Drops of blood everywhere...
I followed the trail up a dead-end alleyway...
Where I found you curled up ...
Hm?
Aren't these yours, sir?
Thanks...
Did you see the fight, boy?
You were awesome, sir.

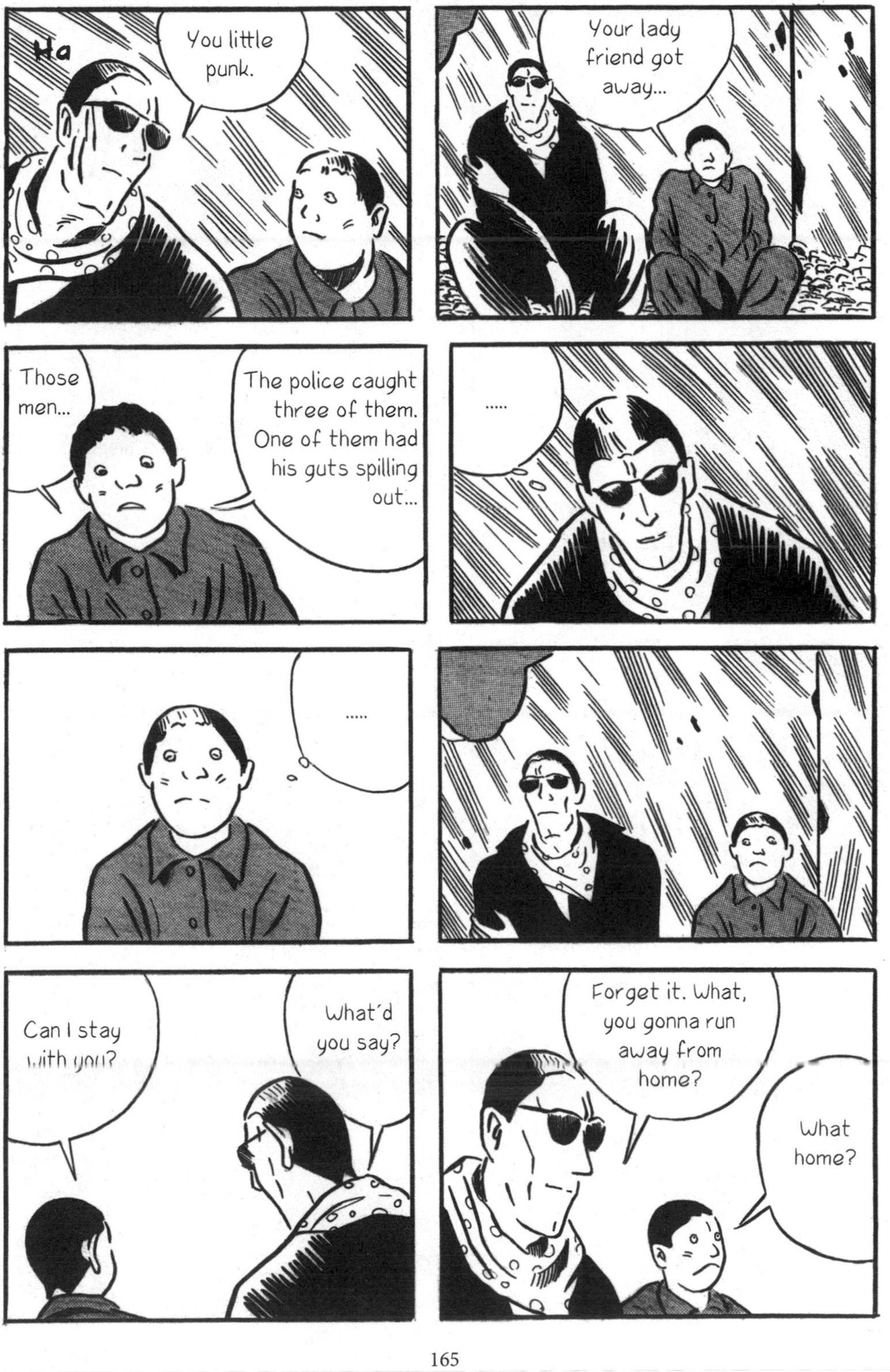
Ha
You little punk.
Your lady friend got away...
Those men...
The police caught three of them. One of them had his guts spilling out...
.....
.....
Can I stay with you?
What'd you say?
Forget it. What, you gonna run away from home?
What home?

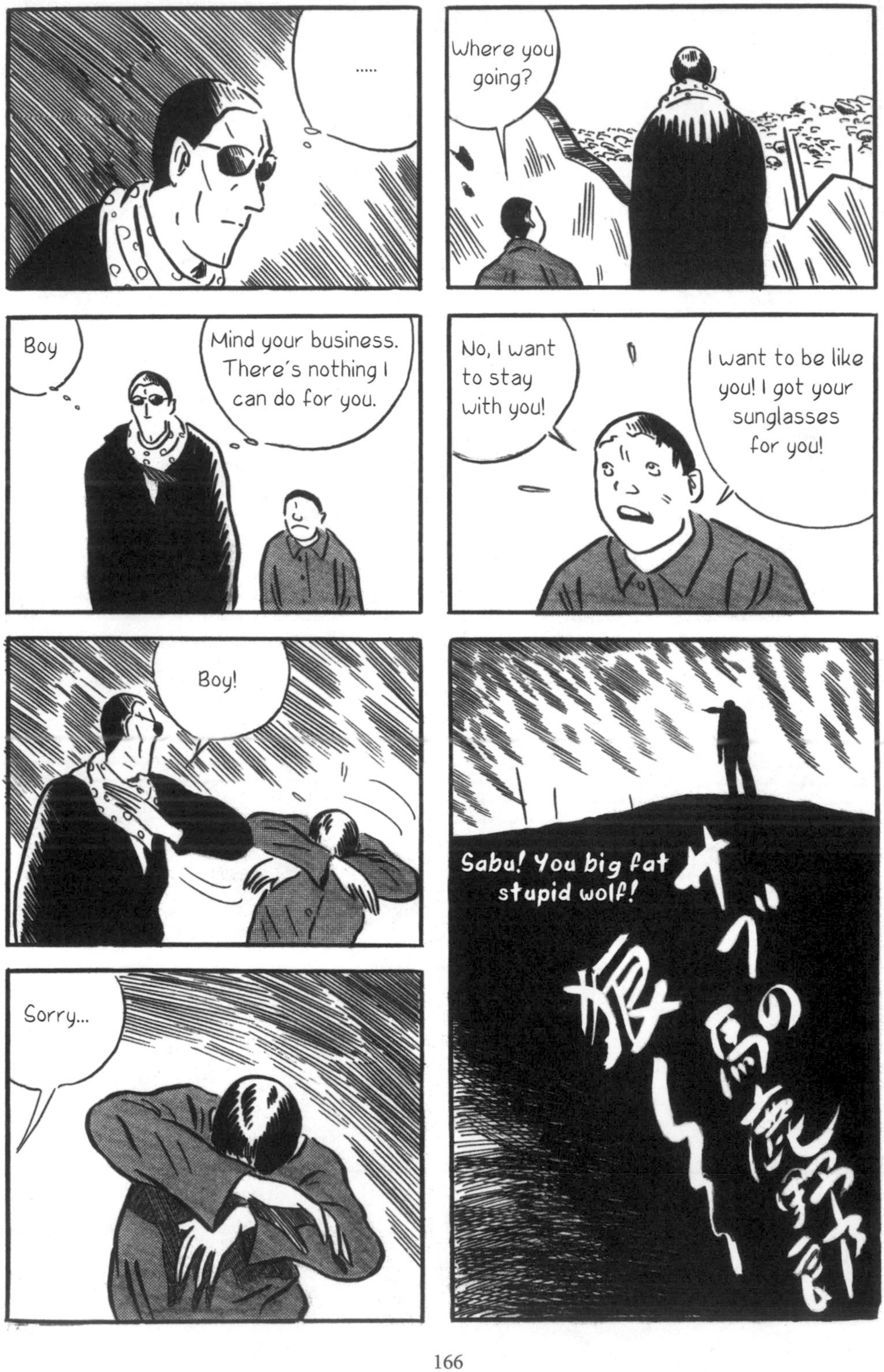
.....
Where you going?
Boy
Mind your business. There's nothing I can do for you.
No, I want to stay with you!
I want to be like you! I got your sunglasses for you!
Boy!
Sorry...
Sabu! You big fat stupid wolf!
サブの馬鹿野郎
狼〜〜

No one knew what happened to you...

Some people said you were in jail...

Others said some hoods stabbed you to death...

Both stories sounded plausible...

But tell me, where did you go?

Brother, the rain's about stopped. I'm heading out.

.....

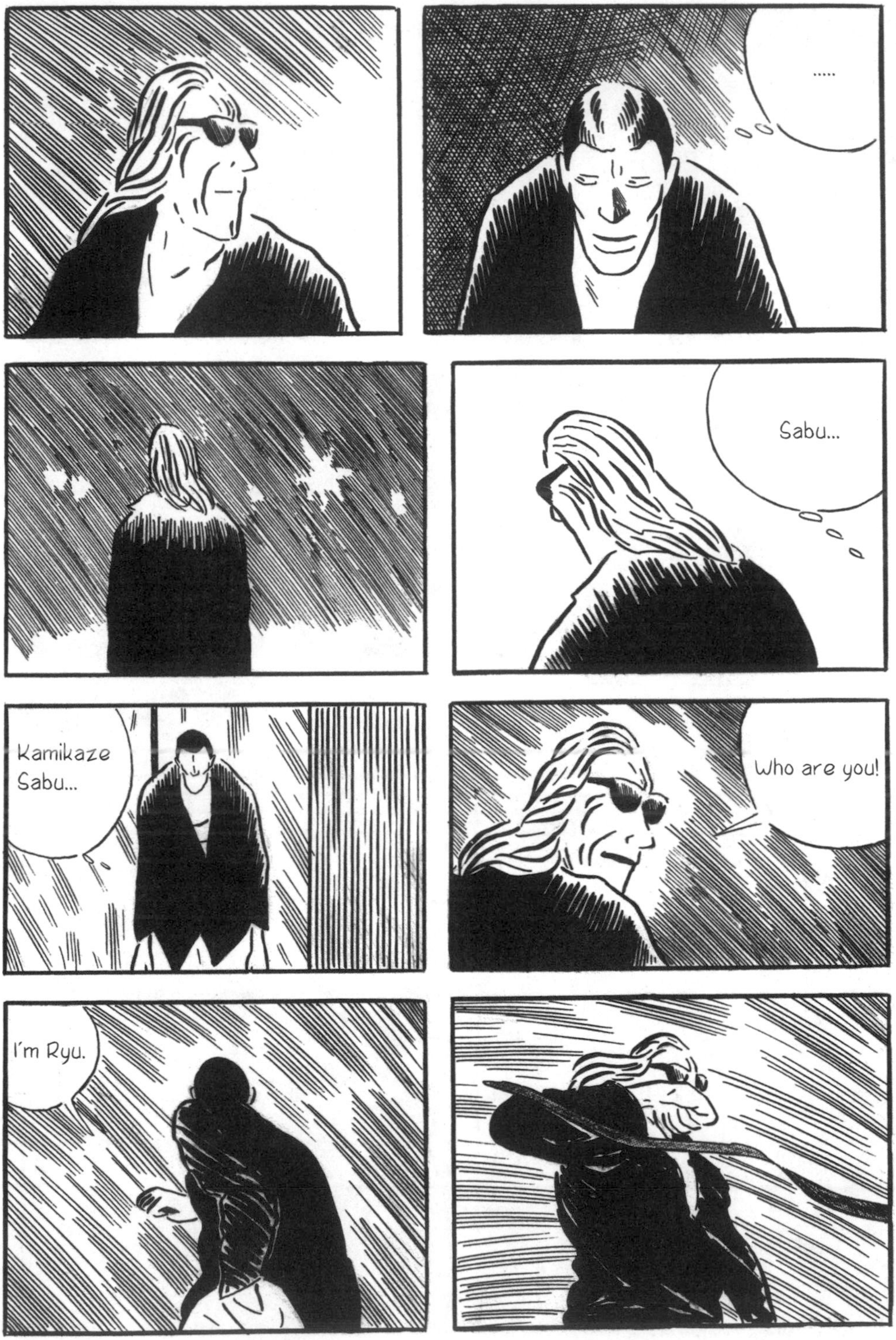
.....
Sabu...
Kamikaze Sabu...
Who are you!
I'm Ryu.

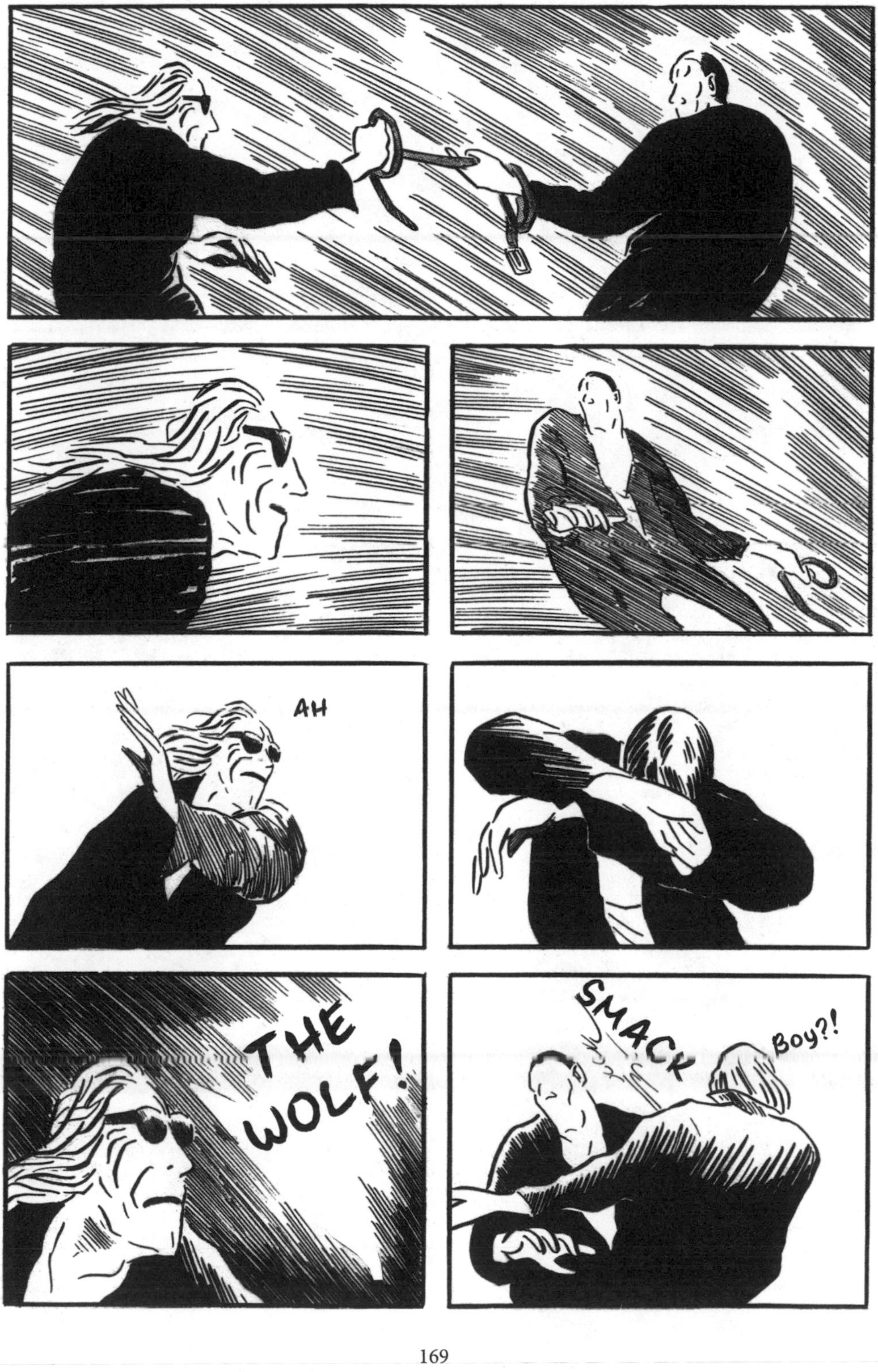
AH
THE WOLF!
SMACK
Boy?!

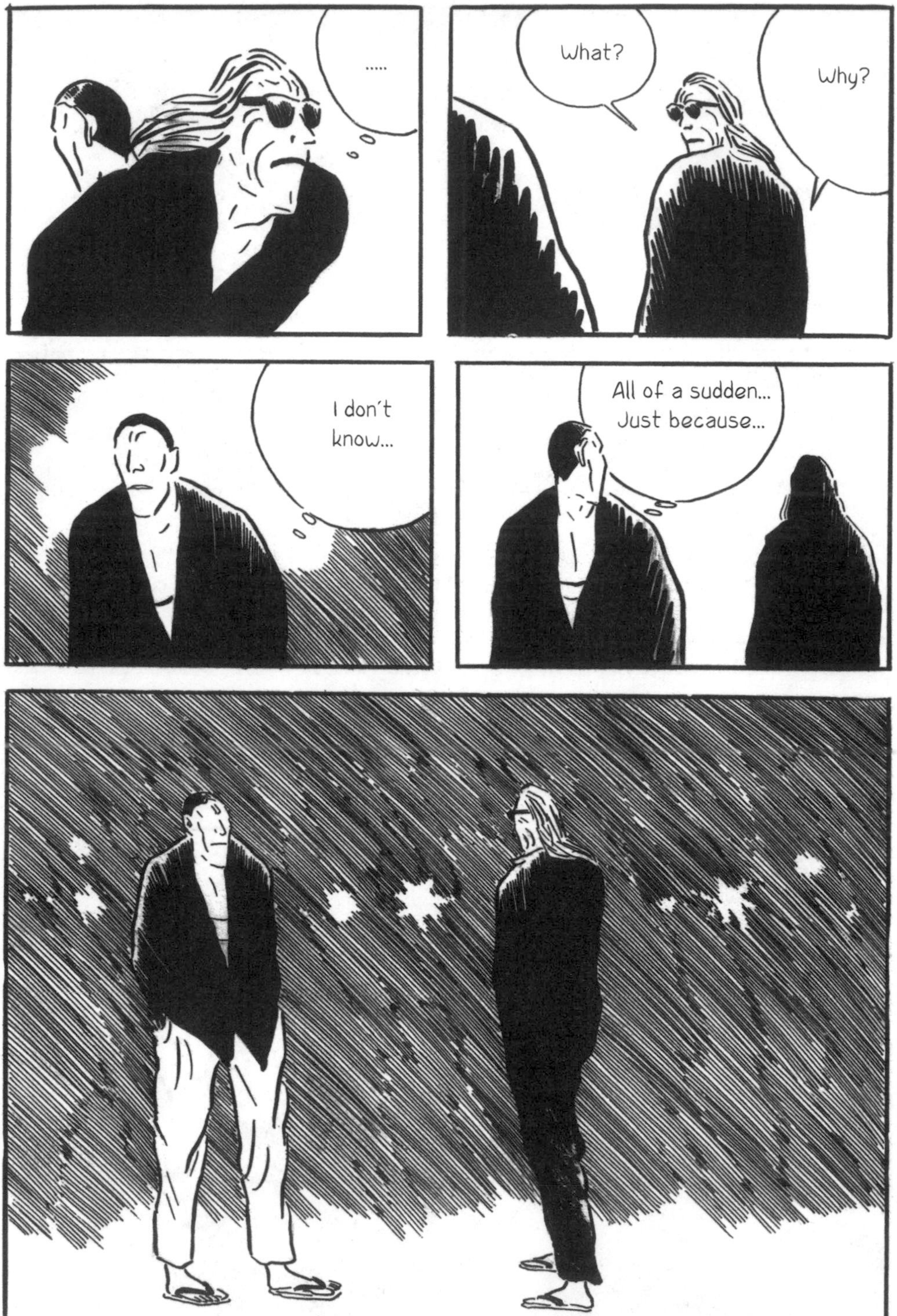
.....
What?
Why?
I don't know...
All of a sudden... Just because...

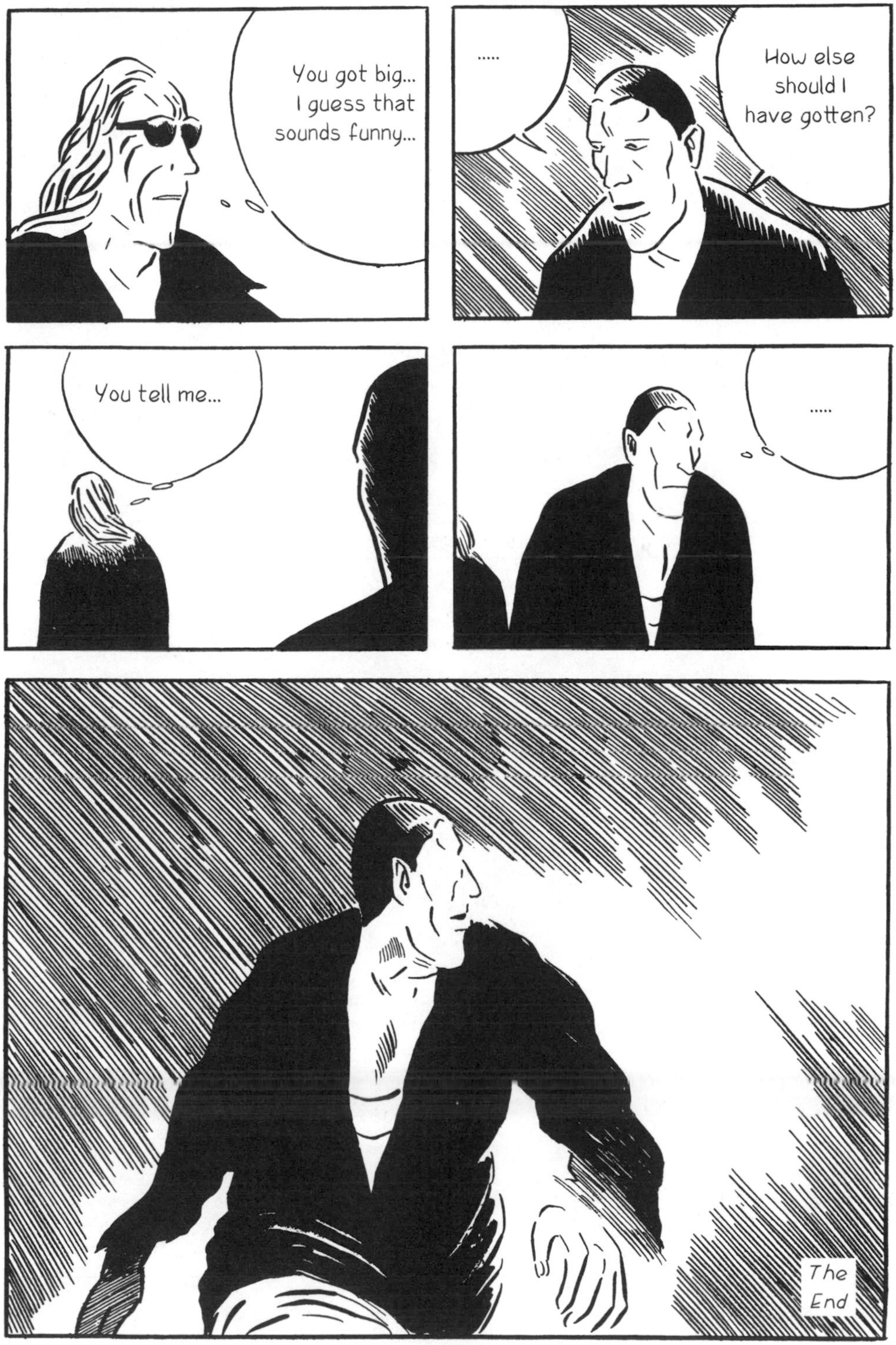
You got big... I guess that sounds funny...
.....
How else should I have gotten?
You tell me...
.....
The End

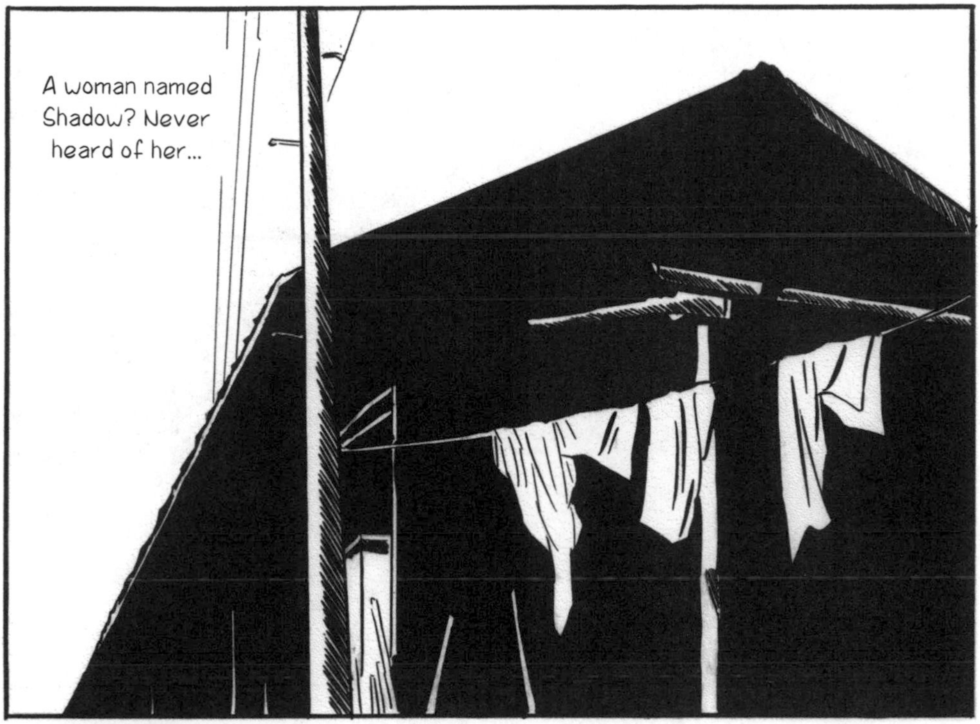
A woman named Shadow? Never heard of her...
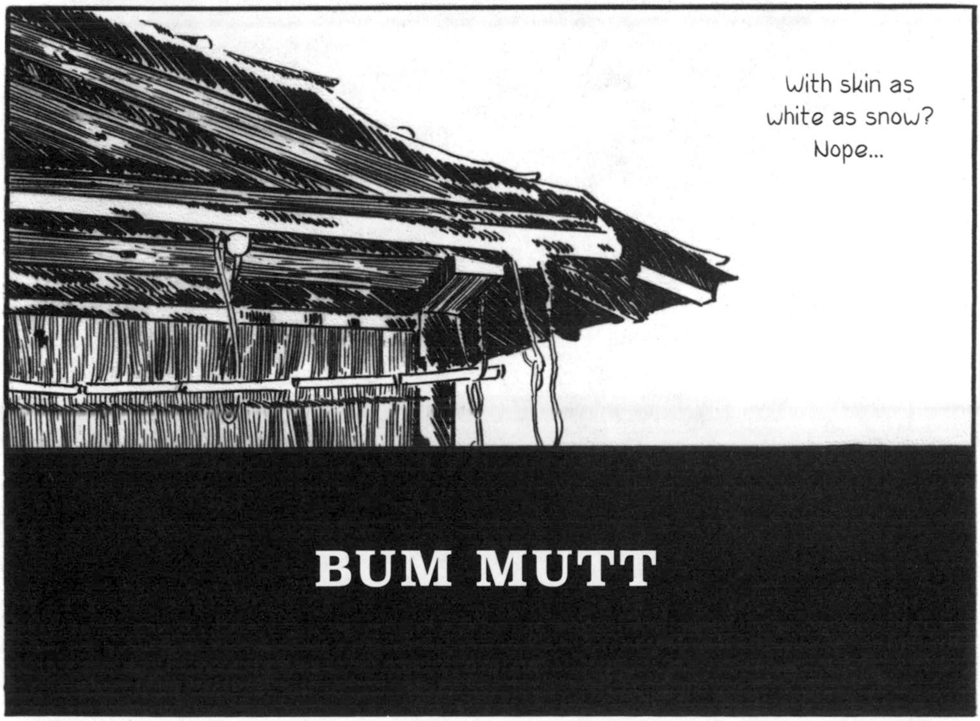
With skin as white as snow? Nope...
BUM MUTT

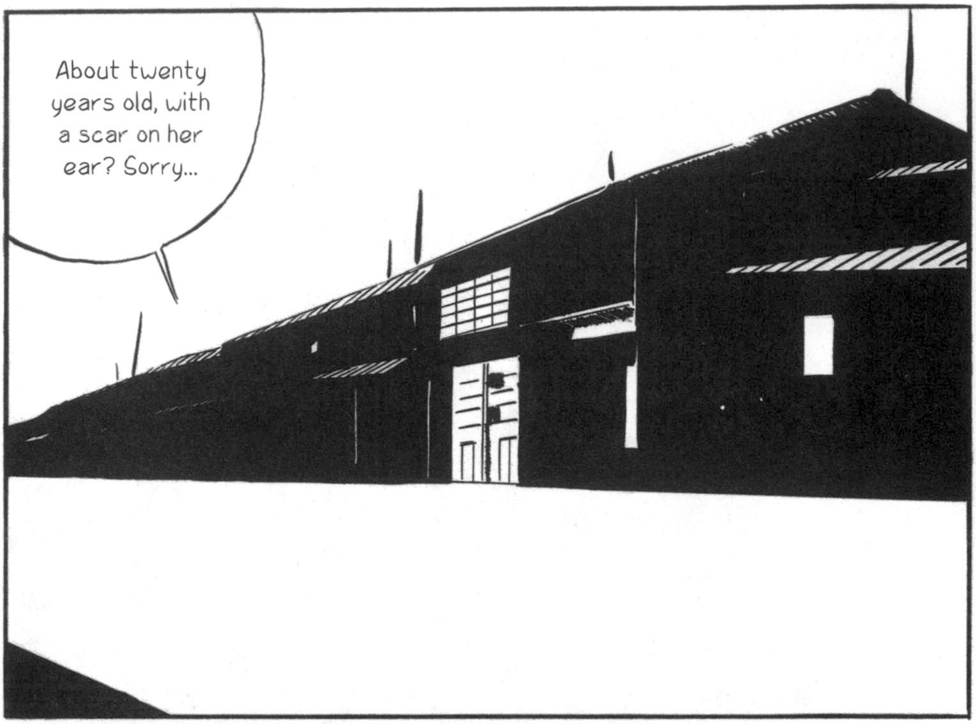
About twenty years old, with a scar on her ear? Sorry...

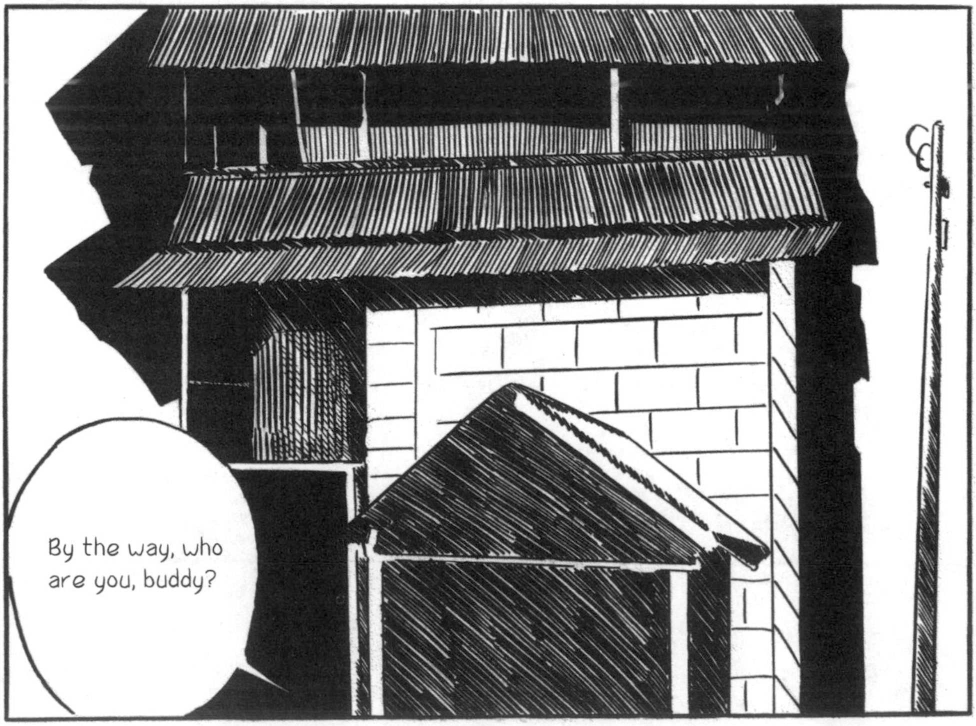
By the way, who are you, buddy?

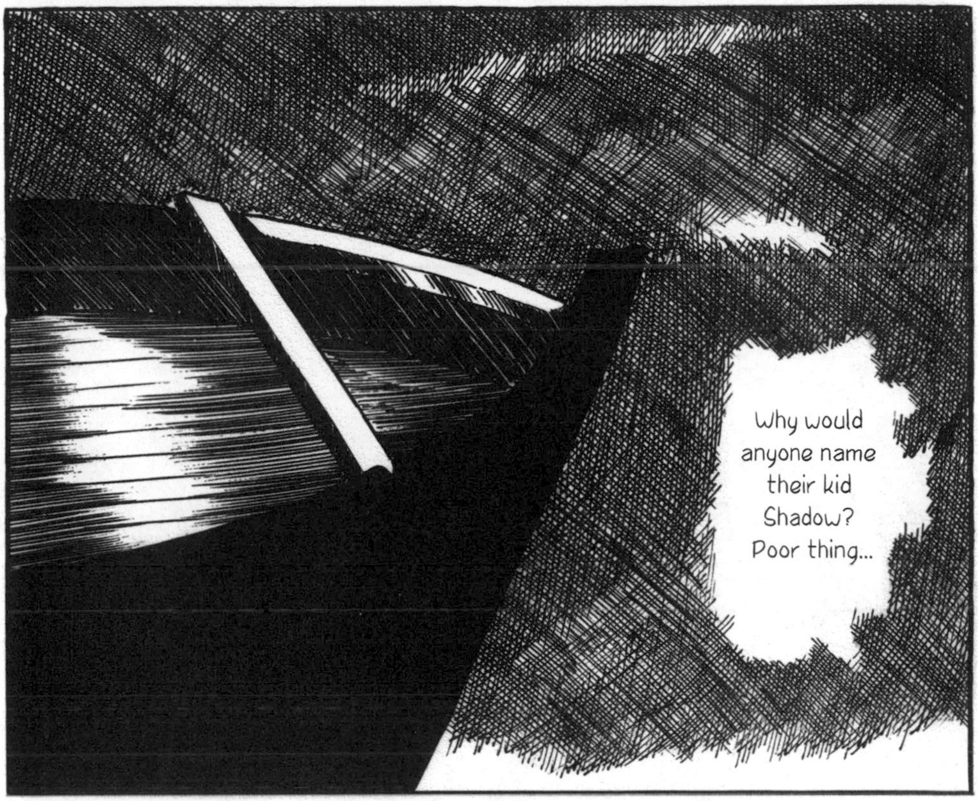
Why would anyone name their kid Shadow? Poor thing...

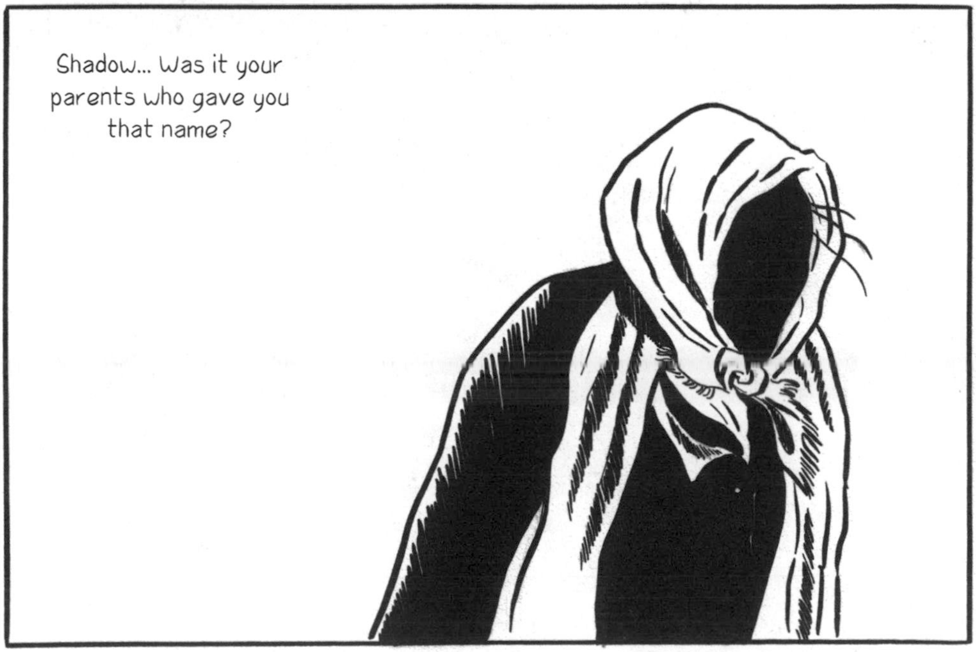
Shadow... Was it your parents who gave you that name?

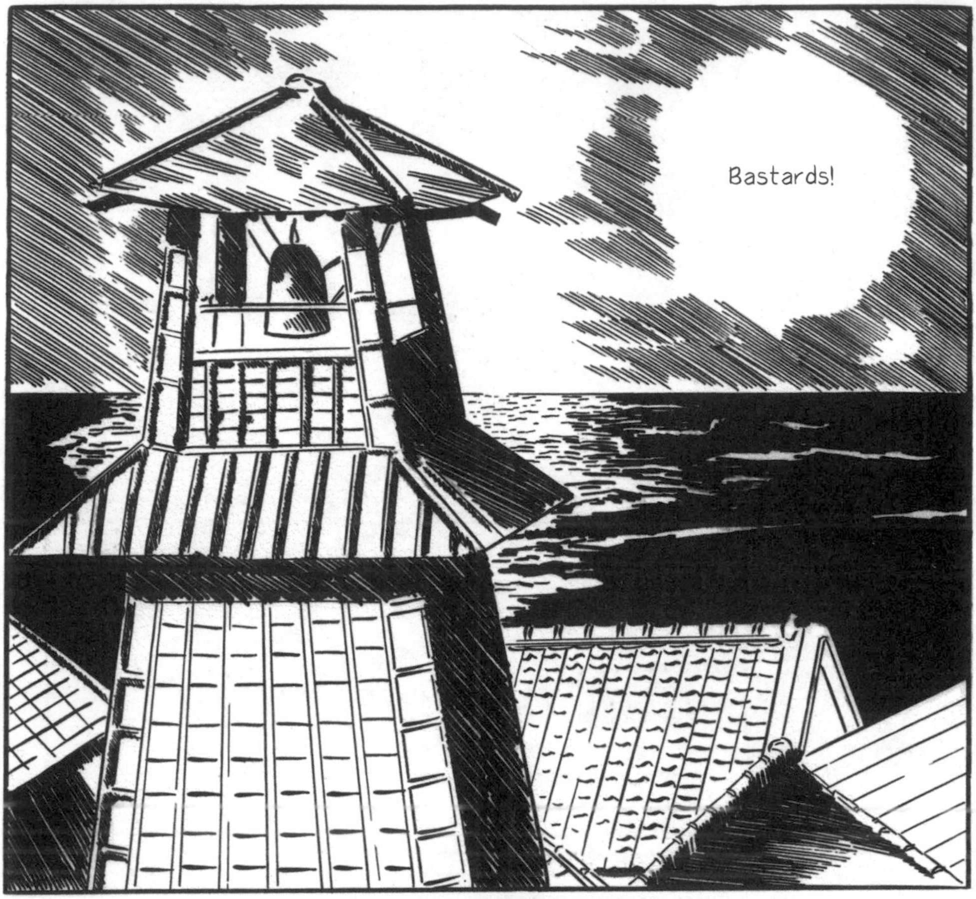
Bastards!
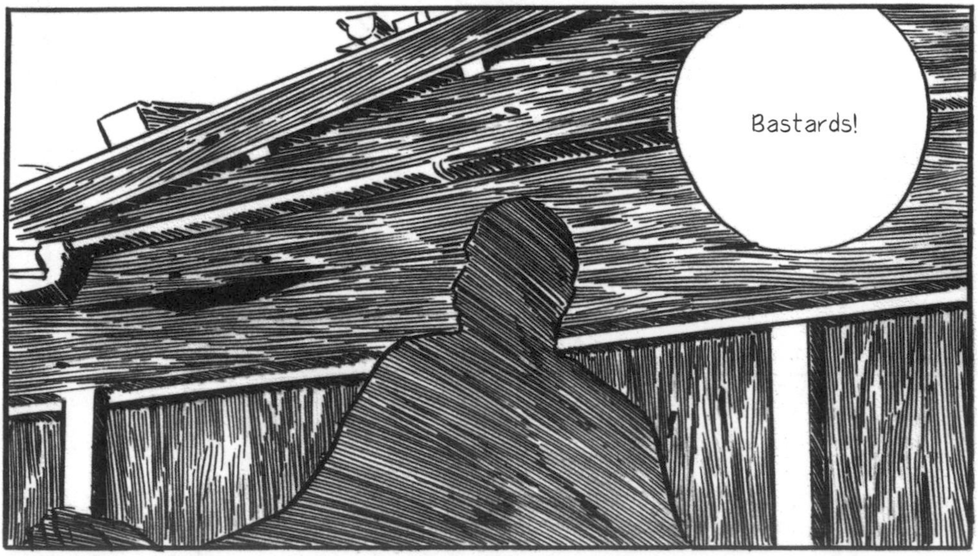
Bastards!

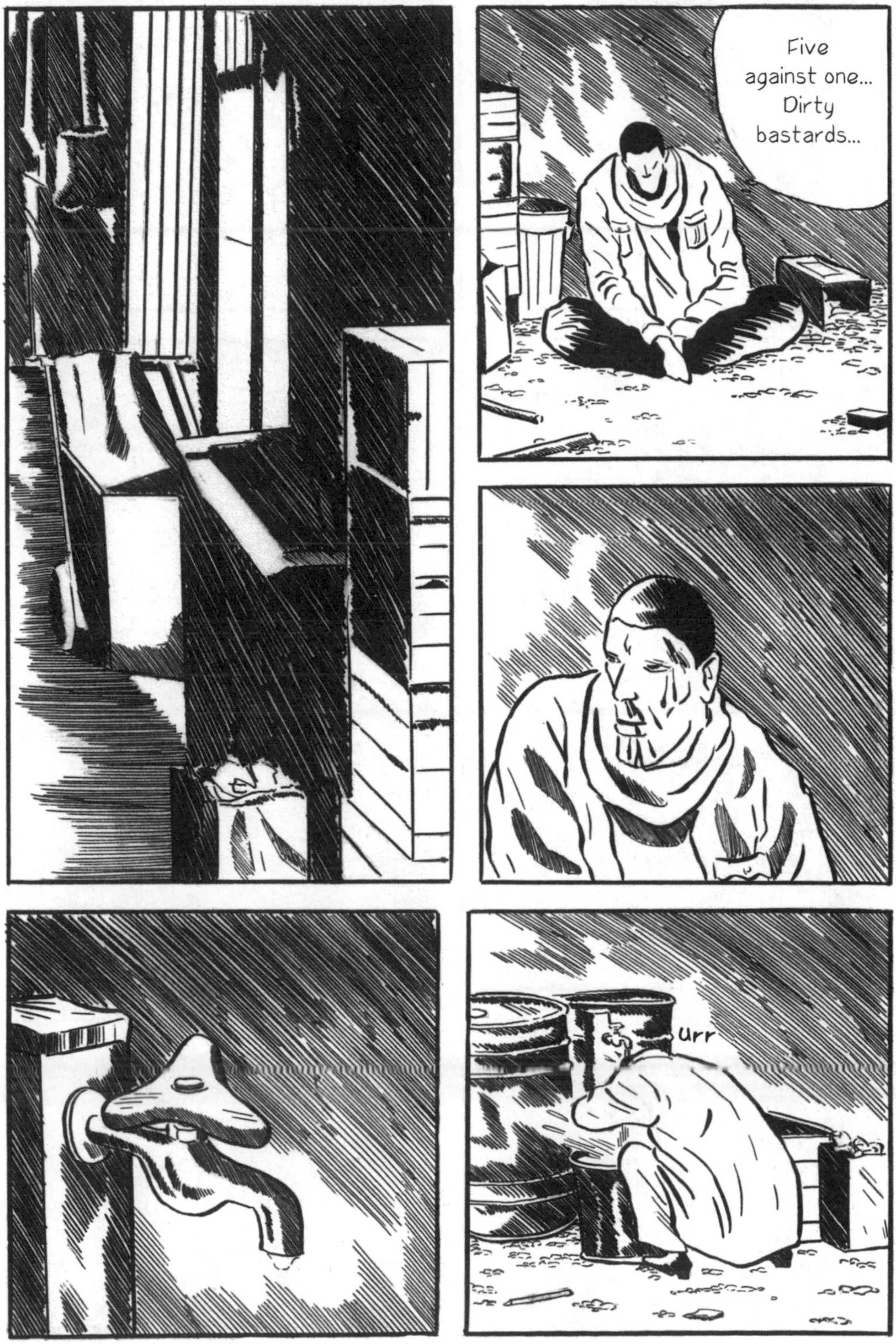
Five against one... Dirty bastards...
urr

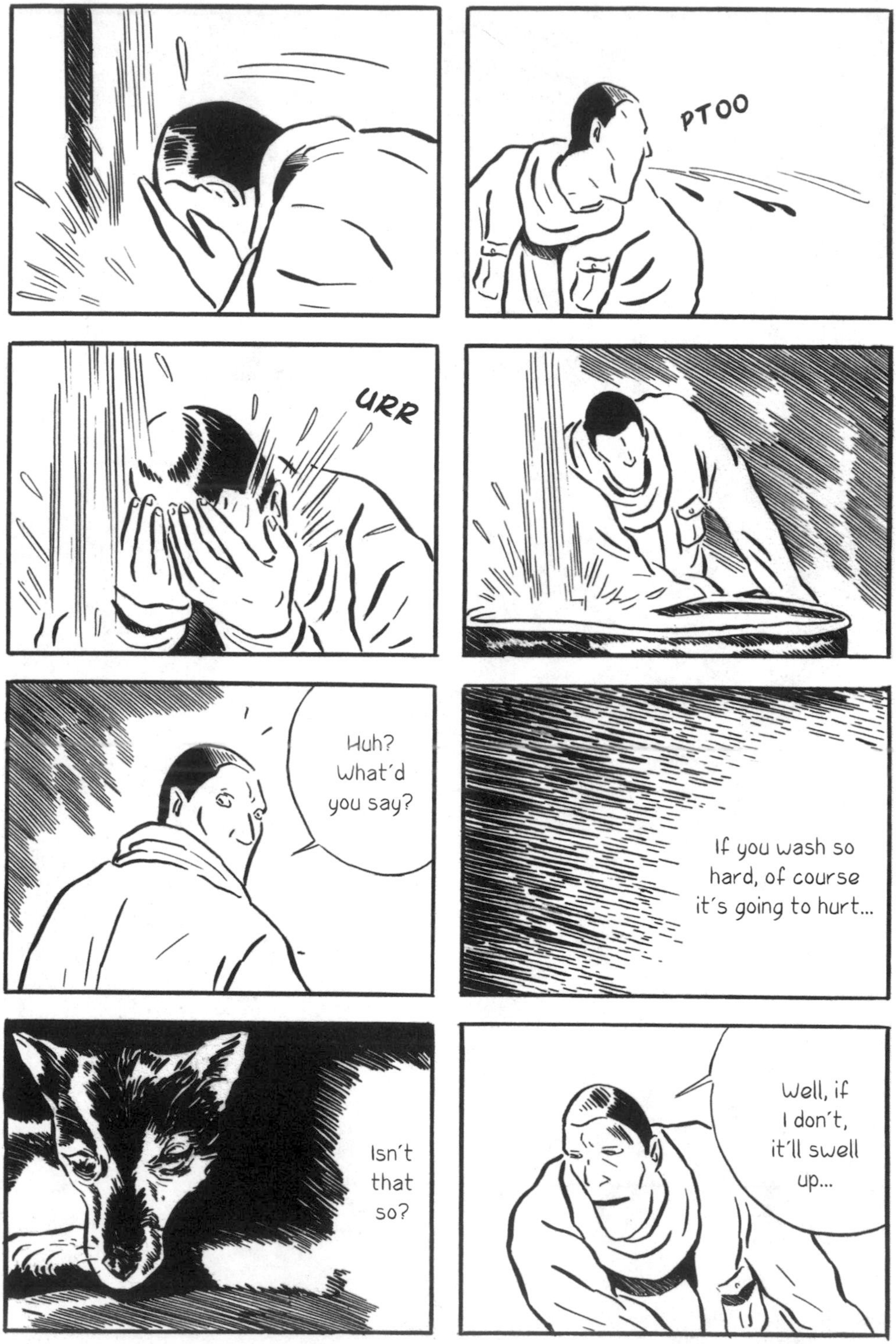
PTOO
URR
Huh? What'd you say?
If you wash so hard, of course it's going to hurt...
Isn't that so?
Well, if I don't, it'll swell up...

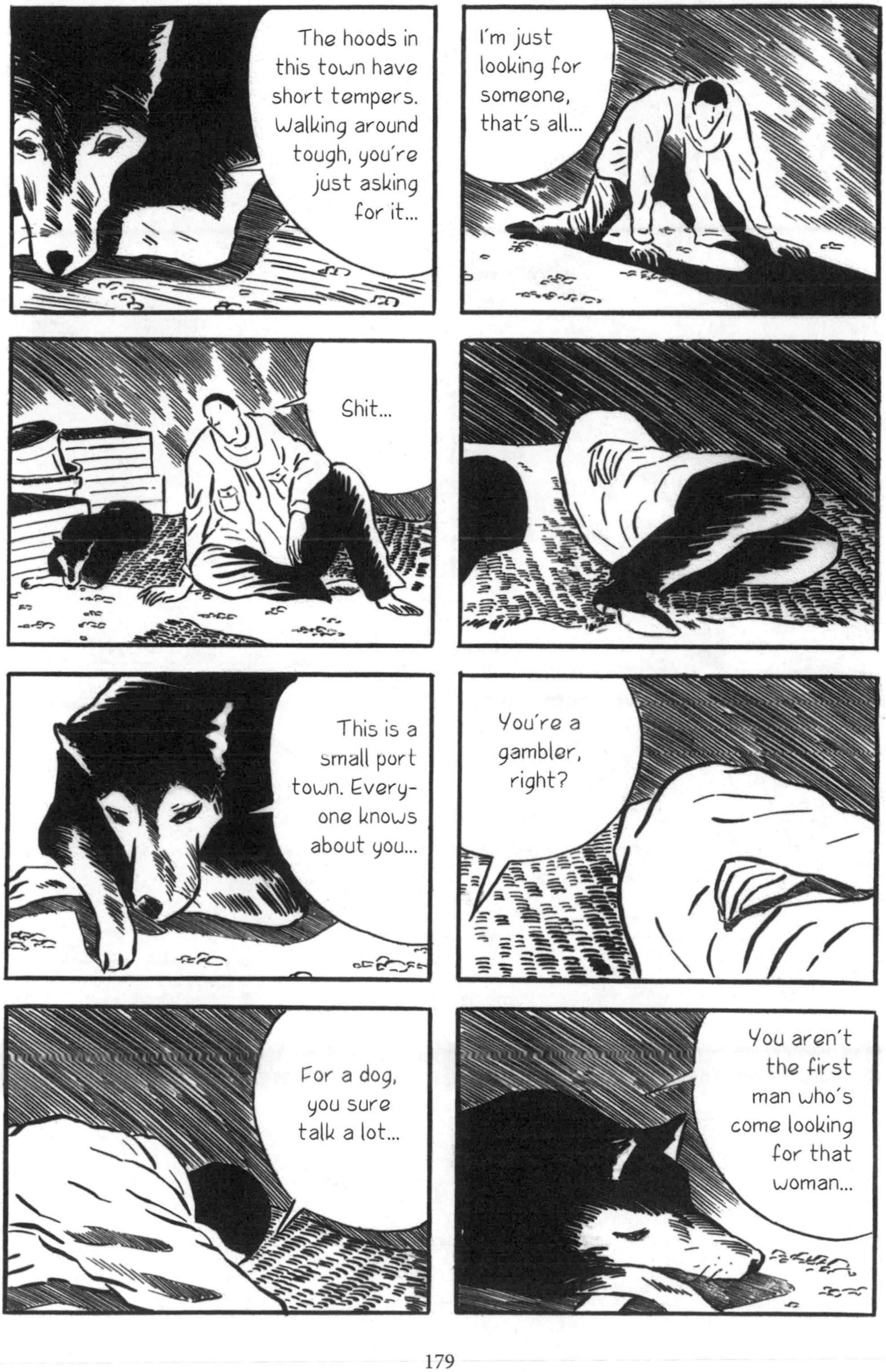

The hoods in this town have short tempers. Walking around tough, you're just asking for it...
I'm just looking for someone, that's all...
Shit...
This is a small port town. Every-one knows about you...
You're a gambler, right?
For a dog, you sure talk a lot...
You aren't the first man who's come looking for that woman...

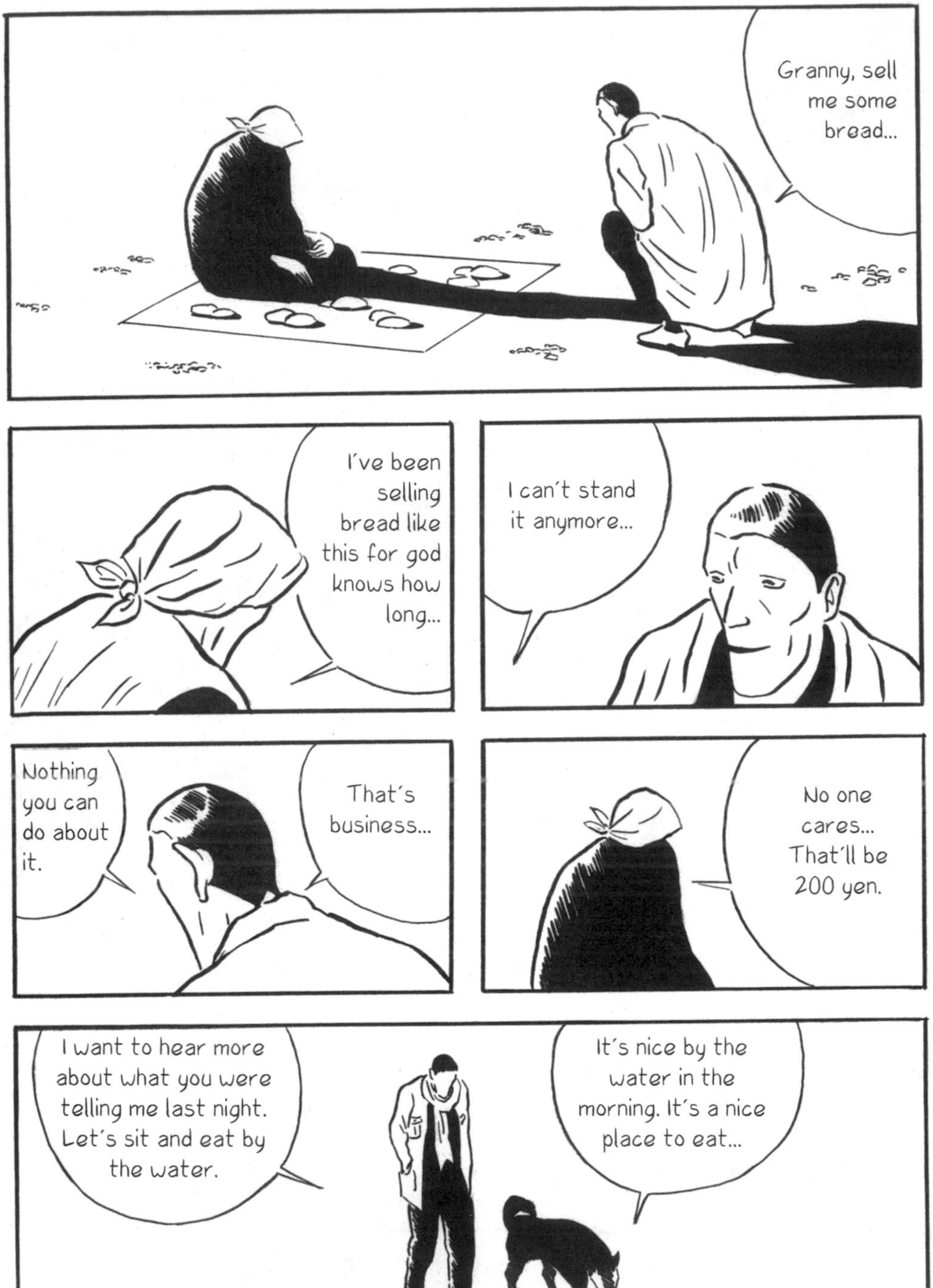
Granny, sell me some bread...
I've been selling bread like this for god knows how long...
I can't stand it anymore...
Nothing you can do about it.
That's business...
No one cares... That'll be 200 yen.
I want to hear more about what you were telling me last night. Let's sit and eat by the water.
It's nice by the water in the morning. It's a nice place to eat...

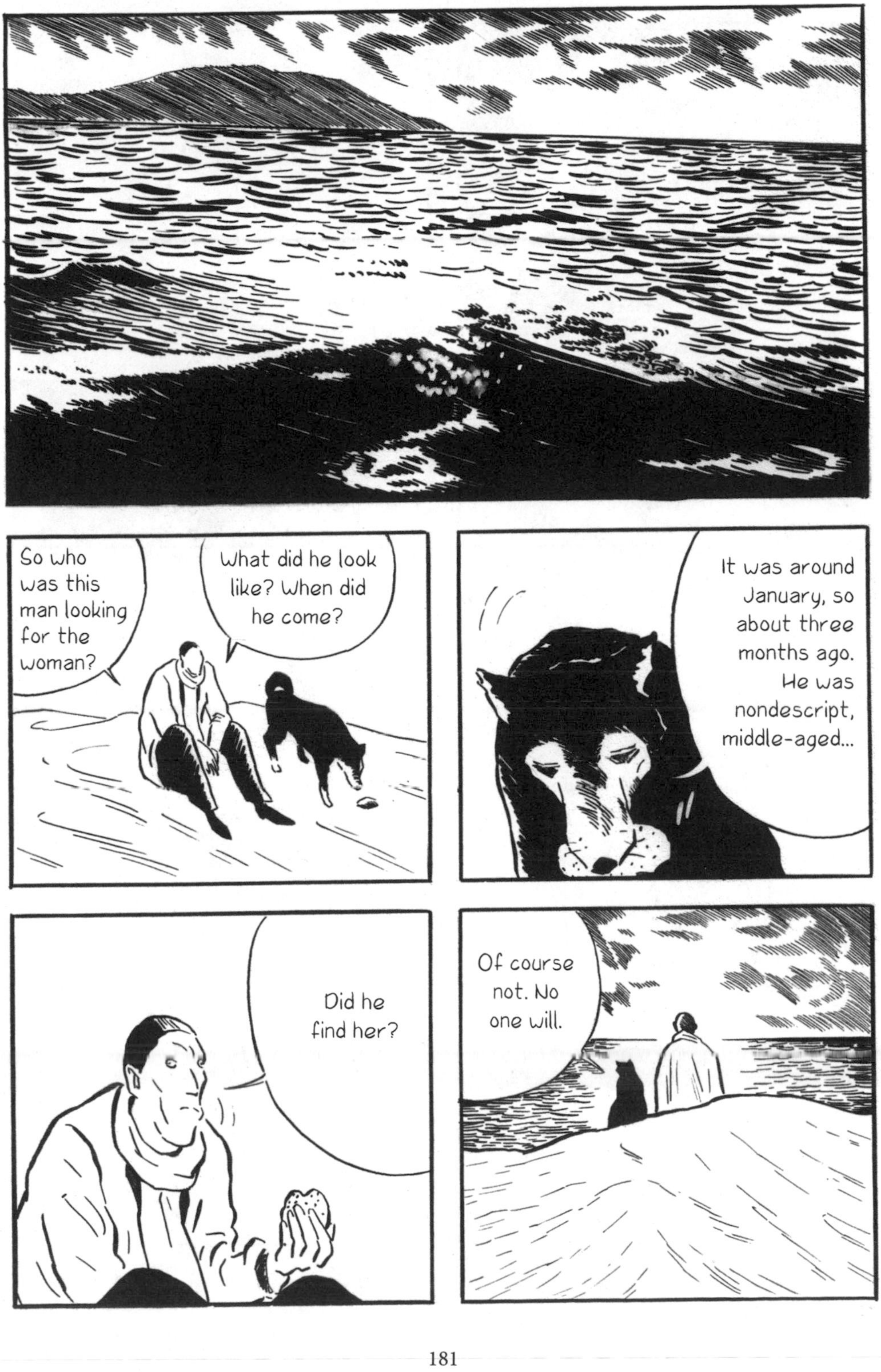
So who was this man looking for the woman?
What did he look like? When did he come?
It was around January, so about three months ago. He was nondescript, middle-aged...
Did he find her?
Of course not. No one will.

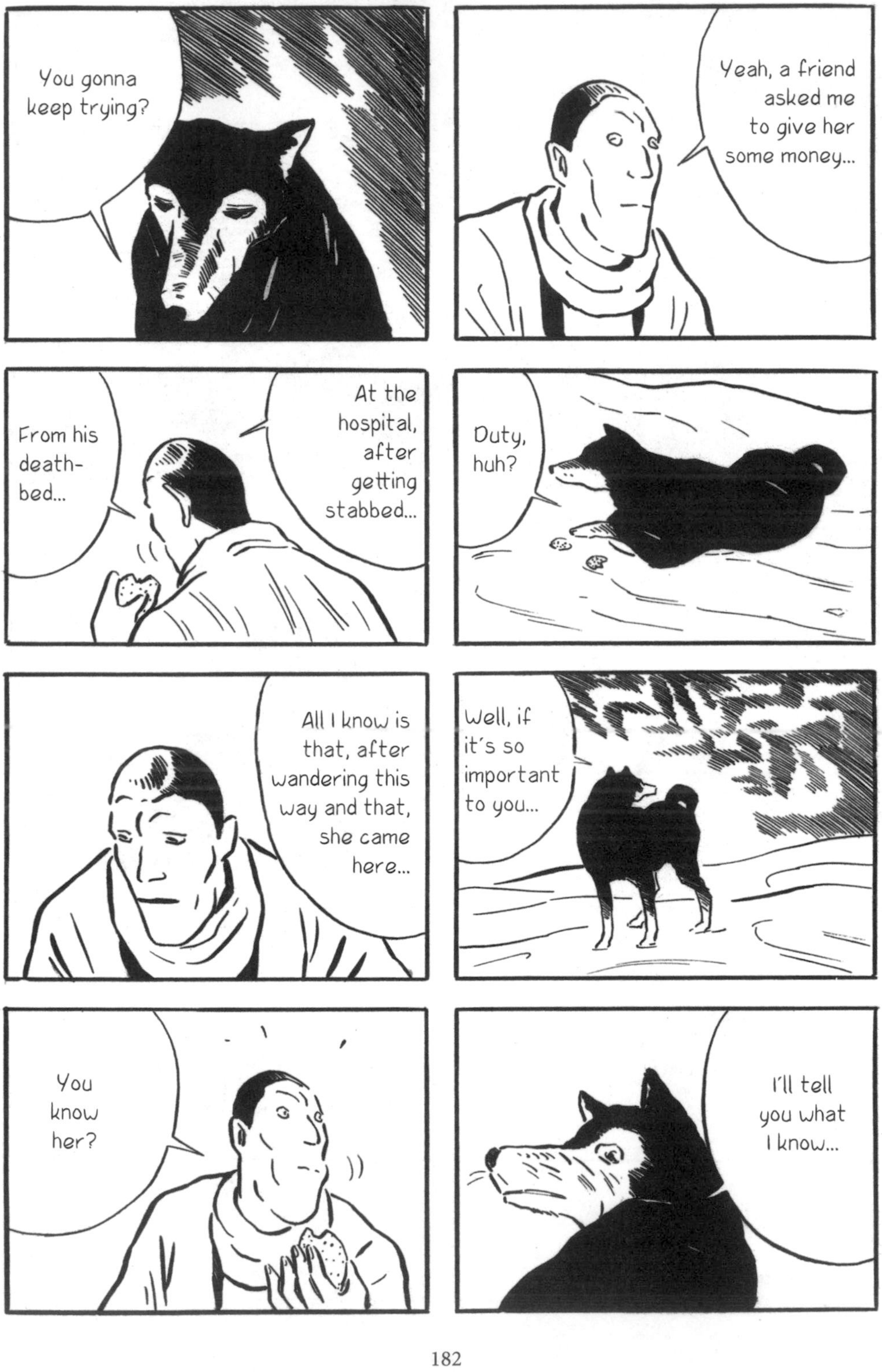
You gonna keep trying?
Yeah, a friend asked me to give her some money...
From his death-bed...
At the hospital, after getting stabbed...
Duty, huh?
All I know is that, after wandering this way and that, she came here...
Well, if it's so important to you...
You know her?
I'll tell you what I know...

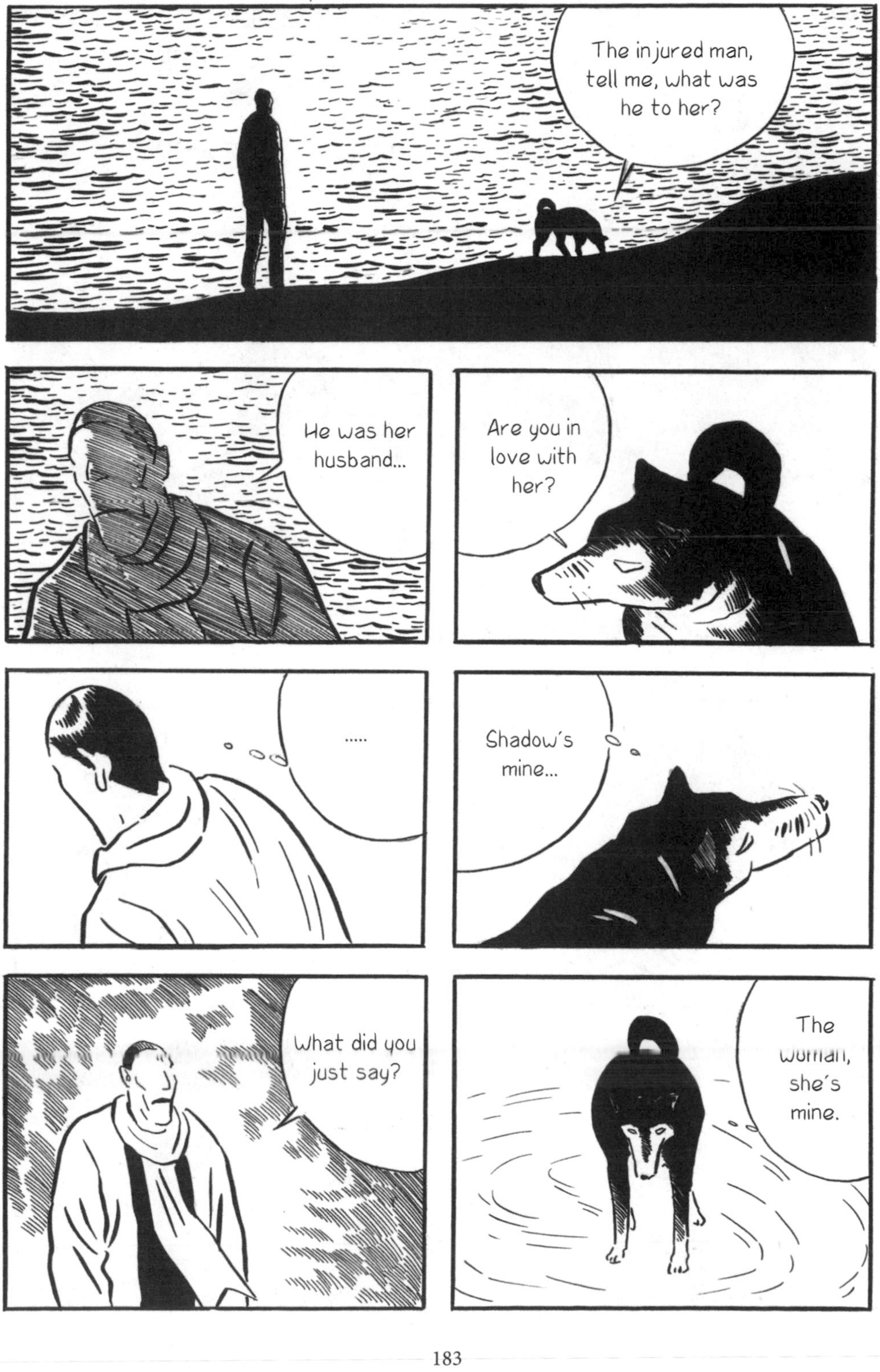
The injured man, tell me, what was he to her?
He was her husband...
Are you in love with her?
.....
Shadow's mine...
What did you just say?
The woman, she's mine.

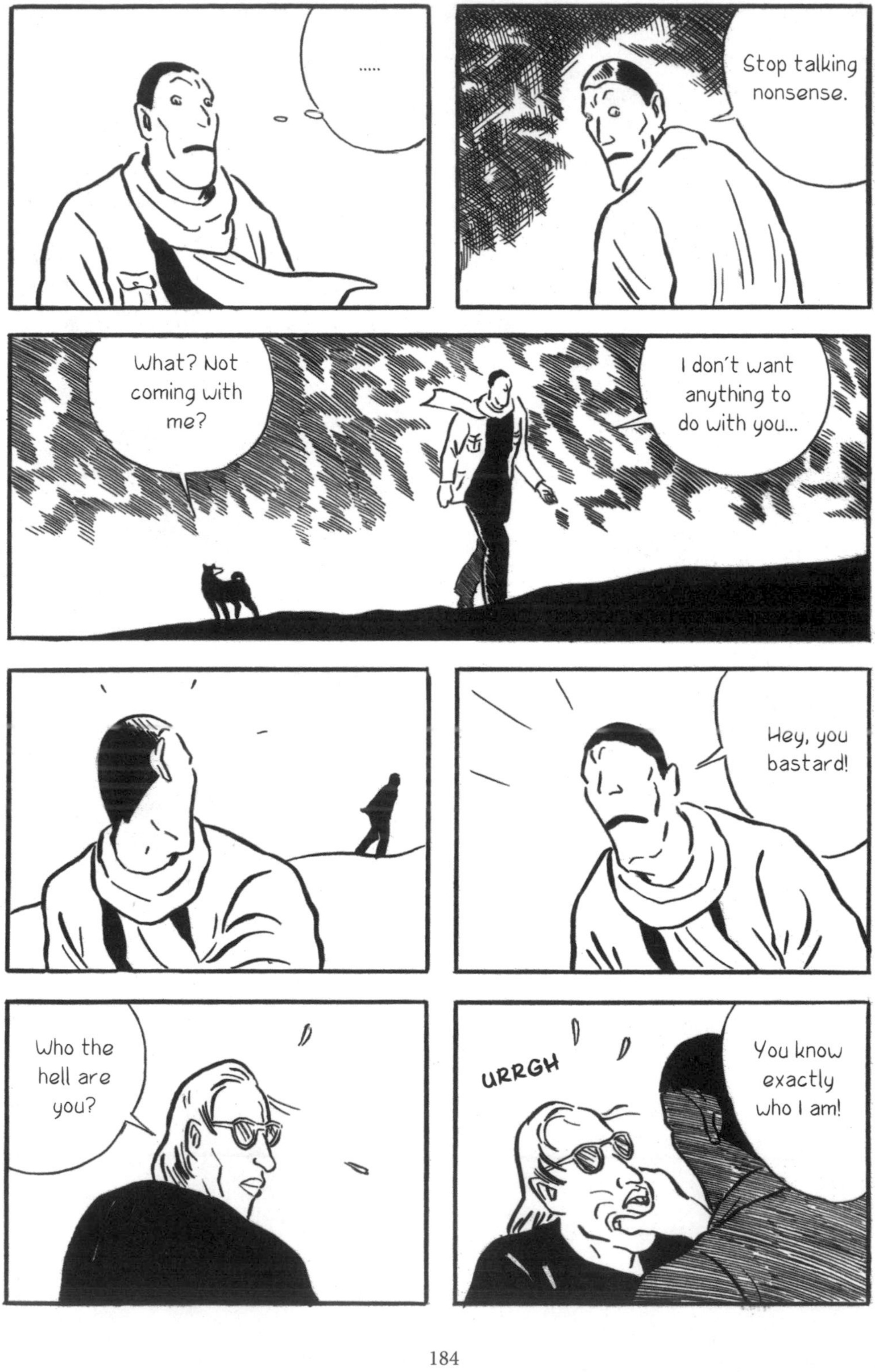
.....
Stop talking nonsense.
What? Not coming with me?
I don't want anything to do with you...
Hey, you bastard!
Who the hell are you?
URRGH
You know exactly who I am!

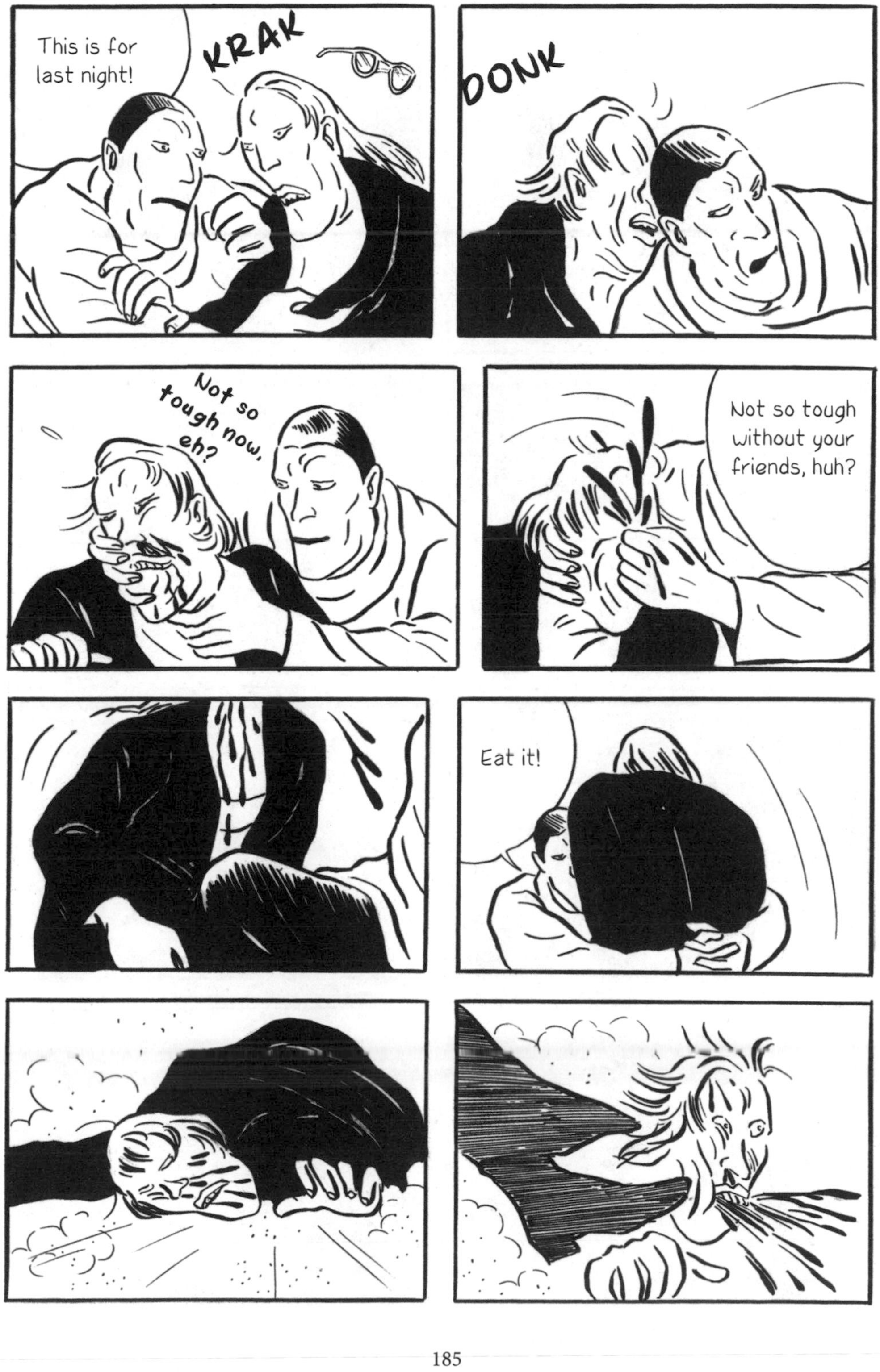
This is for last night!
KRAK
DONK
Not so tough now, eh?
Not so tough without your friends, huh?
Eat it!

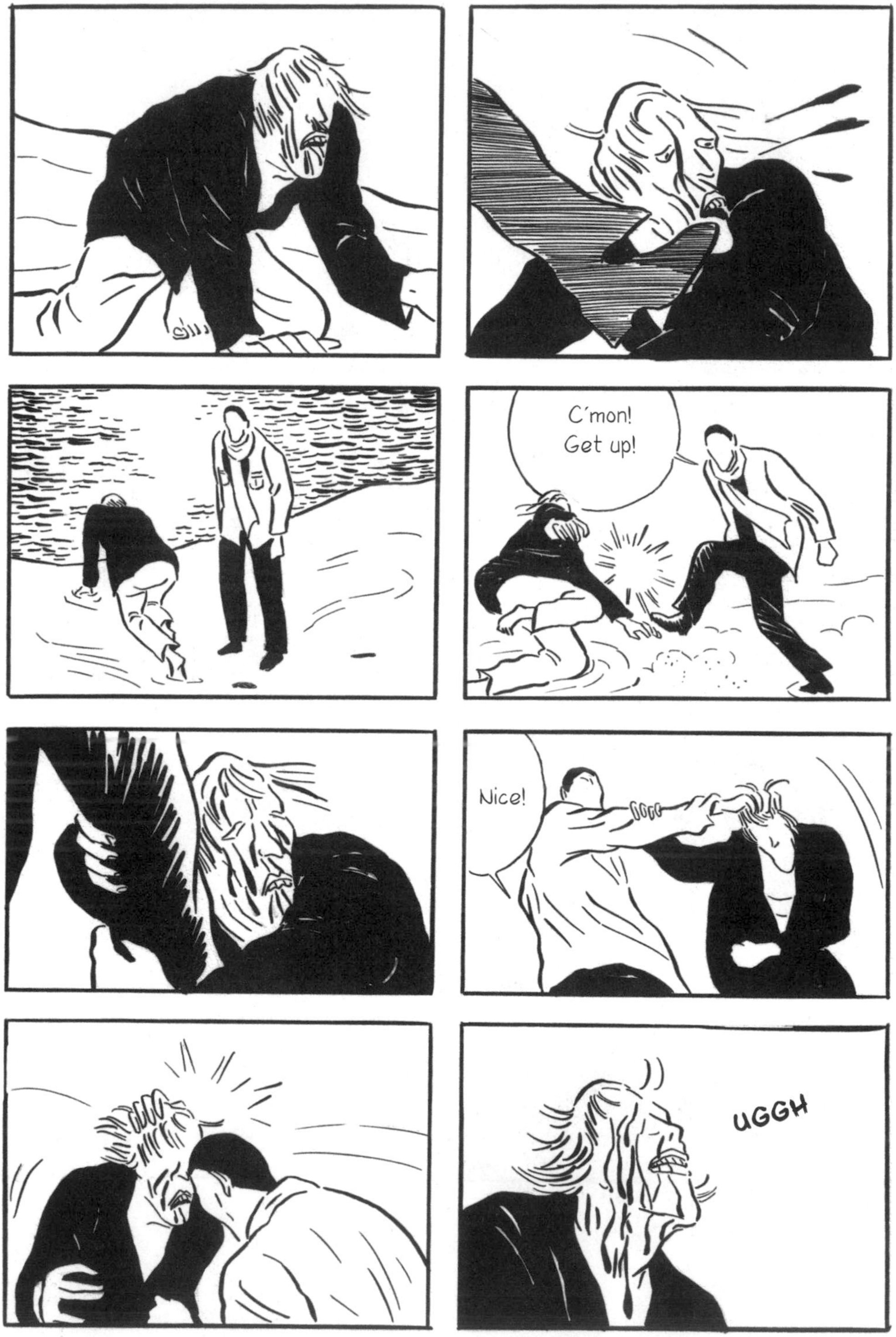
C´mon!
Get up!
Nice!
UGGH

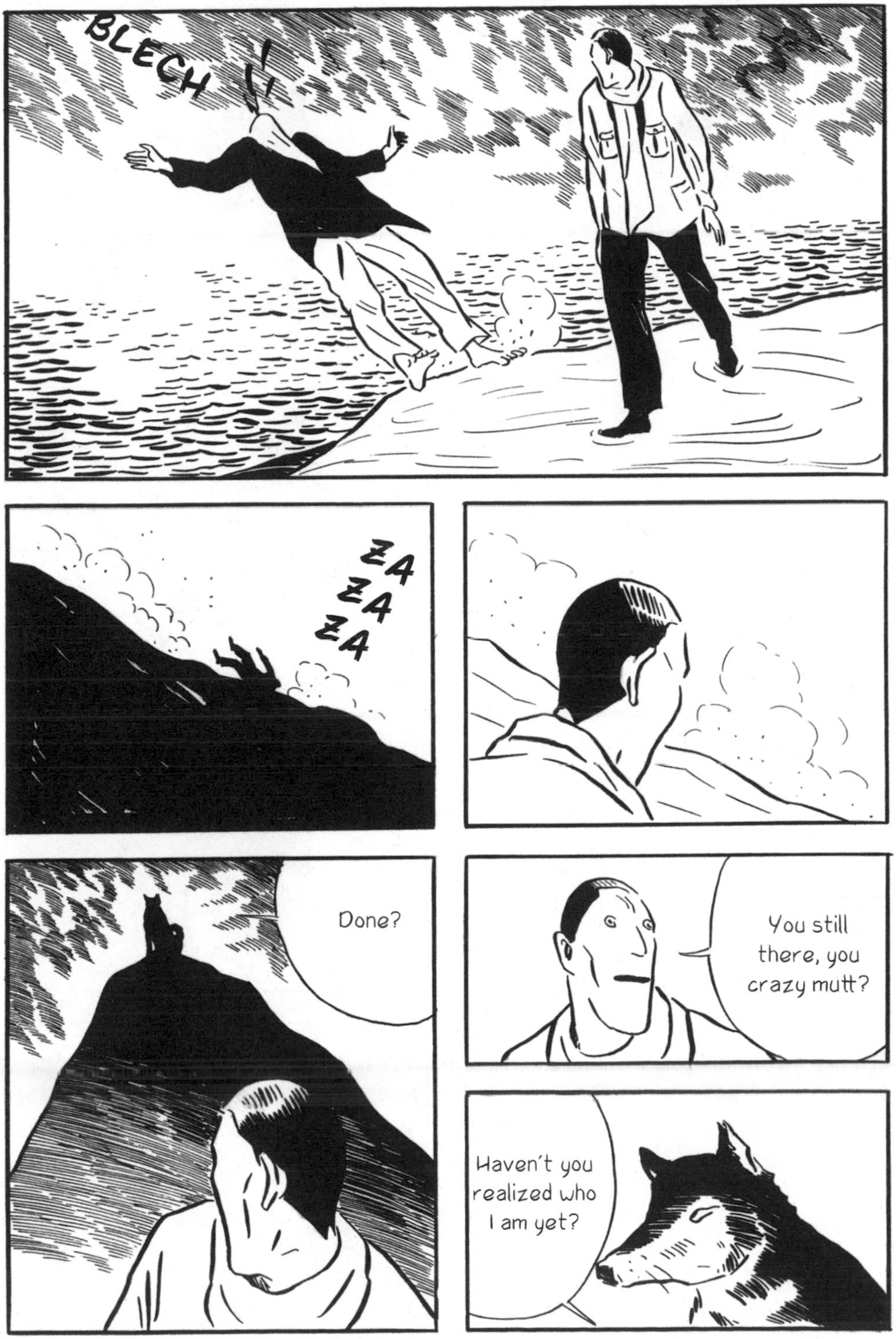
BLECH
ZA
ZA
ZA
Done?
You still there, you crazy mutt?
Haven't you realized who I am yet?

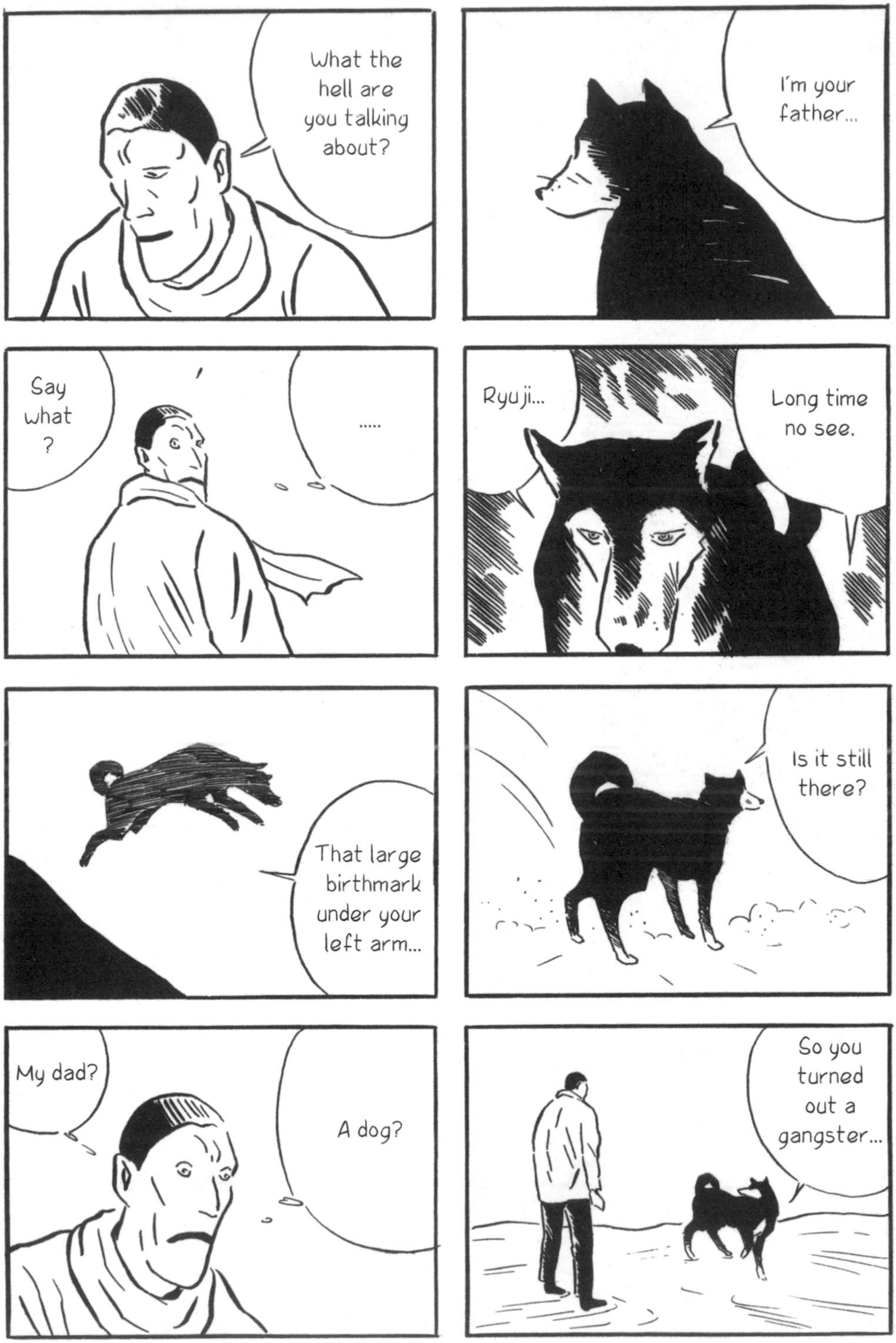
What the hell are you talking about?
I'm your father...
Say what ?
.....
Ryuji...
Long time no see.
That large birthmark under your left arm...
Is it still there?
My dad?
A dog?
So you turned out a gangster...

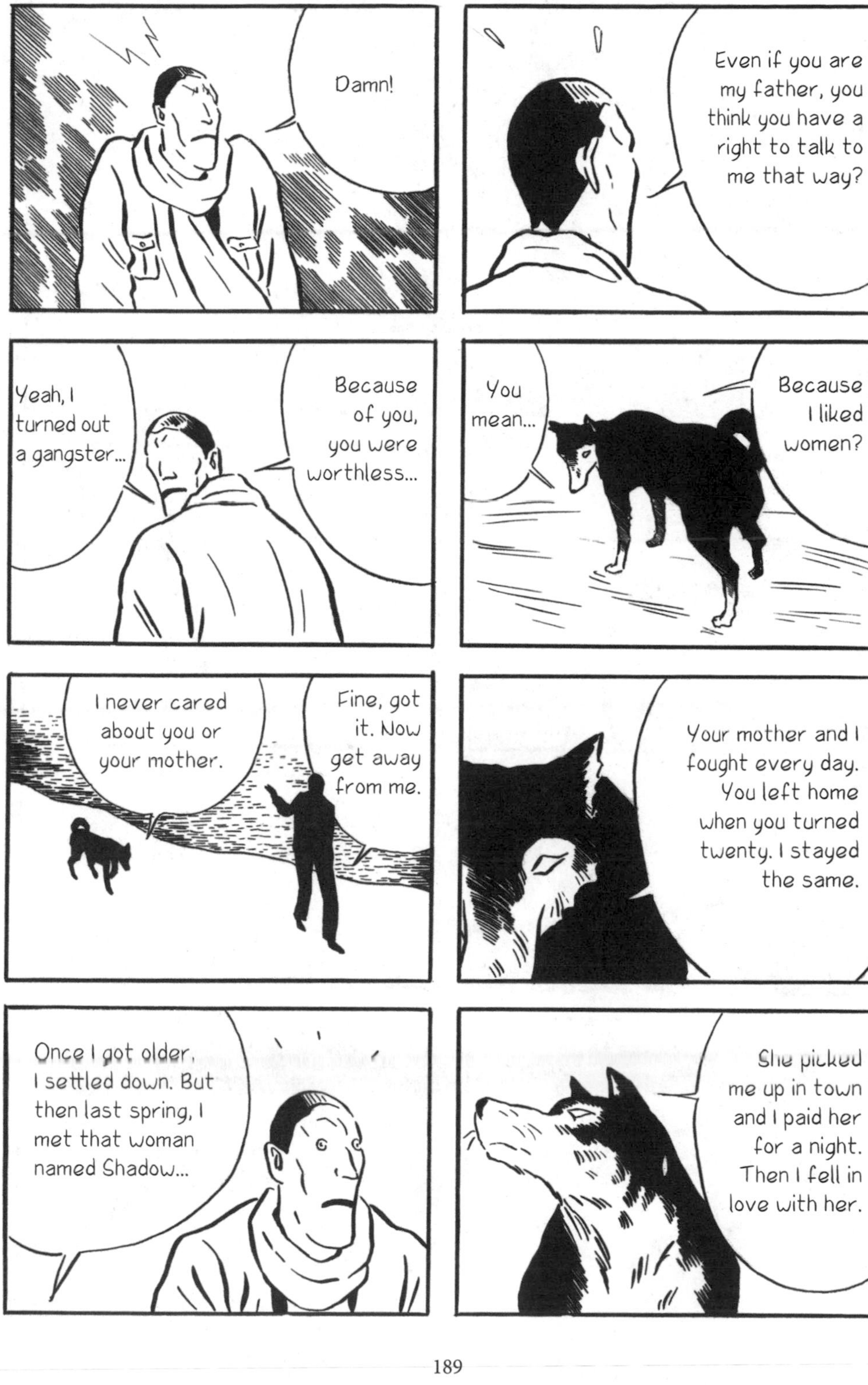
Damn!
Even if you are my father, you think you have a right to talk to me that way?
Yeah, I turned out a gangster...
Because of you, you were worthless...
You mean...
Because I liked women?
I never cared about you or your mother.
Fine, got it. Now get away from me.
Your mother and I fought every day. You left home when you turned twenty. I stayed the same.
Once I got older, I settled down. But then last spring, I met that woman named Shadow...
She picked me up in town and I paid her for a night. Then I fell in love with her.

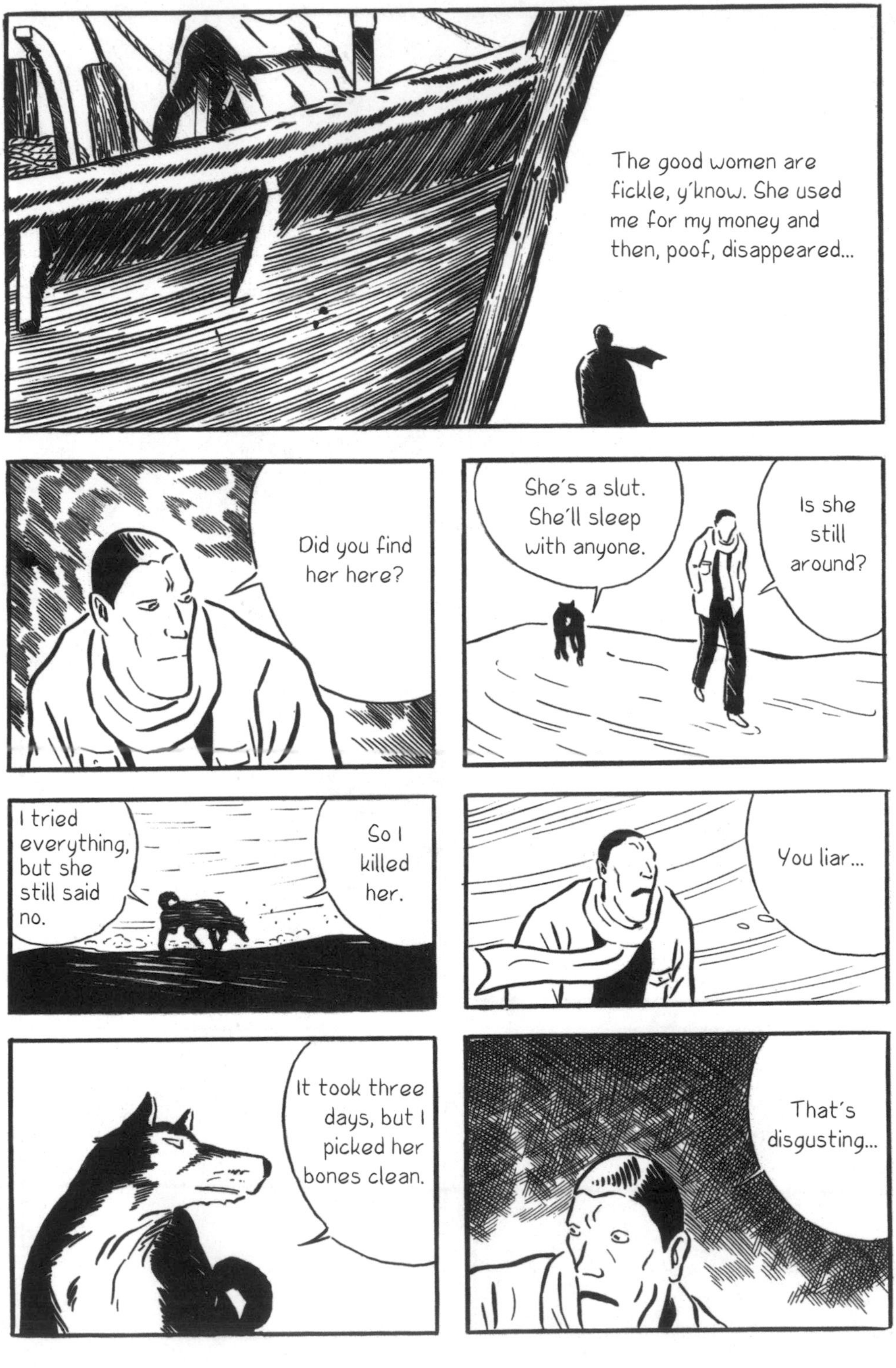
The good women are fickle, y'know. She used me for my money and then, poof, disappeared...
Did you find her here?
She's a slut. She'll sleep with anyone.
Is she still around?
I tried everything, but she still said no.
So I killed her.
You liar...
It took three days, but I picked her bones clean.
That's disgusting...

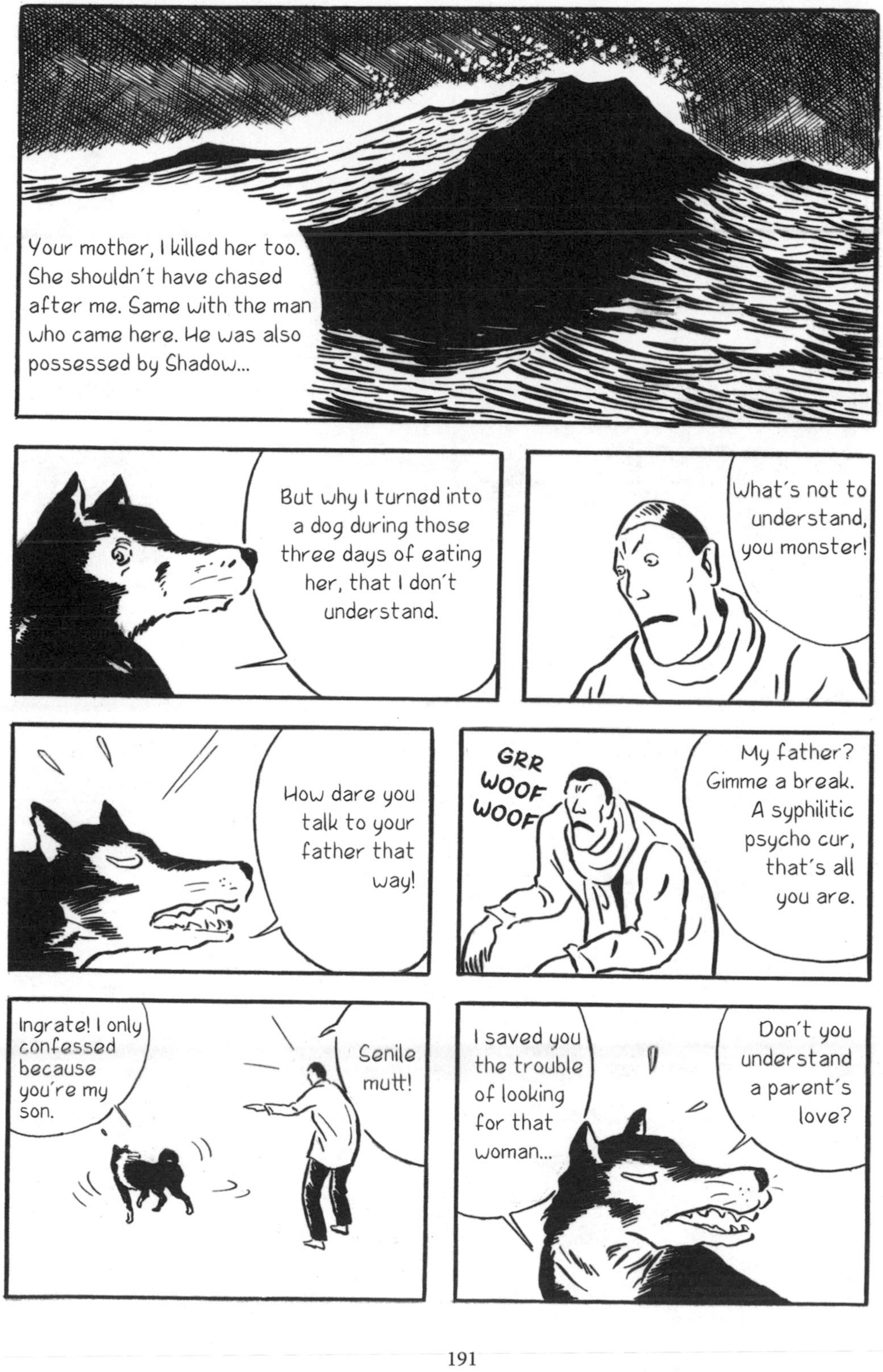
Your mother, I killed her too. She shouldn't have chased after me. Same with the man who came here. He was also possessed by Shadow...
But why I turned into a dog during those three days of eating her, that I don't understand.
What's not to understand, you monster!
How dare you talk to your father that way!
GRR WOOF WOOF
My father? Gimme a break. A syphilitic psycho cur, that's all you are.
Ingrate! I only confessed because you're my son.
Senile mutt!
I saved you the trouble of looking for that woman...
Don't you understand a parent's love?

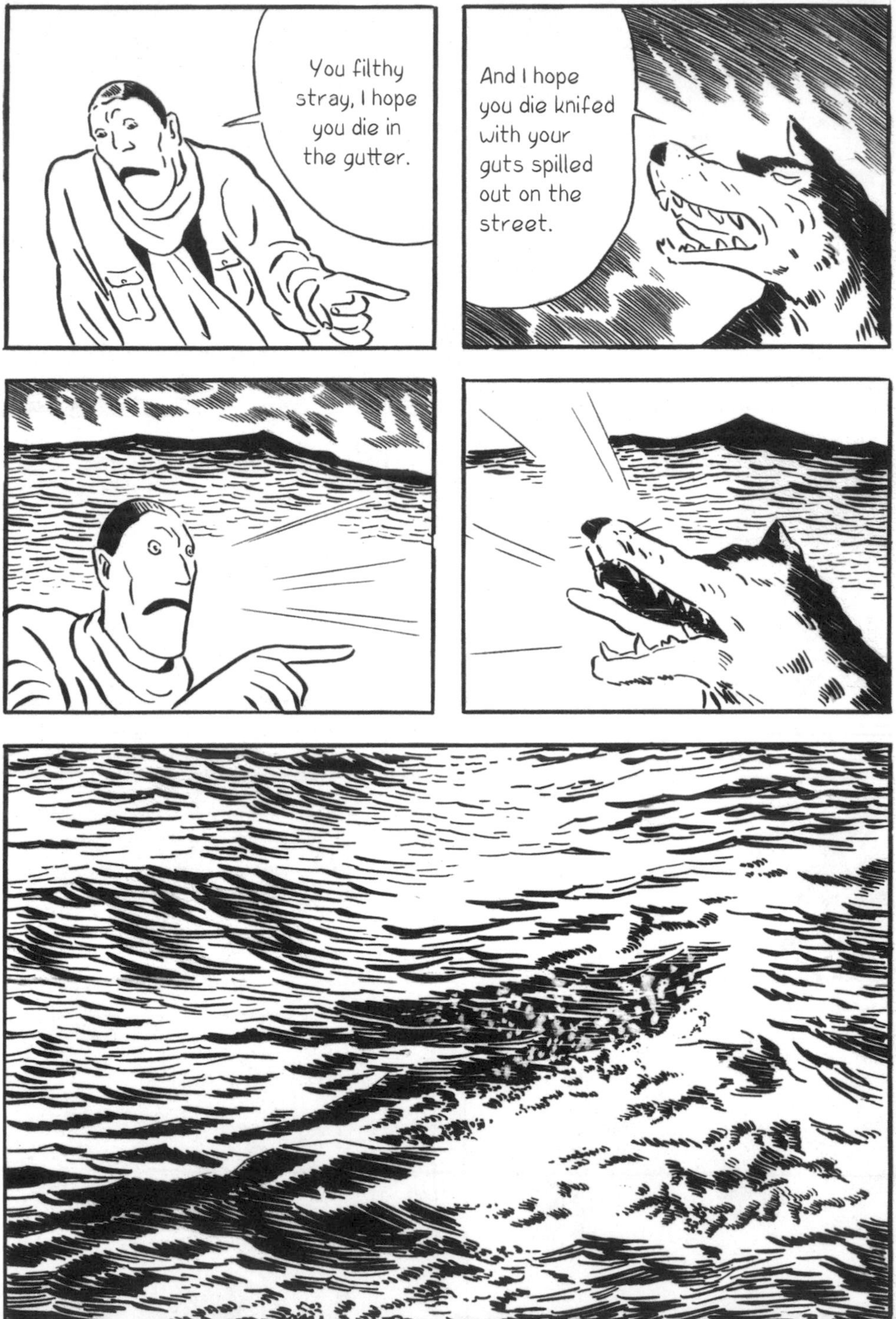
You filthy stray, I hope you die in the gutter.
And I hope you die knifed with your guts spilled out on the street.
THE END

VAGABOND PLAIN

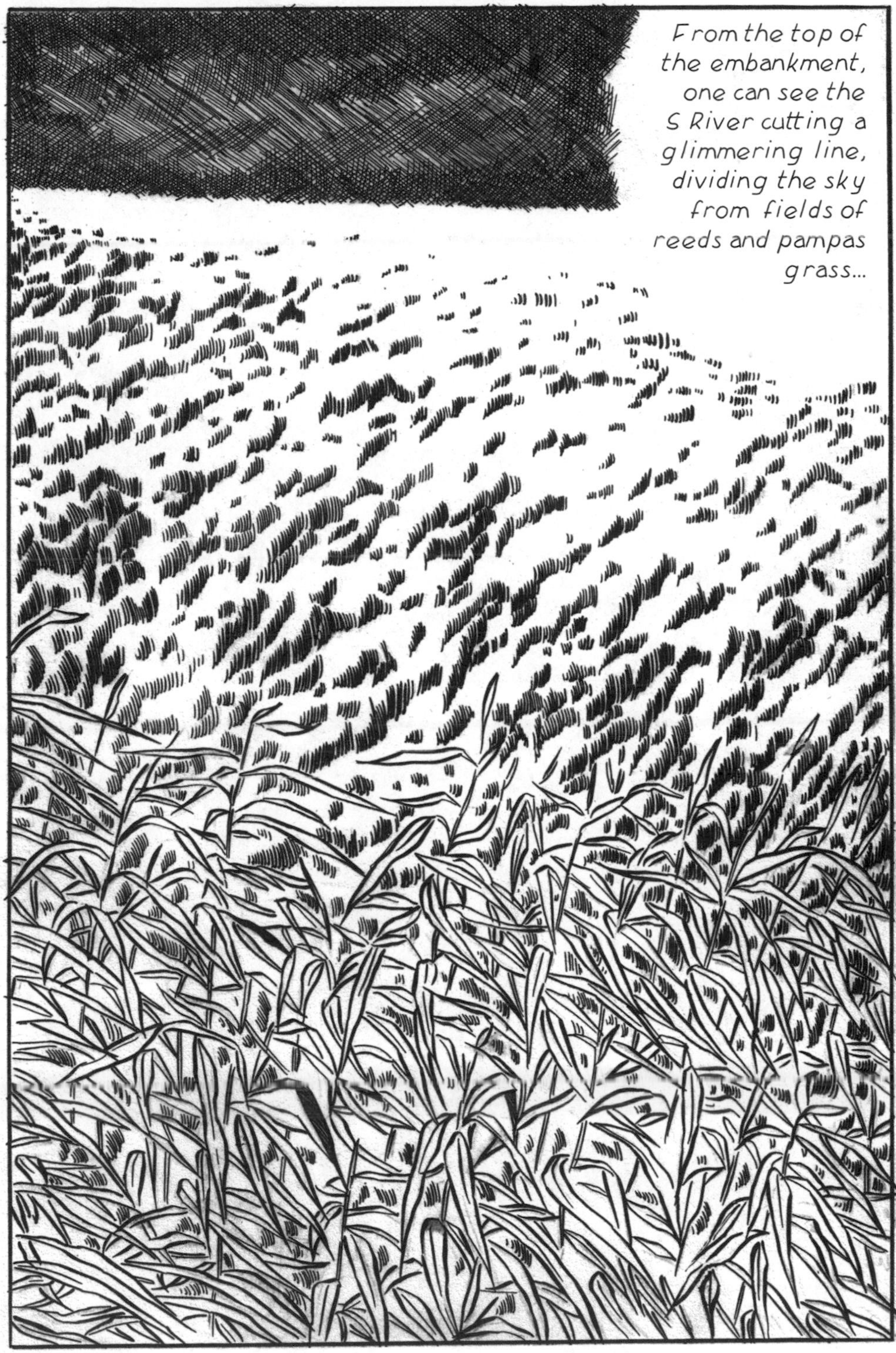
From the top of the embankment, one can see the S River cutting a glimmering line, dividing the sky from fields of reeds and pampas grass...

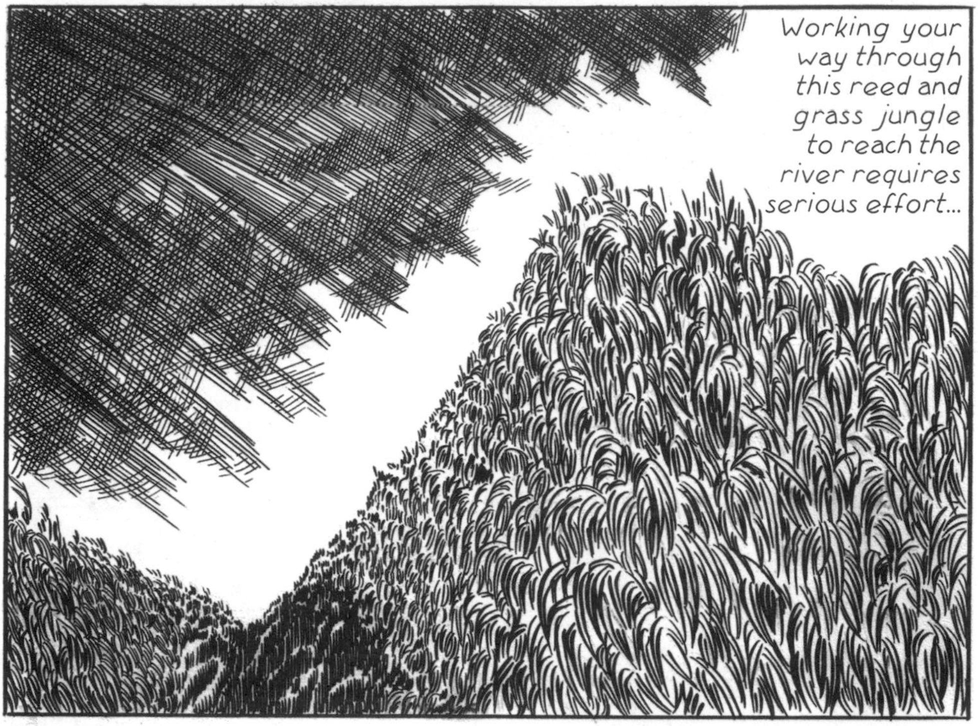
Working your way through this reed and grass jungle to reach the river requires serious effort...

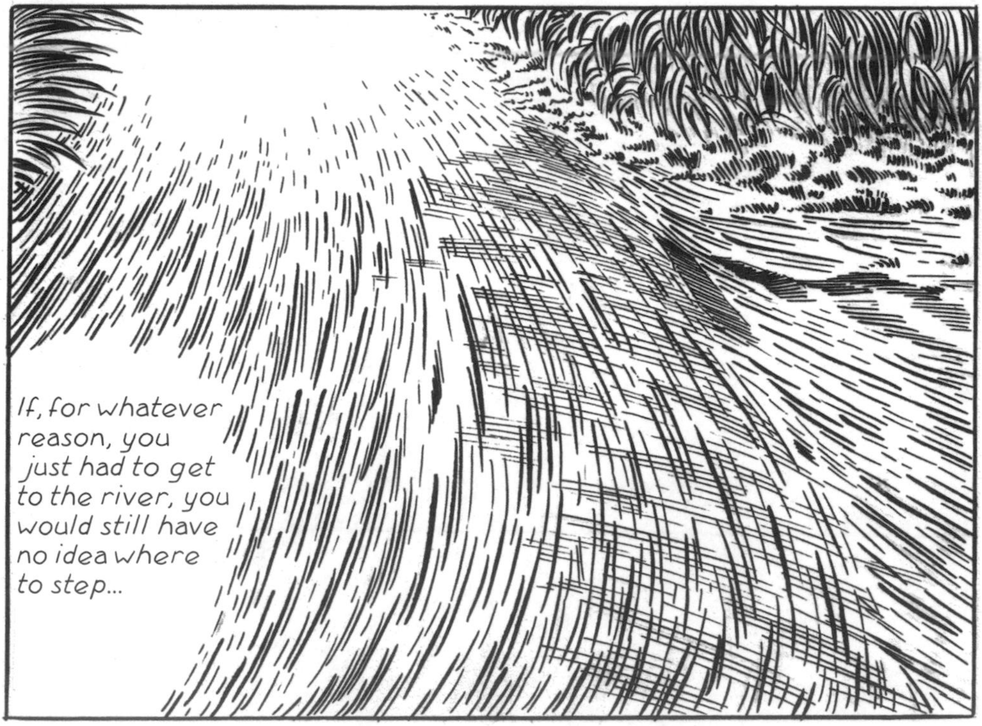
If, for whatever reason, you just had to get to the river, you would still have no idea where to step...

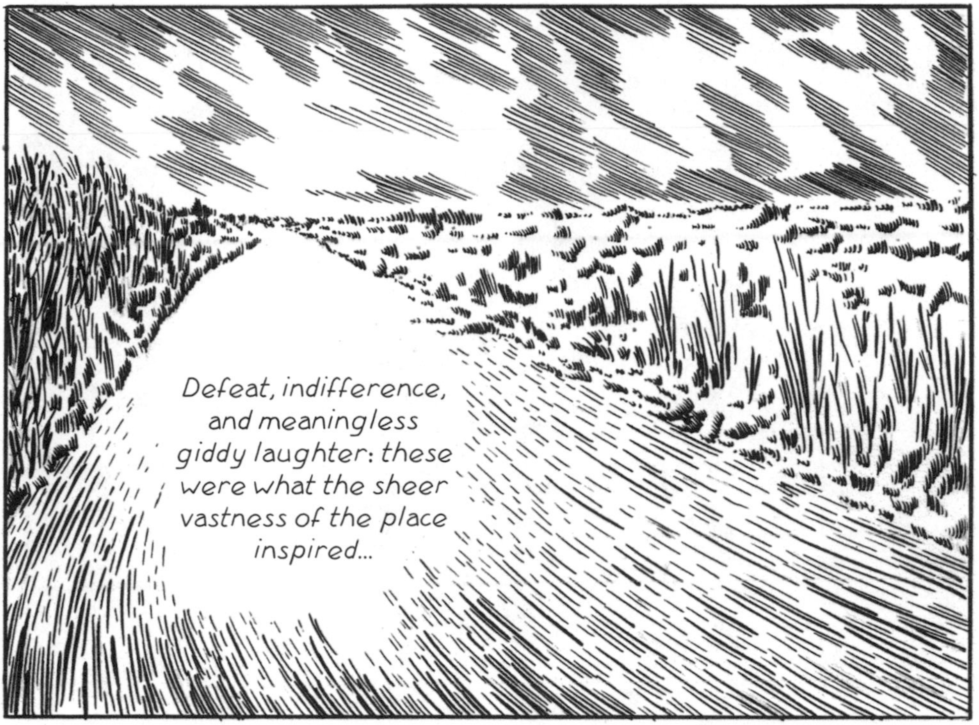
Defeat, indifference, and meaningless giddy laughter: these were what the sheer vastness of the place inspired...

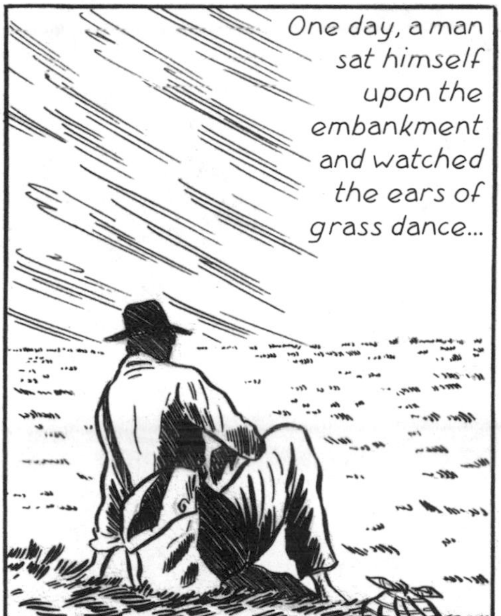
One day, a man sat himself upon the embankment and watched the ears of grass dance...

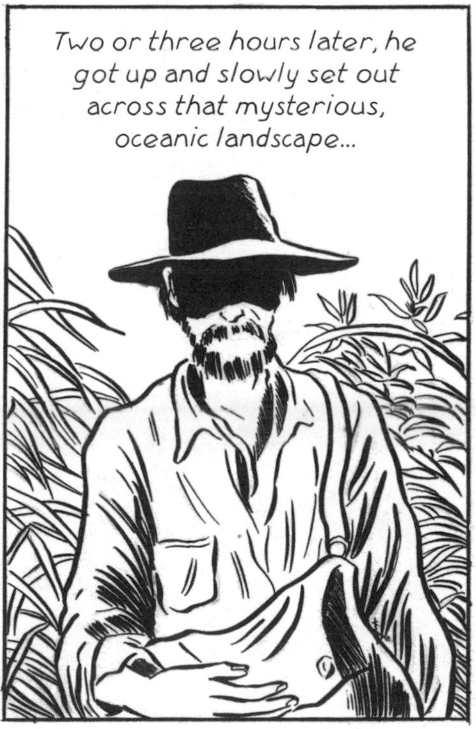
Two or three hours later, he got up and slowly set out across that mysterious, oceanic landscape...

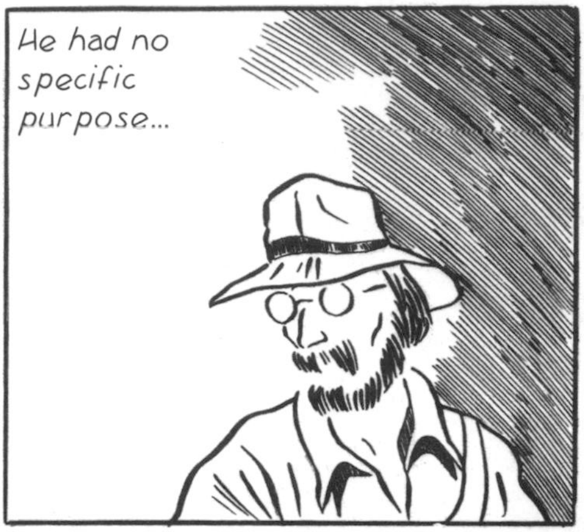
He had no specific purpose...

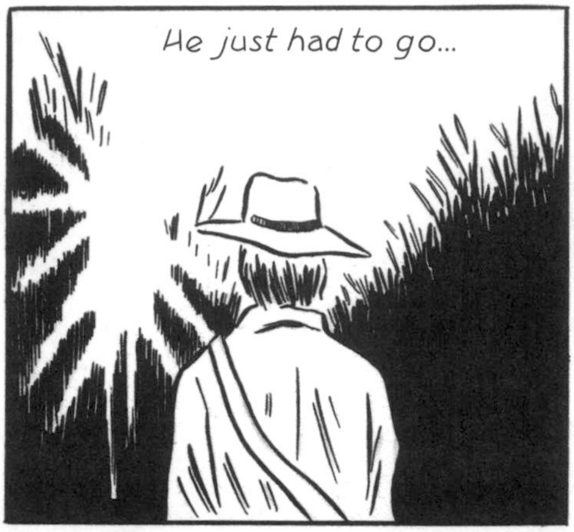
He just had to go...

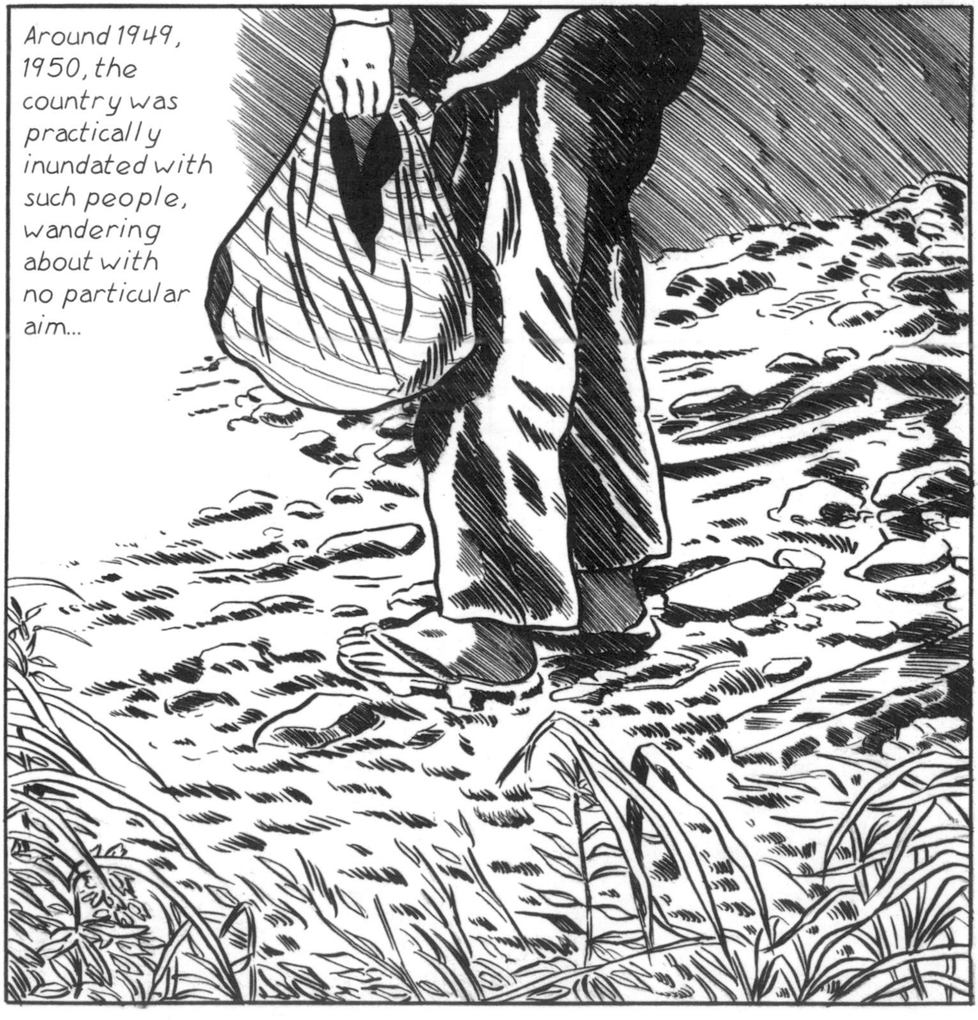
Around 1949, 1950, the country was practically inundated with such people, wandering about with no particular aim...

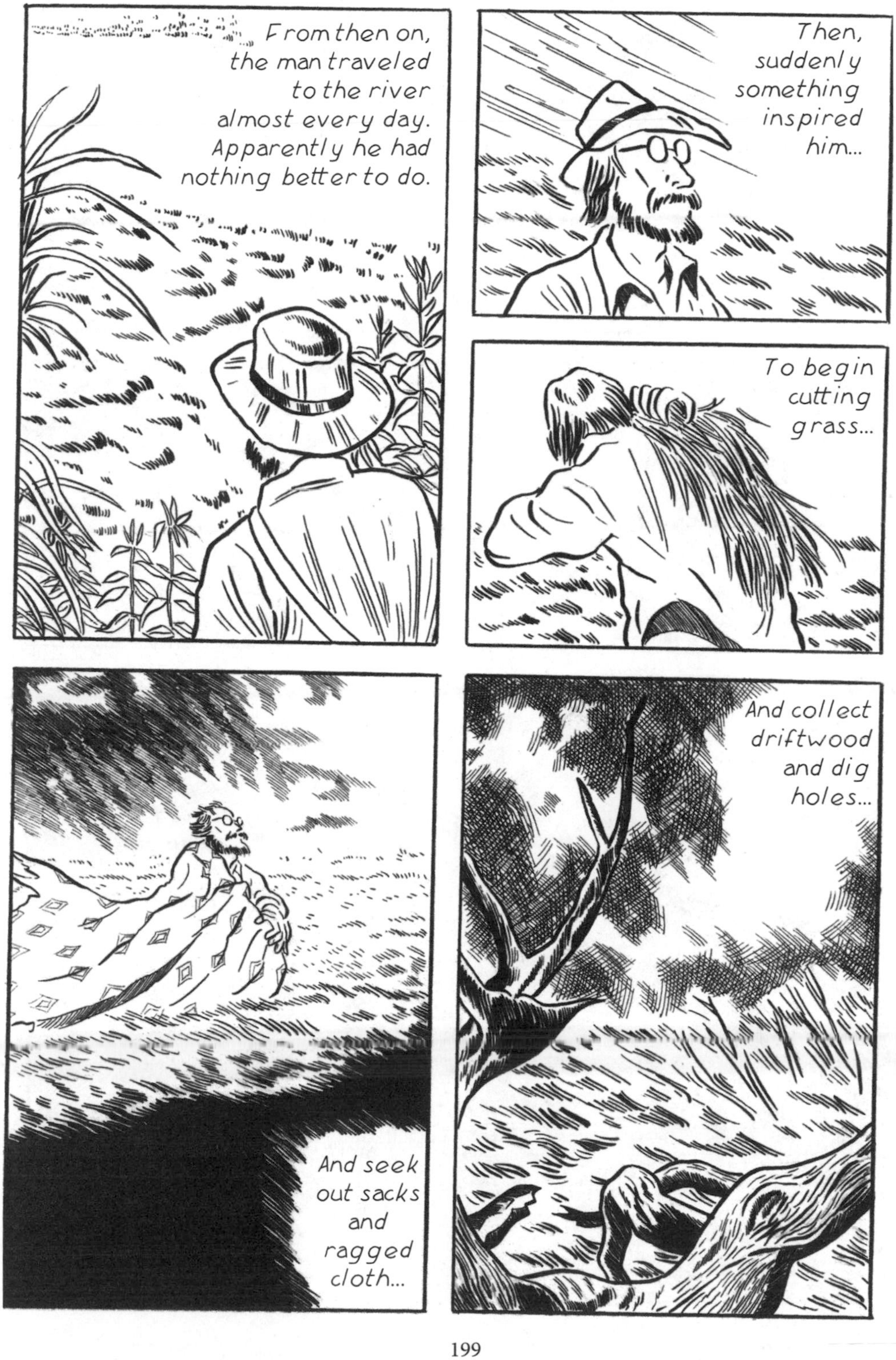
From then on, the man traveled to the river almost every day. Apparently he had nothing better to do.
Then, suddenly something inspired him...
To begin cutting grass...
And seek out sacks and ragged cloth...
And collect driftwood and dig holes...

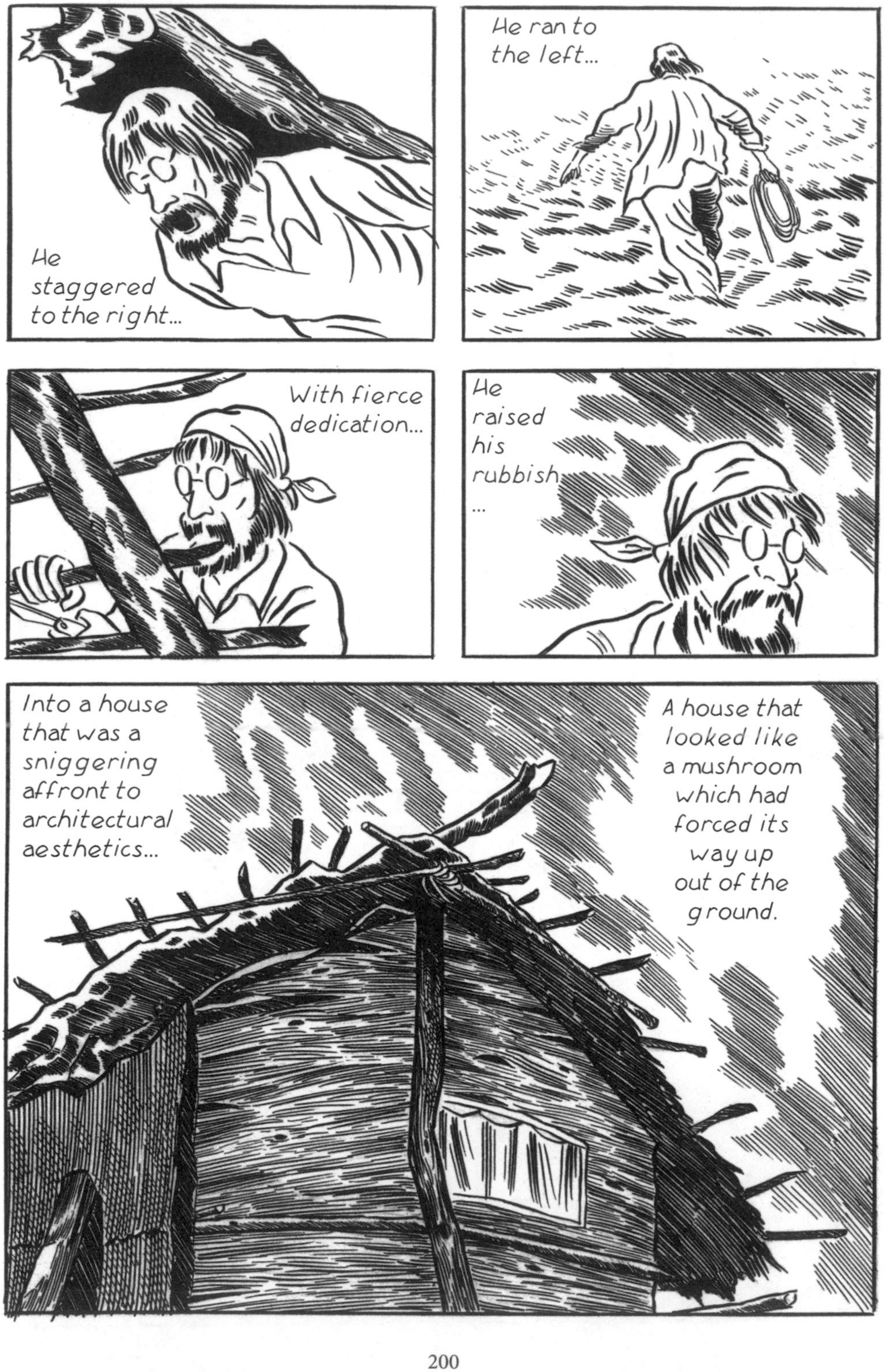
He staggered to the right...
He ran to the left...
With fierce dedication...
He raised his rubbish ...
Into a house that was a sniggering affront to architectural aesthetics...
A house that looked like a mushroom which had forced its way up out of the ground.

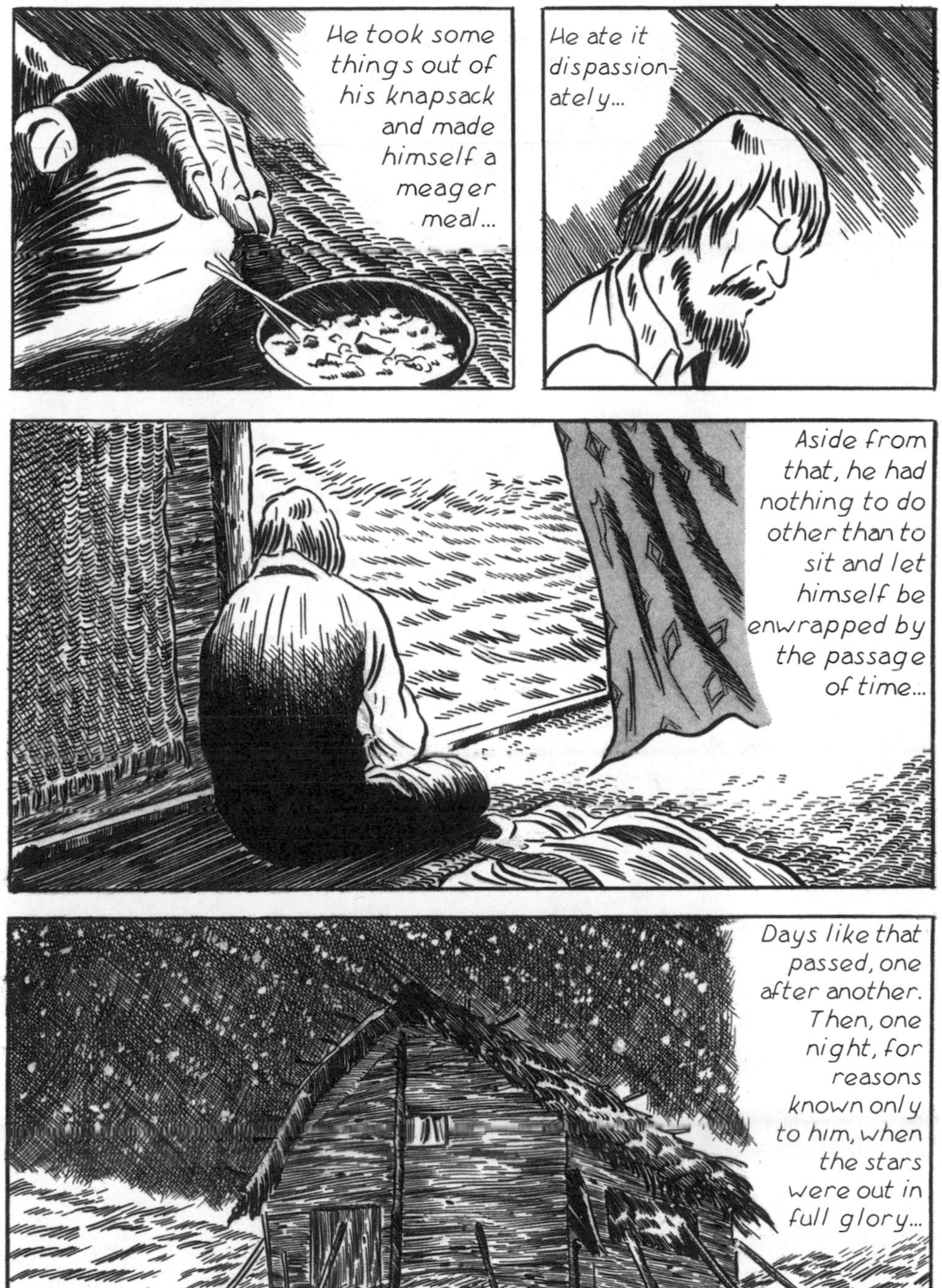
He took some things out of his knapsack and made himself a meager meal...
He ate it dispassion-ately...
Aside from that, he had nothing to do other than to sit and let himself be enwrapped by the passage of time...
Days like that passed, one after another. Then, one night, for reasons known only to him, when the stars were out in full glory...

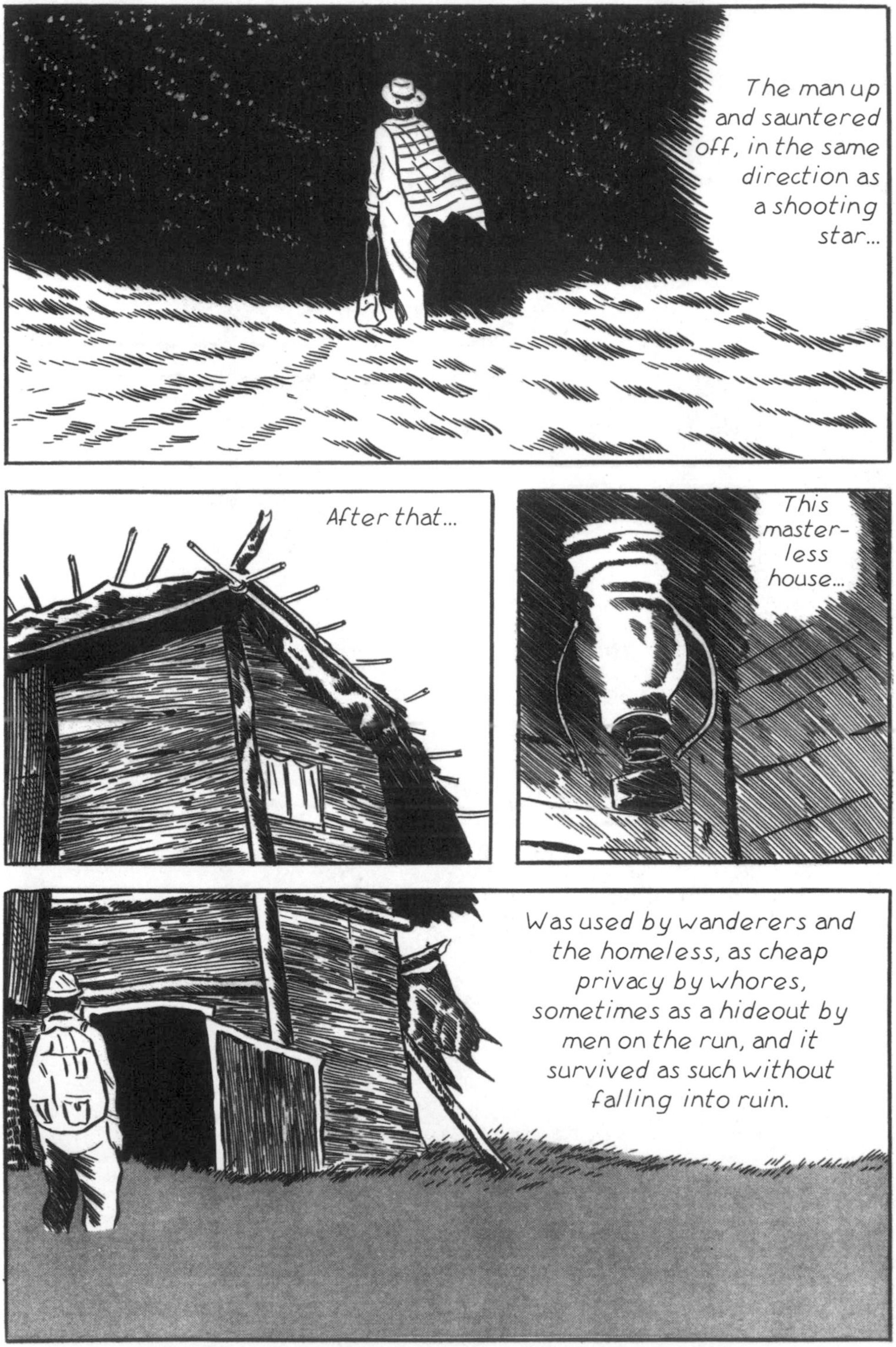
The man up and sauntered off, in the same direction as a shooting star...
After that...
This masterless house...
Was used by wanderers and the homeless, as cheap privacy by whores, sometimes as a hideout by men on the run, and it survived as such without falling into ruin.

Not only did this house continue to stand...
As men without money, without homes, with nothing, began to trickle in...
Oversized mushroom homes proliferated more and more.
Over time...
This sea of grass...
Which once seemed beyond the reach of man...
Was occupied by wild men...
It was filled by their disconcerting laughter...
Thus, in a matter of a few months, appeared a settlement of a hundred or so shelters...

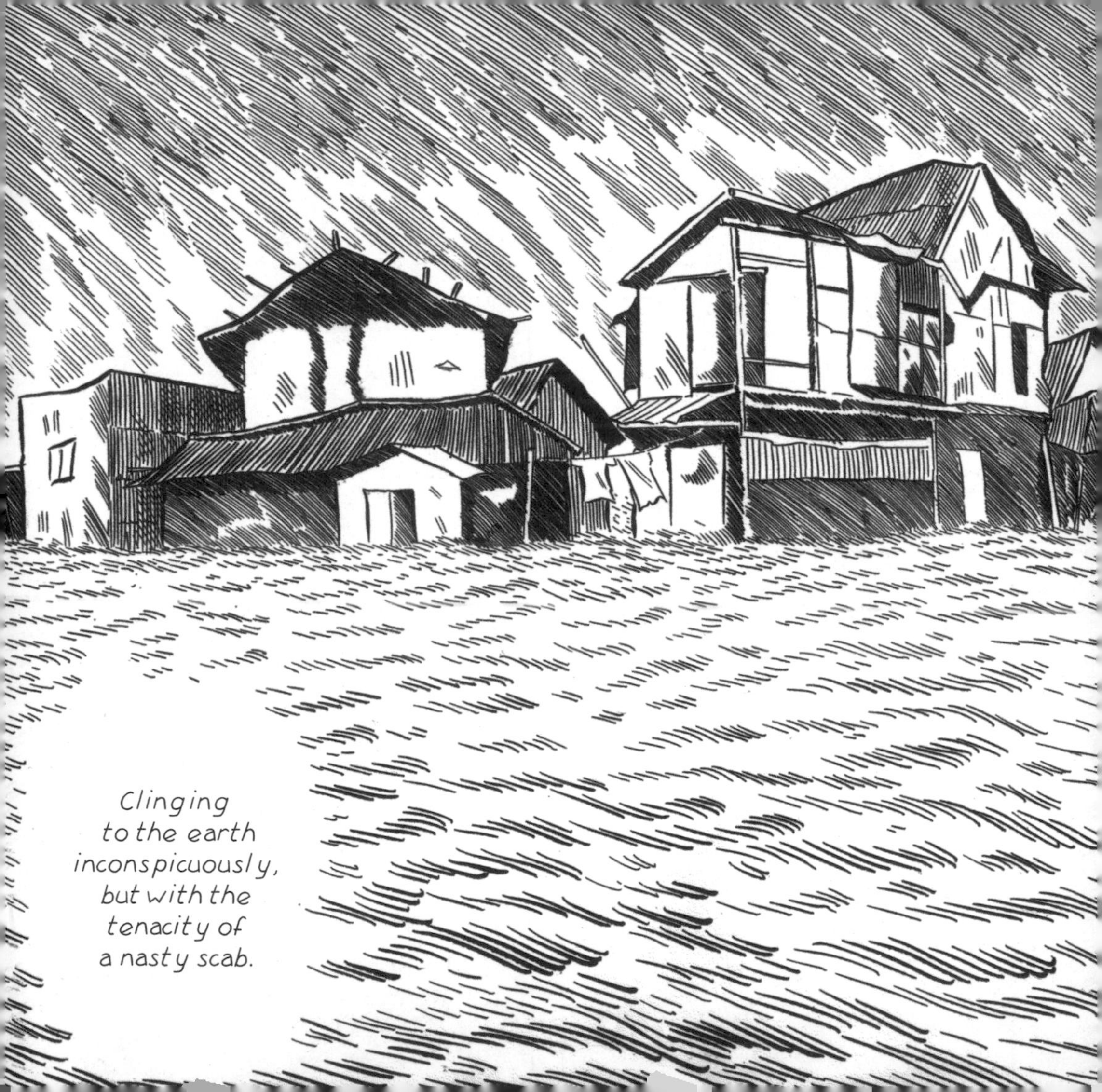
Clinging to the earth inconspicuously, but with the tenacity of a nasty scab.

VAGABOND PLAIN
PART 1

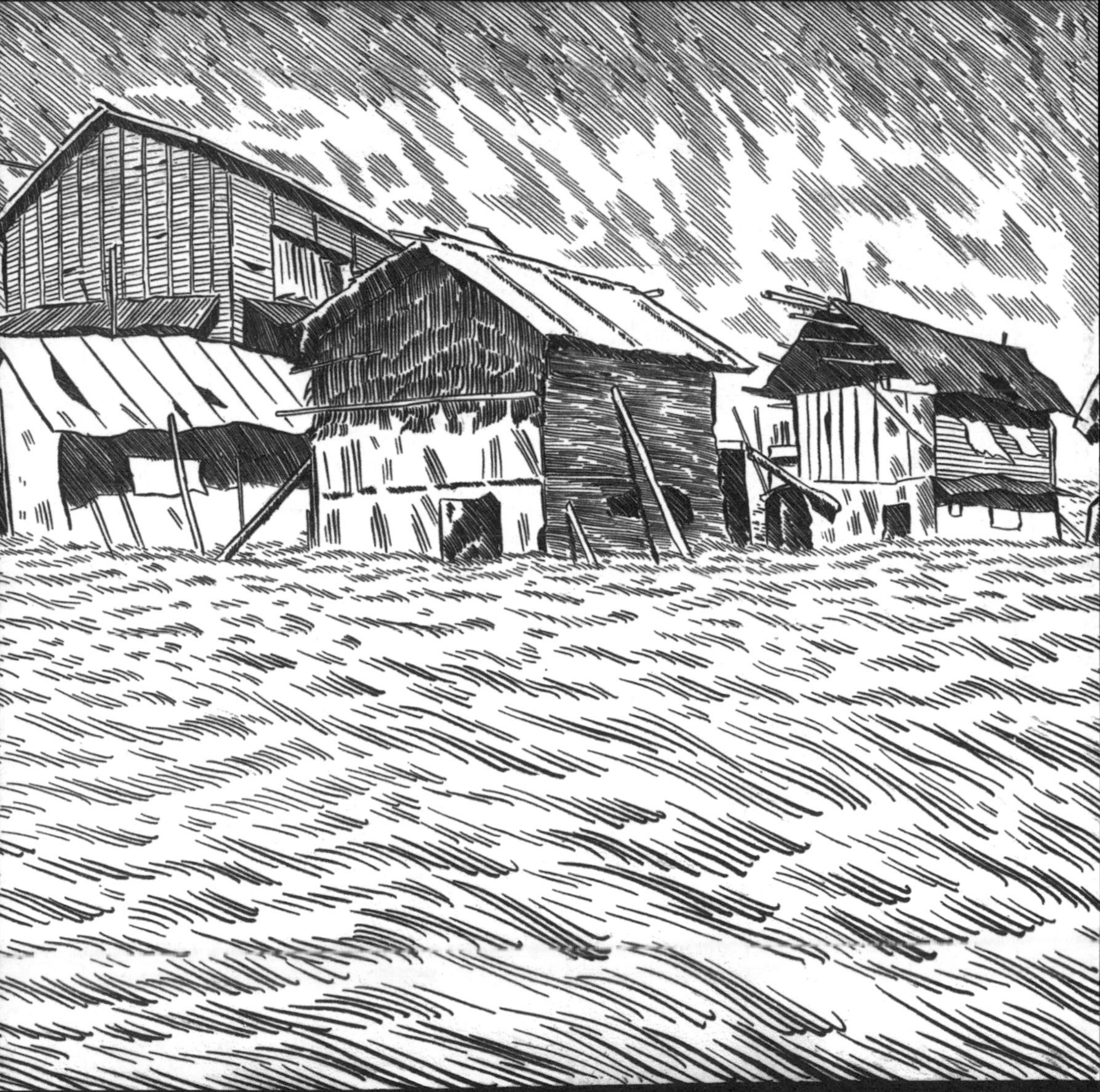

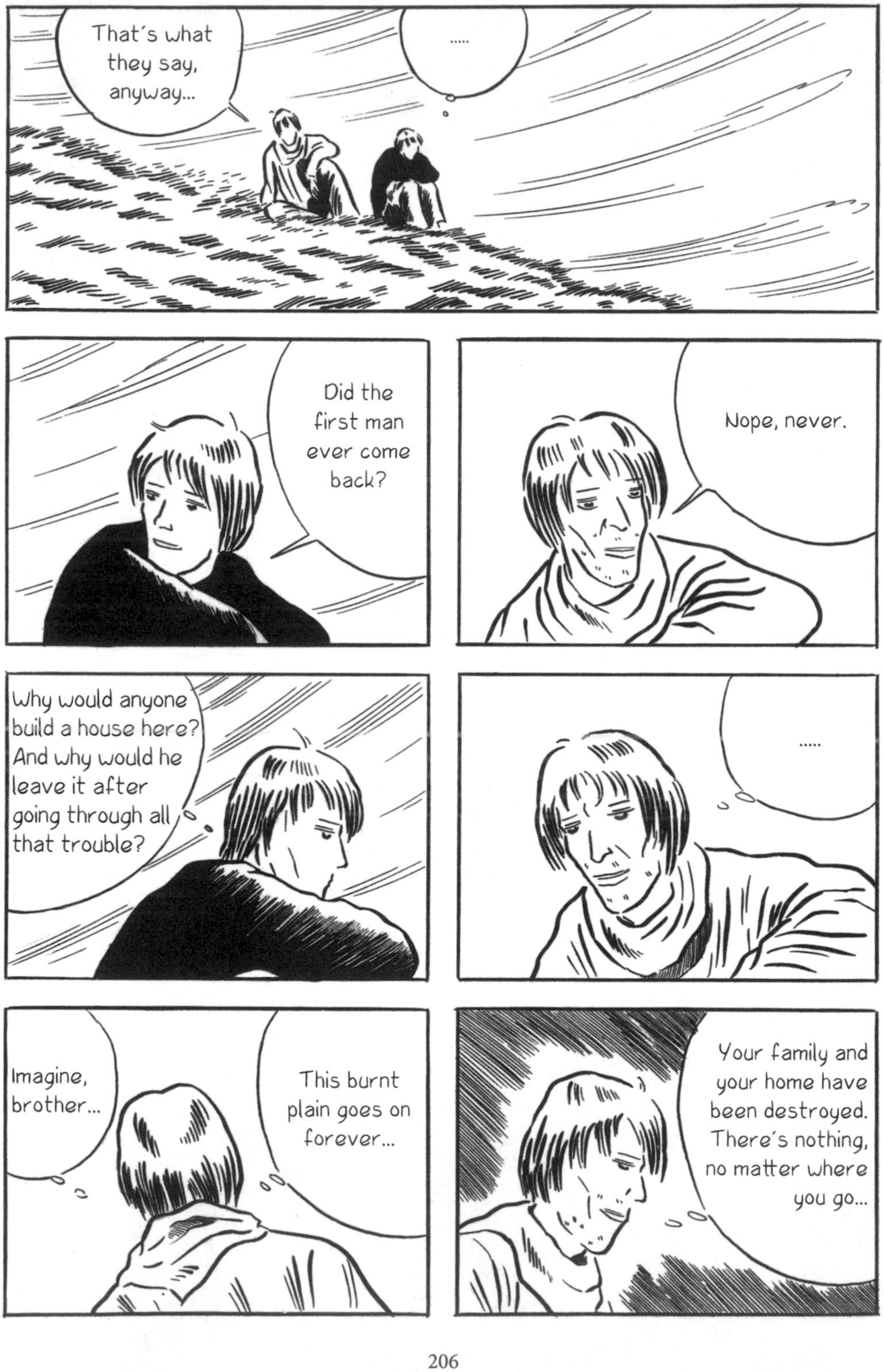
That's what they say, anyway...
.....
Did the first man ever come back?
Nope, never.
Why would anyone build a house here? And why would he leave it after going through all that trouble?
.....
Imagine, brother...
This burnt plain goes on forever...
Your family and your home have been destroyed. There's nothing, no matter where you go...

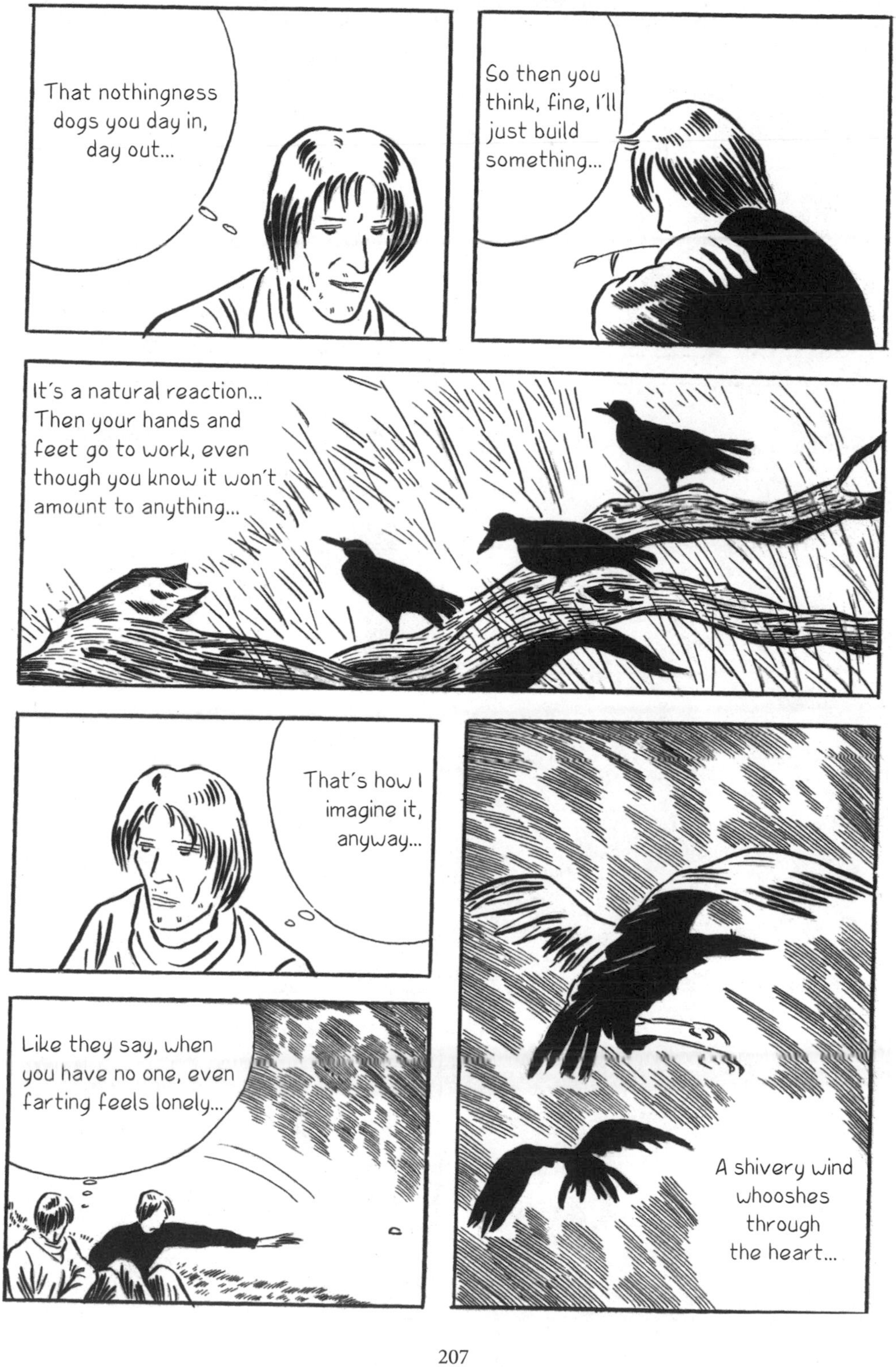
That nothingness dogs you day in, day out...
So then you think, fine, I'll just build something...
It's a natural reaction... Then your hands and feet go to work, even though you know it won't amount to anything...
That's how I imagine it, anyway...
Like they say, when you have no one, even farting feels lonely...
A shivery wind whooshes through the heart...

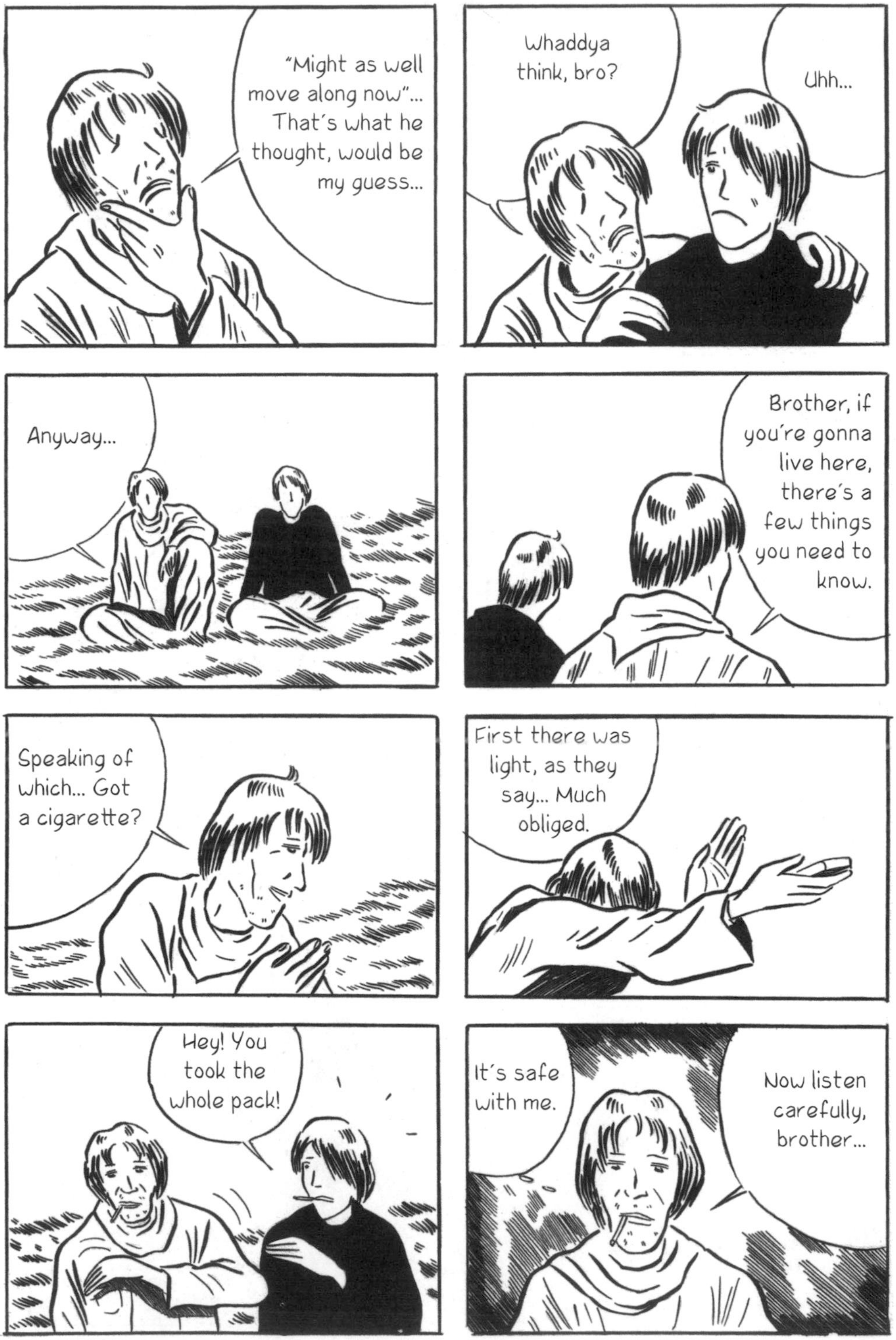
"Might as well move along now"... That's what he thought, would be my guess...
Whaddya think, bro?
Uhh...
Anyway...
Brother, if you're gonna live here, there's a few things you need to know.
Speaking of which... Got a cigarette?
First there was light, as they say... Much obliged.
Hey! You took the whole pack!
It's safe with me.
Now listen carefully, brother...

Look at this map.

I drew it with my own sweat and blood.

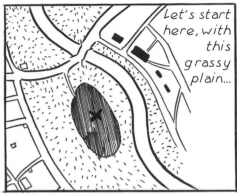

Let's start here, with this grassy plain...

Any normal person would think that only a fool would choose to live in a place like this.

The mere thought of diving in here is enough to make one depressed...

Not far in... heh heh... it's pretty neat, actually... crisscrossed with roads...

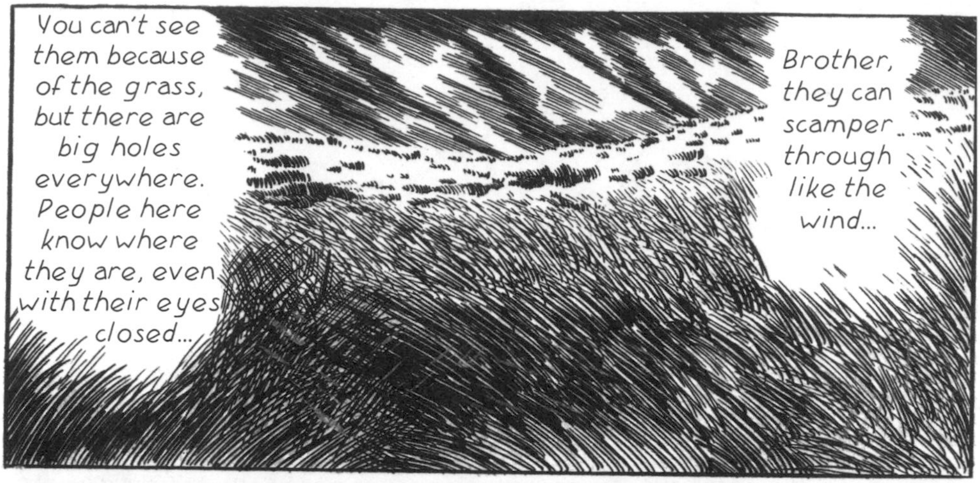
You can't see them because of the grass, but there are big holes everywhere. People here know where they are, even with their eyes closed...
Brother, they can scamper through like the wind...

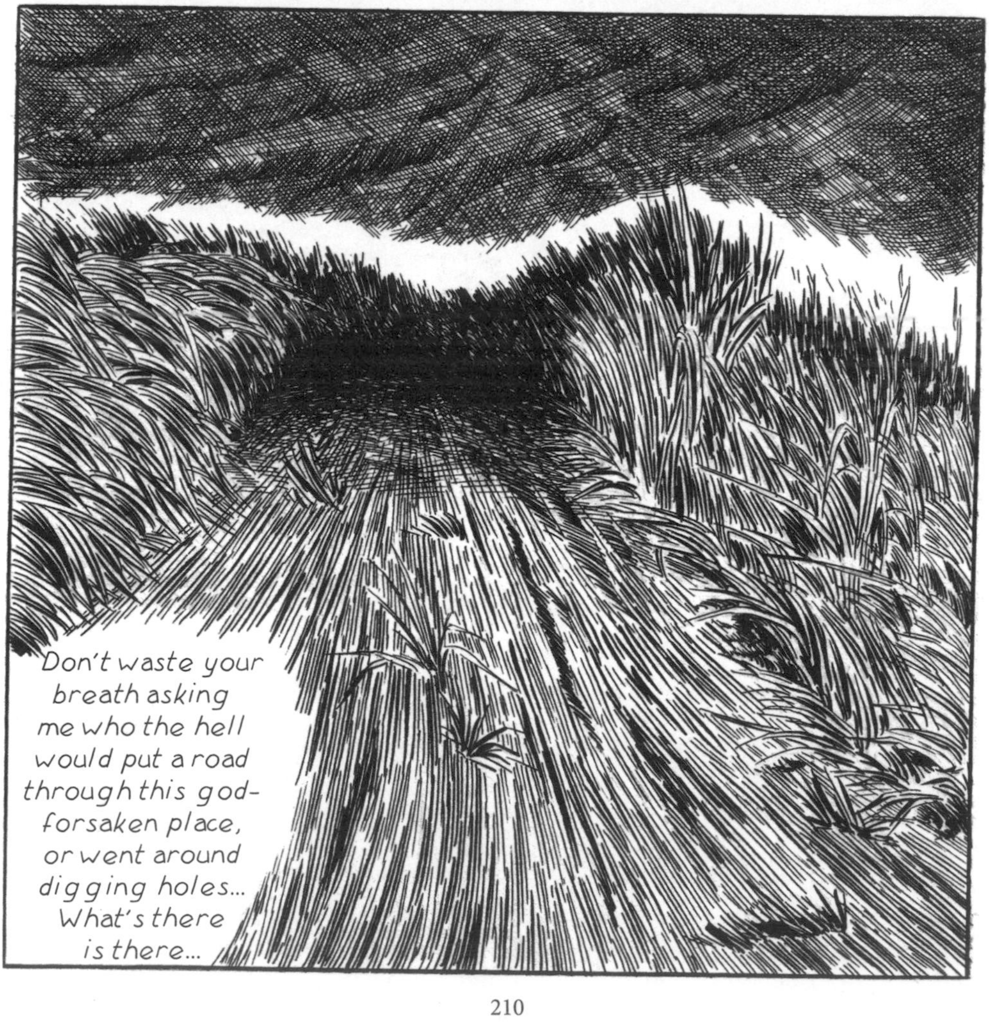
Don't waste your breath asking me who the hell would put a road through this god-forsaken place, or went around digging holes... What's there is there...

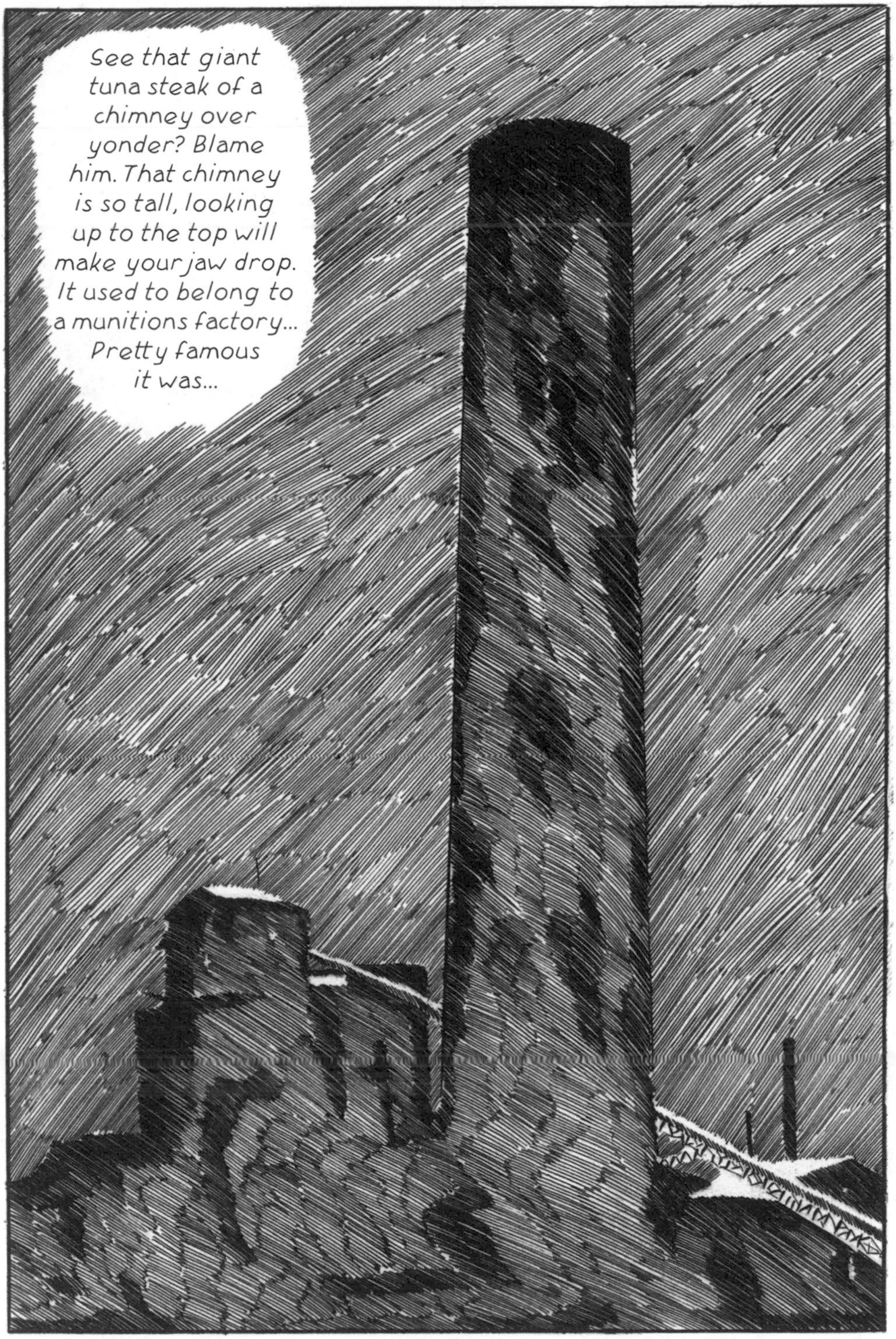
See that giant tuna steak of a chimney over yonder? Blame him. That chimney is so tall, looking up to the top will make your jaw drop. It used to belong to a munitions factory... Pretty famous it was...

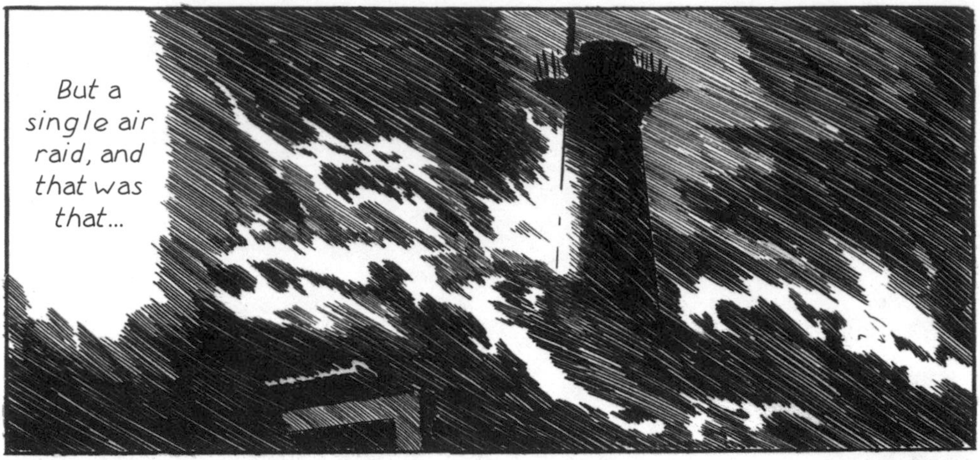
But a single air raid, and that was that...

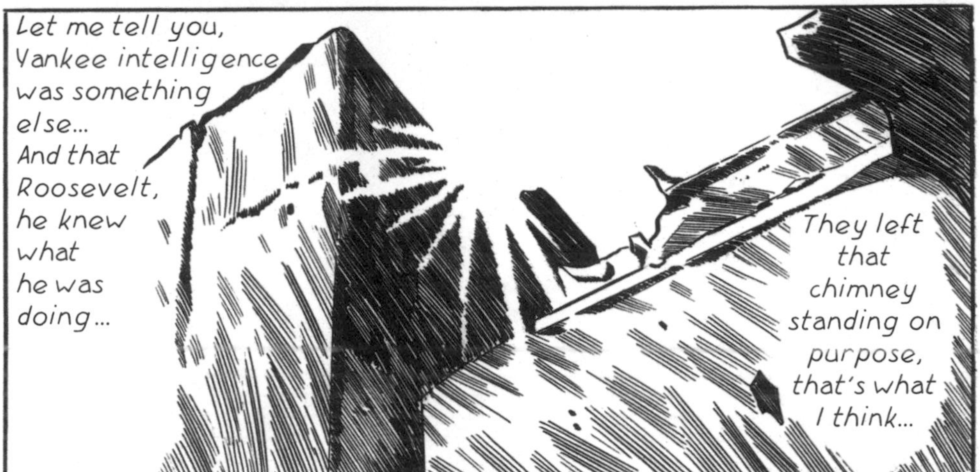
Let me tell you, Yankee intelligence was something else... And that Roosevelt, he knew what he was doing...
They left that chimney standing on purpose, that's what I think...

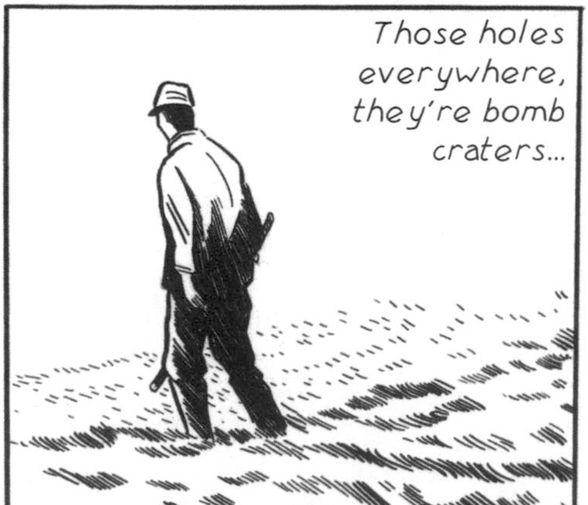
Those holes everywhere, they're bomb craters...

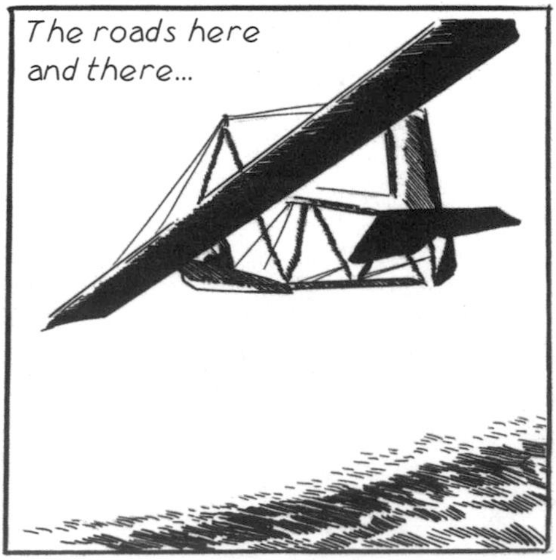
The roads here and there...

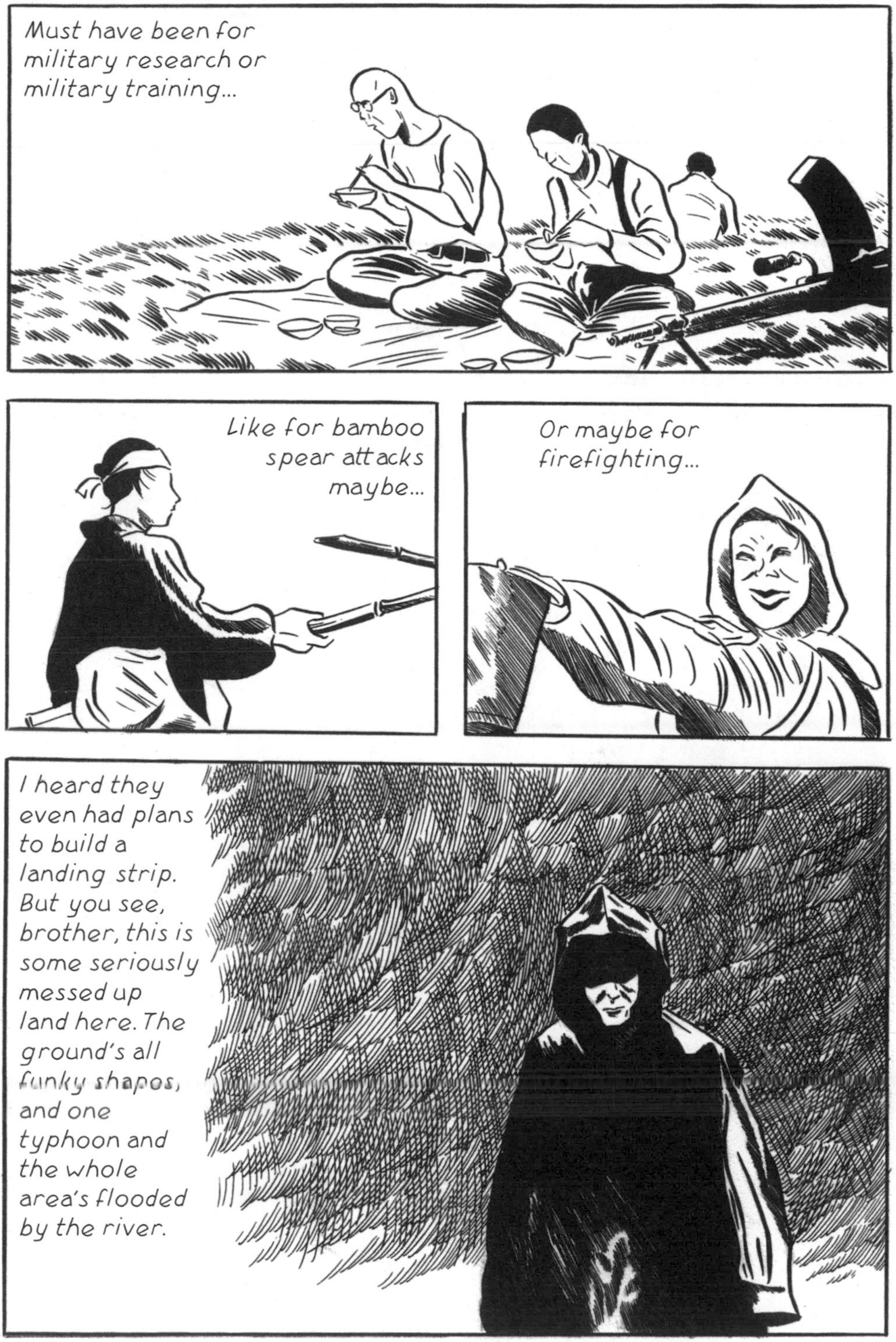
Must have been for military research or military training...
Like for bamboo spear attacks maybe...
Or maybe for firefighting...
I heard they even had plans to build a landing strip. But you see, brother, this is some seriously messed up land here. The ground's all funky shapes, and one typhoon and the whole area's flooded by the river.

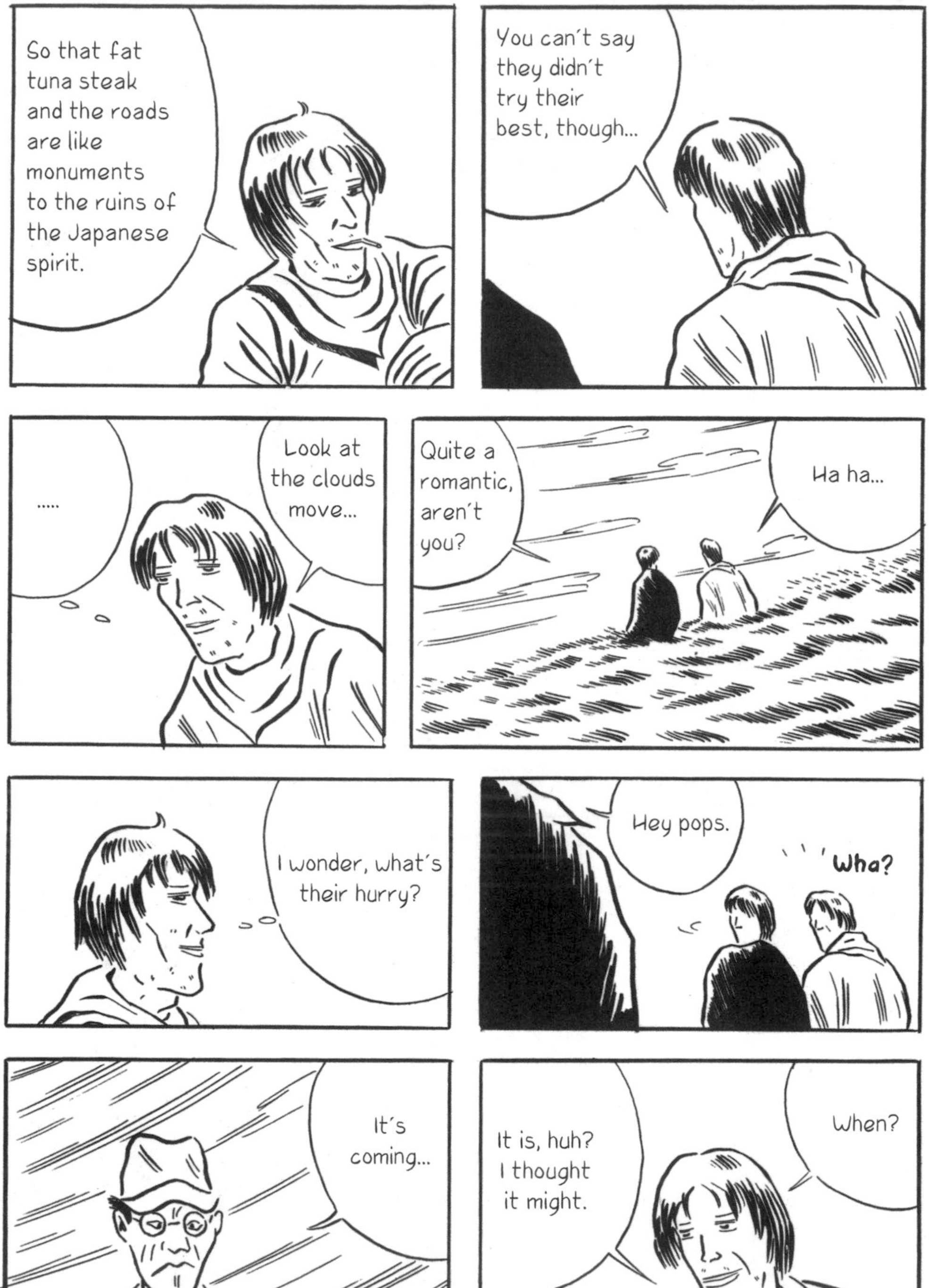
So that fat tuna steak and the roads are like monuments to the ruins of the Japanese spirit.
You can't say they didn't try their best, though...
.....
Look at the clouds move...
Quite a romantic, aren't you?
Ha ha...
I wonder, what's their hurry?
Hey pops.
Wha?
It's coming...
It is, huh? I thought it might.
When?

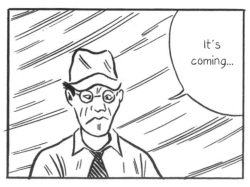

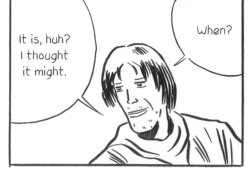

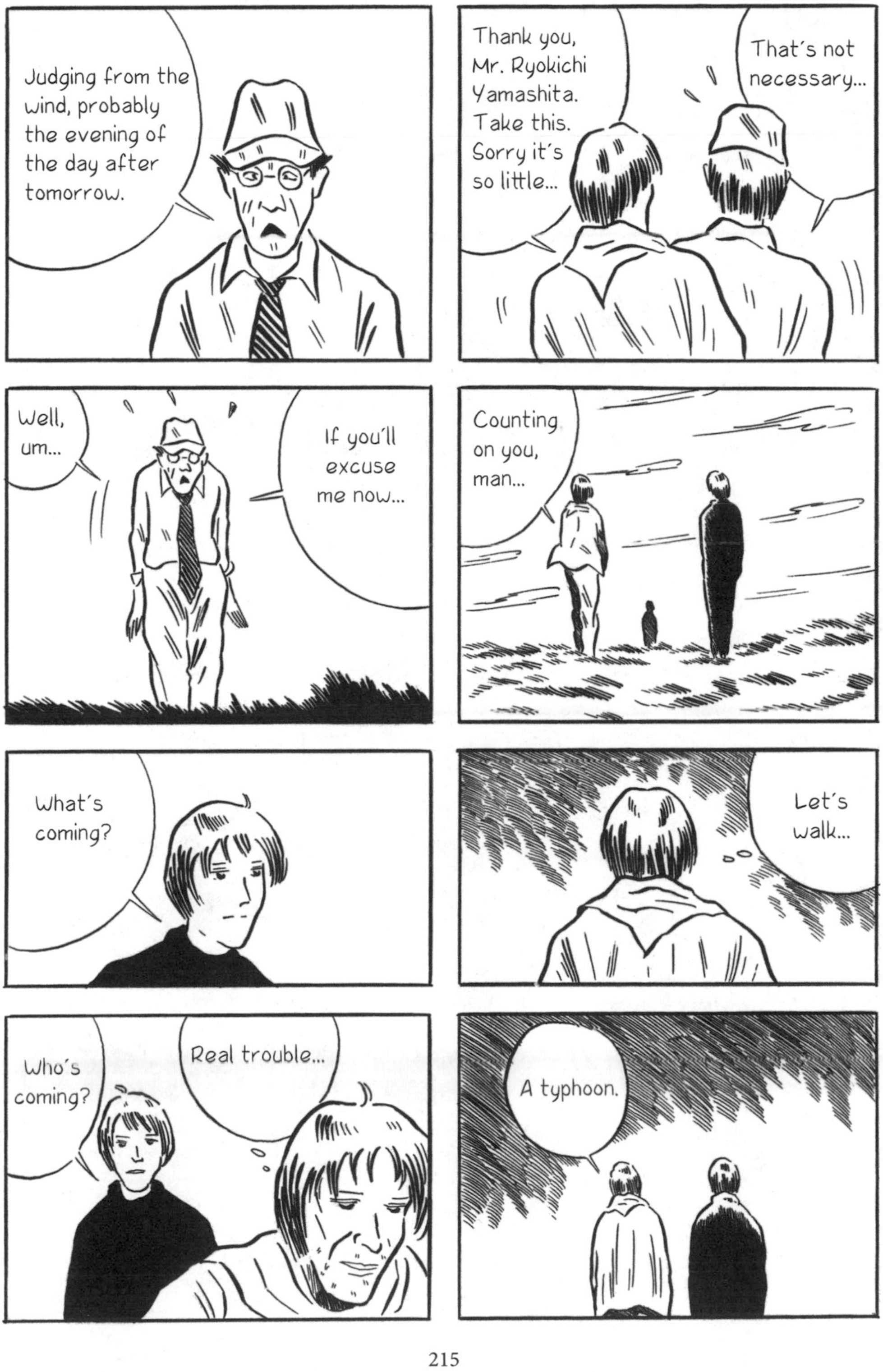

Judging from the wind, probably the evening of the day after tomorrow.
Thank you, Mr. Ryokichi Yamashita. Take this. Sorry it's so little...
That's not necessary...
Well, um...
If you'll excuse me now...
Counting on you, man...
What's coming?
Let's walk...
Who's coming?
Real trouble...
A typhoon.

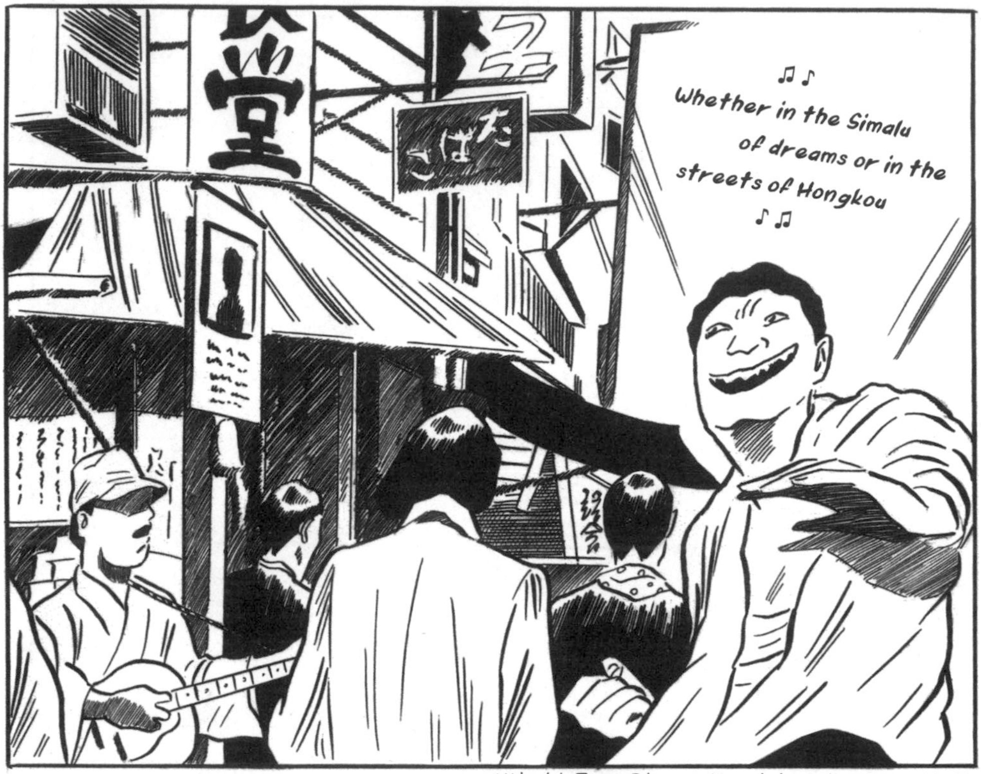
♫♪
Whether in the Simalu of dreams or in the streets of Hongkou
♪♫

song: "Night Fog Blues" (Yogiri no buruusu, 1947)

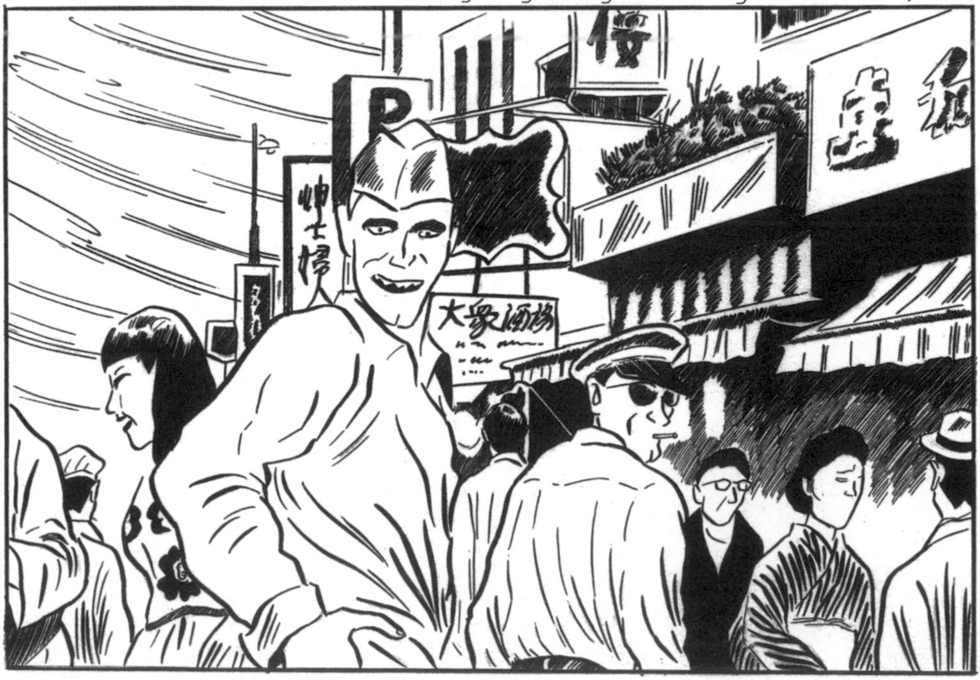

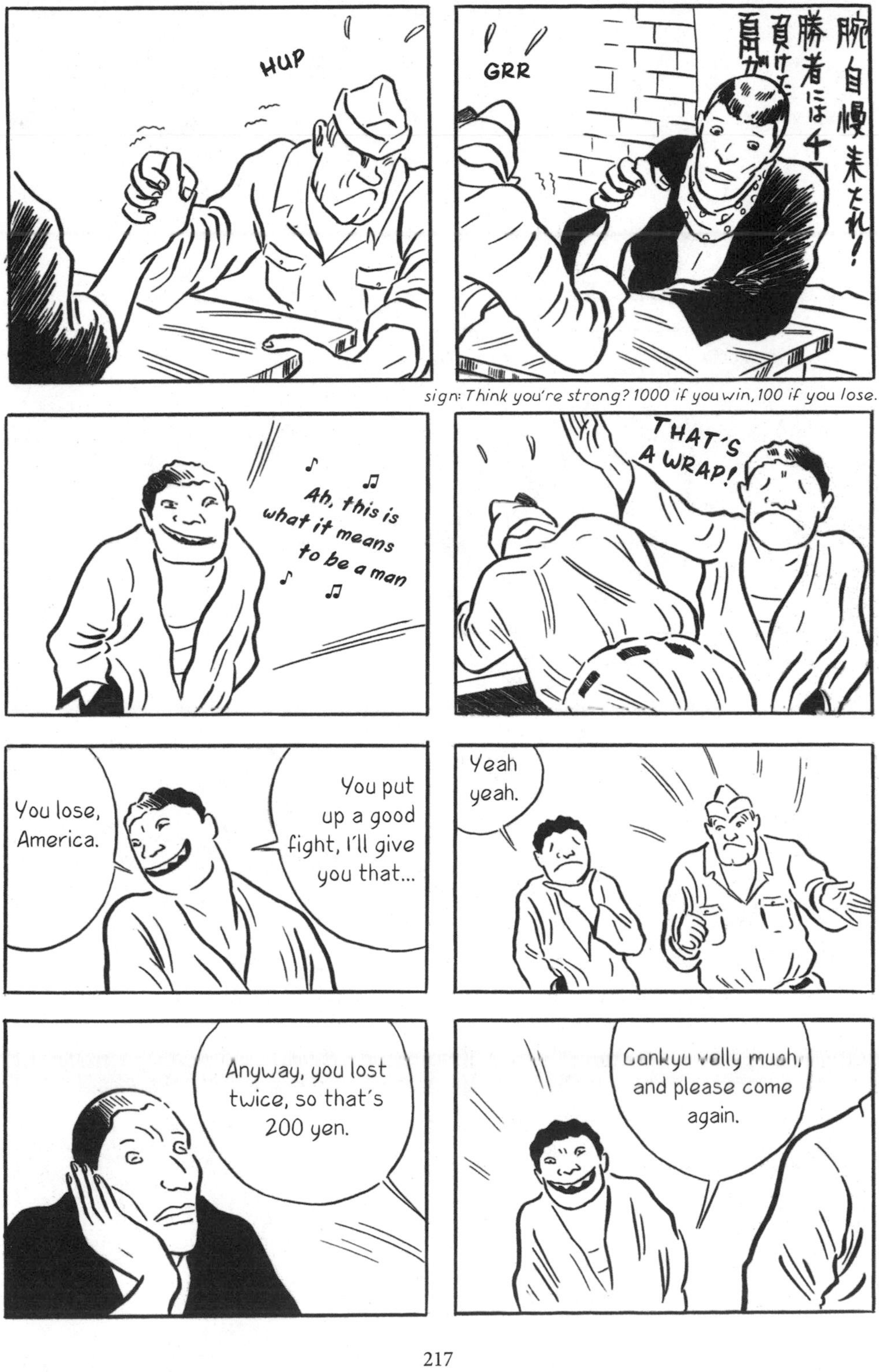
HUP
GRR
腕自慢来たれ!
勝者には千
sign: Think you're strong? 1000 if you win, 100 if you lose.
Ah, this is what it means to be a man
THAT'S A WRAP!
You lose, America.
You put up a good fight, I'll give you that...
Yeah yeah.
Anyway, you lost twice, so that's 200 yen.
Gankyu volly much, and please come again.

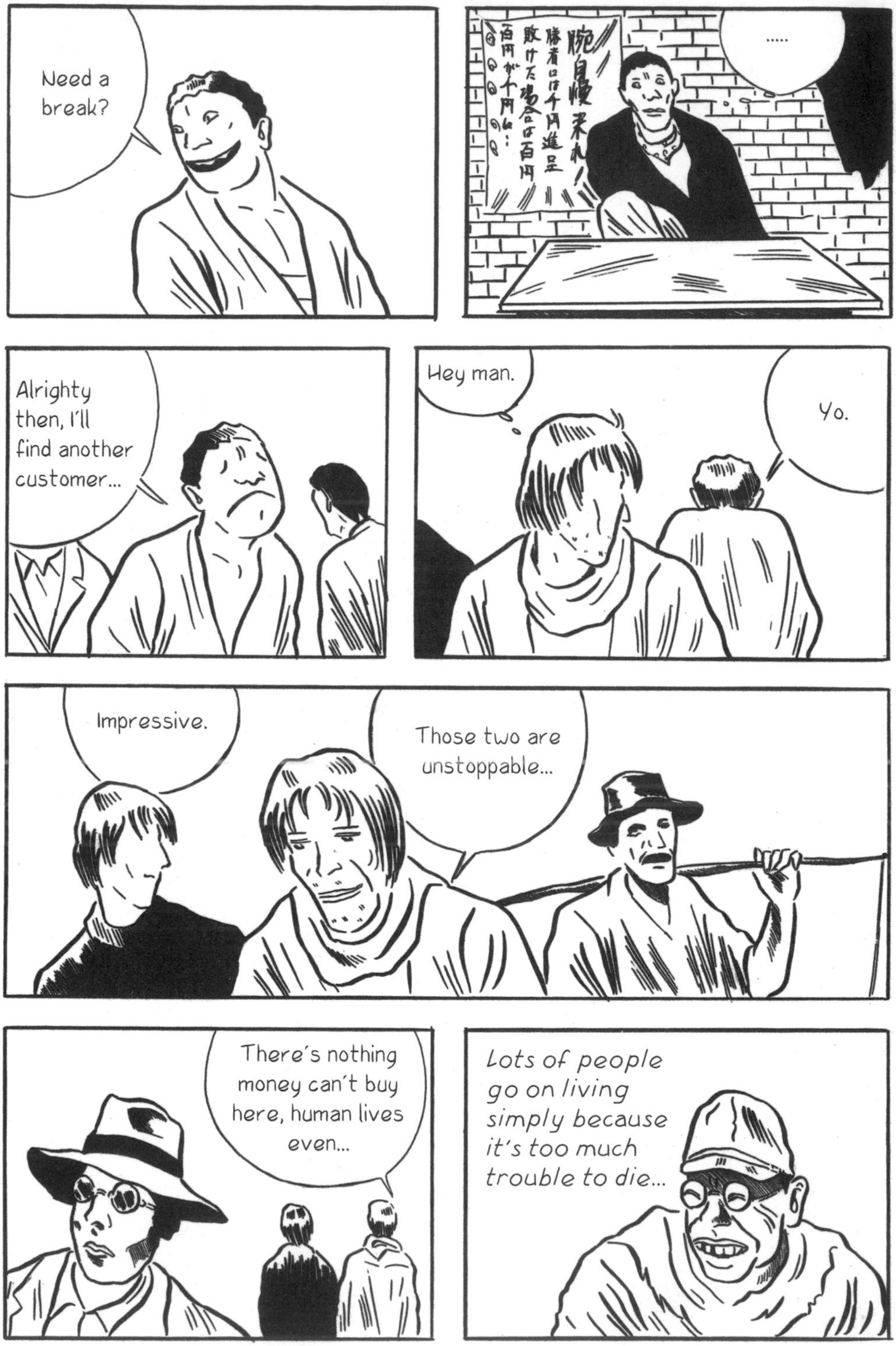
Need a break?
腕自慢来れ！
勝者には千円進呈
敗けた場合は百円
百円が千円に…
.....
Alrighty then, I'll find another customer...
Hey man.
Yo.
Impressive.
Those two are unstoppable...
There's nothing money can't buy here, human lives even...
Lots of people go on living simply because it's too much trouble to die...

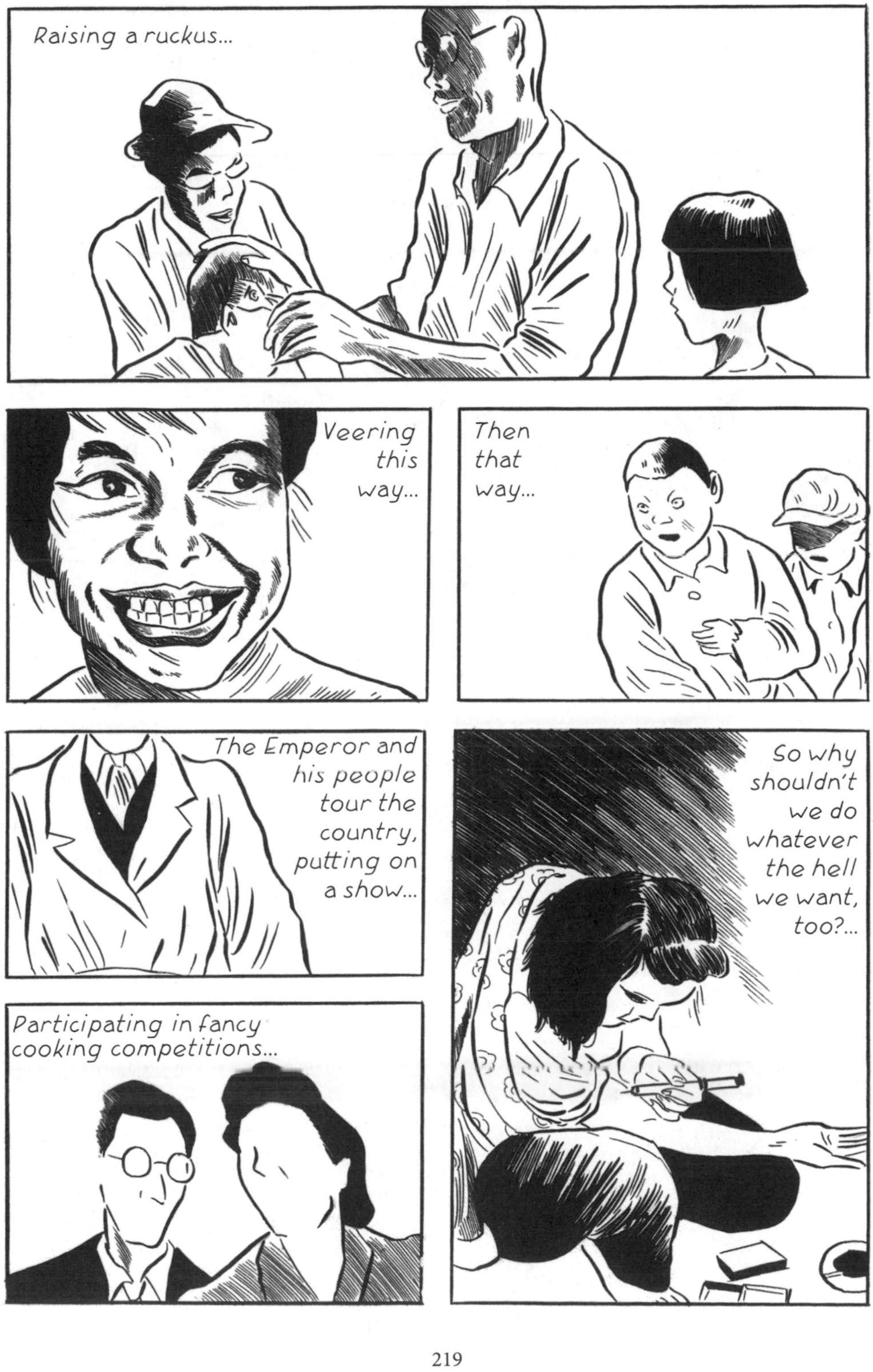
Raising a ruckus...
Veering this way...
Then that way...
The Emperor and his people tour the country, putting on a show...
Participating in fancy cooking competitions...
So why shouldn't we do whatever the hell we want, too?...

What choice do we have?

Teeth bared...

Living it up...

What right do they have to tell us any different?

Y'know what I'm saying?

You know
what I'm
saying!

To be continued...

VAGABOND PLAIN
PART 2

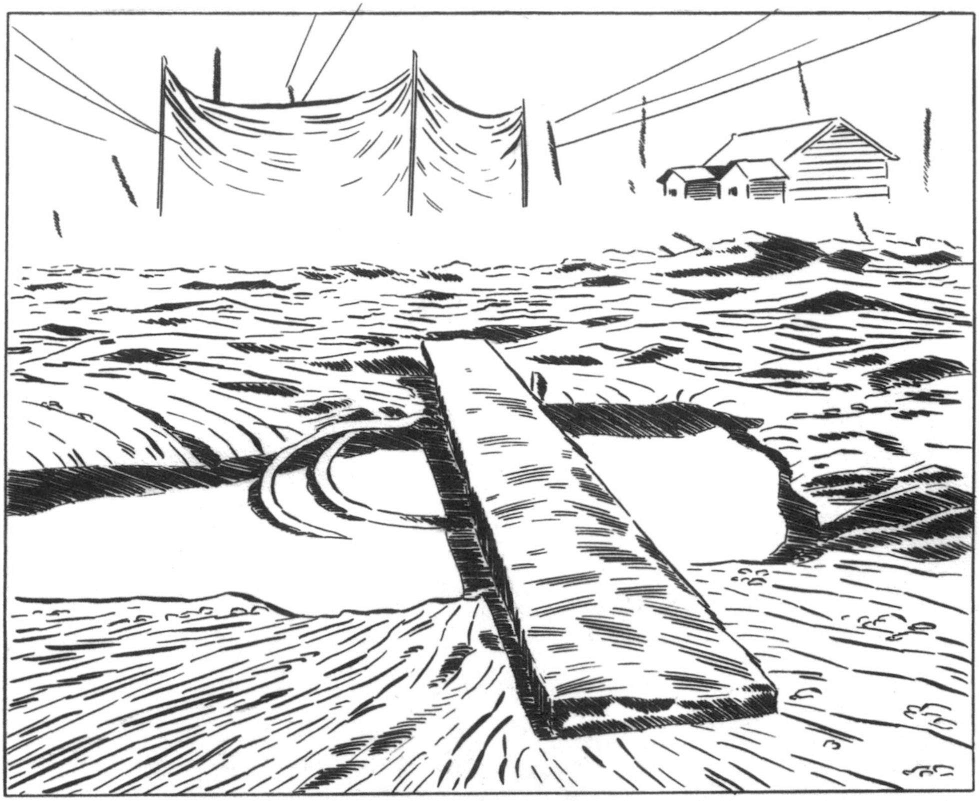

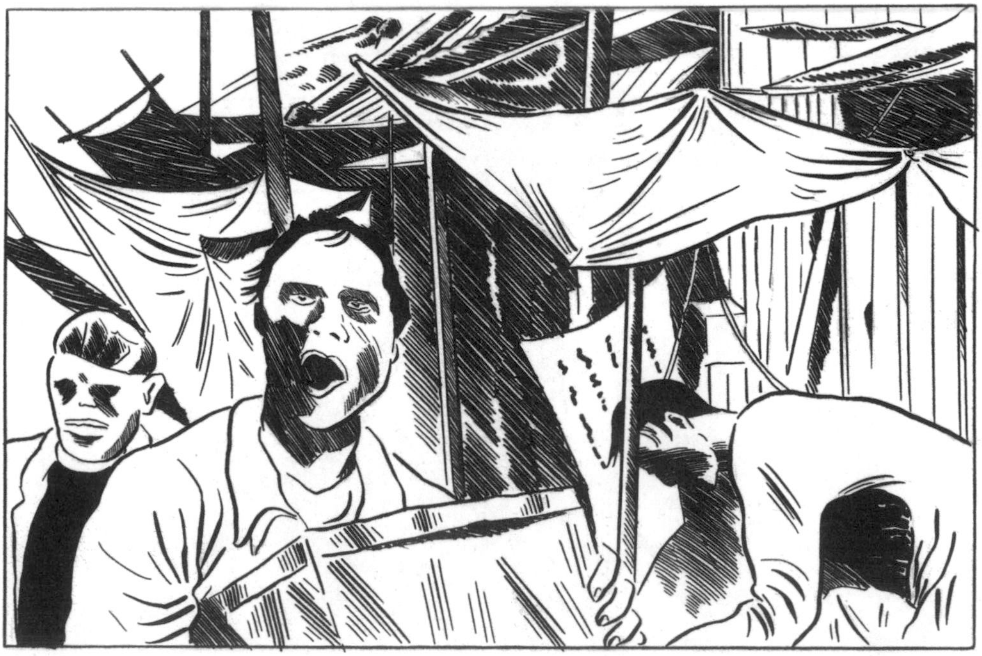

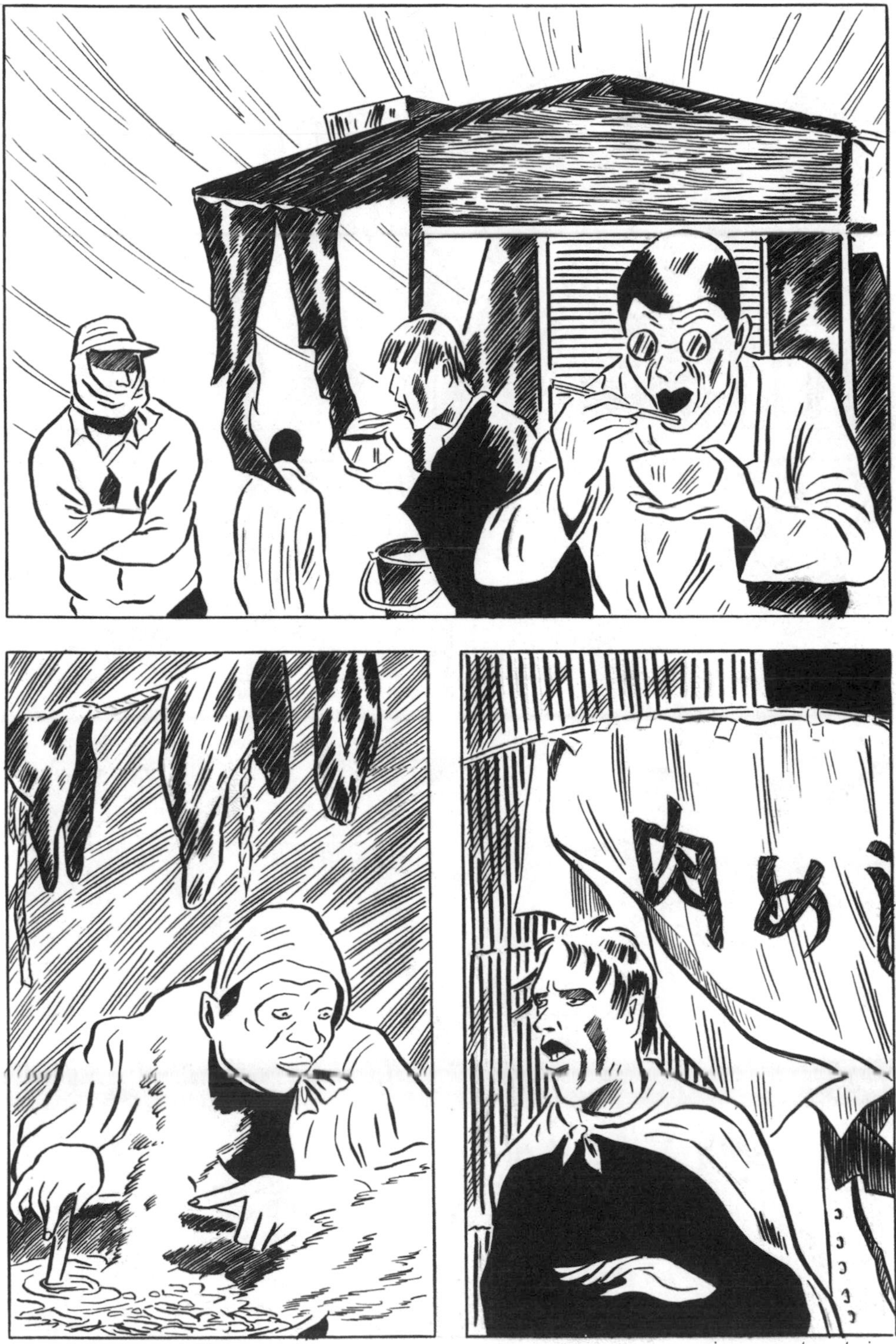
肉め

sign: meat and rice

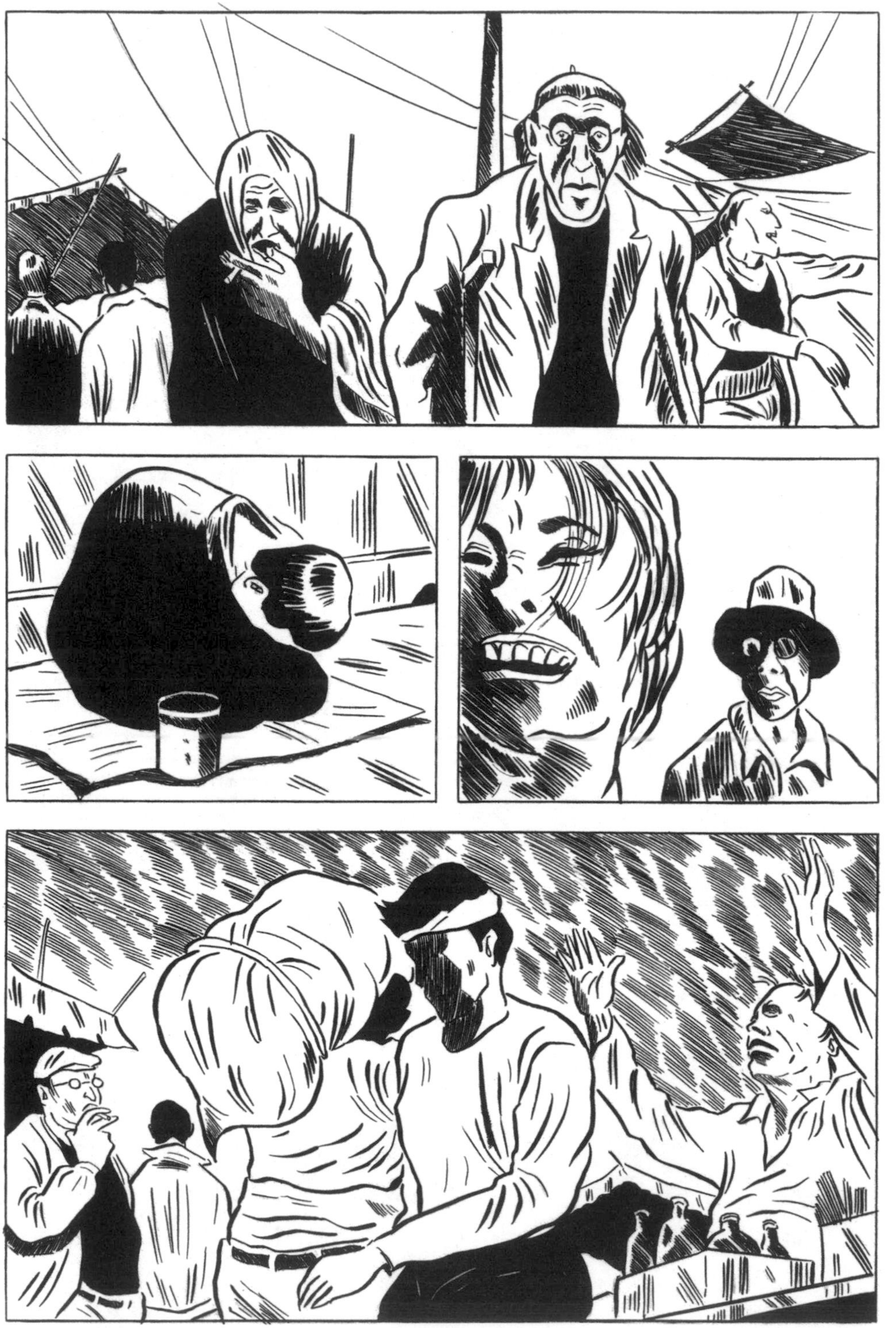

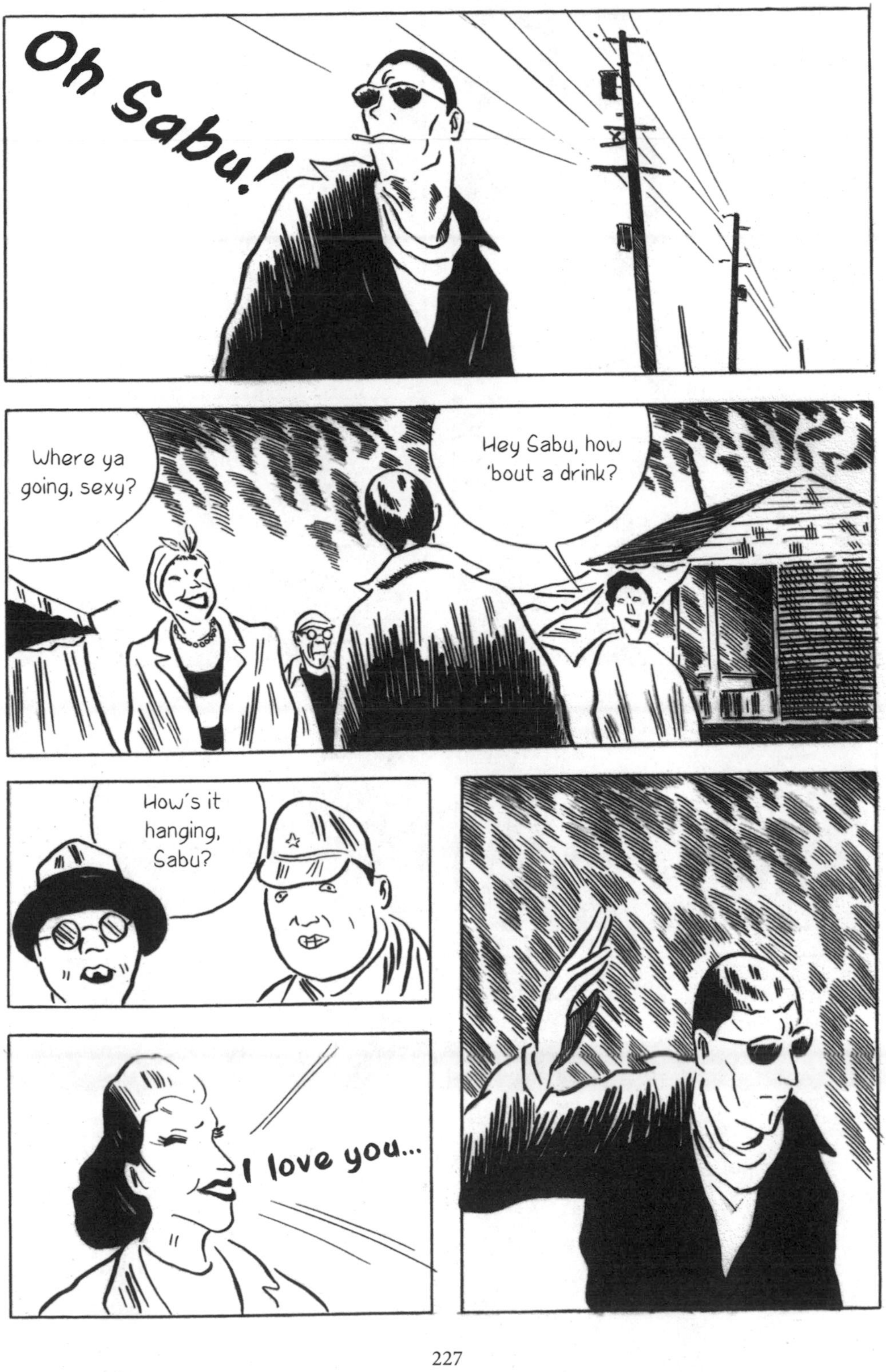
Oh Sabu!
Where ya going, sexy?
Hey Sabu, how 'bout a drink?
How's it hanging, Sabu?
I love you...

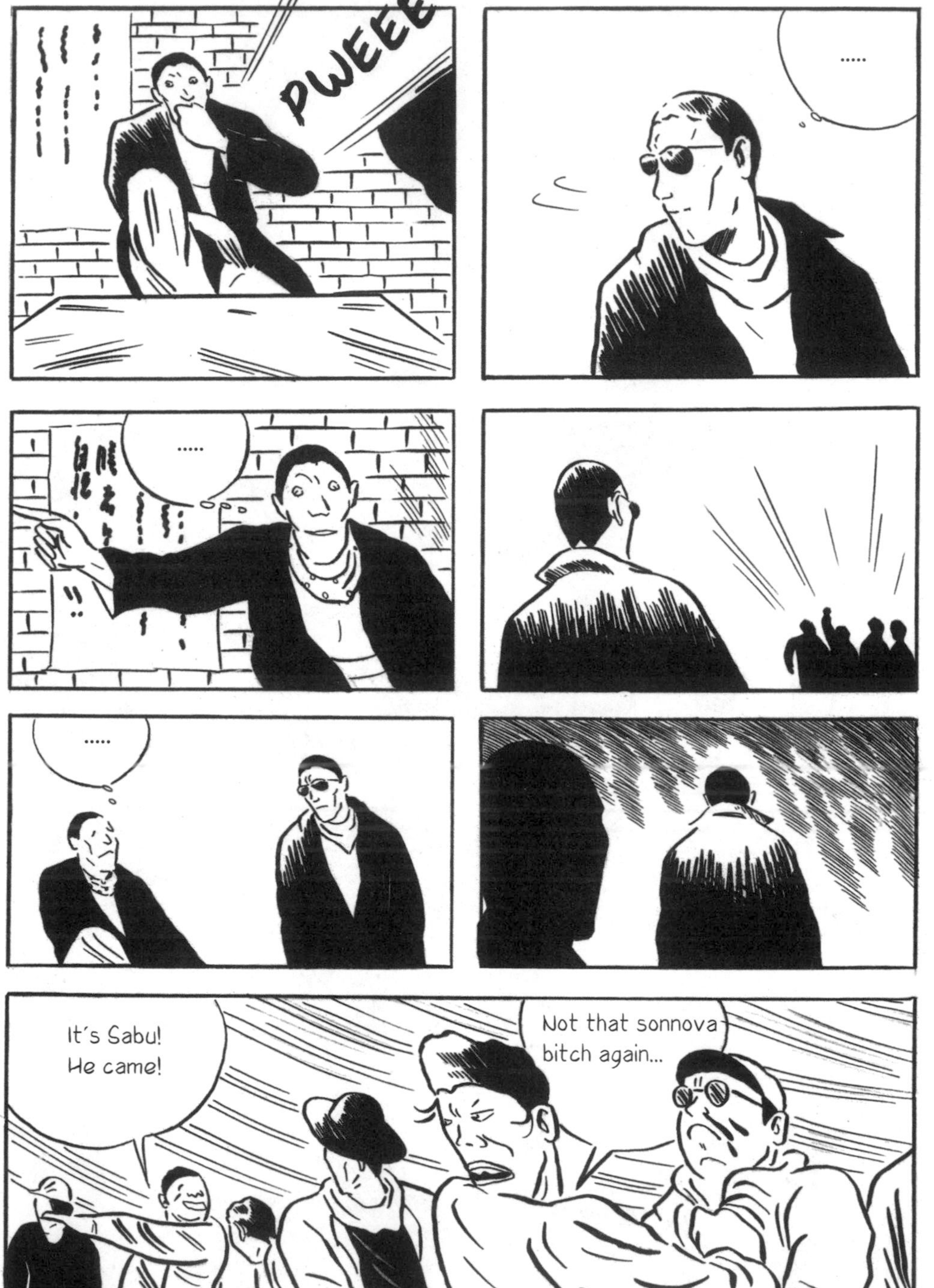
PWEEE
.....
.....
.....
It's Sabu! He came!
Not that sonnova bitch again...

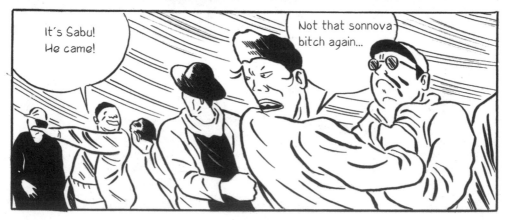

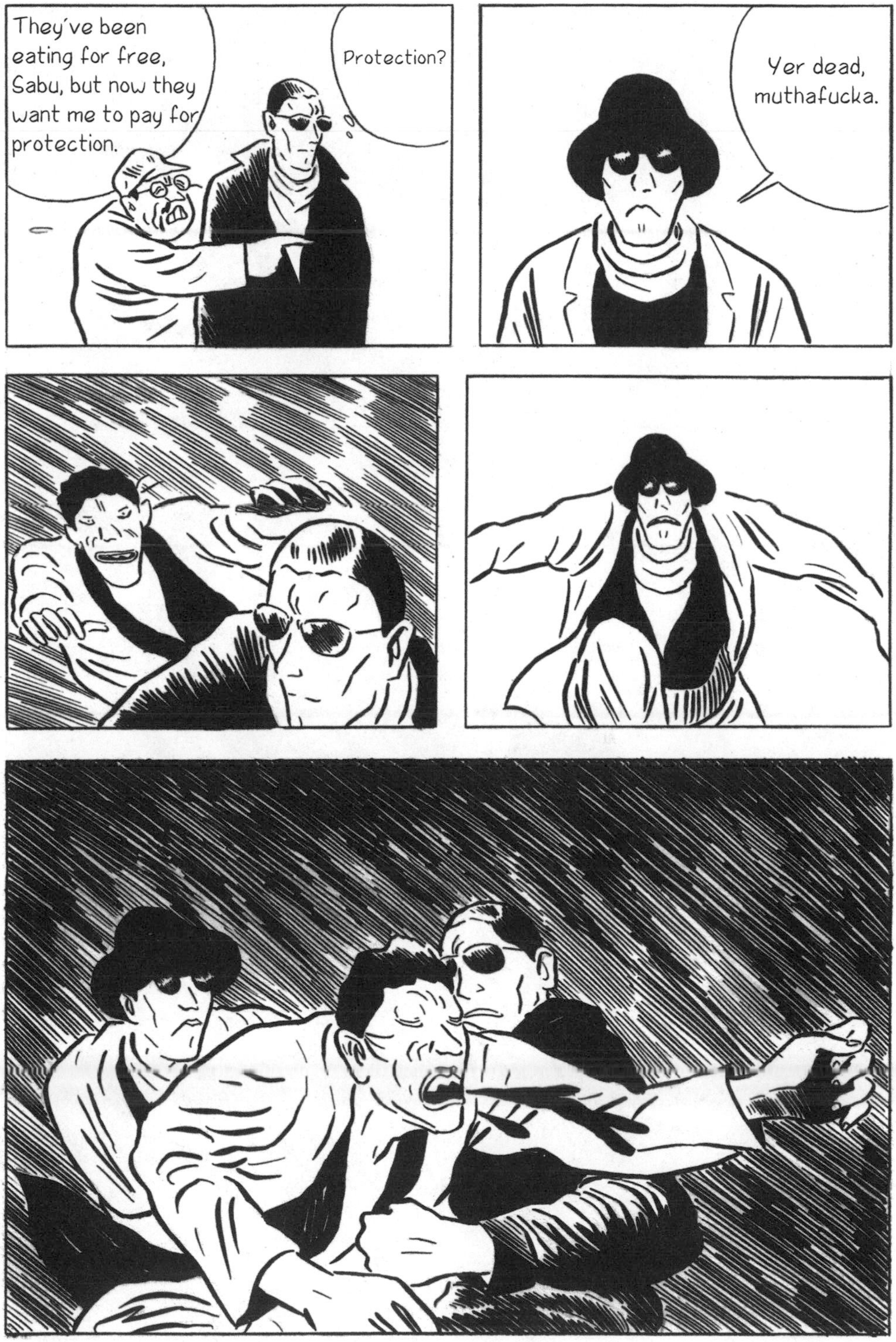
They've been eating for free, Sabu, but now they want me to pay for protection.
Protection?
Yer dead, muthafucka.

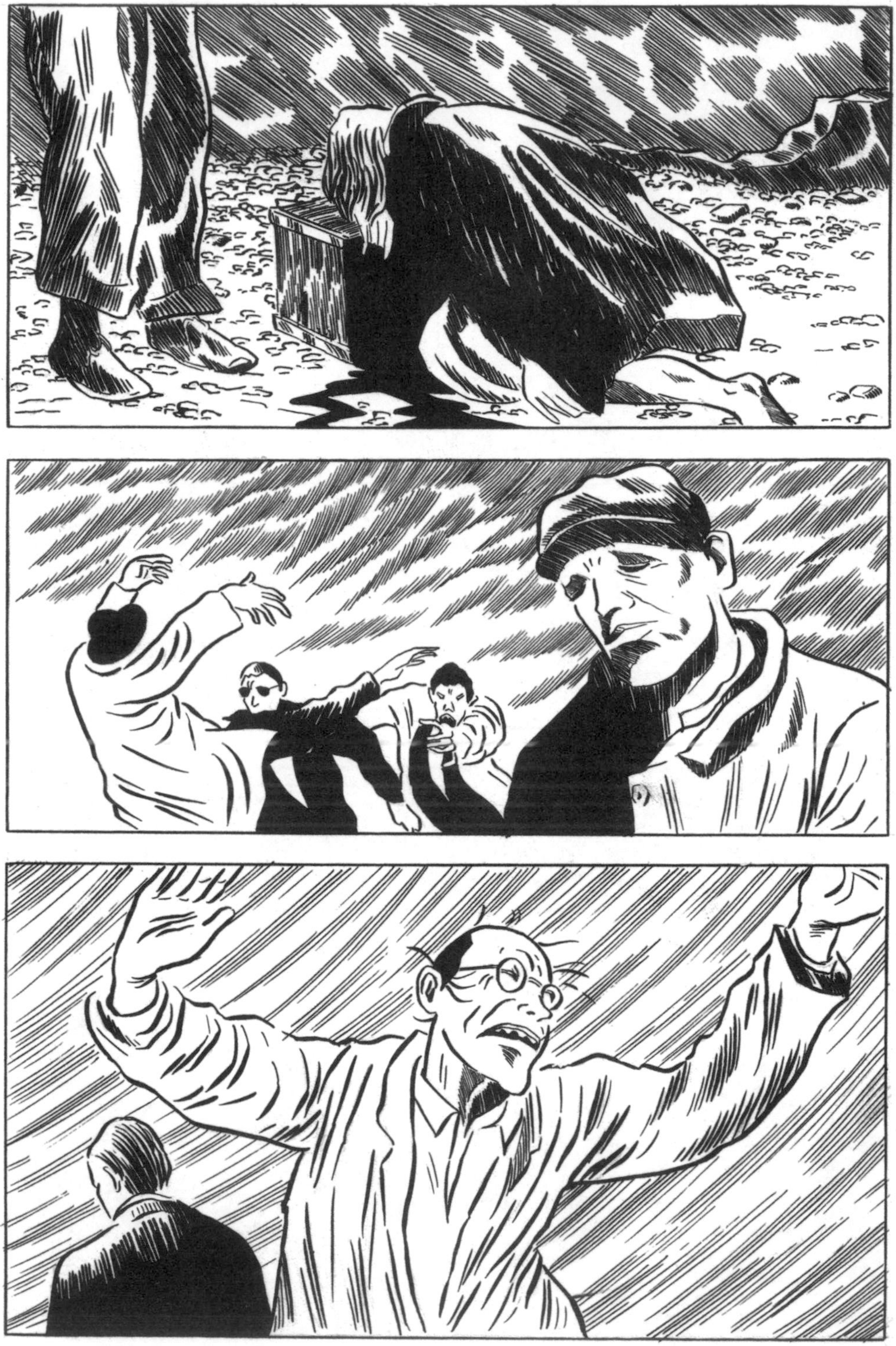

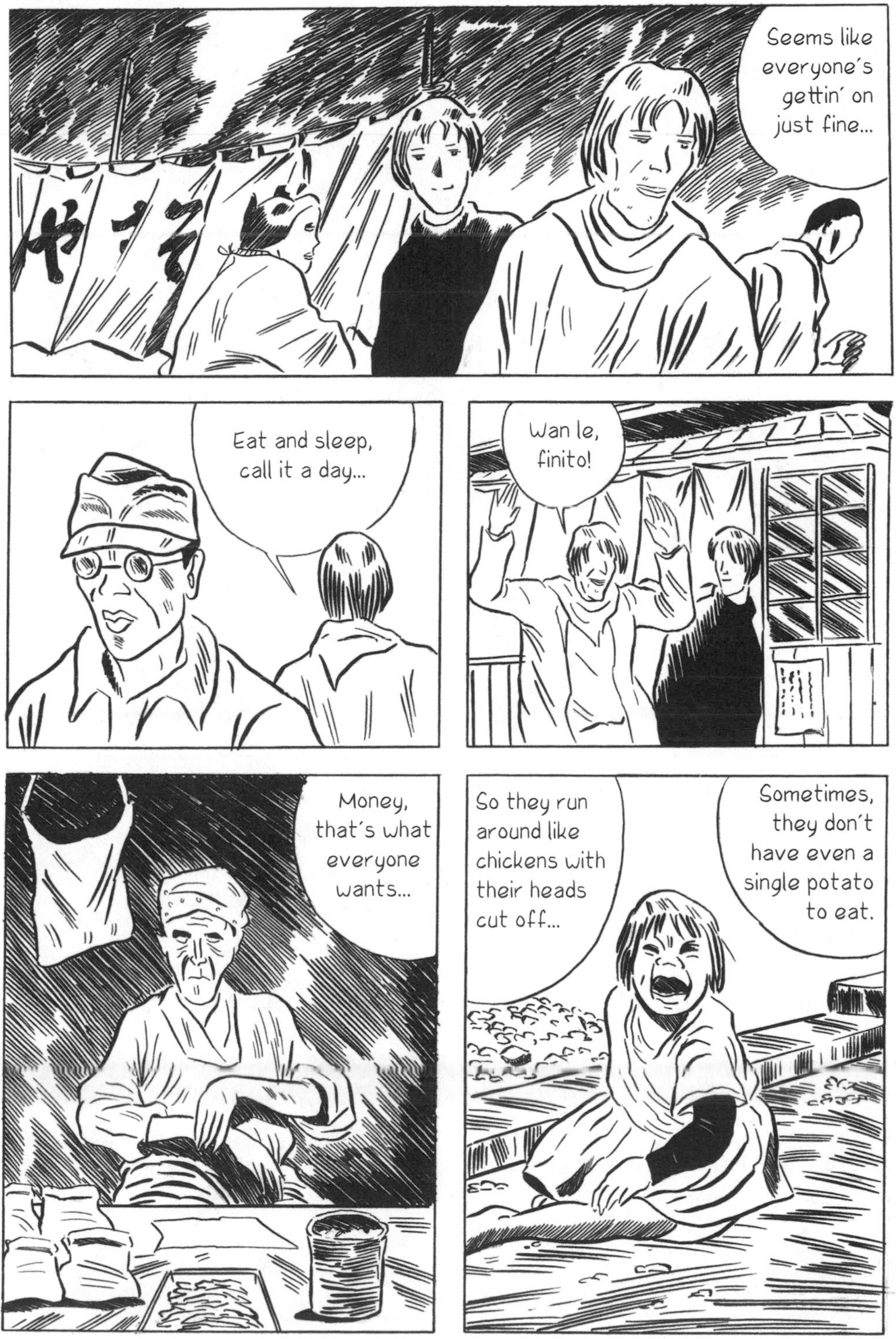
Seems like everyone's gettin' on just fine...
Eat and sleep, call it a day...
Wan le, finito!
Money, that's what everyone wants...
So they run around like chickens with their heads cut off...
Sometimes, they don't have even a single potato to eat.

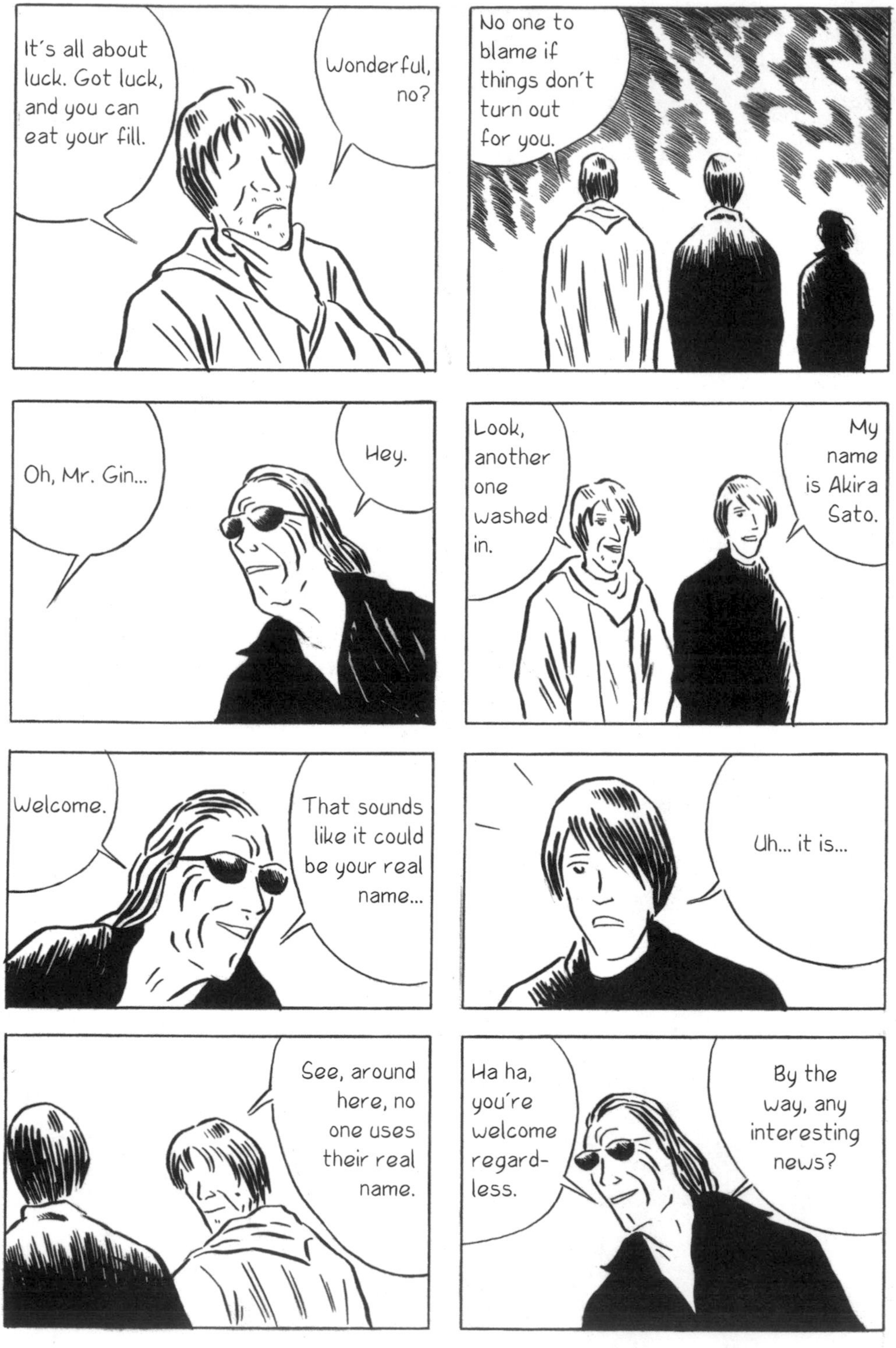
It's all about luck. Got luck, and you can eat your fill.
Wonderful, no?
No one to blame if things don't turn out for you.
Oh, Mr. Gin...
Hey.
Look, another one washed in.
My name is Akira Sato.
Welcome.
That sounds like it could be your real name...
Uh... it is...
See, around here, no one uses their real name.
Ha ha, you're welcome regard-less.
By the way, any interesting news?

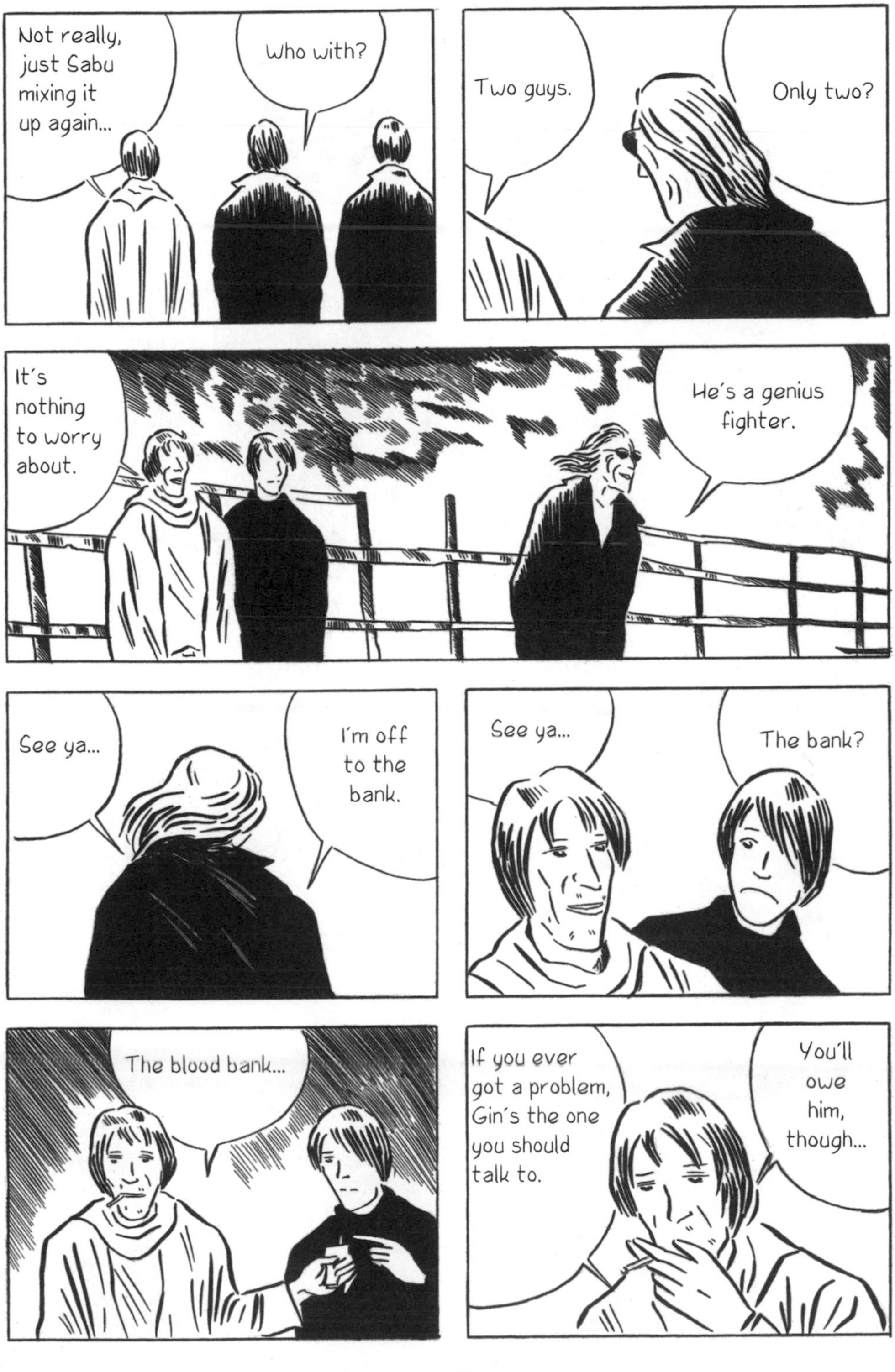
Not really, just Sabu mixing it up again...
Who with?
Two guys.
Only two?
It's nothing to worry about.
He's a genius fighter.
See ya...
I'm off to the bank.
See ya...
The bank?
The blood bank...
If you ever got a problem, Gin's the one you should talk to.
You'll owe him, though...

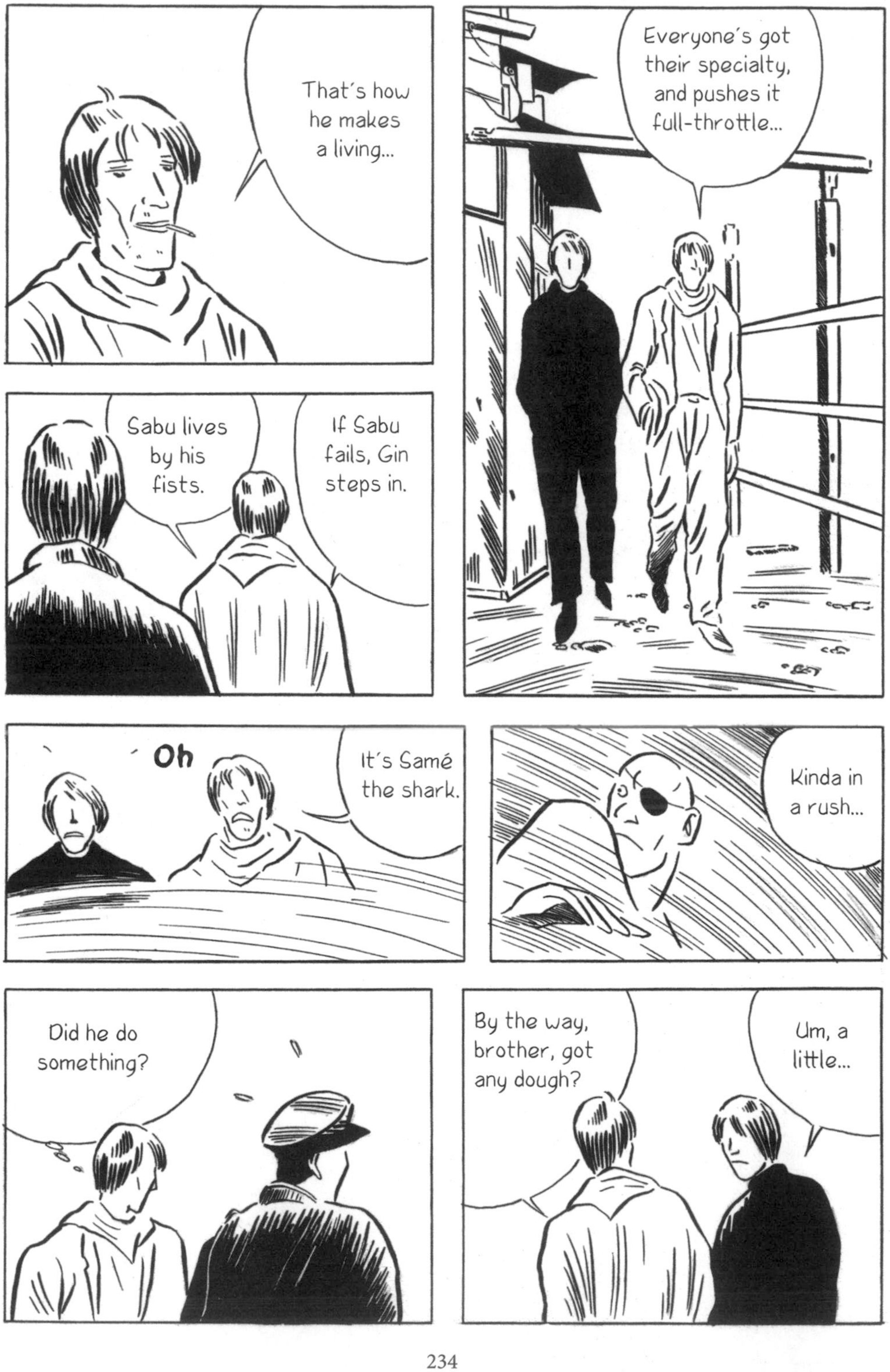
That's how he makes a living...
Everyone's got their specialty, and pushes it full-throttle...
Sabu lives by his fists.
If Sabu fails, Gin steps in.
Oh
It's Samé the shark.
Kinda in a rush...
Did he do something?
By the way, brother, got any dough?
Um, a little...

Ah, good to hear.
So, where we gonna put your head, brother? Can't build a house yourself...
You'll need a hand for that...
Even a hovel is a serious undertaking!
Then again, can't leave you out in the cold... You could stay with me, if it suits you.
Anywhere would be—
HA HA HA
It's settled then. My place is called the Clear Wind Retreat.
Moving on to business, a room is 350 yen a month...
With meals, 500.
In principle, you get white rice. But please, no complaints over the occasional substitute.
For first-timers, I ask a half-month's rent up front...
Just a room is fine.

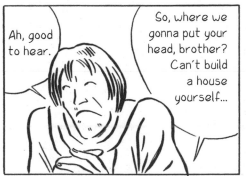

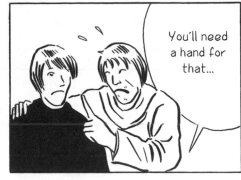

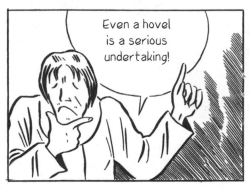

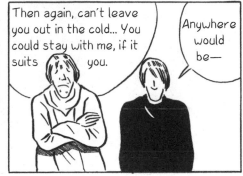

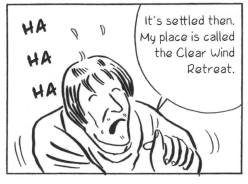

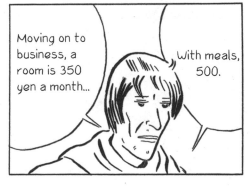

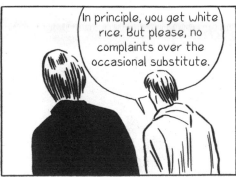

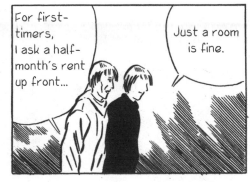

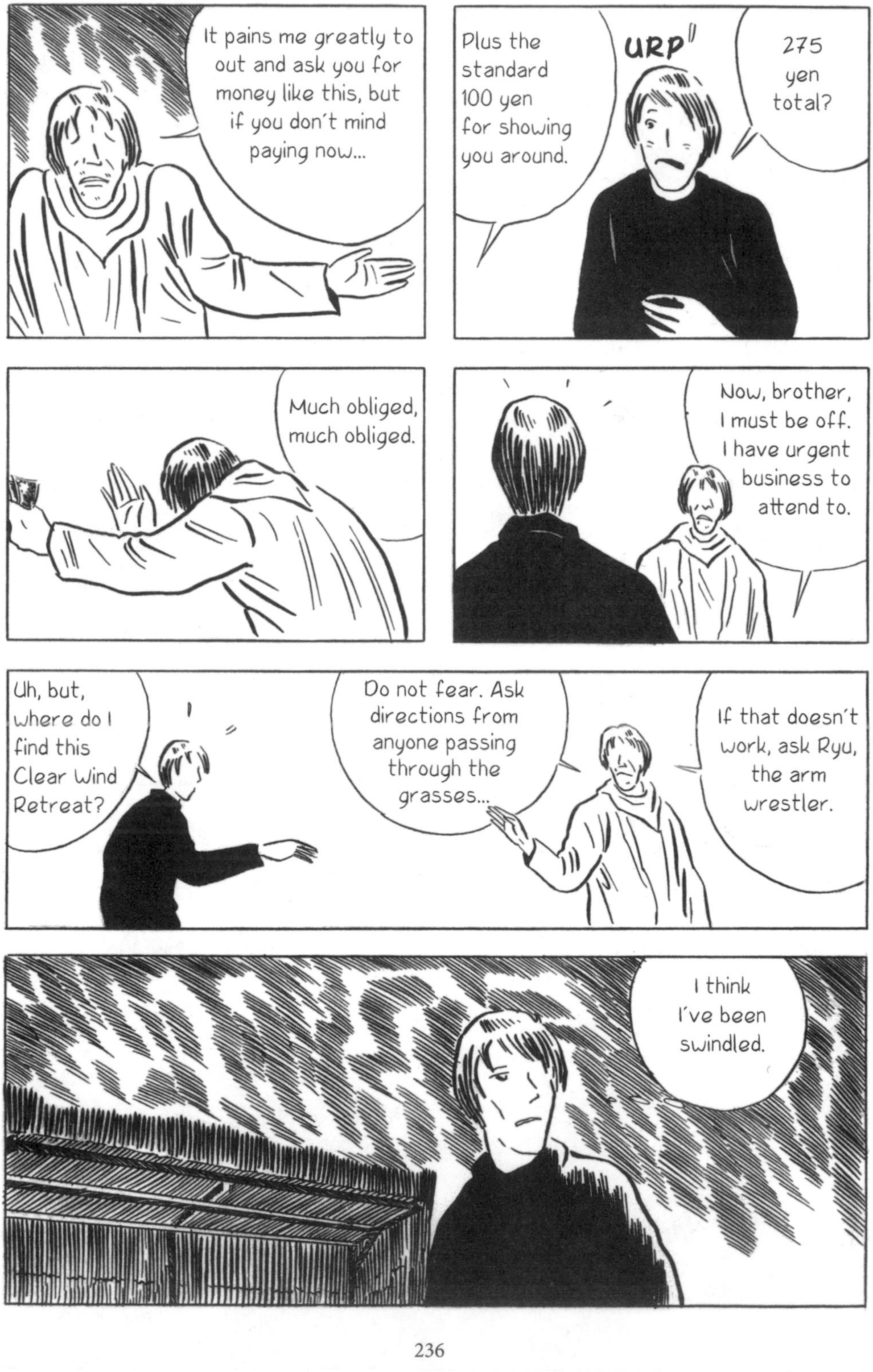
It pains me greatly to out and ask you for money like this, but if you don't mind paying now...
Plus the standard 100 yen for showing you around.
URP
275 yen total?
Much obliged, much obliged.
Now, brother, I must be off. I have urgent business to attend to.
Uh, but, where do I find this Clear Wind Retreat?
Do not fear. Ask directions from anyone passing through the grasses...
If that doesn't work, ask Ryu, the arm wrestler.
I think I've been swindled.

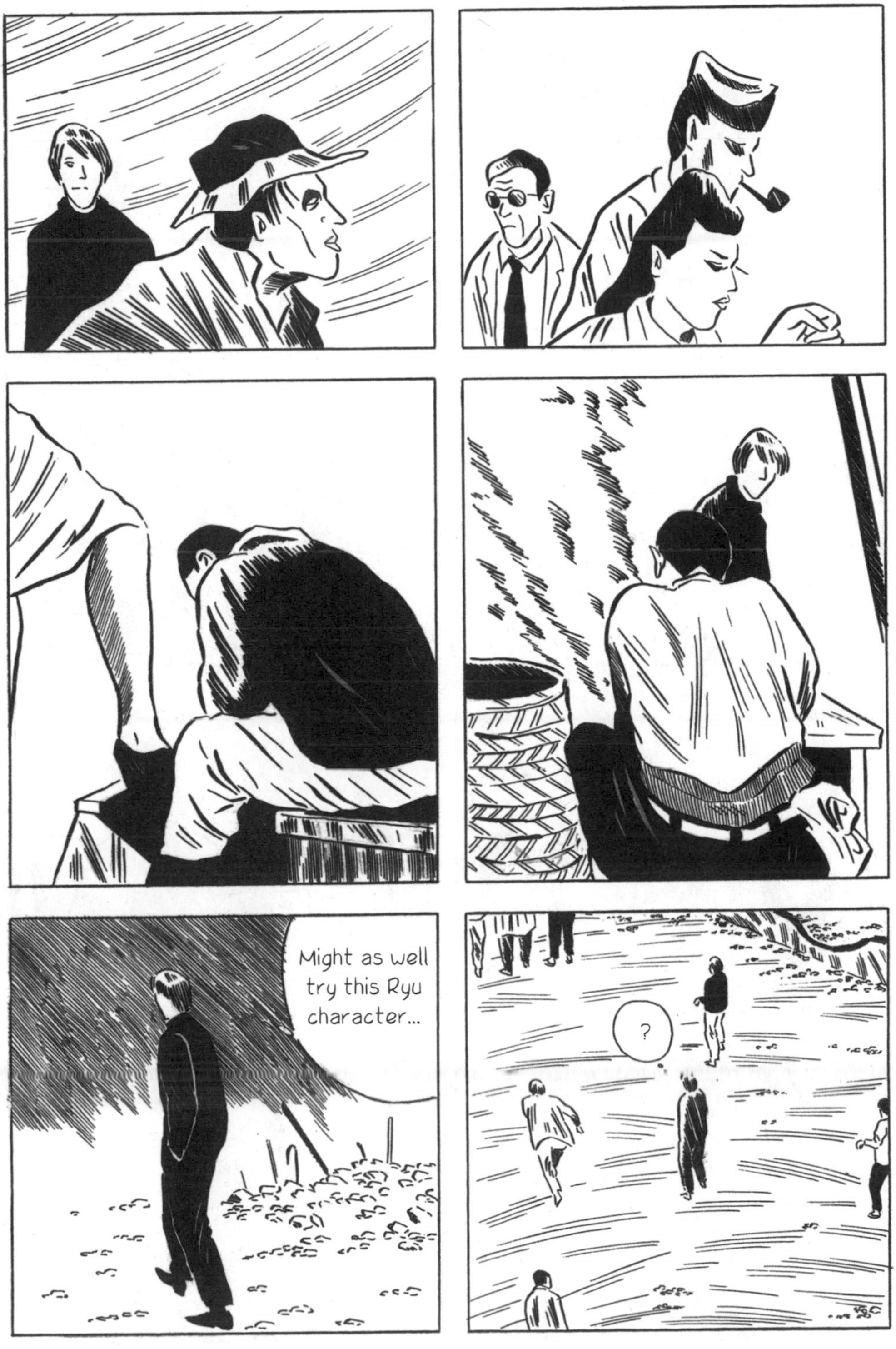
Might as well try this Ryu character...
?

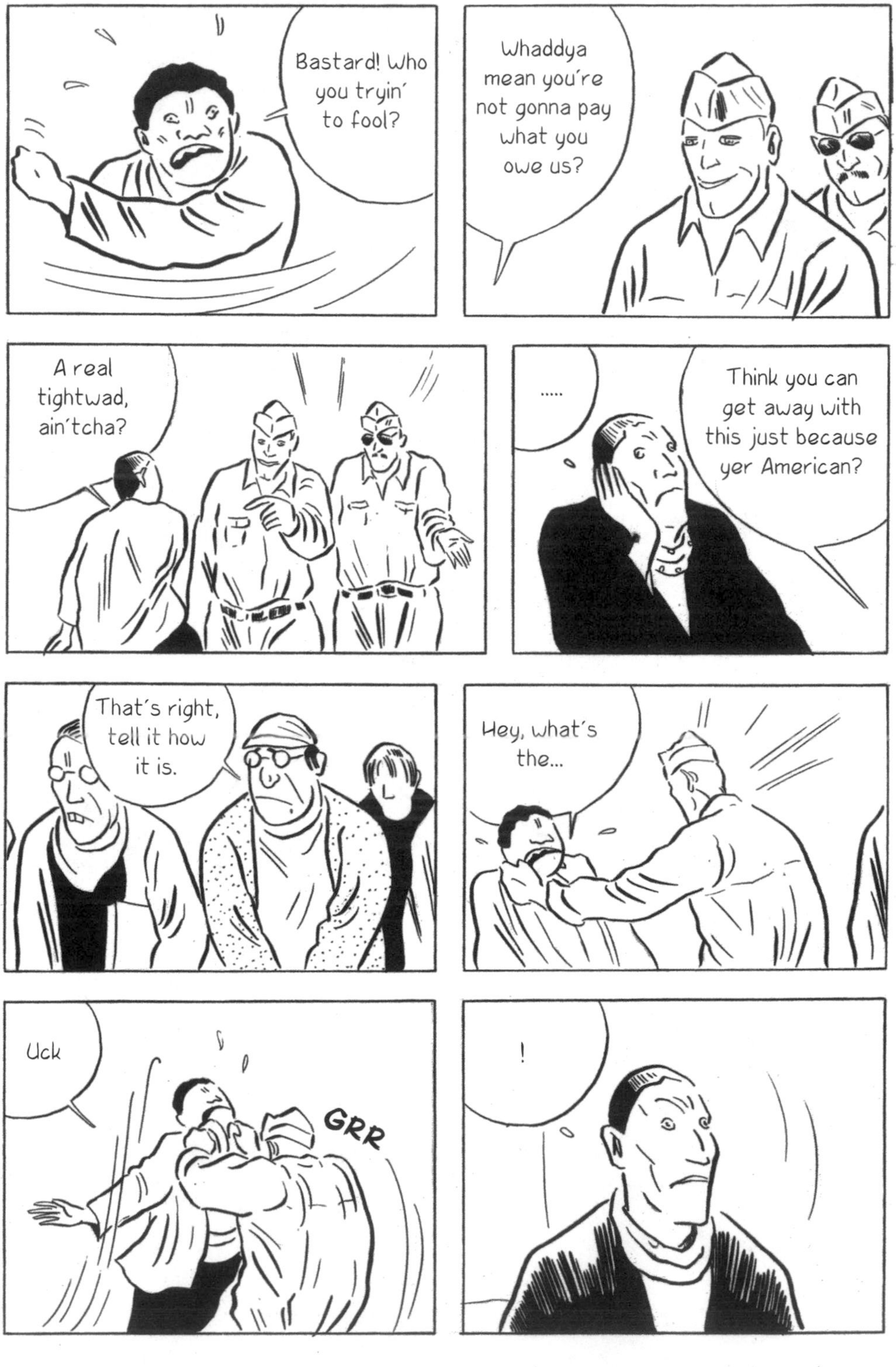
Bastard! Who you tryin' to fool?
Whaddya mean you're not gonna pay what you owe us?
A real tightwad, ain'tcha?
.....
Think you can get away with this just because yer American?
That's right, tell it how it is.
Hey, what's the...
Uck
GRR
!

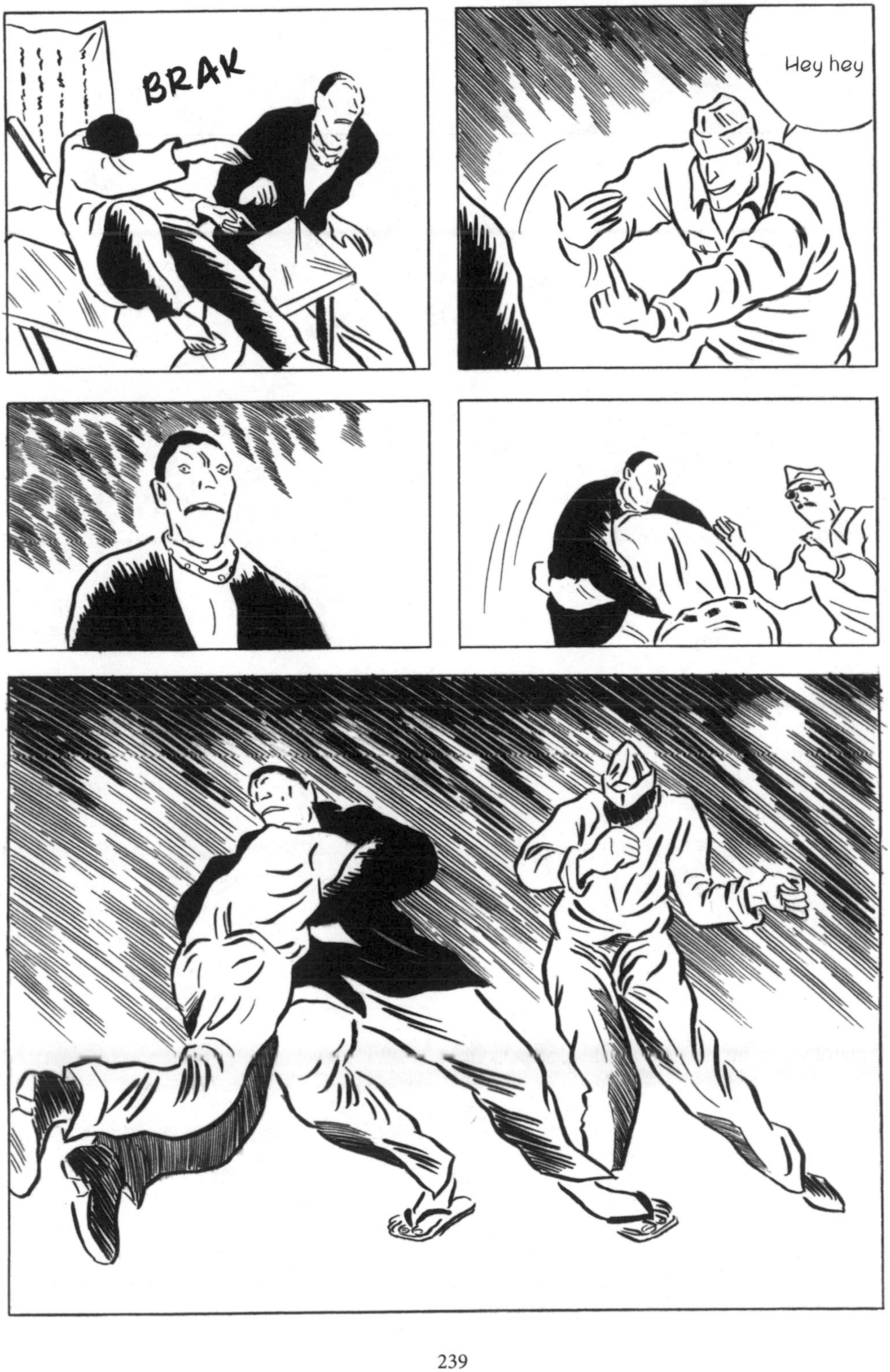
BRAK
Hey hey

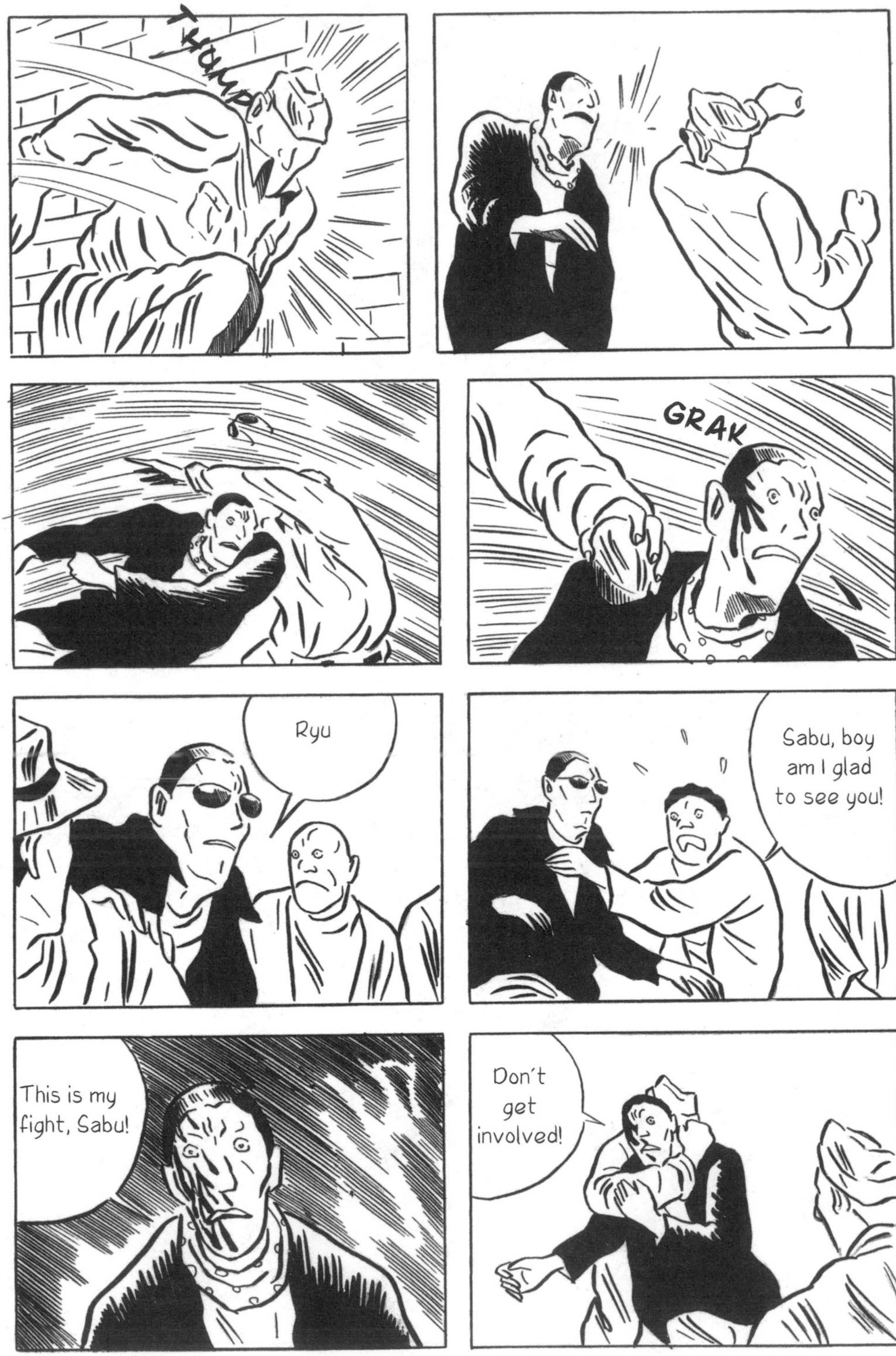
THUMP
GRAK
Ryu
Sabu, boy am I glad to see you!
This is my fight, Sabu!
Don't get involved!

owww

Kyu!

Don't...

Stay where you are.

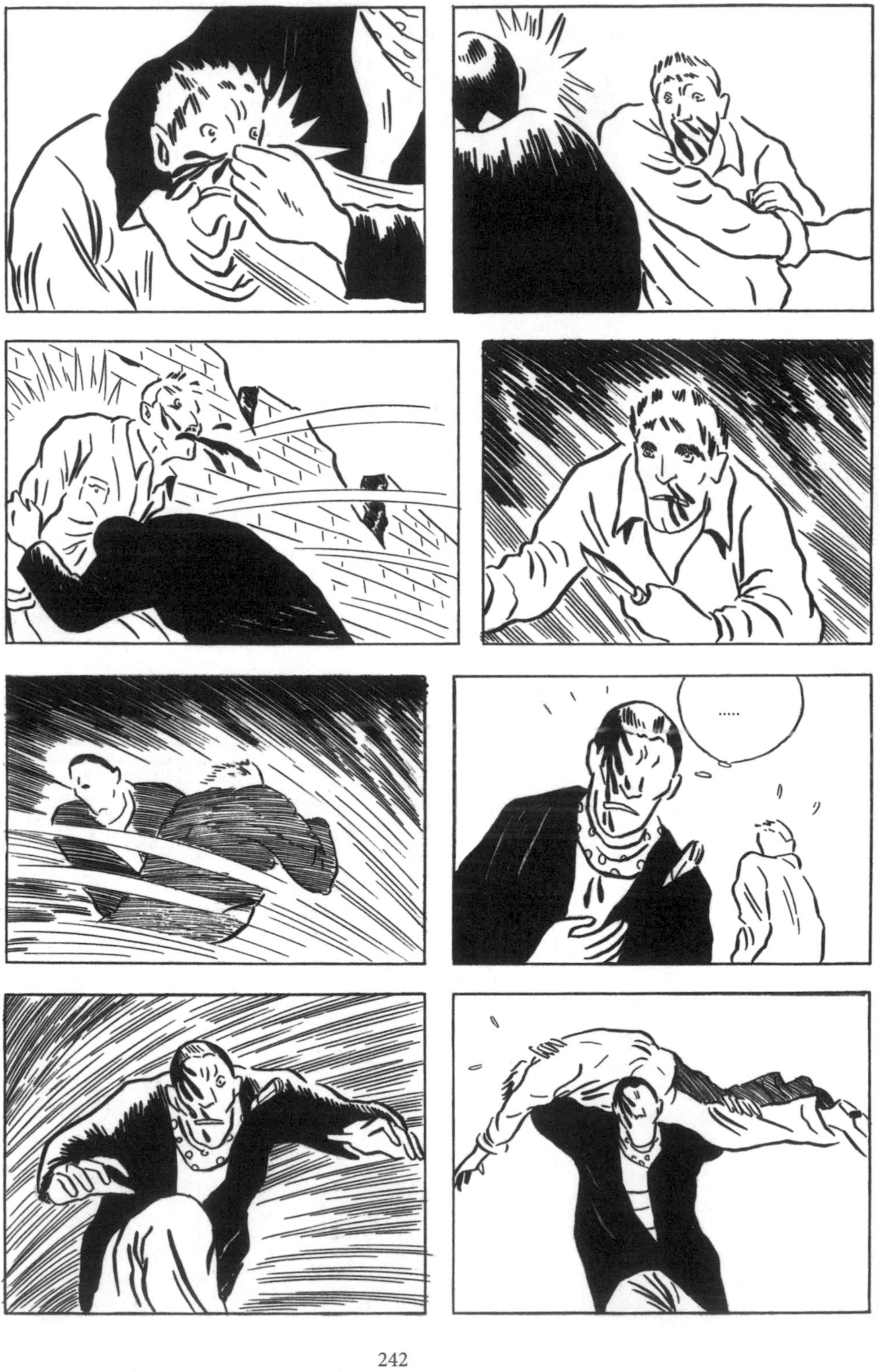
.....

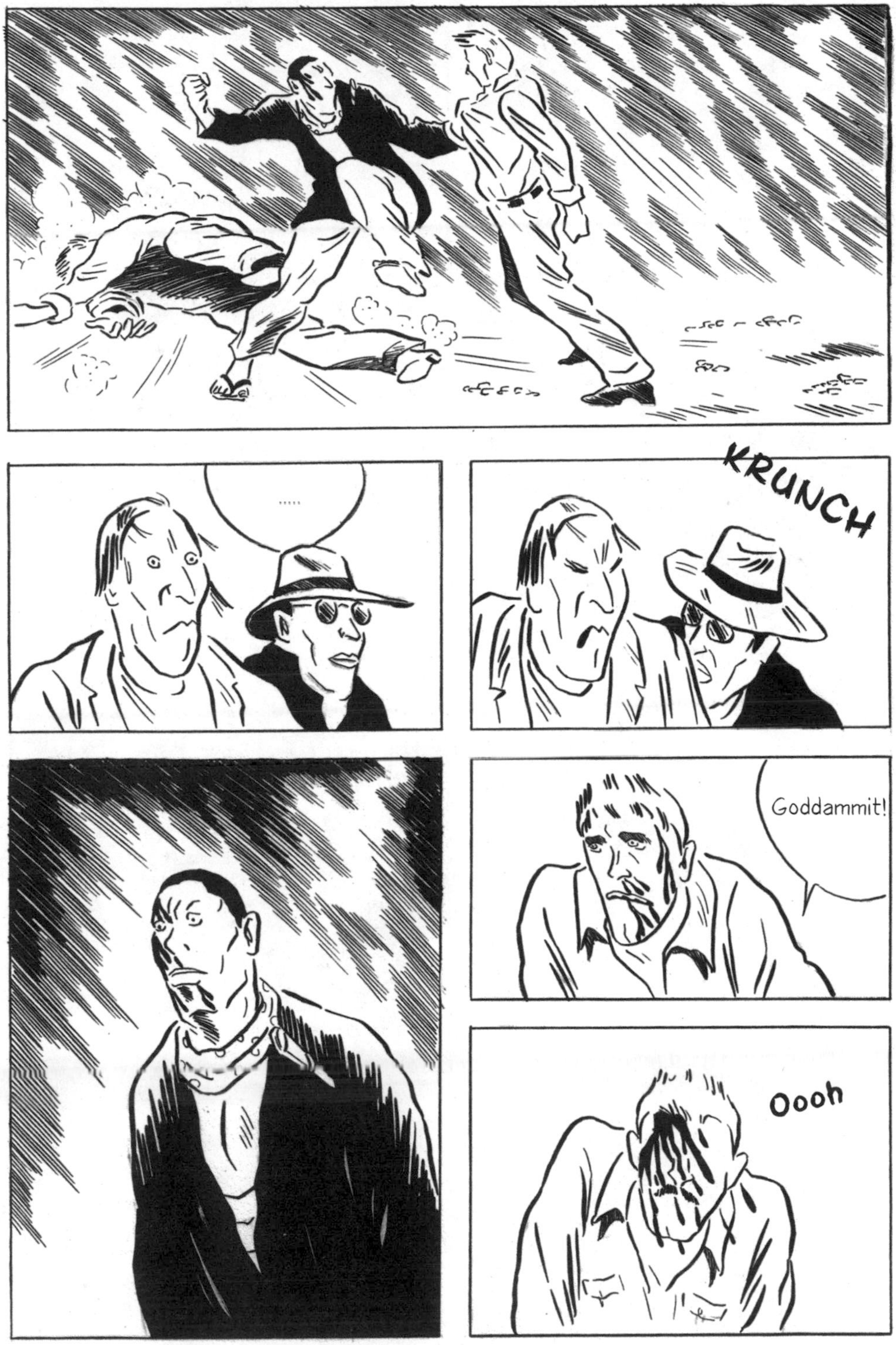
.....
KRUNCH
Goddammit!
Oooh

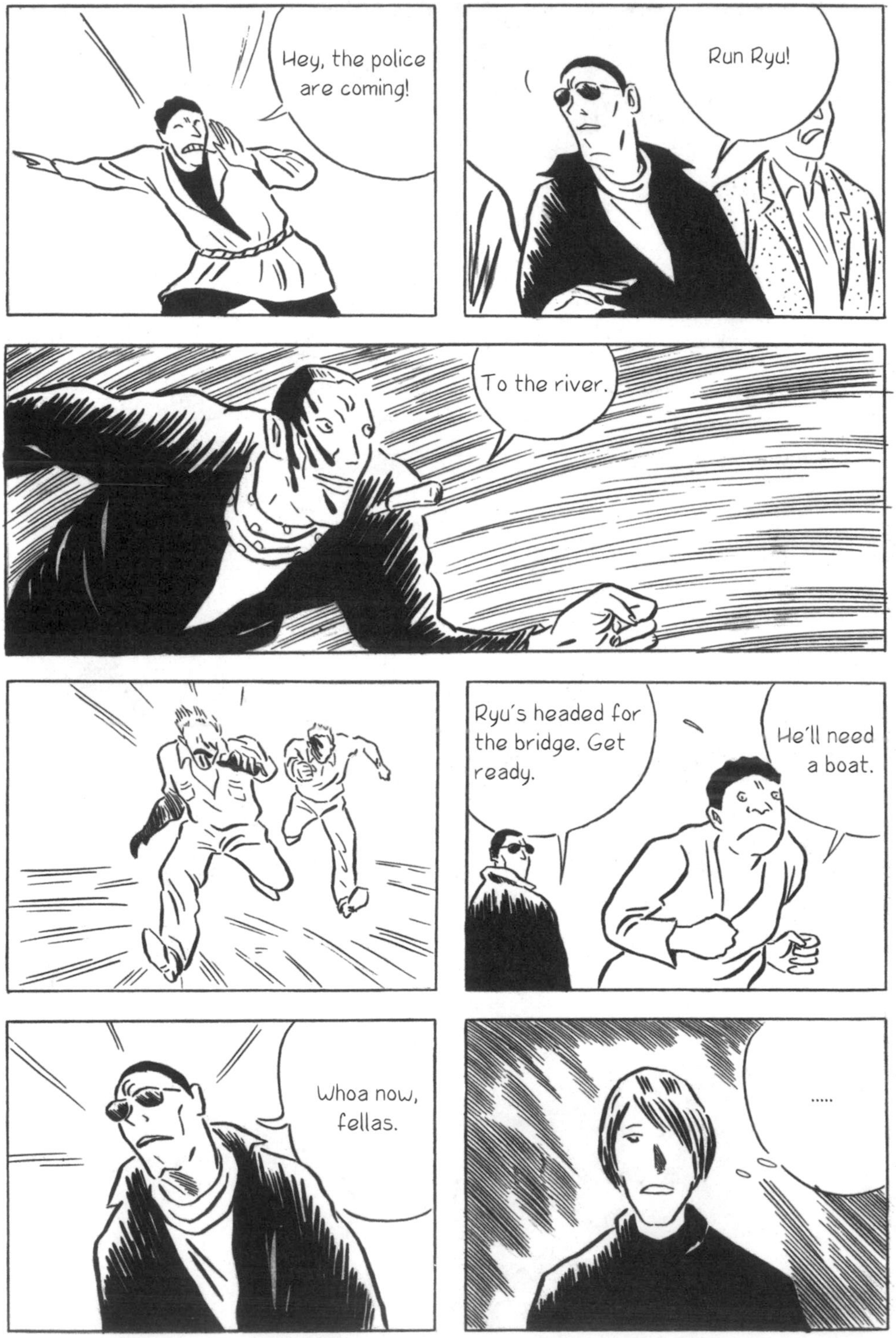
Hey, the police are coming!
Run Ryu!
To the river.
Ryu's headed for the bridge. Get ready.
He'll need a boat.
Whoa now, fellas.
.....

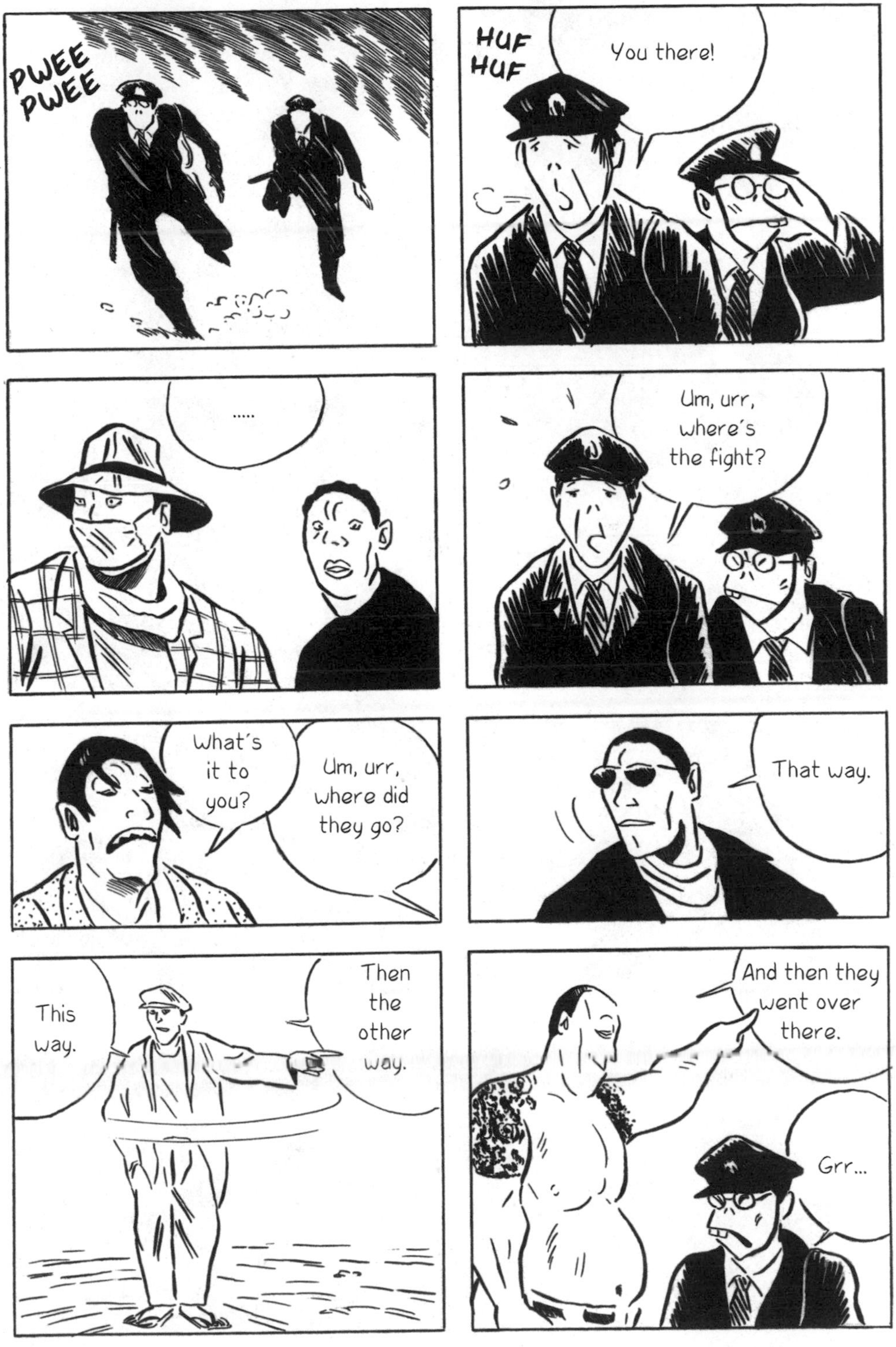
PWEE PWEE
HUF HUF
You there!
.....
Um, urr, where's the fight?
What's it to you?
Um, urr, where did they go?
That way.
This way.
Then the other way.
And then they went over there.
Grr...

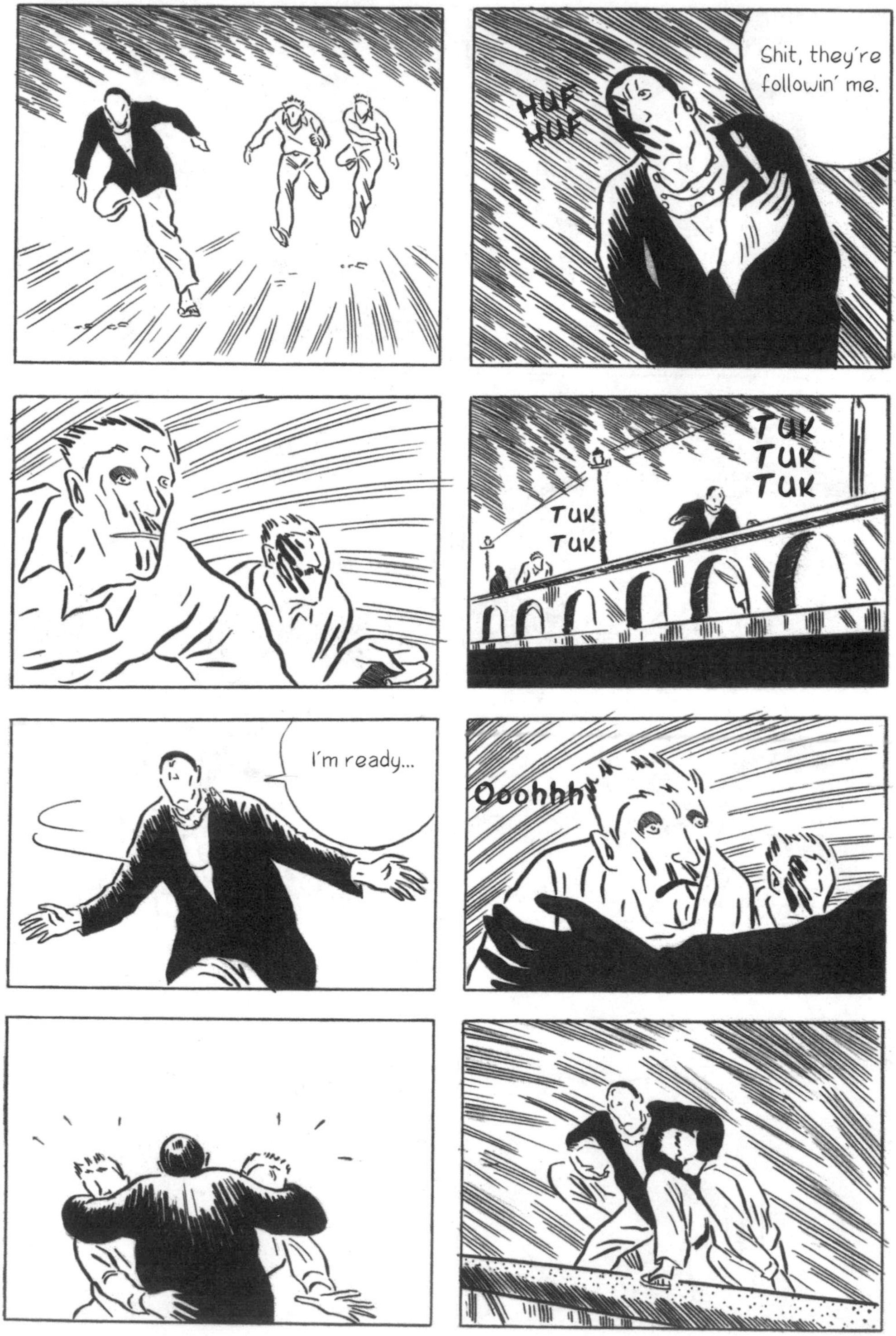
HUF
HUF
Shit, they're followin' me.
TUK
TUK
TUK
TUK
TUK
I'm ready...
Ooohhh!

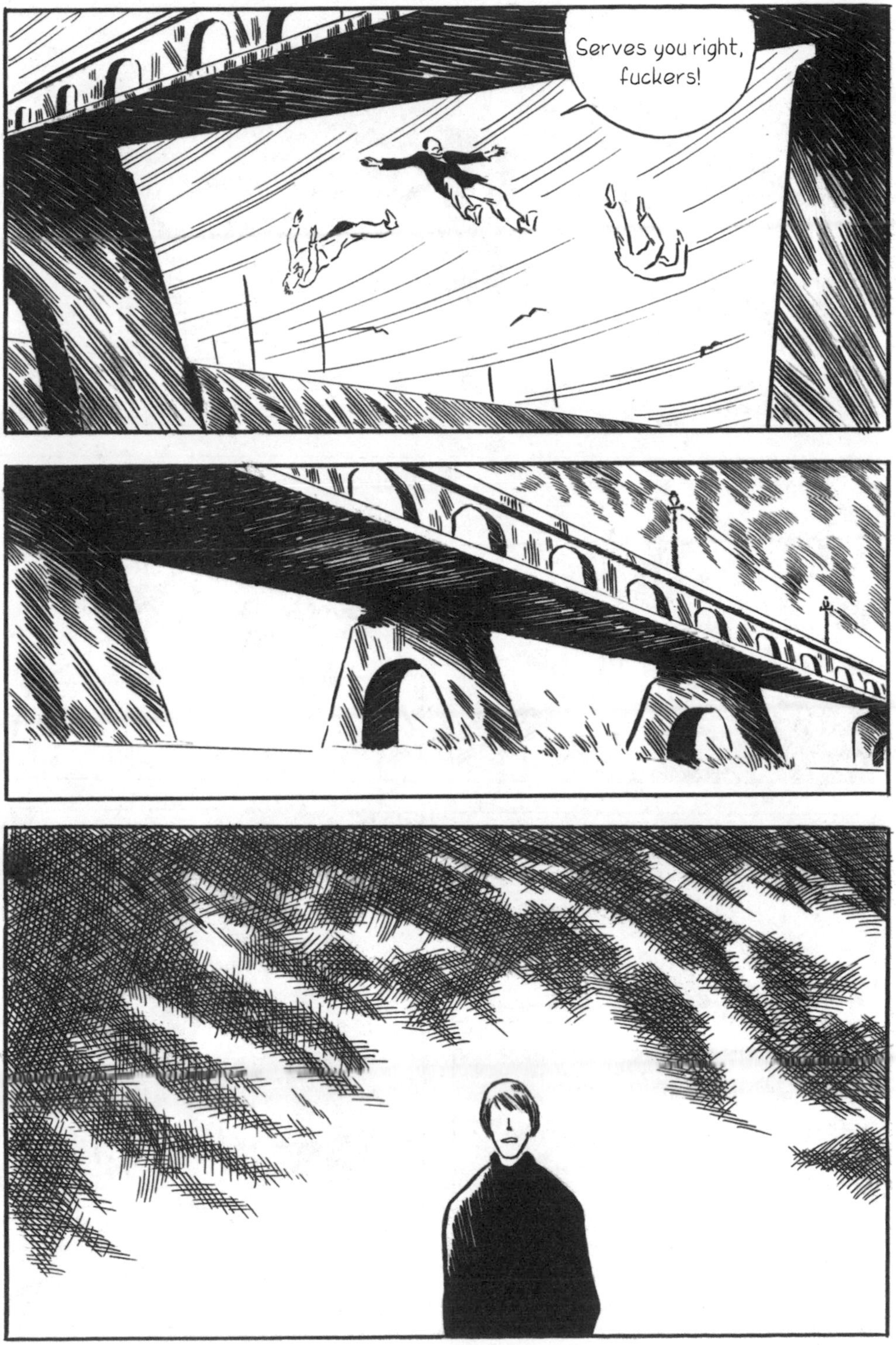
Serves you right, fuckers!

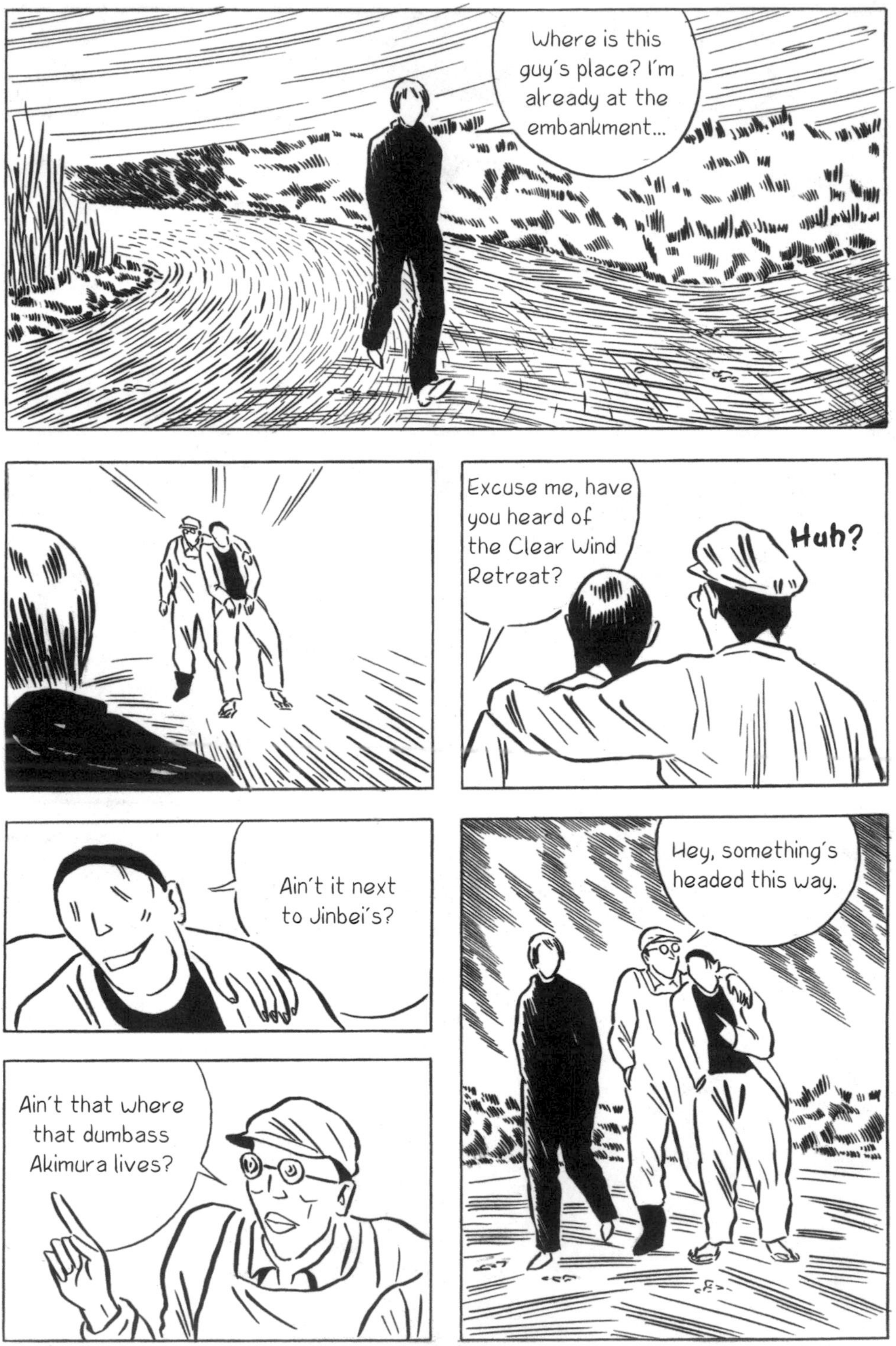
Where is this guy's place? I'm already at the embankment...
Excuse me, have you heard of the Clear Wind Retreat?
Huh?
Ain't it next to Jinbei's?
Ain't that where that dumbass Akimura lives?
Hey, something's headed this way.

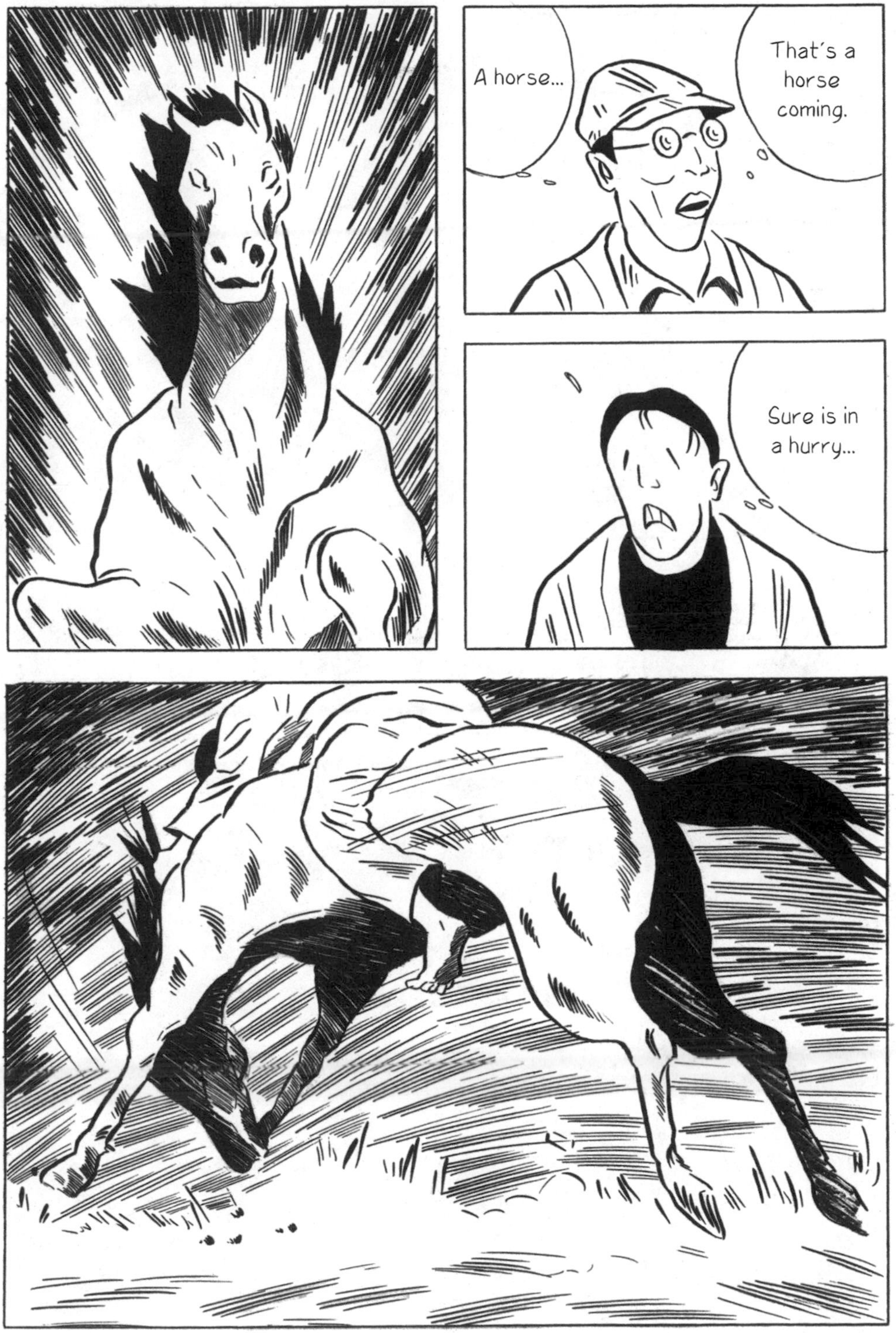
That's a horse coming.
A horse...
Sure is in a hurry...

Whaaa
Whaaa

HARUPH

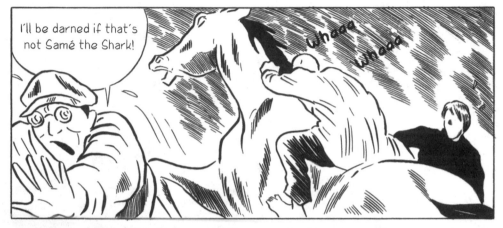

I'll be darned if that's not Samé the Shark!

Whaaa

Whaaa

The men here are mad, raving mad, every last one of them...

Whaaa

Whaaa

To be continued...

THE DEATH OF
RYOKICHI AOGISHI

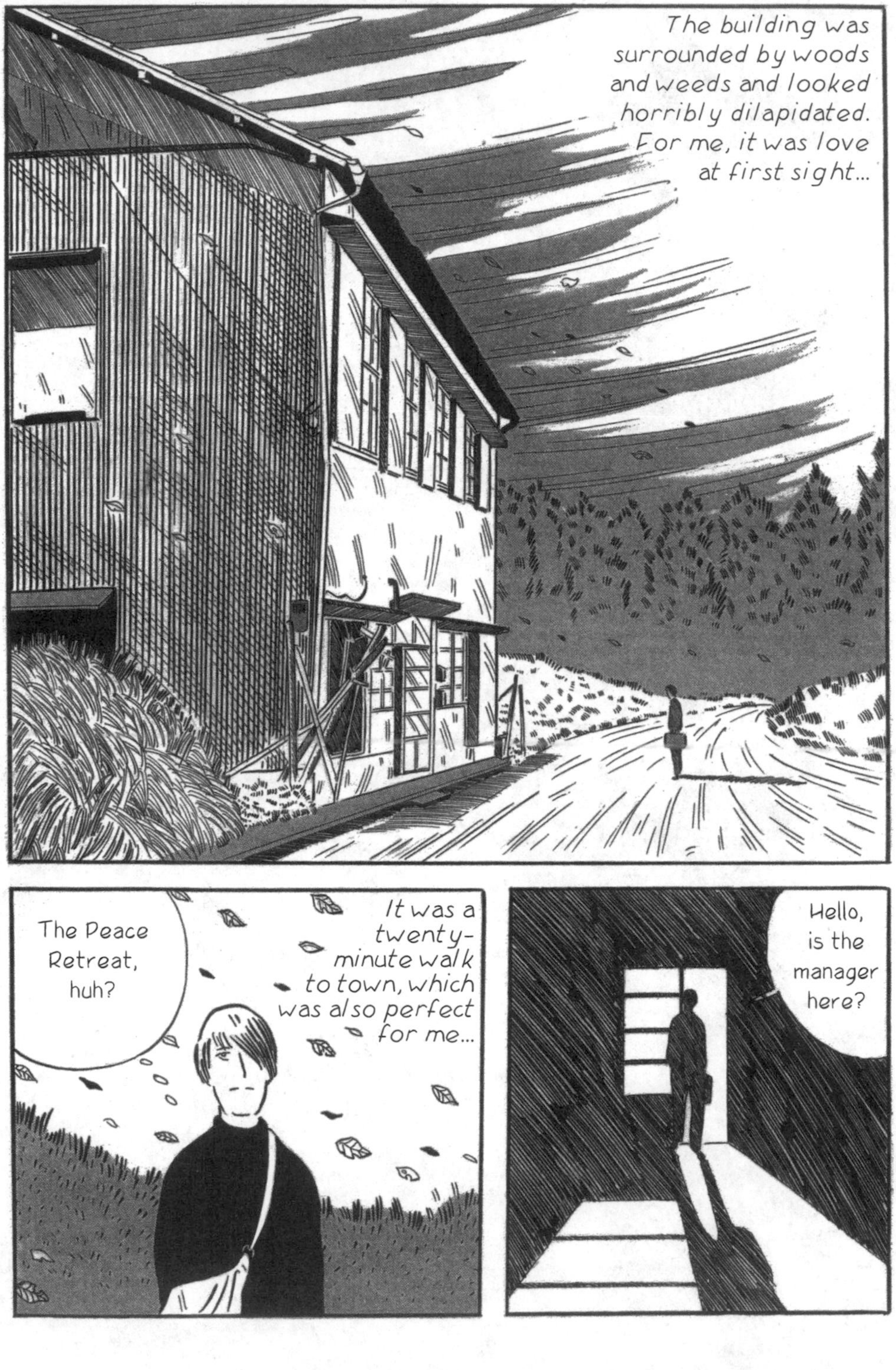
The building was surrounded by woods and weeds and looked horribly dilapidated. For me, it was love at first sight...
The Peace Retreat, huh?
It was a twenty-minute walk to town, which was also perfect for me...
Hello, is the manager here?

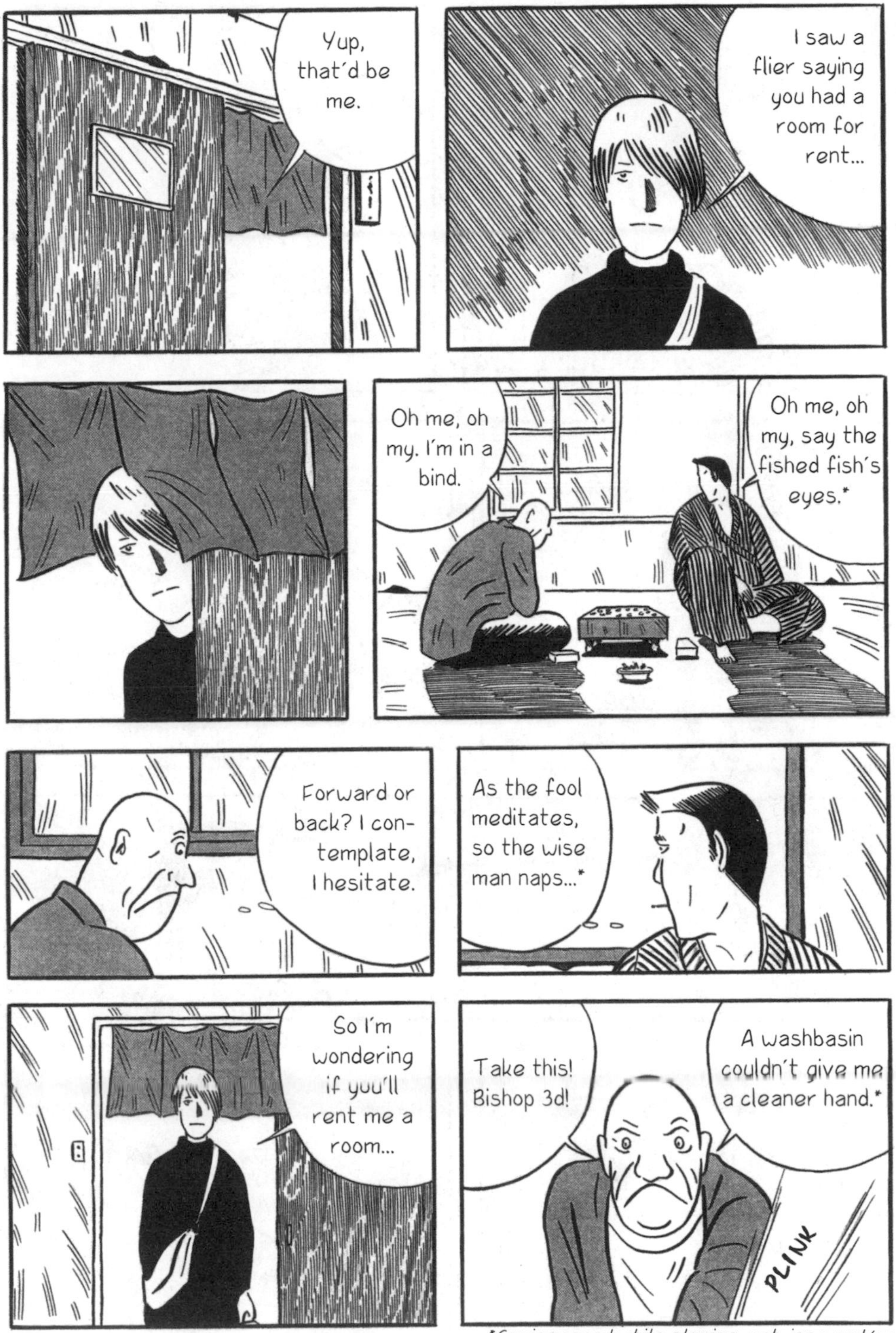
Yup, that'd be me.
I saw a flier saying you had a room for rent...
Oh me, oh my. I'm in a bind.
Oh me, oh my, say the fished fish's eyes.*
Forward or back? I contemplate, I hesitate.
As the fool meditates, so the wise man naps...*
So I'm wondering if you'll rent me a room...
Take this! Bishop 3d!
A washbasin couldn't give me a cleaner hand.*
PLINK

*Sayings used while playing mah jong and (as here) shogi, Japanese chess.

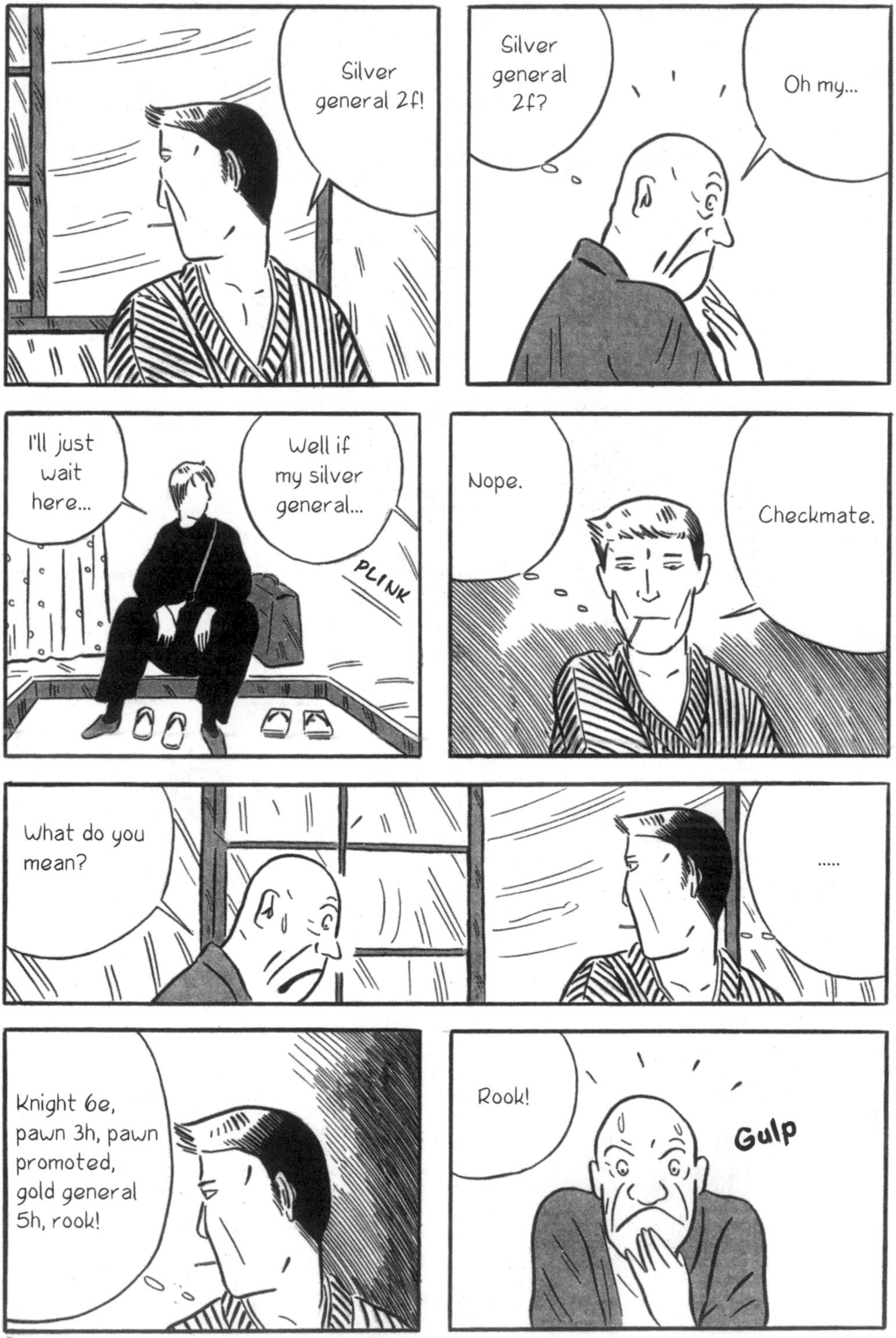
Silver general 2f!
Silver general 2f?
Oh my...
I'll just wait here...
Well if my silver general...
PLINK
Nope.
Checkmate.
What do you mean?
.....
Knight 6e, pawn 3h, pawn promoted, gold general 5h, rook!
Rook!
Gulp

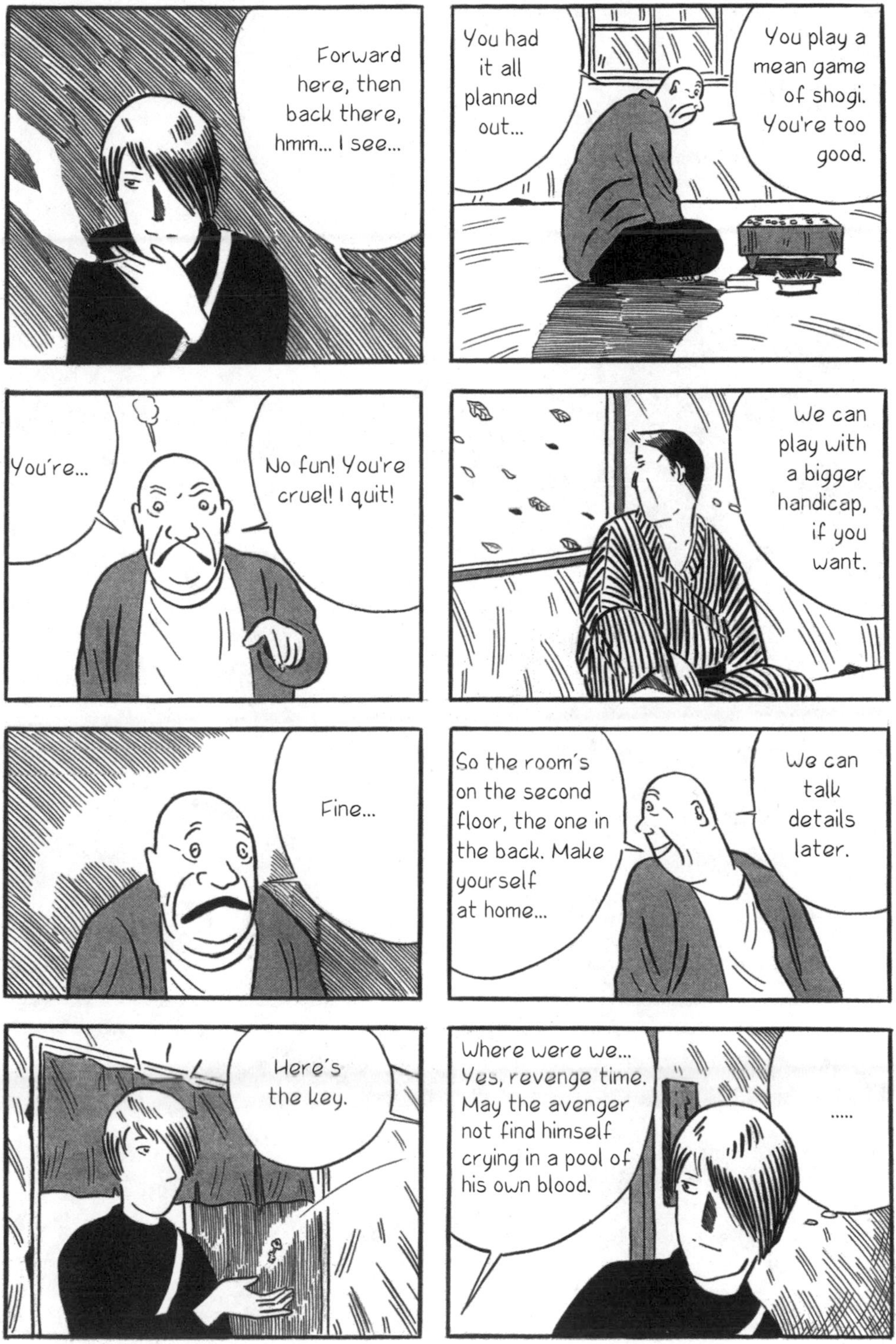
Forward here, then back there, hmm... I see...
You had it all planned out...
You play a mean game of shogi. You're too good.
You're...
No fun! You're cruel! I quit!
We can play with a bigger handicap, if you want.
Fine...
So the room's on the second floor, the one in the back. Make yourself at home...
We can talk details later.
Here's the key.
Where were we... Yes, revenge time. May the avenger not find himself crying in a pool of his own blood.
.....

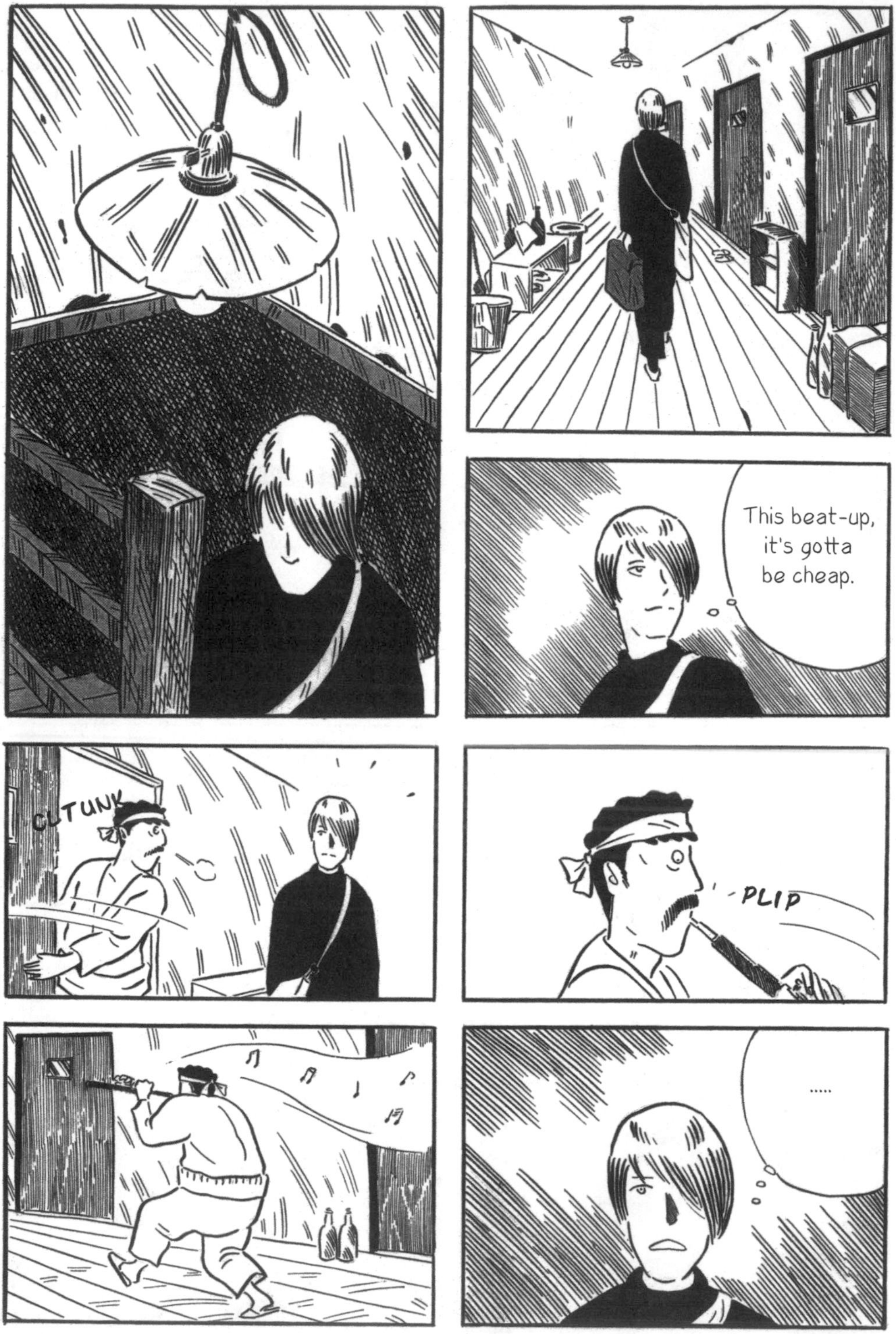
This beat-up, it's gotta be cheap.
CLTUNK
PLIP
.....

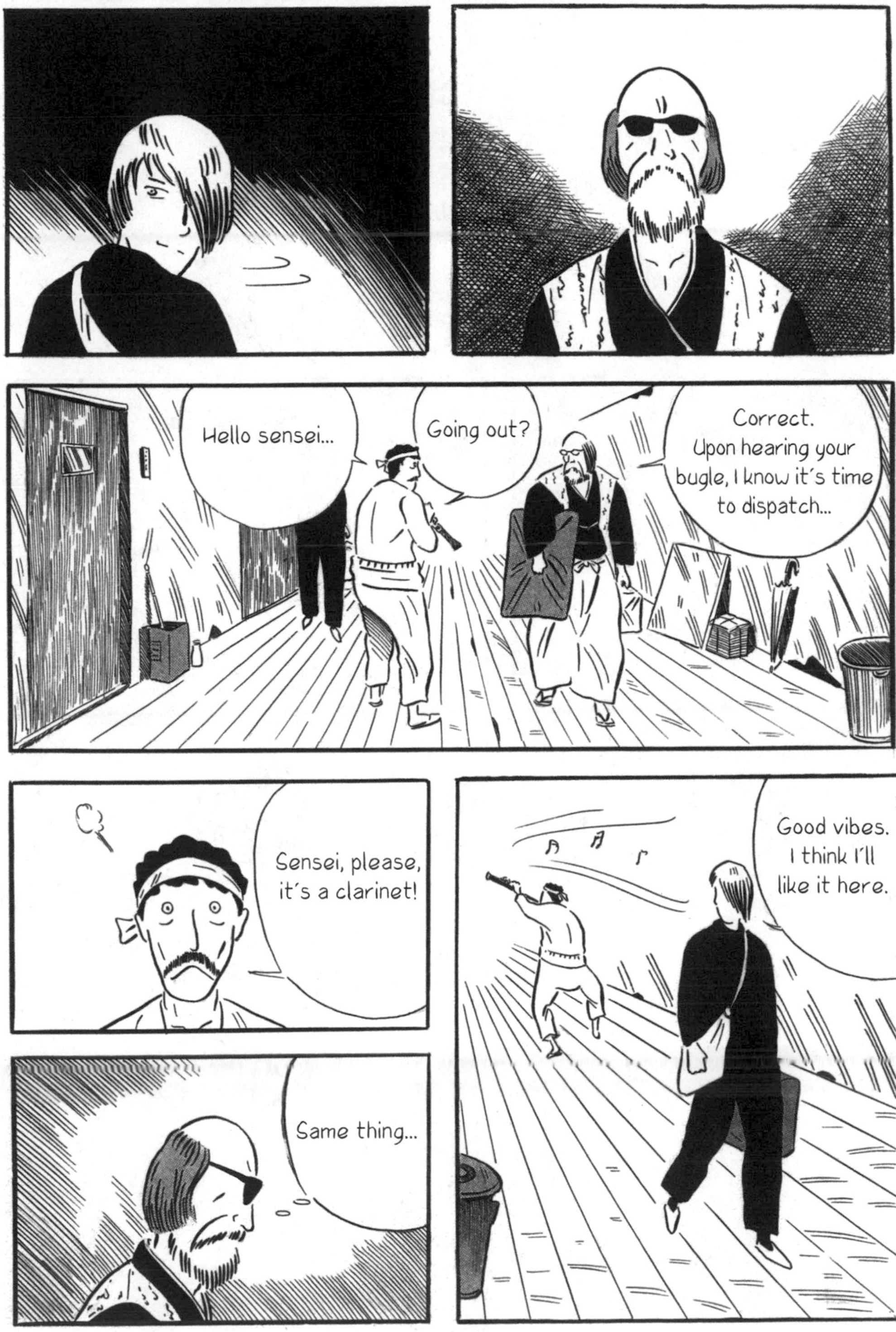
Hello sensei...
Going out?
Correct. Upon hearing your bugle, I know it's time to dispatch...
Sensei, please, it's a clarinet!
Same thing...
Good vibes. I think I'll like it here.

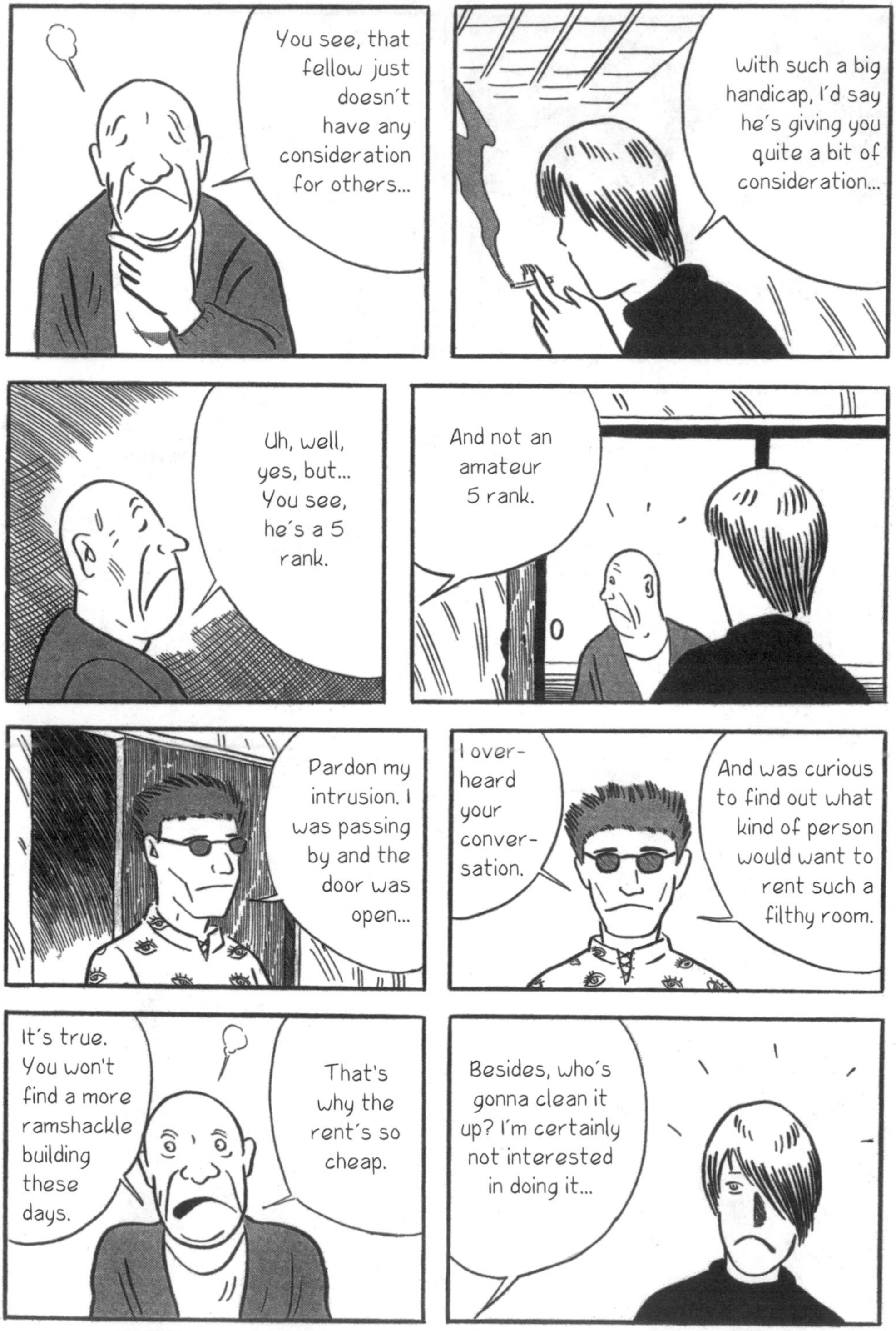

You see, that fellow just doesn't have any consideration for others...
With such a big handicap, I'd say he's giving you quite a bit of consideration...
Uh, well, yes, but... You see, he's a 5 rank.
And not an amateur 5 rank.
Pardon my intrusion. I was passing by and the door was open...
I overheard your conversation.
And was curious to find out what kind of person would want to rent such a filthy room.
It's true. You won't find a more ramshackle building these days.
That's why the rent's so cheap.
Besides, who's gonna clean it up? I'm certainly not interested in doing it...

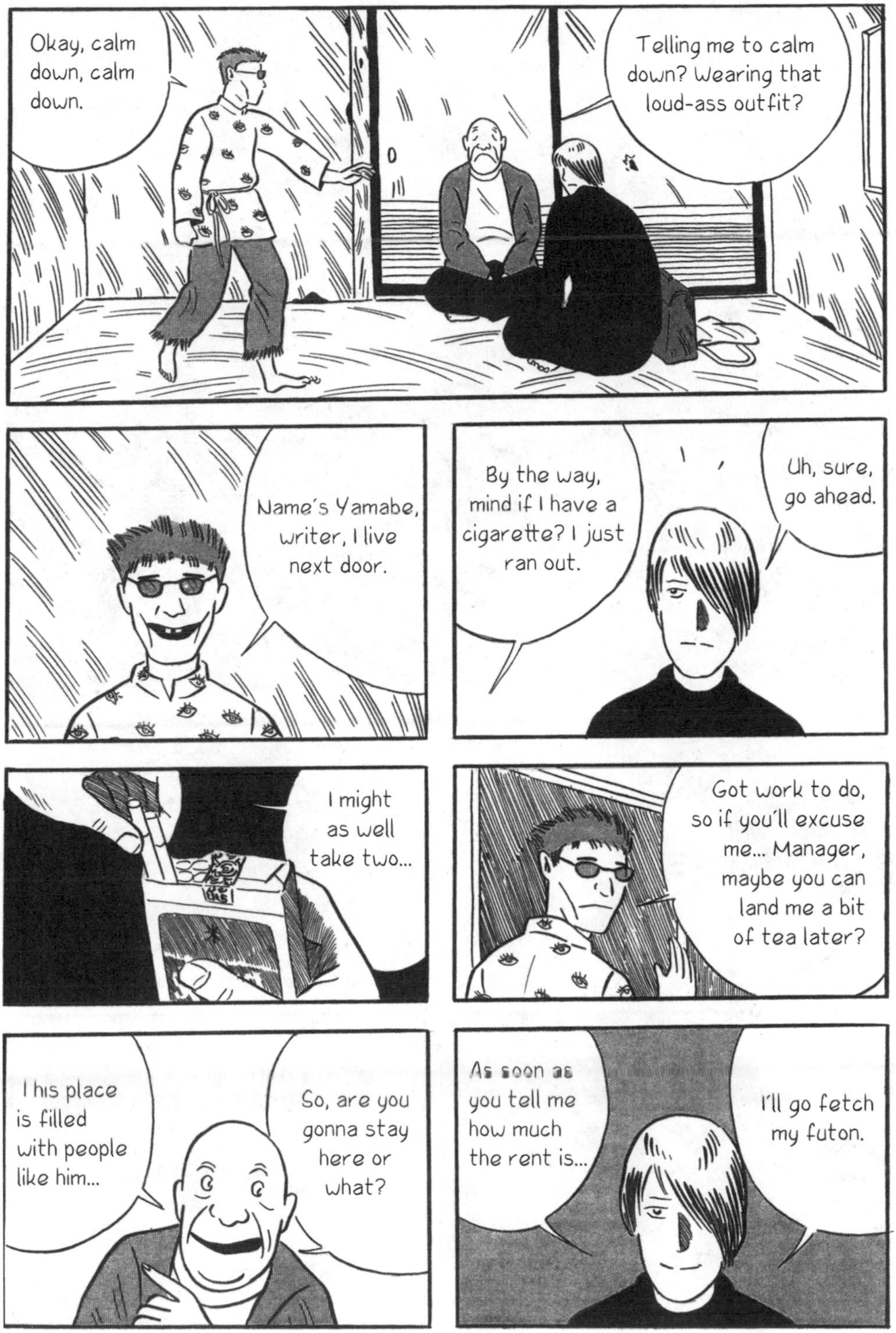
Okay, calm down, calm down.
Telling me to calm down? Wearing that loud-ass outfit?
Name's Yamabe, writer, I live next door.
By the way, mind if I have a cigarette? I just ran out.
Uh, sure, go ahead.
I might as well take two...
Got work to do, so if you'll excuse me... Manager, maybe you can land me a bit of tea later?
This place is filled with people like him...
So, are you gonna stay here or what?
As soon as you tell me how much the rent is...
I'll go fetch my futon.

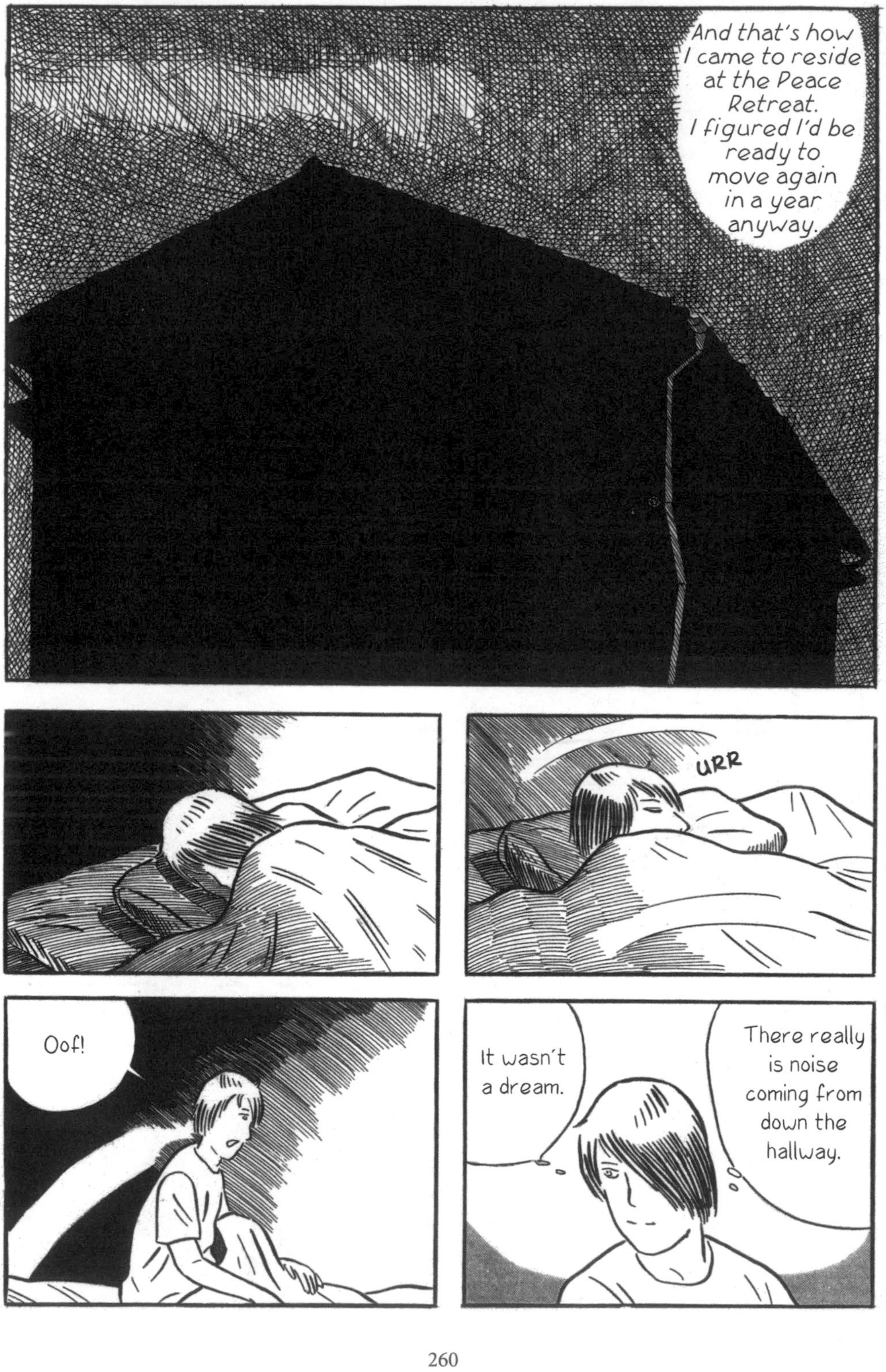
And that's how I came to reside at the Peace Retreat. I figured I'd be ready to move again in a year anyway.
URR
Oof!
It wasn't a dream.
There really is noise coming from down the hallway.

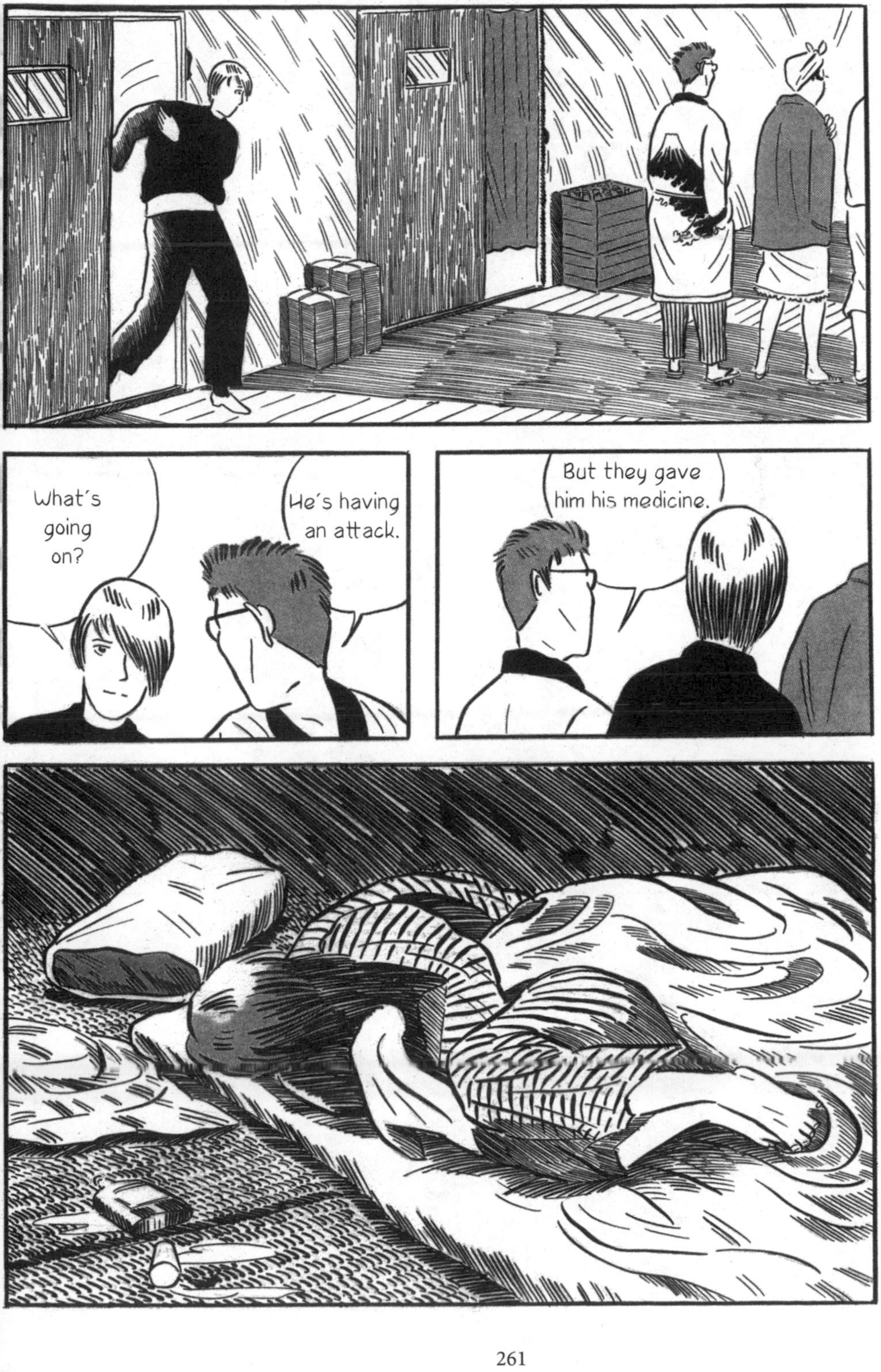
What's going on?
He's having an attack.
But they gave him his medicine.

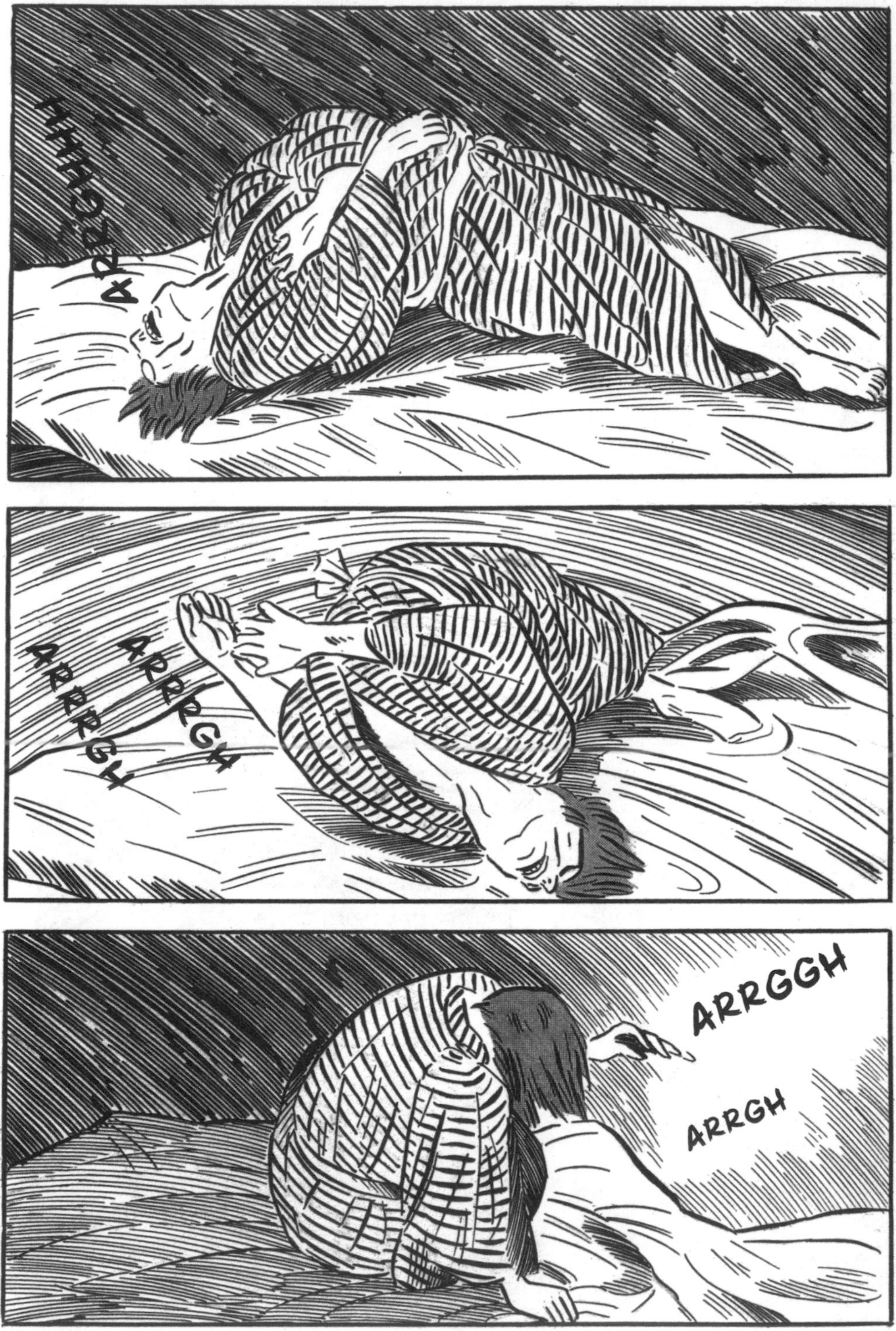
ARRGHHHH
ARRRGH
ARRRGH
ARRGGH
ARRGH

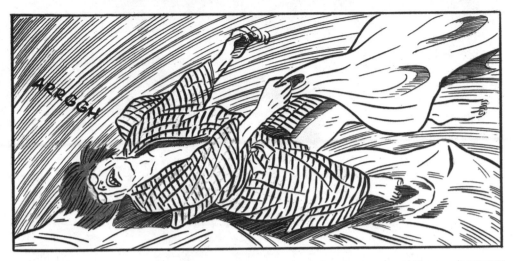

Dear, can't you do something? It's giving me the creeps.

No

You're always bragging about how you know everything.

Be quiet...

Isn't anyone going to call a doctor?

His attacks are getting worse. Next time he's going to need a priest, not a doctor.

N-n-no d-doctor...

URGGH

Looks like the medicine's finally working...

He'll be okay in a minute.

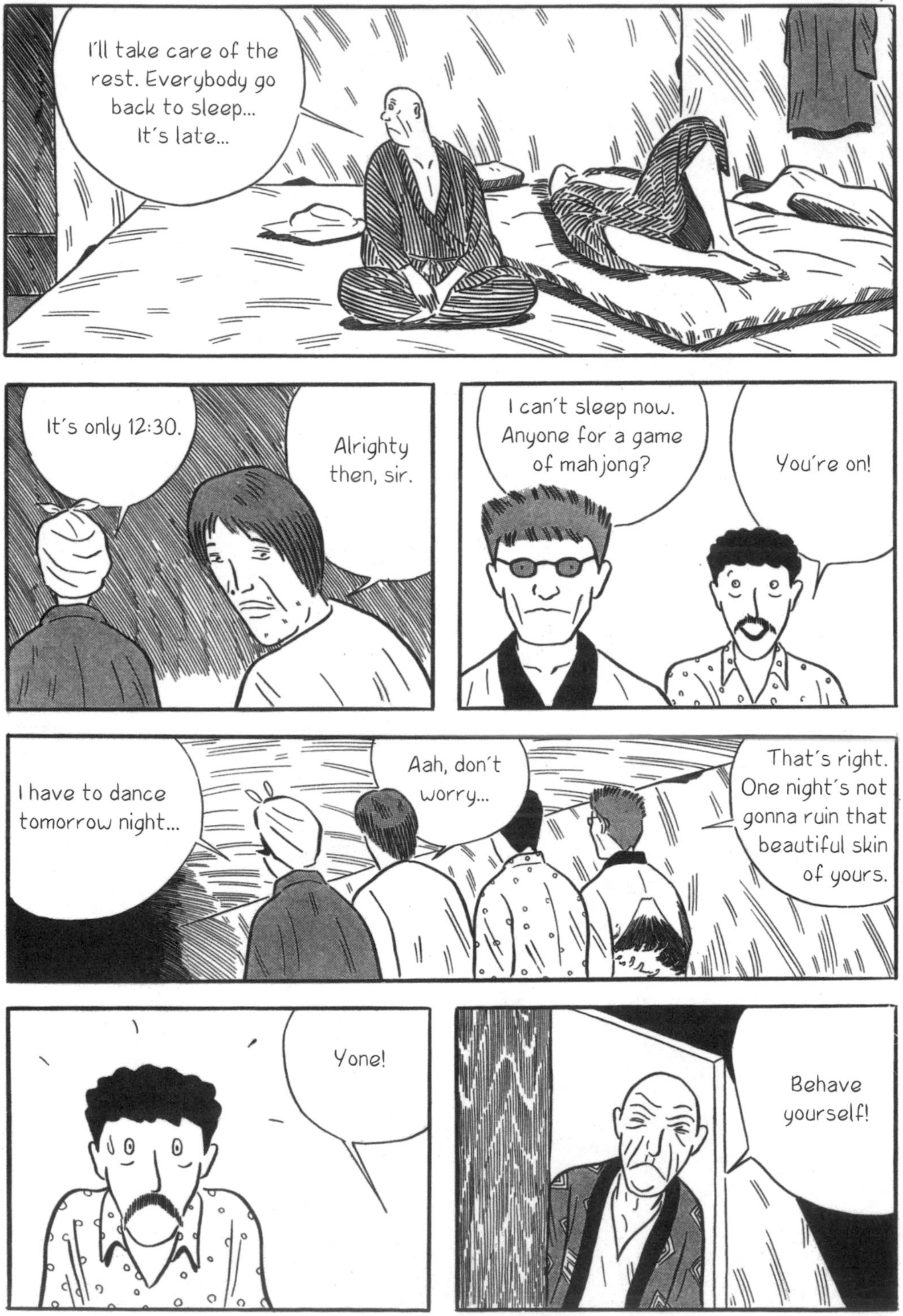
I'll take care of the rest. Everybody go back to sleep... It's late...
It's only 12:30.
Alrighty then, sir.
I can't sleep now. Anyone for a game of mahjong?
You're on!
I have to dance tomorrow night...
Aah, don't worry...
That's right. One night's not gonna ruin that beautiful skin of yours.
Yone!
Behave yourself!

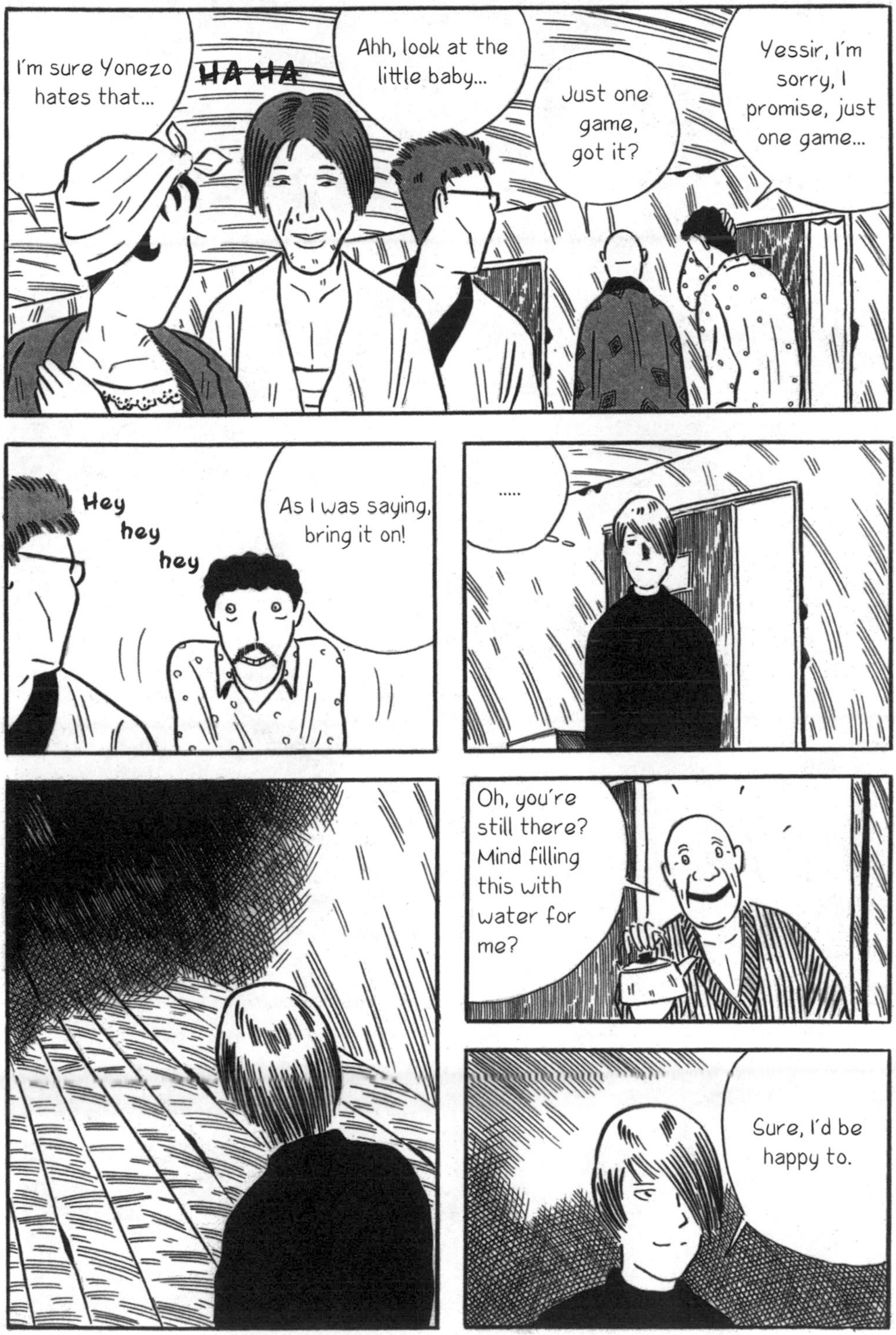
I'm sure Yonezo hates that...
HA HA
Ahh, look at the little baby...
Just one game, got it?
Yessir, I'm sorry, I promise, just one game...
Hey hey hey
As I was saying, bring it on!
.....
Oh, you're still there? Mind filling this with water for me?
Sure, I'd be happy to.

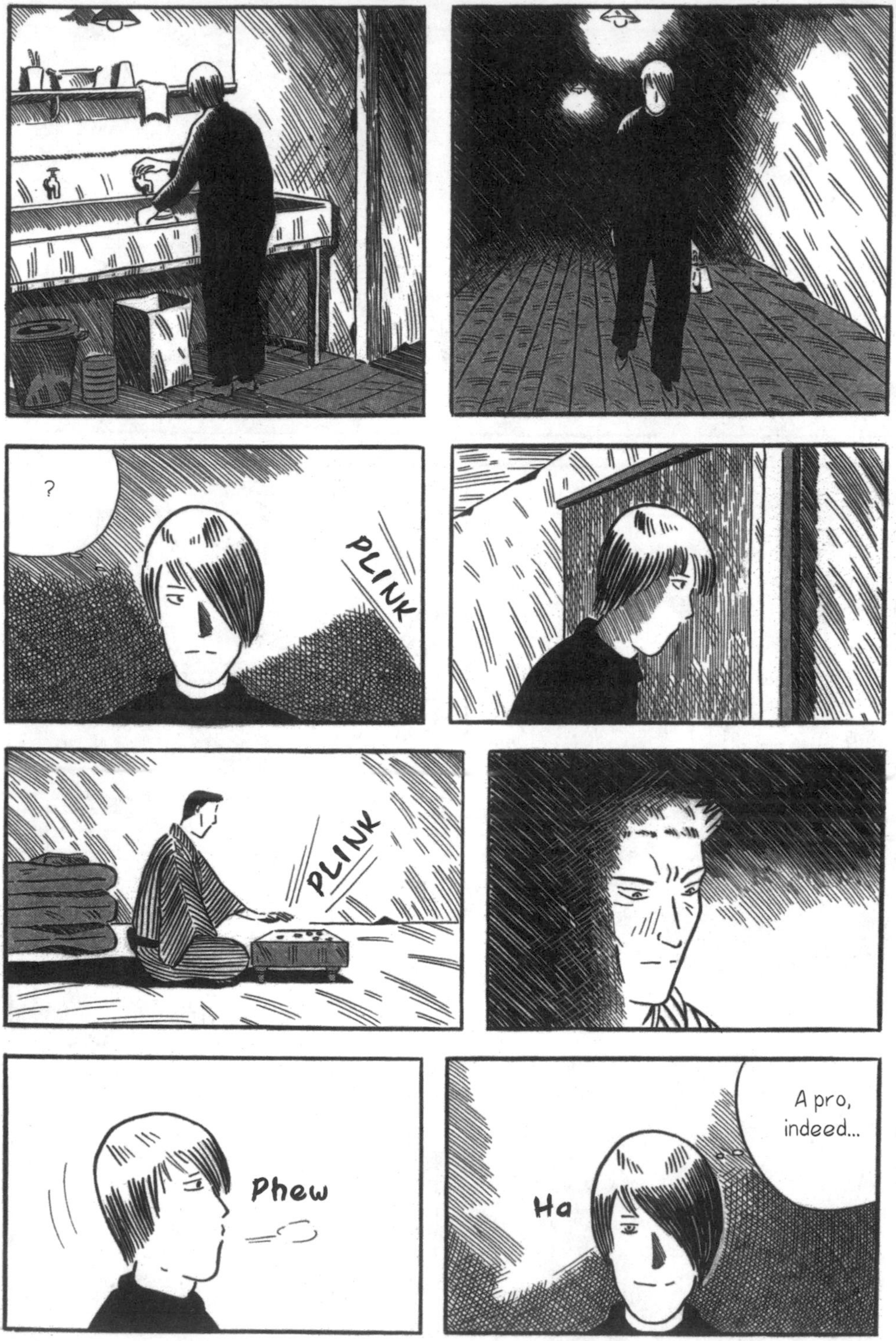
?
PLINK
PLINK
Phew
Ha
A pro, indeed...

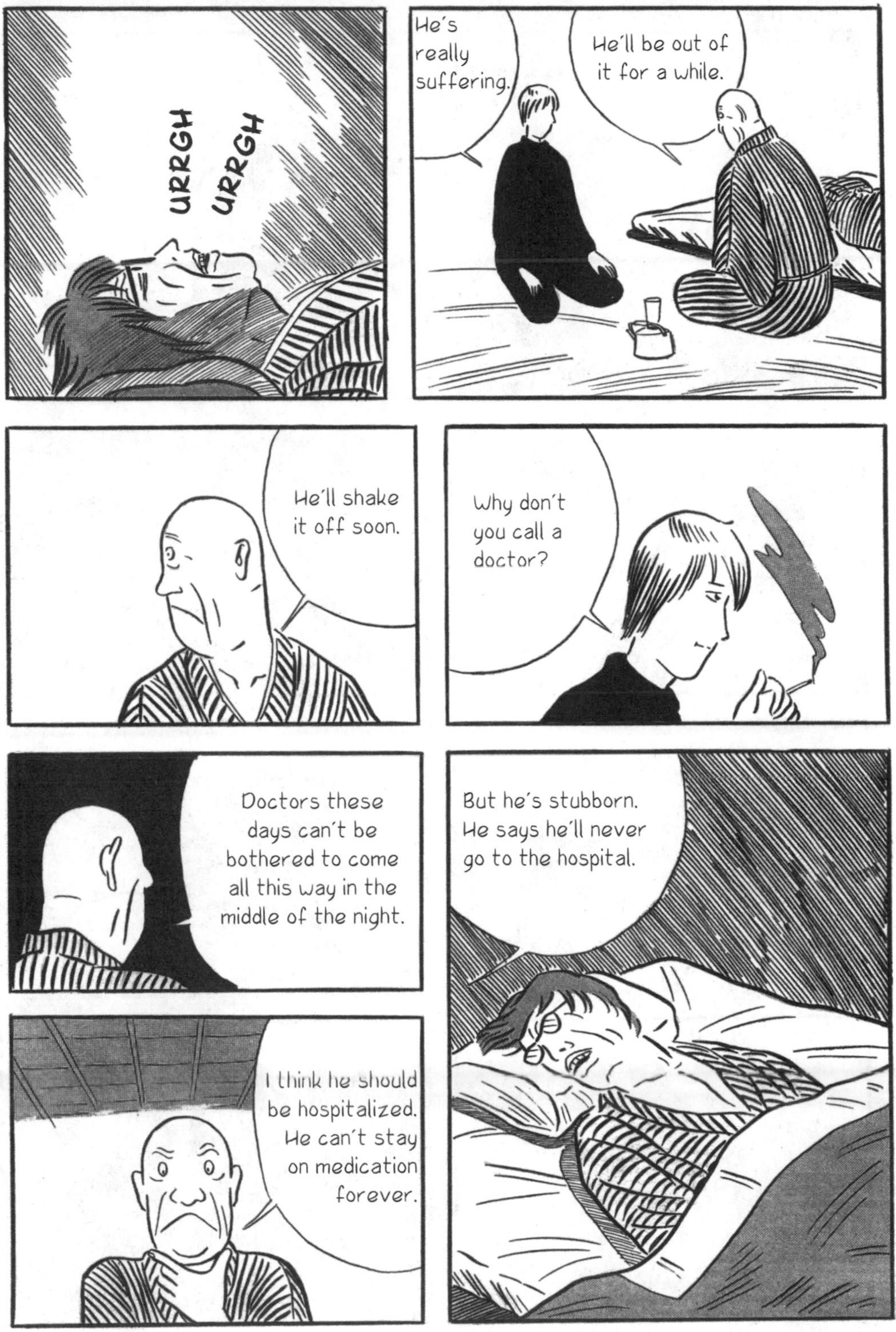
URRGH
URRGH
He's really suffering.
He'll be out of it for a while.
He'll shake it off soon.
Why don't you call a doctor?
Doctors these days can't be bothered to come all this way in the middle of the night.
I think he should be hospitalized. He can't stay on medication forever.
But he's stubborn. He says he'll never go to the hospital.

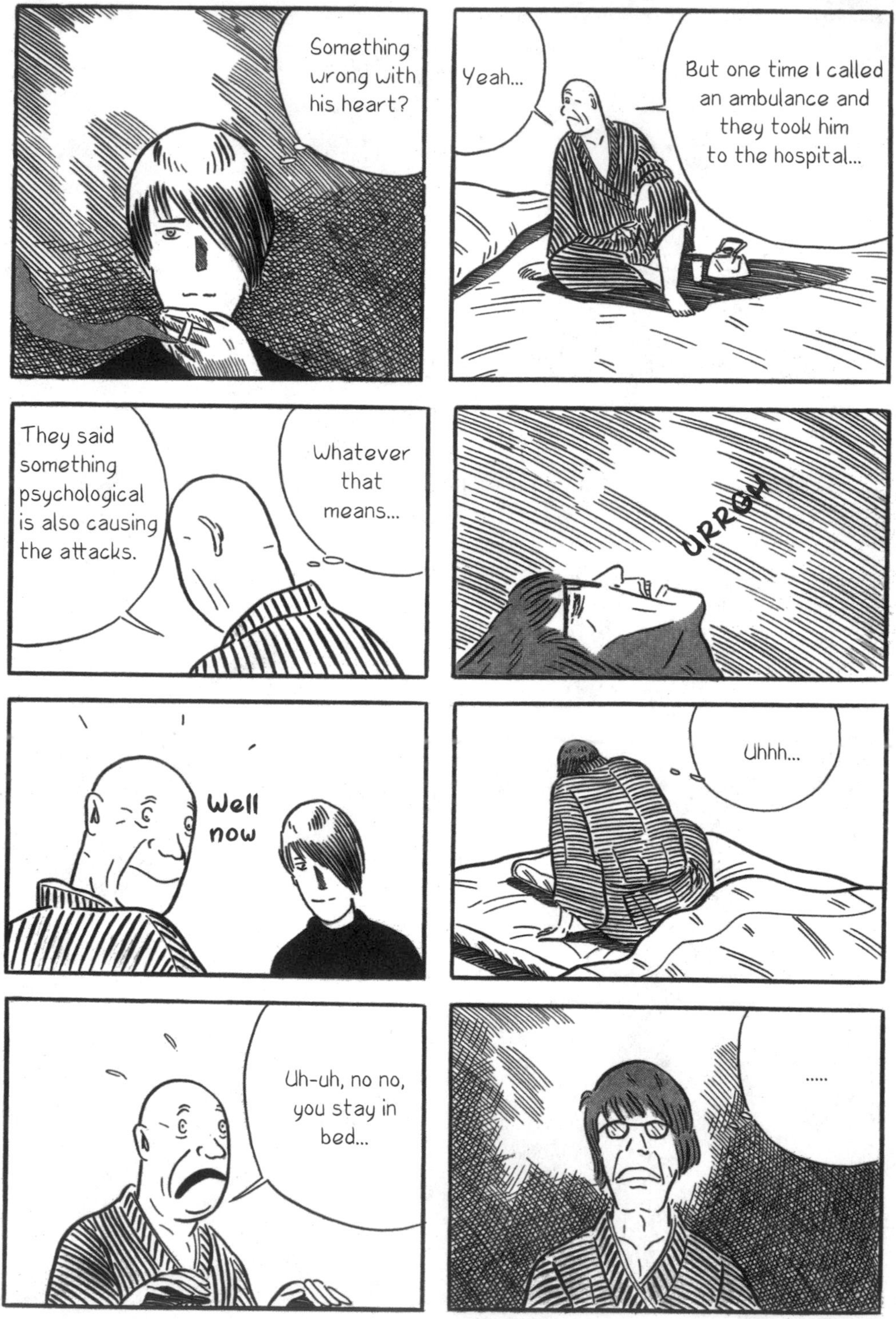
Something wrong with his heart?
Yeah...
But one time I called an ambulance and they took him to the hospital...
They said something psychological is also causing the attacks.
Whatever that means...
URRGH
Well now
Uhhh...
Uh-uh, no no, you stay in bed...
.....

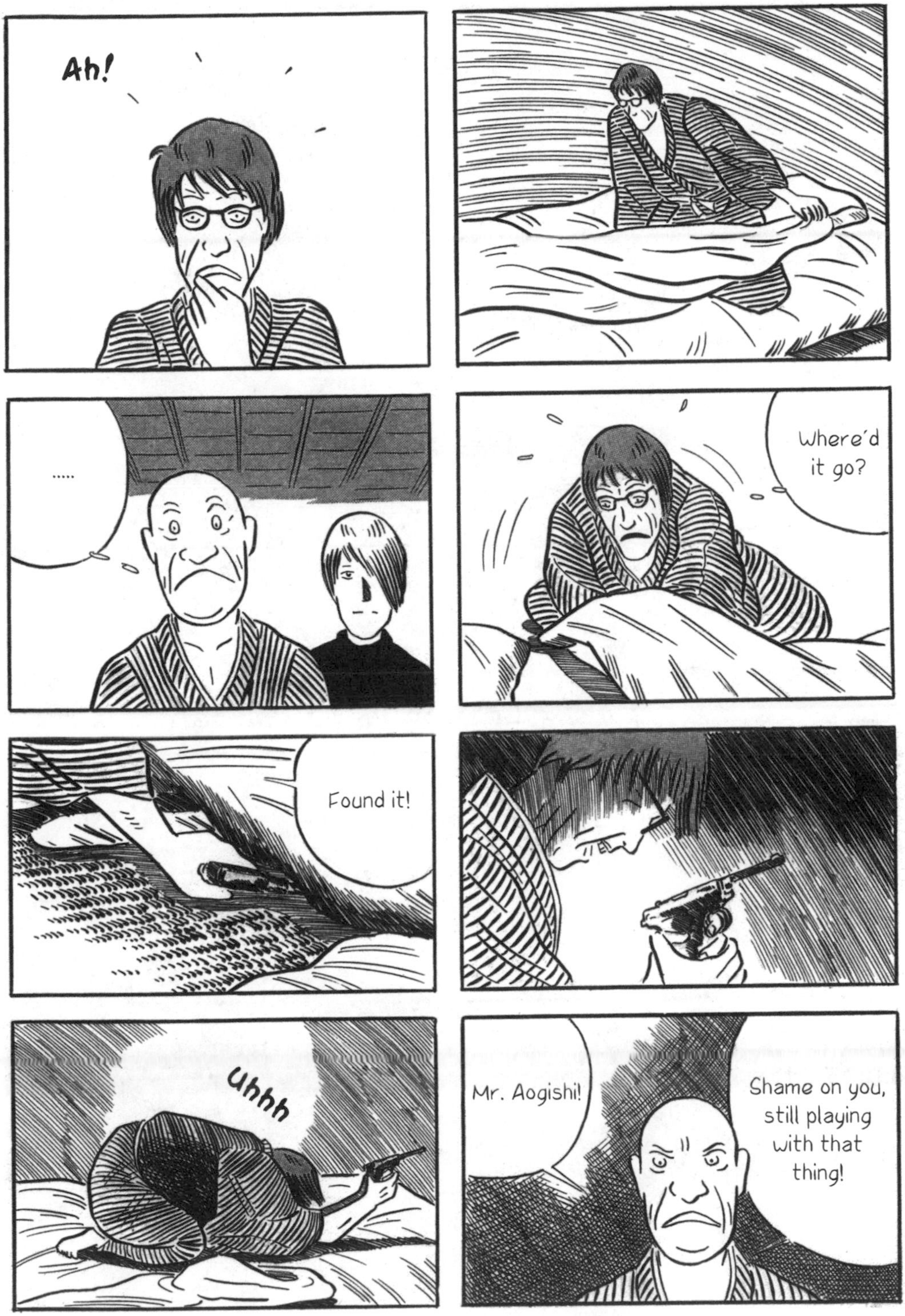
Ah!
.....
Where'd it go?
Found it!
Uhhh
Mr. Aogishi!
Shame on you, still playing with that thing!

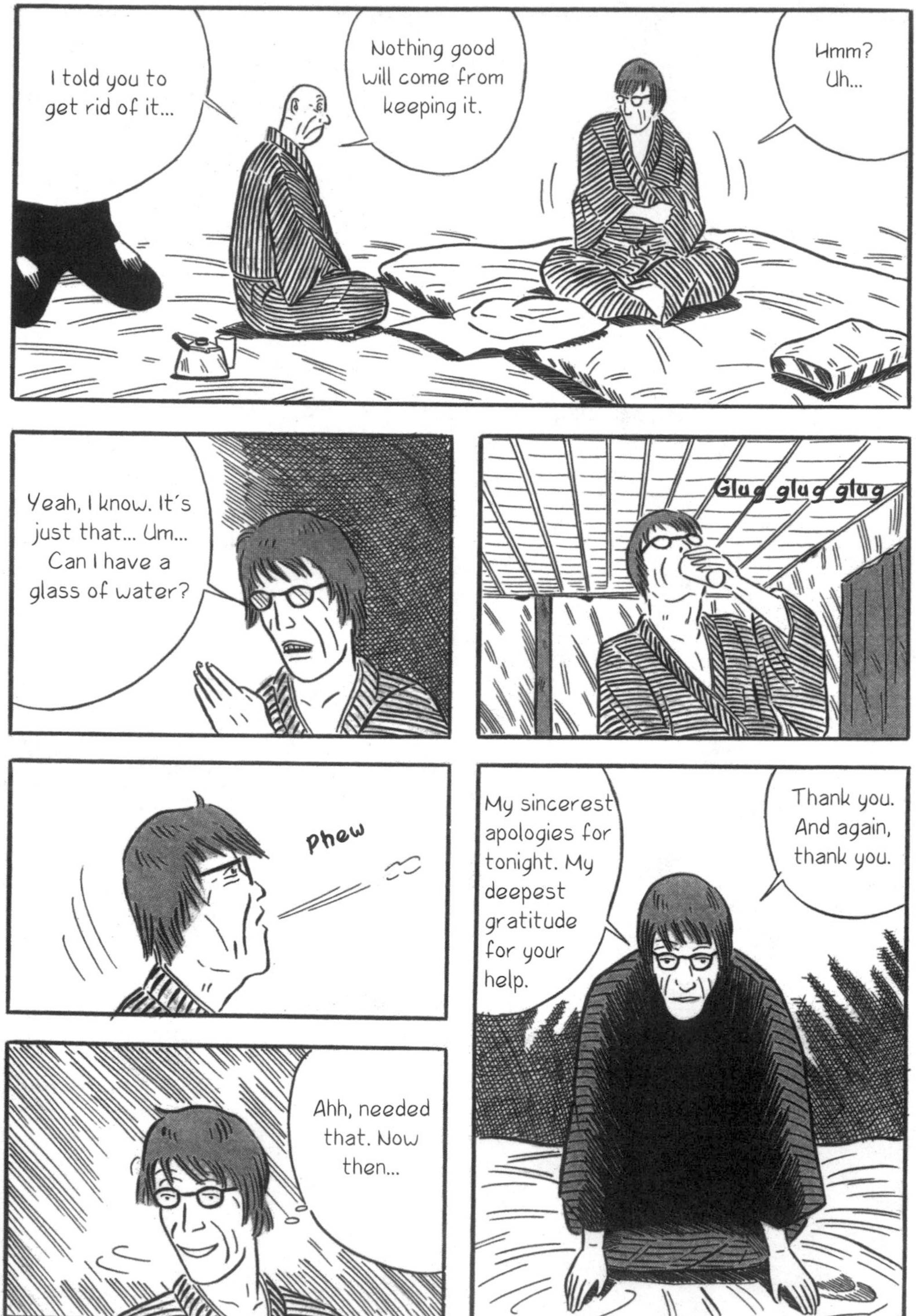
I told you to get rid of it...
Nothing good will come from keeping it.
Hmm? Uh...
Yeah, I know. It's just that... Um... Can I have a glass of water?
Glug glug glug
Phew
Ahh, needed that. Now then...
My sincerest apologies for tonight. My deepest gratitude for your help.
Thank you. And again, thank you.

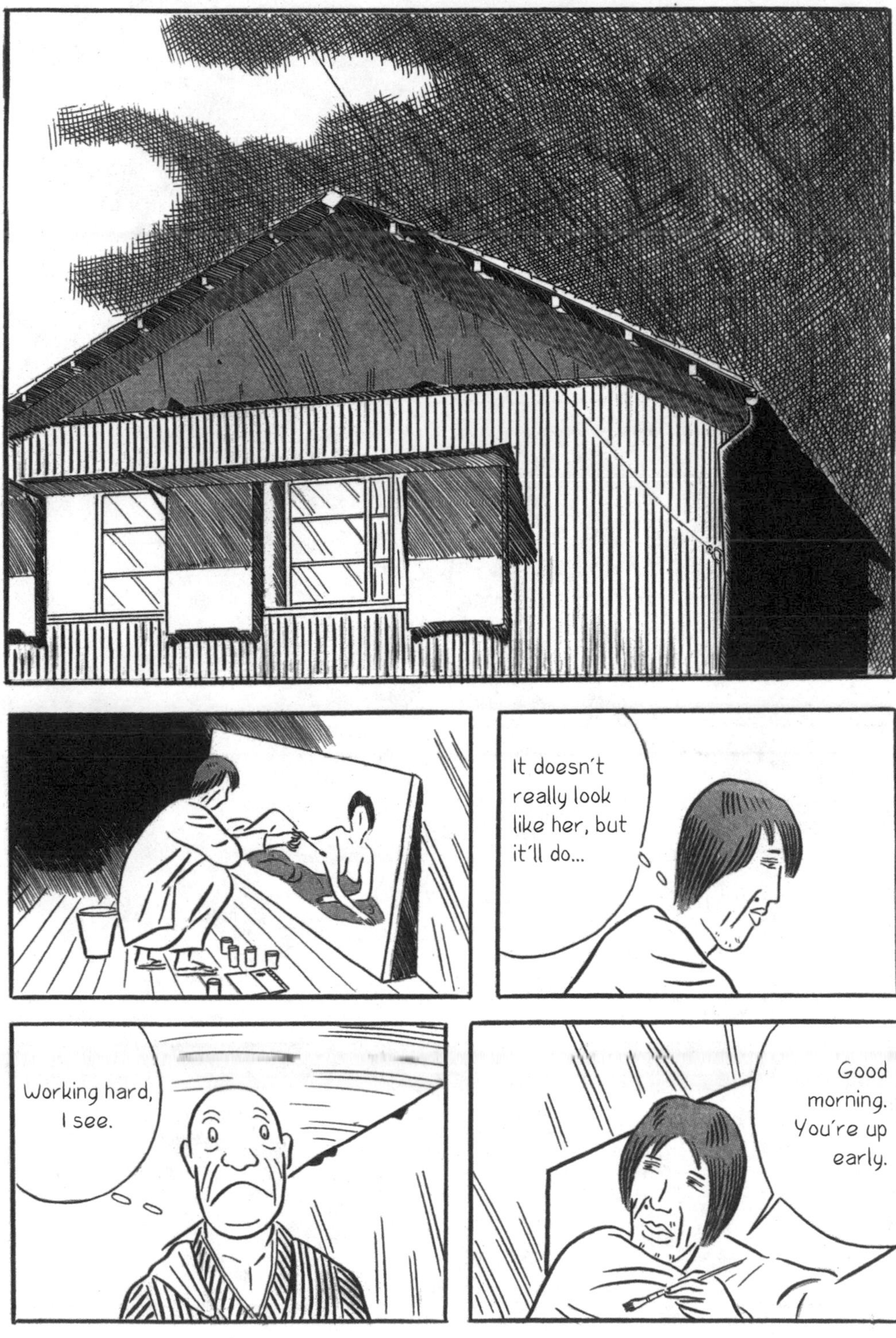
It doesn't really look like her, but it'll do...
Working hard, I see.
Good morning. You're up early.

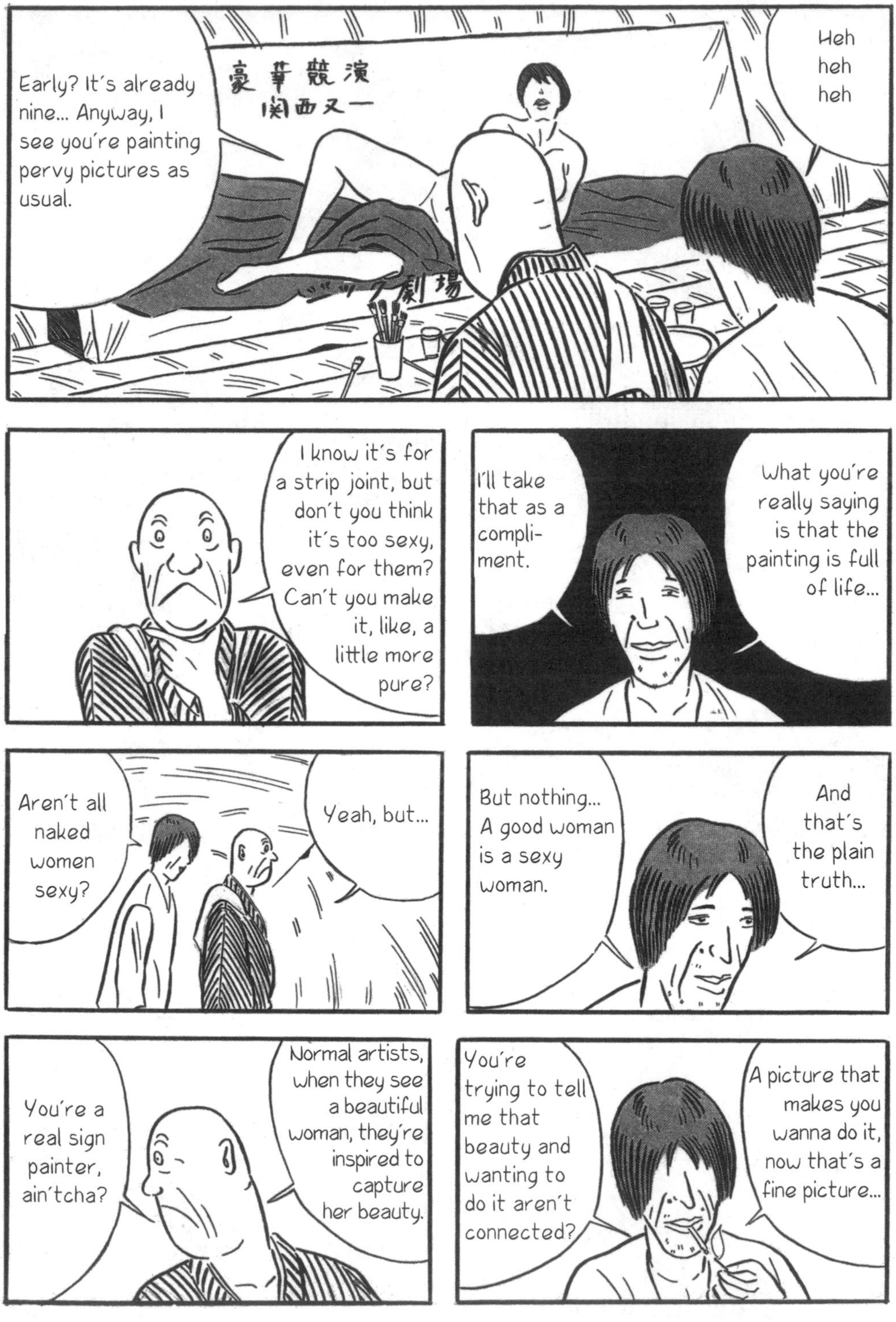
Early? It's already nine... Anyway, I see you're painting pervy pictures as usual.
豪華競演
関西又一
Heh heh heh
I know it's for a strip joint, but don't you think it's too sexy, even for them? Can't you make it, like, a little more pure?
I'll take that as a compliment.
What you're really saying is that the painting is full of life...
Aren't all naked women sexy?
Yeah, but...
But nothing... A good woman is a sexy woman.
And that's the plain truth...
You're a real sign painter, ain'tcha?
Normal artists, when they see a beautiful woman, they're inspired to capture her beauty.
You're trying to tell me that beauty and wanting to do it aren't connected?
A picture that makes you wanna do it, now that's a fine picture...

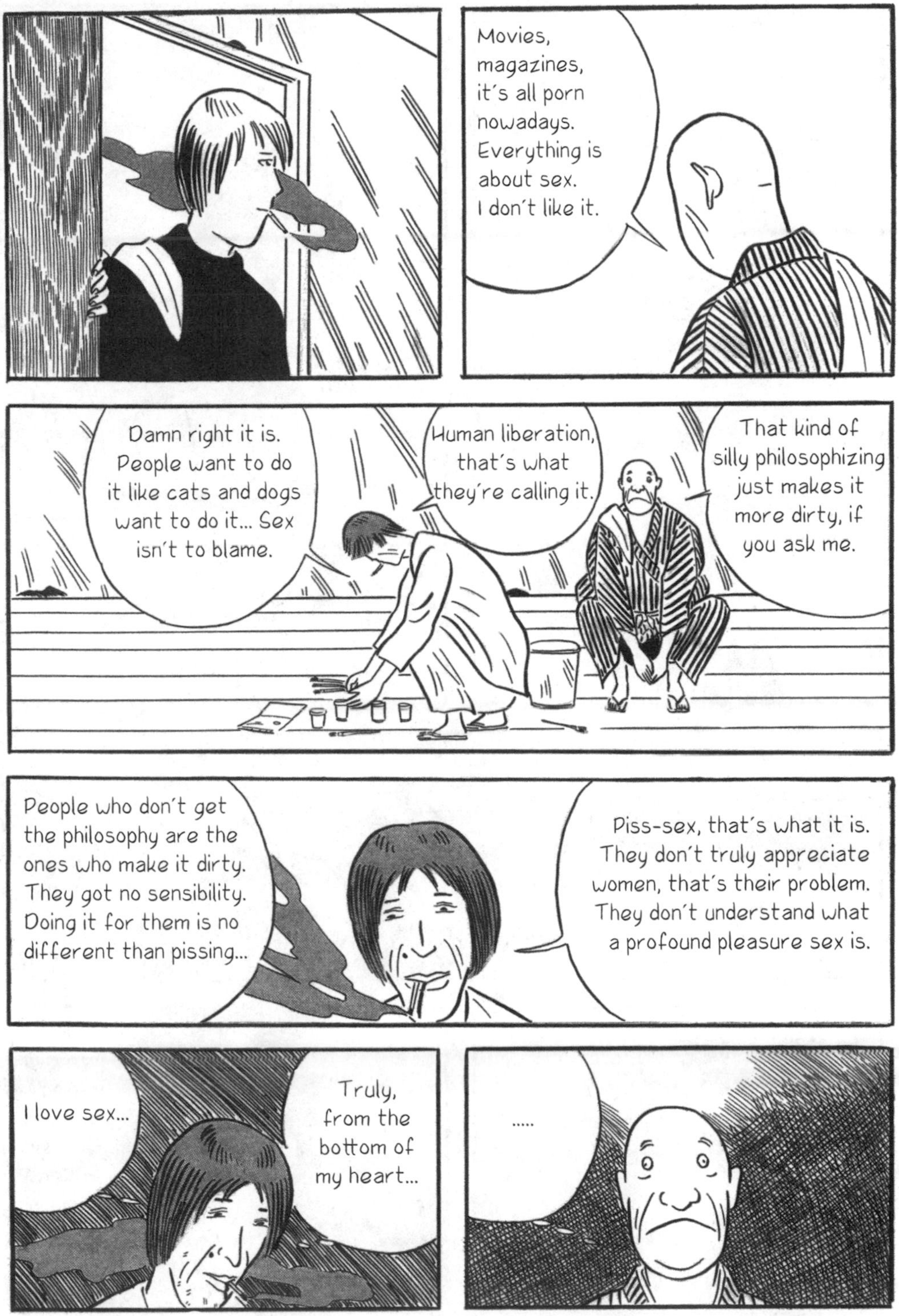
Movies, magazines, it's all porn nowadays. Everything is about sex. I don't like it.
Damn right it is. People want to do it like cats and dogs want to do it... Sex isn't to blame.
Human liberation, that's what they're calling it.
That kind of silly philosophizing just makes it more dirty, if you ask me.
People who don't get the philosophy are the ones who make it dirty. They got no sensibility. Doing it for them is no different than pissing...
Piss-sex, that's what it is. They don't truly appreciate women, that's their problem. They don't understand what a profound pleasure sex is.
I love sex...
Truly, from the bottom of my heart...
.....

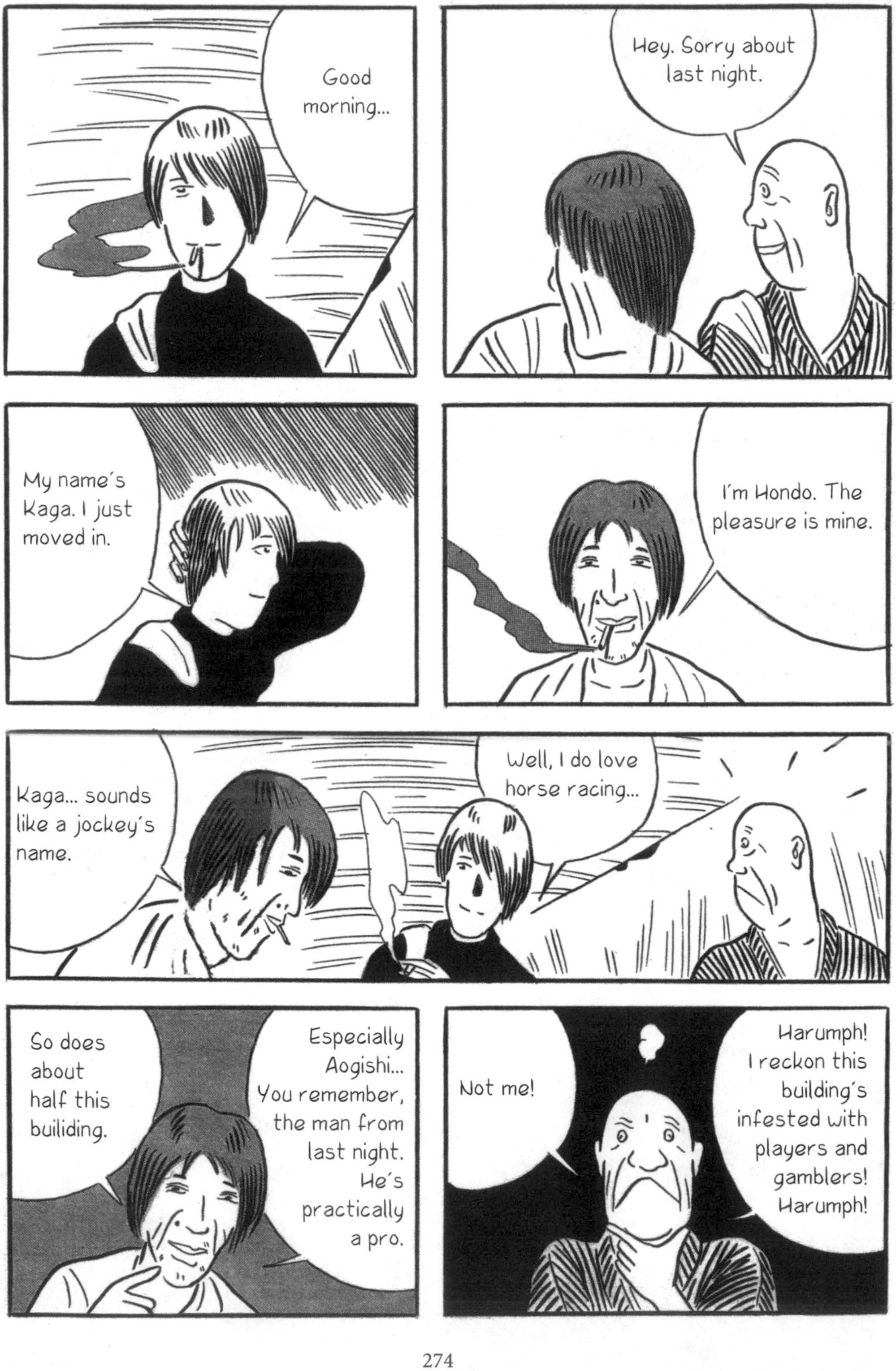
Good morning...
Hey. Sorry about last night.
My name's Kaga. I just moved in.
I'm Hondo. The pleasure is mine.
Kaga... sounds like a jockey's name.
Well, I do love horse racing...
So does about half this builiding.
Especially Aogishi... You remember, the man from last night. He's practically a pro.
Not me!
Harumph! I reckon this building's infested with players and gamblers! Harumph!

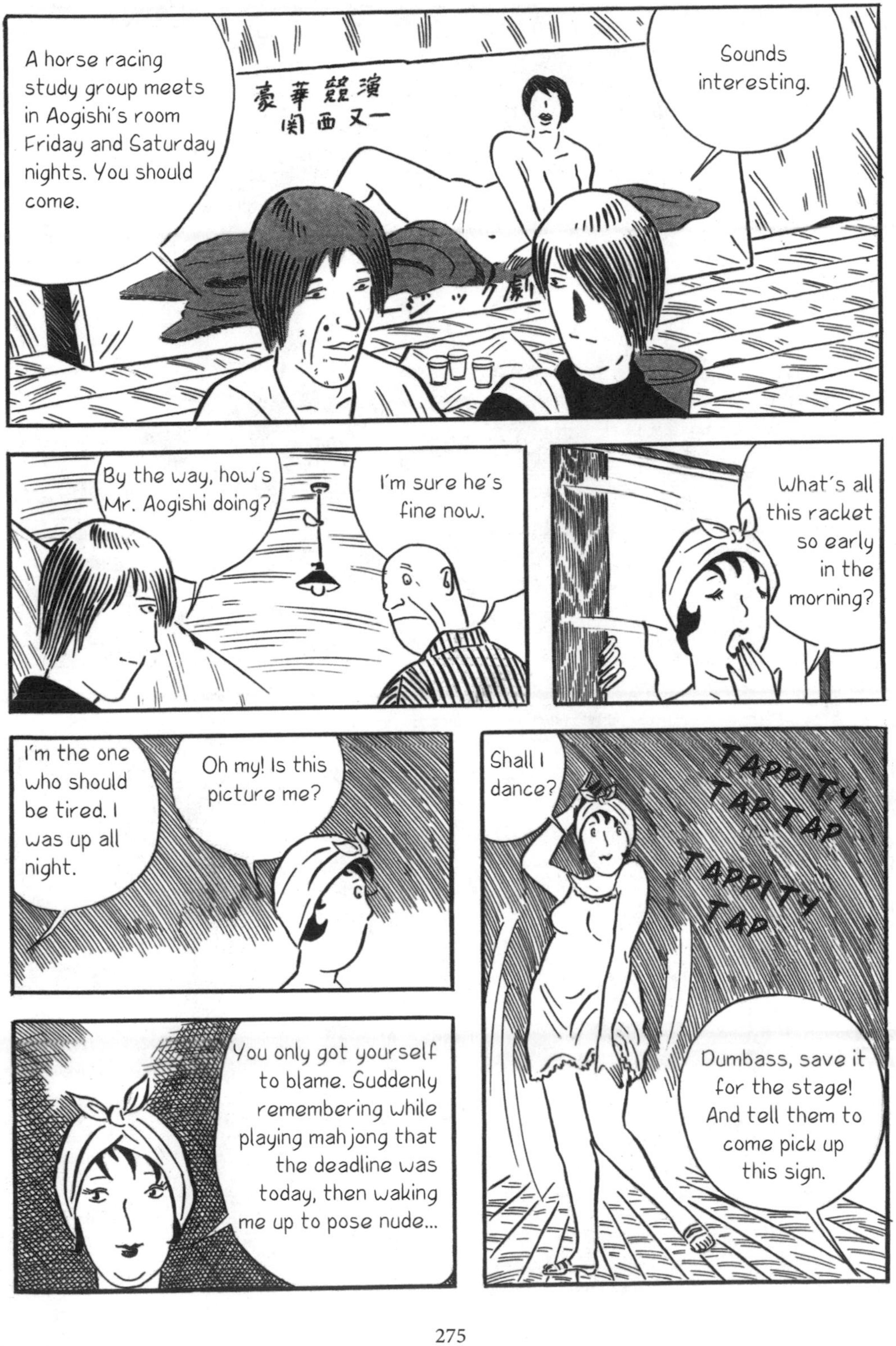
A horse racing study group meets in Aogishi's room Friday and Saturday nights. You should come.
Sounds interesting.
By the way, how's Mr. Aogishi doing?
I'm sure he's fine now.
What's all this racket so early in the morning?
I'm the one who should be tired. I was up all night.
Oh my! Is this picture me?
You only got yourself to blame. Suddenly remembering while playing mahjong that the deadline was today, then waking me up to pose nude...
Shall I dance?
TAPPITY TAP TAP
TAPPITY TAP
Dumbass, save it for the stage! And tell them to come pick up this sign.

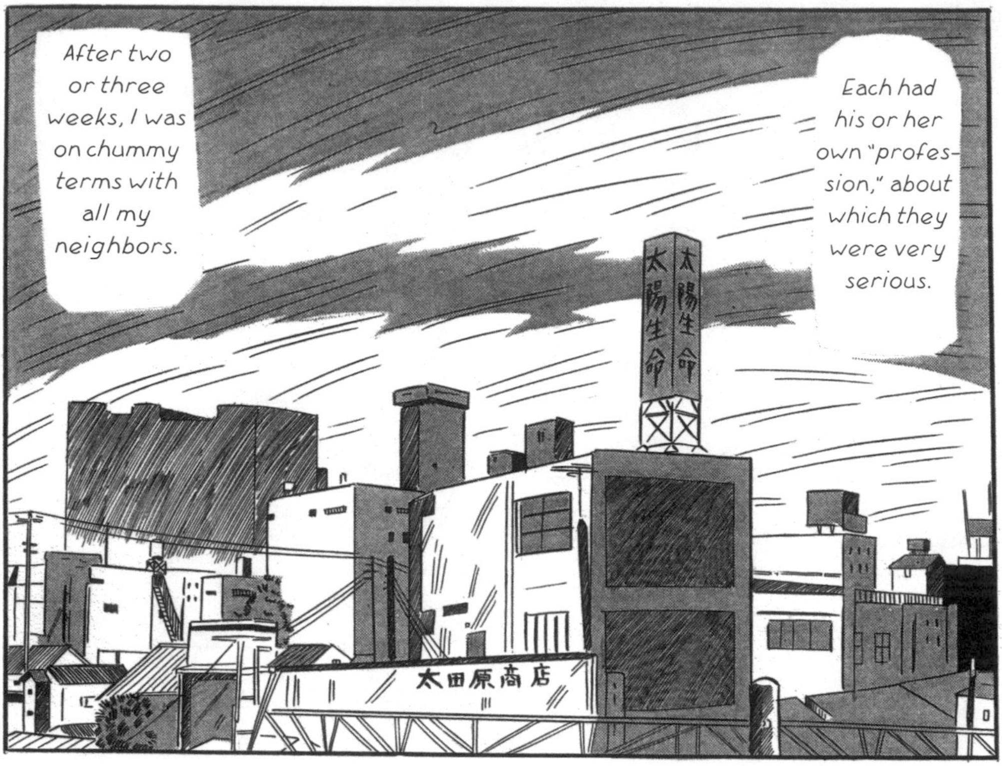
After two or three weeks, I was on chummy terms with all my neighbors.
Each had his or her own "profes-sion," about which they were very serious.
太陽生命
太陽生命
太田原商店

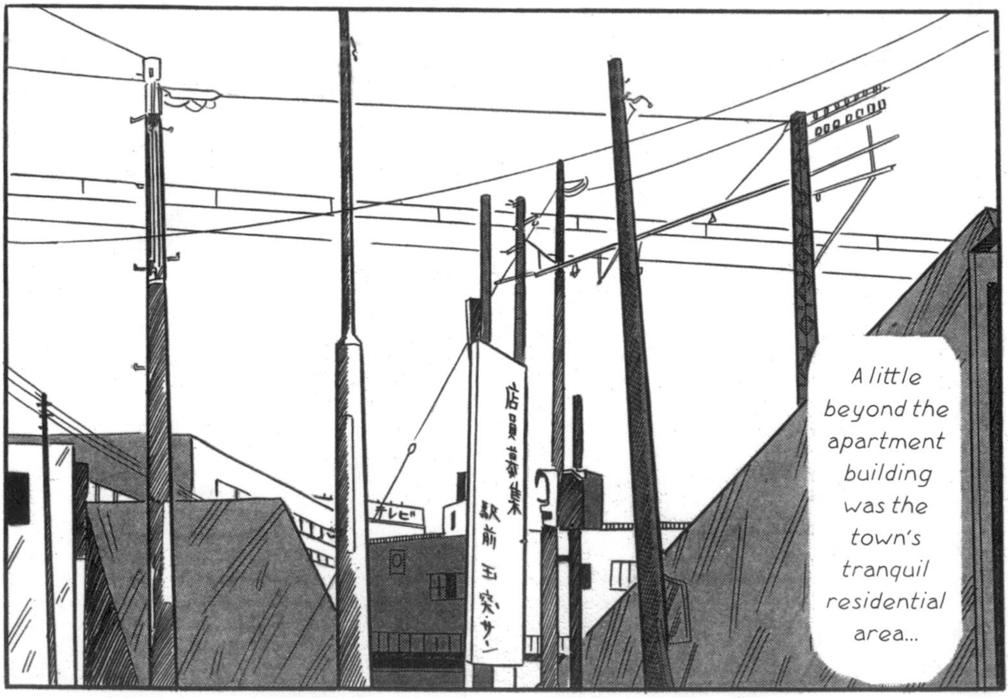
店員募集
A little beyond the apartment building was the town's tranquil residential area...

While punks prowled the area near the station, located in the center of town...

Their mere presence was a sign that the town's entertainment district was thriving.

Yo!

sign: Keihoku pachinko

Hello, Mr. Tokuma.

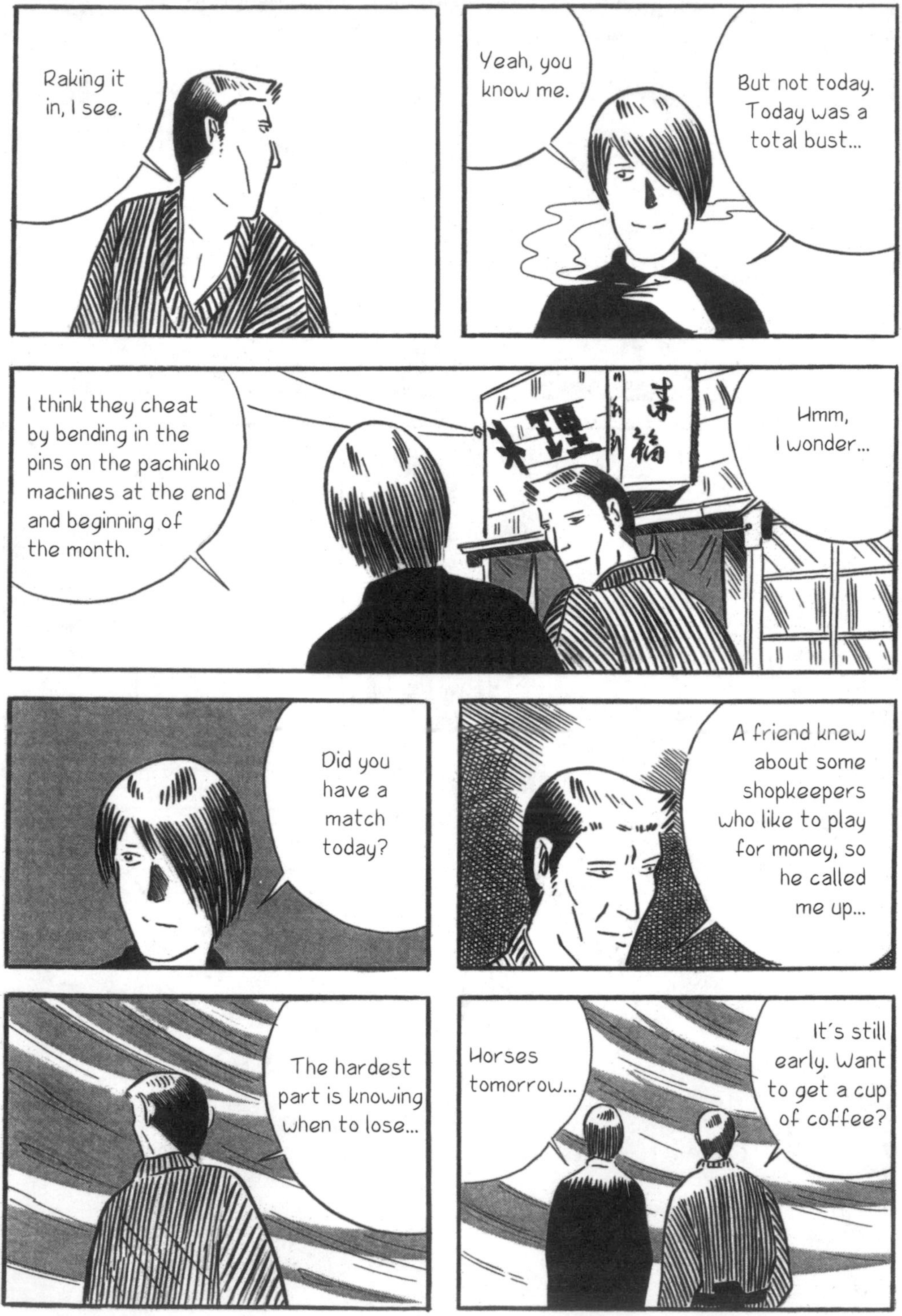
Raking it in, I see.
Yeah, you know me.
But not today. Today was a total bust...
I think they cheat by bending in the pins on the pachinko machines at the end and beginning of the month.
Hmm, I wonder...
Did you have a match today?
A friend knew about some shopkeepers who like to play for money, so he called me up...
The hardest part is knowing when to lose...
Horses tomorrow...
It's still early. Want to get a cup of coffee?

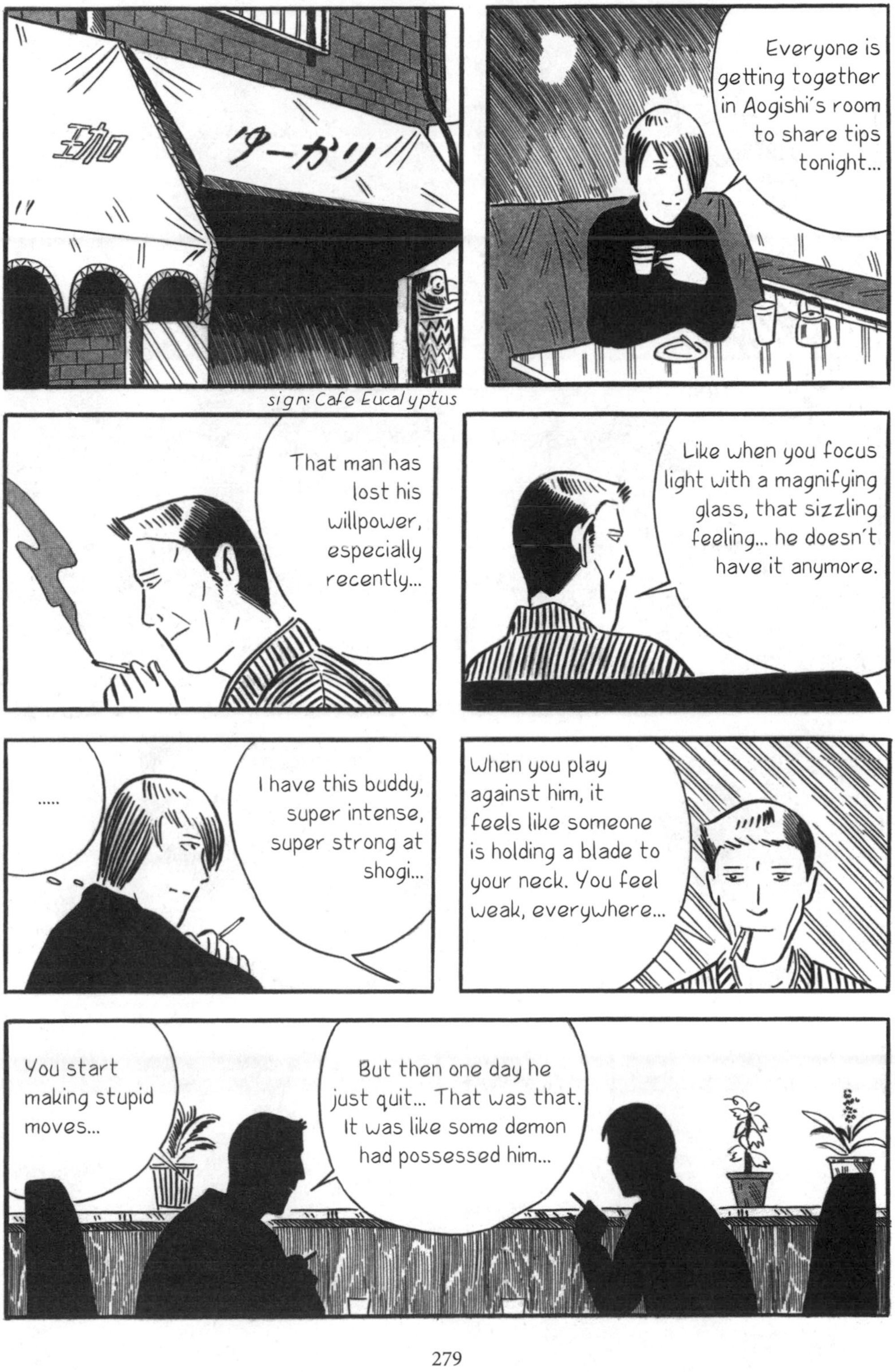
ユーカリ
sign: Cafe Eucalyptus
Everyone is getting together in Aogishi's room to share tips tonight...
That man has lost his willpower, especially recently...
Like when you focus light with a magnifying glass, that sizzling feeling... he doesn't have it anymore.
.....
I have this buddy, super intense, super strong at shogi...
When you play against him, it feels like someone is holding a blade to your neck. You feel weak, everywhere...
You start making stupid moves...
But then one day he just quit... That was that. It was like some demon had possessed him...

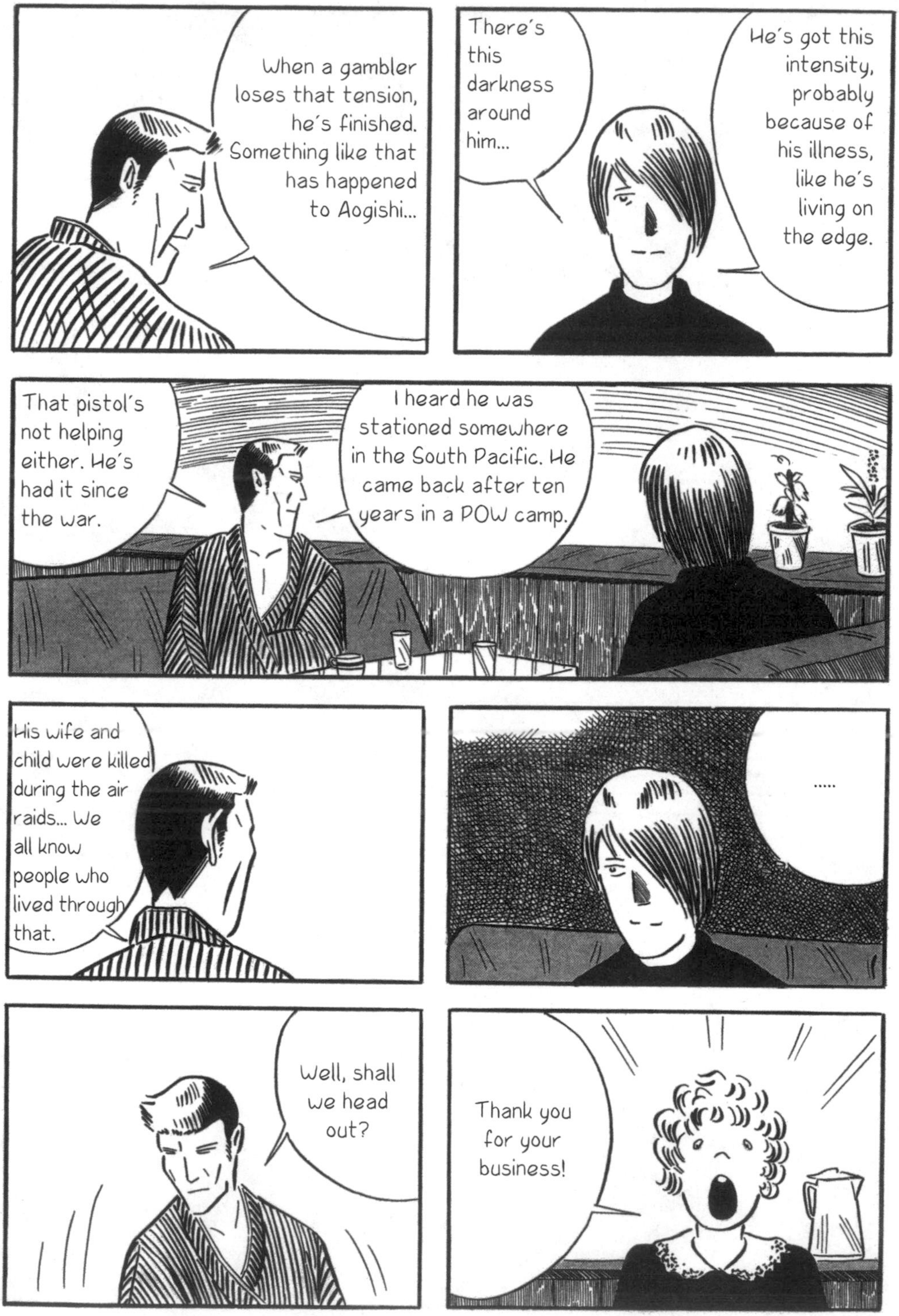
When a gambler loses that tension, he's finished. Something like that has happened to Aogishi...
There's this darkness around him...
He's got this intensity, probably because of his illness, like he's living on the edge.
That pistol's not helping either. He's had it since the war.
I heard he was stationed somewhere in the South Pacific. He came back after ten years in a POW camp.
His wife and child were killed during the air raids... We all know people who lived through that.
.....
Well, shall we head out?
Thank you for your business!

Yamabe told me that...

A former officer lives near our building?

That's right...

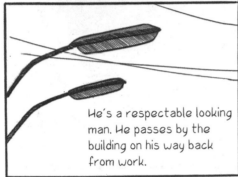

He's a respectable looking man. He passes by the building on his way back from work.

Is it just a coincidence that he lives nearby? Or...

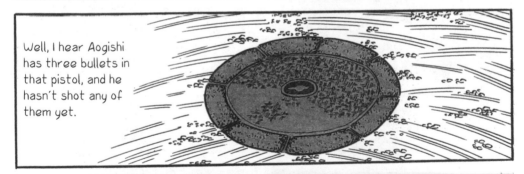

Well, I hear Aogishi has three bullets in that pistol, and he hasn't shot any of them yet.

After saying goodbye to Tokuma, I decided to hit another pachinko parlor.

When night fell, the drizzling rain...

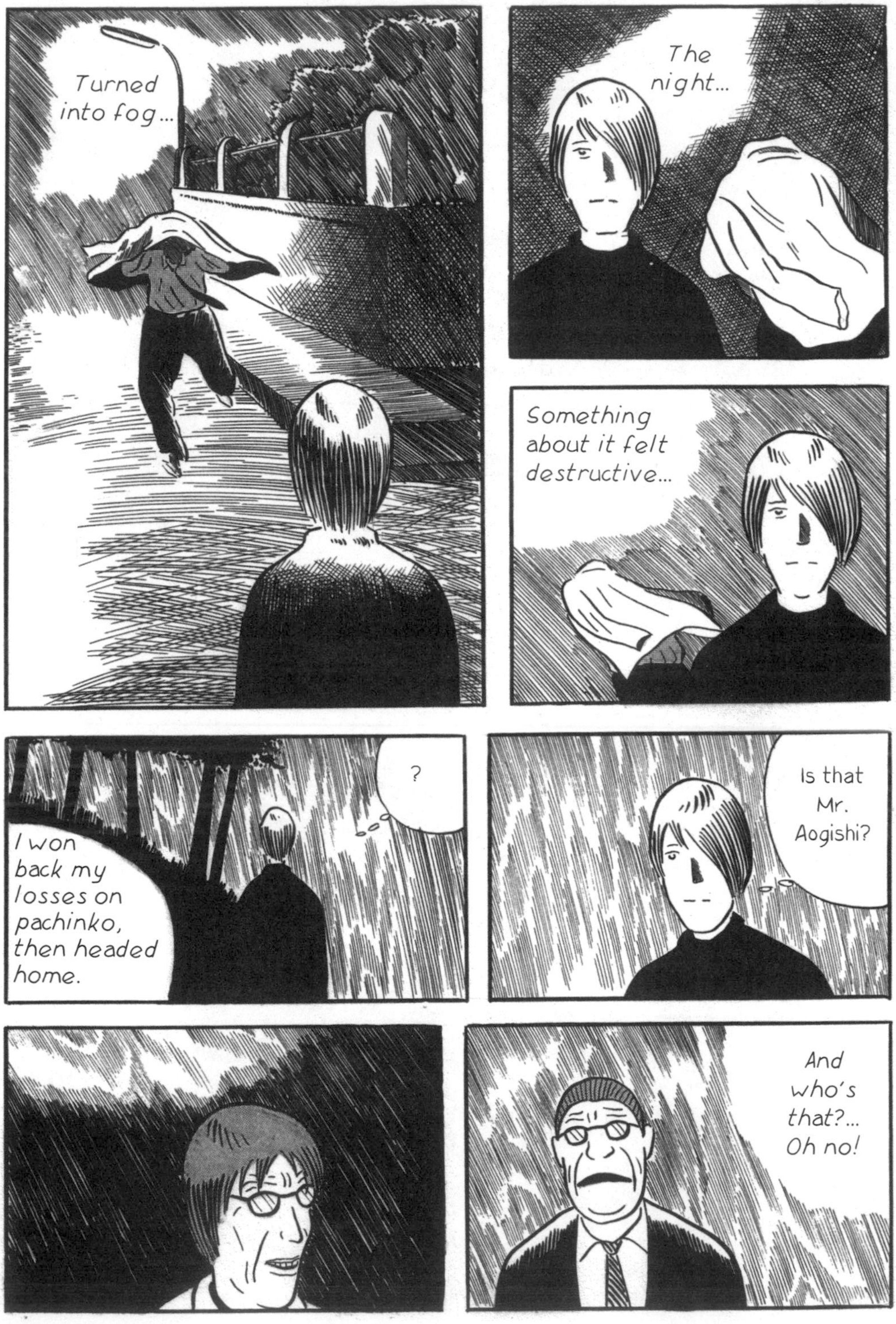
Turned into fog...
The night...
Something about it felt destructive...
I won back my losses on pachinko, then headed home.
?
Is that Mr. Aogishi?
And who's that?... Oh no!

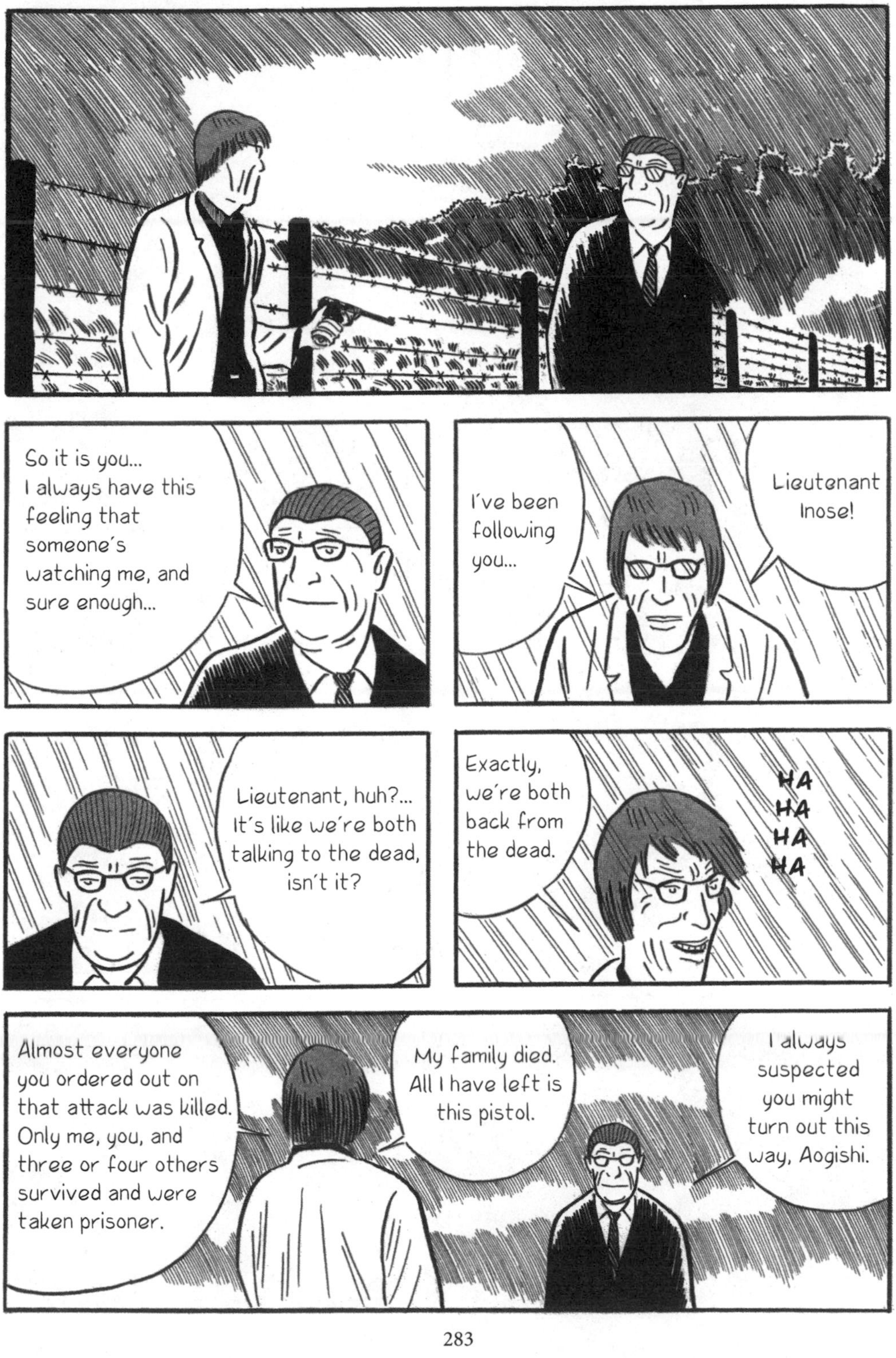
So it is you...
I always have this feeling that someone's watching me, and sure enough...
I've been following you...
Lieutenant Inose!
Lieutenant, huh?... It's like we're both talking to the dead, isn't it?
Exactly, we're both back from the dead.
HA HA HA HA
Almost everyone you ordered out on that attack was killed. Only me, you, and three or four others survived and were taken prisoner.
My family died. All I have left is this pistol.
I always suspected you might turn out this way, Aogishi.

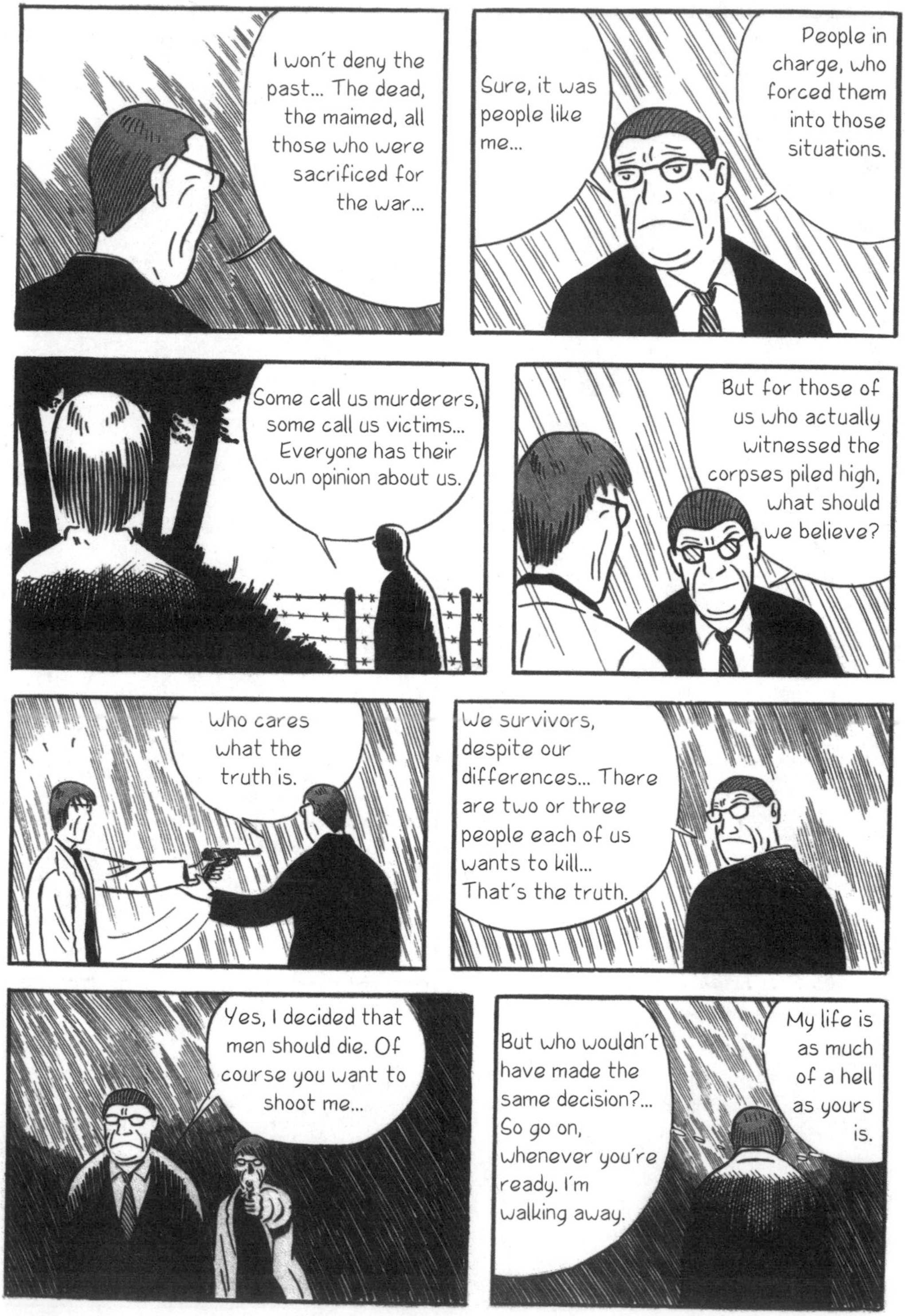
I won't deny the past... The dead, the maimed, all those who were sacrificed for the war...
Sure, it was people like me...
People in charge, who forced them into those situations.
Some call us murderers, some call us victims... Everyone has their own opinion about us.
But for those of us who actually witnessed the corpses piled high, what should we believe?
Who cares what the truth is.
We survivors, despite our differences... There are two or three people each of us wants to kill... That's the truth.
Yes, I decided that men should die. Of course you want to shoot me...
But who wouldn't have made the same decision?... So go on, whenever you're ready. I'm walking away.
My life is as much of a hell as yours is.

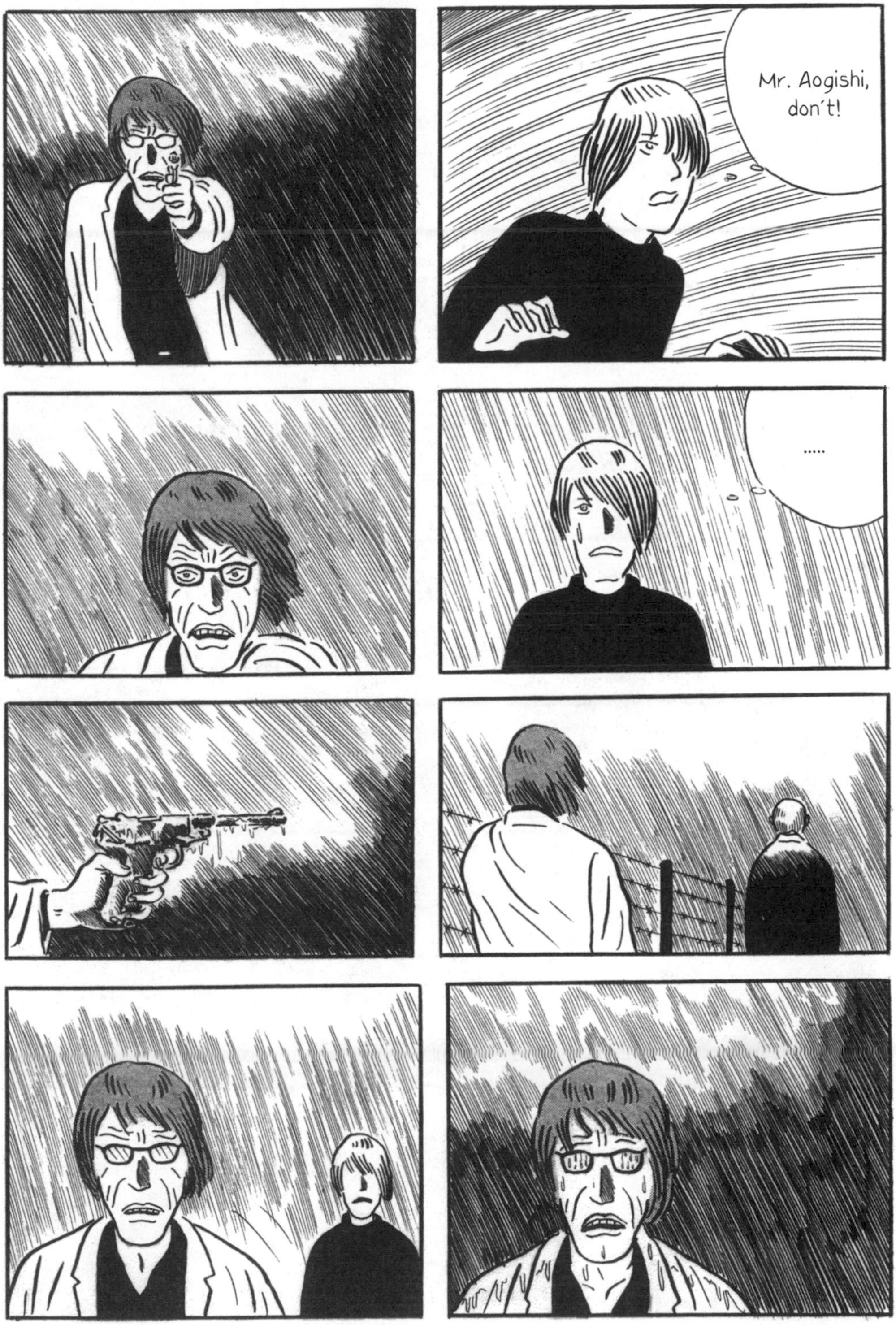
Mr. Aogishi, don´t!
.....

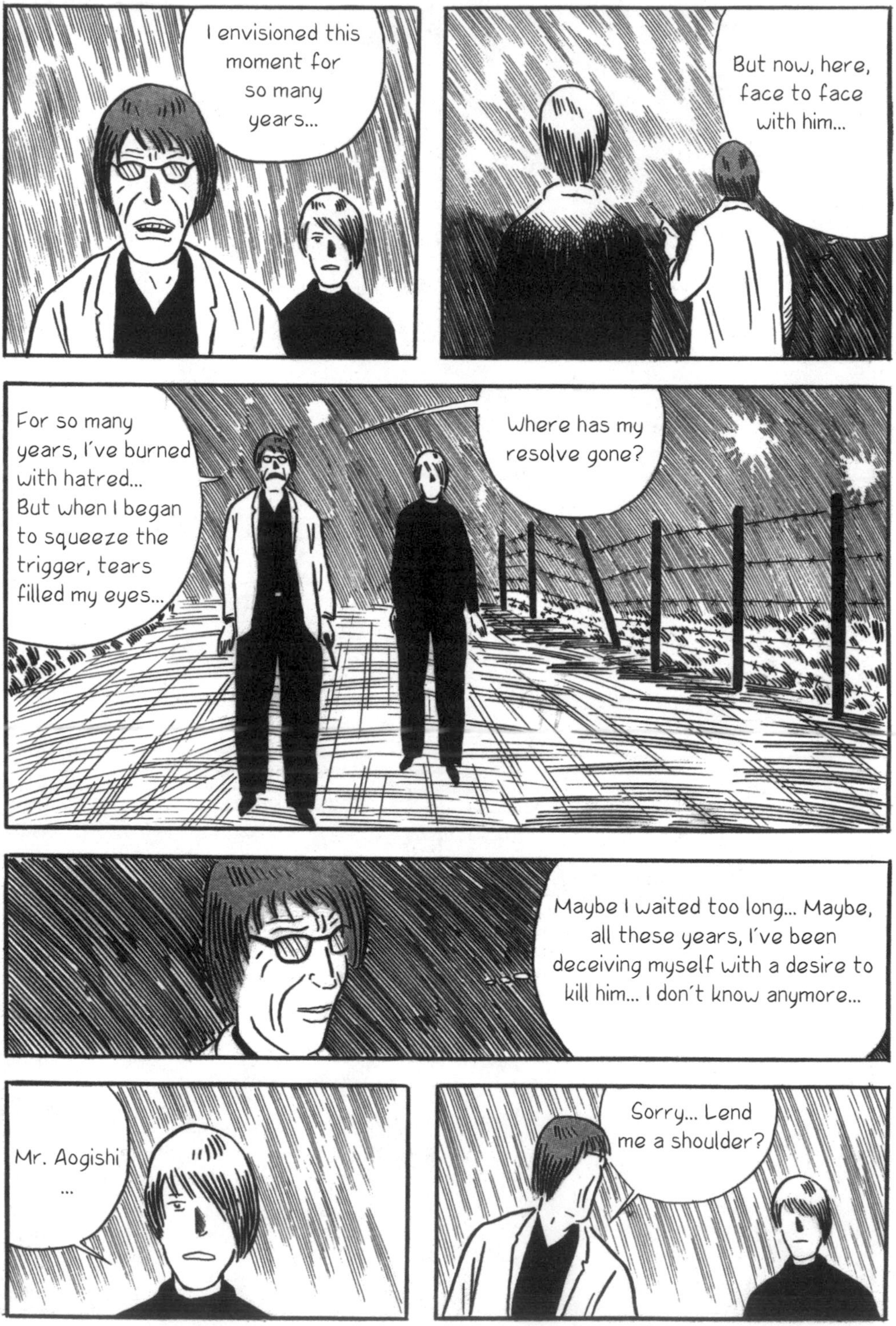
I envisioned this moment for so many years...
But now, here, face to face with him...
For so many years, I've burned with hatred... But when I began to squeeze the trigger, tears filled my eyes...
Where has my resolve gone?
Maybe I waited too long... Maybe, all these years, I've been deceiving myself with a desire to kill him... I don't know anymore...
Mr. Aogishi ...
Sorry... Lend me a shoulder?

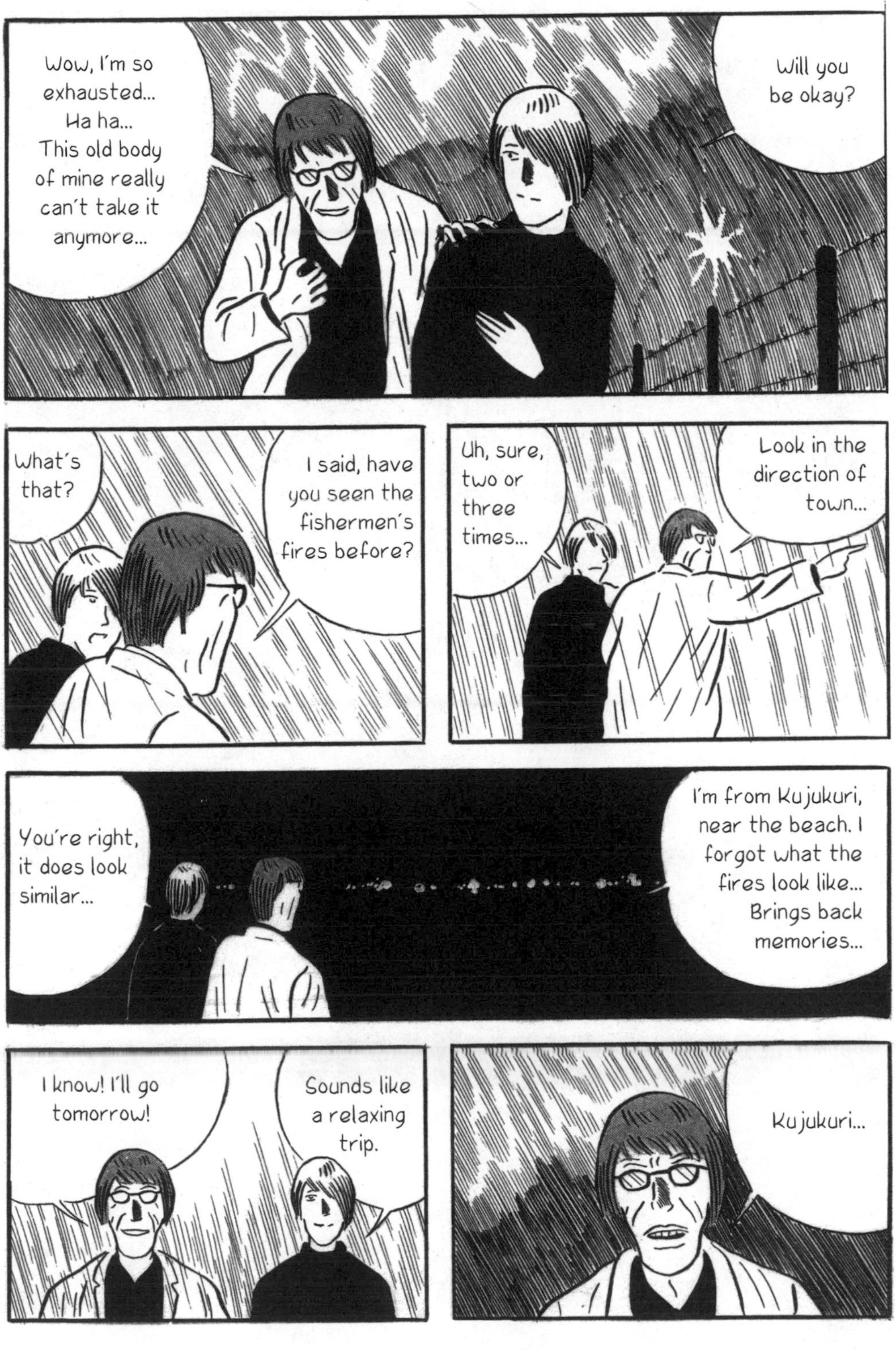
Wow, I'm so exhausted... Ha ha... This old body of mine really can't take it anymore...
Will you be okay?
What's that?
I said, have you seen the fishermen's fires before?
Uh, sure, two or three times...
Look in the direction of town...
You're right, it does look similar...
I'm from Kujukuri, near the beach. I forgot what the fires look like... Brings back memories...
I know! I'll go tomorrow!
Sounds like a relaxing trip.
Kujukuri...

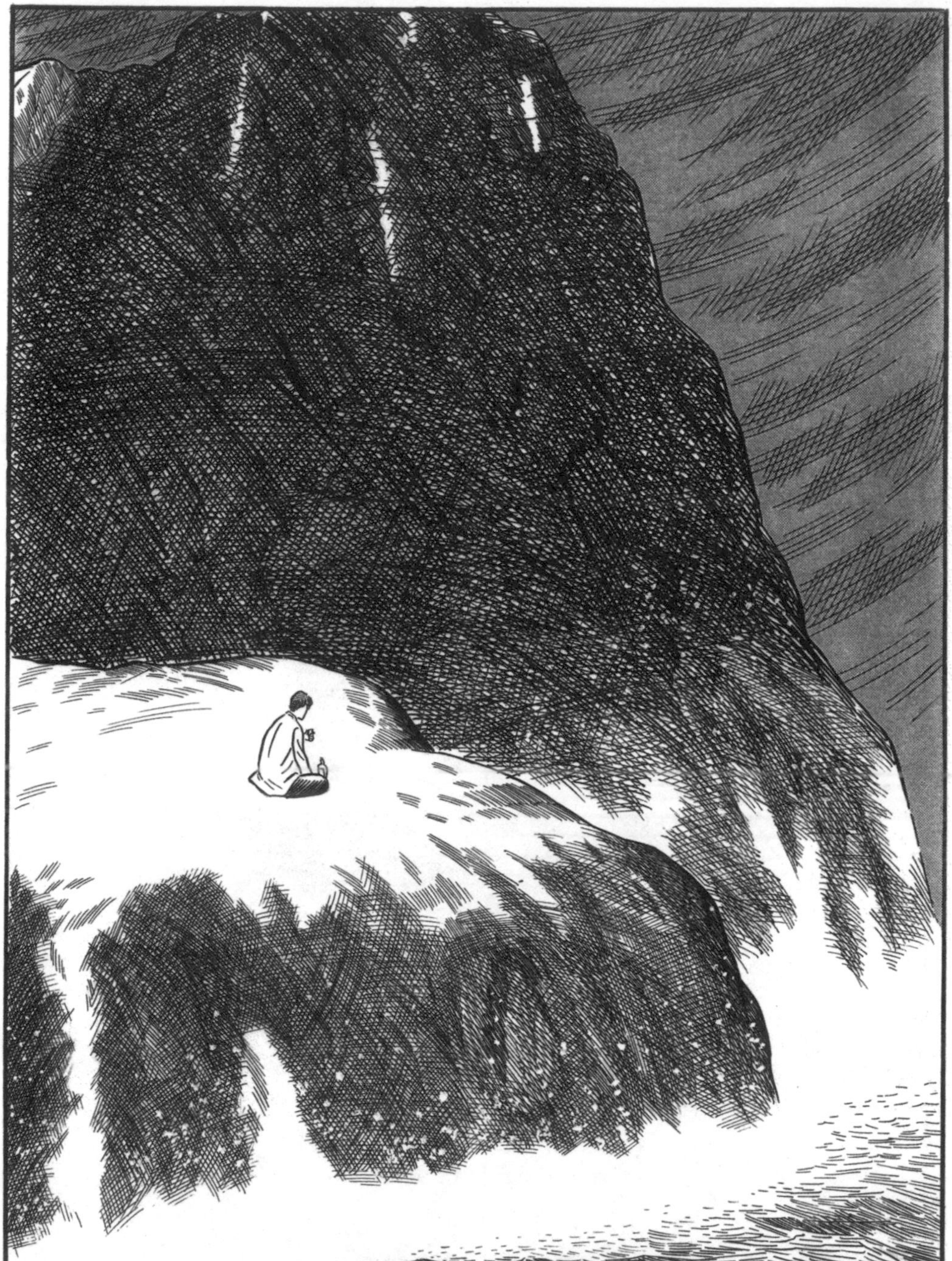

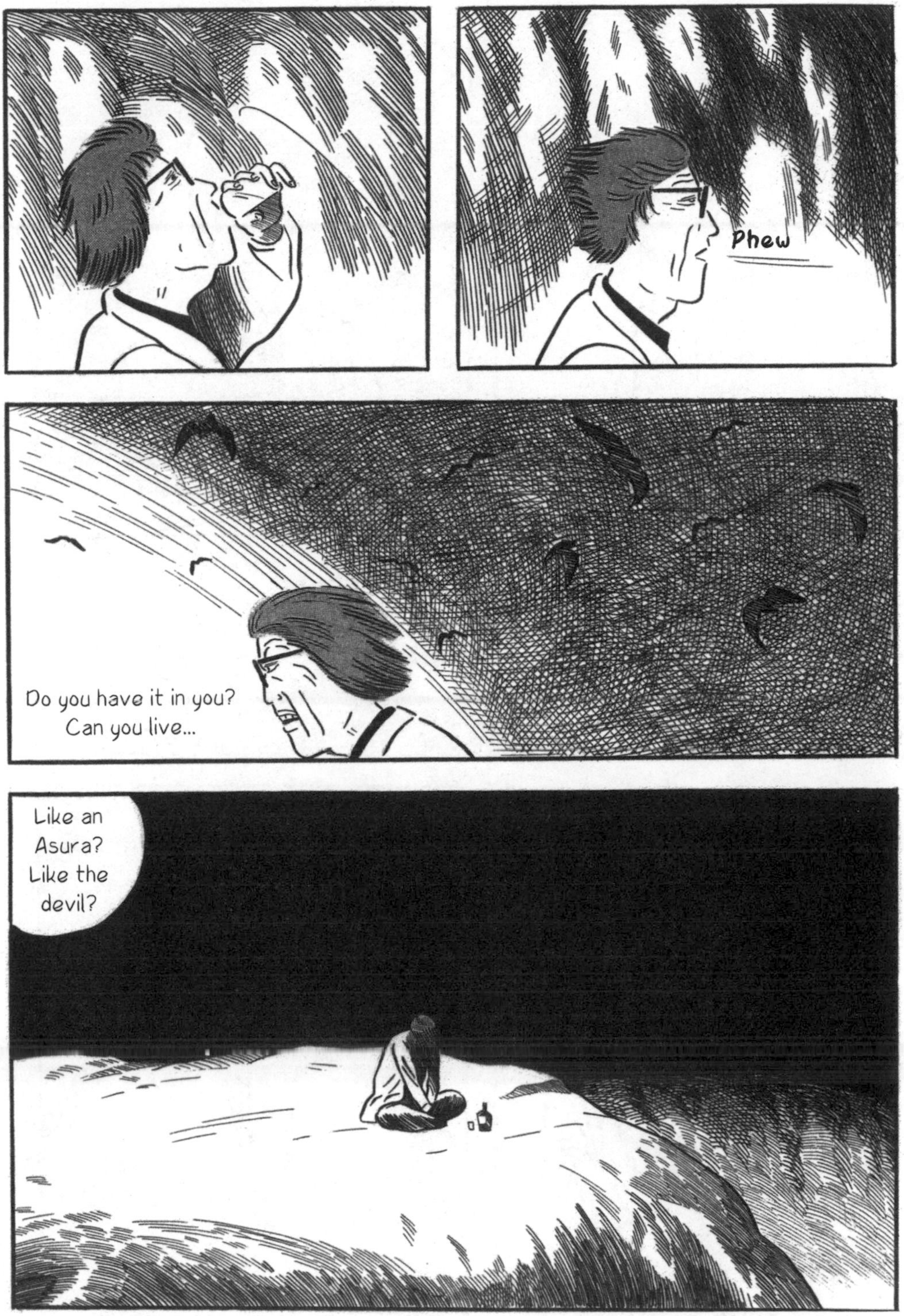
Phew
Do you have it in you? Can you live...
Like an Asura? Like the devil?

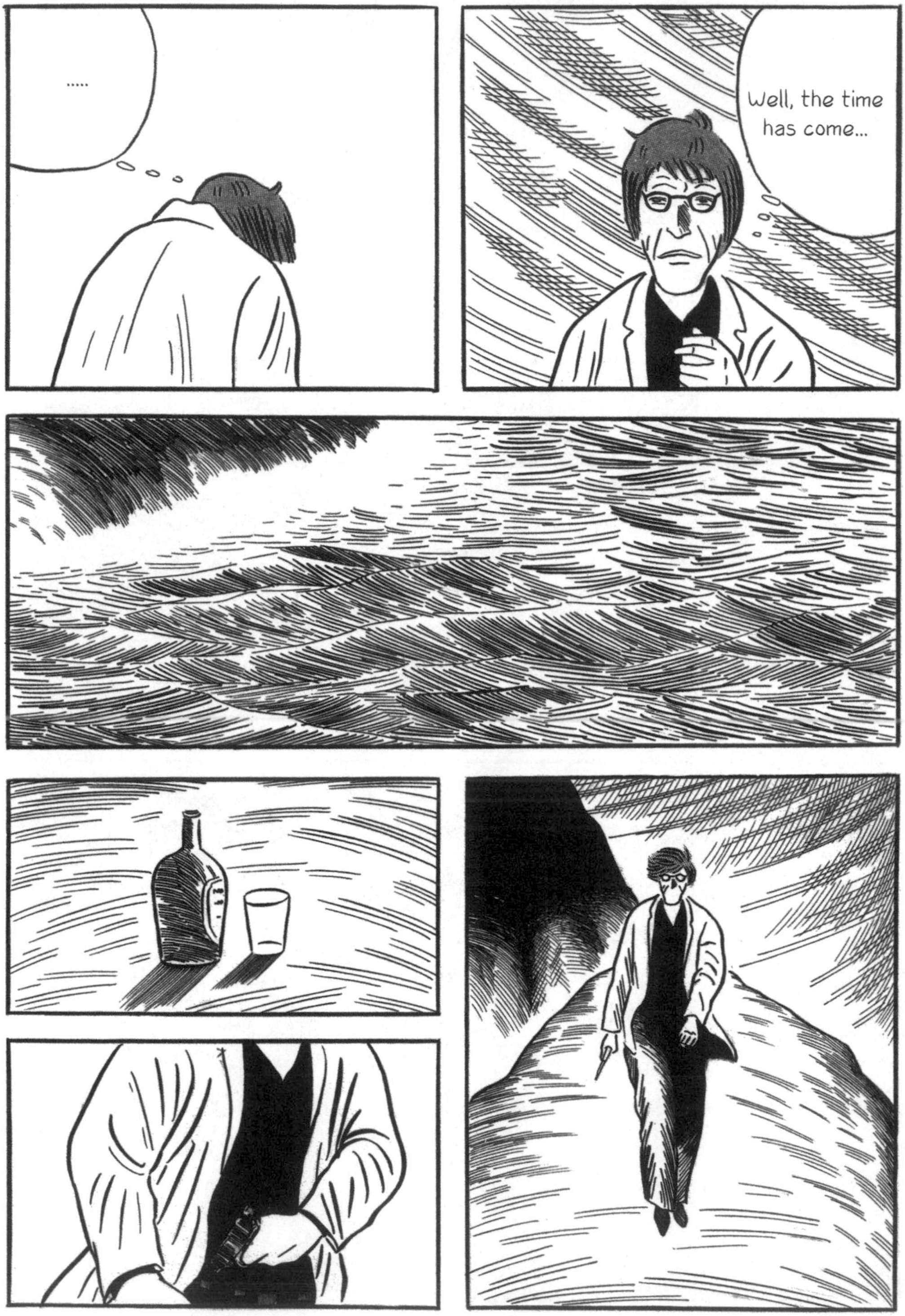
.....
Well, the time has come...

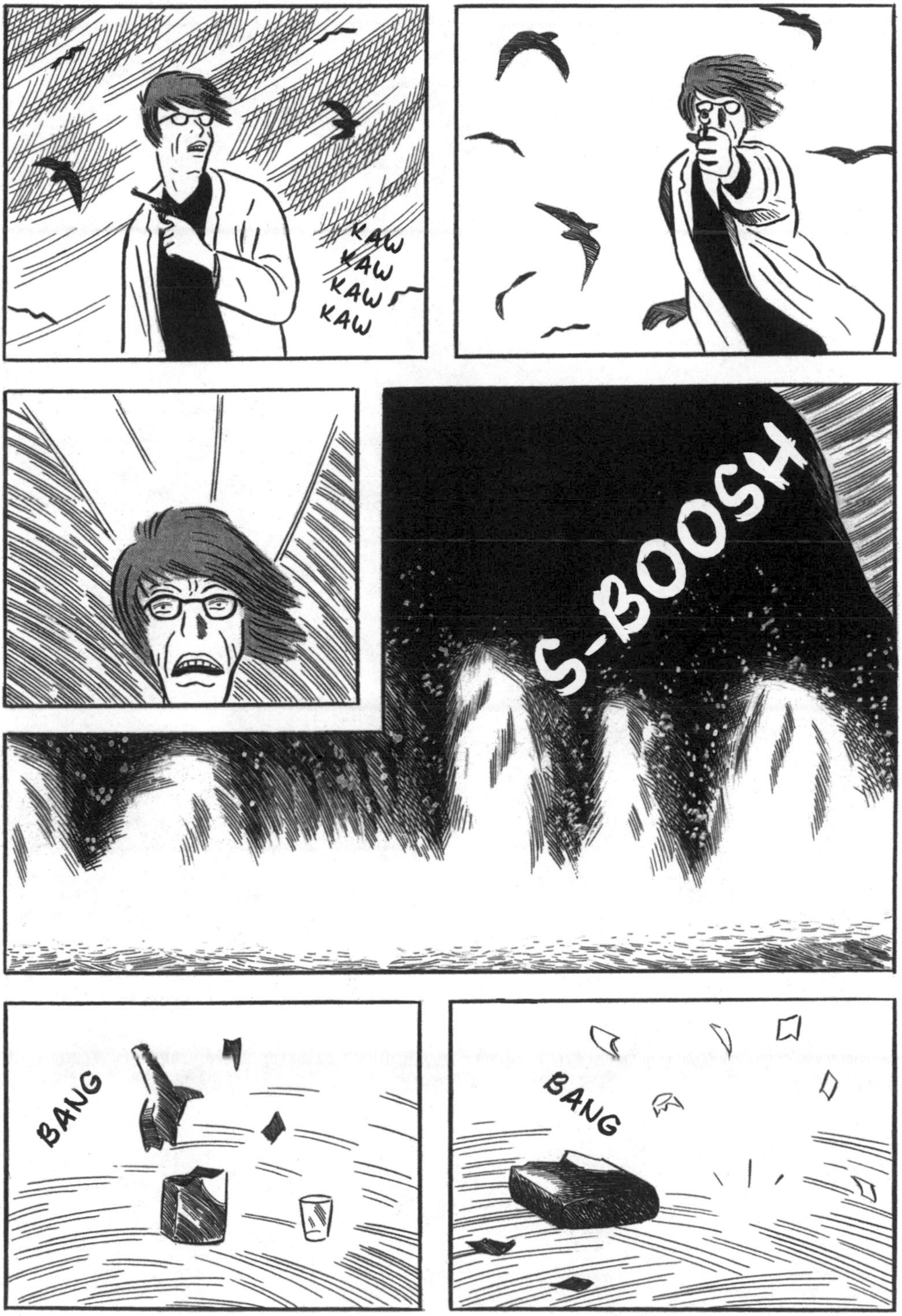
KAW
KAW
KAW
KAW
S-BOOSH
BANG
BANG

KAW
KAW
KAW
B-BANG
KAW
KAW
KAW

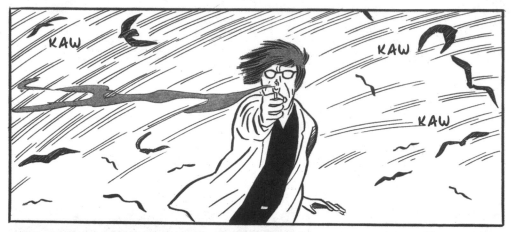

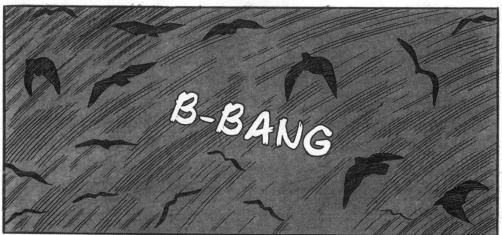

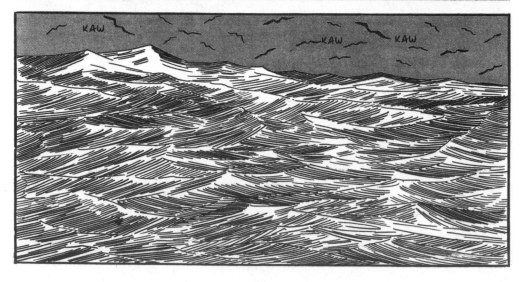

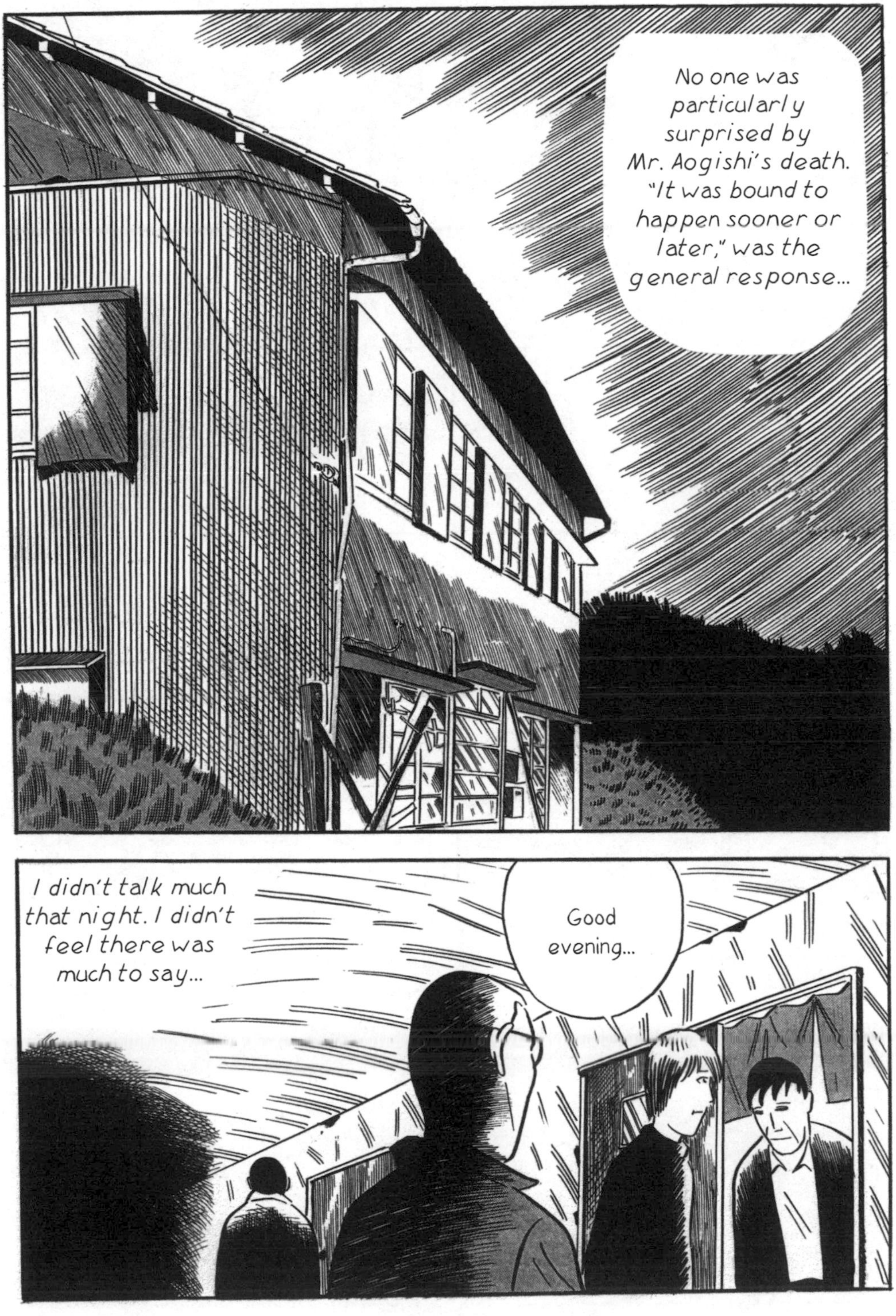
No one was particularly surprised by Mr. Aogishi's death. "It was bound to happen sooner or later," was the general response...
I didn't talk much that night. I didn't feel there was much to say...
Good evening...

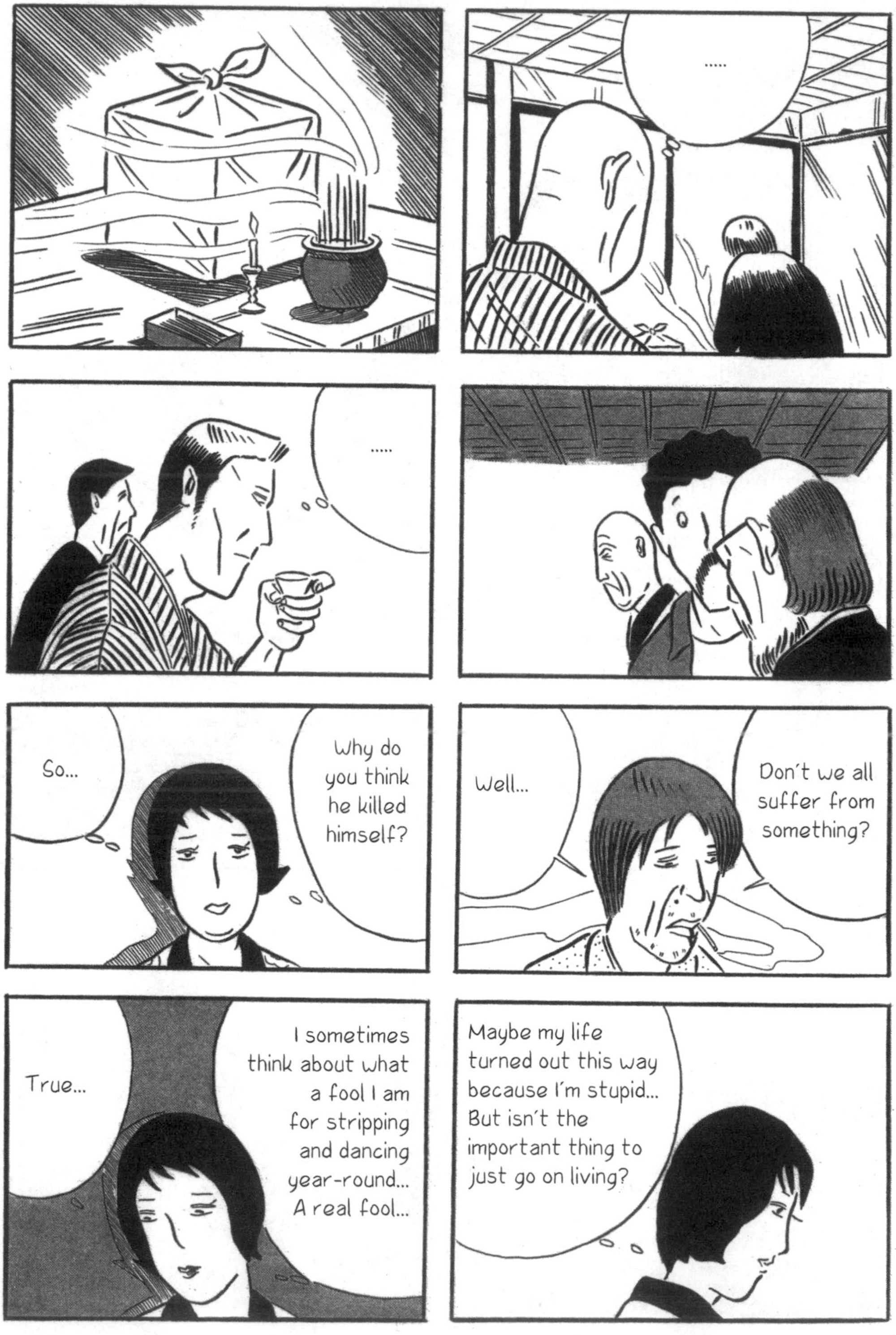
.....
.....
So...
Why do you think he killed himself?
Well...
Don't we all suffer from something?
True...
I sometimes think about what a fool I am for stripping and dancing year-round... A real fool...
Maybe my life turned out this way because I'm stupid... But isn't the important thing to just go on living?

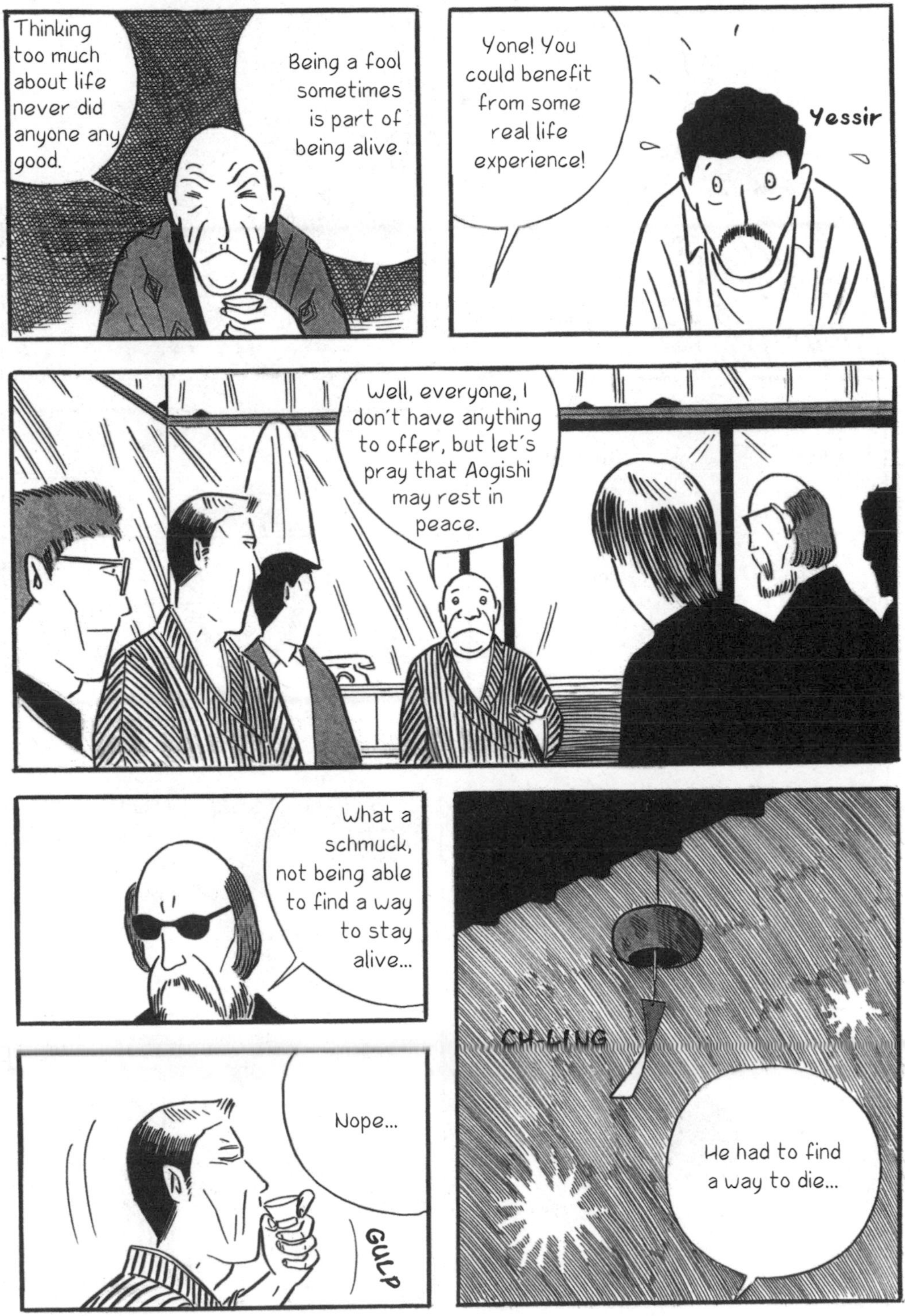
Thinking too much about life never did anyone any good.
Being a fool sometimes is part of being alive.
Yone! You could benefit from some real life experience!
Yessir
Well, everyone, I don't have anything to offer, but let's pray that Aogishi may rest in peace.
What a schmuck, not being able to find a way to stay alive...
Nope...
GULP
CH-LING
He had to find a way to die...

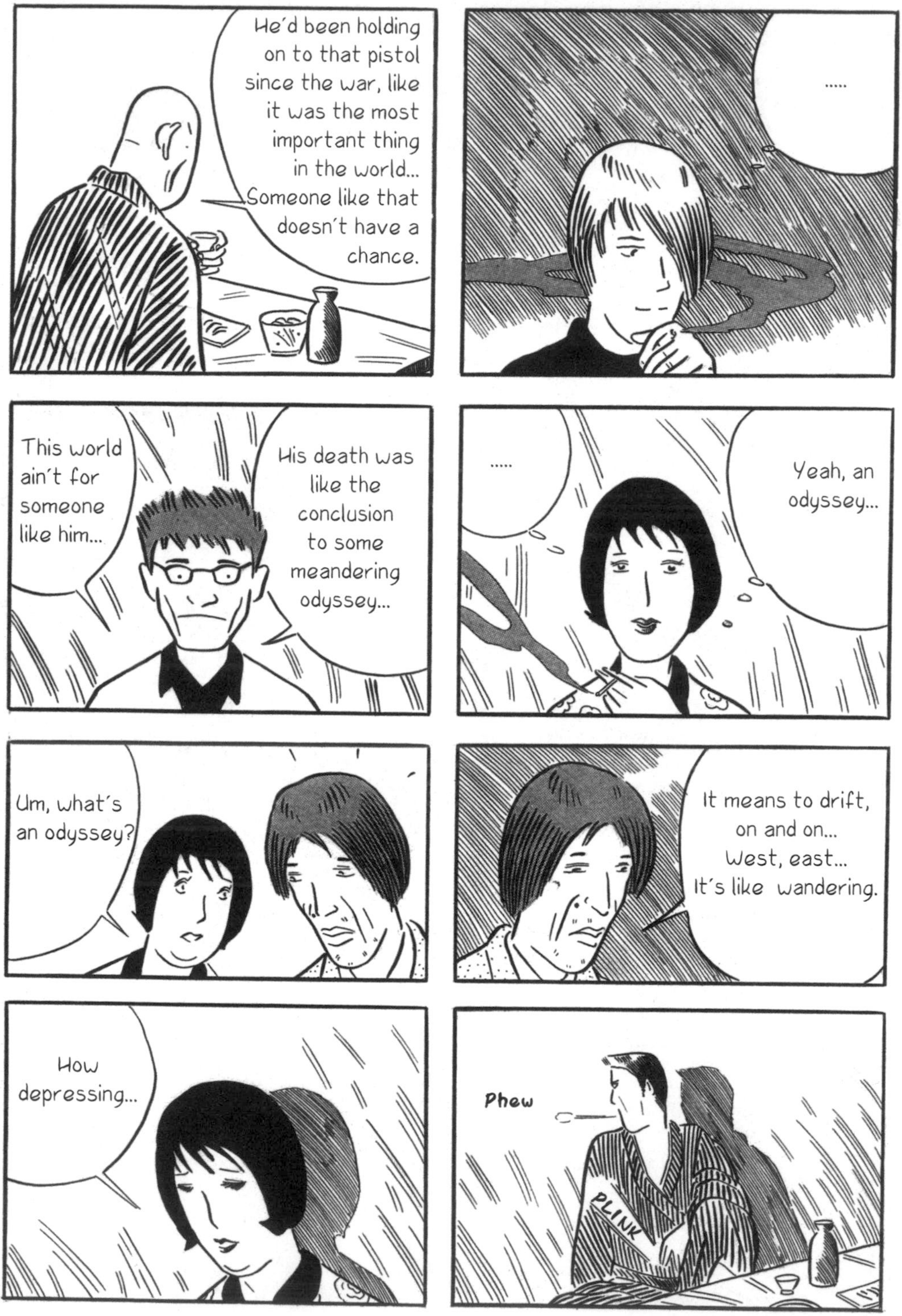
He'd been holding on to that pistol since the war, like it was the most important thing in the world... Someone like that doesn't have a chance.
.....
This world ain't for someone like him...
His death was like the conclusion to some meandering odyssey...
.....
Yeah, an odyssey...
Um, what's an odyssey?
It means to drift, on and on... West, east... It's like wandering.
How depressing...
Phew
PLINK

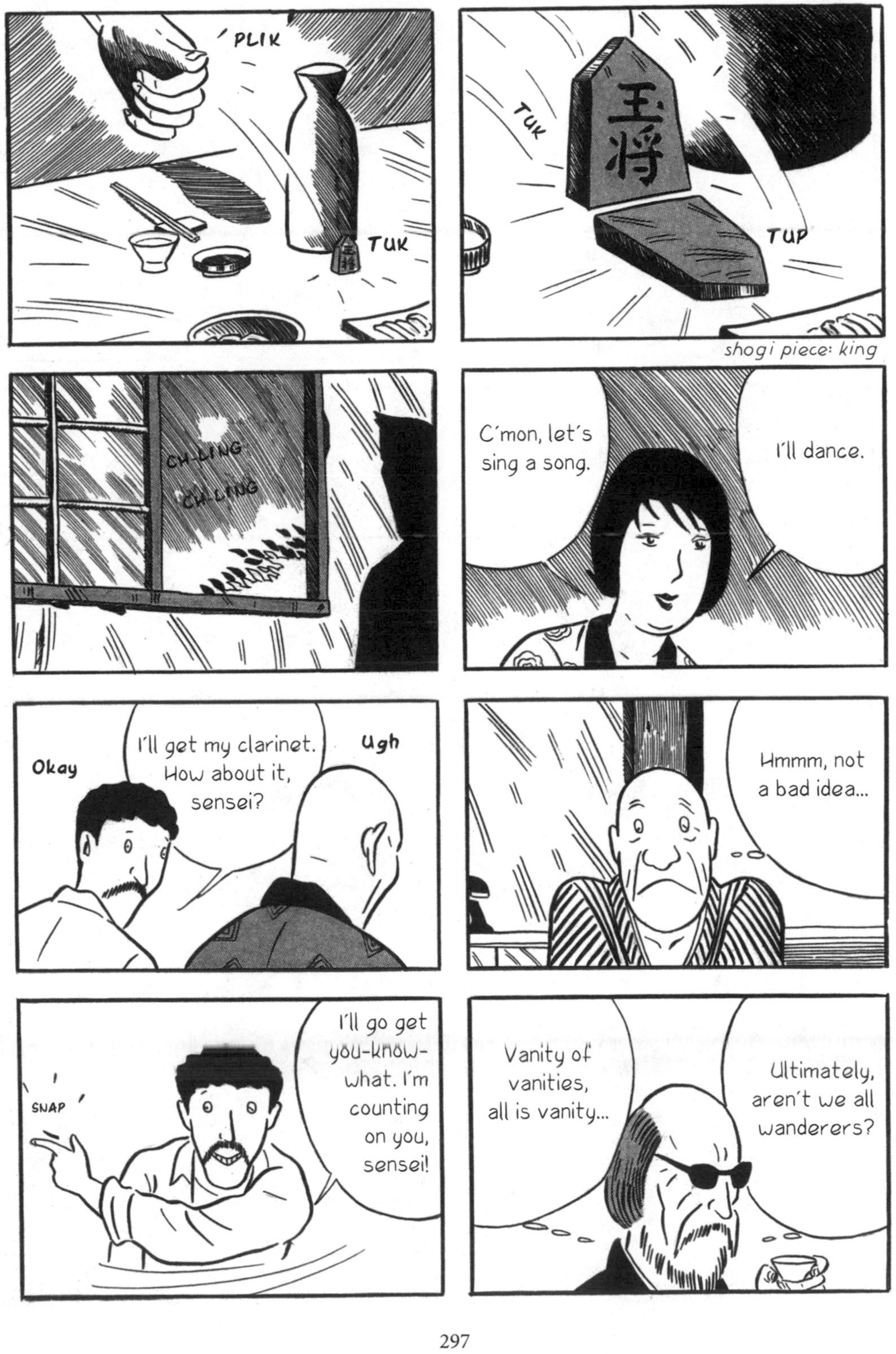
PLIK
TUK
TUK
王将
TUP
shogi piece: king
CH-LING
CH-LING
C´mon, let´s sing a song.
I´ll dance.
Okay
I´ll get my clarinet. How about it, sensei?
Ugh
Hmmm, not a bad idea...
SNAP
I´ll go get you-know-what. I´m counting on you, sensei!
Vanity of vanities, all is vanity...
Ultimately, aren´t we all wanderers?

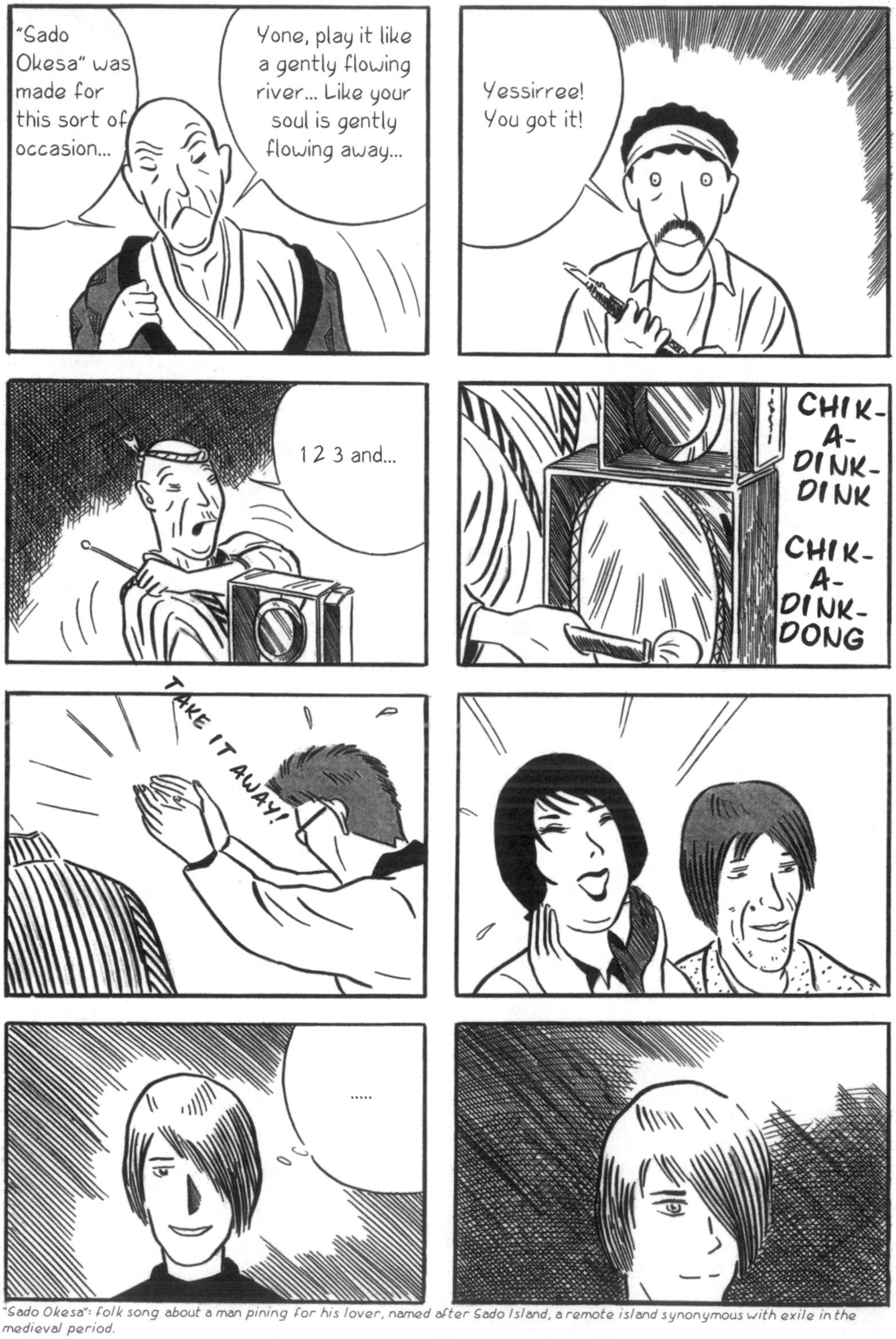
"Sado Okesa" was made for this sort of occasion...
Yone, play it like a gently flowing river... Like your soul is gently flowing away...
Yessirree! You got it!
1 2 3 and...
CHIK-A-DINK-DINK
CHIK-A-DINK-DONG
TAKE IT AWAY!
.....

"Sado Okesa": folk song about a man pining for his lover, named after Sado Island, a remote island synonymous with exile in the medieval period.

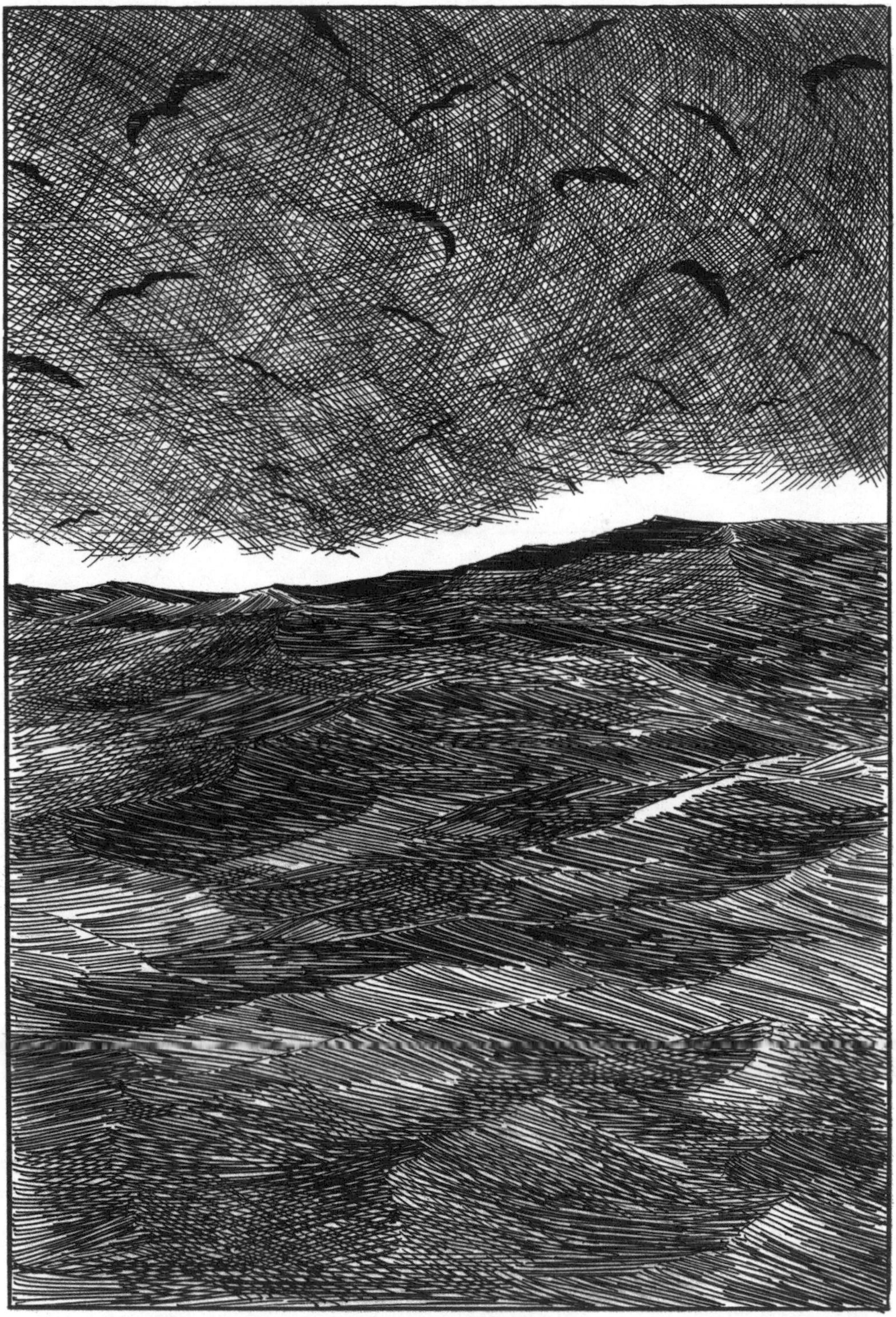

The End

ALWAYS A TOUGH GUY AT HEART

TADAO TSUGE

Between 1994 and 1997, Tadao Tsuge wrote a series of autobiographical articles under the collective title "The Tadao Tsuge Revue" ("Tsuge Tadao gekijō") for Even Flowers and Storms (Arashi mo hana mo)*, a nostalgic youth-culture magazine whose historical cover-age stretched back to the prewar period and across material for both boys and girls. Trans-lated here are four installments related to the characters and themes of the present book, accompanied by some of the original illustrations. Other translated chapters can be found in* Trash Market *(Drawn & Quarterly, 2015).*

TO DESCRIBE, IN THE most basic terms, my impressions of Keisei Tateishi, the neighbor-hood in Tokyo where I grew up, I would say that it was a red-light district and a plywood market and a town of hoodlums in one. I'll add one more thing: The whole place stunk of sewage.

The housing was chopped up randomly by narrow alleyways, which only increased the number of sewers. In the backmost alleyways, there weren't even concrete gutters. You'd often find nothing more than a cut gouged out of the earth. Legions of thin and pitiful, capillary-like worms (we called them *botta* [tubifex]) stuck their bodies half up out of the sludge and undulated in the sewage's current. Today, it's hard to imagine such sights being anywhere but in a slum of a foreign country. But from 1950–1951 to mid-decade, pretty much all of the *shitamachi* [eastern "low city"] areas of Tokyo were like this.

At any rate, I said earlier that my neighborhood was like a red-light district with a plywood market and a town of hoods. Thinking about it more carefully, however, I wonder about those hoods. I'm not sure there were enough of them loitering to warrant naming the area after them. Then again, I doubt my memory is completely failing me.

Hoods, yakuza, thugs...one usually thinks of violence and blood. When I was a kid,

I did witness some big fights where the blood really flew, but I can count those instances on two or three fingers. There weren't too many bloodbaths, and the neighborhood probably wasn't large enough to attract yakuza organizations.

In short, there was nothing special about Keisei Tateishi. It was a neighborhood like so many during the postwar recovery. What was it, then, about the place that left me with so many indelible impressions? There were no jobs in those days. Everything, even food, was in short supply. Many adults squatted or stood around looking lost with nothing to do. Most likely, to my third- or fourth-grader eyes, these men just looked like hoods and thugs.

That said, my memory was probably most shaped by the figure of this one thug—Keisei Sabu. I don't know his real name or what his story was. Where his strange nickname came from is obvious enough. Though I lived in Tateishi for more than ten years, I laid eyes on him only twice, and one of those times was from the back. It was in the middle of the day, in the red-light district. "Hey, that's Keisei Sabu," said someone to his buddy in hushed tones as they walked past. Like a fish on a hook, my head yanked back to take a look. I can't recall exactly, but I must have been in about third grade.

The other time was on a road that passed through the market area. Sabu was stinking drunk and dragging two guys down the street, one under each armpit. "It's just Keisei Sabu," some shop owner blurted dully. That's how I knew who it was. I remember distinctly that I was a second-year student in middle school at the time. However, I couldn't see him well, as his face was turned down.

That's it. Just those two times. Pretty meager for fixing a memory, yet perfect for allowing the imagination to run wild. Only shadows without substance can dart about so rampantly.

No legends of any sort circulate about Keisei Sabu. Perhaps he was nothing more than a ruckus-raising boor, a good-for-nothing thug. Actually, I'm sure that's exactly what he was, just like the Keisei Sabu in my comics, the character whom I sometimes call Ex-Kamikaze Pilot Sabu. He is certainly not the kind of hero one finds in the movies, the man who bares his fangs at life's circumstances, or at institutions, organizations, or the system, or at the powers that be. At most, he's taken it upon himself to be the bodyguard of some prostitute, blundering into unwinnable brawls with more men at once than he can handle. The average person can only be amazed by how this worthless thug keeps making one stupid decision after another.

I'm not interested in heroes.

The illustration here shows the Sabu of my imagination. No one made him how he is. Nothing will change him. He was bound to turn out the way he did no matter what. Not through Tateishi, nor through any other neighborhood in postwar Japan, but rather through the neighborhoods of fiction, does this thug race, like wind across rippling ears of rice in the fields.

. . .

My comics have been turned into a movie. It's titled *Vagabond Plain*.

The script and the direction are both by veteran director Teruo Ishii. Officially, I am "author of the original story." But to be honest, I feel a bit guilty about receiving that honor. Upon reading the script, my initial reactions were "?" and "..." and also some "!!" My crude and naked stories had been dolled up and transformed into something bold and wonderful.

The script was super fun. Director Ishii had laced together a number of my short and medium-length stories, then embellished them with his own wild-spirited sections, to spin a yarn that is truly bizarre. I hesitate to call myself the original author precisely because I am so impressed with Ishii's additions. His parts are the overall narrative's true jewels. Had the script followed my manga faithfully, the resulting movie would surely have been too bleak. It's presumptuous of me to think this, but I wonder if Ishii consciously set out to combat the darkness of my work.

I couldn't wait for the movie to be completed. The shooting of *Vagabond Plain* was wrapped up early last December [1994]—which means it took all of one month!

I went to see the initial cut at the Togen Laboratory in Chōfu [west of Tokyo]. The movie was more fun than I expected. It had singing and dancing and eros and daring action scenes and the bizarre and grotesque. It had anything and everything, and all the charm of the "grand motion pictures" of yore. It wasn't a movie that required difficult philosophizing. If you tried too hard to make sense of it, you would probably just get knotted up inside your own clever thinking.

I am not going to summarize the story here. Suffice to say that it's set in an anonymous *shitamachi* neighborhood soon after the war. The landscape and customs of those days flash across the screen one after another. Men crossing paths on their way to the

red-light district. People loitering in front of a blood bank. The mixed magnificence and shabbiness of the revue clubs. The alleys stinking of sewage, and a thug charging through them. Prostitutes squatting beneath the train tracks.

I must have been in second or third grade...

Suddenly a scene from the past comes to me. It's a summer night. I am with my two brothers selling ice pops on the street that goes through the red-light district. We did this on all festival days. We had an icebox and next to it a vessel holding prize tickets folded into triangles. On a cloth spread over the ground, we set celluloid duck toys as prize giveaways. This open-air business we inherited from our stepfather's friend, who couldn't bear seeing us destitute after my stepfather got sick and became too weak to work.

One day, two or three girls from a nearby brothel skipped over to buy ice pops. One of their tickets was a winner. The girl let out a scream and pressed the toy duck to her chest with great joy. I couldn't pull my eyes away from their faces, caked with white powder and accentuated with bright red rouge. I thought they looked beautiful, truly beautiful. Leaving behind echoes of cheerful laughter, the girls disappeared back into the house tinted by a naked red lightbulb. I watched them spellbound all the way. It's not like I had a special relationship with those specific girls. Any number of girls could have left me with such limpid memories.

And over the years, any number of them did. Once I was old enough to better understand the circumstances of their lives, those girls imparted yet more memories. For various reasons, there were times when I couldn't stand being at home. My feet always took me to the street where the girls hung out. Eventually society decided such places were unacceptable, and quietly disappeared them.

There, on the silver screen, were the streets of Tateishi, the neighborhood in Katsushika ward where I once lived. From yonder, beyond *Vagabond Plain*, distant memories came back to life. I huddled up on the chair in the screening room, my mind shuttling back and forth between past and present. Don't laugh, but when I was a kid I really thought that, once I became an adult, I would protect those girls from the shadows, just like Sabu and Ryū, the two thugs in the film, do. How easily those dreams were quashed.

Nevertheless, even today, when I am sitting around by myself doing nothing, my heart softly, timidly mutters excuses to itself. "Don't worry," it says, "you really are a tough guy at heart."

. . .

Though I have watched countless movies, the following are my oldest memories.

Night. A boy in (I think) about the first year of elementary school is walking frightened, oh so frightened, along a road passing (I think) through some trees or a forest. There's something there. Something scary is going to happen. His chest pounds with anxious expectation. On cue, a ghostly spirit appears, floating through the trees.

I screamed and shut my eyes. I plugged my ears. I have no idea what happened to the boy...

Another memory. This one takes place in the middle of the day on some country road (I think), where a rickshaw driver and his passenger are quarreling about something. What led up to this, I have no idea. Anyway, when the driver then lets out a hi-yah! and begins pulling his rickshaw, the passenger bops him on the head from behind with his cane. The driver is knocked out cold on the road and then... I can't recall what happens after that either.

Those two fragments are all I can remember. How the stories unfolded has been stripped from my memory, like an old and crumbling mud wall.

The title of the movie is *Wild Man Matsu* (*Muhōmatsu no isshō*, [also known as *Rickshaw Man* in English]). It was directed by Hiroshi Inagaki, starred Tsumasaburō Bandō, and was released by Daiei Studios during the war, in 1943. I must have seen this film around 1947 or 1948, when I was about six. It was definitely after the war, though I don't remember who took me to go see it. I only learned that it was called *Wild Man Matsu* ten or so years later. Allowing for a bit of dramatic license, let's say that that was when my movie-going career began.

In 1949–1950, I saw *The Lonely Whistle* (*Kanashiki kuchibue*, 1949 [starring Hibari Misora]) and *Blue Mountain Range* (*Aoi Sanmyaku*, 1949 [starring Setsuko Hara]). As for Western films, there wasn't an installment of Johnny Weissmuller's *Tarzan* or Abbot and Costello that I missed. There was plenty I didn't understand, thanks to the illegible characters produced by old subtitling technology. Like with *Wild Man Matsu*, I only remember a few scenes from those films. Tarzan's strange trademark yell, however, still rings clearly in my ears. Similarly, I'll never forget Bruce Lee's eerie birdlike cry.

Yes sir, I sure saw lots of movies. From when I was seven to about twelve, I must have managed to see two or three a week. Our family's poverty was top-ranked in the neighborhood, so there was no chance that we children would get an allowance. Nevertheless, getting into the movies was easier for me than obtaining gum or candy drops. It

simply required knowing the ins and outs of each theater.

Though my little neighborhood had nothing more than a red-light district, a plywood market, and a bunch of small bars, it boasted four or five theaters (some showing Japanese films, some foreign) and they were usually full. Even the aisles were packed with standing customers. "Hey, you in the front!" someone would complain from the rear, "Put your head down! We can't see!" They say that movies reigned as the "king of entertainment" back then, and they sure did.

They had a deal in those days in which preschool-age kids got in for free if they accompanied a paying adult. Me being a runt, I exploited this frequently. What you did was walk right behind a stranger and try to look like their kid, then disappear inside with the crowd. But as I got older, my body also changed and so naturally this trick stopped working. That's where "Operation Looking for My Parent" came in.

"There's been an emergency! My mom's here somewhere! Can I go in and look for her?" Go up to the ticket girl and say that with a serious face while a movie is playing, and she'd usually let you in. Back then, you were allowed to enter in the middle of a movie, and they didn't clear out the theater between screenings. So once you were in, you were golden. I pulled this trick at all four neighborhood theaters. But it wasn't long before it, too, stopped working. That left the "bum rush."

Scope out the ticket girl's blind spot, then bolt for it like a rabbit. I am ashamed to say that there wasn't a law I didn't break to get into the movies

The movies are pure joy. Their ability to lure us into their world of dreams and illusions, however temporarily, is simply a miracle. When I was a kid, home life was a tangled mess of problems. Nothing was more certain than fists flung at my head frequently and for no reason at all. Movie theaters were my emergency refuge. The only time I felt safe was while sitting in their dim glow. Yet even then, in those moments of happiness, bitterness gnawed at a back corner of my mind.

These days, foreign films are shown all the time, with the result that now everyone is familiar with Western culture. I no longer find it odd to occasionally see a foreign man and a Japanese woman walking arm in arm. As this year [1995] marks a hundred years since the birth of cinema, I will talk about movies again next time.

. . .

By the time I was a sixth-grader, films from the West took absolute priority in my movie-watching. For starters, foreign stars were just too cool.

Male or female, they had chiseled facial features, they were tall, and their legs were ridiculously long. Their hair, eyes, and skin came in different shades. They were literally colorful. And their presence was all the more magnificent when they appeared on the screen in that dye-based process known as Technicolor.

Foreign films, especially those made with American money, were big and impressive in every way. Whether or not one considers *Gone with the Wind* a true masterpiece, its unprecedented production costs guaranteed that it would be the movie of the year [when it was released in Japan] in 1952–1953.

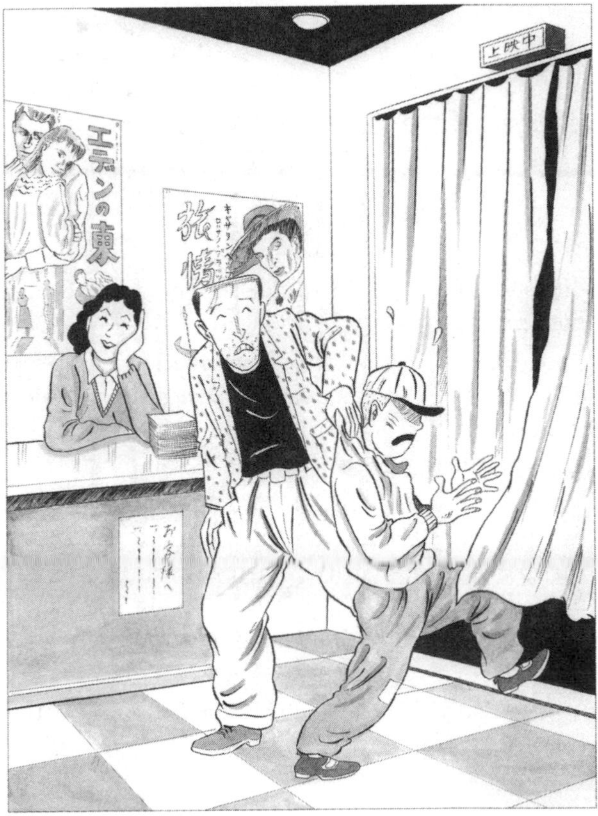
上映中
エデンの東
旅情
お客様へ

When America emerged as the world's number one superpower after World War II, that all-too-self-assured Americanism and that forthright, openhearted, and stubborn "we-first" American spirit took charge of the world—cheerfully, generously, but also, to a degree, by force. The same can be said for the movie industry. Not just the people who made them, but also the beautiful stars and starlets in them, brimmed with confidence and pride. With their chests puffed out, they strutted across the screen.

That, anyway, is how it looks with a slightly cynical eye. But the eleven- or twelve-year-old kid that I was back then couldn't have cared less about such things.

シェーンになりたい
…………

I gravitated toward Western films simply for their large scale, the fun of their showy action, and the coolness of their stars.

Fairly early on—let's see, probably by fourth grade—I was borrowing and reading adventure and mystery novels, as well as all kinds of *kōdan* [classical hero] books and biographies, from my friends and the library. I thus naturally learned a lot of difficult Chinese *kanji* characters. And so, by the time I was in middle school, I could easily read film subtitles and—"Oh, I see!"—understood quite well what was happening.

I read anything and everything. How I got my hands on them, I don't remember, but erotic magazines also came my way. On such occasions, my friends and I would giddily steal away into the shadows. "Oh, I see, I SEE!"—and thus I learned about yet other matters.

Meanwhile, I was still employing the "bum rush" technique to get past the ticket girls. But there was no way my lawlessness would be excused forever. There were four theaters in my neighborhood, but only one showed Western films. I bum-rushed every visit, so I imagine they had their eye on me.

One day, as I charged in and attempted to hide in the crowd, someone grabbed me by the collar. "Gotcha this time, you little punk!" So said a middle-aged man, probably the manager or security. Where do you live? What's your name? Where else have you been doing this? And so on, battering me with questions in rapid fire. I answered him meekly—lying about the important points—while the ticket girl looked on with amusement.

"Oh really? You go to K Middle School? Good old K Middle…How's Mr. Y doing? Does he still teach there?"

"Huh? Uh…yes."

The man looked at me silently, then grumbled, "Dumbass, how would you know? I was just making that shit up."

The earth stopped in its tracks. Was I headed for prison? I was utterly beside myself.

But then the man and the ticket girl burst out laughing. "Don't do it again" is all he said, and let me go. After that, I properly paid to see movies. Well...you bet I did!

No movie made a greater impression on me in those days than *Shane* (1953). Generally, I loved Westerns and saw more of them than of any other kind of film. But this one took the cake. I still think so. If you ask me my top three Westerns, I won't hesitate to answer: *Shane*, *My Darling Clementine* (1946), and *The Wild Bunch* (1969). Everyone raves about *Stagecoach* (1939), but I'm not so crazy about it.

I want to be like Shane! I dreamed of being like him. Quiet, strong, dark, and a little lonely, a wanderer—that was my idea of a hero back then. Can't say for sure, but the reason Shane said so little and looked so impassive must have been because he bore some horribly heavy and heartbreaking "something" on his shoulders. I could feel it even back then.

Alan Ladd was on the small side for a foreign star. It was like he was made for that role. Still, that one film was it. Nothing he made after that is worth mentioning.

As for me, the man who failed to become Shane, you ask what's happened to him? He plays hooky from work and squanders his time addicted to fishing.

THE VAGABOND ZONE

RYAN HOLMBERG

HAD IT BEEN FEASIBLE, this book would have been constructed out of overgrown shredded paper. The corners would crest around eye height. Entering the book, you would have made a loud rustling as you pushed aside the tall, dry pages to progress through something like, but never quite, a story.

As you stand there mid-page, wondering which way to go, you spot small areas in the near distance where the tousled tangle does not grow. Approaching, you find the earth scattered with ruins—cracked concrete slabs, toppled brick walls, bent iron rods and beams—which accrete as you proceed, until rising into a knocked-out edifice and maybe a chimney, whose construction from afar (though you know it should be brick) looks like the paper grass and the crosshatched sky woven together.

Suddenly, from behind, a burst of shuffling jolts you out of your reverie. You turn and see a man. He pauses for a moment to return your gaze, then continues on his way. Curious, you follow him as best you can. He knows the terrain, deftly sidestepping the shrapnel on the ground that keeps tripping you up. Further on, to your right, you notice a man fishing at a river. Next, to your left, a man smoking leisurely and leaning against a broken parapet. Then you see a makeshift shelter, and then another and many more, as you realize that the high unkempt grass is high and unkempt by design rather than neglect. It is camouflage for a city of men who wish to be invisible together.

You have arrived at the spiritual center of the book. You find yourself in a clearing—like that on pages 204–205, in the unfinished story "Vagabond Plain" ("Burai Heiya," 1975–1976)—filled with pop-up habitats of plank and tarp and corrugated metal. You think it a slum, until you realize that its rotating inhabitants fastidiously maintain

Tadao Tsuge, circa 1971; photograph taken at Seirindō, Tokyo

the structures in a state of dereliction. This is the duty they pay for the privilege of disappearing here from time to time, into this world of manicured ruins and artificially preserved beginnings. You think that the author of this world, Tadao Tsuge (born 1941), is something like the Stalker of Tarkovsky's film: a guide to a guarded utopia known for its wish-granting powers and its otherworldly ability to transform fears and desires into breathing omens.

You, it should be clarified, are a Japanese man (there are no women in this world) who lived through and probably fought in World War II. As horrible as it was, and as close as it came to taking your life, the war is lodged in your heart as a repository of nostalgia. Despite its physical and human devastations, the war for you was a life filled with equal parts uncertainty and intensity, where the firebombs of the 1940s did not fully extinguish the fervor of the 1930s, where burning down also meant the chance to rebuild from different blueprints. The war for you is a trauma—but, depending on your personal constitution (witness the poles in this book), trauma became either a way to die little by little or an opportunity for living anew.

As towns have historically sprouted around rivers, mines, industries, ports, and trading junctions, so Tadao's settlement, too, is constructed upon that which nourishes it: the moment when nearly all was annihilated and it seemed that the only hope was to embrace the anarchy of starting over. A moment when wrong was relative, since what the war had celebrated as just was now considered criminal, since what it touted as heroic now lay decaying upon forfeited battlefields and lightless seafloors. A moment when military forms of masculinity, dominant since Japan's imperial enterprise launched magnificently in the late nineteenth century, were so thoroughly humiliated that they had to be either exorcised or reconstructed in disguise. A moment when a fortunate family was one with only a handful of dead members. "It's true... It really is true... There really is nothing left," broods the star of Tadao's "Sabu the Bruiser" ("Buraikan Sabu," April 1974), back in Tokyo after the war to find his home gone, his girlfriend missing, and his mother and brother nothing but ash.[1]

"World War II did not really end for the Japanese until 1952, and the years of war, defeat, and occupation left an indelible mark on those who lived through them," writes the historian John Dower in *Embracing Defeat: Japan in the Wake of World War II* (1999). "No matter how affluent the country later became, these remained the touchstone years for thinking about national identity and personal values."[2] This was certainly so for

Tadao Tsuge, who made a gritty fantasy world out of post-surrender retrospection, filling his story-vignettes with landscapes and characters derived from the war's ruins and the black markets and slums that flourished around them.

A great many Japanese movies, television dramas, novels, comics, and photography collections wax nostalgic about the Occupation period. Most of them look to the era as a way to appreciate how far the country has come. What distinguishes Tadao's work is the added attention he gave to how, even after the ruins of empire had been cleared away and gleaming corporate buildings and consumer culture institutions built in their place, the weeds continued to grow and proliferate in the form of the many Japanese men (again, Tadao's world is narrow in gender) whose war experiences hampered their integration into postwar society, and the many more who, as low-level manual laborers, were grist for the mill of Japan's reconstituted industrial capitalism yet reaped few of the benefits of growth.

One might, in today's English, group such people under the term "precariat." Anti-establishment writers in Japan have a more cutting and encompassing word: *kimin*, or "abandoned peoples." Since it implies that a polity or society has neglected certain people to the point of dispossession, *kimin* is as much about the ethics of a community's leaders as it is about the plight of its abandoned members. To describe someone as *kimin* is to call them a victim in a structural sense. It is to blame local and national government, industry, heads of households, and even the institution of the Emperor for allowing (if not actively supporting) the dispossession of citizens from whom they otherwise expect loyalty.

Since the 1960s, *kimin* has been used variously for the pariah *burakumin* caste, crippled war veterans, former colonial subjects of the Japanese Empire, non-Japanese victims of Hiroshima and Nagasaki, citizens discriminated against because of Korean descent, Okinawans sacrificed to Japan's military alliance with the United States, day laborers and the homeless, rural girls sold into prostitution, farmers driven from their ancestral land by policies favoring industrialization and urbanization, married salary-men who up and disappear, stateless people from around the world—and, most recently, refugees of the Fukushima Daiichi nuclear

Tadao Tsuge, "Sabu the Bruiser," Yagȳo no. 5 (April 1974), as translated in Sabu the Bruiser *(Tokyo: Black Hook Press, 2017).*

meltdowns, whom the Japanese government refuses to compensate adequately and is trying to force back into their contaminated homes.

The men of Tadao's vagabond zone rarely divulge their biographies or occupations. We usually do not know if they are really *kimin* or simply dropouts—but that is exactly the point: The zone is a society where men, regardless of their personal backgrounds, can go and be assured that the overgrowth will screen them from prejudice, economic predation, and (less justifiably) family obligations. The zone is, in that sense, a utopia. It is, of course, utter fantasy. But as an exclusive realm for fallen men alone, and one created by an artist who was personally familiar with life on the margins, it should not be confused with the sentimental and self-affirming portrayals of defeat and recovery that dominate Japanese mass culture.

Usually, representations of how the "common person" maintained his or her dignity amid indiscriminate destruction and widespread hardship in the 1940s assume too much about a baseline of shared experience. These representations typically ignore how Japanese society was strongly shaped by class, caste, and geography, which influenced not only how one suffered the war but also how one benefited from the postwar recovery. If Tadao concedes that the war's ruins were a common starting point for most Japanese, he also insists that the burden of starting over was greater for some people than it was for others. And since that is the case, since some people were not able to escape the ruins, either as a material condition or as a state of mind, as quickly or cleanly as mainstream narratives would have you believe, it is to them—and not the "common person," who is really just a figment of Japanese middle-class imagination—that the right to appropriate the ruins as memory, identity, and fantasy should go.

Tadao's zone is thus a special iteration of *la bohème*. It shares with many fictional and nonfictional texts dealing with *kimin* the idea that life on the margins was more authentic, not only because that is where the contradictions of Japanese capitalism crystallized, but also because invisibility to mainstream society meant that one might at least live unburdened by mainstream mores. The collapse of the Left in the 1960s meant that heroic depictions of the proletariat were all but dead in Japan, and one finds very few such images in *kimin* literature, art, or photography, even when they are specifically about labor. What remained to activists was to help protect the most vulnerable, fight for social support structures and better labor laws, and celebrate the life that thrived despite oppression and self-destructive behavior.

Tadao, in contrast, had no political commitments—disdain for union activities and left-wing discourse simmers in his manga, writings, and interviews—so his response to this demographic was different: sympathetic but not political in a didactic way. He surveyed the fallout of war and recovery, appropriated the precariousness, rootlessness, and nihilism of Japan's marginalized men, polished those qualities with the aesthetics of bohemia, and built for them a refuge in the remnants and memories of the war's ruins.

. . .

Where was Tadao's vagabond zone constructed? Most of the comics translated here—a sampling of the artist's most famous—were published in *Garo*, a monthly manga magazine that was founded in 1964 and is celebrated as the fountainhead of experimental and literary comics in Japan. Others come from *Garo*'s torchbearer, *Yagyō* (*Night Wandering*), a semi-annual periodical created in 1972 by Shinzō Takano (born 1940), who was previously managing editor at *Garo*, and as a publisher and critic has been one of Tadao's greatest supporters since the artist's first contribution to *Garo* in 1968.

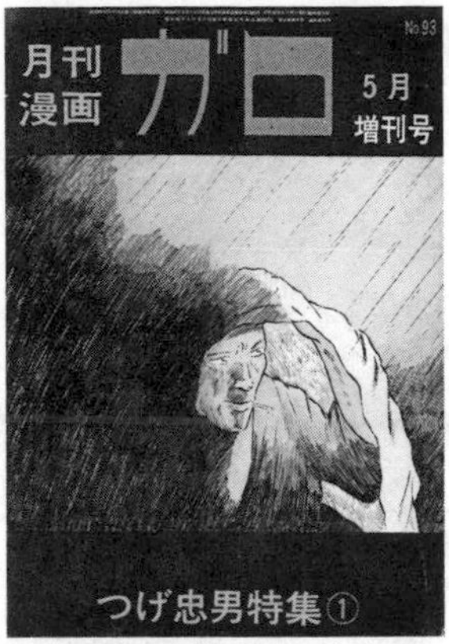
月刊
漫画
ガロ
5月
増刊号
つげ忠男特集①
Garo no. 94 (May 1971), cover of special issue on the work of Tadao Tsuge.

For the nearly forty years of its existence (it folded in 2002), *Garo* was a magazine of many and changing faces. During its first decade, its content ranged from left-wing historical epics and avant-garde send-ups of Japanese militarism to quasi-autobiographical travel narratives and experimental Godardian melodramas.[3] Its first wave of artists grew up during the deadliest years of the war and the meanest years of postwar recovery, with the result that homes and cities decimated by firebombs, and individuals and families scrappily trying to piece their lives back together, assumed a central position in the landscape of *Garo*, if not as explicit subject matter then at least as spiritual touchstone.

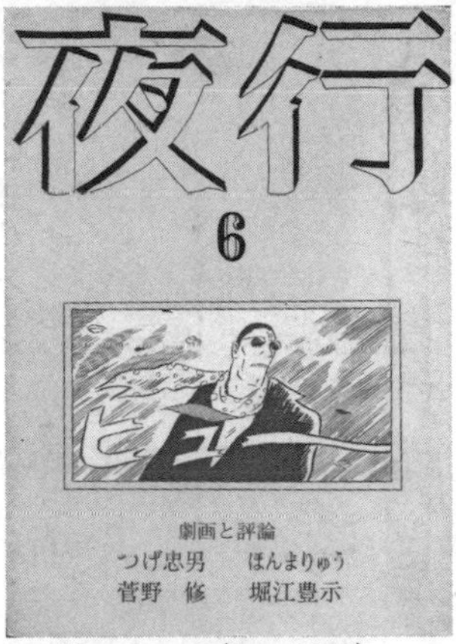
夜行
6
劇画と評論
つげ忠男
Yagyō no. 6 (June 1976), cover art by Tadao Tsuge.

The ascendance of middle-class values that came with the government and business world's single-minded focus on rapid industrial growth estranged artists across the visual and literary arts in Japan. This was the case even for those who, like Tadao, were not visibly moved by the threats state-backed productivism posed to civil society, human rights, and the environment. Like many people who grew up poor after the war, he looked askance at the government's announcement in 1956 that "the postwar era is now officially over," marking the achievement of a GDP higher than that before the war. As Tadao wrote in the 1990s, "My family knew nothing about these changes. We didn't benefit from them whatsoever. Looking back on things more closely, it's true that we no longer worried about whether or not we could eat, so I can't say we were unaffected entirely. Still, at the level of lived experience, the influence of the

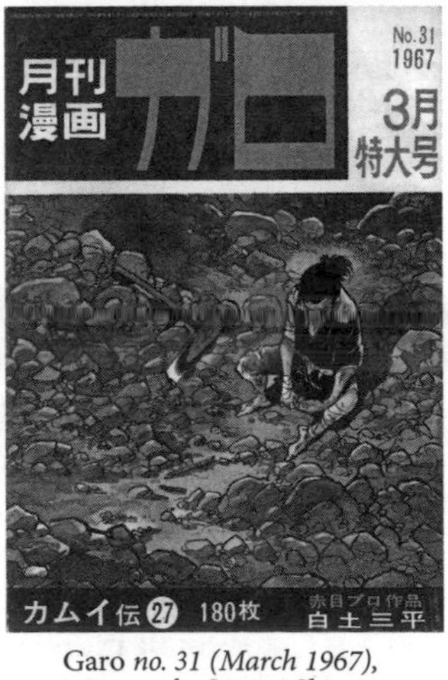
月刊
漫画
ガロ
No.31
1967
3月
特大号
カムイ伝27 180枚
赤目プロ作品
白土三平
Garo no. 31 (March 1967), cover art by Sanpei Shirato.

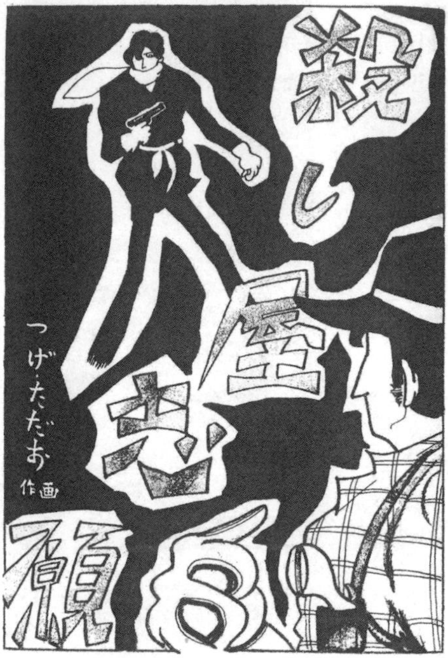
殺し屋志願
つげ・ただお
作画

Tadao Tsuge, "Wanted: An Assassin," Black Shadow, *supplemental volume (Tokyo: Sanyōsha, July 1960), title page.*

recovery felt altogether too light. To learn after the fact how things had been changing actually just makes me more irritated."[4]

While originally funded by cartoonist and cofounder Sanpei Shirato's (born 1932) success in the mainstream children's entertainment market, *Garo* maintained multiple connections to this *après-guerre* milieu. Shirato himself had strong political sympathies for the downtrodden of Japanese history. The eldest son of a leader of the prewar proletarian arts movement, Shirato participated in the "Bloody May Day" protests in Tokyo in 1952 and emerged as a major manga artist in the late 1950s with stories treating subjects like mixed-race children, Hiroshima *hibakusha* (atomic bomb victims), conscript Korean labor under the Japanese Empire, and sixteenth-century peasant rebellions. His *The Legend of Kamuy* (*Kamui-den*, 1964–1971), an epic about discrimination and oppression in premodern Japan, carried *Garo* until 1971.

Tadao, meanwhile, belonged to a contingent of *Garo*-related artists and critics for whom resentment was protest enough. When they complained in print at all, it was usually only to express sympathy for underclass bitterness and resignation, or to insinuate that the margins were blessed with a superior *joie de vivre*. Political demonstrations and ideological grandstanding—so common on the streets and on campuses at the time—were the butt of many jokes. Around 1970, Tadao frequently lampooned union activity in stories set in small factories and businesses. State power was too entrenched, and the struggle to make a living was too exhausting, to waste time and energy on gestures. Left-wing discourse was both too idealistic and too formulaic. Such was the general mood within the early alt-manga milieu, where holding a high school degree was considered a sign of privilege and interpreting a story by a *Garo* artist with reference to organized protest or high culture was often derided by insiders as intellectual masturbation.

Many *Garo* cartoonists, including Shirato and Tadao, cut their teeth on the rental *kashihon* market. From the mid-1950s to the mid-1960s, *kashihon* cartoonists cranked out gritty mystery, murder, gangland, horror, and bloody samurai and ninja stories for fat anthologies and single-artist volumes rented out by children and adolescents for pennies per day. As long as they stuck to the assigned genres, *kashihon* authors could pretty much draw what they wanted. Functional artwork was good enough. Though Shirato's diatribes against discrimination and exploitation were an anomaly in the field, more than a few *kashihon* manga were set in bombed-out cities and feature angry vets, dead parents, and other victims of the war. This is not surprising, considering that the war's wounds were still ten years fresh when the *kashihon* market hit its stride. Freedom of expression and sympathy with *les misérables* had their costs, however. Small and unreliable paychecks were the norm, with even prolific artists living hand to mouth. Tadao was not prolific. He was a minor figure, and supported himself mainly by working at one of the many ooze-for-booze blood banks in Tokyo that both subsidized and exploited the city's poor.[5]

The *kashihon* spirit lived on in *Garo* until the early 1970s. The magazine was published and edited by a former *kashihon* publisher, Katsuichi Nagai (1921–1996), and many of its early artists were refugees from the fast-sinking lending library ship, which was practically defunct by 1969. *Garo* never boasted an impressive print run, at least by manga industry standards: It topped out at around 80,000 in the late 1960s. Nagai paid what he could to his contributors, which was enough to get by in the Sixties and practically nothing by the early Seventies. On the other hand, he allowed even greater artistic freedom—with the result that *Garo*'s legacy of innovation has touched not only most of manga, but also sectors of anime, theater, filmmaking, and contemporary art. Hayao Miyazaki and Haruki Murakami, for example, were *Garo* fans in their youth, and the influence shows in their work.[6]

Despite its broad cultural influence and many of its contributors' subsequent professional success, an aura of bohemian romance continues to surround *Garo*'s name today. To be sure, poverty (not just the externally inflicted kind, but also the self-willed kind) was a leitmotif of the magazine's comics. Stories of the down-and-out proliferated in *Garo* and its latter-day copycats to the point of becoming an "alternative manga" cliché, while what one Japanese critic has described as "the poor man's method" (*binbō mesoddo*) of manga drawing—characterized by loose strokes and heavy crosshatching exercised upon the depiction of small and squalid apartment rooms, dingy factories, and dive bars—is strongly associated with the aesthetics of early *Garo* and, before it, *kashihon* manga.[7]

"Poorest" of them all was arguably Tadao's work. Not only does his drawing often devolve into rickety contours and fields of scratches, but there are probably more slums and bums in his work than in that of anybody else associated with *Garo*, except perhaps the professional vulgarians Takashi Nemoto and Kataoka Tōyō (both born 1958). More importantly, Tadao was also the most sensitive to the details of living on the bottom rungs of Japanese society as a vagrant or low-level laborer. This was partly thanks to biography: Tadao grew up in a slum in Katsushika ward, on Tokyo's working-class east side, and worked with and among Tokyo's bottom crust for most of his adolescence and young adulthood.

At first glance, his work for *Garo* and *Yagyō* appears to ply a limited number of themes and characters. Upon closer look, it reveals itself as an oeuvre with an array of genre-breaking features that one would be hard-pressed to find in any other cartoonist's work, anywhere in the world. Tadao created quasi-documentary comics about working at iffy blood banks and small, struggling companies, as well as an early example of extended comics journalism ("Uranishi Village," April 1971) about poverty and depopulation in the countryside, still dire issues in Japan. He also created surreal deconstructions of the police procedural ("Manhunt," May 1969), and violent fantasies of underclass resentment that, in one case ("A Tale of Absolute and Utter Nonsense," February 1972), flirted dangerously with Japan's greatest political taboo by criticizing Emperor Hirohito.

Some of this material can be found in *Trash Market*, published by Drawn & Quarterly in 2015. The present volume, meanwhile, presents a sampling of what the artist is best known for: portrait sketches of vagrants, vagabonds, punks, and war veterans who will not or cannot accommodate themselves to the social organizations (family, workplace, or criminal) of post-postwar Japan. Were *Slum Wolf* comprehensive on that count, it would be maybe five hundred pages rather than the three hundred you now hold in your hands.

. . .

"I'm not interested in heroes," says Tadao in his essay "Always a Tough Guy at Heart" (1994–1995). Still, there are definitely stars in his zone.

They either strut about in sunglasses or an eyepatch like Sabu the Wolf, the kamikaze trainee who dodged a fate of death to live thereafter only for himself, who embodies the anarchy of the black-market era well into the age of retail commerce and high-rises. Or they flap about in near hysterics like Ryōkichi Aogishi, the middle-aged man who is unable to square what he saw and did during the war with the settled middle-class life that awaited him upon returning to Japan. Sabu and Aogishi were the two paradigms of Japanese masculinity that Tadao kept returning to while drawing for *Garo* and *Yagyō* in the Sixties and Seventies. As different as they are—one an essay in machismo, the other in impotence—they are two sides of the same coin. They are complementary responses to the ruins of the Japanese Empire and the soulless, workaholic life that flourished in its place. Sabu and Aogishi are, each in his own way, attempts by Tadao to imagine what the rubble and vegetal camouflage of the zone might look like if it could walk and talk, and throw an angry elbow or psychic dagger of guilt into the flanks of a society that preferred to bury the unhappier legacies of Japan's past.

Note that Tadao chose two very different types of ex-military man to conduct this interrogation. While hobos in sullied military caps are standard human furniture of the noir city in mystery manga of the Fifties, as desperate soldiers and kamikaze pilots are in war manga of the Sixties, it was only with literary-inclined manga of the late Sixties and early Seventies that the social alienation and psychological tribulations of combat veterans emerged as a recurring theme. *Garo* played a central part in this developing genre, propelled by a wider critical inquiry into war memory, as well as by a fascination with the figure of the "vanishing person" (*jōhatsu ningen*): someone (typically a man) who one day disappears from work and family without a trace, and oftentimes without any apparent motive. The novelist Kōbō Abe (1924–1993) and the filmmaker Shōhei Imamura (1926–2006) both produced works on this subject in the Sixties. Tadao's older brother, the legendary Yoshiharu Tsuge (born 1937), drew many works on this theme for *Garo* and *Yagyō* in the same years covered by the present book.

While unsolved mystery pervades the "vanishing men" genre, combat vets had understandable reasons to hide. Even if an enlisted man was lucky enough to survive the war—an estimated 2.3 million died, roughly half perishing from starvation and disease—other battles awaited him upon returning to Japan. Officially deified during the war as *gunshin* (military gods), many found themselves scapegoated for their country's near annihilation. Some people blamed Japan's defeat on the soldiers' lack of will. Sneers and worse were cast at their ragged uniforms, scars, and missing limbs, as they combed the black markets for food and work, or begged or played music on street corners for change. Tadao recalled their gothic appearance as a child in Tokyo in the early Fifties. "While adults tended to look down or away from the man, we kids surrounded him and stared at his prosthetic leg with bated breath. We stared at him for too long one time and he yelled at us. 'Get away!' he said in a deep growl. His eyes burned with a color fierce beyond hatred or anger."[8] History books offer reports of more callous kids throwing stones.[9] Turn to page 50: According to "The Flight of Ryōkichi Aogishi" ("Aogishi Ryōkichi no haisō," March 1969), injured vets could still be found asking for money on Tokyo streets in the late Sixties, more than twenty years after the war.

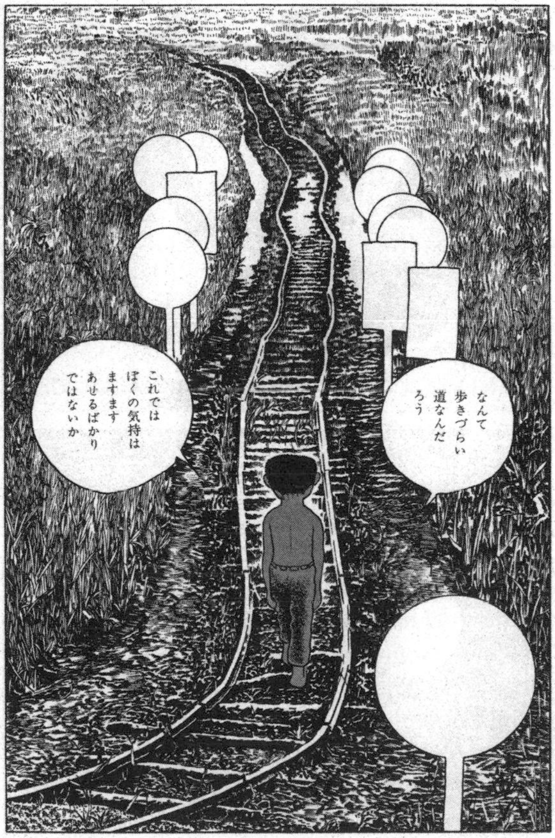
これではぼくの気持はますますあせるばかりではないか
なんて歩きづらい道なんだろう
Yoshiharu Tsuge, "Nejishiki," Garo *no. 47 (June 1968).*

Tadao also had contact with veterans while working at the blood bank in the late Fifties and Sixties. The hard-up were not only low-ranking foot soldiers. While cleaning the toilets, Tadao was shocked by graffiti he saw on the wall of a stall: "Even I, a former lieutenant in the navy, have been reduced to selling my blood." He recalled, "At that moment, as if peeping through a crack, I caught my first glimpse of the true meaning of what they called 'the postwar.'" He also remembered a tall man with hideous injuries, presumably from the war. "From his mouth up, it looked like a volcano had exploded. All you could roughly make out in that red-black mass of flesh were eyes and a nose, more or less where you would expect them to be." The female staff at the blood bank could not bear to look at him.[10]

Though rarely interpreted as such, Yoshiharu's surreal "Nejishiki" ("The Screw Ceremony," June 1968), a crucial work in the establishment of manga as literature and experimental art, featuring an injured young man who rises mysteriously from the sea and unsuccessfully beseeches villagers for care, reads like an allegory about the homefront's inability to come to terms with the deaths of the young men it sent to die in the war. Tadao seems to have recognized that in his brother's work: His creepy "Sounds" ("Oto," February 1971), published initially in a special issue of *Bijutsu Techō* (*Art Handbook*), Japan's leading contemporary art magazine, rewrites the alienating landscape and cryptic dialogue of "Nejishiki" in order to articulate the depths of Aogishi's PTSD. Related works in *Garo* included Seiichi Hayashi's (born 1945) "Red Bird Little Bird" ("Akai tori kotori," May 1969), which mixes soft porn graphics and formerly censored photographs of murder and captivity on the Chinese front in order to burn images of guilt into the psyche of a man in his fifties—in other words, old enough to have participated in atrocities like the Nanking Massacre.[11] English-language readers of manga will be more familiar with Yoshihiro Tatsumi's (1935–2015) many vignettes of middle-aged men suffering from impotence and Aogishi-style workplace and family alienation (only some of which were published in *Garo*); some of these men are explicitly described as war veterans. In Shigeru Mizuki (1922–2015), who wrote copiously about the absurd horrors of the front, *Garo* even had a (one-armed) war veteran in its stable.

Strictly speaking, Sabu, Tadao's other ex-military type, is not a vet, for the simple reason that he never went to war. Yakuza cinema was experiencing a golden age at the time, and one is inclined to read Sabu first in that context. Think of actor Ken Takakura's many films, like those of the *Abashiri Prison* (*Abashiri bangaichi*, 1965–1972) and *Brutal Tales of Chivalry* (*Shōwa zankyōden*, 1965–1972) series, in which the hero struggles with loyalty to his patrons in the world of organized crime while upholding his own personal sense of manly honor. Or the first installment of director Kinji Fukasaku's bloody *Battles Without Honor and Humanity* (*Jingi naki tatakai*, 1973), which opens in a post-surrender black market (this one in Hiroshima) with a combat veteran, played by Bunta Sugawara, protecting Japan's female dignity against arrogant, rapist American GIs—much like Sabu in "Sentimental Melody" ("Natsukashi no merodii," January 1969) and "Legend of the Wolf" ("Ookami no densetsu," June 1976). Bunta later finds himself, like Ken, at odds with his underworld boss. Sabu is cool like these men, with equally Mount Fuji–sized self-respect. But he refuses to have any association with organized crime. Neither the police nor the kingpins, but rather obnoxious and sycophantic *chinpira* (entry-level gangsters) are Sabu's natural enemies.

Sabu's background as a kamikaze trainee is important here. When silver-screen yakuza are presented as veterans, typically that means army vets, who fought on land, starved in jungles, or suffered for years as Russian POWs. Such credentials establish not only that they have faced hell on earth (that they inflicted hell on others is rarely mentioned), but also that their characters were formed in the crucible of Japan's notoriously unforgiving military culture. They are thus able to respect systems of authority, even when that requires dramatic personal sacrifice, which means, in turn, that the true men among them are intolerant of those who abuse the system—hence the explosive outbursts in yakuza movies when codes of duty are exploited by those at the top. The kamikaze trainee, in contrast, experienced a fairly short regime of military induction and was allowed, in

LOOK AT THAT
STUPID ... WONDER HOW IT GOT IN THERE
(BZZ BZZ)
LISTENING?

Seiichi Hayashi, "Flowering Harbor," Garo *no. 60 (May 1969), as translated in* Flowering Harbour *(London: Breakdown Press, 2014).*

exchange for his immediate and certain death, a degree of freedom in his pre-sortie life. If he went to battle, he died, barring some mechanical snafu. Hence, perhaps, why lone wolf Sabu has no affinity for the pack-dog thugs that patrol Japan's entertainment districts. Thus also, perhaps, why Sabu is a free spirit, even to the point of being self-destructive, while the former foot soldier Aogishi is crippled by PTSD even though he follows the rules.

Sabu wasn't the typical ex-kamikaze of postwar literature. In his era-defining "Discourse on Decadence" (1946), the novelist and essayist Ango Sakaguchi (1906–1955) argued that Japan's renewal and self-respect hinged on the wartime state's heroes being rehumanized through humiliation. The Emperor, alas, remained untouchably high. Happily, lower-hanging fruit, like stoic war widows—whose faithfulness to their dead husbands made them paragons of womanhood—could now be found working as prostitutes. What's more, many of them appeared to enjoy their new situation, or so thought Sakaguchi. The equivalent for fallen kamikaze was unglorified work: "The heroism of the kamikaze pilots is really nothing more than an illusion; their real history as humans starts the moment they set up shop in the black market."[12] Tadao did not see the ex-kamikaze pilot's redemption in this way. Sabu is tough and scrappy, and was reborn in the war's ruins, but nowhere does he do an ounce of work in Tadao's many stories about him. He is essentially still a suicide fighter, just now without an airplane or a purpose, and with urban legends and boyish romance taking up the myth-making that state propaganda formerly provided.

Once upon a time, a real Sabu did in fact prowl the ghetto streets of Tokyo, according to "Always a Tough Guy at Heart." Nonetheless, that essay and stories like "Sentimental Melody" readily admit that Sabu is essentially a pastiche of vague memories and fantasy projections. Tadao typically tries to maintain an atmosphere of realism for his vignettes of lone wolf masculinity, like in "Legend of the Wolf" or "Sabu the Bruiser." Elsewhere, the scrim of authenticity falls and the generic inspirations are plain to see. Obvious in this regard is "Wandering Wolf: The Bloodspattered Code of Honor and Humanity" ("Sasurai no ookami: chishibuki jingi," May 1972), which pulls on the world of male rolling stones and pining bar maidens popularized by bluesy *enka* music and related melodrama films. The story appears to be inspired by Tadao's *Garo* colleague Seiichi Hayashi's "Flowering Harbor" ("Hana saku minato," May 1969), an extended homage to *enka* aesthetics set in a lonely port town and similarly featuring a lonely wanderer and lonely female bar owner.[13] Likewise, "Sentimental Melody," even as its characters try to faithfully reconstruct the past, gestures toward contemporary Sixties pop culture. The title is almost identical to the name (*natsukashii merodii*) used for the radio and television programs of the early and mid-1960s that featured old war songs, and which are usually understood as one of the wellsprings of the subsequent *enka* boom as well as one of the ways in which veteran's nostalgia was made a more acceptable part of Japanese everyday life.[14]

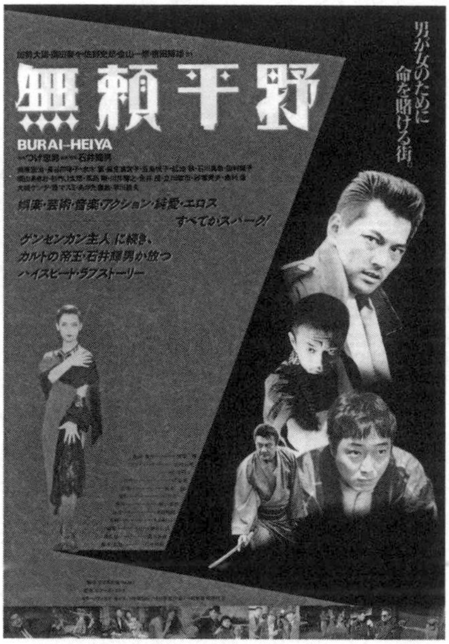
男が女のために命を賭ける街。
無頼平野
BURAI-HEIYA
娯楽・芸術・音楽・アクション・純愛・エロス
すべてがスパーク!
ゲンセンカン主人に続き、
カルトの帝王・石井輝男が放つ
ハイスピード・ラブストーリー
Movie flier for Vagabond Plain *(May 1995), directed by Ishii Teruo.*

Though thus stereotypically Japanese in many ways, Sabu is a curious breed. Consider Tadao's comments on the movies in "Always a Tough Guy at Heart." He confesses to having been addicted to Westerns as a kid, and being enamored with the arrogant airs of white American actors and actresses. He cites *Wild Man Matsu* (*Muhōmatsu no isshō*, 1943, also known as *Rickshaw Man* in English) as his earliest film memory; then he names Alan Ladd's *Shane* (1953), about the gentle wandering gunman who defends wholesome Wyoming homesteaders against gun-slinging evil, as his favorite childhood movie. Both of these films feature reserved manly types who unleash their brawn only when the situation leaves them no other choice. They both feature young boys who look up to the adult male stars as surrogate father figures. Was Sabu, for Tadao, a black-market Shane? The tough guy a kid could admire, the man who sacrificed a settled place in the world so that that the prostitutes and the good shopkeepers could live their lives unmolested by the scary Jack Palances and greedy yakuza ranchers of postwar Japan? A strange view, indeed: a Japanese boy gazing upon a man who gallantly fights the salacious American Occupation forces, through eyes enamored with Hollywood's white dreams.

In 1994, Tadao's black-market hero made his way back into celluloid. That year, cult director Teruo Ishii (1924–2005)—who, not incidentally, broke out in the Sixties by directing the first ten installments of Ken Takakura's *Abashiri Prison* series—made the film *Vagabond Plain* (*Burai Heiya*). Composed of a medley of fragments from various Tadao manga, including "Legend of the Wolf," Ishii's film not only includes no reference to its namesake manga, it also ignores the alienation that leads into Tadao's zone. The Shōwa period (which began in 1926) had just ended with the death of Hirohito in 1989, marking the symbolic closure of one of the most exhilarating and painful eras in Japanese history. Baby boomers were turning fifty, while those who witnessed and fought in the war were rapidly passing away. For those who grew up immediately before or after the war, it was a ripe time to be nostalgic about their childhoods and the watershed years of the Occupation. The power of sentimentality was such that even black-market fantasies that offered a more complex and less redeemable version of postwar society, like those by Tadao in *Garo* and *Yagyō*, were easily bowdlerized as kitsch.

. . .

While Tadao's work is a unique intervention into the literature of war memory, it also speaks to issues of class, geography, and the built environment. The artist's apathy toward political organizing was overt. Nonetheless, his late Sixties and early Seventies comics were fairly close in spirit to the work of labor activists, anarchist writers, and photojournalists who were concerned about the neglected armies of men who manned the lower echelons of Japan's booming construction, manufacturing, and energy industries, often via yakuza-mediated day-labor markets in big cities like Tokyo, Yokohama, and Osaka.

Until the late Sixties, such informal labor markets (known as *yoseba*) were also where blood banks like the one where Tadao worked went to recruit when supplies were low. They were where major corporations like Toyota scouted men to work their assembly lines, usually on grueling shifts and under dangerous conditions for terrible pay. Corrupt day-labor markets were also where the fledgling nuclear power industry and their yakuza go-betweens went to find short-term janitorial and maintenance workers, to be shipped off to places like the Fukushima Daiichi station (already notorious as a dirty and dangerous facility in the 1970s) to wipe up radioactive spills and remove radioactive corrosion from valves and vents, so that Japan's nuclear power plants were clean *enough* to pass inspection and reopen with *tolerable* efficiency and without *too great* a risk of accident. Many writers took to calling these exploited laborers *kimin*—"abandoned peoples"—thereby identifying the day-labor markets, and the alliance between industrial capitalism and organized crime that governed them, as one of the major engines of dispossession in Japan.

As time passed, Tadao's work moved away from actual *kimin* sites and peoples. His careful depiction of Japan's human "trash markets" (his name for the blood banks and the colorful riffraff that congregated there) in the late Sixties and early Seventies mutated into generalized fantasy zones situated vaguely on the undeveloped fringes of Tokyo. "Vagabond Plain" offers the most detailed such rendering, though one finds nondescript riverside embankments and wastelands as settings for social flight and perverse sex even in his earliest works for *Garo*. A further twist on the zone's evolution was provided twenty years later, with his two-volume graphic novel *Dwelling in a Boat* (*Fune ni sumu*, 1996–2000). Almost the entire story takes place in a real-life grass zone on the Tone River in Chiba prefecture, twenty miles north of Tokyo, near where Tadao has lived since the 1970s. One character, a stand-in for the artist, wishes to spend his last years

へ
へ
ッ
いい
いじ
ゃ
ね
え
か

Tadao Tsuge, Dwelling in a Boat *vol. 1*
(Tokyo: Waizu shuppan, 2000).

living on a small, rickety houseboat, allowing the current to take him where it will. Meanwhile, his friend has developed a taste for modernist junk sculpture, and spends his days hauling rubble into an overgrown field, smashing it with hammers, and then carefully burning the vegetation to create a simulation of a bombed-out city. "It sends shivers up my spine," sighs one of the characters as he gazes upon this wonderfully anachronistic outdoor installation. With this page, Tadao pulled the plug on the zone's black magic. Back in the mid-Seventies, at the time of "Vagabond Plain," elaborating a world of ruins called for no such irony.

Popular images of a nation composed of neon-lit cities and industrious white-collar workers notwithstanding, ruins and ruined people remain an important part of Japanese national identity. One of the country's top tourist sites, after all, is the skeletal brick-and-steel remains of a former government exposition hall near ground zero in Hiroshima—the Atom Bomb Dome—while the *hibakusha* (those exposed to the blast and radiation in Hiroshima and Nagasaki) have long stood as Japan's emissaries of world peace. Though *Garo* founder Sanpei Shirato was committed to peace activism and used the magazine as a platform to that end in the mid-Sixties, most other artists and critics associated with *Garo* shrugged their shoulders at the kind of humanism the *hibakusha* and their supporters stood for, just as they dismissed organized politics. As explained earlier, many of them were drawn instead to the ambivalent figure of the combat veteran: the killer who was also a victim of reckless imperial ambitions and an inhuman military culture.

They were also intrigued by the ambivalence that many people of their parents' generation expressed (though usually in hushed tones) about life during the war. In a 1969 interview with *Garo* editor Shinzō Takano, Tadao reflected: "People our age, we only really comprehend what happened at the end of the war. At night, from the air-raid shelters, we witnessed airplanes in flames streaking across the sky. That's all the war was for us. But for them [people who were adults during the war], they had to deal with a variety of problems when the bombs fell.... There must be a lot we don't know about. Talking to people, you often hear them say that they never want to go to war again, that the war was really horrible. Yet, I feel like that's not the whole picture.... War war war consumes one's life like a fever, then all of a sudden it's over. How does someone live life after that? Were they able to just, snip, start fresh? They don't look bothered now, but who knows what they're really feeling..."[15]

This preference for moral ambivalence can be seen clearly in Tadao's taste in architectural ruins. While generally his wastelands suggest firebombed Tokyo, at the center of "Vagabond Plain" stands a monument from another city, the wrecked masonry edifice with a "giant tuna steak of a chimney" on page 211. The narrator describes it as belonging to a famous munitions factory, referring most likely to the ruins of the Osaka Artillery Arsenal, a forgotten but important facility that once stood in the heart of Japan's second city. Situated just east of Osaka Castle, the arsenal was the largest such factory in Asia until American bombers obliterated it on August 14, 1945, the day before Japan surrendered. "That Roosevelt, he knew what he was doing," muses the story's narrator. "They left that chimney standing on purpose," meaning, presumably, with the intent of rubbing superior power in the Japs' faces.

While Occupation authorities liquidated most of the surviving machinery and weaponry at the Osaka Arsenal, a treasure hoard of scrap steel and other metals still remained when Japan regained national sovereignty in 1952. It was so valuable that the site was known colloquially as the Sugiyama Gold Mine, after the district in which it was located. Over the next few years, the arsenal's carcass was picked apart and sold on the black market by teams of scavengers who lived in a shantytown across the river that ran beside it.

Among the literary works inspired by news coverage of the arsenal's plundering was one of Tadao's favorite novels: Takeshi Kaikō's *Japan Threepenny Opera* (*Nihon sanmon opera*, 1959), which focuses on the social organization of the scavenger's settlement. Kaikō calls the place "Osaka's Casbah," as it is led by stateless Koreans and filled with "ex-convicts, wanderers, the formally unemployed, and illegal aliens, all of whom come like the wind and go like water."[16] He presents the place as a kind of *kimin* utopia where freedom and order were promised by a meritocratic anarchy that did not recognize the social hierarchies, class privileges, or prejudices of the outside world. He calls its inhabitants "Apaches," after the name the Osaka police used in real life to honor the scavengers' speed and muscle, and their choreographed hit-and-run attacks—"Apaches" as in John Ford's Apaches, who were well known to Japan's many fans of Hollywood Westerns like *Stagecoach* (1939) and *Fort Apache* (1948). The appellation was presumably meant as an innocent pop culture reference, but was apposite given Native Americans' fate as the United States' own colonial *kimin*.[17]

Though Tadao's ruin fantasies are rarely political in an admonitory way, they do stake a claim on memory, on who should get to remember what and how. The shadow appearance of the Osaka Arsenal in "Vagabond Plain" reaffirms what the slum wolves and traumatized men elsewhere in his work establish: that the war's ruins did not belong equally to everyone, and could not be appropriated so simply as monuments of melancholic peace. Even a place like Hiroshima was guilty on this count. As many historians have argued, a singular focus on Japanese *hibakusha* as World War II's exemplary victims obscures much about Hiroshima's history and the selective nature of Japanese war memories. For example, many *hibakusha* of Korean descent, brought to Japan as conscript laborers, were, until recently, refused the benefits provided to Japanese atomic bomb victims. The Hiroshima area's repressed history as a major military center is also frequently highlighted.[18]

Closer to the concerns of the present inquiry is the fate of the so-called "atomic bomb slum" (*genbaku suramu*) that once neighbored the Atom Bomb Dome. A sprawling and labyrinthine settlement of rickety shacks on land that previously housed various military structures, it provided shelter to an assortment of *kimin*: pariah *burakumin*, Koreans, and ailing and disfigured *hibakusha* who feared going out in public and whose care was hampered by government bureaucracy. In the honorable tradition of urban renewal, Hiroshima progressively cleared the atomic slum in the Sixties and Seventies and replaced it with parks, museums, and other municipal leisure facilities, as well as with a fancy, modernist public housing project. Because they were technically squatters on government land, the slum dwellers were compensated little or not at all for their displacement. *Kimin*, and the challenges they posed to a monovocal narrative of Hiroshima's identity, had no place in the new City of Peace. Tadao, meanwhile, was erecting new slums in pen and paper around uncelebrated war ruins precisely so that the rootless could continue to have a homeless home, at least in fantasy.

With a good-natured smile, Tadao often laments his work's lack of wide readership, blaming its bleakness and loose drawing. He should take it as a compliment instead. It is a reflection of his art's refusal to pander to popular Japanese tastes for upbeat and redemptive depictions of economic hardship and social marginalization, its refusal to give in to the compulsion to cast Japan's defeat as a long-gone event still capable of moving the masses emotionally but without any material or social legacies worth thinking about critically. Tadao should, in other words, take pride in his zone's integrity as an exclusive and well-fortified utopia. He invites you to visit. He will even show you in. But do not expect him to make you feel at home.

NOTES

RYAN HOLMBERG would like to acknowledge the generous support of a Postdoctoral Teaching Fellowship in the Department of Art, Art History, and Visual Studies at Duke University during the research and writing of this essay.

1   Tsuge Tadao, "Buraikan Sabu," *Yagyō* no. 5 (April 1974), in *Sabu the Bruiser*, trans. Ryan Holmberg (Tokyo: Black Hook Press, 2017).

2   John W. Dower, *Embracing Defeat: Japan in the Wake of World War II* (New York: Norton, 1999), p. 25.

3   On *Garo* in this period, see Ryan Holmberg, *Garo Manga: The First Decade, 1964–1973* (New York: The Center for Book Arts, 2010), and the various essays I have written for *The Comics Journal* online and for translated volumes from PictureBox Inc., Drawn & Quarterly, and Breakdown Press.

4   Tadao Tsuge, "The Tadao Tsuge Revue" [1994–97], as translated (with modifications) in Tadao Tsuge, *Trash Market*, trans. and ed. Ryan Holmberg (Montreal: Drawn & Quarterly, 2015), pp. 247-8.

5   On Japan's blood banks in this era, see Ryan Holmberg, "Blood Plants: Mizuki Shigeru, Kitaro, and the Japanese Blood Industry," *The Comics Journal* online (May 2015). Tadao wrote and drew much on the subject: in translation, see "Trash Market" (1972) and "The Tadao Tsuge Revue" in D&Q's *Trash Market*.

6   On Garo's influence on Hayao Miyazaki and the Japanese animation industry, see Ryan Holmberg, "Seiichi Hayashi's Nouvelle Vague," in the paperback edition of Seiichi

Hayashi, *Red Colored Elegy*, trans. Taro Nettleton (Montreal: Drawn & Quarterly, 2018), pp. 249–63. Haruki Murakami has written about his love for the work of *Garo* artist Maki Sasaki numerous times: in translation, see the bellyband of Sasaki Maki, *Ding Dong Circus*, ed. and trans. Ryan Holmberg (London: Breakdown Press, 2015).

7. Itō Gō, "Binbō manga no pentacchi o kaisetsu suru" (1999), *Manga wa kawaru: 'manga katari' kara 'manga ron' e* (Tokyo: Seidosha, 2007), pp. 79–86.

8. Tsuge, "The Tadao Tsuge Revue," pp. 244–5.

9. On the post-surrender reception of veterans, see Yoshida Yutaka, *Heishi tachi no sengoshi* (Tokyo: Iwanami shoten, 2011), pp. 9–50, and passim. See also Yoshikuni Igarashi, *Homecomings: The Belated Return of Japan's Lost Soldiers* (New York: Columbia University Press, 2016).

10. Tsuge, "The Tsuge Tadao Revue," pp. 251–2.

11. This work is available in English translation in Hayashi Seiichi, *Red Red Rock and Other Stories*, 1967-1970 (London: Breakdown Press, 2016), pp. 207-14.

12. Sakaguchi Ango, "Discourse on Decadence" [1946], trans. James Dorsey, in Dorsey and Doug Slaymaker, eds., *Literary Mischief: Sakaguchi Ango, Culture, and the War* (Lanham, MD: Lexington Books, 2010), p. 181.

13. See Ryan Holmberg, "Enka Gekiga: Hayashi Seiichi's Pop Music Manga," *The Comics Journal* online (June 2014), and Hayashi Seiichi, *Flowering Harbour*, trans. Ryan Holmberg (London: Breakdown Press, 2014).

14. On the recuperation of veteran experience through war songs in the 1960s, and the related rise of veteran associations, see Yoshida, pp. 89–144.

15. Tsuge Tadao and Takano Shinzō, "Sengo no sei no omomi," *Garo* no. 69 (August 1969), translated as "The Weight of Postwar Life," *The Comics Journal* online (May 2018).

16. Kaikō Takeshi, *Nihon sanmon opera*, in *Kaikō Takeshi zenshū* vol. 2 (Tokyo: Shinchōsha, 1992), p. 274.

17. On writings related to the Osaka Arsenal, see Takayuki Tatsumi, *Full Metal Apache: Transactions Between Cyberpunk Japan and Avant-Pop America* (Durham & London: Duke University Press, 2006), pp. 151–70.

18. On the politics of war memory in Hiroshima, see Lisa Yoneyama, *Hiroshima Traces: Time, Space, and the Dialectics of Memory* (Berkeley: University of California Press, 1999), and Ran Zwigenberg, *Hiroshima: The Origins of Global Memory Culture* (Cambridge: Cambridge University Press, 2016).

ALSO AVAILABLE
FROM NEW YORK REVIEW COMICS

YELLOW NEGROES AND OTHER IMAGINARY CREATURES
Yvan Alagbé

ALMOST COMPLETELY BAXTER
Glen Baxter

AGONY
Mark Beyer

PEPLUM
Blutch

THE GREEN HAND
Nicole Claveloux

WHAT AM I DOING HERE?
Abner Dean

PRETENDING IS LYING
Dominique Goblet

VOICES IN THE DARK
Ulli Lust

FATHER AND SON
E.O. Plauen

SOFT CITY
Pushwagner

THE NEW WORLD
Chris Reynolds